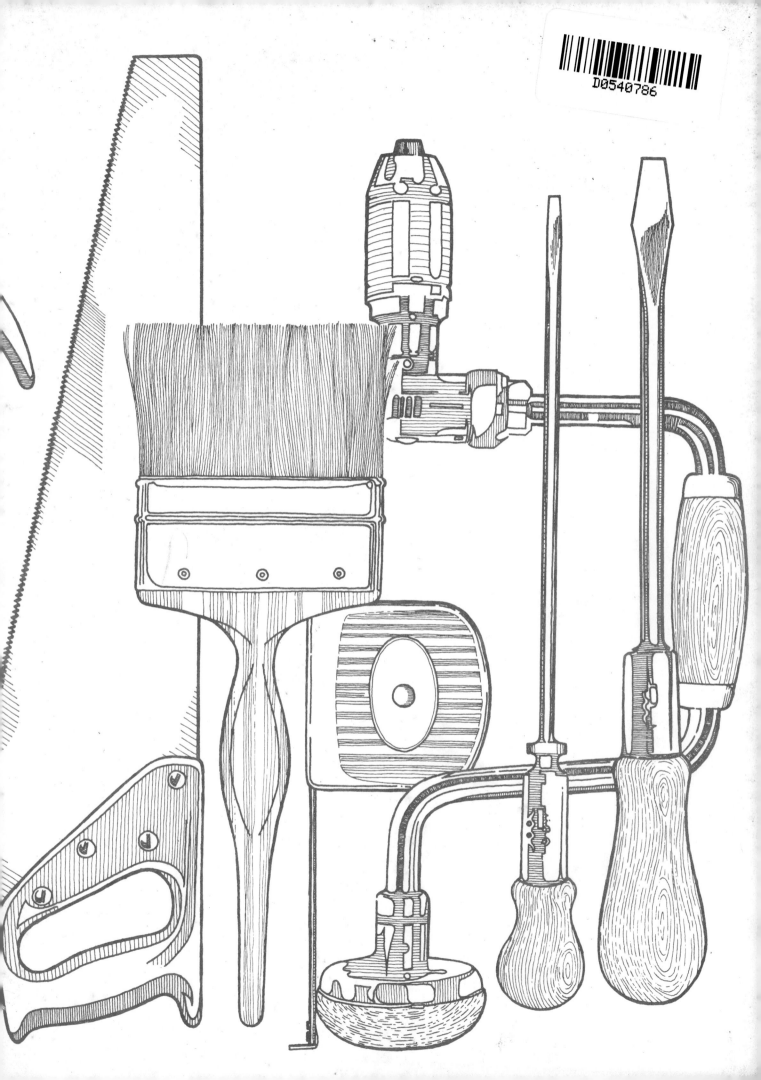

The Golden Homes Book of

The Complete Home Carpenter

A Golden Hands book

Marshall Cavendish, London

Edited by Phil Hutchinson
Published by Marshall Cavendish Publications Limited,
58 Old Compton Street, London W1V 5PA

© Marshall Cavendish Limited, 1972, 1973, 1974, 1976

This material was first published by Marshall Cavendish
Limited in the partwork *Golden Homes*

First printed in 1973
Reprinted 1976

Printed by Henri Proost, Turnhout, Belgium

ISBN 0 85685 040 3

About this book . . .

Carpentry is one of the few do-it-yourself skills that offers something for everyone. Even the inexperienced carpenter can make attractive and functional furniture and carry out repairs to timber in the home. And carrying out a simple job gives you the skills and techniques to tackle more ambitious projects.

This book covers all aspects of carpentry. There are full instructions for making originally designed furniture for every room in the home . . . superb kitchen units, a beautiful gate legged dining table and a Welsh dresser, modern bed platforms, a cocktail bar and built-in units for the living room, and a compact 'mini' office for the study. If storage is a problem in your home there's a military chest to make, space saving wall units, and shelves and cupboards to make use of those awkward alcoves.

There are projects involving structural carpentry — a stylish open riser staircase to give a modern look to your home, or, for a more traditional look, there are instructions on fitting a bow window. And if your family is outgrowing your home, you can build a mansard roof that will give you a valuable extra 'floor'. The book also tells you how to repair household timbers — the simple and the more complex jobs that can both be expensive if done by a tradesman.

There is carpentry to decorate your home too, with full instructions on timber panelling walls, room dividers, panelled doors and applying veneers. The sparkling colour photographs show just how good these features will look in your home.

Step by step photographs show you how to undertake the projects in the book and with the full directions and easy to follow diagrams you can't go wrong. There are a host of useful hints too that will simplify your work.

Data sheets tell you exactly what tools to use for a job, what the different types of screws, nails and bolts are used for and the variety of carpentry joints. In addition, two chapters tell you about the power tools that will speed up your work.

This book is a collection of information and ideas that you are unlikely to find elsewhere in one place and as such it is invaluable to both the beginner and the advanced carpenter.

Contents

Storage box on wheels: 1

Storage boxes can make very attractive items of furniture, in addition to being extremely practical. The modern tendency towards smaller houses and rooms means that storage planning becomes increasingly important. When articles are inconvenient to store in one place, the problem can often be overcome by using storage boxes. This basic unit affords scope for personal design and it is easy and inexpensive to make.

This unit, because of its simple structure, is a good introduction to carpentry. The work involved provides practice in the basic technique of glued and pinned butt joints, and the use of some important tools. Basically all furniture is of either frame or box construction. As the storage box uses both methods, the experience of making it will assist the handyman in a wide variety of projects later on.

If the box is required for some purposes its interior may have to be divided. Three different uses are illustrated here, and many more variations could be added. Handles can be attached, and the surfaces can be painted, polished, or covered with material or wallpaper.

Buying tools

When buying tools, quality is a prime consideration. With percussion or impelling tools, such as a hammer or screwdriver, an inexpensive item will often serve—although there is nothing more annoying, when you are half-way through a job and the shops are closed, than having a hammer head part permanently from its handle. But with saws, chisels and other cutting tools, the best buy is the best you *can* buy. In the long run, you will save money.

In this and subsequent chapters, the tools listed have been chosen to give the maximum versatility for the handyman who wants real 'mileage' for the money he spends on equipment.

Tools required

The tools needed for making the wheeled storage box are:

Carpenter's folding rule either 3ft or 1m long. Since (in Britain) some building materials come in metric sizes and some still in imperial sizes, a rule marked with both is handiest. For longer measurements, as when making fitted furniture, a *steel tape* is used. The best sort has a square case measuring exactly 2in. across; it is handy for taking 'inside' measurements—for example,

across the back of an alcove.

Try square with a fixed blade. This is essential for seeing that timber is square and for marking lines at right angles to the edges. Eight inches (203mm) or 9in. (228mm) is the most useful size; it is wide enough to cover most shelves, for example, but not too unwieldy to use on a narrow moulding.

Marking knife for scoring lines across the grain of the wood. It marks more accurately than a pencil and, by severing the fibres on the wood surface, helps ensure a clean cut with saw or chisel. A handyman's knife, such as the Stanley model with replaceable blades, will serve both as a marking knife and for several other jobs.

Panel saw about 22in. (550mm) long with ten points (teeth) to the inch. It is designed for finishing work, such as cutting mouldings, but will serve at a pinch for almost anything—from ripping (down the grain) or cross-cutting (across the grain) in heavy timber down to quite fine bench work.

Tenon saw about 12in. (305mm) long with 14 points to the inch. The tenon saw has a stiffening rib along the back of the blade to help you cut a dead straight line. Used for fine cutting, it is essential if your ambitions lie in furniture making.

Bench hook to hold timber steady when using a tenon saw. It is usually home-made (see instructions below).

Plane. There are many different types of plane,

but the handyman's best 'all-rounder' is a smoothing plane about 9¾in. (250mm) long with a 2in. (52mm) cutting edge. The Stanley No.4 is a good example.

Claw hammer for driving and removing nails. Hammers come in several patterns and weights, and should be chosen to suit the individual's strength. An 8oz or 10oz will probably be best.

Bradawl for making 'start holes' for screws, in the absence of a drill.

Screwdriver about 10in. (254mm) long, to fit No.6 screws.

Nail punch to drive pin or nail heads below the surface of the wood. When the punch holes are filled and smoothed down, a better surface is obtained than one with exposed nail heads. Nail punches are also used for a variety of other jobs, for example:—to make 'start holes' for the electric drill in awkward situations; to loosen the heads of old screws that the screwdriver cannot budge; and in skew-nailing, to prevent the hammer head from bruising the side of the timber. Since punches cost only pence, a range of three or four sizes is a useful investment.

The bench hook

Carpenters use the bench hook (Fig.1 is an exploded diagram) to hold timber steady while they are cutting it with a tenon saw. The length of batten or planking is held firmly against the upper 'lip' or edge, while the lower lip prevents the hook from slipping across the table or workbench. Since the upper lip is cut at an exact right angle, the experienced carpenter uses it as a guide while he cuts a straight line 'by eye'.

Although bench hooks can be purchased, they are so simple to make that it is usual to see the home-made variety in a workshop. And if you are starting off at carpentry, making a bench hook will show you how to measure, mark, cut and fasten timber without a disaster—if you make a bad job, you can afford to throw it away and start again.

For materials, you need a rectangle of wood about 12in. x 10in. x 1in. thick (or 300mm x 250mm x 25mm) and two pieces of batten 2in. x 1in. (or 50mm x 25mm) about 8in. (or 200mm) long. But the dimensions are not critical; somewhere about this size will do.

Offcuts of wood are quite good enough, but make sure that none is warped; otherwise, the hook will rock and cause inaccurate cutting.

Measuring and marking

'Measure twice, cut once' is the first principle of carpentry. It saves a lot of waste!

When measuring with a folding rule (or any other measuring stick of considerable thickness), always stand the rule on edge so that the lines on the rule actually touch the timber at the points where you want to mark it (Fig.2). This will avoid sighting errors of the kind shown.

Timber is almost never exactly straight. So you will find, if you try to mark right round a

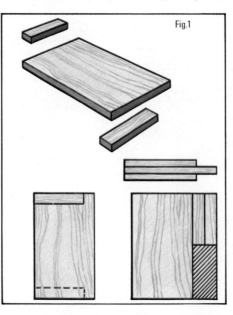

Fig.1

Right. Hessian for the 'bar', paint for the toy box, felt for the sewing box—each box is finished to suit its intended use.
Fig. 1 (left). An exploded view of the bench hook. This can be cut from offcuts of any reasonably good timber.

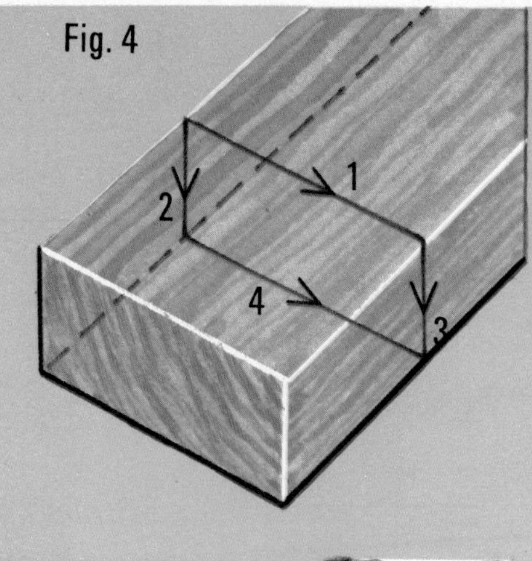

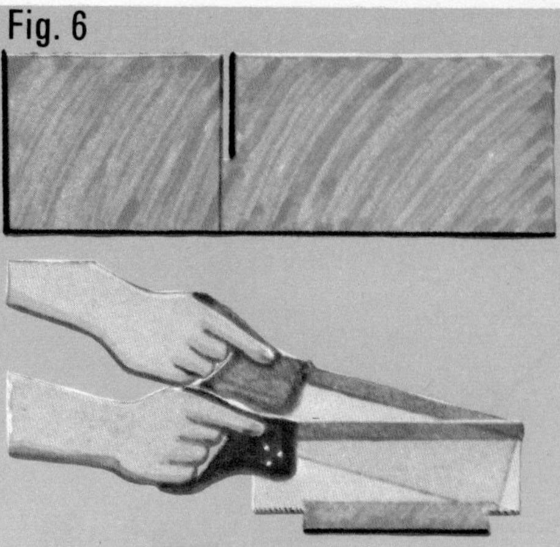

Measuring and sawing timber

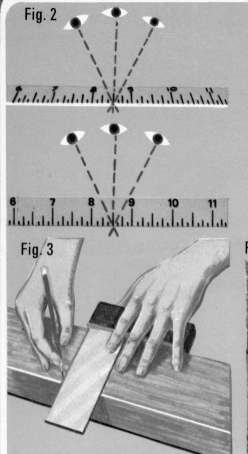

Fig. 2. If the rule markings are not touching the surface of the wood, inaccuracies will result. A folding rule, because of its thickness, is more likely to create this problem.
Fig. 3. The correct method of using the try square and marking knife or pencil.

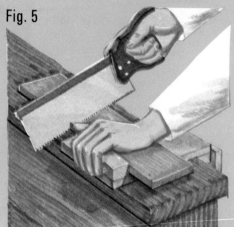

Fig. 4. How to mark a sawing line round a piece of timber. Note that lines *1* and *4*, and *2* and *3*, run in the same *direction*. This helps ensure a dead square cut.
Fig. 5. Using the tenon saw and bench hook. Start by steadying the blade with your left thumb while you draw it back a few times.

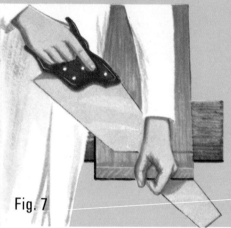

Fig. 6. Start the saw cut with the blade at an angle of 45°. As you proceed, gradually lower it until it is almost horizontal.
Fig. 7. Using a panel or cross-cut saw. Steady the work with your left hand until the offcut is nearly severed, then hold the offcut to prevent it splintering away.

board in a continuous line before cutting it, that you usually finish at a different point from where you started; the slight error caused by the curve in the board has 'compounded'. On a piece of planed 'inch by inch', the variation will probably be negligible. But on rough-sawn heavy timber—a 'four by two', say—you could easily find yourself $\frac{1}{8}$in. or even $\frac{1}{4}$in. out of line. The problem then becomes, 'Where *do* I cut?', and some poor joints can result.

So it is good practice to get into the habit of marking always in the correct order, (Fig.4).

The first stage of making the bench hook, then, is to mark a 'good' end on each of the battens. Use the try square as shown in Fig.3, pushing it against the timber with the thumb of your left hand and holding the blade flat with your fingers. Hold the blade of the marking knife against the blade of the try square, and score a line towards you across the timber. Working in the order given above (you will have to swap hands at one stage), score lines on the other three surfaces.

Using the tenon saw

The next stage is to use the tenon saw to cut the batten. Since you have no bench hook—

yet—you will need a substitute (the chopping board, clamped to the table with the mincer?) and perhaps some help to hold the work steady. What you will try to do is to saw on the waste ('wrong') side of the marked line, so that the line is just barely visible after the cut is made. In fact, you should *always* cut on the waste side of the line, not down the middle; this avoids the possibility of cutting 'short'.

Hold the tenon saw with its teeth almost parallel with the surface of the wood (Fig.5). Use your left thumb to guide the blade while you make your starting cut by drawing the saw backwards two or three times. Now try to saw smoothly and easily, using as much length of saw as possible for each stroke and letting the weight of the saw do the work. (Short, jerky strokes and heavy pressure will simply carry the saw off line.) Keep your line of vision over the saw to help you cut straight. When you reach the bottom of the cut, use three or four extra strokes to make sure you do not leave a fringe of fibres protruding.

If at your first attempt you have cut a squared line, the marking line will still be faintly visible all round. If not, call this the 'bad' end of the batten—and start again!

Once you have two battens with true ends, use the same marking and cutting process to square the ends of the 12in. x 10in. board. This time, use the panel saw, holding it at a slightly 'steeper' angle.

Nailing

If you 'can't drive a nail straight', do not worry—carpenters seldom do, either. A nail driven straight does not always have great holding power. So, in most jobs, alternate nails are driven at opposing angles for greater strength. For the bench hook, you should use the technique known as 'dovetail nailing' (Further details of nailing techniques are in the next chapter). Since the hook will have to withstand considerable pressure in use, you will need six 1$\frac{1}{4}$in. (31mm) panel pins, plus wood adhesive, for each batten.

Start by placing one batten along the top left-hand corner (as you look down at it) of the hook board, and drive one nail at each end until it is just catching the board below. Make sure you hold the nail firmly between thumb and forefinger, because the greater the length of nail that is held firmly the less likely it will be to bend. Drive with a short upswing and a full

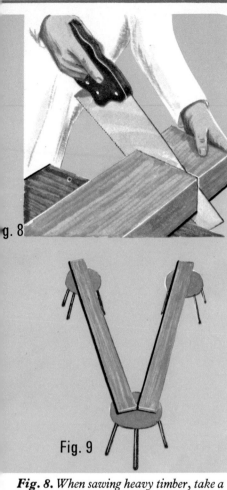

Fig. 8. *When sawing heavy timber, take a firm grasp of the off-cut when you are near the end of the sawing line.*
Fig. 9. *A suitable temporary support for sawing a large panel. There are many other ways in which you could improvise an adequate support.*

'follow-through', for the same reason. If the hammer tends to 'skid' off the pins it is probably because the face is dirty; clean it by rubbing it with a piece of sandpaper.

With your first two nails part-driven, lift the batten off the base and spread some pva adhesive thinly along it. Replace the batten, check that it is properly aligned—the part driven nails will stop it skidding about on the glue—and drive home the two nails. On the last few hammer strokes in particular, try to keep the face of the hammer parallel with the wood surface, to lessen the risk of hammer 'bruises'. Now drive in the four intermediate nails.

The opposite batten is fastened on in the same way as the first. Note that it, too, goes on the left-hand side and not (unless you are ambidextrous!) diagonally opposite the first one.

Materials for the storage box

The storage box has dimensions of 2ft 2in. x 1ft 6in. x 1ft 4in. (661mm x 457mm x 407mm). The complete carcase can conveniently be cut from a piece of 6ft by 3ft (or 2m by 3m) plywood, although a partitioned box would need a larger sheet. For a box this size plywood, $\frac{1}{2}$in. (13mm) thick is required. If cutting the

panels is too daunting a proposition, ask your DIY dealer to cut them, using the dimensions in Fig. 10 as a guide.

In addition to the panels, you will need two 7ft 6in. (2.4m) lengths of 2in. by 1in. (or 50mm by 25mm) wood batten; several dozen 1¼in. (31mm) panel pins; four castor wheels with screws; one tube of pva wood adhesive.

Cutting the panels

The panels are first marked out on the sheet plywood; then cut; then planed down slightly to the marked size.

If you intend cutting the panels from a single sheet, measure the outlines according to Fig.10 Use the try square and marking knife for marking at right angles to the edges. Then extend the lines with the rule and marking knife. You must allow between the panels enough space for both the saw cut and for planing—$\frac{1}{8}$in. should be adequate. If you have no other straight-edge long enough to cover the longer dimensions, use the 'manufactured' edge of the first panel you cut out as a check that your other lines are straight.

The fine-toothed panel saw listed above is well suited for cutting plywood. A coarser saw, with fewer teeth or 'points' to the inch, would produce bad splintering along each side of the cut. Before beginning to cut, ensure that the plywood is placed on a suitably smooth surface that will not rock or slip, and that the line the saw blade has to travel is clear of obstructions. Accurate sawing requires a good working

position. Your feet should be slightly apart and your body balanced so that your sawing arm is free to move without hitting your body; if this should happen, the saw will wobble and work away from the marked line. Like the tenon saw, the panel saw demands an easy, flowing movement. Your job is to guide, withdraw and steady the saw; the cutting action comes from the saw's own weight.

As you near the end of the saw cut, you will need someone to hold the panel you are cutting off so that it does not wrench away from the sheet and leave great splinters. You cannot solve this problem by laying the sheet across two planks and sawing down the middle; the sheet will merely sag inwards into a slight V-shape and jam the saw.

Cut the two sides, two ends, and transverse partition (matching the ends) if wanted, but do not cut the top or bottom yet. Leave these until the box is assembled, when you can adjust their size to match any slight variation in your outer 'walls'.

Fig. 10. *The plywood sheet: an exploded view showing the cut panels in order of assembly. 'Label' each panel with a pencil before starting work. Note that the end panels must be shorter than the side panels by the thickness of the lid. Check this before cutting, otherwise the finished lid will not sit flush with the side panels, and you will have unnecessary planing to do.*

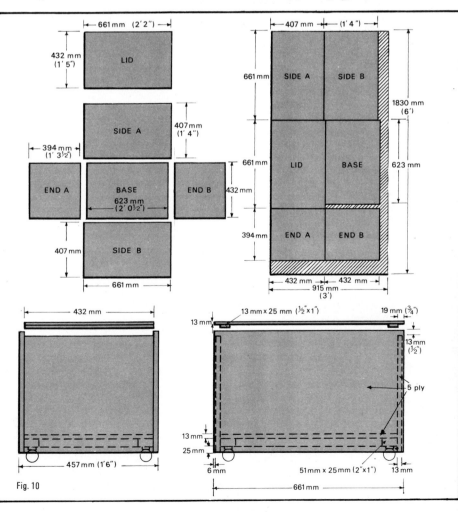

Fig. 10

Storage box on wheels: 2

Planing is one of the most important arts in carpentry. It isn't just done to remove surplus wood; most really superb woodwork finishes depend on the plane for essential preparatory work. The second stage of building the wheeled storage box introduces one of the most basic techniques in planing—the edge cutting and trimming of plywood sheets. It also introduces joining techniques for sheet materials.

Planing the panels

Using the plane, smooth the edges of all four panels down to your knife-marked lines. A sharp plane blade is essential. Blunt cutting tears the surface of the wood, making it unsightly and sometimes unusable. Set the plane blade to 'fine' (with very little blade showing). When planing, take a firm stance behind the work, making sure the panel is secure. In the absence of a vice or clamp, this is best done by wedging the panel, upright, into the corner of a room. The panel is held in place with the inside of your foot, and you can comfortably plane the top half nearest to you. The panel is then reversed, and the other half can be planed.

Hold the plane firmly with both hands and glide the plane forward over the panel, making the strokes as long and as even as possible. It is most important to maintain even pressure throughout the planing. Too much pressure at the beginning will 'round off' the corner of the panel, while too much pressure at the finish of the stroke will 'bow' the panel inwards. Test frequently by holding the panel up so that your eye can sight down the edges being planed; a deviation of even a fraction of an inch can be seen this way.

As you plane, make sure your edges are kept at right angles by frequent checks with the try square. To do this, fit the square snugly into the corner of each panel; the inside of the handle and the inside edge of the blade should line up exactly with the edge on the panel. Make sure that each pair of panels is identical in size.

Assembling the carcase

Next, you must mark the panels for assembly. The two end panels will be set in (recessed) by

Opposite. Another use for the box-on-wheels. This is a storage unit for records, avoiding the necessity of carrying piles of records to and from the record player. The range of alternative uses is limitless.

¼in. or 6.5mm, so a nailing line must be drawn along the outside of each side panel opposite where the end panel butts. Measure a point ½in. or 13mm inward from the edge of each panel, then line the ruler along the points and draw a line through. With the bradawl, make start holes along the line for the nails at 2in. or 50mm intervals, then drive each nail through the panel so that the tip is just protruding through the opposite side; this will help locate the side panel to the end panel.

Nailing is much easier when the wood to be nailed is resting on a solid surface. For this job, the easiest way is to make a kind of 'table' out of the two end panels, with the side panel resting on top of them. If you place the farthest end panel against a wall (Fig. 2), it is easy to steady the side panel while you nail it.

Use dovetail nailing. Spread a thin film of pva adhesive over both surfaces. Now locate an end panel, make sure that there is an even ¼in. or 6.5mm overlap by measuring from the end, and hammer home the nails.

When you have nailed on both sides, use the hammer and nail punch to punch the nail heads just below the surface of the wood. Do this before the adhesive starts to set as the punching action helps bring the surfaces closer together, ensuring a stronger joint.

Once the box is assembled, before leaving it for the adhesive to set, measure the diagonals to ensure that the box is square. Run the ruler across from corner to corner; each diagonal should measure the same. If not, slight hand pressure will adjust the corners. The assembly must be left on a level surface to set, otherwise twisting will occur.

Fitting the bottom frame

Battens are fitted as a frame round the underside of the base panel to stiffen the box and provide a mounting for the wheels. Do not measure the lengths of batten with a ruler; instead, use the 'direct' method. Hold the batten along the inside edge of the box and mark the inside length on the batten with the blade of the marking knife (Fig.3). This eliminates mistakes in transferring measurements from a ruler. Cut the four lengths of batten with the tenon saw, using the bench hook to steady the timber. Remember to cut on the 'waste' side of the line. Check that the four battens fit together snugly inside the carcase.

Now use the same 'direct' method, by placing the carcase on your sheet of plywood, to measure and mark the bottom panel. Cut it out with the panel saw. Make sure that it, too, fits snugly, paring it down with the plane if necessary.

Fig. 1 (*top*). *Checking a frame for squareness. Each diagonal is measured from corner to corner, and both sets of measurements should be identical. If they are not, the 'long' corners' must be pressed inwards. A smaller frame or unit could be checked with the try square to ensure that the edges are at right angles.*
Fig. 2 (*middle*). *Three panels can be formed as a 'table' for nailing the butt joints. One upright panel and the far end of the top panel should be placed against a wall and the whole assembly kept rigid by the pressure of your hand pushing it against the near end of the top panel. This keeps the panels firm against the wall.*
Fig. 3 (*bottom*). *A batten is marked 'direct' over the carcase into which it will be fitted. Direct marking eliminates errors in transferring measurements from the rule to the working surface of the wood. Because of the greater accuracy achieved, this method should be used whenever possible in preference to the rule transfer method.*

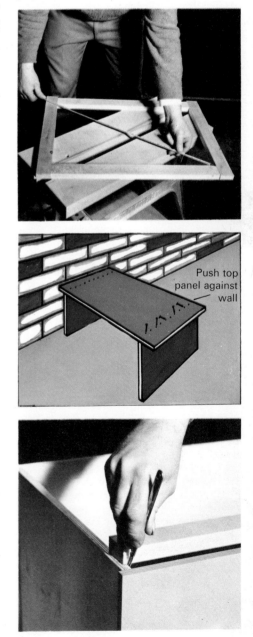

Push top panel against wall

11

The next step is to fasten the battens and bottom panel together so they can be fitted into the box as one unit. Mark a nailing line 1in. or 25mm inwards from the edge all round the top face of the base panel and make start holes for nails at 2in. or 50mm intervals along the line. Drive the nails in so that the tips are fractionally protruding through the other side. Spread adhesive on both panel and batten surfaces to be joined, place battens in position and nail into place. (The nails are driven in through the ply panel first because this ensures that the nail grips the full thickness of the panel, while still leaving an adequate length through the batten. It is a general rule in nailing that the thinner timber is nailed to the thicker timber when possible.)

When the adhesive on the base panel 'sub-assembly' has set, fit it in the bottom of the box, planing down any edges that make fitting difficult. The base is inset or recessed by 1in. or 25mm. Check that this recess is the same depth all round by making a mark on the inside of each side or end panel about halfway along. Then see that the battening of the base panel is level with these marks all round.

Before nailing the base in position, make sure that the recess is not too deep for the castor wheels. If it is, and the castors cannot move round freely, the depth of the recess will have to be reduced.

Now nail the base in place through the outside of the side and end panels. To make a neat job, mark a line round the outside of the carcase at a depth equal to the depth of the recess, plus half the depth of the batten. In this case the line would be drawn 1½in. or 38mm deep.

Making the lid

(If you intend covering the box with wallpaper or fabric, leave the lid until the covering has been completed, otherwise the thickness of the material may make the lid too tight.)

The lid fits *between* the side panels and *over* the end panels and is, in effect, countersunk. This is a removable lid—without hinges—and battens will have to be joined to the bottom of the lid, and recessed, so that the lid will not slip off in use. As the lid fits between the two side panels, it needs only two battens slotting inside the two end panels to make it secure, although you may like to fit battening all round for a neater finish.

Cut and plane the lid to shape, making it a loose fit (about $\frac{1}{16}$in. or 2mm undersize) to leave room for the paint. Then carefully mark lines on the underside of the lid just inside each end panel; this can be done using the 'direct' method of marking. Cut two (or four) lengths of batten to fit, not too tightly, inside this line. Spread adhesive on the surfaces to be joined and place in position on the lid. Using only one nail per batten, lightly nail in position. You can now place the lid in position to check whether it fits. If it does not, it is easy to re-place the batten(s). When the fit is perfect, nail the battens securely, as before, through the ply lid.

Finishing off

Every nail head must be punched in. Carefully fill all the holes left by the recessed nail heads with a cellulose filler such as Polyfilla and,

when it is dry, sand smooth with grade 0 glasspaper. If you intend to paint it, the storage box should be finished by the same method used for whitewood furniture—painted with primer, undercoat and the top coat. If it is to be wallpapered, or covered in fabric, thinly coat the whole surface of the box with pva adhesive and leave it to dry. This prevents stains coming through from the wood, and provides a good 'base' for applying the covering.

The castors are screwed in position after the finishing and decorating work has been done.

Making the partitions

The partitioning has been omitted from the general construction details, because in a general purpose box none might be needed, while boxes for specific purposes would require differing numbers of partitions.

Constructing a partition to divide the box in half (across its width, for example) is quite easy. Measure and cut the partition and check that it fits. On the outside of the side panels, mark the exact middle at the top and bottom edges. Draw a nailing line between the two marks. Drive a nail through about 2in. or 50mm inwards from each end of the line, so that the points are just protruding on the inside. The partition panel can now be located on the nails, and the nails driven home. This method ensures that the nails are driven into the middle of the partition, and avoids splitting the edges. A further two nails can now be placed at equal distances inside the first two.

Any number of parallel partitions can be added, using the same procedure. For T-shaped, H-shaped or more elaborate forms of partitioning, make up the partitions as a complete sub-assembly before dropping it into the box and fixing from the outside.

Storage tray

A useful fitment, especially for a toolbox or sewing box, is a tray that fits inside the top of the box so that small items can be stored there, leaving room for larger items underneath. This is begun by fitting lengths of 1in. x 1in. or 25mm x 25mm batten below the inside top

edge of the side panels. The battens will provide a lip, or rail, to hold a panel of ¼in. or 6mm plywood on which the tray is built up.

To fit the rail batten, mark a line along the inside of the side panels. Remember to allow enough depth to accommodate: the thickness of the plywood main lid; the battening underneath the lid; the thickness of the tray base itself; and the depth of the partitions or receptacles fixed to its surface. The *top* of the rail batten must be on the *lower* side of the line.

Some kind of support will be needed while the batten is glued and pinned from the inside—otherwise you risk knocking out the side panel. The best idea is to lay the box on its side on a table. Hammering in a confined space is difficult. Two tips to make it easier: **1,** drive the nails through the batten before you put it in the box. **2,** Use the nail punch to drive the nails home, hitting with the *side* of the hammer.

Wood or plywood tray partitions are measured (to dimensions suiting the items you will store), marked, cut and fitted to the tray base by the same methods you used in making the wheeled box itself. Since the joints are carrying little weight or stress, pva adhesive is quite strong enough to hold them together, provided the edges are straight. So you need use only tiny nails to fasten the joints while the glue dries.

Alternatively, you can fit a plastic sewing box to the tray base with small screws or bolts. To punch the necessary holes in the plastic, first mark the hole positions on the bottom of the box, keeping them well clear of the partitions. Now hold a nail or skewer in a pair of pliers while you heat it red-hot—a gas cooker flame will do the job in seconds—and quickly, before it can cool, drive the nail through the plastic. Be careful that the heated end of the pliers does not rest on the plastic, or the hole may be somewhat over-sized!

If the storage tray covers only half the inside area of the box, it can slide across the rail in the manner of a sliding door, providing access to the contents underneath without your having to remove the tray. But if it is to cover the whole inside area, handles may have to be attached at either end so that the tray can be lifted out.

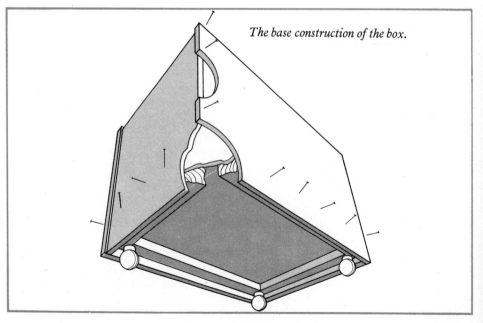

The base construction of the box.

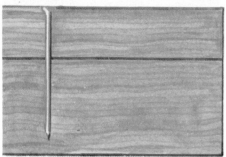

1: Always nail the thinner piece of timber to the thicker.

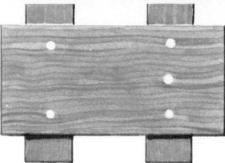

2: Do not over-nail. In this situation, two nails hold as well as three.

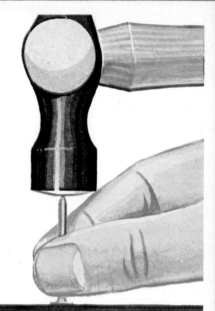

5: Blunt nail points help avoid splitting the wood.

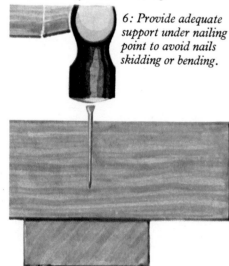

3: Nailing overhead, lean backwards and use normal 'forehand' nailing stroke.

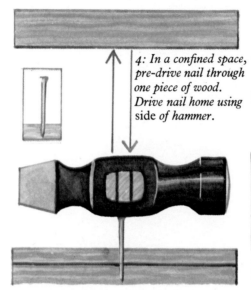

4: In a confined space, pre-drive nail through one piece of wood. Drive nail home using side of hammer.

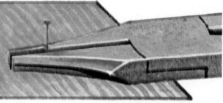

8: Pincers or pliers hold nails too small to be gripped by finger and thumb.

6: Provide adequate support under nailing point to avoid nails skidding or bending.

7: Block of wood under hammer avoids bruises while extracting nails. For big nails, extend hammer handle with length of pipe for extra leverage.

10: For 'secret' nailing, lift surface with chisel and drive nail under the paring.

11: Iron and damp cloth lifts hammer bruises from new woodwork.

9: Dovetail nailing — nails at opposing angles — makes stronger joint than straight nailing.

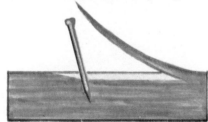

Glue paring back in place after nail is driven.

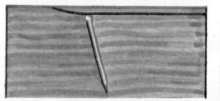

12: Skew nailing locks timber framing firmly in place.

Build a roomy bookcase

This bookcase is practical, attractive, and easy to make. The chipboard, available in a selection of veneered surfaces, enables you to match the finish with your existing furniture.

The bookcase is made in 9in. by ⅝in. or 230mm by 15mm chipboard, with the rear panel in ¼in. or 6.5mm gaboon plywood.

Making it will introduce you to two new tools, the plough plane and the paring chisel; and to the techniques for making a rebate joint and a stopped housing joint.

About chipboard

Chipboard is a versatile material that is a cheaper alternative to solid wood. It is produced by bonding wood chippings with synthetic glue under heat and pressure. Available in a wide variety of lengths, widths and thicknesses, the unsurfaced board is termed chipwood in Britain (the names vary in other countries), but this project uses the type that has the surfaces veneered with hardwood (or laminated plastic) and, as such, is called chipboard.

Veneered chipboard is available in a variety of wood surfaces, but for reasons of manufacturing economy you cannot always get the same veneer on all sides and edges. For instance, a relatively expensive wood such as teak might be surfaced on five sides of a board, with one face in mahogany. This is fine if you are making furniture that has an 'under' or 'inside' surface that will not be seen; but for this project you need to start with all facings in the same wood— or fit the 'odd' face inside the case and tone it to balance.

Working in chipboard

Chipboard, although easy to work, is easily bruised. Even small wood chippings on a bench cause indentations if a board is placed over them and pressed down. Always provide a clean, smooth surface to work on.

The veneer will tend to flake or chip during sawing—this is more apparent on the underside of the cut—and the coarser the teeth of the saw, the worse the flaking will be. So always use the finest saw blade possible.

Flaking can be eliminated if the veneer is scored with the marking knife before you start sawing. When marking out any lines that will be

Left. The finished bookcase, an attractive addition to any home. The unit could also be used as a china cabinet.

sawn or chiselled, cut right through the veneer, using several light strokes rather than one heavy one. Then, if you follow the correct procedure and saw on the waste side of the line, the veneer will not chip at all.

Tools required

Some of the tools have been introduced in earlier chapters—a light hammer; fine tooth panel saw; 12in. or 300mm tenon saw; try-square; marking gauge; marking knife; ¾in. bevel edge chisel; and a fine nail punch. In addition you will require:

Plough plane. This plane 'ploughs' a groove through wood. The width of the groove is set by the size of the plane blade. The plough is guided along the groove by a fence or runner, which can be adjusted.

Paring chisel, ½in. or 15mm, for forming and cleaning out housing joints.

Materials

The quantity of chipboard can easily be estimated from the drawing (Fig. 1). Allowing about an inch or 25mm of wastage for each section of board, you require six 31in. lengths. Other materials :–

A 22in. by 31in. sheet of gaboon plywood, ¼in. or 6.5mm thick.

A small roll of veneer strip, for replacing veneer where the chipboard has been exposed.

Panel pins, 1½in. or 40mm.

Pva wood adhesive.

Proprietary wood stopper to match the veneer. If you cannot get a matching colour, buy two tubes of stopper, one darker and one lighter, and blend to match; or use ordinary putty, tinted. (If you make a practice of keeping on hand three tubes of tint for oil-based—one dark brown, one red and one yellow—you will be able to match most timber colours.)

Sliding glass doors, if required, have to be made up by your glass merchant. Do not order until the case is finished, and the runners inserted. Then measure carefully.

The final finish will require turpentine substitute (mineral turps); clear matt polyurethane; fine glasspaper; grade 0 steel wool, and teak oil.

Marking out

All the lines that are to be sawn or chiselled out must be cut with the marking knife. Any lines used for location, and which will not be cut, are marked with the pencil—the lines can then be rubbed out when no longer required.

Carefully measure each length of chipboard, double-checking each measurement. For each length, score a line heavily across the veneer using the try-square and marking knife. Repeat this until you have cut straight through the veneer. Follow this line right round the board, using the method which is given in CHAPTER 1, 'Measuring and Marking' to ensure that the lines on both sides of the board correspond with each other.

You will now have a line which, if sawn properly, along the waste side, will allow the board to fall neatly apart without damage to the veneer.

It is best at this stage to cut all the lengths you need—two sides, top, two shelves, and plinth (the panel below the bottom shelf). This allows you to lay out the panels in rough form to check that all dimensions are correct.

The rebate joint

Joints in carpentry have two quite separate objectives—strength, and appearance. Many are designed to conceal the end-grain of timber, which is less attractive than side grain and often more difficult to finish smoothly.

The rebate—sometimes spelled or pronounced 'rabbet' or even 'rabbit'—is a stepped joint. It is often used to hide the sawn edges of panelling, as in panelled doors and the backs of furniture. It is also used, as in fitting the top of this bookcase, to provide a joint which is both more rigid than a butt joint (because there are three separate touching surfaces) and neater in appearance.

In this project, you start by marking out the rebate joints for the top. These are located at the top inside edges of the two side panels, and the inside ends of the top panel.

Set the marking gauge to half the depth of the chipboard. Holding it firmly against the top inside face of one of the end panels, lightly scribe a line along the veneer. Do not press too hard or the veneer will chip. Repeat on the opposite side panel. With the gauge set to the same depth, run a line along the top end of each side panel. Now lay the blade of the try-square along the scribed lines, and sever the veneer with the marking knife.

The marks for the same joint are now made along the inside face of the ends of the top panel, and along the extreme ends of the top panel. Fig. 7 shows how the joints will match after waste material has been cut away.

The same procedure is carried out along the edges of the side and top panels, and of the bottom shelf, where the inside back of the case will be located. This rebate is for the plywood back.

The housing joint

Housing joints, like rebates, are used both for extra strength and for better appearance. In a bookcase, they provide a solid support for the shelves, which otherwise would rest solely on the strength of nails driven through the sides. At the same time, the cut ends of the shelves are tucked neatly out of sight.

A 'stopped' housing joint is one which, instead of running for the full width of the board, stops just short, giving a neater finish at the most conspicuous point—in this project, at

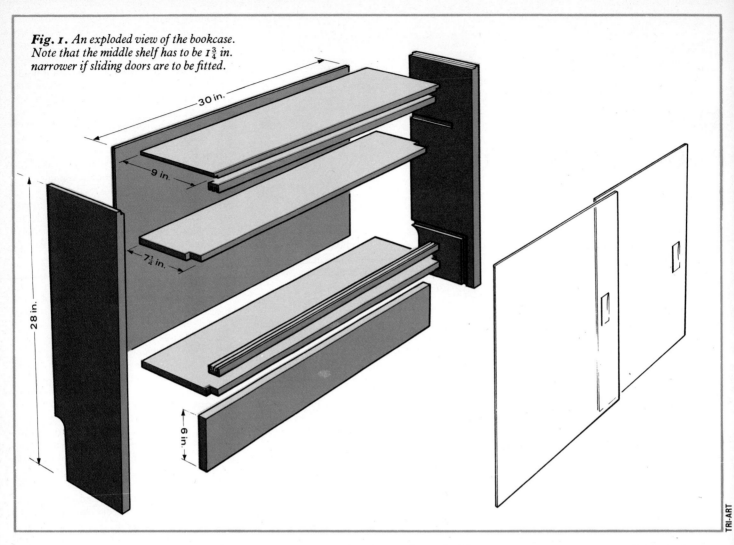

Fig. 1. *An exploded view of the bookcase. Note that the middle shelf has to be 1¾ in. narrower if sliding doors are to be fitted.*

30 in.

9 in.

7¼ in.

28 in.

6 in.

the front edge.

To mark out for the stopped housing joints, start by clamping the two side panels together. The lines marked for the rebate along the inside faces should touch each other; this end of the pair of panels represents the top of the bookcase. Decide where the joint for the first shelf will be and, with the try-square, mark two lines across the panel the thickness of the chipboard. Use the direct marking system for this by using another piece of board.

These marks run across what will be the back of the case.

Repeat the two marks at the point where the bottom shelf will be located.

Separate the side panels. Lay the try-square blade along the inside of one panel, and draw a line, with the marking knife, from the topmost mark, along the face, to within 1½in. of the opposite edge of the board. Repeat this with the next mark, and you will have twin parallel lines, ⅝in. apart, running from the 'back' of the panel, and stopping 1½in. short of the opposite side. At this point run the marking knife between the two lines, joining them. You now have a clearly defined outline that will have to be chiselled out to house the ends of the top shelf.

The same procedure is carried out for the bottom shelf. But in this case, when the outline has been marked out, an additional pair of lines are marked, beginning at the point where the housing joint 'stops', and running down to the bottom of the panel at right angles to the joint (Fig. 2).

Making the joints

Start with the stopped housing joint for the top shelf. Place one of the side panels on a clean bench, with the markings upwards. With the ¾in. chisel held vertically, lightly tap along the marking lines at the stopped end. The bevel edge of the chisel should be inside the joint. The idea is to remove the veneer for about 1½in. along the joint (Fig. 2). Once you have done this, the chipwood beneath must be removed down to half the thickness of the board. Do this by starting in the middle between the marked lines, chipping gently with the chisel and working outwards. It will chip quite easily. Blow into the joint as you work, to keep the space clear. You now have a rectangle, ⅝in. wide, about 1½in. long, and 5/16in. deep. Check the depth carefully —the whole joint depends on its being accurate.

The remaining two lines will be worked along with the tenon saw, the recess you have just made providing a clear area for the end of the saw blade.

Extend the width of the remaining marking lines with the chisel, so that you have a channel wide enough to take the tenon saw blade. This is done by running the chisel along the marked lines slightly inside the joint (Fig. 3), removing a sliver of veneer.

With the tenon saw, carefully saw along the

lines (Fig. 4) down to half the depth of the board.

Then, with the paring chisel, starting at the 'open' end of the joint, carefully chip a groove right along the joint (Fig. 5). Start with the chisel 'upside down'—that is, with the bevelled end facing downwards—and turn it over only to pare out the last few slivers of wood. (The reason for doing this is that, held 'right way up', the blade tends to dig in deeper and deeper, rather than to cut straight, because of the wedging action of the bevel.)

You have now made a stopped housing joint. Check with the edge of the try-square that it is flat along the bottom. Repeat this for the lower shelf. The only difference here is that once you have completed the stopped section of the joint, work out the section to take the plinth (Fig. 2).

The rebate Joints—for fitting the top panel to the sides, and the plywood sheet to the back— are slightly simpler to make. The plough plane cuts a rebate out of the edge of a piece of wood by cutting a deep narrow groove, to the depth required, along one side (Fig. 6). This is repeated along the other marking line, which is at right angles to the first one. The two grooves, when they meet, remove a square of wood, forming a step-shaped recess, or rebate (Fig. 7).

The most important point in cutting the rebate is to set the plane fence or guide to the correct width (Fig. 6). When using the plane, start the cutting near the *far* end of the line. For each short stroke you push the plane away from you, but the starting point of each successive stroke is a little nearer to you than the one before. In short, you work in a series of overlapping movements.

Assembly

Once you have made all the joints, you will have all panels ready to fit together like a jigsaw. Before you go any further, trial-assemble them, without glue, to make sure that they fit.

At this stage it is best to finish all the surfaces that will be on the inside of the bookcase. The method for this finish is given below.

To assemble, start by placing one of the side panels on the bench, 'inside' upwards. Spread adhesive along the housing joints where the shelf ends will be located, and stand each shelf end in the joint. Spread adhesive on the exposed ends of the shelves, and place the opposite side panel over the ends. You now have the shelves housed in the side panels.

While the assembly is in this position, drive panel pins through the outside of the side panel, which is resting on top of the upright shelves into the ends of the shelves. Place the pins at approximately 1½in. or 40mm intervals. With the punch, drive all heads below the surface.

Carefully lay the assembly down, and turn the whole unit over so that the opposite side panel can also be nailed to the shelves. With a damp cloth, remove immediately all traces of any glue that has been squeezed from the joints.

Next, stand the assembly upright. This will enable you to glue, place and pin the top panel to the side panels.

Now lay the unit down again, spread adhesive in the joints to take the plinth, and slide or tap this into place. Again be sure to wipe off any excess glue.

Check the frame for squareness by measuring diagonally from corner to corner. If the two diagonals are not identical, adjust by pressing the 'longer' side.

Leave it for the adhesive to set.

The back of the case frame has a rebate groove running round the inside edges. With the panel saw, cut the plywood sheet to fit snugly into this. As with the side panels, the plywood is fixed with adhesive and panel pins, but in this case the pins can be spaced more widely—say, at 3in. or 75mm intervals.

Sliding doors

If sliding doors, in glass or wood, are to be fitted, these should not be cut or ordered until the runners have been fixed. There are many types of proprietary runner, the most usual being

plastic channels that are nailed to the top and bottom panels. The top runner is deeper than the bottom one, so that doors, when fitted, can be inserted into the top runner first, then dropped into the bottom runner and still leave enough room to hold the top of the door.

For this reason, vertical door measurements are taken by measuring the distance between the base of each channel, and deducting the depth of the bottom channel.

When fitting plastic channelling especially, remember that it is easily bent out of line, and that jammed doors can result. So check carefully for straightness as you go.

Applying veneer

At certain points—the skirting recess, both ends of the top panel, and the bottoms of the side panels—the veneer will have been removed, exposing the chipwood. This is replaced from the roll of veneer strip.

Veneer strip is made with either an adhesive backing or a plain backing requiring pvc. Another type has a dry adhesive that melts when heated; this must be applied, and then pressed with a warm iron.

If any exposed areas are narrower than the adhesive strip, cut the veneer back with the marking knife until it fits. Then cut the strip to size and fix it according to the method advised by the supplier.

Fig. 2 (above). The end of a stopped housing joint, chiselled out ready for the next stage. This is the shelf-plinth junction.

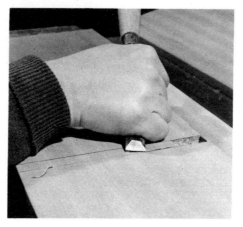

Fig. 3 (above). When the end of the stopped housing has been chiselled out, a groove for the saw blade is cut with a chisel.

Fig. 4 (above). With the tenon saw, carefully cut along the lines, down to half the depth of the board.

Fig. 5 (above). The stopped housing joint is completed by chiselling out the material between the lines cut by the tenon saw.

Fig. 6 (above). The plough plane cutting the first groove for the rebate joint. Another groove is then cut at right angles.

Fig. 7 (above). When the two rebate grooves have been cut, they are fitted to form the joints at the top of the bookcase.

17

Marking for a true fit

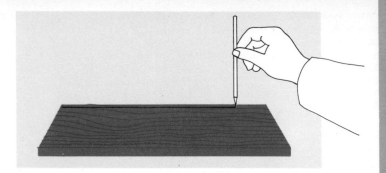

1: *A simple example of direct measuring is making a diagonal brace for a frame. The length and angle of the ends are marked by using the frame itself as a ruler.*

2: *To scribe the back of a shelf to a wall, run a pencil along the wall to trace its shape on to the shelf. Cut along the pencil line.*

3: *Shelves should be scribed to alcoves by making them slightly too large and jamming them in diagonally at the right height.*

4: *Fitting a shelf to a corner: scribe it first to one wall, then to the other (below). Use a block behind the pencil on irregular walls.*

This method is slightly inaccurate, because the second scribing and cutting process throws the first one slightly out of true.

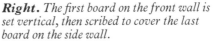

5: *Three stages in fitting T&G boarding to a chimney breast.* **Left.** *The first board is set upright with a spirit level and scribed to the back wall.* **Centre.** *The last board on the side wall is scribed flush with the corner, using the point of the pencil.*

Right. *The first board on the front wall is set vertical, then scribed to cover the last board on the side wall.*

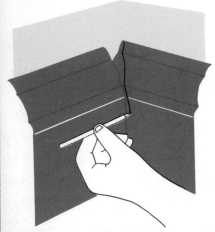

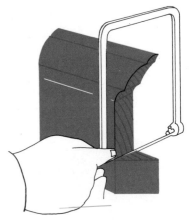

6: *Don't mitre skirtings at the corners; if they shrink, it leaves an ugly gap. Cut one piece off square and scribe the other to fit it.*

An alternative method: cut the end of one piece at exactly 45 degrees. Then use a coping saw to cut down the line the slanted

cut makes with the front surface. This will produce the right profile automatically, without the need for scribing.

If you always wanted to make your own furniture, but were frightened off by the apparent complexity of the job, here is your chance. You can make this elegant, professional-looking coffee table simply in a few hours, with a minimum of fuss and bother.

This project introduces a *halving joint* and a *'T' halving joint,* and the use of *screws and screw cups.* It begins by showing how to make a shooting board, a simple but necessary device that allows you to plane the end of a piece of wood exactly at right angles to the sides. Resist the temptation to make the coffee table first, because you will need the shooting board to help make a good job of it.

Modern coffee table: 1

Tools required

In addition to the tools listed in earlier chapters, the following will complete this project and set you up for most carpentry jobs you are likely to encounter.

Set of bevel-edge chisels. In this type of chisel, the sides of the blade are sloping, and so will not stick when being used to make a narrow crevice. It is a good idea to buy a matched set of chisels in sizes from $\frac{1}{4}$in. to $1\frac{1}{2}$in. (6mm-38mm, but chisels are not yet made in metric sizes). You will need only the widest of these at the moment, but the others will be useful later. Buy chisels with smashproof plastic handles that can be hit with a mallet. These are more expensive than the wooden kind, but will last longer because they do not split or fray.

Hand drill (the type that looks like an egg-beater) and a range of *twist drills* (cutters) which cut metal as well as wood, in all the sizes between 1/16in. and $\frac{1}{4}$in., or 1mm and 6mm. It is cheaper to buy each size separately, and not to get a made-up set. Drills fit into the *chuck* (holder) of the hand drill and are fixed in place by turning the outer ring of the chuck clockwise.

Countersink bit, for making recesses in wood to take the heads of screws.

No.10 'screw mate' cutter, such as the Stanley No. 1542A, for making the wide but shallow hole needed for a screw cup. These useful cutters are numbered in the same sizes as the screws they are for.

Edging cramps for holding the glued joints of the table together while they dry. G-cramps can be used, but edging cramps are more useful as they have an additional device to hold a third

edge to the main parts being clamped. Buy large ones. You can use large cramps for small jobs, but not small cramps for large jobs.

Woodworker's vice. Buy a simple vice that clips on to the edge of any table or bench. This type of vice comes with unpadded metal jaws, so cut two wood blocks about $\frac{1}{2}$in. (13mm) thick and fit them between the jaws to keep them from making marks on wood clamped in the vice. Glue or tape them lightly in place to stop them from falling out when the jaws are undone.

Marking gauge. This simple wooden tool scribes (scratches) a line parallel to the edge of a board. It consists of a wooden shaft with an adjustable crosspiece sliding up and down it. At one end of the shaft there is a small metal spike. You set the crosspiece with a rule to the desired distance from the spike, and slide the

Fig. 1 *(above, left). Chamfering the corner of the stop with a chisel. The tool should be held upright.*

Fig. 2 *(above, centre). Using a drill punch. The small dent it makes keeps the drill from slipping sideways.*

Fig. 3 *(above, right). The top plate held in place on its bearers by a cramp with jaws padded with scrap wood.*

Figs. 4-5 *(left). Two stages in marking the position of the bearers on the top plate. The line is squared first up the back edge of the plate, and then along the top face.*

tool up the edge of the piece of wood to be marked. The crosspiece keeps the spike a constant distance from the edge, and the spike scribes a straight line.

Making a shooting board

A shooting board is a device that overcomes the problems of planing the end grain of a piece of wood. If you try to do this without a shooting board, you will run into two problems. After a few strokes you will find that you have planed the far side of the wood lower than the near side. And the far edge of the wood will almost certainly split as the plane blade drags across it.

A shooting board surmounts the first problem by holding the plan and wood firmly at right angles to each other. It helps deal with the second by placing a *stop*, or wood block, against the far side of the piece you are planing.

You can make a shooting board out of any old wood you have around, provided that it is not warped. It does, however, have to be made accurately, or it will not plane at right angles. Size is not important. The dimensions given below should be taken as minimum sizes, except for the thickness of the top and its bearers, which should not be exceeded.

Plywood or blockboard are the most suitable materials for the two largest pieces, because they are both cheaper and less likely to warp than solid timber. The large bottom plate measures 9in. x 24in. (230mm x 610mm). The smaller top plate is 7in. x 24in. (180mm x 610mm). The wood for making these pieces should be ¾in. or 20mm thick, unless you have a very narrow plane, when it should be ½in. or 12mm thick.

The three bearers that space the top and bottom plates apart are ½in. thick in either case (though they can be less for very narrow planes), and measure 6½in. long by 2in. wide (or 165mm x 51mm). The stop should be made of a piece of good quality hardwood or hardwood ply 7in. x 2in. x 1in. (or 180mm x 51mm x 25mm). The grip on the bottom, which holds the device steady in use, should measure roughly 9in. x 2in. x 1in. (or 230mm x 51mm x 25mm) and can be made out of any timber. You will also need some adhesive and screws: nine 1in. No. 8s and four 1½in. No. 10s.

Mark out the pieces, and cut them out as described fully in CHAPTER 1. Make sure, by looking along each long edge, that none of them is in the least warped. Test the two large pieces for *winding* (twisting) by laying them down flat, putting a straight lath across each end and checking that the laths are parallel. If any piece of wood fails any of these tests, throw it away and cut another. This is particularly important in the case of the stop, which must be cut and finished with great accuracy.

Planing the pieces

The next stage is to plane an absolutely straight, accurate front edge along the top plate. The edge must be at right angles to the flat faces of the plate, because the plane slides along it and must have its cutting edge dead upright. When planing along the grain of a piece of wood, you can improve the accuracy of your work by pressing on the front of the plane at the beginning of each stroke, and

Fig. 6 (top). The parts of the shooting board — from top to bottom, the stop, the top plate, the three bearers, the baseplate and the 'hook' for fixing it to the bench.

Fig. 7 (next to top). Ensure that the stop is on straight before you screw it down. The slightest inaccuracy will affect everything planed on the board.

Fig. 8 (above). Using the shooting board to plane a piece of timber. The board keeps plane and wood exactly at right angles to each other.

gradually transferring the pressure to the rear during the stroke. Always hold the plane parallel with the line you are cutting along. The grain of wood never runs exactly straight. Plane with the slope of the grain (see Fig.9) and not against it, or the plane blade will catch on the ends of the fibres and produce a rough result.

When planing the end grain of a piece of wood, do not run the plane over the far edge of the surface, or it will split the wood. Plane from one edge to the middle and stop there (see Fig.10). Then turn the wood around and plane the other edge to the middle to finish the piece off. This will keep the end of the wood straight and symmetrical, though it will not be as well-finished as if you had used a shooting board.

Check the angle of the planed surface with a try square, and make sure of its straightness by looking along it from one end. Any curve in the wood is magnified when seen from a low angle.

Plane one of the narrow sides of the stop with particular accuracy. Then use a chisel to *chamfer* one corner of the opposite side (Fig.1). This means cutting the corner off at an angle of 45°. You will not need to hammer the chisel to cut the wood; just scrape the corner off bit by bit until you have removed about ⅛in. (6mm) from each side of the corner.

Marking up and assembly

Next, use a try square, ruler and marking knife to draw two lines on the base plate at right angles to its accurately planed edge, and 2in (51mm) from each end. These mark the position for the outside edges of the two outer bearers. Mark the inside edges another 2in. farther in. Then draw another line halfway along the board and two more lines 1in. (25mm) either side of it. These mark the position of the third bearer.

Draw a line up the centre of each bearer along its wide face and cross it at right angles with three lines, one in the middle and one 1in. (25mm) from each end. Then make a small x on the outer cross lines halfway between the centre line and the edge of the wood on one side of the centre line only, and mark the middle cross half way between the centre line and the opposite edge (you are in effect making a triangle). Punch a small dent on each x with a drill punch, nail punch or old blunt nail, to give the drill a spot to start on (see Fig.2). Put each bearer in turn on the baseplate accurately on its lines with its far end flush with the rear edge of the plate. Holding the bearer in place, drill a 5/64in. or 2mm hole through each x almost through the baseplate. Then remove the bearers and enlarge the holes in them (but not those in the baseplate) with the 11/64in. or 4.5mm drill. Use a countersink bit to open out the tops of the holes so that the screw heads will be level with the wood.

Spread a thin film of pva adhesive, such as Evo-Stik woodworking adhesive, on the bottom of each bearer and its place on the baseplate. Then put the bearers down in position and immediately screw them into the baseplate, using 1in. No. 8 countersink-head screws. It will help the screws to go in if you put a little wax polish or soap on them.

Now lay the top plate on the bearers exactly in position and hold it there while you mark the

position of the bearers on the plate's rear edge. Draw lines from that edge forward along the top to show where the bearers lie under the plate. Sketch in the position of the bearer's screws—freehand if your are confident enough (this is a precaution against putting the next screws on top of the bearer screws). Then mark the centre line of each bearer on the top plate. Make two x's on this line—one 1½in. (40mm) from the rear edge, and one 2in. (90mm) from the front edge.

Clamp the top plate in position with one of your G-cramps, 'padding' the jaws on each side of the board with a small square of scrap wood. Then drill a 3/32in. or 2.5mm hole through each x through the bearer and deep into the base. Enlarge the holes with a 13/64in. or 5mm drill in the top two pieces of wood only. You can drill to the exact depth (1in. or 25mm is about right) if you stick a piece of tape to the drill bit that distance from the end and stop drilling when the tape reaches the wood. Countersink the holes and unclamp the top

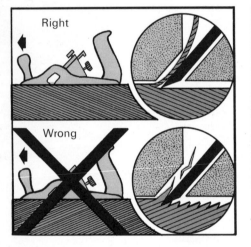

plate. Glue it to the bearers and screw it home with 1½in. No. 10 countersink-head screws.

The stop should be mounted on the top board with its centre just in from the centre of the right-hand bearer (to keep the screws from hitting each other). If you are left-handed, put it at the other end. Its exact position is not important, but what is vital is that its inside edge, on which the wood rests, is *exactly* at right angles to the front edge of the top plate. Check this with the try square. The stop should project 1/10in. (2mm) over the front edge. The chamfered corner should be at the front on the outside. Screw the stop down as you did the top plate, using the same size screws and holes. Do not glue it, because you will want to take it off sometimes for replacement or adjustment.

The final stage of the assembly is to glue and screw a grip on to the bottom of the plate. You can put it at the opposite end of the board from the stop, so that you can hook the board over the bench like a bench hook and plane away from you. If you prefer to plane from side to side, put the grip below the front of the board so that you can lock it in a vice sideways-on. Exact positioning is not important.

To finish the board, rub wax polish on the surfaces on which the plane slides to enable it to glide easily. The plane slides on its side on the baseplate, with its cutting edge touching the

near edge of the top plate. The first planing job is to plane the stop level with the top of the front board, but before you begin, make sure your plane is sharp and properly set, or you will wreck everything. Wood to be planed is set against the inside of the stop to hold it. You should occasionally check that the stop is still on straight.

The coffee table

The choice of wood for the table depends on you. The construction is suitable for both hardwood and softwood. A really elegant version for the living room can be made out of teak, using solid teak for the frame and teak-veneered blockboard for the top. The wood can be given a natural oiled finish with a subtle sheen which will blend in with any type of furniture, old or new.

A less expensive version of the table can be made out of softwood and a manufactured board. The frame can be made of good-quality pine, which has a clearly marked grain that

Fig. 9 (above left). Always plane with the grain of wood, and never against it, so that the plane iron cuts cleanly.

Fig. 10 (centre). When planing end grain without a shooting board, always plane from the outside edges to the middle, first from one edge, then from the other.

Fig. 11 (right). Slide a marking gauge against the grain, so that the slope of the grain holds it in place.

looks well when varnished; or it can be made of the cheapest type of softwood and painted. The top can be made from a chipboard with a top and bottom of plastic laminate such as 'Formica'; this comes complete with its own stick-on edging strip. Alternatively, you can use ordinary chipboard or blockboard and laminate it yourself; or a blockboard with a good quality surface; or (in some countries) a wide pine planking. If the top is made of chipboard or blockboard, it should be edged with a narrow wood strip to match the frame.

The lengths and sizes of the timber you will need are: for the top, a piece 18in. (457mm) wide, 44in. (1.13m) long, and ¾in. (63mm) thick. For the frame, a 7ft length of 2½in. x ¾in. (dressed, or planed, size). 2½in. is not a standard

width, but can generally be bought; otherwise, buy 3in. x ¾in. and plane it down. (The metric equivalent is a 2m length of 76mm by 19mm.) Also for the frame, a 12ft length of 2in x ¾in., or 3.5m of 51mm x 19mm.

These lengths allow 10 per cent extra for wastage, but you may find that the dimensions vary slightly from the measurements given—and not always by the same amount. Watch out for this and measure everything yourself.

You will also need seven 2½in. No.10 screws and screw cups, and four 1¾in. No. 8 'mirror' screws with decorative heads. If you are using teak, the screws must be brass or the natural oils in the wood will attack them. Buy a steel one of each size as well, to put in the screw holes first.

Starting work

Once you have bought the timber for the table, the next stage is to cut it roughly to length. Using the plan in CHAPTER 5, cut each part of the frame, making it ½in.-1in. (13mm-25mm) longer than it will finally be.

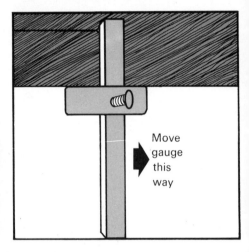

Move gauge this way

You may have had to buy timber 3in. (76mm) wide for the parts of the table 2½in. (63mm) wide. Reducing it to the correct width is quite simple. First, find out how wide your '3in.' timber actually is—planed timber, as bought from timber merchants, is generally narrower than its stated width because of the planing. Set your marking gauge to 2½in. (63mm), and slide it along each piece on both sides of the wood—but make sure it is next to the same edge on both sides. When using a marking gauge, always work *against* the grain (Fig. 11) so that the grain cannot carry the point of the gauge into the 'good' area of wood. If one edge of the wood looks better than the other, cut off the worse edge.

Clamp each piece of wood in turn in the vice and saw the edge off, keeping the inside edge of the saw at least ⅛in. (3mm) from the marked line on the waste side. Then plane down to the line, making sure you touch it exactly on both sides of the wood. Test that the edge is at right angles to the sides with a try square. Then, using a pencil, lightly mark the best-looking side of the wood with a looped 'l' and the best looking edge with a little 'x'. These conventional carpenter's marks are to show which side and edge will be on the outside of the work, where they can be seen. These surfaces are called the *face side* and *face edge*.

Modern
coffee table: 2

The halving joint is one of the most useful joints in carpentry. It is a means of joining the corners of a frame where moderate strength and a neat appearance are called for. The marking, sawing and chiselling techniques needed to make it are introduced at this stage.

Marking up the pieces

Once the pieces are cut a little over-size, mark them up accurately for final cutting. The pieces of the frame come in pairs, one at each end or side. Mark up each pair of pieces together, to make sure they come out the same length.

The marks made by a marking knife are quite deep and, of course, will not come out of the wood. For this reason, it is essential to mark only where you intend to cut. The halving joints used in this frame will be spoiled if marks are visible on the side of the wood opposite the cutout you make for the joint.

The four pieces that make up the rectangular central part of the table's frame are visible from both sides of the table. The face side (good side) of each piece should be the side that is cut out to make the joint, and the face edge the edge towards the inside of the rectangle.

Lay each matching pair of pieces in the vice, face edges uppermost. Measure them for length, but mark the upper surfaces only. Now measure 2in. (51mm) in from each of the end marks, and rule another two lines across both pieces of wood. Take the wood out of the vice and use a try square to continue the end marks right round the wood. Take the other pair of marks only part-way — across the face side, and halfway down each edge. These lines mark the cutouts for the halving joints (see Fig. 2).

Using the marking gauge

To 'halve' the timber, set your marking gauge as exactly as you can to $\frac{3}{8}$in. (9.5mm), and use it to scribe a short test line on one of the edges, but somewhere less than 2in. from the end, so that it will be covered up later. Then turn the gauge around and mark the same surface from the opposite side. If the two marks merge into one, you have set the gauge right. If they do not, adjust the gauge till they do.

Now scribe around the end of each piece, starting from one end of the cutout mark, continuing the 2in. (51 mm) to the end of the wood, around it and back up to the other end of the mark. Keep a wary eye on the grain of the

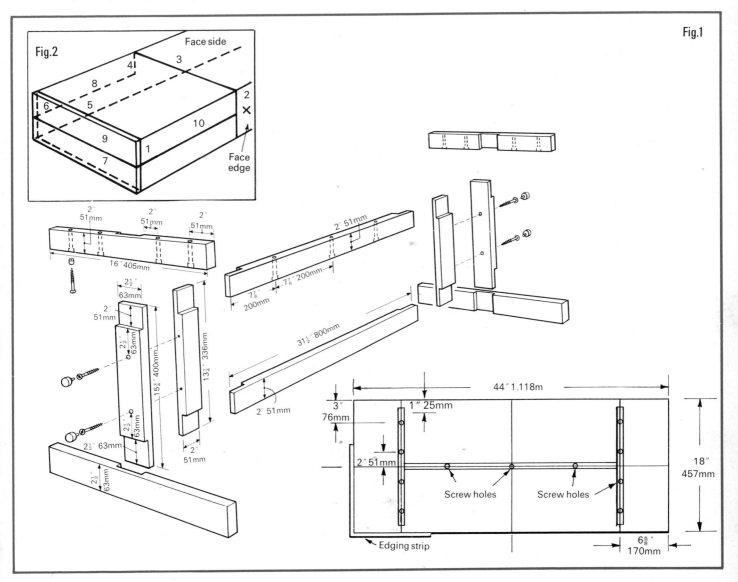

Fig.1

Fig.2 — Face side — 4 — 3 — 8 — 5 — 2 — 6 — X — 10 — 9 — 1 — Face edge — 7

wood as you use the gauge, because the grain can carry the gauge point off line. If you show signs of getting stray marks on the 'good' side (instead of 'waste' side) reverse the direction in which you are gauging so the grain helps keep you *on* line.

Sawing for a halved joint

When sawing a section out of a piece of timber, the 'rip' cut (running in the same direction as the grain) is done before the 'cross' cut (running across the grain). If you try to reverse the order, you will find that, before the rip cut is complete, the timber will split down to the cross-cut mark, leaving you with an unnecessary clean-up job with the chisel.

Really fine sawing depends largely on how you position your body. You should not stand square-on to the work, because your right elbow would hit your body as you draw the saw back. Stand with the work at your left side and cross your right arm over your stomach to reach it, moving your arm from side to side to saw. This position sounds a bit twisted, but will soon become familiar.

Keep the waste side of the sawing line on the far side of the saw, so that the scribed line is not masked by the saw blade, and keep your eye above the line of the saw. The near side of the saw blade should just cut the line in half.

To start your halved joint, set the wood upright in a vice with the face side away from you. Put your left thumbnail on the far end of the marked line. Lower the tenon saw until the blade just touches your thumbnail. Then make a tiny notch on the corner next to your thumbnail by drawing the saw blade back (see Fig. 5).

Continue to saw very gently, dropping the saw handle slowly until the blade is horizontal, and cut a groove about $\frac{1}{8}$in. (3 mm) deep along the end of the wood. The near side of this groove should just touch the marked line. (A common 'first time' mistake is to forget that the cut itself has width, and thus take out too much wood.)

Now lower the handle of the saw until the blade is at 45° to the end of the wood, as in Fig. 6. (You may prefer to tilt the wood instead of the saw, to keep your hand in a comfortable position.) Saw down until the deep end of the cut you are making almost touches the line drawn across the wood 2in. (51 mm) from the end. Then turn the wood around in the vice and make a similar cut from the other side. Finally, straighten the saw (and the wood, if you have tilted it) and saw out the V-shaped piece of wood left inside the cut.

Now that you have a clean, straight 'rip' cut, finish the cutting out with a cross cut. Start this cut the same way as when ripping, but when you have lowered the saw blade so that it is parallel with the surface of the wood, continue to saw with the blade level until you have reached the right depth. Keep checking the angle of the saw from both sides to avoid cutting too deeply.

When you have made an L-shaped cut in the end of each piece of wood, clean out the angle of the L with a chisel, used *across* the grain. Then saw the piece of wood to only $\frac{1}{16}$ in. (1 mm) longer than its correct length at each end. This slight projection will be smoothed off later.

Finishing the pieces

Once all four pieces of the rectangular centre frame are cut to shape, drill three screw holes in the top horizontal piece. They are to hold the table-top on, so they should be drilled through the wood from edge to edge – a job that needs a vice for the wood and a steady hand with the drill. One hole should be in the middle of the piece, and the other two halfway between the middle and the end (see Fig. 1.). Mark the position of the holes lightly in pencil, so that the marks can be rubbed off afterwards. Punch a small dent on each mark and drill the holes with a $\frac{13}{64}$in. (5 mm) drill. Sight along the length of the wood, rather than across it, so that if you drill slightly off line the drill point will not come out through the side of the wood. Do not countersink; instead, enlarge the end of the hole away from the tabletop with a No. 10 'screw mate'. Cut to a depth that allows you to insert a screw cup with its top just below the surface.

Put the pieces together without glue to make sure they are a good fit. If they are not, you can probably improve the fit by switching the pieces around.

Finish the face edges of each piece of wood (which will be on the inside of the frame, and hard to get at later) before you put the frame together. This finishing is done in various ways, depending on how the wood is to be treated. All methods start by levelling any irregularities in the wood, usually with a plane (remove as little wood as possible). Then lightly sand the wood with a piece of fine glasspaper wrapped around a block of scrap wood.

If you are using teak, and mean to give it an oiled finish, you need do nothing more at this stage. The same applies if the wood is to be painted. If, however, you are going to wax-polish the wood, give the face edges a light coat of cellulose sanding sealer or, failing that, clear shellac. When it is completely dry, re-sand the surface. Then apply a thin coat of wax polish to stop glue from sticking to the wood in places where it cannot be sanded off.

Glueing up the frame

Squeeze out a fairly generous amount of pva adhesive on both surfaces to be joined, and spread it thinly with a piece of scrap cardboard. Fit the frame together and hold each glued corner in place with an edging cramp. All the cramps should be put on the same way round, so that the frame will sit level on a level surface. To avoid marking the wood, pad the jaws of the cramps with pieces of scrap wood or hardboard, all of which must be of the same thickness to keep the frame level.

Before the glue sets, check that the joints are tight-fitting. Wipe away any excess glue with a damp cloth – even a spot of pva left on the surface will show through most finishes. Check also that the frame is square by measuring the diagonals between opposite corners; the two diagonals should be exactly the same. The measuring can be done with an ordinary steel tape rule, but a more accurate way is to sharpen the ends of two laths, each slightly longer than half the distance to be measured (see Fig. 8). Then put one pointed end in each inside corner and grip the laths firmly where they overlap.

Lift the laths out of the frame, without disturbing their setting, and lay them across the other diagonal. The points should fit into the corners exactly. If the frame is not square, slacken off the cramps and adjust it.

Look at the frame from the side and end to check that it is not twisted. Lay it down on a flat, level surface to dry. If it is twisted, weight it to hold it flat. Leave the frame to dry overnight.

Using the chisel

The next job is to make the two end frames. They are made in the same way as the centre frame, except that the joints are in the middle of the two horizontal members of each frame instead of at the ends. This means that the chisel must be used to cut out for these joints.

The upright members have cutouts at the ends only. Make them first, remembering that the bottom cutout of each is 2½in. (63 mm) deep instead of the usual 2in. (51 mm).

To make the cutouts in the centre of each horizontal piece, first measure the exact width of the upright members – it may be less than the nominal 2½in. (63 mm). Then divide the measurement in half and, using a pencil, mark a line that distance on either side of a centre line drawn across the face edge of each piece. Check that your pencil lines are accurate by 'direct measuring' – that is, laying the upright on the area where it is supposed to fit – before using the marking knife. Mark so that each upright will fit its own pair of cross-pieces; timber components cannot always be cut so accurately that they are interchangeable.

Having established accurate widths for the cutouts, use the marking knife and gauge, still set to $\frac{3}{8}$in. (9.5 mm), to complete the outlines of the cutout.

Put each piece of wood separately in the vice in a horizontal position, with the back edge uppermost. Saw down the lines running across each piece, cutting halfway through the wood and stopping at the marking gauge lines. Try to saw just inside the lines you have marked, to make the joint a tight fit. But do not go more than $\frac{1}{32}$in., or a 'mean millimetre', inside the marked lines, since enlarging an under-sized cutout with a chisel is difficult to do accurately. Add a pair of saw cuts inside the first two, dividing the area roughly into thirds, and not quite as deep as the main cuts. These extra cuts will make it easier to chisel out the wood.

To chisel away the surplus wood, angle the chisel blade at 45°. Push the chisel across the grain with your hand so that you cut a slanted piece out of each end of the section to be removed (see Fig. 3). The lower (outer) side of the cut should reach almost to the full depth of the proposed cutout. Cut halfway across from each side, turn the wood round and cut from the other side. This will leave a roughly tapered piece of wood in the middle of the cutout. To remove this lump, turn the chisel blade upside down and knock out most of the wood by hitting the chisel with a mallet. (If you have no mallet, use the *side* of the hammer.) Finish off by turning the chisel right way up, holding it flat and (pushing by hand instead of using the mallet) working from both sides to the middle. Check the straightness of the cutout with a try square.

Finishing the end frames

Drill two $\frac{11}{64}$in. (4 mm) holes through each upright member, one $2\frac{1}{2}$ in. (63 mm) from the shoulder (the edge of the cutout) of each joint and both on the centre line of each face. These holes are for fixing the end frames to the centre frame, and should be countersunk if the 'mirror' screws you are using require it (not all 'mirror' screws are the same shape).

Drill four $\frac{13}{64}$in. (5 mm) holes from edge to edge of each top horizontal member, two 2in. (51 mm) from each end, and two 2in. from each shoulder of the centre cutout. These holes are for fixing the end frame to the tabletop, and should be drilled out for screw cups with the 'screw mate', like the holes in the centre frame.

Saw the pieces of the end frame to $\frac{1}{16}$in. (1 mm) longer than their marked length. Plane the outside ends of the horizontal members to their exact marked length, using the shooting board, but leave the uprights over-size for the time being.

Finish the inside surfaces of the pieces as you did those of the centre frame. Include all edges that adjoin inside corners – that is, both edges of the uprights, the bottom edge of the top, and the top edge of the bottom. Finish also the back sides of all the pieces of the end frames. If you are using wax polish, keep it off the middle $\frac{3}{4}$in. (19 mm) of the width of the upright member, which is going to be glued. You can do this by

Top left. *A teak frame and teak-veneered top give this table a touch of luxury.*

Top right. *In this version, a plain white frame sets off a rich rosewood-veneered top.*

Above left. *An ultra-modern table with glass top supported on small rubber pads.*

Above right. *A tough plastic laminate protects the top of this pine table.*

sticking a $\frac{3}{4}$in. wide strip of cellulose tape down the middle.

Now fit the pieces of each end frame together. If your sawing has been accurate, they should be a tight fit. If the fit is too tight, you can chisel a bit out of the cutouts, but rule a line first to keep you straight, and take out only a little at a time. Glue and clamp the parts together, and measure them to ensure they are straight. Leave them to dry overnight, with both ends of the horizontal members propped up straight and level – not with the cramps resting on the floor, which might give the parts a twist as they dry.

When the glue on all three frames is properly set, plane, finish and polish the outside surfaces of all of them. The end grain showing at each joint will be protruding slightly beyond the wood on either side, because you have sawn slightly over-size. Plane off the excess, sliding the plane

from the outside corner of the frame towards the inside. Sand and polish (if required) in the usual way.

Assembling the frames

The rectangular centre frame is slightly shallower than the end frames because it is not meant to touch the ground. Turn all the frames upside down, hold the end frames one at a time to the centre frame in the exact position they will occupy, and mark the position of the screw holes in the centre frame by tapping a blunt nail through the holes already drilled in the end frame. Take the end frame away and check that the nail dents are exactly centred. If not, make new dents in the correct positions.

Drill a hole 1in. (25 mm) deep and $\frac{5}{64}$in. (2 mm) wide through each dent. Then glue and screw all three frames together with your No. 8 'mirror' screws. Some types of 'mirror' screw have non-countersunk heads and a washer that goes under the head before the screw is put in. The decorative cover is then fixed to the washer. In other types, the screw is countersunk flush with the wood and the cover screwed into a small hole in the screw head. If you are using the brass screws needed for teak, put a waxed steel screw of the same size into each hole first, screw it home, and then remove it. This makes it easier to put the brass screw in, for if too much pressure is applied to brass, it may break.

Fig. 3 (*above*). *Chiselling out wood for a 'T' halving joint. First a slanting slice of wood is removed with the angled blade.*

Fig. 4 (*above*). *Then the wood between the slanting cuts is removed with the chisel blade held bevel edge downwards.*

Fig. 5 (*above*). *Starting the 'rip' (along the grain) cut for a halving joint. A small notch is made in the far edge of the wood.*

Fig. 6 (*above*). *The saw handle is lowered and the wood tilted in the vice to make a deep diagonal cut.*

Fig. 7 (*above*). *Laying an end frame out to dry. The wood is resting on its ends and not on the two edging cramps. Note how the cramps are padded with scrap wood.*

Fig. 8 (*above*). *Testing the centre frame for squareness. The two sharpened laths are laid first across one diagonal, then across the other.*

Check that the table frame is sitting straight and true in all directions. Small adjustments can be made by slackening off the screws a little, moving the pieces and tightening the screws up again.

While the frame is drying, prepare the top. Cut it to its finished size and trim its edges with the plane. Mark the position that the frame will occupy on the underneath of the top, using Fig. 1 as a guide. If you are gluing laminate to the top, glue on the backing layer (underneath of the board) before you mark the frame position. (See below for instructions.)

Drill seven $\frac{3}{32}$in. (2.3mm) holes for the mounting screws to a depth of $\frac{1}{2}$in. (13mm), being careful not to drill through the top. A piece of tape round the drill $\frac{1}{2}$in. from the end is a useful guide to the depth of the hole.

The method used to finish the top depends on what it is made of. The simplest type to finish is the one made of ready-laminated chipboard. This can be bought in a standard width of 18in. (457mm), so that only the ends need planing smooth. Edging strip to match the plastic laminate is supplied with the board. Stick it down with an impact adhesive.

If you are laminating a chipboard or block-card top yourself, it is best to laminate both sides to ensure that it does not warp. Cheap, thin laminate is used for the backing. Remember to buy enough good-quality top laminate to cover the sides as well as the top, unless you are edging them with wood strip.

More finishing techniques

If you are using a veneered blockboard top, the edges can be finished with wood strips. Do the ends first. These should be cut slightly over-size, put on with woodworking adhesive, and held down with edging cramps while the glue sets. Clamp the cramps to the edge of the table, padding the jaws with scrap wood. Then do up the cramp's extra screw (padded with wood) on to the strip to hold it down. (If you have no edging cramps, tack the edging on with small panel pins, punch their heads below the surface and, after the first coat of paint or other finish, fill the holes with plastic wood.)

When the glue is dry, trim off the ends of each strip with a plane. Plane inwards, so that the plane presses the strip down on to the table edge and thus prevents splitting. Now glue on the side strips so that they overlap the end strips. Finally, trim the sides to length and finish all the edging with fine glasspaper—held tightly around a sanding block.

If the frame is to be finished differently from the top, now is the time to paint, varnish or polish it. When the finish is dry, turn the top upside down and screw the frame to it — and the table is complete.

If the table is made of teak, it can be finished simply by rubbing in teak oil. A tougher finish that looks exactly like oiled teak can be achieved by painting the teak with a 50/50 mixture of clear polyurethane varnish and turpentine substitute. Allow it to dry, sand it down with fine glasspaper, and put on another coat. It is important to paint along the grain to avoid leaving brushmarks. Finish with Grade 0 (very fine) wire wool and a little teak oil.

Timber panelled walls

Natural timber boarding can be used to decorate any room in a house—from a living room to a bathroom. The colours and patterns which can be achieved with different wood grains and board profiles are almost limitless, and since timber is long-wearing, redecorating problems will be minimized.

Most woods used for building purposes can be used for decorating interiors. The choice of timber, therefore, should depend on cost, availability and appearance. Many softwoods are very pale in colour, while hardwoods range from the creamy yellow of ash, beech or sycamore to the richer browns of mahogany, cherry and walnut.

When choosing a wood for timber lining, it is important to consider the moisture content of the wood; timber which has a high water content will shrink and warp in a heated room.

Solid timber planks, or boarding, are cut to

Below. A small, rather confining bedroom can be made to look rich and cosy with timber lining on all walls.

MICHAEL BOYS

one of several standard profiles. Square-edged planks may be used, but tongued and grooved—or 'T and G'—planks are more commonly used for internal timber linings, as they allow for easy formation of interlocking joints. Different groove designs, such as rebated, V-jointed, squared and extended shiplaps, are available in lengths which will fit the height of an average room. On a long wall, however, horizontal boarding may need to be joined end-to-end.

Planks may be between $\frac{1}{2}$in. and 1in., or 13mm and 25mm, thick. Normally, they are between 3in. and 6in., or 76mm and 152mm, wide. The thickness determines both the rigidity of the boarding and the spacing of the fixings. Allowance for movement of the planks is made when the tongues and grooves are originally machined. As shown in Fig. 5, the tongue is made not to extend the full depth of the groove.

Design considerations

So much depends on the use of the room, its size, shape and lighting, and on personal choice, that it is difficult to lay down rules for choosing internal linings. The basic factors which should be considered are : whether to line the walls and ceilings in wood (a later chapter explains how to line ceilings with timber boards) or only one or the other ; whether to cover all the walls with timber or to leave some in a contrasting finish ; what kind of wood to use ; the angle at which to fix the boards—vertical, horizontal, or diagonal ; and the extent of coverage that is desired—the full or partial height of the walls.

Another point to consider is that if furniture in a room is a jumble of pieces of different heights, horizontal boarding will tend, unfortunately, to accentuate this aspect by providing guidelines for the eye. On the other hand, rooms such as kitchens and laundry rooms, which usually have worktops and appliances all about 3ft. high, will usually look better with

horizontal boarding. It helps make their (usually small) walls look longer.

A final consideration is your own skill. A beginner will find it quite easy to board one plain wall to make a 'feature wall'. But covering a whole room involves a range of problems—replacing door and window architraves, for example—and requires a bit more skill, or experience, or patience at any rate.

Preparatory work

Before fixing any planks to new walls, be sure that the walls are dry ; newly plastered walls will take at least two months to dry and concrete walls will take at least four months to dry before planks can safely be fixed to them.

The method of fixing internal timber linings will depend primarily upon the type of wall to which they are to be fastened.

Masonry walls, such as unfaced or plastered bricks or lightweight building blocks, will need to have a timber framework of battening

attached directly to their surfaces. The linings will then be fixed to these.

Timber frame walls will also need battening, unless the studs (vertical members) and noggins (horizontal members) are close enough to make battens unnecessary. You can find the studs and noggins by driving nails at intervals across, and up and down, the walls. Mark a pencil x every time you strike solid timber ; soon you will be able to rule a grid pattern on the wall to show where solid 'nailing' is available.

Re-wiring and re-plumbing

You may want to put in some new light fittings or move existing ones or, if you intend to line a kitchen or bathroom, you may need to rearrange the pipework. Any work of this sort should be carried out at the 'bare wall' stage rather than later, to avoid damaging the wall planking. Also, it is advisable to mark the wall surface where any new wiring has been buried under plaster. This will help you to avoid

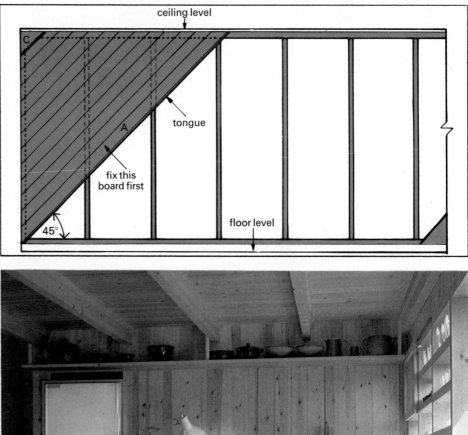

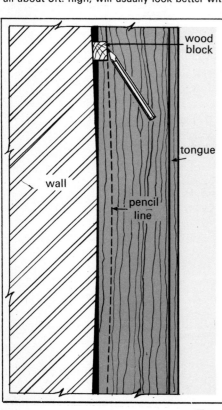

TRANSWORLD FEATURE SYNDICATE

accidentally severing or damaging cables when drilling or nailing the battens.

Wall preparation

Protection against damp. If the walls to be panelled have a tendency to dampness or will be subject to condensation—as they would in a kitchen or bathroom—you may prevent this from affecting the panelling by treating the boards with a special damp-proofing compound. There are many proprietary, damp-proofing compounds available, both liquid and solid, including bitumen-based emulsions, siliconized resin-based liquids, and pva-based sealants. Select one which is easy to apply and follow the makers' instructions. You can also use 500-gauge polythene sheeting as a vertical damp-proof membrane, or aluminium foil, or heavy-duty bitumen-impregnated paper, glued to the wall with neat pva adhesive.

Alternatively, treat the panels and the battens, before fixing, with a wood preservative. (Be sure to buy a clear, not a coloured variety.) This will protect the timber from damp, and fungal and insect attack—particularly important in warmer climates where insects are more prolific and damaging.

Insulation. If necessary, you can insulate against heat and sound by inserting a quilt or blanket of thick, flare-free expanded polythene sheeting, fibreglass, mineralized rock-wool quilting, or cork panels between the wall surface and the new panelling.

Conditioning the timber

Ideally, keep all timber in a dry, damp-free store, preferably in the room in which it is to

Fig. 1 *(far left). When an adjoining wall is 'out of true' (shown here in exaggerated form) the first board must be scribed to fit the curve or slope. See that the board is vertical—it too may have a curve which you must straighten—as you nail it temporarily. Then trace the outline of the wall by running a wood block and pencil down the wall. Cut the board down the pencil line, and move it over into its correct position.*
Fig. 2 *(above left). Fixing diagonal boards to vertical battening. Note that you must also have top and bottom battens: these are to give you nailing for the ceiling moulding and the skirting board, as well as for the ends of the T & G boards. Whichever way your boarding is to run, you always need to 'frame' the wall with the outside battens.*
Fig. 3 *(left). Timber boarding used as in this kitchen, for walls, storage units and a dining shelf, will help disguise awkward features and unify the room's appearance.*
Fig. 4 *(top right). A plain room can be given a distinctive appearance by the use of T & G boards, in this case fixed diagonally.*
Fig. 5 *(centre right). Cramping vertical boarding. Drive the chisel point into the batten and pull it upright to squeeze the board against its neighbour. This helps to eliminate ugly gaps as the timber dries.*
Fig. 6 *(bottom right). Since the last two or three boards cannot be cramped, fit them together into a bow shape and 'spring' them into place with your fist.*

ELIZABETH WHITING

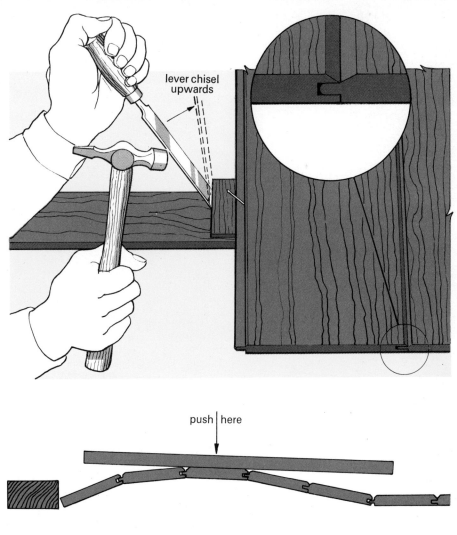

lever chisel upwards

push here

be used. Store it for at least a week before using it, to allow the wood to acclimatize to the room's general temperature and to permit excess moisture to evaporate from it.

Calculating quantities of battening

Estimating the amount of wood needed for the battens is a fairly simple procedure. Battens are continuous lengths of sawn softwood, sometimes available insect-proofed, about 2in. (50.8mm) wide x 1in. (25.4mm) thick. If using boarding about ½in. (12.7mm) thick, battens should be fixed at 2ft (610mm) centres when horizontal. (ie. for vertically-fixed boards)

Above. Natural grained furniture combined with timbered walls for a striking effect.

and 16in. (457mm) centres when vertical (ie. for horizontally-fixed boards). If using boarding about 1in. thick, horizontal battens can be at 2ft 6in. (762mm) centres, and vertical ones at 2ft (610mm) centres.

Either way, remember that there is always one more batten than there are spaces between battens. Allow also for two pieces running in the opposite direction to the battens—these are to form a 'frame' round the outside of the wall (Fig. 2). Allow 10 per cent extra for waste.

Fixing the battens

The positioning of the battens will depend on the style of boarding you want to use. For *horizontal* tongued-and-grooved boarding, the main battens should be fixed to run vertically. For *vertical* boarding, you will require horizontal battens. For *diagonal* boarding, either vertical or horizontal battens may be used.

It is desirable that battens present a plane (dead flat) surface for the planks to fit evenly over, but it is not necessary, and normally not practical, to go to great lengths to achieve such a level surface. Neither walls nor timber are ever perfectly true. Any major irregularities in

Above. A narrow hall and archway gains warmth and richness from all-over timber.

Above. One timbered wall, plus matching shelf unit, makes a pleasant kitchen.

a wall can be corrected by packing the battens with scraps of wood to the correct level, or by shaping a batten to fit over a 'high spot'.

There are several methods of fixing battens to walls, depending upon the type of wall you have.

On *masonry walls,* battens may be fixed with 2in. or 50mm No.10 masonry screws and fibre or plastic proprietary wall plugs such as Rawlplugs. Space the screws about 15in. (381mm) apart. If the walls are made of concrete

or very hard brick, you may wish to hire a percussion drill, especially if you are covering a large area. Otherwise, an ordinary electric drill set to run at a slow speed and fitted with a high-speed masonry bit, or a Rawlplug tool for tapping holes, may be used.

Houses which have a *timber framework* may need additional noggins (cross members) between the studs (vertical framing members), or vice versa. If after examining your wall, you find that noggins are too far apart to take vertical planking, you have two choices: 1, to batten the whole wall as for a masonry house, nailing the battens with 2½in. (or 63mm) flathead nails; or 2, to remove the existing wall lining and provide extra noggins between the studs.

If, on the other hand, the studs are too far apart to take your proposed horizontal boarding, battening across the face of the whole wall is the best course.

When putting up battening, it is necessary to treat each wall separately. Begin by removing the skirting boards and protruding ceiling mouldings from the wall.

The first thing you need is a 'frame' of battening right round the wall (Fig. 2). Start by loosely fixing a horizontal batten across the top of the wall, an inch or two (or 25mm to 50mm) down from the ceiling. Use a spirit level to check that it is reasonably level, and fix it permanently in place. Now fix a second batten about 3in. (or 76mm) up from the floor, checking that it too is reasonably level.

Next, cut two vertical battens to fit between the horizontal ones. Theoretically, these go right at the ends of the wall. But before fixing them permanently, check with a spirit level held vertically to see that they are plumb (straight up and down). If not, your wall is slightly out of plumb; bring each batten back into plumb by fixing it (or one end of it) slightly out from the corner.

Once the 'frame' round the outside of the wall is completed, you need only to fill in the intermediate spaces with battens at the correct intervals, as given above. Try to keep them reasonably level (or plumb, as appropriate), because straight battening will make nailing easier when you come to the top boards.

When you come to doors and windows, battens will be needed around the edges or frames to secure the ends or edges of the planking. (See 'Doors and windows'). Batten offcuts should also be used where new light switches or power points are to be fixed. If surface wiring is to be bridged by battens, notch them to fit over the wires. Remember to fix additional battening where wall-hung furniture or units are to be positioned.

Selecting and matching panelling

All natural timbers vary in colour, grain and figuring, so there may be some slight variation from plank to plank. To get the most pleasing effect, stand the boards against the wall and arrange them to suit your own taste before cutting and fixing them.

Fixing the boarding

There are three important points to note when fixing: 1, Always begin panelling from a corner

to avoid wastage, and to establish a 'true' board, so that following boards can be correctly joined on and do not 'stagger' out of line. 2, Always 'square off' the first board with the adjoining wall and ceiling before nailing, as few ceilings and walls are ever perfectly straight. 3, Always leave a ¼in. (6.35mm) gap between the panelling and the floor and ceiling for air to circulate freely behind—this allows the panels to expand slightly in damp or humid atmospheres.

Scribing

If the wall is out of plumb or is slightly curved, it may be necessary to trim your first board to fit exactly into a corner. To do this hold the board against the corner, flush to the butting wall and the ceiling; use the spirit level to make sure it is truly vertical. The exact contour of the wall is then traced off on to the board with a pencil (Fig. 1) and the board trimmed or cut accordingly. This process of tracing an angle or contour directly on to a board is called *scribing.* The advantage of scribing over measuring is that any unevenness in a surface will automatically be transferred in outline to the piece being traced.

For trimming the edge of a board, use a sharp plane with a fine set. Then sand over with fine glasspaper to smooth the edge.

Fixing T & G boards

Vertical positioning

Begin at an internal corner of a room and scribe to fit the groove side of the first board into the corner, as described above. Remember to leave about a ¼in. (6.35mm) gap at the ceiling and floor levels for air to circulate. Keeping this first plank vertically true, begin pinning about ¼in. (6.35mm) away from the corner edge. Skew pin the board at about a 45° angle into the support framework behind, using 1¼in. or 32mm lost-head nails, a small hammer, and a nail punch to push the nailhead well below the surface of the board. Work down the plank from ceiling to floor, pinning at intervals to correspond with the battening behind. Any holes can be filled with a suitable wood filler.

On the other side of the plank, place pins along the tongue of the board and skew pin with a hammer and nail punch (Fig. 5). Fit the groove of the next board over the tongue, thereby hiding the nail heads. Next, part drive the nails in this board, and *cramp* the board up close to the preceding one using a chisel (Fig. 5). Cramping should always be done on the tongue of a T and G board, as any marks will be covered by the groove of the next board. It is necessary to cramp tightly; otherwise gradual shrinkage of the timber will make your wall open up at the joints. When you come to the third board, cramp and nail from the bottom up instead of from the top down—cramping always in the same order will gradually 'skew' your boards out of line.

When you reach the last two or three boards to be fixed along a wall and into a corner, do not cramp them. Instead, cut them a little oversize and fit them together in a slightly bowed shape (Fig. 6). Then bang or 'spring' them into place with your fist. These last boards will need to be pinned through their surfaces, and the holes filled with wood filler.

All about joints

1. The butt joint is the simplest of all joints in carpentry. It may be made straight or right-angled, and needs nails, glue or screws to hold it together.

2. The dowelled joint is basically a butt joint reinforced with dowels—lengths of wooden rod. Both halves of the joint are drilled at once to make the holes line up.

3. The secret dowelled joint is better-looking, because the ends of the dowels do not show. The two rows of holes are drilled separately, so great accuracy is essential.

4. The mitred joint has a very neat appearance, because no end grain is visible. Unfortunately, it is a very weak type of joint unless it is reinforced in some way.

5. The halving joint is used at the corners of a rectangular frame. It is simple to make, has a reasonably neat appearance, and is quite strong if glued together.

6. The T halving joint is a variant of the usual L-shaped halving. It is used in conjunction with the previous type of halving in the construction of simple frameworks.

7. The X halving joint is the third member of this versatile family. It is used where two pieces of timber have to cross without increasing the thickness of the frame.

8. The dovetail halving joint is an extra-strong halving. Its angled sides make it impossible to pull apart in a straight line, though it still needs glue to hold it rigid.

9. The through housing joint is used for supporting the ends of shelves, because it resists a downward pull very well. It, too, must be reinforced with glue or screws.

10. The stopped housing joint has a neater appearance, but is harder to make because of the difficulty of cutting out the bottom of the rectangular slot neatly.

11. Tongued-and-grooved joints are most commonly found along the edge of ready-made boarding. But a right-angled version is also found, for example at the corners of boxes.

12. The lapped joint has a rebate cut in one side to hide most of the end grain. It is often found in cheap cabinet work, because it is easy to make with power tools.

13. The mortise-and-tenon joint is a very strong joint used to form T shapes in frames. The mortise is the slot on the left; the tenon is the tongue on the right.

14. The through mortise-and-tenon joint is stronger than the simple type. It is generally locked with small hardwood wedges driven in beside, or into saw cuts in, the tenon.

15. The haunched mortise-and-tenon is used at the top of a frame. The top of the tenon is cut away so that the mortise can be closed at both ends, and so retain its strength.

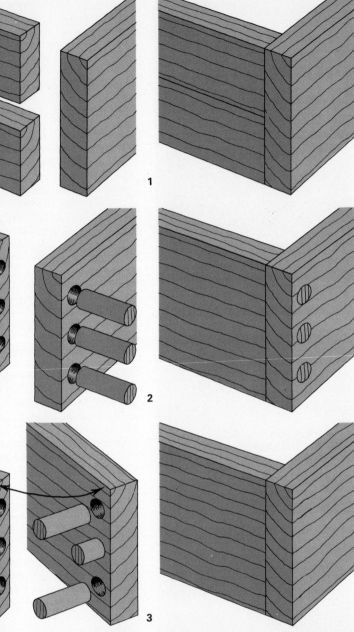

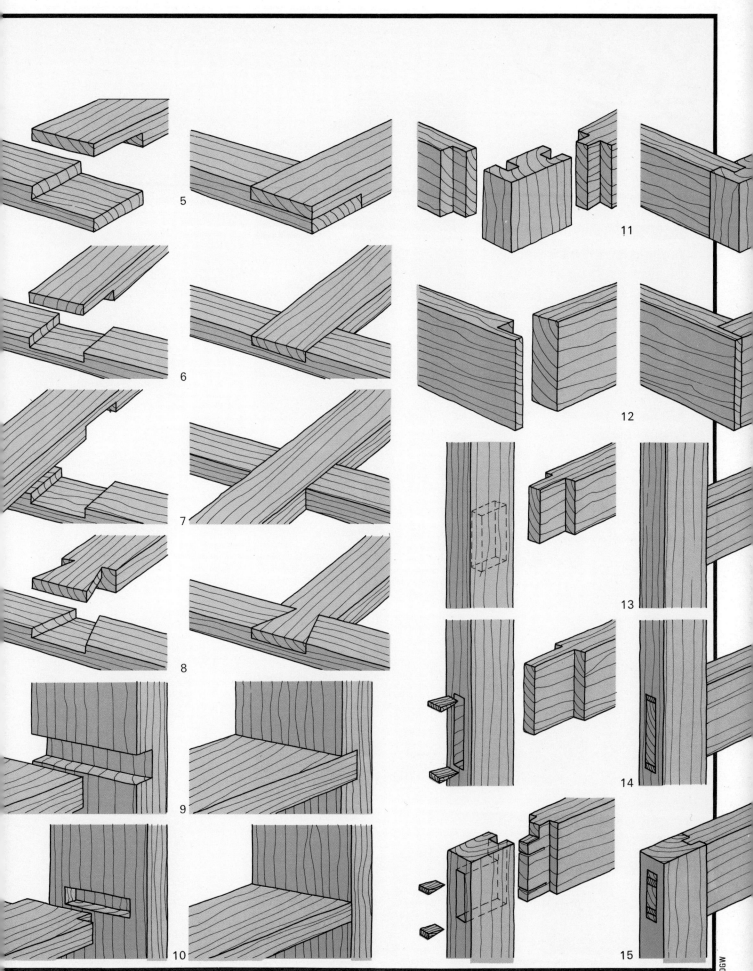

5

6

7

8

9

10

11

12

13

14

15

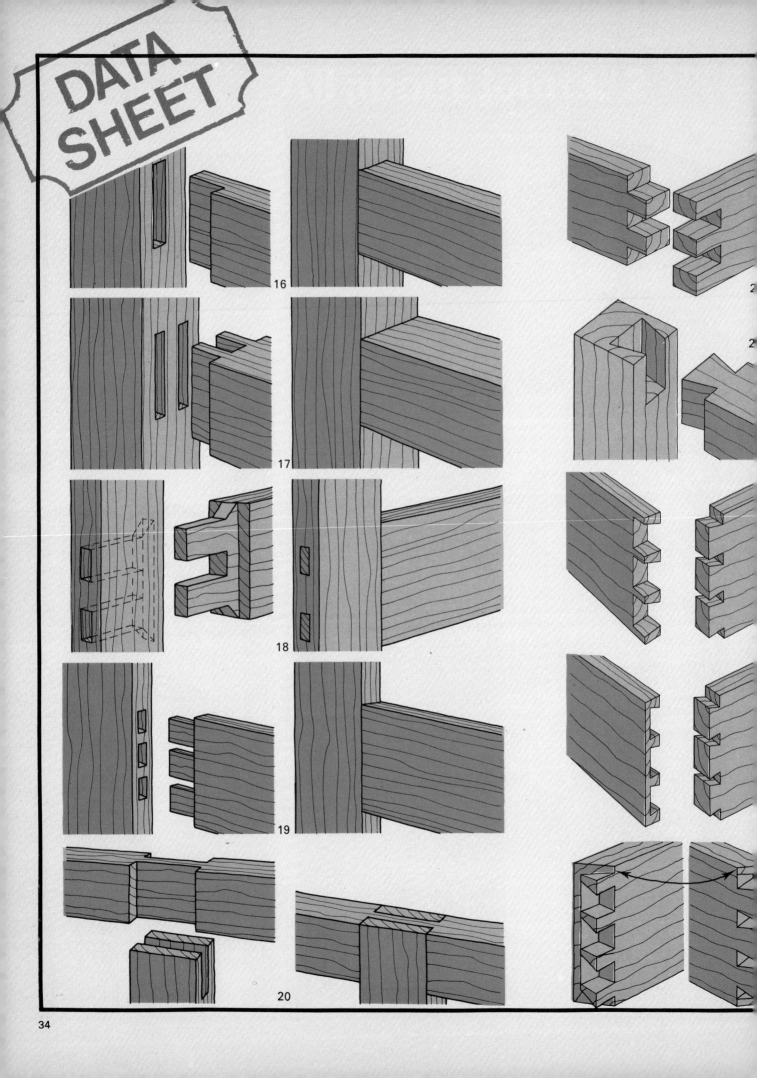

16

17

18

19

20

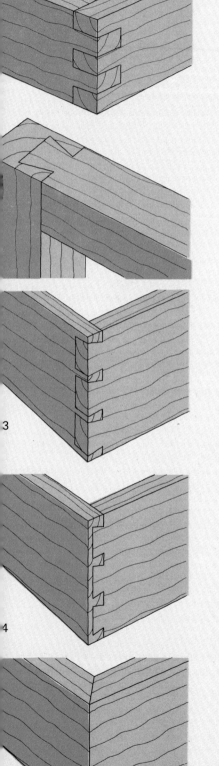

Four more kinds of mortise-and-tenon joint:

16. The bare-faced tenon is offset, with a 'shoulder' on one side only. It is used for joining pieces of different thicknesses.

17. Twin tenons are used in very thick timber. They give the joint extra rigidity and do not weaken the wood as much as usual.

18. Forked tenons add rigidity to a deep, narrow joint. The angled edge of the tenon is sometimes found in a haunched m-&-t joint.

19. Stub tenons are used on even deeper joints, but are weaker and less rigid than the forked tenons shown above.

20. The bridle joint is used where a long horizontal piece has to be fitted into the tops of several vertical pieces.

21. The box joint is quite strong and has a decorative appearance. It is used for the corners of wide frames and boxes.

22. The single dovetail, like all dovetails, is extremely strong and hard to pull apart. It is used at the corners of heavy frames.

23. The through dovetail is used at the corners of boxes where great strength and a good appearance are required.

24. The lapped dovetail is nearly as strong, but also has one plain face. It is used in very high-quality cabinet work.

25. The mitred secret dovetail is also used in very high-quality work. It looks like a mitred joint, but grips like a dovetail.

26. The lapped secret dovetail looks like a lapped joint. It is slightly easier to make than a mitred secret dovetail.

27. The cogged joint is like a dovetail with the tails subdivided into smaller tails. It is extremely strong and rigid.

28. The scarfed joint is used for joining frame members end-to-end where only moderate strength is required.

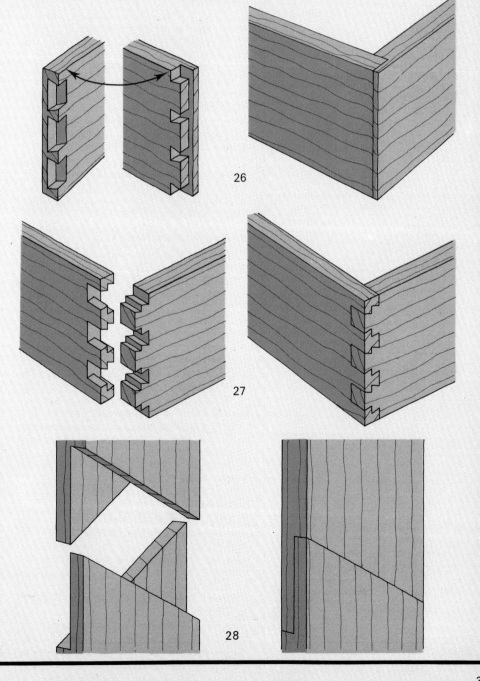

26

27

28

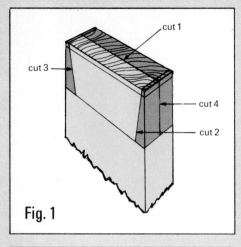

Fig. 1

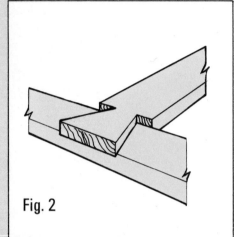

Fig. 2

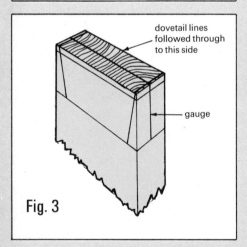

Fig. 3

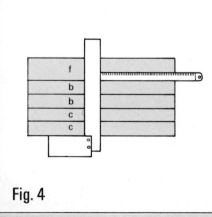

Fig. 4

Versatile work platform

One of the most useful and versatile of work aids is the sawing stool, or horse. Used with a staging platform or scaffold board, it is particularly handy for those out-of-reach decorating and repair jobs. In giving details for both a sawing horse and lightweight staging platform, this article introduces the bevel gauge, used for marking timber to be cut at an angle, and the dovetail halving joint, used to lock together sections of timber which otherwise come apart under stress in the course of everyday general use.

This sawing horse may be one of a pair and can be used with a staging platform or scaffolding. The horse, or stool, is compact and light to carry. It consists of a top platform, used for sawing and for trestle support, a fixed leg, and a hinged leg which is held open to the correct position by two rope braces on each side. The horse folds flat to save valuable space when put away in a garage or workshop. The staging platform provides a convenient bench when larger sheets of material have to be handled.

The dovetail halving joint

The dovetail halving joint is used on both sides of the lower rails of the horse. The joint strengthens the legs and will prevent them from splaying apart.

The male half of the joint is made by marking out the angles with a bevel gauge (see below) and then proceeding as you would for cutting out a half lap joint. Note that the male dovetail runs only halfway through the thickness of the timber (Fig.10) The timber is placed vertically in a vice and, cutting to the waste side, a tenon saw is used to make those cuts running with the grain (Fig.1). The rail is then placed on a bench hook and the remainder of the waste is removed by cutting *across* the grain (to form the 'shoulder').

The female half of the dovetail is marked out from the cut male joint. (Fig.2).

The bevel gauge

A bevel gauge is used for accurately marking out cutting angles, on dovetail joints and elsewhere. It consists of a slotted metal blade attached to a wooden handle, either by an adjustable screw or by a quick-release locking lever. The blade is adjustable to any angle.

When using the gauge to mark out dovetails, it is advisable to use a ratio of 3 to 1—that is, for every 3in. (76mm) of timber width, the dovetail should angle inward by a *total* of 1in. (25mm), ie, ½in. on either side. This is to ensure that the dovetail will withstand strain. When making the

dovetails for the 2in. rails, a bevel of about ¼in. or 6mm is suitable. (Fig. 3).

Countersinking

In order to prevent screw heads from protruding, screws must be countersunk. To countersink, you first bore a pilot hole to the size of the tip of the screw, using a wood twist drill. Then you enlarge the hole with another drill to the thickness of the shank of the screw, and drill to the depth of the shank. Then, using a rose bit or a countersinking bit, you drill to a depth just below the thickness of the screw head. Finally, you drive the screw home until the head is below the timber surface. All the screws on the sawing horse should be countersunk.

Matching the pieces

As two horses are needed for the platform, you will obviously need to cut out double the number of everything listed below.

All timber is cut slightly oversize to leave a ¼in. or 6mm piece of waste at each end. Ends are always vulnerable, and the excess provides protection while the timber is being worked. The waste is removed afterwards with a tenon saw and by planing the timber from each edge and, finally, right across.

Waste material protruding from a joint is planed smooth to match the surrounding surface. To steady it while planing, the joint should be placed in a vice. On an open end, the waste is planed away on a shooting board before assembly.

For the sake of clarity, the instructions below show how to make each section of the sawing horse separately, and then assemble the sections. However, where a number of boards have to be cut to the same length, or joints kept in a straight line over several components, it is usual to mark all the boards at the same time—at least with the important dimensions. For an example, see Fig.4.

Materials required

Ordinary standard, planed softwood is used. This should be straight-grained and free from twist. Avoid purchasing timber with knots as they can create weak points. particularly on legs. Planed-all-round timber (PAR) is slightly under the nominal 2in. (50mm) size; it measures 1 13/16 in. (47mm). Pre-planed timber is generally of consistent quality, but inspect it carefully. Select the best face and side, and mark these with the appropriate carpentry symbols to show 'face' and 'face edge'.

The platform

Fig.10 shows the unit with the sections

numbered for identification. Mark and cut one piece of 6in. x 1in. (152mm x 25mm) to a length of 24in. (610mm) to make the top platform A. Find the centre of this piece of timber and, using the try square, mark a pencil line lightly across the surface, lettering this X.

To mark out the waste, measure out $11\frac{3}{4}$in. (298mm) from the centre to one side and, with the marking knife, score a line across the timber (Fig.5). Reverse the timber and measure and mark back $23\frac{1}{2}$in. from the end and score a line (Fig.6). Follow this and the previous line round the timber with marking knife and try square, and then lightly run over the score marks with a sharp pencil. This will make the line easier to see when you are cutting away the waste.

For the top assembly (on which the platform sits) cut four pieces of 2in. x 1in. (50mm x 25mm) timber and one piece of 4in. x 1in. (100mm x 25mm), all 23in. (584mm) long. On one surface of each, mark the centre line. Letter the pieces F, BB and CC (Fig.4) to identify them.

Next, for legs D, cut four pieces of 2in. x 1in., 19in. (483mm) long and for rails E, two pieces of 2in. x 1in., $18\frac{1}{2}$in. (470mm) long. On one surface of each timber, mark the centre line and letter the pieces to identify them (Figs.4 & 10).

Using the same method as for platform A for marking out waste, mark out final lengths of $22\frac{1}{2}$in. for the five pieces of timber in the top assembly, $18\frac{1}{2}$in. for the legs, and 18in. for the bottom rails.

Marking off the joints

(1) The male dovetail halving joints.

To determine the length of the male dovetail halving on rails E, take one leg D and place it at right angles on one edge of the rails. Position the leg against the $\frac{1}{4}$in. waste, and mark off its width on the rail (Fig.7). Do this at both ends of each of the two rails. Follow the cut marks around the rails with the try square and marking knife and mark them lightly with a pencil. Crisscross the surface to show the waste portion. The marked surfaces will be the backs of the rails.

(2) The half lap joints.

Next, mark the positions of the half-lap joints which are used to secure the legs to the top assembly. Place the end of each leg at right angles on section C, and mark the waste on the back face of the legs. To mark the position of the half-lap on section C centre them with both bottom rails E. Mark in lines across C from the depth of the dovetail markings on rails E (Fig.8).

(3) The female dovetail halving joints.

The next step is to mark the female dovetail halving joints on the legs. Place a rail $12\frac{1}{2}$in. down from the waste-marked end of the legs. Mark the width of the rail on to the legs to indicate where the female dovetail halving should be made. Make certain that you mark the width on the *opposite* side of the waste marking on the legs ie, the waste for the half-lap joint is on the *back* of the legs, the waste for the dovetail joint is on the *front* of the legs).

Gauging the thickness

Now, use the marking gauge to mark the thickness of the joints. Set the gauge to half the thickness of the timber, less a fraction consisting of $\frac{1}{64}$in. or 0.4 mm, and gauge the depth of the half-lap joints. Test the setting of the gauge by marking from both sides of the wood. There should be a $\frac{1}{32}$in. (0.8 mm) gap in the middle. If it does not measure $\frac{1}{32}$in., the setting is incorrect and you will have to reset the gauge. Repeat the procedure for each of the rails and the legs in turn.

Note that the gauge mark runs only halfway through the timber; the piece on one side of the mark is cut away. Once you have cut each male dovetail, place it on the leg to which it will be fitted and mark its position with a pencil (Fig.2). Number each joint with an individual number in case there are slight discrepancies between different joints.

Then cut out the female dovetail halving joints to fit the male joints.

When you have cut out all the joints, trim all the pieces to length (other than at the joint ends) using the tenon saw and bench hook. Smooth the ends with the smoothing plane and the shooting board.

Assembly

The top-rail section is assembled from sections B and F. Carefully line up the top edges and glue and pin the sections together, using pva adhesive and $1\frac{1}{2}$in. (38mm) steel pins (Fig.9). The pins should be driven in fairly low down in order to provide clearance for the screws which are used to fix the top platform to the frame. Allow the glue to dry and then square up the top surface with a plane.

The next stage is to bevel the top so that the platform is level when the sawing horse is in use. Set your marking gauge to a depth of $\frac{1}{4}$in. and mark all the way round the timber. Then set the gauge to $1\frac{1}{4}$in. (31mm) depth and mark along one face of the timber only. Use the bevel gauge and marking knife to join this line to the previous one on the other side of the timber (Fig.9).

Place the section in a vice and set your smoothing plane at a medium setting. Plane the timber to the marked angle.

The top end rails C and F are then cut slightly—about $\frac{1}{4}$in. or 6.5mm—inwards on both sides with a tenon saw and planed smooth. This is to remove any protruding edges. Fig. 12 shows how the marking out is done.

With the plane at a very-fine setting, clean up the inside edge of each rail and leg. Remember as well to clean up the waste from those edges which cannot be planed after final assembly.

Frame and rail assembly

Line up the legs and the rails and check that the letters on the sections relate to one another.

Apply pva glue to each surface and tap the assembly together with a mallet (or a hammer and a piece of wood). After checking carefully, by measuring across the diagonals that each section is 'in square', two No. 6 $\frac{3}{4}$in. (19mm) screws are countersunk in each dovetail to consolidate the joint.

One 'gate' is then permanently fixed to the top assembly at the sloped side of platform A with glue and four countersunk 1$\frac{1}{2}$in. (38mm) screws. Drive a screw into each half-lapped joint and space the remaining two equally between these.

The other 'gate' is hinged, using 1$\frac{1}{2}$in. (38mm) backflap hinges fixed by $\frac{3}{4}$in. (19mm) screws. The size of screws chosen must suit the countersinking in the backflap. First, secure the hinge to the top rail C through the half-lapped joint and then, carefully squaring the hinge, fix it to the top assembly. Secure at first with only one screw in each hinge flap while checking that the hinge is square.

Next, clean up the frame generally, using the smoothing plane at a fine setting, and finish off, using a No. 1 grade glasspaper.

Platform A is then centred and fixed on to the top frame. To position the platform accurately, turn A upside down, stand the trestle top on it, and pencil in the correct position. The platform oversails the centre framework by about $\frac{1}{4}$in. or 6.5mm. Turn everything right side up and hammer in a temporary holding pin. Peer underneath to make sure that the platform has not slipped off line and, finally, drill and countersink three evenly spaced No.10 1$\frac{1}{2}$in. screws. Remove the pin and then plane the ends of the platform smooth. Rough edges may be smoothed away using a medium grade of glasspaper.

Levelling and bracing the legs

The next job is to true up the bottom of the legs so that the trestle stands firmly. Place the assembled trestle on a level surface and open its legs until the top platform is parallel with the ground. Use a spirit level to establish this. Take a short piece of timber, about $\frac{1}{2}$in. thick by 2ft long, and set this in front of and against each leg. Mark a pencil line on each leg as in Fig.13.

Place the trestle sideways on a bench and saw off and plane each leg accurately to this line. The bottom of the legs should now be at the correct angle when the trestle is opened.

Finally, fix the securing ropes. Close the trestle and drill a small pilot hole through the centre of each dovetail joint and into the second leg. Enlarge the holes to $\frac{3}{8}$in. (10mm) to admit the rope.

Open the legs on a level surface so that the trestle is standing evenly, and thread the rope through the holes on both legs. Leave one knot loosely tied in order to adjust the rope to the proper length.

Repeat the procedure with the other leg. Test that the ropes are bracing the trestles properly by applying an even downward pressure, then by standing on it to make sure. Correct any variation by adjusting the feet or the rope.

If you are using nylon rope, check that the knots are tied firmly, as nylon tends to slip more readily than ordinary rope. Sear the rope ends with a lighter or match.

Making the platform

Platforms must be strong enough for maximum security and are therefore often quite heavy. This one has been designed to be strong yet light in weight. It consists of a planed 2in. x 1in. softwood framework with a $\frac{3}{8}$in. (10mm) plywood decking. Double outer rails provide added reinforcement. To prevent sagging, the maximum length should be no more than about 9ft 9in., or 3m. The inner framework, excluding the two reinforcing rails, is 12in. (315mm) wide. All its cross members are half-lapped for greater strength. A 12in. wide plywood decking fixes to the top of the inner framework (the detail is shown in Fig.11).

Constructing the staging

Set up the four side rails in the vice and mark an initial $\frac{1}{4}$in. for waste. Mark the position of the cross members, spacing these equally over the distance, and leave another $\frac{1}{4}$in. for waste at the far end. Square round the waste and cut out the rails.

On the two side surfaces, square a line across for the cross members. Set the marking gauge to half the depth of the timber and gauge mark to the depth of the half-lapped joints for the cross members.

Cut out the joints with the tenon saw and a 1in. chisel.

Next, cut the five cross members 12in. (305mm) in length in the vice, allowing $\frac{1}{8}$in. (3mm) at either end for waste, and square the cut lines. Measure in 1in. (25mm) below the waste line on each rail and mark this across with the cutting knife on the face and on the back. Gauge and mark to a depth of 1in. Cut out this half section of the housing joint. Repeat the procedure on all five sections.

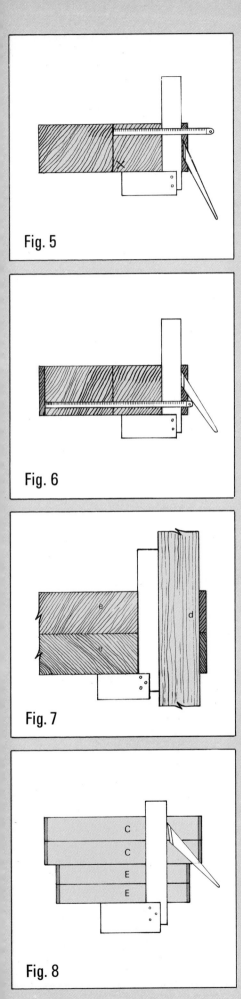

Fig. 5

Fig. 6

Fig. 7

Fig. 8

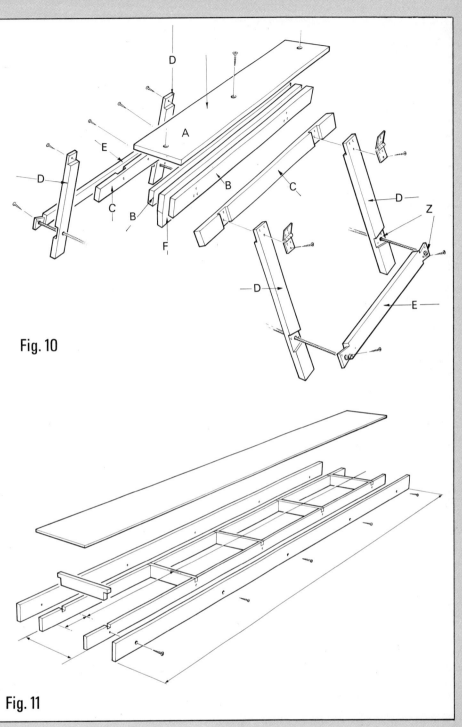

Fig. 10

Fig. 11

TRI-ART

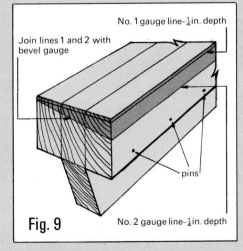

No. 1 gauge line–$\frac{1}{4}$in. depth

Join lines 1 and 2 with bevel gauge

pins

Fig. 9

No. 2 gauge line–$\frac{1}{4}$in. depth

Figs. 10 and **11.** (*above*) *show exploded views of the sawing horse and the lightweight staging platform. The sections of the sawing horse are lettered for identification and described in the article. The diagram shows the two types of joint used—the halving and the dovetail halving. The remaining joints are pinned or screwed together and glued. Rope braces hold the legs open at the correct angle. The lightweight platform should support average weights over a length of about 10ft or 3m. Its strength is derived from the double set of rails, which provide firm structural bracing. The cross-members are half-lapped to the inner rails and the decking is fixed on to these sections, countersunk and glued.*

The inner framework is then glued and pinned together. Steel 1½in. (38mm) oval pins are knocked into each joint at an angle to avoid screws which are used to attach the outside members to the main frame.

Check carefully that all joints are sound and allow the glue to dry thoroughly. Glue the outside rails and screw them into the lower portion of the cross members using 1½in. No. 10 countersunk screws.

The plywood decking is fixed on to the framework using countersunk screws and glue.

All surfaces, other than the top, can be given a coat of clear polyurethane varnish for protection. The top surface should be left untreated to prevent the working surface from becoming slippery.

Below. *The correct way of planing timber true to size. Press down firmly at the start of each stroke; slow down as you reach the far end, to avoid 'bowing off' there. The correct order of work: 1, Plane one face. 2, 3, Test both ways for straightness. 4, Test for any twisting. 5, Make 'face mark' with pencil. 6, Plane one edge. 7, 8, Test for straightness, and squareness with face. 9, Make edge mark. 10, Gauge across the thickness, on both sides, and plane the second face to the gauge marks. 11, Gauge across the width, on both sides, and plane the second edge. 12 shows how the gauge is tilted to make a fine line, and the direction in which it is moved. 13 shows one way of holding the gauge when you have to use it across a wide board.*

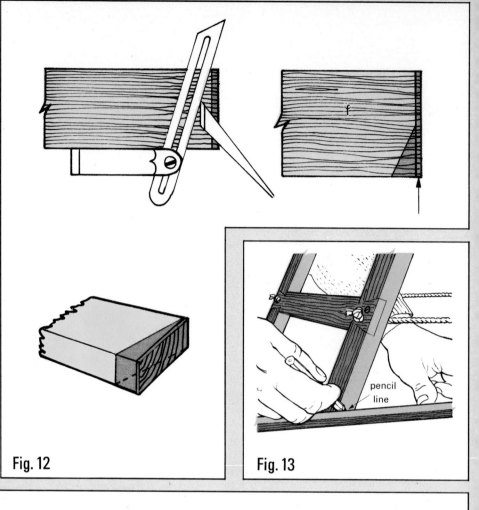

Fig. 12

Fig. 13

pencil line

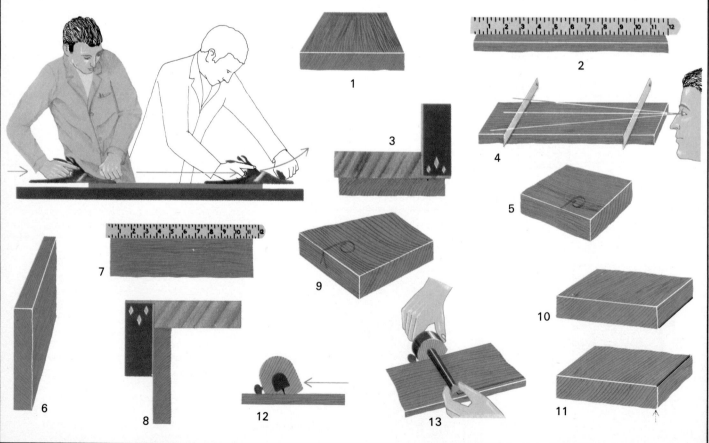

Built-in alcove units

Most old houses, and many new ones, have alcoves in their walls. Too often the space they provide goes to waste in the room layout, when it could be usefully filled with a fitted cupboard.

A fitted cupboard can be built in an alcove of any size from a small niche to a huge recess twenty feet long. If it is built so that its front is flush with the wall on either side of the alcove, it completely hides the alcove and gives the effect of a flat wall. For this reason, it is a popular fitting on either side of an old-fashioned chimney breast, where in a typical British house there is a pair of alcoves anything from 3ft. 6in. (1.1m) to 5ft. (1.5m) wide x 18in. (450mm) deep. In a bedroom, this provides two roomy built-in wardrobes, and at the same time simplifies the shape of the room so that it is easier to decorate, furnish and clean.

All built-in cupboards can be made in one of two ways. For reasonably square alcoves with straight walls in good condition, all you need to do is fasten shelves to the walls and face the alcove with a flat frame to carry a pair of doors.

Below. A wide, decorative frame with an inset arch makes a feature of this alcove cupboard topped with a display shelf.

If the walls are irregular, it is easier to build a frame-and-plywood cupboard as described opposite. The frames are made into a box that fits the alcove only loosely; plywood covers any gap between frames and adjacent walls.

Scribing

All parts that have to fit against a wall or floor should be scribed to the right shape. The technique is fairly simple—once you understand the principle.

For scribing part of, say, a plinth to a floor, you will need a couple of pairs of *folding wedges*. You can make these yourself. They are just pairs of identical wooden wedges which are laid on top of each other nose to tail. By sliding one wedge over the other, anything resting on the wedges can be raised or lowered.

To scribe a part to the floor, lay it on two pairs of wedges immediately above the position it will occupy when it is installed. Place a spirit level on top of it and slide the wedges back and forth until it is exactly horizontal. Then take an ordinary school-type pair of compasses with a pencil in, and set them to the size of the largest gap between the wood and the floor.

Now comes the difficult part. Hold the compasses with the point touching the ground and the pencil touching the wood, and the pencil vertically above the point. Then, *without tilting the compasses,* run them along the ground so that the pencil traces the outline of the floor on the wood. If the compasses tilt, so that the pencil is no longer directly above the point, the line will be inaccurate.

You can ensure accuracy by using, instead of a compass, a pencil and a wood block cut to exactly the right height. This arrangement cannot tilt, because the block slides flat along the ground. But you have to cut a new block for every part scribed.

Cut away the part below the scribed line with a coping saw, pad saw, power jigsaw, or, if there is very little wood to remove, a plane or spokeshave. The piece of wood should then fit the floor.

If you are scribing two pieces that fit together, and the floor is more irregular under one piece than the other, you may find that both pieces fit the floor but meet each other at different heights. The remedy is simply to saw or plane a straight strip off the higher piece parallel to the edge, which is easier than sawing the irregular contour of the bottom edge.

To scribe a horizontal board—a shelf, say—into an alcove with total accuracy, you would ideally insert an undersized board into the alcove at the desired height, scribe sheets of cardboard to fit each part of the wall, and pin them to the board so that it formed a template. Then you would trace round this shape on to the board you were cutting.

This is an ideal method, but slow. Provided the wall is not too irregular, you can use a less accurate but perfectly adequate method that takes much less time (see Fig.1). Measure the length of the alcove in several places and choose the longest reading. Cut the wood to a bare $\frac{1}{8}$ in. or 3mm longer than this. Do the same with the depth of the alcove, so that you have a board just too long and just too wide.

The side of the board that touches the smoothest and straightest wall should be scribed first, and the most irregular wall last. If all the walls look about the same, do the ends of the board first.

Scribe the board by jamming it into the alcove as near horizontal, and as near in the right place, as you can. Don't use compasses to rule the line, but a pencil held directly against the wall. Try to remove the absolute minimum amount of wood. If you scribe and cut the ends of the board first, it will then fit into the alcove horizontally, and you can scribe the rear edge normally.

Box cupboard

This design consists of three plywood-lined rectangular frames made of 3in. x 1in. (75mm x 25mm) timber joined by *slotted mortise-and-tenon* joints—that is, joints where the mortises do not go right through the wood. These can be made by following the instructions for a through mortise-and-tenon joint given in CHAPTER 40. The only differences are (a) that the mortise does not go right through the wood—make it and the tenon, say, 1in. (25mm) deep—and (b) that the mortise has straight sides, and the tenon is not held in by wedges. Put pins through the joint to hold it instead.

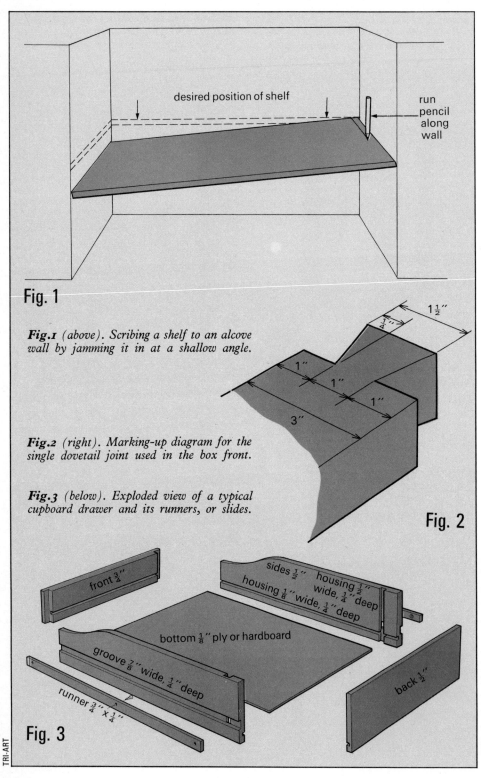

Fig. 1

Fig.1 (above). Scribing a shelf to an alcove wall by jamming it in at a shallow angle.

Fig.2 (right). Marking-up diagram for the single dovetail joint used in the box front.

Fig.3 (below). Exploded view of a typical cupboard drawer and its runners, or slides.

Fig. 2

Fig. 3

TRI-ART

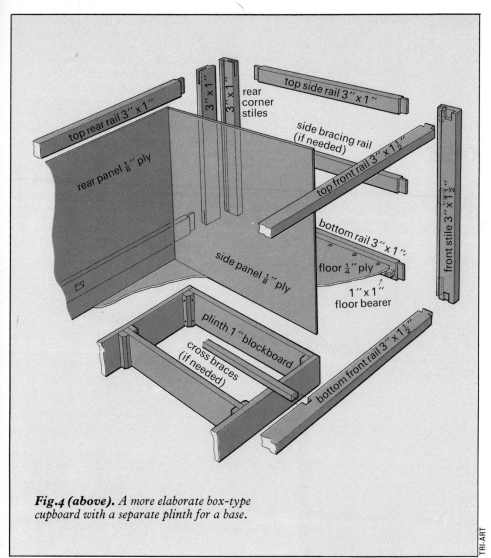

Labels on the diagram:

top rear rail 3″ x 1″

rear panel ⅛″ ply

3″ x 1″ 3″ x 1″

rear corner stiles

top side rail 3″ x 1″

side bracing rail (if needed)

top front rail 3″ x 1½″

front stile 3″ x 1½″

bottom rail 3″ x 1″

side panel ⅛″ ply

floor ¼″ ply

1″ x 1″ floor bearer

plinth 1″ blockboard

cross braces (if needed)

bottom front rail 3″ x 1½″

TRI-ART

Fig.4 (above). A more elaborate box-type cupboard with a separate plinth for a base.

The three frames—rear and two sides—are joined by tongues and grooves which must be cut with a plough or combination plane.

If the frames are for a full-height cupboard, it is a good idea to put a horizontal brace in each frame at an angle of 45°.

The front stiles, the vertical members on which the doors are mounted, are made of 3in x 1½in. (75mm x 38mm) timber. The extra width is not strictly necessary, but it does have two functions. One is to make the front stiles the same width as the top and bottom rails, which must be this thick because they are unsupported. The other is to hide the unsightly front edge of the ply lining, which is sunk in a ½in. (13mm) deep rebate on the rear edge of the stile.

The box has a floor made of ¼in. ply. If you want a flush floor that is easy to sweep clean, it should be mounted on bearers screwed to the bottom rails of the frames to bring the floor level with the bottom front rail, into which it can be rebated if you don't want the edge to show.

The cupboard unit stands on a rectangular plinth scribed to the floor to ensure that the unit is level. The plinth is fastened together with glue blocks and nails inside the corners. If it is more than, say, 4ft. (1.2m) wide, it is a good idea to put a cross-brace in it, and another one in the cupboard to strengthen the floor.

There is no need to screw the cupboard to the plinth, or the plinth to the floor (unless you live in an earthquake zone). The cupboard's weight should be sufficient to hold it steady.

The procedure for making a cupboard of this type is as follows:

1. Measure the alcove carefully all over and draw a plan and elevation of it to scale, showing any irregularities. Determine what is the largest box that will fit the space.

2. Draw out, to scale, the complete cupboard and its three constituent frames. This way you can determine what their measurements are.

3. Mark up, cut out and assemble the three frames. Then glue and pin the frames to each other. Pin a temporary batten across the front to hold it to the right width.

4. Cut the top and bottom front rails to 1½in. (38mm) longer than the gap they will have to bridge. Square lines across each piece ¾in. (19mm) from the ends to mark the shoulders of a single dovetail joint as shown in Fig.2. Cut the shapes out and use them to mark the socket into which they will fit on the side frames. Chisel out the sockets and insert the front rails.

5. Line the walls of the box with ⅛in. (3mm) ply reaching down to the level of the floor of the cupboard. Glue and pin the ply in place.

6. Glue and screw the floor bearers in place. Install the cross brace for the floor, if there is one.

It should be dropped into slots cut in the bottom front rail and the bottom rear rail. The rear slot will be in the shape of a square mortise. Glue and screw or pin the floor to its bearers.

7. Scribe the plinth parts to the floor and make up the plinth. Put it in the alcove.

8. Put the cupboard on its plinth. If it reaches to the ceiling, it will not need a top. If it reaches above head height, you can roof it with ⅛in. ply before installing it. If it is worktop height, scribe a worktop to the alcove walls and screw it to the top of the cupboard.

9. Hang doors on the cupboard, as described earlier for the other cupboard.

If the cupboard incorporates a vertical division, this should be screwed on from the outside, screwing through the plywood walls into the edge of a chipboard or blockboard panel. Shelves should be mounted on angle strip.

Bridging the gap

When the box cupboard is installed there will be a gap all round it between the edge of the frame and the irregular alcove wall. One way to deal with this is to nail blocks to the side of the frame so that they are 1in.–2in. (25mm–50mm) behind the level of the wall front, and cover them with ⅛in. (3mm) ply scribed to reach from the frame edge to the wall. The ply and adjoining surfaces can then be painted in a dark colour, so that the irregular edge on the wall side, or any crack, is not noticeable. There are other ways to disguise edges but this is the simplest.

Drawers

A typical drawer is shown in Fig.3. It is a wardrobe 'shirt drawer' with a dropped front, but a straight-fronted drawer is made in the same way.

The front is made of ¾in. (19mm) thick solid timber. It is grooved at the bottom to take the ⅛in. (3mm) plywood or hardboard drawer floor, and rebated at the ends to take the ½in. (13mm) sides without their end grain showing.

The sides should be made of solid timber or 'drawer side' plywood, which has three plies running the same way. Ordinary ply makes drawers stick on their runners because whichever way it is turned, it has rough end grain showing. The sides are grooved at the bottom for the floor, vertically at the rear end for the back, and horizontally along the outer sides for the runners.

Since the grooves reach half-way through the wood, the runner grooves may break into the vertical grooves on the other side of the wood. Provided that no glue gets through the hole into the runner grooves, and the drawer back does not project into them, this does not matter.

The drawer back is also ½in. (13mm) thick. It is grooved at the bottom only, to take the floor. The drawer runners are slightly smaller than their grooves in the drawer sides. They are screwed to the side wall of the cupboard and to the vertical division, and must be exactly parallel and the right distance apart to work. The screws should be countersunk well below the surface of the wood.

The drawer is assembled by glueing the back to the bottom first, then the sides, then the front. It is impossible to put it together any other way.

Spacious bathroom cabinet

Modern bathrooms are often limited in size—and storage space for the wide range of items that have to be kept readily to hand is, therefore, at a premium. This compact bathroom cabinet affords ample storage space and its simple good looks add an attractive touch to any bathroom.

This bathroom cabinet is a glued and nailed construction made, in the main, from WPB plywood, with the exception of the cupboard doors, which are blockboard. Carried out carefully, this job is not beyond the capabilities of even the very inexperienced woodworker.

The joints are simple—either housing joints or, at each of the four outside corners, rebate joints. The back panel fits into a rebate cut into the two short sides and is screwed into place. The front edges of the cabinet are covered with a decorative edging; apart from this, the finished cabinet is painted. The cabinet has ample storage space, with two cupboards and two glass shelves which are easily fixed in place using chrome screw eyes. It is fitted with a large mirror. The light above the mirror is optional.

Cutting the sides

All the plywood horizontal and vertical members are 5in. (127mm) deep from front to back, with the exception of the short outer sides which are $\frac{1}{2}$in. deeper to allow for the rebate into which the back fits, and the centre division in the top cupboard, which is $4\frac{5}{8}$in. (118mm) deep. When the $\frac{1}{4}$in. (6.3mm) edging is applied to the other members, this central division will accommodate the $\frac{5}{8}$in. (15.8mm) thick blockwood doors.

First cut all the horizontal and vertical pieces slightly longer than the lengths given in the cutting list to allow for waste. Mark the exact lengths required and square lines through these points. Plane down to these lines. You should clamp a waste piece of wood to the edge of the board so that the plane does not damage the corners. Check that the ends of the boards are exactly square.

Now cut the rebates into which the back panel will fit, down the edge of the two short sides. The method of cutting rebates is described fully in CHAPTER 3. Cut the rebates $\frac{1}{2}$in. (12.1mm) deep to allow the back panel to fit in flush, and $\frac{3}{8}$in. (9.5mm) wide, leaving a tongue $\frac{1}{8}$in. (3.2mm) wide protruding.

Now mark out the positions of the housings. The most accurate method of doing this is to lay edge to edge the two parts into which a third is to be jointed. Then mark the positions of the housings down both the faces of both pieces of timber—this will ensure that the housings are perfectly matched. For example, to mark the position where the long vertical piece (piece F in the exploded drawing) is to be jointed into the long sides (pieces A and C), lay the long sides together edge to edge with their ends exactly in line with each other. Mark the position of the housing on both surfaces.

To mark the position where the long horizontal piece (H) is jointed into pieces D and F, butt the edges of these two pieces together. Then slide piece F so that its end is exactly $\frac{1}{4}$in. (6.35mm) inwards from the end of piece D. This is done because the top of piece D in the finished cabinet is $\frac{1}{4}$in. (6.35mm) above the top of piece F, which is in a housing joint. Measure where the housing is to come from the end of piece D and mark the position on both boards.

When you mark the position where the dividing piece in the top cupboard (G) will joint into pieces A and H, remember that the front edge of this piece is set back $\frac{3}{8}$in. (9.52mm) from the fronts of the other pieces. After the $\frac{1}{4}$in. (6.35mm) edging is added at a later stage, this space will allow the $\frac{5}{8}$in. (15.8mm) blockboard doors to fit in flush with the cabinet front.

Now cut all the housing joints and the stopped housing joint for the centre partition in the top cupboard to a depth of $\frac{1}{4}$in. (6.35mm). The method of cutting housing joints is described in CHAPTER 3.

The next step is to cut rebates on each end of the two short sides to receive the long sides of the cabinet. Cut the rebate $\frac{1}{2}$in. (12.7mm) deep, so that the long side will fit flush, and $\frac{3}{8}$in. (9.52mm) wide. The shape of the rebate will leave a tongue of wood only $\frac{1}{8}$in. (3.2mm) wide projecting. This will allow greater room for you to pin the pieces together by pinning from the longer sides into the shorter. It also reduces the

area of end grain to be painted and, therefore, improves the decorative effect of the cabinet.

Applying the edging

The decorative edging can now be applied to all the edges that will face in the finished cabinet, apart from the edge of the central division in the top cupboard. Before doing this, however, stand the pieces on their edges on a flat surface in roughly the arrangement of the finished cabinet. Mark all the facing edges with a pencil. This will ensure that you do not apply the decorative edging to the wrong edges of the pieces by mistake, and also check that you have cut all the components accurately.

The finished size of the edging will be $\frac{1}{4}$in. x $\frac{1}{2}$in. or 6.35 x 12.7mm, but it should be bought and applied slightly wider than $\frac{1}{2}$in. to allow for final cleaning up. The type of wood used is a matter of personal taste—the cabinet in the photograph is edged with rosewood.

The edging is glued with a pva adhesive to the front edges of the cabinet components. It then has to be cramped in place while the adhesive dries.

There are three ways of doing this. The first is to use edging cramps. These are shaped like G cramps but they have an additional threaded bar through the long side of the G which will apply pressure to the narrow edge of a piece of wood. Cramp the edging as shown in Fig.3. The second method uses sash cramps. Take matching pieces, for example, the two short sides of the cabinet. Butt the two edges where the decorative edging has been applied. Cramp the components together using sash cramps (see Fig.4). Either way, be careful to wipe off with a damp cloth any smears of adhesive.

The third way of applying pressure is to pin through small plywood blocks and the edging, into the component. Use $1\frac{1}{2}$in. (38mm) panel pins and small blocks of $\frac{1}{4}$in. (6.35mm) ply, about 1in. (25mm) square. Place the blocks on the edging and pin through them. Angle the nails as in dovetailed nailing, which is described and shown in CHAPTER 1 (see Fig.5). The disadvantage of this method is that it leaves pin holes in the edging. These are, however, only the size of the nail shank (and not the head) and can be filled with a matching filler.

When the adhesive has dried, use a sharp smoothing plane to clean off the edging so it is level with the plywood components.

Next mitre the edging on the ends of the long and short sides. Arrange the four sides on the floor in the shape in which they will finally fit together. Set a bevel gauge to an angle of 45°. On the ends of each piece mark a diagonal line from the outer edge along the blade of the bevel gauge. Carefully saw through the edging down these lines until you reach the plywood. Remove the waste edging.

Now, at the edged ends of each internal dividing component, except piece G, cut a small step. The application of edging strip to the front of the components has, in effect, created stopped housing joints at the points where through housing joints were cut. Thus a small step, the depth of the housing, has to be cut through the edging on the pieces which fit into these joints. On the edged side of each dividing member, except piece G, measure inwards $\frac{1}{4}$in.

(6.35mm)—the depth of the housing. Square a line through this point, around the edging. Carefully cut down this line through the edging until you reach the edge of the plywood board. Do this at both ends of each internal component, except piece G. Remove the waste edging.

Assembling the cabinet

Now assemble the cabinet. The long and short sides are glued and dovetail pinned together (described in CHAPTER 1) and the internal divisions are glued into the housings. Wipe any excess adhesive from around the area of the joints with a soft cloth.

Check that the cabinet is square by measuring each set of diagonals. The measurement of each diagonal should exactly match that of its intersecting diagonal.

The cupboard doors

The next step is to cut the cupboard doors and fit them. Mark out and cut the doors to the size indicated in the cutting list. One door is $\frac{1}{4}$in. (6.35mm) wider than the other, to allow for a matching rebate down the ends of the two doors in the top cupboard where they meet at the centre division. To cut the rebate, set the rebate plane to a width of $\frac{5}{16}$in.—half the thickness of the doors (see Fig.2).

Before fitting the doors, remember that there should be a thin coin's width between the edges of the doors and the cabinet sides. Plane the doors to a size that will suit but do not, of course, plane the rebated edges of the top cupboard doors.

Fix each door with a pair of $1\frac{1}{2}$in. (38.1mm) brass butt hinges and brass screws. Remember, though, that when using brass screws the thread hole in the wood should be cut first with steel screws. This will avoid the danger of the brass screws breaking in the hole.

The cabinet back

The back of the cabinet can now be fitted. The back is made from $\frac{1}{2}$in. (12.7mm) plywood and is screwed into place. This enables it to be easily removed when you want to repaint the interior of the cupboard. Use No. 6 countersunk brass screws to fix the back. Space them about 7in. (178mm) apart and screw into the back (rebated) edges of the two short sides. Be careful to drill straight; you have little margin for error.

The mirror frame

The next step is to make the frame for the mirror. This is a simple box construction, made from 2in. x $\frac{3}{4}$in. (50mm x 19mm) timber, rebated at the corners. The four pieces are glued and dovetailed pinned together. So that the mirror screws can be set in from the corners of the mirror, two pieces of the same timber are fixed to the inside of the box. Position them vertically, with their wider surfaces facing outwards (Fig.6) to provide the greatest possible area for the screws.

When the mirror frame is made, it has to be glued and screwed in position. It is fixed centrally in the bottom left-hand panel of the unit—that is, $2\frac{1}{2}$in. (63mm) from the side, and $2\frac{1}{2}$in. from the bottom.

The most difficult part of this job is that,

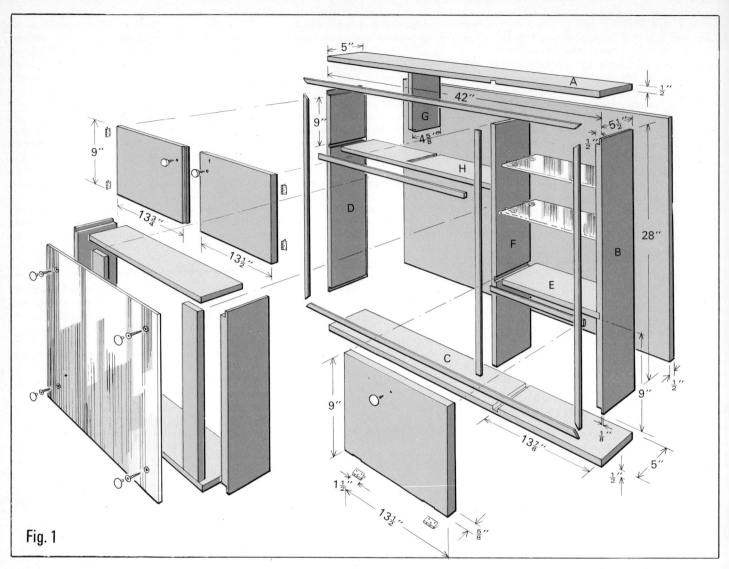

Fig. 1

Cutting list

Part	No.	Size
Short sides	2	28in. x $5\frac{1}{2}$in. x $\frac{1}{2}$in.
Top side	1	$41\frac{3}{4}$in. x 5in. x $\frac{1}{2}$in.
Bottom side	1	$41\frac{3}{4}$in. x 5in. x $\frac{1}{2}$in.
Back	1	$41\frac{1}{4}$in. x 28in. x $\frac{1}{2}$in.
Vertical division	1	$27\frac{1}{2}$in. x 5in. x $\frac{1}{2}$in.
Horizontal division	1	14in. x 5in. x $\frac{1}{2}$in.
Horizontal division	1	$27\frac{1}{2}$in. x 5in. x $\frac{1}{2}$in.
Top cupboard division	1	$9\frac{1}{2}$in. x $4\frac{5}{8}$in. x $\frac{1}{2}$in.
Mirror 'bearers'	2	$11\frac{1}{2}$in. x 2in. x $\frac{3}{4}$in.
Short sides of mirror frame	2	13in. x 2in. x $\frac{3}{4}$in.
Long sides of mirror frame	2	22in. x 2in. x $\frac{3}{4}$in.
Edging strip (for sides)	2	42in. x $\frac{1}{2}$in. x $\frac{1}{4}$in.
Edging strip (for sides)	2	28in. x $\frac{1}{2}$in. x $\frac{1}{4}$in.
Edging strip for internal divisions	2	$27\frac{1}{2}$in. x $\frac{1}{2}$in. x $\frac{1}{4}$in.
	1	14in. x $\frac{1}{2}$in. x $\frac{1}{4}$in.
Door	2	$13\frac{1}{2}$in. x 9in. x $\frac{5}{8}$in.
Door	1	$13\frac{3}{4}$in. x 9in. x $\frac{5}{8}$in.
Other requirements :		
Shelves, plate glass	2	$13\frac{1}{2}$in. x 5in. x $\frac{1}{2}$in.
Mirror	1	22in. x 13in. x $\frac{1}{4}$in.
Shelf supports	8	Chrome screw eyes
Brass butt hinges	6	$1\frac{1}{2}$in. x $1\frac{1}{4}$in.

You will also need 3 knobs for the cupboard doors, and a door stay and magnetic catch for the lower cupboard door.

The sides, internal divisions and back of the cabinet are plywood, the mirror frame and bearers are softwood, the doors are made from blockboard and the edging strip is a hardwood. The measurements given do not include any allowance for waste.

Fig.1. *An exploded drawing of the cabinet.*
Fig.2. *A cross section through the top cupboard showing the matching rebate in the cupboard doors.*

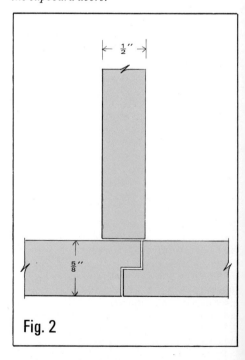

Fig. 2

Fig. 3. *One method of cramping the hardwood edging to the cabinet components once it has been glued in place is to use edging cramps. These force the edging up against the edges of the components while the glue dries.*
Fig. 4. *Another method is to take matching parts of the cabinet, for example, the two short sides, and butt the edges to which the edging has been applied. The two parts are then sash cramped together.*
Fig. 5. *The third method of cramping the edging is to pin through waste plywood blocks into the edging and the cabinet component. The pins are angled as in dovetail nailing to provide greater cramping pressure.*
Fig. 6. *A simple box construction, the mirror frame is rebated at the corners and the pieces glued and dovetail pinned together.*

although the screws have to be driven through the back of the back panel, the only way to site the frame accurately is to work from the front. To overcome this, place the frame in position, and draw a light pencilled line right round it. Remove the frame, spread pva adhesive over its back edge, replace it, and weight it down with a few books until the adhesive dries.

Next remove the back panel from the unit, and turn it upside down. Measure carefully from the outside edges to give accurate screw positions. Drill for, and fix, No.6 screws at about 7in. centres. Once again, use No.6 countersunk steel screws first to cut the thread. Then remove the steel screws individually and replace them with brass screws of the same size.

The glass shelves

Next fix the supports for the two glass shelves. The shelves are plate glass with ground edges—your glass stockist will probably prepare these for you. The shelf supports are chrome screw eyes. Mark the position of the supports on the short side B and on the long vertical dividing piece F. Bore small holes at these points with a bradawl and screw in the supports.

Finishing the cabinet

The cabinet can now be cleaned up and painted. Remove the shelf supports, the back panel and mirror frame. Sand the face of the decorative edging to remove any irregularities at the corners, and place masking tape over it. Paint all the component parts. For the very best results use a primer, followed by an undercoat and finished with the topcoat.

When the paint has dried, reassemble the cabinet. Remove the masking tape and to the decorative edging apply two coats of clear polyurethane. Fix knobs to each of the cabinet doors and a brass door stay and magnetic catch on the lower cupboard door.

Now fix the mirror in place. Your glass merchant will supply a mirror exactly to size. The mirror is fixed with four mirror screws each set in 1½in. (38mm) from the corners as shown in the exploded diagram. It is fairly easy to drill holes in glass with a slow speed drill but your glass merchant will probably be willing to do the job for you.

Screw the finished cabinet to the bathroom wall. Position the screws so that they are as inconspicuous as possible.

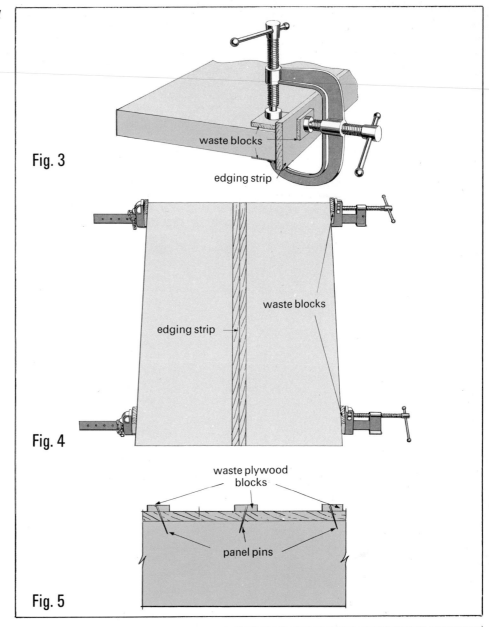

Fig. 3

Fig. 4

Fig. 5

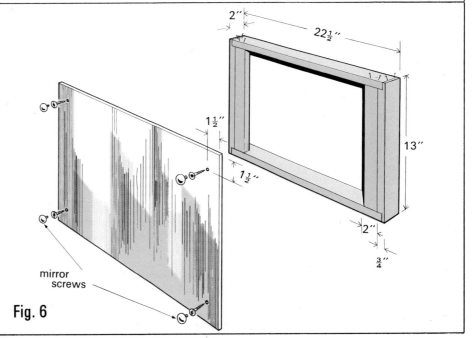

Fig. 6

Nails

The number of different kinds of nails and other hammered-in fasteners is staggering—and each one has a different function. Here is a list of all the main types, and what they are generally used for.

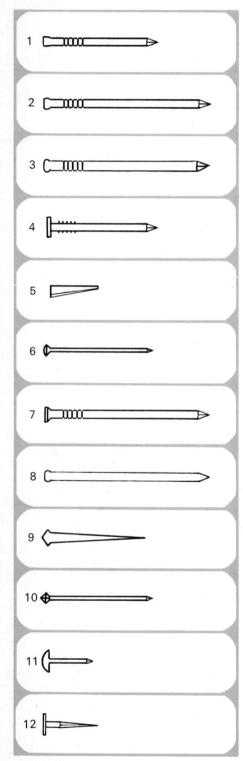

Commonly used nails:

1 Lost head nail. Head can be punched below surface for a neater finish in fine work.

2 Round wire nail. For work where strength is more important than a neat appearance.

3 Oval wire nail. Oval cross-section makes nail less likely to split wood.

4 Clout nail. Large-headed, for fixing roofing felt, etc., to wood.

5 Picture sprig. Headless, holds glass to picture frames; also for fixing down lino.

6 Panel pin. Small nail for securing light pieces of wood; used in conjunction with glue.

7 French nail. For rough carpentry work: large, ugly head ensures a firm grip.

8 Masonry pin. Hardened steel nail for fixing wood direct to masonry.

9 Wrought nail. Soft iron nail: point can be 'clenched' (turned over) for extra grip.

10 Hardboard pin. Unusual head shape countersinks itself in hardboard, can be filled over.

11 Chair nail. Decorative head for fixing leather, etc., in upholstery work.

12 Tack. Small nail with broad head, for fixing down carpets and fabrics.

13 Staple. For securing wire, upholstery springs, etc., to woodwork.

Special-purpose nails:

14 Corrugated fastener. For butt-jointing timber quickly and easily: not very strong.

15 Screw nail. For fastening sheet materials to wood. Great holding power.

16 Floor brad. Holds down floorboards. Great holding power, but now obsolete.

17 Joiner's brad. Small carpentry nail used where extra holding power is needed.

18 Cut clasp nail. Obsolete general-purpose nail superseded by oval wire nail.

19 Needle point. Steel pin for fixing small mouldings: head broken off flush.

20 Annular nail. Used like the screw nail (15), but larger and stronger.

21 Duplex head nail. For concrete formwork: double head permits easy removal.

22 Dowel nail. For end-to-end hidden joints in high-quality work.

23 Chevron. For joining corners of frames where strength and appearance are unimportant.

24 Insulated staple. For securing telephone and other low-voltage wiring.

25 Saddle tack. For wiring: first tacked down, then folded over and fastened.

26 Roofing nail. For securing corrugated iron or asbestos roofing to wooden rafters.

27 Chisel-headed nail. For fastening gutters, etc., direct to mortar.

Easy to build workbench

Every carpenter needs a workbench. Without it, he is severely restricted in the range of jobs he can tackle; with it, he can build advanced projects quickly and easily. Here is a design for a full-size professional-type bench—and the best thing about it is that you don't need a bench to make it.

This workbench has three important advantages over other benches. First, it is extremely simple to make. No advanced carpentry techniques are required, and yet the result is just as strong and long-lasting as a more complicated structure.

Second, it has been designed not to require expensive equipment to make it. The main parts of the frame are held together by bolts, so no sash cramps are used in assembling them. Everything can be done easily and quickly with ordinary hand tools.

Third—and unlike any other workbench—it has a replaceable top. The design calls for high-density flooring grade chipboard to be used, and this should last for years; but when it does wear out, all you have to do is undo a few screws and put in a new piece. Chipboard is not expensive.

This project introduces the simple but useful technique of rubbing 'glue blocks' into the corners of a frame—a technique much used in furniture-making to give a square frame extra rigidity and strength.

For the timber and accessories you will need, see the cutting list, Fig.15. The vice shown in the pictures is a Record 52E, a type extremely suitable for the amateur woodworker, but any woodworking vice can be fitted to the bench.

A *bench stop* is also a recommended fitting. This is a small projection that can be raised from the flat surface of the bench top, and used to rest wood against when sawing or planing it. Various kinds of stop are made, but one of the hinged type shown in Fig.14 is easiest to fit. It is just let into a shallow, chiselled-out recess in the chipboard and secured with screws.

To save time and trouble in construction, ask your timber merchant to machine-plane the wood you buy to the exact widths given in the cutting list. He can do this a lot faster and more accurately than you can, and he will not charge you much for the service. It might not be a bad idea to have the chipboard and plywood cut to exact size as well—though you will then have to work accurately to be sure they fit.

The end frames

The 'legs' of the bench are two simple upright frames, one at each end, made of two heavy pieces of timber screwed to a sheet of plywood. Mark out the plywood by drawing a pencil line down each of the long sides $1\frac{1}{4}$in. (32mm) in from the edge. Then make crosses on the line 2in. (51mm) from each end, and another two crosses $8\frac{1}{8}$in. (206mm) further in from the first two. These crosses mark screw holes. As a check on their accuracy, the second pair of crosses should be $8\frac{1}{8}$in. (206mm) from each other, as shown in the exploded drawing. Bore and countersink through the crosses for $1\frac{1}{2}$in. (38mm) No. 10 screws.

Mark out all four legs together to a length of $30\frac{1}{2}$in. (775mm). Square the lines right around each end and saw them to length.

Put each frame together 'dry', lining up the legs carefully so that their outer edges are flush with the edge of the plywood panel, and their tops flush with its top. Mark the position of the screw holes through the holes already drilled in the ply. Take the frame apart and drill the holes in the legs, using a depth stop (such as a piece of adhesive tape) on the drill bit to ensure that the holes are not more than 1in. (25mm) deep.

Glue and screw both frames together, doing the screws up very tightly so that they hold the pieces together firmly while the glue dries. Wipe off any surplus glue with a damp cloth and set the frames aside on a flat surface to dry.

The top and bottom frames

The top and bottom frames are almost identical, and their parts can be marked up together. There are two differences between them: the top is $5\frac{1}{2}$in. (140mm) deep, while the bottom is only $3\frac{3}{4}$in. (95mm) deep; and the side members of the bottom frame are $8\frac{1}{2}$in. (216mm) shorter than those of the top frame. The first difference does not affect cutting out

the pieces, because they are already planed to their finished width. As for the second, it is easiest to mark up all four side members 4ft 6in. (1372mm) long, and cut $4\frac{1}{4}$in. (108mm) off each end of the bottom frame after you have assembled it.

Put the wood for the six cross-members together in the vice, and mark them all up at the same time to a length of $23\frac{3}{4}$in. (603mm). Do the same with the four side pieces, marking them up 4ft 6in. (1372mm) long. Cut all the pieces to length.

Mark the positions of the housing joints on the side pieces, where the cross-members fit into them. The outer edge of the two outside cross-members is 7in. from the end of the side piece—provided you have followed instructions and cut them all to the same length—and the third cross-member is mounted centrally. Mark the width of the housings directly from one of the cross-members by the simple method of holding it against the side piece, squaring it with a try-square, and drawing a marking knife down both sides. Using a ruler leads to inaccuracy in cases like this.

Set a marking gauge to $\frac{3}{8}$in. (9.5mm) and mark the depth of the housings on the side of the wood. With a tenon saw, saw down to the depth marked, making the cuts very slightly inside the marked lines to make the joints a tight fit. Clean out the housings with a $\frac{3}{4}$in. (19mm) paring chisel, working from the ends to the middle to avoid splitting the wood. A router, if you have one, speeds up the job considerably, but it is not necessary.

It is a useful check on accuracy to make one complete joint before starting any of the others, and fit it together dry. Then you can adjust your sawing of the other housings.

Glue blocks

Before you finally assemble the housing joints, make sixteen glue blocks to brace them. These can most easily be made from a single strip of $\frac{7}{8}$in. x $\frac{7}{8}$in. (22mm x 22mm) timber 4ft 8in. (1422mm) long, and then cut it into eight $4\frac{1}{2}$in. (114mm), and eight $2\frac{1}{2}$in. (64mm) long blocks.

Plane a chamfer off one corner of the strip along its whole length, so that it loses $\frac{1}{4}$in. off each side (see Fig.1). Plane a much smaller chamfer of about $\frac{1}{16}$in. off the corner diagonally opposite. This corner fits into the inside corner of the housing joints, and the tiny chamfer helps it to fit well.

Cut this long strip into separate glue blocks. Then assemble the frames by glueing and pressing together the housing joints, and fastening them firmly with nails driven in diagonally as shown in Fig.3, and with their heads punched below the surface. Three nails a side is enough. Check the frames for squareness, and if satisfied, spread more glue in the corners of the joints— the inside corners of the two outer cross-members, and both sides of the centre cross-member. The glued area should extend about 1in. (25mm) from the corner on either side, along the whole length of each housing.

Spread glue on the two surfaces of the glue blocks adjacent to the smaller chamfered corner. Then press a glue block into the inside corner of a housing joint—the longer glue

blocks fit into the wider top frame, the shorter ones into the bottom frame. Rub the block backwards and forwards to get most of the glue out of the joint, and to make the block sit firmly. Then use thin nails to nail the block to the side-piece and to the cross-member (see Fig.4). Use the minimum number of nails— one each way if this makes a tight fit—and, if the first block shows signs of splitting, drill nail holes through the others. Repeat this with all the other glue blocks, then recheck both frames for squareness and set them aside to dry.

Assembly

While the glue is drying on the top and bottom frames, drill holes for the coach bolts in the end frames. There are two rows of three holes at the top, and one row at the bottom. Drill the outside holes of each row 2in. (51mm) in from the inside edge of the legs, and the centre holes in the exact centre of the frame. The top row of holes should be 2in. (51mm) from the top edge of the frame, and the second row another 2in. (51mm) below the first row. The bottom row should be 2in. (51mm) up from the lower edge of the plywood panel. The size of the drill should, of course, be the same as the size of the shank of the bolt.

When the glue on the other frames is dry, assemble the whole framework without glue and mark the position of the bolt holes on the top and bottom frames by poking a pencil through the holes in the end frames. Also mark how much wood you will have to cut off the projecting ends of the bottom frame to make them flush with the legs of the end frames. This should be about $4\frac{1}{4}$in. (108mm).

Take the framework apart, drill out the bolt holes you have marked, and trim the end frame to length. Then spread glue on all the contact surfaces of all the frames, and bolt them together with the coach bolts. As each bolt is put into its hole, its head should be hammered to make the square collar under it sink into the wood. Put a washer on the other end of the bolt and then do up the nut really tight to hold the glued joint together. When you have tightened all 18 bolts, check the complete framework for squareness and leave it to dry.

Glue and screw the $1\frac{1}{2}$in. x $\frac{7}{8}$in. (38mm x 22mm) edging to the larger of the two pieces of chipboard. It should be positioned so that its *lower* edge is flush with the under-surface of the chipboard and its top edge projects $\frac{3}{4}$in. (19mm) above it. Put the edging on the ends of the board first, plane the ends of the edging flush with the sides of the board, then apply the edging to the sides and plane its ends flush. It is not worth the trouble to mitre the corners.

Screw the chipboard sheet on to the top of the frame. The sheet and edging together are $\frac{7}{8}$in (22mm) wider than the frame (though exactly the same length) and should be allowed to project this distance off the *back* of the table, so that the front of the edging is flush with the front of the frame.

The vice

At this stage the vice should be installed. The type of vice you choose is, of course, up to you, but the instructions here are for a Record 52E, and you can adapt them to the vice you choose.

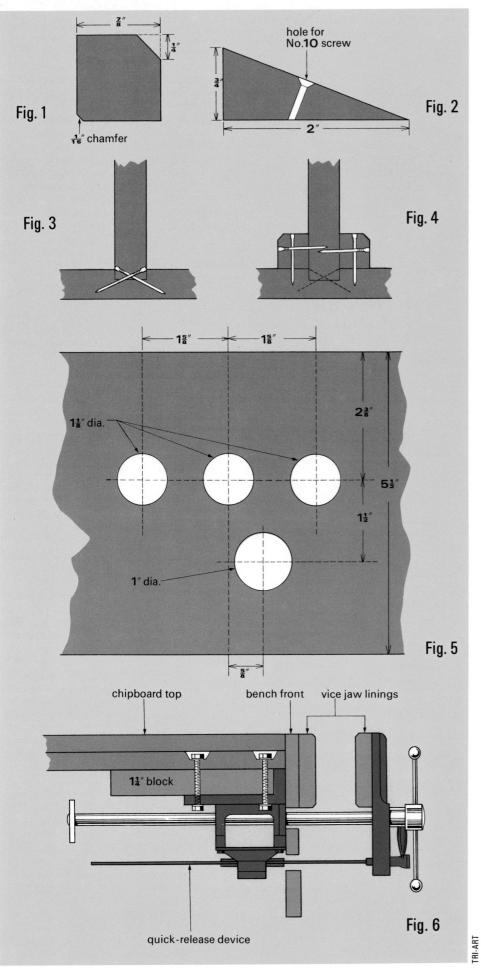

Fig. 1

$\frac{7}{8}''$

$\frac{1}{4}''$

$\frac{1}{16}''$ chamfer

hole for
No.**10** screw

$\frac{3}{4}''$

$2''$

Fig. 2

Fig. 3

Fig. 4

$1\frac{5}{8}''$ $1\frac{5}{8}''$

$1\frac{1}{8}''$ dia.

$2\frac{3}{8}''$

$5\frac{1}{2}''$

$1\frac{1}{2}''$

1" dia.

Fig. 5

$\frac{5}{8}''$

chipboard top   bench front   vice jaw linings

$1\frac{1}{4}''$ block

quick-release device

Fig. 6

TRI-ART

Woodworking vices arrive without the wooden lining that goes inside their jaws, so you will have to make it yourself. Sizes are given in the cutting list. The smaller piece is screwed to the moveable jaw; the larger piece to the front of the bench.

A cross-section of the vice mountings is given in Fig.6, and a marking-out diagram for the four holes that have to be drilled is in Fig.5. Note that the holes are very large—1in. (25mm) and $1\frac{1}{4}$in. (32mm) in diameter—and will have to be drilled out with a very large flat bit or a hole saw (see CHAPTER 38 if in doubt).

The recommended procedure for mounting the Record 52E is as follows: Mark out the front edge of the frame, anywhere along its length, as shown in the diagram and drill the holes. Make sure the rods and screws on the outer jaw of the vice fit into the holes.

Place the inner jaw lining piece against the front of the bench at the place where you want to install the vice, and with its top edge level with the top of the bench. Make sure it is the right way up. Screw it firmly to the front of the bench with four screws, one at each corner, out of the way of the vice's outer jaw. The screws should be countersunk so that their heads are slightly *below* the surface of the wood, to avoid damaging objects clamped in the vice.

Prop the bench up on one end. Poke the outer part of the vice through the holes from outside and attach the inner part temporarily to it. With most vices, you will need to put wood blocks between the inner part of the vice and the underside of the bench top to mount it firmly. In the case of the 52E, the blocks will be about $1\frac{1}{4}$in. (32mm) thick.

Mark the position of the inner part of the vice clearly; its front edge should lie against the inside of the bench frame. Remove the outer part of the vice. Cut out some blocks of a suitable size, put the inner part of the vice on them in the correct position, and drill a hole the size of the vice mounting bolts through the mounting holes on the inner part, the blocks and the chipboard bench top.

Turn the table right side up and chisel a small recess around each hole to allow the bolt heads, with a good, large washer under them, to be let in flush with the surface of the chipboard. Do not over-recess the heads or you will weaken the mounting. Bolt the inner part of the vice and the blocks firmly to the table, passing the bolts through from the top.

Screw the outer jaw lining to the outer part of the vice at such a height that, when the vice is assembled, the top of the wood will be level with the inner jaw lining and the edge of the bench. Then assemble the vice.

The Record 52E has a quick-release device that enables you to move the jaw without turning the screw. There is a cheaper version, the 52, without this device. It only needs the three 1in. (25mm) holes drilled to mount it, and not the single $1\frac{1}{4}$in. hole. This applies to many other makers' vices as well.

Final assembly

Once the vice is installed, there is not much else to do. The smaller piece of chipboard should be dropped into the top of the table at the front, so as to leave a $5\frac{7}{8}$in. wide well at the

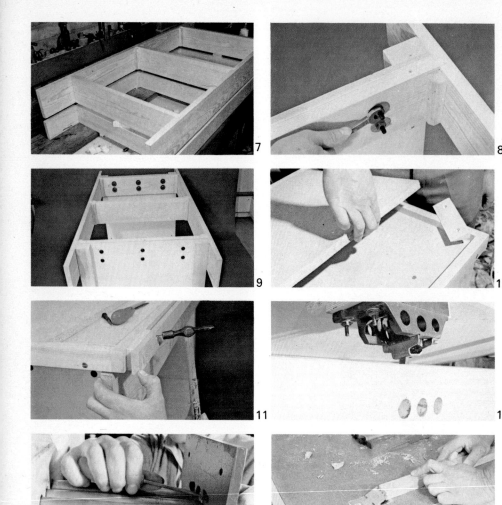

7

8

9

10

11

12

13

14

Fig.7. (left). The top and bottom frames are similar in width and length, and should be marked out and cut to length together.
Fig.8. Fastening the end frame to the top frame with glue and coach bolts.
Fig.9. The complete frame assembly, finished except for installing the top.
Fig.10. The replaceable front part of the top fits over three-quarters of the width of the lower part, and is wedged in place with triangular blocks to form a well behind it.
Fig.11. Nailing on the tool rack at the rear of the bench. Tools and unfinished parts can also be stored in the well on the top.
Fig.12. The top of the bench raised to show how the rear part of the vice is mounted. Only the first three holes have been drilled.
Fig.13. Passing the other half of the vice through the holes in the front of the bench.
Fig.14. The metal bench stop in use.
Fig.15 (below left). A list of parts.
Fig.16 (right). Exploded view of the bench.

back, which can be used to stop tools from rolling about. The two well-blocks with a triangular cross-section (see Fig.2) fit at each end of this well. They have two functions: their sloping shape allows the well to be swept out when it gets full of sawdust, and they stop the replaceable chipboard top from slipping backwards. They should be a very tight fit, so cut them out over-length and trim them to length on the spot. Then screw them to the lower piece of chipboard with two 1in. (25mm) long screws. Screw the lower piece of chipboard to the top replaceable piece from underneath with a few 1½in. (38mm) screws. When the top needs replacing, all you will have to do is remove these screws. Grease them so that they don't rust in place.

The tool rack on the rear edge of the bench should be fitted by glueing and pinning the three blocks in place, then glueing on the rail and screwing it to the bench through the blocks with 1½in. (38mm) screws. It provides a useful storage space for chisels, screwdrivers and saws.

Glue and pin the remaining sheet of ½in. (13mm) plywood to the top side of the lower frame. This will provide a storage shelf for larger tools and half-completed projects.

To finish the bench, give it two coats of polyurethane varnish. Give the top a third coat, just to make it last longer.

The bench is now complete, unless you want to install a bench stop (which is a good idea). There are many types of stop, but all are simple to fix. The type shown here (see Fig.14) can be fastened on in a few minutes by laying it on the table, drawing round it with a pencil, and chiselling out the outlined area to a depth of about ½in. (13mm). A hole is also drilled to give clearance to a large screw that projects below the rest of the stop. Then the stop is dropped into the recess; it should fit flush with the bench top. It is held in with two ¾in. (19mm) No. 6 countersunk screws, and can be raised or lowered by turning the large screw.

If you do not want to use a proprietary bench stop, buy a piece of hardwood about 1½in. or 38mm square and about 6in. or 300mm long, and install it in a square hole chiselled right through both pieces of chipboard.

Fig.15 CUTTING LIST   All planed finished sizes

		inches	millimetres
Good quality softwood			
4 legs		30½ × 2½ × 1⅜	775 × 64 × 35
top frame:	2 rails	54 × 5½ × ⅞	1372 × 140 × 22
	3 cross rails	23¾ × 5½ × ⅞	603 × 140 × 22
	8 glue blocks	4½ × ⅞ × ⅞	114 × 22 × 22
bottom frame:	2 rails	54 × 3¾ × ⅞	1372 × 95 × 22
	3 cross rails	23¾ × 3¾ × ⅞	603 × 95 × 22
	8 glue blocks	2½ × ⅞ × ⅞	64 × 22 × 22
top edging:	2 sides	54 × 1½ × ⅞	1372 × 38 × 22
	2 ends	23⅞ × 1½ × ⅞	606 × 38 × 22
tool rack:	3 blocks	3 × 1½ × ½	76 × 38 × 13
	1 rail	54 × 1½ × ½	1372 × 38 × 13
2 well blocks (approx. size)		7 × 2 × ¾	178 × 51 × 19
13mm (½in.) plywood			
2 end panels		28½ × 23	724 × 584
1 bottom panel		40 × 24¾	1016 × 629
19mm (¾in.) high-density chipboard			
top (permanent part)		52¼ × 23⅞	1327 × 606
top (replaceable part)		52¼ × 18	1327 × 457
Hardwood (preferably beech)			
vice jaws (for Record 52E or similar type): 1 piece		15 × 3 × ¾	381 × 76 × 19
	1 piece	9 × 3 × ¾	229 × 76 × 19

Also needed
18 coach bolts 1¾in. × ⁵⁄₁₆in. (44 × 8mm), 18 large 'mudguard' washers, 3 dozen 1½in. (38mm) No. 10 countersunk screws, and a bench stop, vice and mounting bolts to choice.

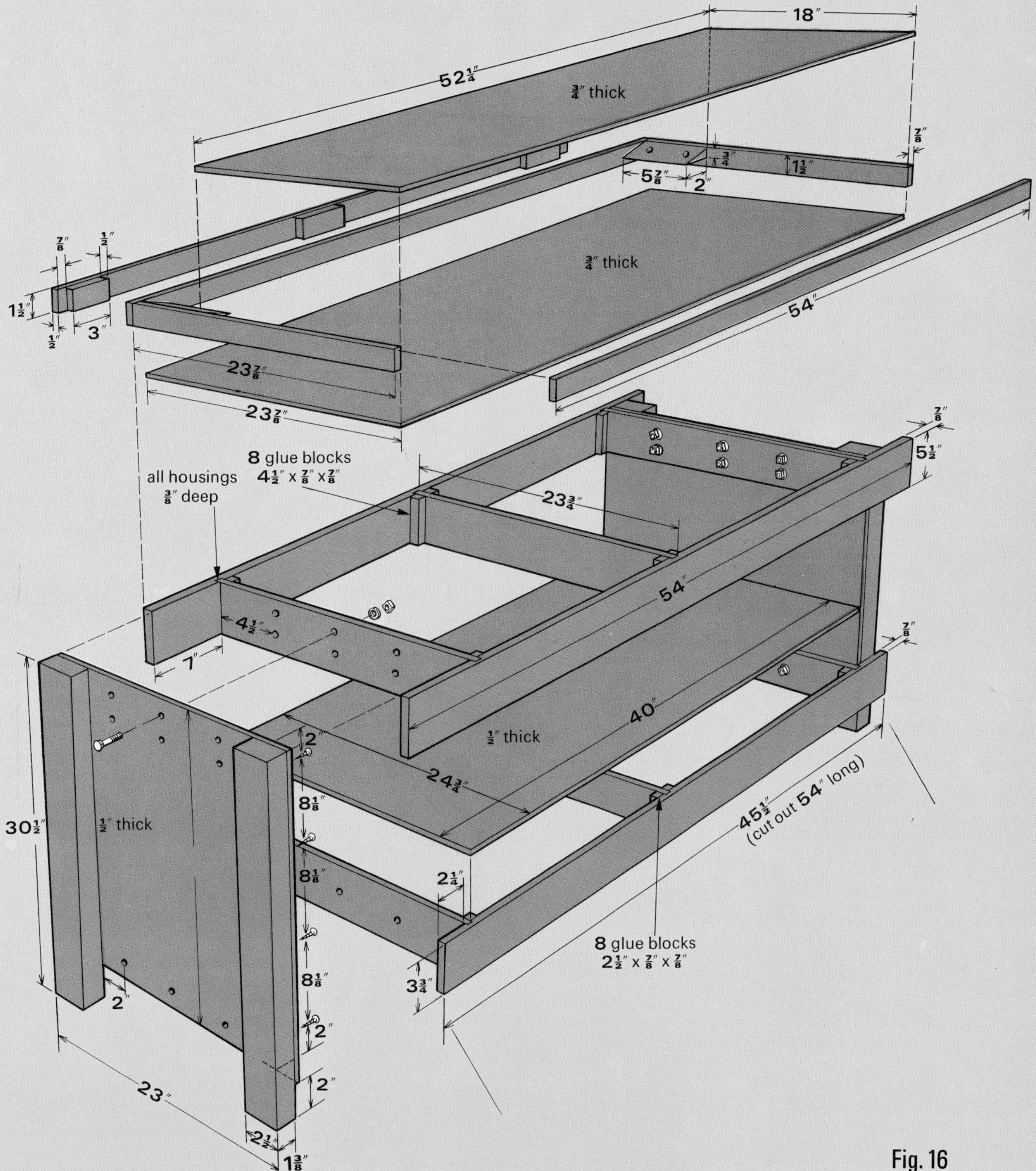
18″
52¼″
¾″ thick
⅞″
¾″
1½″
5⅞″
2″
⅞″
½″
1½″
½″
3″
¾″ thick
54″
23⅞″
23⅞″
⅞″
5½″
8 glue blocks
4½″ x ⅞″ x ⅞″
all housings
⅜″ deep
23¾″
54″
4½″
7″
⅞″
40″
½″ thick
2″
24¾″
8⅛″
45½″
(cut out 54″ long)
30½″
½″ thick
8⅛″
2¼″
8 glue blocks
2½″ x ⅞″ x ⅞″
8⅛″
3¾″
2″
2″
2″
23″
2½″
1⅜″

Fig. 16

TRI-ART

Build a toolbox
and sawhorse

There are a lot of jobs around the house that are done just above head height—putting up pelmets, repairing door and window frames, and so on. A stepladder is too tall for this kind of work, and a chair unsafe. What you need is a stable, horizontal support—and here's how to make one.

This versatile unit combines a roomy storage box for your carpenter's tools with a *hop-up*—a stand that you can use for supporting the end of a plank, or just for standing on. If you have already built the sawhorse which is described in CHAPTER 7, the hop-up and the sawhorse, which are exactly the same height, make a useful pair of trestles.

The project introduces the *through dovetail* joint, one of the strongest joints in carpentry—and the most impressive looking. In fact, it is much easier to make than it looks.

Materials needed

The sides of the box and the hop-up frame are made of 19mm ($\frac{3}{4}$in.) pine. You will need: 2 pieces 21$\frac{1}{2}$in. x 7in (545 x 178mm), 2 pieces

20in. x $6\frac{1}{4}$in. (506 x 161mm), 2 pieces $18\frac{1}{4}$in. x 5in. (463 x 128mm), 1 piece 25in. x 6in. (635 x 153mm) and 2 pieces 25in. x $1\frac{3}{4}$in. (635 x 44mm).

The lid is made of 19mm ($\frac{3}{4}$in.) birch plywood:
2 pieces $18\frac{1}{4}$in. x $8\frac{1}{4}$in (463 x 209mm), 1 piece $18\frac{1}{4}$in. x 5in. (463 x 128mm).

The bottom is made of a piece of 9.5mm ($\frac{3}{8}$in.) birch ply $21\frac{1}{2}$in. x 20in. (545 x 506mm).

You will also need four 9in. (229mm) and two 21in. (532mm) pieces of 19 x 9.5mm ($\frac{3}{4}$in. x $\frac{3}{8}$in.) beading, and two 20in. (506mm) pieces of 19 x 13mm ($\frac{3}{4}$in. x $\frac{1}{2}$in.) beading.

The fitting for the unit are:
4 'strut' hinges—which are easier to get from a leathergoods shop than a hardware store—and some $\frac{3}{4}$in. (19mm) No. 6 screws for mounting them, 8 coach bolts 2in x $\frac{3}{16}$in. (50 x 5mm) with 8 nuts and 8 washers, 4 rubber seat buffers (the small rubber 'feet' used on furniture), two dozen $1\frac{1}{2}$in. (38mm) No. 10 screws, $1\frac{1}{4}$in. (32mm) panel pins (for fixing the bottom of the box), 1in. (25mm) panel pins (for fixing the beading) and adhesive.

If the box is to be used out of doors—as it probably will—all metal fittings should be brass, or lacquered, plated or galvanized. The adhesive should be a waterproof urea formaldehyde type.

All sizes given for timber are exact finished sizes. The pieces should, of course, be originally cut slightly oversize.

Marking out for a dovetail joint

The corners of the tool box part of the unit are dovetailed together. Since this type of joint must fit perfectly to work, it is essential that the ends of the boards are cut exactly at right angles to give you an accurate start.

Mark out the pieces for the opposite sides of the box together in pairs, to ensure that they are exactly the same length as each other. Then plane the ends dead square with a shooting board, leaving only $\frac{1}{8}$in. (3mm) waste overall—$\frac{1}{16}$in. at each end of the board. Check the angle of the ends to the sides and edges of the wood with a try square.

Choose the face side and edge of each piece and arrange them as they will be in the finished box. Then mark and number the adjacent corners as shown in Fig.1, using a pencil. This is important, for it is all too easy to make a dovetail joint backwards if you don't know which way round the wood is to go.

The shape that the dovetail joint will eventually have is shown in Fig.7. Each side of the joint is different, and also assymetrical in its own right. There are two shapes of interlocking teeth: *pins* and *tails*. The tails are made first and the pins marked directly from them to ensure accuracy.

First mark a line to indicate the depth to which the dovetails will be cut. Set a marking gauge to the thickness of the timber plus $\frac{1}{16}$in. (1.6mm) for the waste—this comes to $\frac{13}{16}$in. (20.6mm). Then, working from the squared end of the box sides and the ends, *lightly* mark the line all the way round the end of each piece.

The sides of the pins and tails are sloped to lend greater strength to the joint, and the slope in this particular case is 1 in 7. This should be marked with an adjustable bevel gauge, which must be very accurately set.

To set the gauge, take one of the 7in. (178 mm) wide pieces of wood and lightly square a line across it anywhere along its length in pencil (see Fig.8). Then mark a point on the edge of the piece 1in. (25mm) along from the squared line, and draw a sloping line from the mark to the far end of the first line. This sloping line and the edge of the wood form the angle to set your bevel gauge to. Rub out the lines afterwards.

Take the two narrower pieces of wood—the box ends—which will have the tails of the joints on them, and mark them up carefully with the bevel gauge as shown in Fig.6. Mark on both sides, using the bevel gauge for each slope and squaring the lines across the end of the wood with a try square. Do not mark the pins yet.

Cutting for a dovetail joint

As in all carpentry, the saw cuts for the joints must be made on the waste side of the marked lines. It is easy to forget which *is* the waste side when cutting out a complex shape, so draw diagonal pencil lines through the waste wood to identify it.

The most accurate way to cut the tails is put the timber upright in a vice and make all the cuts sloping one way first (see Fig.2), then turn the wood round and make the other halves of the cuts. In this way you will always be tilting the saw blade the same way, and so you will be able to gauge the angle you are cutting at with greater ease. A right-handed person should cut on a slope from top right to bottom left for the greatest accuracy; a left-handed person the other way. This will enable you to see the line you are sawing to.

Cut out the majority of the waste with a coping saw (see Fig.3), and then cut back to the marked line with a $\frac{1}{2}$in. (13mm) *bevel-edged* chisel. A square-edged chisel blade cannot cut right into the acute-angled corners, so it is no use here.

Once all the tails are cut to your satisfaction, transfer their shape to the pins in the following way. Put the piece in which the pins are to be cut upright in the vice. Lay on top of it the adjacent piece with tails to which it will fit, check the numbers you have marked on both pieces to ensure that they are the right way round.

The top piece must be square on to the bottom piece so that the markings can be accurately

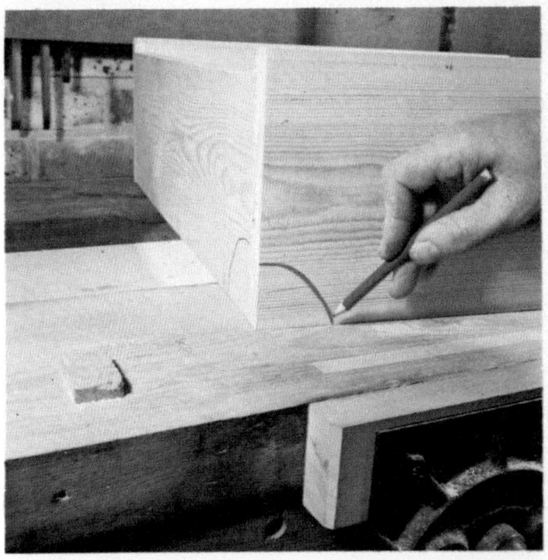

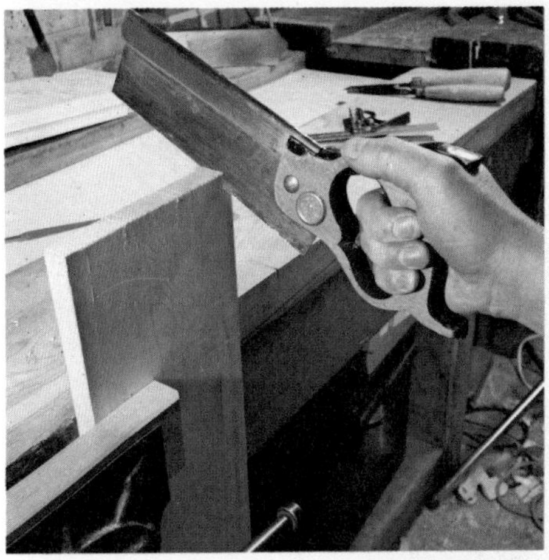

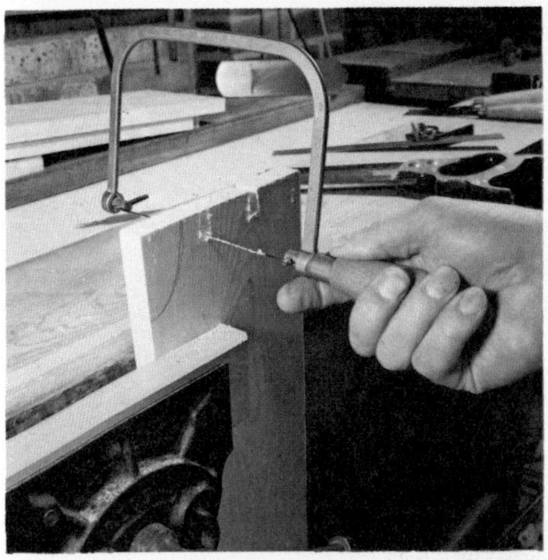

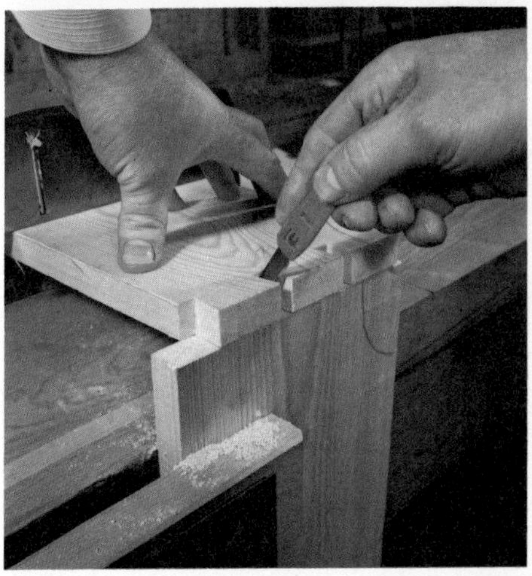

***Fig.1** (top). Mark the adjacent corners of all the pieces that are to be dovetailed together. They should be numbered as well.*

***Fig.2** (second from top). It will improve the accuracy of your sawing if you cut all the right-hand slopes, then turn the wood round and cut all the other slopes.*

***Fig.3** (third from top). When all the slopes are cut, remove most of the surplus wood with a coping saw, and chisel out the rest.*

***Fig.4** (bottom). Transfer the outline of the tails to the other piece with a marking knife pressed well into the corners.*

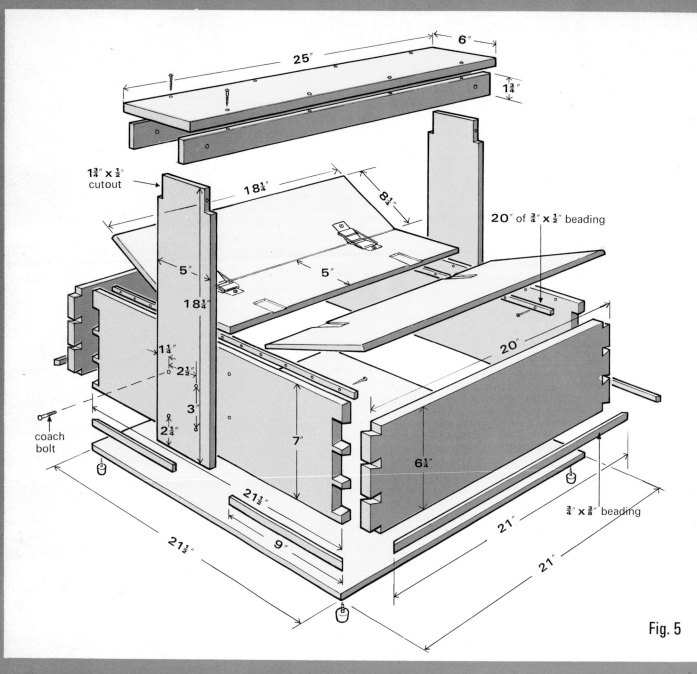

Fig. 5

transferred. The best way to do this is to prop it up on a big wood block—for example, a wooden plane on its side, and put a weight on top to hold it steady (see Fig.9). Then you can move the other piece up or down in the vice until you have got the two pieces correctly arranged.

The piece on which the pins are to be marked is slightly wider than the piece with tails in this unit, so make sure that the extra width is at the side that will form the top edge of the box. When everything is lined up right, trace around the outline of the tails with a marking knife (see Fig.4). Then remove the wood from the vice and square the marks down each side as far as the gauge line.

Saw out the sides of the pins as before, the only difference being that the slope is the other way—tilted in relation to the edge of the wood instead of to the end. Cut out the waste with a coping saw as before, and finish with a chisel—a 1in. or 25mm bevel edge is better than a ½in.

or 13mm one, since there is more wood to remove this time. Be very careful not to cut through the pins.

Test the first joint you finish by tapping the pieces together with a block of wood. If it is a very tight fit you may be able to improve it by chiselling away a little wood from the tails. If it is too loose, there is no remedy but to start again.

Assembly of the box

Once the dovetail joints are cut, everything else is fairly straightforward. Glue the joints together—if they are well made they should not need cramping. If they are a bit loose, chisel out pieces of scrapwood to press only on the tails (not the pins), and put them under the jaws of the cramp to press the tails down on to the pins (see Fig.10). You will have to use sash cramps. Check the diagonals to make sure the box is square and leave it till the glue sets.

Plane the bottom edge of the box frame lightly to level it off, then glue and pin the

ply base in position. Plane off the excess ply, and then plane down the $\frac{1}{16}$in. (1.6mm) waste sticking out of each side of the dovetail joints.

Glue and screw the two thicker pieces of beading to the inside of the longer sides of the box, with their top edges $\frac{3}{4}$in. (19mm) below the top edge of the box. These pieces act as bearers to hold up the lids. Glue and pin the centre fixed part of the box top in place, resting on the bearers and secured by panel pins driven into its ends through the outside wall of the box.

Plane the moveable lids for the box to shape. They should have at least $\frac{1}{16}$in. (1.6mm) gap down each side to stop them from jamming shut when varnished. If you can get a thin coin between each side of the lid and the box wall, that is about the right clearance. Plane the outer edge of the lid off at an angle (see Fig.11) so that you can hook your fingers under it to lift it.

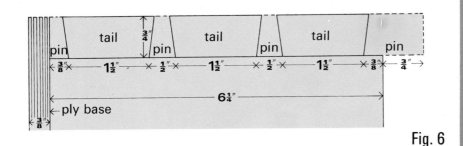

tail | tail | tail
pin | pin | pin | pin | pin

$\frac{3}{4}$"

$\frac{3}{8}$" — 1$\frac{1}{2}$" — $\frac{1}{2}$" — 1$\frac{1}{2}$" — $\frac{1}{2}$" — 1$\frac{1}{2}$" — $\frac{3}{8}$" — $\frac{3}{4}$"

6$\frac{1}{4}$"

ply base

$\frac{3}{8}$"

Fig. 6

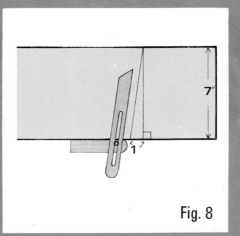

pins

tails

Fig. 7

7"

6

1"

Fig. 8

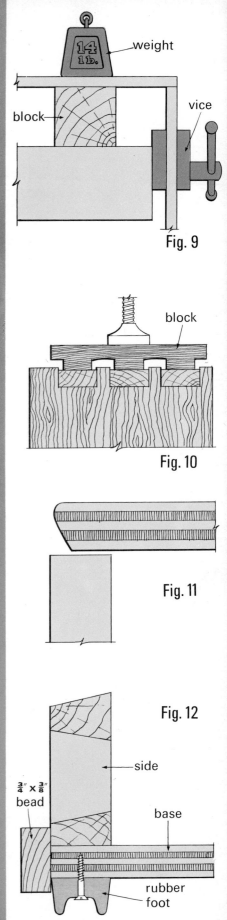

weight

14 lb.

block

vice

Fig. 9

block

Fig. 10

Fig. 11

Fig. 12

side

$\frac{3}{4}$" × $\frac{3}{8}$" bead

base

rubber foot

Fig.5 (left). An exploded view of the unit, showing the shape and dimensions of the pieces, and how they fit together.

Fig.6 (top). The measurements of the dovetail joints, seen from the tail side of the joint. Use this diagram as a guide for marking out the tails (it is not to scale).

Fig.7 (above, left). The same joint seen in perspective, to show how it fits together.

Fig.8 (above, right). How to set the bevel gauge to a 1 in 7 slope. It is vital that the line running straight across should be at right angles to the edge of the wood.

Fig.9 (top, far right). Prop the two halves of each joint up in this way when transferring markings from one piece to another.

Fig.10 (second from top). If the dovetail joints need cramping while the glue dries, make four of these special blocks to press down only on the tails of the joints.

Fig.11 (third from top). The outside edge of each lid should be planed off at an angle to allow you to lift it easily.

Fig.12 (bottom). A cross-section of the base of the unit, showing the position of the rubber foot and the beading.

The hop-up

The hop-up is a simple square frame bolted to the sides of the box. There are two reinforcing strips under the horizontal top to stop it from sagging when you stand on it. Make a $\frac{1}{2}$in. x 1$\frac{3}{4}$in. (13 x 45mm) cutout in each side of the top of the two vertical frame members to accommodate these reinforcements.

Assemble the three pieces of the top first, glueing and screwing them together with four screws a side for extra strength.

While the glue is drying, bolt the vertical pieces to the sides of the box. This is done by laying the pieces against the box in the correct position and drilling straight through vertical piece and box at once with a drill the same size as the shank of the bolt. There are four bolt holes a side, as shown on the exploded view, Fig.5.

Press each bolt through from the outside and hammer the head until the square flange under it has sunk completely into the wood. Then apply a washer and nut to the shaft on the inside.

Before you tighten the nuts, check that both vertical frame members are upright and parallel.

Slide the horizontal top down on to the vertical frame members. Centre it and screw it on with screws passed through the reinforcing strips into the edge of the vertical members.

Glue and pin the beading to the lower edge of the box (see Fig.12.) This can be mitred at the corners if you prefer, but an easier method is to butt-joint it.

Complete the assembly by screwing the lids on to the box with strut hinges 3in. (76mm) from each outside edge. This type of hinge holds the lid open, and also prevents it from falling over backwards and getting in the way of the other lid. Make sure that the planed finger-grip on each lid is the right way up. Screw a rubber foot to each corner of the box base.

Finally, plane down any rough spots, lightly glass-paper the unit all over and finish it with three coats of polyurethane varnish, rubbing down lightly between coats.

Making picture frames

Have you ever wanted a special picture frame for one of your favourite paintings? Shops have only a limited range of frames, but you can quickly and easily make a frame to suit any picture and any room decor—at a cost of a few pence, using nothing but inexpensive mouldings.

This project introduces *mitring*, a technique used for making a neat-looking L-shaped joint. The ends of two pieces of wood are cut at 45° and fastened together so that their two angles make up a 90° right angle. The mitred joint is symmetrical, and so is particularly convenient where a rebate or moulding has to be carried round a corner without interruption (see Fig.7).

Great accuracy is essential when making a mitre, particularly in angling the 45° cut. If one or both of the angles is not 45°, the resulting corner joint will not be a right angle, or there will be an unsightly gap in it. For this reason the

angled cut is made with the wood held in a simple sawing guide called a *mitre box* (Fig.1). You can make your own out of scrap timber, but since professionally-made ones cost just a few shillings in Britain it is easier to buy one at a tool shop. More accurate, but expensive, metal types are also made.

Mitred frames are normally glued and pinned together, and must be held in cramps while the glue dries. Ordinary cramps are not suitable. You can buy metal corner cramps like those in Fig.2, which often have a saw slot so that they can be used for cutting mitres as well as holding them. But they tend to be expensive, particularly if you have to buy four. A far cheaper alternative is the simple plastic device illustrated in Fig.5, which consists of four corner pieces, a length of nylon cord and a clip for holding it tight.

Buying mouldings

The choice of mouldings used to make your frame depends on personal taste and the type of picture you are framing. A plain, narrow

frame can be made from a single moulding, or you can make up a complex one from a lot of mouldings stuck together. Some ideas are shown in Fig.8.

The only feature all frames must have is a rebate around the inside rear edge to accommodate the thickness of the picture, a hardboard backing and the glass (if any), plus about $\frac{1}{8}$in. or 3mm extra depth. This rebate can be cut with a rebate plane, though you may find it less trouble to arrange the mouldings so that a rebate shape is built up at that point without the need for cutting. It is difficult and tiresome to cut a long rebate in a narrow moulding.

The amount of moulding you will need for each picture can be found by measuring the circumference of the picture and adding eight times the width of the moulding itself, plus a generous allowance for waste.

For a frame made up of several mouldings, use this formula for determining the amount of each moulding.

You will also need a piece of hardboard the same size as the picture, and some thin glass if the picture is to be covered. The only other materials you will need are some picture sprigs (tiny, headless nails), panel pins (small ones, except for a huge frame), some pva glue, and a roll of brown-paper tape.

Preparation and measurement

An oil painting, or a picture on a stiff backing, will need no preparation before you start work. A picture or print on paper should be stuck carefully on to a stiff card backing. Use a rubber solution adhesive such as 'Cow' gum, which

will not damage the paper and which allows the picture to be peeled off if you lay it down crooked. The only type of picture that could be damaged by this type of adhesive is one done in spirit-based ink such as 'Magic Marker' ink. For this type, use a white paper glue.

Now decide whether you want any of the mount or backing around your picture to show when it is framed. If not, trim it down until it is $\frac{1}{4}$in. or 6mm larger all round than the size of your picture, using a handyman's knife (this does not apply to oil paintings). Very small pictures can be trimmed to within $\frac{1}{8}$in. or 3mm of their final size. This margin will also be the width of the rebate on the back of the frame. It is impossible to frame an oil painting without covering up a little of the edge.

As a general rule, oil paintings should not be covered by glass—their varnish protects them. Water-colours are generally covered with glass and pastels must be, because they smudge easily. Covering prints is optional, but it is not recommended where the glass might catch the light from a window and hide the picture with reflections.

Before starting work, check that the corners of your picture and mount are perfectly square, and that the opposite sides are the same length. Mark the width of the rebates clearly at each corner.

Assembling the mouldings

If your picture frame is to be made out of several mouldings stuck together, you should assemble them before cutting the mitres. The best way to do this is to fasten, with glue and temporary pins, a whole length of moulding in the size in which you bought it. In brief: assemble first, cut later.

The pins cannot be left in because they may get in the way of the saw later. In any case, picture frames do not have to be particularly strong, so glue alone will do for the mouldings. The best way to hold the glued joints together is with pins driven through from the back, so that the holes do not show later. If the frame is to be painted, you can put pins in the front too, and fill the holes with stopping after you have removed them.

Put a small piece of scrap plywood or hardboard under the head of each pin. This will protect the wood from hammer marks, and also make the pins much easier to remove.

Leave the glue to dry to its full strength (overnight at least) before doing anything else, then remove the pins.

Cutting the rebates

The rebates are cut with a plough plane, which cuts a deep narrow groove to the depth required along one edge of the wood. Then another groove is cut at right angles to the first. The two grooves, when they meet, remove a square or oblong section of wood to leave a step-shaped recess, or rebate.

To ensure uniformity of your rebates, set your marking gauge first to the width required and mark all your lengths of moulding. Then re-set the gauge to the depth required, and again mark all the lengths. This avoids any error through repeated re-setting.

In cutting, the most important thing is to set the fence, or guide, on the plane to the correct width. The next most important thing is to start cutting towards the *far* end of the line, pushing the plane away from you in a series of short, overlapping strokes. (Further details on rebating are in CHAPTER 3.)

Cutting mitres

From your standard moulding or collection of glued-together mouldings, cut out the four sides of the frame, leaving a generous waste allowance in addition to the allowance for the width of the mitre at each end (see Fig.9).

Then transfer the marks you have made at each corner of the picture to the inside edge of the moulding, using a pencil and aligning the pair of marks carefully on each piece (see Fig.10). These marks indicate the length of the shorter inside edge of the frame.

Put a piece of moulding, front side up, in the mitre box so that the mark at one end of the moulding lines up with one of the 45° slots on the top of the mitre box, and the marked inside edge lies along one side of the box (see Fig.11). Fasten it firmly in place with a G-cramp, its top jaw padded with scrap wood so as not to damage the moulding.

Place a tenon saw blade in the appropriate 45° slot and cut through the moulding. Repeat with the other seven ends, making sure that the mitres are being cut the right way round. The tenon saw you use must have a blade wide enough to reach to the bottom of the box, and it must be *very sharp*. Your local tool shop will sharpen it for you quite cheaply.

If you are not confident of your ability to do

59

Fig.1. *The mitre box: a channel-shaped guide to take the moulding, with pre-cut slots to hold the saw at the correct angle.*

Fig.2. *A more expensive and accurate metal mitre guide with built-in screw cramps to hold the wood steady.*

Fig.3. *The mitre shooting board ensures 100 per cent accuracy in cutting a mitre at exactly the right angle.*

this absolutely right first time, you have two choices. One, is to do a 'trial run' on a short offcut of the moulding. The other is to leave $\frac{1}{16}$in. — $\frac{1}{32}$in. waste on the wood when sawing, and finish the mitres with a plane and a mitre shooting board. You can convert an ordinary shooting board (described in CHAPTER 4) to a mitre shooting board quickly and easily by removing the stop and replacing it with a centrally mounted stop cut in the shape of a right-angled equilateral triangle (i.e. with one angle of 90° and two angles of 45°—see Fig.12). Cut this stop on the mitre box and check its angles and position on the board carefully with a bevel gauge or mitre try square. The angles must be *exactly* right, or your frame will end up out of square.

Set the plane very fine to avoid splitting the mouldings, and use the shooting board like an ordinary one—though you will have to move the plane the other way for half the mitres, because you always plane *towards* the stop.

Assembling mitres

Glue and pin the mitres together. The correct way to drive in the pins is to put one side of each joint upright in a vice and to hold the other

horizontally above it, as in Fig.13. Note that the top piece is a little too far 'uphill'—about $\frac{1}{16}$in. or 1mm. This is because the pin will inevitably slide a little to the side as it is driven in, although pre-drilling the pin hole (see below) helps avoid this.

The bottom corners of the frame should be made with the pins driven in horizontally on both sides, to prevent the weight of the picture from pulling the bottom piece of the frame away from the sides.

With very narrow mouldings, there is a risk of the pins splitting the wood. To prevent this, drill a narrow pilot hole in the first piece of wood the pin passes through. If you do not have a drill bit of the correct size, cut the head off one of your pins and file one end to a wedge shape. Do not drill the second piece, because the pin will be going into end grain, and there is little danger of splitting the wood.

Cramp up the frame, check the diagonals to see that it is square, and leave it to dry.

Finishing the frame

The frame can be painted or varnished. Wide flat areas on a frame can be covered in cloth toning with a colour in the picture, or matching

your room decor. It is a good idea to make a painted frame first of all, so that any gaps or mistakes made during construction can be filled up and painted over.

Gloss paint generally does not look good on frames. It is a better idea to use three or four coats of emulsion, allow it to dry thoroughly and burnish it to a smooth satin finish with fine steel wool.

Mount the picture on the frame in the following way: cut the glass (if any) and hardboard backing to the right size to fit neatly into the rebated back of the frame. Put the glass in first, then the picture, then the backing. Secure this 'sandwich' in place with sprigs driven into the edge of the frame almost horizontally, as shown in Fig.14. There should be at least one sprig every three inches (75mm). Finally, cover the join between frame and backing with strips of brown-paper tape for a professional finish and to keep out dust.

The completed framed picture can be hung up invisibly by putting screw-eyes in the back of the frame sides, three-quarters of the way up, and stretching picture wire tightly between them. The wire can then be hooked over a nail or a special picture hook.

Fig.4. *An alternative method of holding mitred corners together—corrugated fasteners driven into the back.*

Fig.5. *This beautifully simple string-and-plastic device holds a frame together as strongly as more expensive corner cramps.*

Fig.6. *To colour the frame but leave the natural grain of the wood clearly visible, use waterproof drawing ink.*

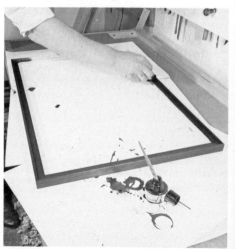

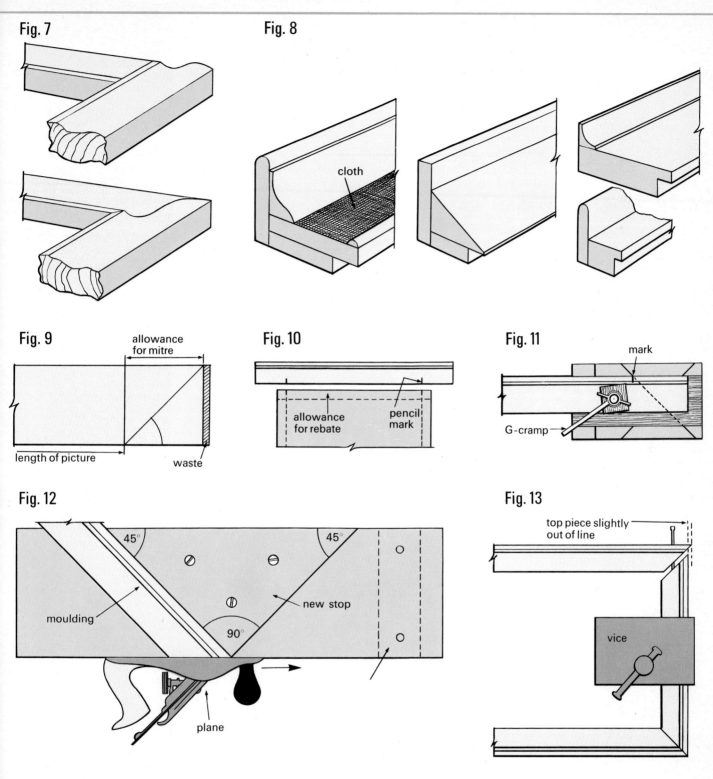

Fig. 7

Fig. 8

cloth

Fig. 9

allowance
for mitre

length of picture

waste

Fig. 10

allowance
for rebate

pencil
mark

Fig. 11

mark

G-cramp

Fig. 12

45°

45°

moulding

new stop

90°

plane

Fig. 13

top piece slightly
out of line

vice

Fig.7. *Shaped mouldings look messy when butt-jointed (above); the neat mitred joint (below) solves the problem.*
Fig.8. *Several ideas for joining standard mouldings to make a wide frame—but the possibilities are endless.*
Fig.9. *When cutting the mouldings to length, you should allow for the width of the mitre as well as for waste.*
Fig.10. *The inner corner of the mitre is marked directly from the corner of the central, visible area of your picture.*

Fig.11. *The mark at the inner corner is then lined up with one of the 45° slots in the sides of the mitre box.*
Fig.12. *Top view of a mitre shooting board, showing the angles at which the corners of the new stop should be cut.*
Fig.13. *When pinning the frame together, the top piece should be set slightly out of line to allow for slippage of the pin.*
Fig.14. *A cross-section of the framed picture. The sprigs should be driven in as near horizontal as you can manage.*

Fig. 14

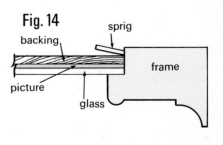

sprig

backing

frame

picture

glass

A classic Welsh dresser

The clean lines of this Welsh dresser add a modern touch to the traditional design and enable the unit to blend well with any style of decor. An added attraction is the ample storage space the dresser provides with its spacious cupboard, shelves and drawers and the sturdy work surface.

The Welsh dresser in the photograph is made from redwood, but any softwood that can be sanded to a smooth finish will do. The dresser has two spacious drawers and a large cupboard with a shelf. The doors of the cupboard and the short sides of the dresser are made by the same techniques. The unit has a large, solid work surface and an upper part, with two shelves for the storage of plates or jars.

The construction is simple, the joints being either through or stopped housings or secret-dowelled joints. Some grooves have to be made, but if you have a combination plane, this is easy work.

Another advantage of the type of construction used in the Welsh dresser is that nearly all the components can be cut out and partly assembled before any major assembly work has to be undertaken. For example, while the adhesive that joins the planks that form the work surface is drying, you can be making another component. In this way the dresser can be made quickly—though you should be careful not to spoil the job by working *too* quickly.

Because most of the components can be made independently of each other, the order in which they are made is not really important.

The cupboard frames

These are the easiest components to construct. They form the skeleton of the front and back of the cupboard part of the dresser. The drawers fit into the front frame, and the cupboard doors are hinged to it. The plywood panel that forms the back of the cupboard is pinned to the near frame.

The arrangement and dimensions of the components used in the frames are shown in Fig.2. The components of the frame are butted together and strengthened with one dowel pin in each joint. **CHAPTER 15** describes the secret-dowelling method that is used.

When making these frames it is essential that the final construction is square. You can test this with a large try square or by measuring the

Left. A functional and attractive unit, the Welsh dresser has ample storage space for food, crockery and table linen.

diagonals. The components are glued together and sash cramped while the glue dries, so if the frame is slightly out of square you may be able to correct it by doing up one sash cramp more tightly than the others.

The sides and cupboard doors

The construction of the two side panels of the cupboard and of the cupboard doors is the same; only the dimensions are different. Each door is 23$\frac{3}{16}$in. x 17in. (588mm x 432mm) and the finished size of the side is 31$\frac{1}{8}$in. x 21in. (790mm x 533mm). The rails and stiles of doors and sides alike are made of 2$\frac{3}{4}$in. x $\frac{7}{8}$in. (69mm x 22mm) timber.

The rails and stiles are fastened together at the corners by halving joints. A $\frac{5}{16}$in. (8mm) thick infill of T & G matching is fitted into grooves cut in the inside edges of these pieces.

First cut the rails and stiles a little oversize. Mark a point in the centre of each piece along its length and take all measurements for the halved areas from this point. Mark out the area of the joints with the four rails of the two doors laid together with their long edges butting. Do the same for the four rails of the two sides. Mark out the stiles for the doors and the stiles for the sides in the same way. Then cut the joints in the manner described fully in **CHAPTER 5.**

When the joints are cut, lay the pieces together in roughly their finished position. Mark the top faces. This ensures that when you cut the grooves into which the matching fits you cut from the correct side of all pieces.

Now cut the groove on the inside edge of the stiles and rails. You will need a combination plane to do this. You will also have to make stopped grooves on some of the pieces to avoid encroaching on the halving joints. You can make most of each cut with the plane and finish the ends with a chisel. Cut the groove to a depth of $\frac{1}{2}$in. (13mm) using a $\frac{5}{16}$in. (8mm) wide blade. Make the cut from what will be the front of the doors or sides and set the fence on the plane to $\frac{3}{16}$in. (4.8mm)—the distance from the front face of the rails and stiles to the front edge of the groove.

The next step is to fit the matching. This is 2in. x $\frac{5}{16}$in. (50mm x 8mm) tongued-and-grooved boarding; the length of the boards is the distance between the inside edges of the stiles plus $\frac{1}{2}$in. (13mm) at each end. The matching is fitted so that it is parallel to the rails of the doors and side panels.

Before you fit any matching, work out the widths of the first and last pieces. These should be of equal width but they should not be too narrow. You can find the width easily by

dividing the width of the matching into the distance between the inside edges of the rails an exact number of times and halving the remainder.

Cut the first piece of matching to size. If you need to reduce its width, cut from the tongued side. In any case remove the tongue from the first piece. Before fitting it, glue the bottom rail of each door or side piece and the two stiles together. Cramp the assembly with a sash cramp running along the rail and parallel to it. Then fit the first piece of matching before the adhesive dries.

Push the first piece of matching into the groove and lightly tap it into place in the rail with a mallet and scrap wood block. Fit this piece tongued side first. Fit each subsequent piece in the same way, but exert a little more force with the mallet to push the tongue of the new piece into the groove of the previous piece. Push the last piece of matching into place. Apply glue to the joint surfaces at the top of the stiles and on the top rail. Jam the top rail into place on top of the last piece of matching. Release the sash cramp at the bottom rail and check that the assembly is square. If it is, cramp it together again firmly.

When the adhesive has dried, plane off the small pieces of the rails and stiles that protrude from the halving joints.

Cutting the finger holds

The doors (but not the sides of the cupboard) have a finger hold cut into the outside edge of one stile of each door. The stile is, of course, the opposite one to the one that has a hinge fitted to it later.

The finger hold is 5$\frac{1}{4}$in. long and starts 2$\frac{3}{4}$in. down from the top edge of the stile. It enters the narrow edge of the stile to a depth of $\frac{5}{8}$in. (16mm), and the wide inner face of the stile to the same depth. First mark from the top of the stile a distance of 2$\frac{3}{4}$in. (70mm) and from this point mark off 5$\frac{1}{4}$in. (133mm) down the stile. Square lines through these points on the edge of the stile and on the inner face. Then set a marking gauge to $\frac{5}{8}$in. (16mm) and score a mark between these two square lines on both the edge and inner face of the stile, but not quite reaching the lines because of the curved ends of the finger hold. Mark out the curved ends freehand, with the top of the curve ending on the line scored on the inner face of the stile. The top of the curve should be about $\frac{3}{4}$in. (19mm) from the squared lines which indicate the length of the finger hold.

Then use a chisel to cut the finger hold. This will be quite a long process, but the initial chiselling does not have to be particularly careful.

The worktop

The dimensions of the cupboard top are 39in. x 21$\frac{3}{4}$in. x $\frac{7}{8}$in. (991mm x 552mm x 22mm). You will not be able to buy a single plank wide enough for this job so you will either have to butt two planks, each 10$\frac{7}{8}$in. (276mm) wide, along their edges and glue them together or, as in the case of the dresser in the photograph, butt and glue three planks, each 7$\frac{1}{4}$in. (184mm) wide.

First lay the boards on the floor and choose the most attractive combination of grain patterns. Mark the surfaces of the boards with a pencil so that you do not accidentally reverse one of them later.

To join planks along their long edge, first plane the edges that are to butt exactly square. Then spread adhesive on these edges and put the planks together. Cramp them with sash cramps or folding wedges and wipe excess adhesive off of the planks with a damp cloth.

The cupboard drawers

The drawers are made from $\frac{7}{8}$in. or 22mm thick timber. Fig.4. shows the dimensions of the finished drawers. The sides, back and front pieces are fitted together with rebated joints. The front piece has stopped grooves cut into it to accommodate the sides. This is so that the grooves are not visible on the top front edge of the drawer. The bottom of each drawer is a $\frac{3}{16}$in. (4mm) plywood panel which is held in grooves cut near the bottom edge of the side, front and back pieces. The bottom of the inside face of each front piece has a finger hold cut into it.

When making drawers it is essential to work accurately. The final construction must be square or the drawer will be a bad fit, or may even not fit at all.

Cut the side, front and back pieces to the dimensions given in Fig.4. Square the ends with a plane, but take care not to damage the corners of the pieces. Clamp a scrap of wood to the edge to which you are planing to prevent this.

The next step is to mark out and cut the tongues and grooves of the rebated joints. HOME CARPENTER 6 describes this process. Cut rebates along the ends of the side pieces to leave a tongue $\frac{7}{16}$in. (11mm) long and $\frac{3}{8}$in. (9.5mm) wide protruding. On the back piece, cut the groove to these sizes to accommodate the tongue. The face of the groove nearest the end of the pieces should be $\frac{1}{2}$in. (13mm) away from the ends. The front of the drawer is longer than the back piece. Here the stopped grooves are cut $1\frac{3}{16}$in. (30mm) away from the ends. Stop them $\frac{1}{2}$in. (13mm) away from the top edge of the drawer front.

Next cut the groove near the bottom edge of the four pieces that accommodates the bottom $\frac{3}{8}$in. (9.5mm) plywood panel. The groove is $\frac{3}{8}$in. (9.5mm) wide and $\frac{7}{16}$in. (11mm) deep. It begins $\frac{5}{16}$in. (8mm) from the bottom edge of the four pieces. The groove can be cut the whole length of the side and back pieces. On the front piece, however, stop the cut $\frac{3}{4}$in. (19mm) from the ends, so that it does not show.

The next step is to cut the finger hold at the bottom of the inside faces of the drawer fronts. The method of marking out and cutting is the same as that for the door finger holds, but the dimensions are different. The finger hold is in the centre of the bottom inside edge of the front piece. It is $7\frac{1}{4}$in. (184mm) long, enters the bottom edge of the front piece to a depth of $\frac{5}{8}$in. (16mm) and the inner face to a depth of $\frac{1}{4}$in. (6mm).

Cut the bottom plywood panel to size. Glue three pieces of the drawer together. Slide the panel into the groove and glue the fourth side of the drawer in place. Check that the drawer is square and cramp the assembly together.

The drawer runners

The drawers slide on hardwood runners—

pieces of $1\frac{1}{4}$in. x $\frac{3}{8}$in. or 32mm x 19mm timber with a $\frac{3}{8}$in. x $\frac{3}{8}$in. (9.5mm x 9.5mm) rebate cut in them. Four runners are used—two for each drawer. Do not use softwood for the runners as it will wear quickly and the drawers will stick.

Cut the runners to size and use a rebate plane to cut the rebate. The runners, since they run from the front frame to the back frame, cannot be fixed until the four sides of the cupboard, but not the top, have been assembled. They are screwed at the appropriate time to $1\frac{1}{2}$in. x $\frac{3}{4}$in. (38mm x 19mm) softwood blocks which are fixed to the insides of the rear and front frame. Six blocks are fitted, three to each frame. They are fixed to the places where the middle horizontal rail crosses the three vertical members of each rail. Their exact size is not important provided their tops are all at the same level and are long enough to accommodate the runners.

The cupboard base

The cupboard of the Welsh dresser rests on a four-sided plinth a few inches smaller than the length and width of the cupboard. The base is not purely decorative, but acts as a scuff board.

The four pieces are fastened together with rebated joints. The short pieces have a tongue $\frac{7}{16}$in. (11mm) long and $\frac{3}{8}$in. (9.5mm) wide cut on their ends. When grooves of the same size have been cut in the other two pieces, glue and sash-cramp the assembly together, making sure that it is square.

Assembly of the cupboard

The main components of the cupboard have now been constructed. After a few more steps assembly can take place. First, pin the back panel to the rear frame. A $\frac{5}{8}$in. (16mm) wide and $\frac{7}{16}$in. (11mm) deep rebate is cut on the inner face of the bottom rail of each side, and also in the inside face of the bottom piece of both the rear and front frames. This rebate accommodates a $\frac{5}{8}$in. (16mm) plywood panel which forms the base of the cupboard.

The shelf in the cupboard is supported by pieces of $1\frac{1}{4}$in. x $\frac{3}{4}$in. (31mm x 19mm) timber. These are fixed across the inside of the front and back frames parallel to the rails and $11\frac{1}{2}$in. (293mm) from the bottom rail. The pieces have a $\frac{3}{8}$in. x $\frac{3}{8}$in. (9.5mm x 9.5mm) rebate cut in them so that the $\frac{3}{8}$in. plywood shelf panel fits in flush with the tops of the support pieces. The supports are fixed so that their $\frac{3}{4}$in. (19mm) edge butts against the frames.

Fixing for the top is provided by two hardwood bearers $1\frac{1}{4}$in. x 1in. (31mm x 25mm) which are screwed to the inside face of the side stiles. The sides and the front and back frames are fixed together by the secret dowelling method described in CHAPTER 15. They are glued as well, for extra strength.

Fix the doors to the front frame with a length of 1in. (25mm) wide brass piano hinge. They are fitted so that the bottom edge of their bottom rail is flush with the bottom edge of the bottom rail of the front frame.

Fix the blocks which carry the drawer bearers and fix the bearers to the blocks. Then fasten the top in place by secret dowelling.

The shelf unit

The shelf unit, with the exception of its infill

T & G matching, is made from planed-all-round timber with a nominal thickness of 1in. (25mm) —though in fact it is more likely to be about $\frac{15}{16}$in. (24mm) thick. The dimensions of the unit are shown in Fig.1. The horizontal shelves are accommodated in the vertical sides by stopped housing joints. A $\frac{5}{16}$in. (8mm) thick infill matching is set in a groove cut in the back of the cabinet. The unit also has a decorative curved piece of timber which butts against the bottom edge of the top shelf.

The first step is to cut the two sides to length and square their ends. Then mark out the positions of the stopped housing joints. Do this by laying the two pieces together with their long edges butting. Measure a distance of 13in. (330mm) up from the bottom edge of the planks. This indicates where the bottom edge of the lower shelf will be. From this point, measure and mark the thickness of the shelf. From this second point, make another mark 12in. (305mm) up to mark the lower edge of the upper shelf. Again mark off the thickness of the shelf. Mark the thickness of the top of the shelf unit from the top of the side pieces. Square lines through all these points. The housings are narrower than the thickness of the shelves, and cut so that one side of them runs along the lower squared line of each pair that indicates the thickness of the shelves.

Now cut the stopped housings. These are $\frac{7}{16}$in. (11mm) deep and $\frac{3}{8}$in. (9.5mm) wide. Stop the housing $\frac{1}{2}$in. (13mm) from the front edge of the side pieces. You can run the housing right through to the back edge of these pieces. This will leave six small gaps showing when the T & G matching has been fitted, but they are at the back of the unit and not conspicuous.

Next cut the shelves and top piece, to length, remembering to allow for the $\frac{7}{16}$in. (11mm) depth of housing at each end. The top is 7in. (178mm) wide, and the two shelves are $6\frac{1}{4}$in. (158mm) wide. This allows the infill T & G matching, when it is fitted, to butt against the back edge of the lower two shelves and to fit in a rebated groove in the underside of the top piece. Cut a tongue on the end of these pieces to a width of $\frac{3}{8}$in. (9.5mm) and to a length of $\frac{7}{16}$in. (11mm). If you are going to put plates on the shelves, cut a groove $\frac{1}{4}$in. (6mm) deep and $\frac{1}{2}$in. (13mm) wide in the top surface of each shelf near the front edge.

The next step is to cut the rebated groove near the back edge of the sides and under the top shelf to take the matching. The groove is $\frac{5}{16}$in. (8mm) wide and $\frac{1}{2}$in. (13mm) deep. Set the fence on your combination plane to a distance of $\frac{7}{16}$in. (11mm) from the near edge of the plane blade.

Once the rebated groove has been cut, the shelf unit can be assembled. Apply adhesive to the joints and push the assembly together. Check that it is square and then sash-cramp it, the bars of the cramp running parallel to the shelves.

The infill T & G matching can now be fitted. In the shelf unit the matching runs vertically, unlike the horizontal boarding on the cupboard sides and doors. Estimate the number of boards you require and work out the size of the first and last pieces as you did for the cupboard doors and sides.

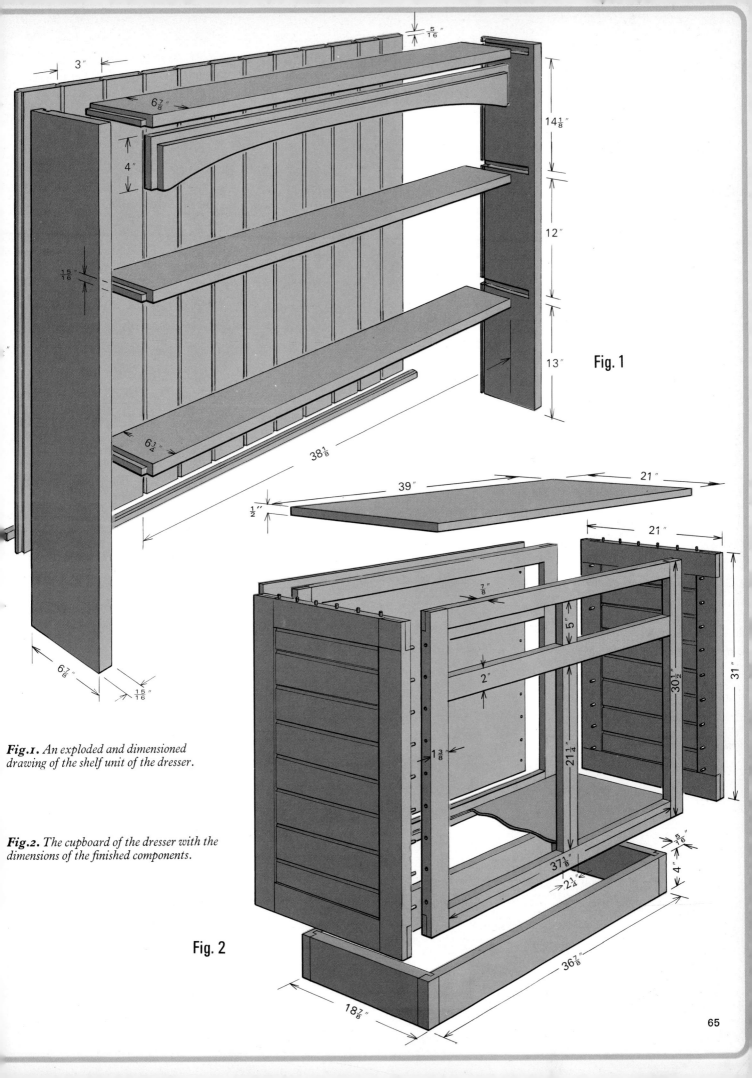

3"

$\frac{5}{16}$"

$6\frac{7}{8}$"

$14\frac{1}{8}$"

4"

12"

$\frac{15}{16}$"

13"

Fig. 1

$6\frac{1}{4}$"

$38\frac{1}{8}$"

39"

21"

$\frac{1}{2}$"

21"

$6\frac{7}{8}$"

$\frac{15}{16}$"

Fig.1. *An exploded and dimensioned drawing of the shelf unit of the dresser.*

$\frac{7}{8}$"

5"

2"

$30\frac{1}{2}$"

31"

$21\frac{1}{4}$"

$1\frac{3}{8}$"

$\frac{5}{16}$"

4"

Fig.2. *The cupboard of the dresser with the dimensions of the finished components.*

$37\frac{1}{8}$"

$2\frac{1}{4}$"

Fig. 2

$36\frac{7}{8}$"

$18\frac{7}{8}$"

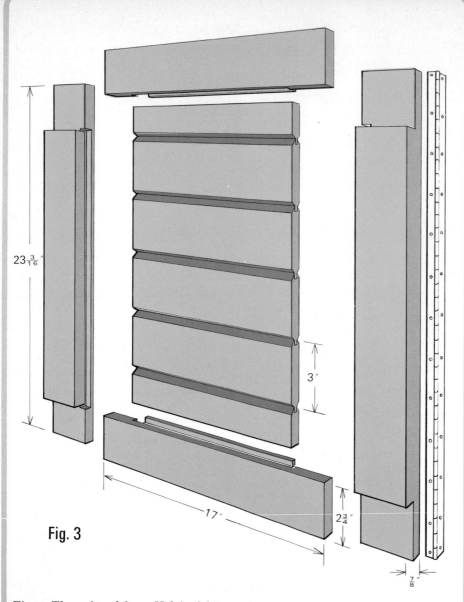

$23\frac{3}{16}''$

$3''$

$17''$

$2\frac{3}{4}''$

$\frac{7}{8}''$

Fig. 3

Fig. 3. The cupboard doors. Halving joints are used to fix the stiles and rails together.

Fig. 4. An exploded drawing of one of the cupboard drawers with the finished dimensions.

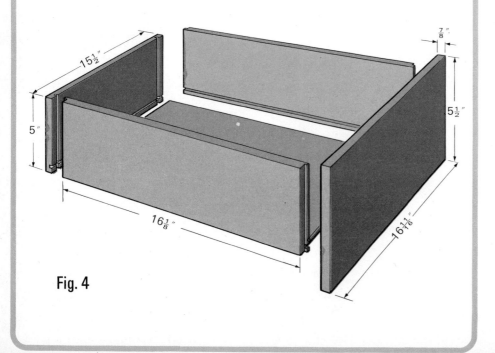

$15\frac{1}{2}''$

$\frac{7}{8}''$

$5''$

$5\frac{1}{2}''$

$16\frac{1}{8}''$

$16\frac{11}{16}''$

Fig. 4

Cut each T & G board about 1in. (25mm) too long. Push the first piece (its tongue must have been removed) into the groove cut in the inner face of one of the side pieces of the shelf unit. Tap it well into the groove with a mallet and waste block used on both the bottom end and the long edge. Insert the subsequent boards in the same way.

When you come to the last few boards, you will have no room to use the mallet on the long edge. The final few boards should be cut very slightly wider than required and fitted together in a slightly bowed shape. Offer them to the assembly with the outside edges of the boards just within the rebated groove in the shelf unit side and in the grooved side of the last board fixed. Spring the bowed boards flat with your fist. They should then fit tightly in place.

Now hit the ends of these last boards with the mallet and waste block until they fit into the rebated groove cut in the top shelf. You will need to knock the boards fairly hard to do this.

When all the boards are fitted, trim them to the exact length required with a panel saw. The cut ends of these boards are disguised by two strips of $\frac{3}{4}$in. x $\frac{1}{2}$in. (19mm x 13mm) timber with a bevelled top facing edge. Glue one strip to the bottom of the boards at the front, and the other to the back.

The decorative curved piece that butts against the underside of the top shelf can now be cut. The piece is $37\frac{5}{16}$in. (948mm) long. Cut it to the length required. Cut a rebate from the front face on the two ends and the top edge. This rebate is $\frac{3}{8}$in. x $\frac{3}{8}$in. (9.5mm x 9.5mm), and is purely decorative.

The curve on the bottom edge of this piece is 2in. (51mm) deep in the middle and begins $\frac{3}{4}$in. (19mm) from the ends of this piece. As the piece has no functional purpose, the curve does not have to be accurate, but it does have to by symmetrical. One way of ensuring that it is, is to make a paper template. Draw a line on a large sheet of paper. On this line mark two points, one that indicates the end of the curve and another that indicates half the length of the curve. From this second point draw a line at right angles and measure a distance of 2in. (51mm). Draw a freehand curve between the point that indicates the end of the curve and the point 2in. above the half way mark. You will probably have to make several attempts to draw a neat curve. Then cut out the paper template and put it in place on the timber. Draw half the curve, turn the template over and draw the other half of the curve.

Cut the curve out with a coping saw. Finish it with a spokeshave and glasspaper. Glue the curved piece of timber in place.

The shelf unit is fixed in place on the cupboard by two brass 'mirror plates' with three screw holes. These are fixed so that two of the screws enter the end grain of the table top and the other goes into the side of the shelf unit. Set the plate about $2\frac{1}{2}$in. (63mm) from the back of the cupboard.

To finish the dresser, sand all the pieces that need it to a smooth finish with glasspaper. Apply several coats of clear polyurethane varnish, rubbing down carefully between coats. Put a couple of extra coats on the worktop, which will suffer the most wear.

Above. *Three typical drawers, one of which is bound to be suitable for any purpose. At the top, a high-quality mahogany drawer; centre, a traditional flush-fronted drawer, and at the bottom, a simple one with a laminate front.*

Making and fitting drawers

Most homes need more storage space than they actually have; families always seem to accumulate huge amounts of possessions, equipment and junk and it has to be put somewhere. The most economical way to store it all—and the most space-saving—is to make your own built-in furniture and fit it with drawers. Here is how to make the drawers.

It is possible to buy ready-made drawer kits at a reasonable price, and they can be quite satisfactory in some situations. But the trouble with them is that they come in a limited range of sizes, and it is hard to fit them in where you want them. If you build your own drawers from scratch, you can make them exactly the size you want, both to fit the space where they are installed and to take any odd-shaped items you might want to store in them.

Basic requirements

Drawers can be built to various designs, some simple and some complicated, but all have the same basic parts and many points in common. All have a four-sided frame (unless they are being fitted into a very strange-shaped piece of furniture) and this normally has runners down the sides, on which the drawer slides. A base, generally of thinner material than the frame, is fitted into it and—as well as supporting the contents—holds the frame in square.

It is essential that the front and back of the drawer are the same size, and thus that the sides are exactly parallel. Attention must be paid to this point when making the drawer, or it will not slide properly. Some types of drawer do in fact have an extra-wide front that is not the same

67

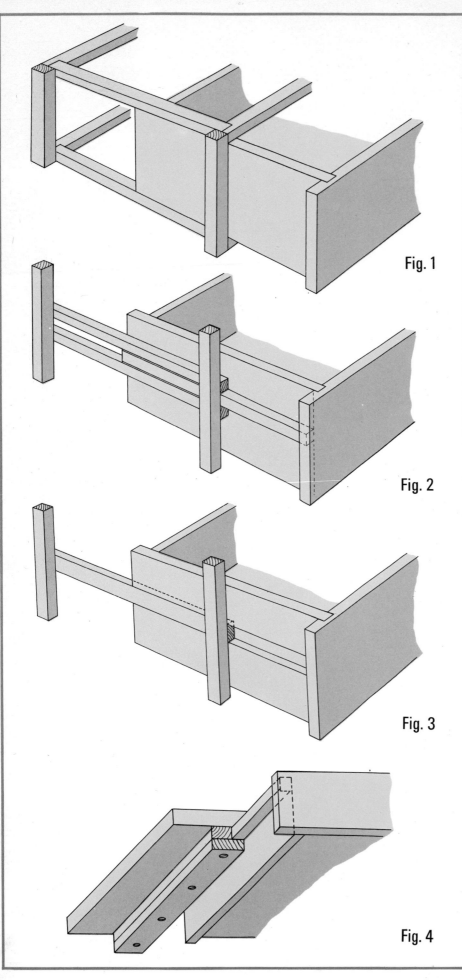

Fig. 1

Fig. 2

Fig. 3

Fig. 4

TRI-ART

Fig.1, left. A drawer mounted on rails or battens in the traditional manner. It is supported by, and slides on, rails underneath it. Rails above stop it from tipping when open. *Fig.2.* A drawer mounted by the three cleat method. This is the easiest technique for mounting drawers, but wastes a lot of space. *Fig.3.* A drawer mounted by the cleat and groove method. This does not waste space, and is the normal method used in modern furniture. *Fig.4.* A top-hung drawer; this method is used for mounting drawers under table tops.

size as the back, but this is often an attached facing and there is a conventional box-shaped drawer behind it. In any case, the sides are still parallel.

The runners must also be parallel and absolutely straight and smooth on their sliding surfaces. Some drawers use the bottom edge of the frame sides as runners, and in this case the base must be recessed a short way above these edges so as not to catch on the drawer mountings.

Drawers are held together by various joints. These must be strong enough to hold the drawer absolutely rigid; if it goes out of square it will stick. They must also be made the right way round to resist the forces acting on the drawer when it is pulled open, or when heavy objects are put in it. For example, it is no use simply nailing the drawer front on from the front side, or a violent tug will pull the nails out and you will be left with a frontless drawer.

The best way of understanding the requirements of drawers in detail is to deal with the various parts one by one.

Drawer runners

The design of the runners of a drawer, and the way it slides on the supporting framework, are the most important factors affecting the design of the drawer.

The *rail technique* is the way that drawers are mounted in traditional furniture. It is shown in Fig.1. The basic framework of the furniture is made out of battens, which form a frame round the front of the drawer into which it fits flush when closed. More battens stretch back horizontally from this front framing, both above and below the drawer. The battens under the drawer are used as rails to support it; there is a wide rail below each side of the drawer on which it slides, and further rails attached to this at each side of the drawer to stop it from slipping sideways.

The drawer is not fitted with separate runners, as it slides on the bottom edge of its sides. For this reason also, the base must be recessed a short way.

Drawers mounted in this way must be made very accurately, since if they are too narrow, there will be a noticeable gap at the front, and if too large, they will not go into their supporting frames.

The *three cleat technique* requires much less accuracy and is a method commonly used with modern drawers fitted with over-width fronts. It is shown in Fig.2. A cleat, or wood strip, is fitted to each side of the drawer. Two parallel cleats are attached to each side of the space into which the drawer fits. The cleat on the drawer

Fig.5, right. A flush-fronted drawer is most easily made with lapped joints at the front, and the back housed into the sides.
Fig.6. A drawer with a modern over-width front, and the sides housed into it.
Fig.7. A very simple drawer with a false front screwed on invisibly from inside, and butt joints used throughout the structure.
Fig.8. Joints used in drawer-making: *a* butt with false front, *b* butt with plain front, *c* lapped, *d* housing, *e* through dovetail for rear, *f* lapped dovetail for front.

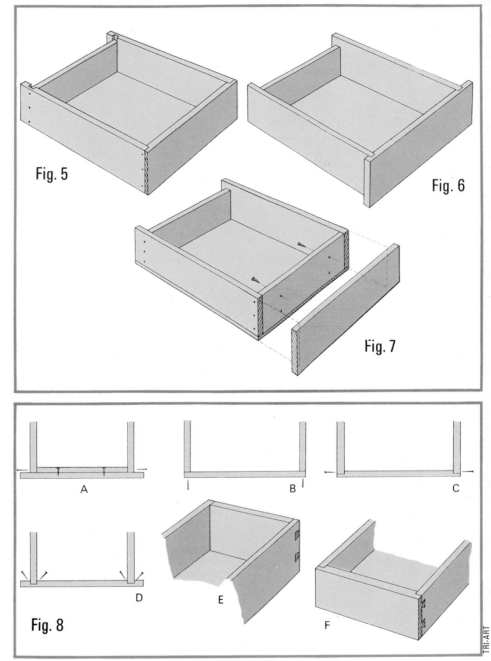

Fig. 5

Fig. 6

Fig. 7

Fig. 8

A   B   C

D   E   F

TRI-ART

runs between the two cleats on its supporting framework, and in this way the drawer is held straight and level and there is no need for any other support. Sometimes there are two cleats on the drawer and one on the frame.

This method is very suitable for drawers fitted between two vertical boards, a situation often met with in built-in furniture or when fitting extra drawers to existing whitewood units. It is also good for fitting drawers to frames that are out of square, as the two cleats on each side of the frame can be packed out until they are parallel.

It is not, however, a good method for very heavy drawers, since the whole weight of the drawer is taken on two narrow wood strips. Furthermore, there is a large and unsightly gap down both sides of the drawer, which has to be concealed with an over-width front.

The *cleat and groove technique* is neater, though drawers using this method are harder to build. It is shown in Fig.3. A single cleat is fixed to each side of the supporting framework, and this fits into a groove cut in the side of the drawer. If the groove is made as deep as the thickness of the cleat, the drawer can be made the full width of the space into which it fits, and will not require an over-width front. The groove must stop short of the front of the drawer for the sake of appearance.

A groove cut in a drawer side must not be made too deep, or it will weaken the drawer. As a general rule, its depth should not exceed half the thickness of the wood. It must be cut with a combination plane or by some equally accurate method; if it is just chiselled out it will be too rough and the drawer will stick.

Top hanging is a special technique used for fitting drawers to the underside of a table top without any support underneath. As shown in Fig.4, a pair of cleats with an L-shaped cross section is fixed to the underneath of the top, and a single cleat screwed to each side of the drawer right at the top fits into, and slides in, the angle of the L.

Where two drawers are hung side by side, the cleat between them must be T-shaped, so that it can support the adjacent edges of both drawers.

This method is unsuitable for heavy drawers, which tend to tear the fixings out of the table top. Heavy drawers should always be properly supported from underneath.

Drawer fronts

Drawer fronts can be of two shapes, flush and over-width. The choice is dictated by the desired appearance of the drawer and by the way it is mounted.

The *flush front* is the type used on traditional drawers mounted on rails, and also sometimes with the cleat and groove method. A flush-fronted drawer of a typical design is shown in Fig.5.

The drawer is simply a plain square box, and the front does not project beyond the sides. This allows any inaccuracy in the fit of the drawer to show clearly, so it must be made carefully. It is also rather hard to attach the drawer front both strongly and in such a way that the joint does not show from the front; see below for more on this point.

The *over-width front* is the type generally used on modern furniture. An example is shown in Fig.6. The front of the drawer projects beyond the sides, conveniently concealing the drawer runners as well as any inaccuracies in fitting. It is also very easy to conceal the way the drawer front is fixed on, because the joints are not at the corners and are therefore less visible.

Drawers with over-width fronts must be used if you want your furniture to have a modern look, with the drawer fronts butting edge to edge and no frame showing between them.

Some over-width fronts are not an integral part of the drawer frame. A plain box-shaped drawer is built, and a 'false' over-width front attached to it, as shown in Fig.7. This method is a very simple one for the beginner, as the drawer can be made and fitted in its framework, and the front attached at the last moment to get it in exactly the right place. It is also useful for drawers with fronts made out of pre-decorated materials, such as veneered or laminated chipboard. The front can be glued and screwed on working entirely from the inside, without marking the decorative covering.

Drawer bases

Drawers generally have bases made out of a single sheet of plywood of a suitable thickness. Hardboard can be used in small drawers carrying light loads; drawers in antique furniture have solid (though thin) timber bases.

Bases can be attached in various ways. The simplest, but weakest, method is suitable for drawers with false fronts. The base is cut to the width and depth of the *outside* of the basic box, and then glued and nailed firmly in place before the false front is attached.

Drawers mounted by the rail technique, and drawers that will carry heavy loads, must have the base recessed a short way up the sides to allow for a slight sagging of the base when the drawer is full. The simplest way to do this is to cut the base to the *inside* measurements of the drawer frame and support it on a strip of beading glue and nailed around the inside of the frame.

For extra strength, make the base a little larger and set it in grooves cut in the inside of the frame. This will involve you in more work than the other methods.

The friction problem

Drawer runners, whether they are cleats, grooves or the lower edges of the frame, have to be smooth so that they slide easily, and at the same time be tough enough to resist wear. For this reason, the choice of materials is important.

The ideal material for all types of drawer runner is hardwood with the grain running horizontally. This can be sanded to a beautiful smoothness and resists wear well.

Ordinary plywood must never be used for cleats, or for drawer sides if they are grooved or mounted on traditional rails. This is because at least one veneer of the ply will present its end grain at the edge. End grain cannot be smoothed properly. A special type of ply called *drawer side ply,* which has three veneers all with the grain running in the same direction, may be available in your area. If you can't get it, though, stick to solid timber for all sliding surfaces. Other types of manufactured board, such as chipboard, are obviously quite unsuitable.

If you are painting drawers you should never paint the sliding surfaces—although you may wish to paint the sides of the drawers. Paint on the runners prevents the drawers from opening smoothly.

Joints

Drawers can be assembled with many types of joint, and as a general rule you will want to choose the simplest one that will give you the necessary strength. The joints here are described in increasing order of difficulty. All are shown in Fig.8.

The *butt joint* is the simplest type of joint to make, and quite adequate for most drawers if reinforced with glue and pins or screws. Extra strength can be added by fastening a piece of beading down the internal corner, though this looks rather messy.

Butt joints are simple to make at the back corners of a drawer. At the front corners, however, there is a problem. If you make a butt joint where the front is the full width of the drawer (or wider) and the sides are attached to it from the back, it will be hard to pin or screw it on invisibly and at the same time give it enough strength; a firmer fixing will make a mess of the front. If, on the other hand, you sandwich the

front between the sides, you will achieve the necessary strength but there will be two areas of end grain showing at the front of the drawer in a most unsightly manner. This does not, of course, matter if the drawer is to have a false front, but otherwise it looks terrible.

The *lapped joint* solves the problem neatly and without loss of strength. It is only suitable for flush-fronted drawers. The rebate down each side of the front should not be made with a rebate or combination plane, since it is hard to use these tools across the grain. You will find it much easier to make it with two cuts of a tenon saw.

The *through housing joint* is a good way of fitting an over-width front directly to the sides of the drawer (instead of using a false front). The housings are cut down the rear edge of the front and the sides inserted into them. This joint does not have much resistance to pulling apart, however, and must be carefully reinforced with glue and skew-nailing from the rear, or screws passed through from the front with their heads filled over.

The *through dovetail joint* is very strong and resistant to pulling apart. It is the classic joint used in drawer-making, and is nearly always found in antique furniture.

It is also very laborious to make, and there is not much point in doing it unless exceptional strength is required. Instructions on making a through dovetail are in CHAPTER 11.

Through dovetails are suitable only for the back corners of drawers, since they would be unsightly at the front. If the drawer is to have a false front, this does not matter, of course. One solution for the front corners of a flush-fronted drawer would be to use *lapped dovetail joints* (illustrated at No. 24 of the data sheet on page 35). These are not much harder to make than through dovetails, and have one plain face.

Sample drawers

The three drawers illustrated in Figs.9, 10 & 11 and on the first page of this chapter are typical examples of types of drawers you might wish to construct. The first one is the easiest and simplest, and the third is the most difficult to make.

The first drawer (Fig.9) is extremely simple but reasonably strong. It would be an ideal drawer for use in the kitchen cabinets described in CHAPTER 30, or for any other use where meticulous craftsmanship was not called for.

The basic frame of the drawer is made with butt joints; those at the front are hidden by a fascia made of plastic-laminated chipboard. The ply base is simply nailed on to the underside.

This drawer is made to be mounted on three cleats, but since it has solid timber sides of reasonable thickness, the cleat and groove

technique would be just as suitable.

The second drawer (Fig.10) is a more advanced drawer of the traditional flush-fronted type used in chests of drawers. The front is joined to the sides with lapped joints; the back is housed into the sides.

This type of drawer would normally be mounted on rails, so it does not have any separate runners or grooves. The base is recessed and supported on beading running round the inside of the frame.

The third drawer (Fig.11) is a high-quality drawer of a type suitable for modern furniture. The over-width front has the sides housed into it and fastened with glue and skew-nailing. The rear corners have dovetail joints for extra strength.

The base is recessed and supported by grooves cut into the sides and front. At the back, however, it is nailed on to the underside of the frame, which is shallower at the back than

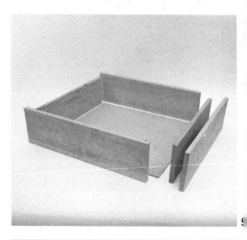

Fig.9 *(above, right). Exploded view of a drawer with an over-width false front, and designed simply to be screwed together.*
Fig.10. *The parts of a traditional flush-fronted drawer, showing the lapped joints at the front and the housings at the rear.*
Fig.11. *Exploded view of a higher-quality mahogany drawer, with the sides housed into the front and dovetailed rear corners.*

the sides. This arrangement allows the base to be slid in after the frame is assembled. You have to be careful in marking out the dovetail joint to ensure the groove for the base passes through a tail and not a pin. This would weaken the joint and spoil its appearance from the side of the drawer.

Another point to watch when making this type of drawer is that you should cut the base to the width of the inside of the drawer frame plus *twice* the depth of the grooves, and to the length of the inside of the drawer frame plus the depth of *one* groove *and* the thickness of the back.

General instructions

The procedure for making different types of drawer will, of course, vary slightly, but the following general procedure should be helpful if you remember to include the modifications for your particular type of drawer.

1. Measure, cut and plane the front and back to size. You may be using ready-planed timber if you are working with certain types of hardwood. If not, plane the faces of the wood flat, then plane one edge and use this for the bottom of the front and back. Next, cut and plane the ends to length. Plane the top edges last. Check that the front and back are identical, or the right relative size in the case of drawers with over-width fronts.

2. Measure, cut and plane the sides in the same way, remembering that their length depends on the type of joints being used. Check that they are identical. Mark the sides 'left' and 'right' to avoid confusion.

3. Cut all necessary joints and grooves on the frame pieces.

4. Trial-assemble the frame, making sure that it fits its intended position (remember to allow for the thickness of any cleats you are using).

5. Mark out and cut the base, and check that it fits the framework. If the base is mounted in grooves, check that it will slide in without catching on the back of the frame.

6. Assemble the frame permanently with glue and pins or screws. Check it for squareness by measuring the diagonals and let the glue dry thoroughly.

7. Plane down and sand any rough spots on the framework. The best way to support it is on a wide board clamped horizontally to your work bench (this is why you have not put the base on yet).

8. Fasten the base in position.

9. Fit any necessary cleats to the piece of furniture to which the drawer will be fitted. Make sure that they are absolutely level and parallel before you insert the drawer.

Design points

As you have already gathered, there is a huge variety of different ways of making drawers. By bearing the following points in mind, however, you should be able to choose the right type of drawer and mounting for your needs.

Most drawers are purely functional and only the front is ever noticed. As long as the drawer is strong enough for the job, the simpler the design the better—unless you actually *enjoy* making dovetails.

Make sure that the features you choose for your particular drawer do not clash with each other. For example, if the drawer is mounted on rails in a framework of battens, do not fit a flush bottom, which will certainly cause the drawer to stick.

Equally, do not mount a flush-fronted drawer by the three-cleat technique, since this will leave large and unsightly gaps on either side of it.

When you are measuring the size of the space into which a drawer will fit, and working out the size of the drawer, remember to allow for the thickness of all cleats and the depth of the grooves, plus at least ⅛in. (3mm) clearance to allow the drawer to expand as the wood absorbs moisture from the atmosphere in wet weather.

There are other points to watch, of course, but most of them are common sense. In fact, drawers are easy things to make provided that you don't allow yourself to be seduced into making complicated joints that you don't need.

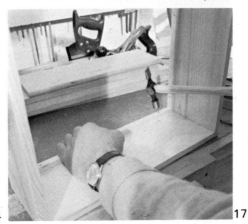

Fig.12 (above, left). Cutting housings with a router, which must be very sharp to cut across the grain. It should be held with both hands and pushed away from the body.
Fig.13. A bevel gauge and marking knife are used to mark the slope of the dovetails at the rear corners of the mahogany drawer.
Fig.14. Using a narrow bevel-edged chisel to clear the slots in the dovetail after they have been roughly sawn out. The chisel is gripped with the left index finger to brace it.
Fig.15. The profile of the 'tails' of the joint is marked directly on to the other half to give the size and position of the 'pins'.
Fig.16. Skew-nailing the drawer sides into the front housings. The nails must be at a 45° angle, or they may come through the front. Pre-drilling the holes makes the job easier.
Fig.17. Strips of beading are nailed around the inside of the drawer to support the base.

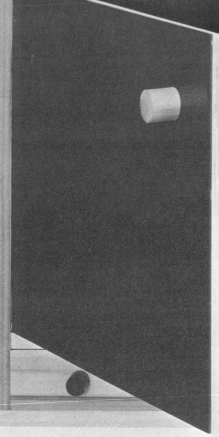

Wall hung kitchen cabinet

The wall hanging cupboard is one of the most useful items of furniture, creating extra storage space at a level which is easy to reach, while preserving the working area of the floor.

This unit is of comparatively simple design and can be made by anyone who has had some experience in carpentry. The main wood used is thick pine planking, with plywood doors faced with sheet acrylics. The thickness of the planking gives the cupboard a bold styling, although this is softened to a certain extent by the light colour of the wood.

Materials and construction

The cupboard carcase, shelves and horizontal partitions (those immediately over the drawers) are all made from 12in. x 1in. or 305mm x 25mm parana pine. The carcasses of the drawers are constructed from 3in. x 1in. or 76mm x 25mm parana pine. The doors are of ½in. or 12.5mm plywood, faced with ⅛in. or 3mm acrylic sheet. A ⅜in. or 9mm plywood sheet lines the back of the shelving and the bottoms of the drawers.

The cupboard shelves are fitted with proprietary fittings which allow them to be adjusted in height. There are many similar fittings on the market. If you want the shelves to be a permanent fixture, you can house them into the sides of the carcase and vertical partitions.

The drawers, as shown in Fig.2, are inset ½in. or 12.5mm at the sides as part of the design, but if you prefer, the sides can be constructed the full width of the drawer recess. In this case the

guide battens along each side are not necessary, but the drawers will need to be precision-finished to avoid jamming.

Handles for the doors and drawers are cut from thick dowelling rod—¾in. or 19mm for the drawers and 1¾in. or 44mm for the doors. These are approximate sizes; it does not matter if they vary slightly.

The doors shown here are both fitted with brass back-flap hinges, two to each door, and closed by means of magnetic catches. If the door (or doors) opens from the side, as shown on the left hand side of Fig.1, no further fitment is necessary, but if you want a drop flap, (Fig.1, right side) some form of stop must be fitted to hold the door horizontal. In this case the most simple method—two lengths of chain—is used, but there are various manufactured items on the market that you may prefer. These are called joint stays and are made to fit either left or right hand sides.

Four types of joint are used in the construction; a *secret dowel* (Fig.2C) which consists of five dowels, inset into the butted ends of each corner of the carcase at approximately 2in. or 50mm intervals, and at the four ends of the vertical partitions that butt on to the top and bottom of the carcase; a *stopped housing* joint, which insets the horizontal partitions in the vertical partition and sides; a *mortise and tenon* for each corner of the drawers; and a *rebate*

round the rear inside edges of each side partition and the bottom inside edges of the drawers to house the plywood bases.

Making a dowelling template

Although a secret dowelled joint is not intricate, it does require care and precision if you do not want to end up with an out-of-square cupboard. For this reason a dowelling template must be made so that each dowel will locate exactly into the drill holes on each end of the timber.

The dowel template is shown in Fig.3. Note that in Fig.3A it can be used to drill the dowel holes for both the end grain and inside edges of planking, while in Fig.3B the template has been turned upside down and in this position it is used to drill the dowel holes on the top and bottom of the carcase (which forms a T-joint with the vertical internal partition panels).

The template is constructed from: a piece of rigid plywood (at least $\frac{3}{16}$in. or 5mm thick) or hardboard, 13in. or 330mm long and about $2\frac{1}{2}$in. or 63mm wide; one length of 1in. x 1in. or 25mm x 25mm battening the same length as the plywood; another piece 1in. or 25mm long, to butt against one end of the long batten as in Fig.3 B; and one piece 2in. or 50mm long for the 'underneath' of the template as in Fig.3A.

The template holes must be marked out and drilled from the B side. Mark a line, exactly $\frac{1}{2}$in. inwards from the inside of the long batten, and drill $\frac{1}{4}$in. holes along the line at 2in. or 50mm intervals. If possible, drill all holes with a vertical drill stand.

Assembling the cupboard

The various timbers, as indicated in the parts list, should be purchased about 10% over-length to allow for wastage. If you have done this, you can trim each piece as the unit is assembled, by planing or cutting, so that precise fitting is obtained throughout.

First cut the top, bottom, sides and internal vertical partitions to size. The sides and vertical partitions must be identical in length, so clamp these four pieces together when measuring. To ensure a perfect fit, all ends—and this applies throughout—must be absolutely square, so use the try square frequently to ensure that all cut ends are at right angles to the edges. Trial assemble the carcase and vertical partitions (this is quite easy with timber of this thickness) to make sure that the fit at each butt is flush all along the join.

Using the dowel template, drill $\frac{1}{4}$in. dowel holes at each joint shown in Fig.2C, *but only drill outside dowel holes* shown in Fig.2C. Leave the other three dowel holes until later. You will now have drilled holes to take 16 dowels, leaving 24 to drill later.

Assemble the components cut so far by inserting a dowel—dry, not glued—into each

Fig.1. The finished cupboard. Note the two different door fittings.

recess and tapping the frame together. Use a block of wood under the hammer head when doing this so that the surface is not marked.

When the basic frame is trial-assembled, you can easily see that everything is square by measuring the diagonals.

Next mark out the housing joints for the fixed horizontal partitions shown in Fig.2A. To do this, take one of the lengths of timber that will be used for the drawer fronts, and lie it along one of the bottom corners as shown in Fig.6. This will enable you to draw a line along the top of the drawer timber to mark out the bottom limit of the housing joint; the pencil thickness should give you clearance between the drawer and shelf. Repeat this at all six of the bottom corners.

Gently disassemble the frame with a hammer and wood block. The 'top' sides of the housing joints can now be marked. Use the direct marking system by placing the edge of one of the planks to be housed along the line previously drawn, then mark along the opposite side.

The stopped housing joints can now be cut and chiselled out. Avoid cutting the channel very deep—about $\frac{1}{4}$in. or 6mm is sufficient—and stop it about 1in. or 25mm from the front of the cupboard.

At this stage cut out the recesses for the back

73

panels of the side compartments (these are the partitions which have doors). This rebate should be cut $\frac{1}{4}$in. or 6 mm along the edge of each board, and $\frac{3}{4}$in. or 19mm along the side or into the cupboard round the rear inside edges of both partitions. This will inset the back panels about $\frac{1}{2}$in. (12mm) to allow room for the wall fixings. Do not carry the rebate where the drawer will be.

Drill out the remaining dowel holes. Put a little adhesive in each dowel hole, spread a little on each dowel, place all the dowels in their recesses along the top and bottom planks, and ease the four vertical panels into position. When the whole frame is fitted, cramp it from top to bottom, square it if necessary, and leave on a level surface to set.

When the adhesive has set on the frame, cut the three horizontal panels to slot into the housing joints. Use the direct marking system for measuring by placing each panel at the back between the two housing channels. Then mark and cut the panels to size. Slide each panel into the channel to the point where the channel 'stops'. Go round to the front and mark both ends of each panel where it butts against the sides, withdraw the panel, and you have accurate marks for cutting the stopped housing recesses.

Spread adhesive along the housing channels and the edges of the horizontal panels, slide into place, wipe off any excess glue and leave to set.

The doors can now be cut to size and planed to a precise fit. As the plywood for the doors has been ordered slightly oversize, you can adopt direct marking to ensure an exact fit. Place one of the doors over the front of the partition to which it will eventually fit. Holding it in position, gradually lay the cupboard over on to its front; the partition edges will now be resting directly over the door. Lift the opposite end of the cupboard slightly and ease the other door underneath so that it covers the edges of the partition at the other end. When they are placed correctly, you can mark a line round the back of the doors from the 'inside' of the cupboard. Saw along the waste or outside of this marked line using a fine-toothed panel saw and you have your two doors tailored for a perfect fit.

The $\frac{1}{4}$in. plywood sheets for the back of the two side partitions can now be trimmed down so that they fit neatly into the rebated recesses; and secured with $\frac{1}{2}$in. panel pins at 2in. or 50mm intervals.

The doors, in this unit, are covered with acrylic sheet, although there is nothing to stop you adopting some other covering such as a matching parana pine veneer, or a laminated plastic. If you want to get a similar, but cheaper effect to the cupboard shown, glasspaper the door fronts down to a satin smooth surface and apply several coats of hard gloss paint, rubbing down with extra fine wire wool after each coat has set hard.

If acrylic sheet is being used as a covering, the safest method by far is to take your doors round to a firm that specializes in cutting and selling acrylic and ask them to supply two panels to fit the doors. Remind them that the doors have already been planed to fit.

If you intend doing-it-yourself right through to the end, then it is quite possible to cut and fit

Part	Description	Quantity	Dimensions or length	Size
Sides	parana pine	2	21in. or 533mm	12in. x 1in. or 305mm x 25mm
Interior verticals	parana pine	2	21in. or 533mm	12in x 1in. or 305mm x 25mm
Top and bottom	parana pine	2	6ft or 1.8m	12in x 1in. or 305mm x 25mm
Interior horizontal timbers	parana pine	2	23in. or 584mm	12in x 1in. or 305mm x 25mm
		1	25in. or 635mm	305mm x 25mm
Rear panels	plywood	2	22$\frac{1}{2}$in. x 17$\frac{1}{2}$in. or 570mm x 444mm	$\frac{1}{4}$in. or 6mm
Doors	plywood	2	22in. x 17in. or 558mm x 432mm	$\frac{1}{2}$in. or 12.5mm
Door covering	acrylic sheet	2	22in. x 17in. or 558mm x 432mm	$\frac{1}{8}$in. or 3mm
Door handles	dowelling	2	2in. or 50mm	1$\frac{3}{4}$in. or 44mm
Hinges	back-flap	4	—	1$\frac{1}{2}$in. or 38mm
Catches	magnetic	2	—	1$\frac{1}{2}$in. or 38mm
Chain or stays	(see text)			
Shelving	parana pine	(quantity as required)		9in. x 1in. or 229mm x 25mm
Drawer fronts	parana pine	2	23in. or 584mm	3in. x 1in. or 75mm x 25mm
		1	25in. or 635mm	
Drawer sides	parana pine	6	11in. or 279mm	3in. x 1in. or 75mm x 25mm
Drawer backs	parana pine	2	22in. or 558mm	3in. x 1in. or 75mm x 25mm
		1	24in. or 610mm	
Drawer bottoms	plywood	2	22in. x 11in. or 558mm x 279mm	$\frac{1}{4}$in. or 6mm
		1	24in. x 11in. or 610mm x 279mm	$\frac{1}{4}$in. or 6mm
Drawer handles	dowelling	3	1in. or 25mm	$\frac{3}{4}$in. or 19mm
Drawer stops	softwood	6	11in. or 279mm	$\frac{1}{2}$in. x $\frac{1}{2}$in. or 12.5mm x 12.5mm

These are the dimensions for finished lengths. When ordering, add 10% for wastage.

the acrylic yourself. Use direct marking again. Buy the acrylic slightly oversize. Lay a door down over one of the acrylic sheets and mark round the edges with a marking knife. Saw carefully round the waste side of this line with a fairly fine-toothed saw such as a panel saw. If you are used to working with plastic sheeting, you might, with luck, be able to achieve a perfect fit first time. But if this is your first attempt, cutting round the waste line will leave a fraction over all round. Glue the oversize plastic sheet to the door and, when the adhesive has set, remove the oversize edges with a fine, broad flat file. For glueing, use only the proper adhesive, in this case an acrylic based one such as Perspex Cement.

A hole will have to be drilled through the acrylic to enable the screw for the handle to pass through. With patience, this can be done with a hand drill, but it is easier with a power drill. Mark the location of the hole and place a drop of heavy oil over the spot. Switch on the drill and lightly drill a recess. Place a little more oil in this recess and continue drilling. Use a light pressure to stop the drill bit seizing, and apply more oil if the drill hole dries up. When the plastic has been penetrated, continue through the plywood. Countersink the hole inside the door, hold one of the door handles over the hole in the plastic, insert a wood screw from the inside or plywood side and screw into the handle. It is useful to fit the handles at this stage because they provide something for you to hold

on to when you are fitting the hinges.

Cut the recesses for the back-flap hinges, and fit the hinges. If you are including a drop-flap door, fit the chain or stays, and the magnetic catches.

Assembling the drawers

First cut and plane the front drawer timbers so that they fit snugly into their respective compartments. Although the drawer partitions are much smaller, you can mark these out by direct marking as you did for the doors.

Next cut the side and back timbers for the drawers.

Plough a groove along the bottom inside edges of all the drawer timbers. The groove should be slightly over $\frac{1}{4}$in. deep so that the plywood drawer bottom will slide easily into place later.

Cut a tenon into both ends of each of the side drawer timbers. Set the marking gauge at $\frac{1}{4}$in. and scribe a line round all four edges of the end grain. Now mark a line, $\frac{1}{2}$in. deep or inwards round all four sides of the same piece of wood. Place one of the sides in a vice, end grain uppermost, and with a tenon saw cut out the tenon. Repeat at the other end of the timber.

When all the tenons, 12 in all, have been cut, mark out the mortise recess on the inside faces of the front and back timbers. Place a back or front piece on edge on a level surface, butt a tenon against it where it will recess, and mark the mortise outline using the tenon as a tem-

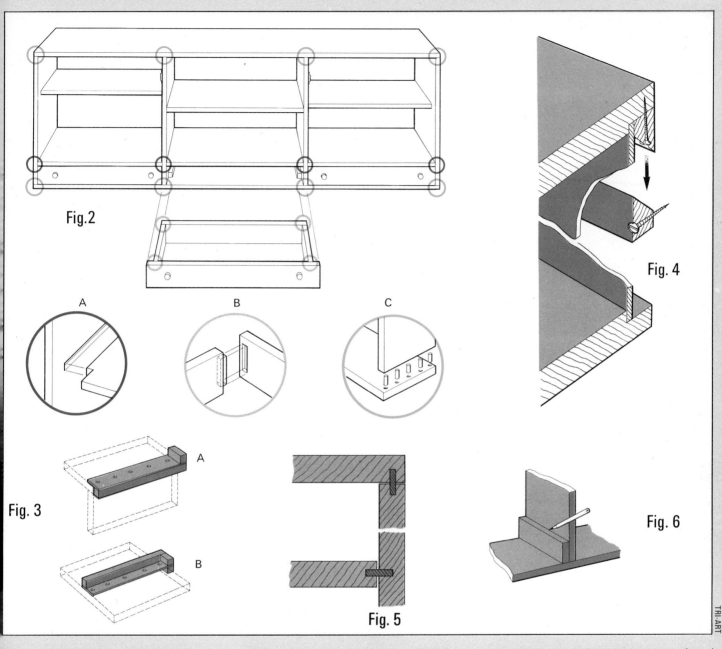

Fig.2

A   B   C

Fig. 4

Fig. 3

A

B

Fig. 5

Fig. 6

TRI-ART

Fig.2. *The cupboard, minus doors, showing the construction. Inset A is a stopped housing joint, B is a mortise and tenon joint and C shows five secret dowels.*
Fig.3. *The dowelling template used to ensure that the dowelling holes match accurately. A shows the template being used on the ends, and B, on the middle of a timber to mark out the holes.*

Fig.4. *One method of fixing the unit to the wall. This method uses a diagonally cut batten, but there are many proprietary fitments on the market that would do equally well.*
Fig.5. *Side section view of the secret dowelled joints at the shelf end and corner sections of the carcase.*
Fig.6. *Marking out the housing joints for the fixed horizontal partitions.*

plate. Chisel out the mortises to a depth of $\frac{1}{2}$in.

Fit all the drawer handles using the same procedure as for the doors. Again, this is done for convenience in handling. Cut and fit the plywood bottoms into their grooves. Apply adhesive to the mortise recesses and smear some round the tenons, fit the joints and cramp them until the glue has set.

The last step is to fit the side battening into the lower drawer partition corners as shown in Fig.2. The purpose of this battening is to act as a stop so that the drawers will not slide right through the partition, and also to ensure that the drawer front pushes in flush with the edges of

the partition.

First, insert all the drawers in place and then, from the back, push a length of batten along each side to ensure that there is sufficient space for them. If there is not, plane the battens down to size. Pull one of the drawers out, and squeeze a little adhesive into the corner where the batten will be fitted, but do not spread any glue along about 2in. or 50mm of the corners at the front of the cupboard. Press the two battens in position until they are almost, but not quite, flush with the front of the cupboard. Now ease the drawer in until it is flush with the front. This has the effect of pushing the battens back to their

correct positions. Pull the drawer out gently and allow enough time for the adhesive to set. If you can manage it, drive a couple of panel pins through the battens into the sides of the vertical panels to 'cramp' them in place while the glue is setting. (A piece of hardboard on the 'floor' will prevent the hammer from marking the timber.)

Hanging the cupboard

There are many fittings on the market for attaching cupboards and shelves to walls, but if you do purchase one of these remember that this cupboard is very heavy and needs a heavy-duty support. It is for this reason that the back panels have been rebated $\frac{3}{4}$in., so that at least $\frac{1}{2}$in. is available for fixing a support.

You can make a wall fitting yourself, and the one used in this project, consisting simply of a length of timber cut slantwise so that one half fits the cupboard and the other fits the wall, is shown in Fig.4. It is a very simple one and has the advantage that the cupboard can easily be removed by merely lifting it off the wall support.

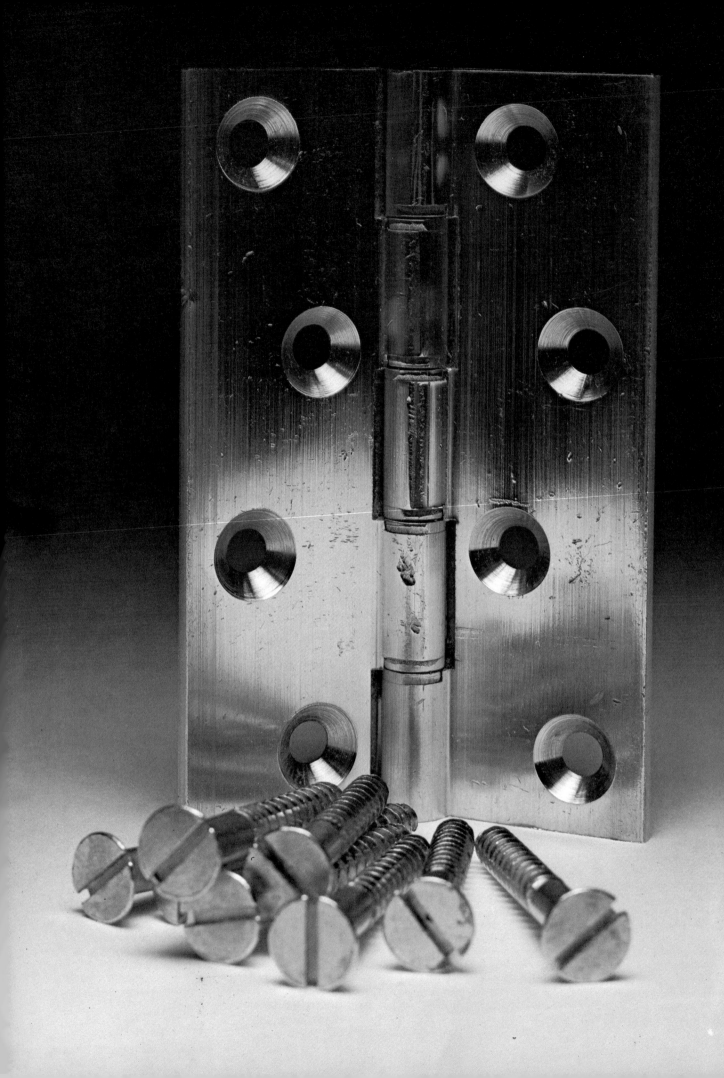

Hanging doors and windows

Doors and windows have two purposes: they open to provide access or let in air, and they shut to keep out rain, draughts and sound. So they must open easily and shut firmly, which means that they must be fitted very accurately into their frames.

Hanging doors and windows is not particularly difficult, and there are only a few facts and procedures you need to know about to get it right every time.

The most important part of the job is getting the door or window to fit properly into its frame. They do not fit exactly; there has to be a clearance all round to allow for expansion in wet weather, and to keep the door from scraping against its frame when it is opened and shut.

Doors do not open straight out as if they were being lifted out of their frame. They swing slightly outwards as they pivot on their hinges, and the lock side of the door, opposite the hinge, has to be cut away to allow for this movement. Different kinds of hinges cause the door to move in different ways, and you have to know how a particular type of hinge will make the door behave.

The hinges themselves have to be installed strongly but accurately, so that the door does not sag or hang at an angle. It is not hard to put them in correctly when you know how.

Fitting doors and windows

These instructions apply to doors and windows alike, except where stated.

Doors (and wood-framed windows) invariably expand slightly when the humidity rises. If they are painted, or sealed in some other way, it slows down the rate at which the humidity affects them, but they still change size.

Outside doors are obviously more affected than inside ones, but even so, inside doors in a house that is centrally heated during the winter or air-conditioned during the summer, may change their size quite noticeably from season to season, perhaps by as much as $\frac{1}{16}$in. (1.6mm).

Panelled doors made of solid timber move more than modern ones made from manmade boards. Softwood ones move more than hardwood ones. And of course, wide doors move more than narrow ones (in actual distance, not in proportion to their width).

The way to estimate the right clearance is to leave a minimum of $\frac{1}{16}$in. (1.6mm) round the top three sides of the door, and at least $\frac{1}{8}$in. (3mm) at the bottom (but more about clearance *under* doors later). Then you can add to this figure $\frac{1}{32}$in. (0.8mm) for each factor that might

make the door expand an extra amount—for example if it is an outside door, in a centrally heated house, or if it is made of solid timber panels. The average clearance for an inside door is about $\frac{1}{8}$in. (3mm) on the top three sides, and $\frac{1}{4}$in. (6mm) at the bottom.

There used to be a British joiner's rule of thumb that you should be able to get an old penny (just over $\frac{1}{16}$in. thick) between a door and its frame all round. This was before central heating, however, and the gap is a bit small by today's standards. But it is a good way of measuring if you can find a coin of the right thickness for the clearance you need.

The method for fitting a standard-sized door into a standard-sized frame is as follows: first, buy a door of the correct size and leave it in the room where it is to be fitted for a couple of days to let it adjust to the prevailing humidity. New doors with solid timber rails and stiles (this includes many flush doors) often have the top and bottom ends of the stiles (vertical side pieces) left uncut, and these projecting *horns*, as they are called, should be sawn off and planed smooth.

When the door has acclimatized itself, offer it up to the hinge side of the door-frame and examine the edge of door and frame to see if they are parallel. Many frames are leaning or curved, even in new houses. If the frame is really irregular you may have to scribe the door to it, but otherwise an ordinary plane and your own judgement should be enough to make it fit. Make sure that you don't remove so much more wood from one end than the other that the door is no longer vertical; an occasional check with a spirit level should guard against this.

If the door is not too tall to fit into the door frame at this stage, hold it up with a couple of wedges underneath it while you check it against the frame. If it is too tall, rest it on the floor and put wedges under it only when it begins to take on the right size and shape (see Fig.1).

After the hanging edge of the door is cut to shape, do the same with the top, then the bottom (remembering to remove more wood than for the sides). Then raise it to its correct height on wedges, and shape the last side, which is the side with the lock.

Finally, run a coin around the top three edges of the door to check that there are no tight spots.

Non-standard sizes

Most door frames in houses less than about a century old are in standard sizes, and you can buy doors that only need a little planing to fit into them. If, however, you are unlucky enough to have a door frame in a non-standard size, you are going to have to alter your new door more

drastically than by merely planing it.

Nearly all doors, including flush (flat-surfaced) modern doors, have some kind of supporting framework of stiles and rails to strengthen them and keep them from sagging or warping. This is held together by mortise-and-tenon or dowelled joints. If you remove more than, say, $\frac{1}{2}$in. (13mm) from any side of the door, there is a danger of cutting into one of these joints, and this could seriously weaken it.

One way round this problem is to order a specially-made door, but this might turn out to be expensive. Ask a builders' merchant and see if you think the job is worth the money. If not, you could just buy a large piece of $\frac{3}{4}$in. (19mm) blockboard, apply an edging strip all round and use that as a door. It might, however, warp a bit because of not having a proper frame.

The best solution is to dismantle a door and re-cut the joints to alter the size—if you can be bothered to do it. The technique for an ordinary panelled door is described fully in CHAPTER 29. It is a laborious job, however, for door manufacturers use good glue and strong joints deliberately to stop their doors from coming apart.

Altering the size of window frames in this way is nearly impossible for the amateur. They will almost certainly have to be made to measure by a professional joiner.

Fitting the hinges

Nearly all doors and casement windows are hung on butt hinges (see Fig.2). These come in a good range of sizes from 1in. (25mm) long, used for cupboard doors, to 6in. (150mm) long, used for heavy front doors. Most ordinary-sized doors use 4in. (100mm) hinges. For really large doors—the front doors of some Victorian houses are a case in point—you can use three hinges instead of two, with the third hinge halfway between the other two. This also helps to prevent warping.

To fit a pair of hinges, first position the door in its frame in the exact position it will occupy, propping it on wedges to hold it steady. Then make a mark on both door and frame (and at the same level on each) 6in. (150mm) from the top of the door and 9in. (230mm) from the bottom. For small casement windows, halve these measurements.

Then take down the door and draw round one flap of the butt hinge with a marking knife to mark its position on both door and frame. Top and bottom hinges should be positioned *inside* the lines you have already marked. The hinges should be set so that the 'knuckle' (pivot) is just clear of door and frame.

When you are satisfied that the position of the hinges is correctly shown, set a marking gauge to the thickness of the hinge flap and mark how deep the cutout for the hinge is to be. Be very careful not to mark it too deep.

Some marking gauges will not adjust far enough to make such a shallow mark. One solution to this is to put in a new metal spike at the other end of the arm of the gauge in such a position that the sliding part of the gauge can move right up to it. You could make a good spike from a small panel pin sharpened with a file.

Now chisel along all the marked lines to ensure that the wood will be removed cleanly (see Fig.3). Then turn the chisel bevel-edge down and make some diagonal cuts to the correct depth to make it easier to remove the wood (see Fig.3 again). Finish the cutout neatly by slicing out the raised wood chips from the spindle with the chisel held right way up. Using a broad chisel improves accuracy.

Place a hinge leaf in each of the cutouts to ensure that it fits with its upper surface flush with the edge of the door or frame. If the cutout is too shallow, and the hinge stands proud, remove more wood. If it is too deep, you will have to pack it out with a piece of veneer or ply —but this is *not* recommended and it is much better to cut too shallow and work down.

When all the hinges leaves are set in properly,

drill *one* hole through each side of each hinge into the door and frame. Drill through the centre hole of each hinge leaf, using a bradawl on small hinges, a drill of the correct size for the mounting screws on large hinges. Don't drill the other two holes in each side yet.

Prop the door up on its wedges and mount it temporarily on its hinges with one screw per hinge leaf. Then open and shut it—gently, so as not to tear the screws out—to make sure that it is not catching on anything. You will almost certainly find it does catch on the lock side, because the projecting hinge knuckle makes it swing slightly wide. The remedy is to bevel the edge of the door slightly with a plane (see Fig.4). Nearly all doors and wood-framed windows are bevelled in this way.

Open the door as far as it will go to make sure

that it does not catch on the floor. If it does, you will have to plane a bit more off the bottom edge.

The door should fit flat into its frame and stay there without having to be held. If it sticks and has to be forced, or swings open of its own accord, the screw holes are wrongly sited. Take the door off and plug the misplaced holes with glued-in dowels. Let the glue dry and try again.

When you are satisfied with the fit, take the door down, drill the remaining holes and refit it with all its screws. Make absolutely sure that all the countersunk screw heads are in the whole way, or the hinge will not fold flat. If they stick out, file the heads flat—this is cheating, but it works. The installation is now completed except for any locks or bolts. These come in a multitude of shapes, sizes and types, but any good-quality lock comes with instructions.

Fig.1. *A door propped up on wedges to bring it up to the right height while it is being fitted into its frame.*
Fig.2. *A typical butt hinge. The screw holes are offset to keep the screws from splitting the wood of the door and frame.*
Fig.3. *Cutting in a butt hinge. First the outline is cut round, then the wood is chiselled out to leave a flat bottom.*
Fig.4. *The edge of a door must be bevelled, because the position of the hinge pivot, or knuckle, makes it swing outwards.*
Fig.5. *A stormproof hinge, which fits into the L-shaped space between some types of casement window and their frames.*
Fig.6. *A rising butt hinge, which raises a door a short way as it is opened.*
Fig.7. *The top of a door on rising butts must be bevelled to allow it to clear the frame as it rises during opening.*

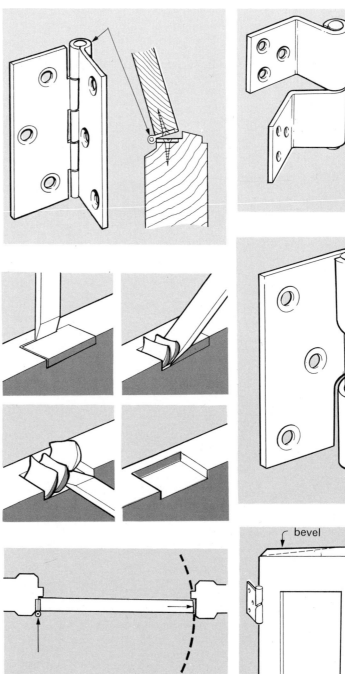

Other types of hinges

Special problems in fitting doors and windows may call for special types of hinge. For example, a door or window that has to fold flat against a wall needs a special type of hinge, known as a 'parliament' hinge. This has an offset pivot that moves the door well away from the frame as it opens, allowing it to be opened much farther than normal. It makes the door swing very wide in the first few inches of opening, so that the lock side needs a heavily angled bevel cut on it.

Casement windows often have a rebated edge and frame to keep the rain out. These must have a special L-shaped hinge called a 'stormproof' hinge (see Fig.5). Unlike butt hinges, these come in left- and right-handed versions, depending on which way the window opens (though of course, they are generally

Above. These two doors must be hung at exactly the same height to avoid giving the installation an untidy appearance.

bought two pairs at a time for paired windows). They are installed in the same way as butt hinges, but the window frame can be a looser fit than usual, since the rebated front seals it.

In houses with irregular floors or thick carpets, there is often a problem with the door catching on the floor as it opens. If enough wood is taken off the door to clear it, the wind whistles through the huge gap underneath. The solution is to use 'rising butt' hinges, which raise the door as it opens (see Fig.6). To stop the top of the door from catching on the frame as it rises, a special tapered bevel has to be cut along one-third of the length of the top edge of the door at the hinge end (see Fig.7).

The only way to get the shape of the bevel right is by trial and error, removing a very little wood at a time. The length, angle and depth of the bevel vary with particular installations. The hinge is installed like a normal butt hinge, so if you hang the door temporarily on single screws and keep taking it off, planing a bit more wood off and replacing it, you should soon get the shape of the top edge right.

Certain types of hinge are installed in plain view on the front (or back) of the door. These include the long sheet-metal hinges found on cottage and outhouse doors, and special self-closing spring hinges, which have such huge pivots that it would be impossible to hide them. Both types are very easy indeed to install, because the screws are exposed and you don't have to keep taking the door off to get them positioned correctly.

Louvred doors and shutters

If you are looking for a way of brightening up your doors and cupboards, why not try louvres? Don't be put off by their complicated appearance. There is no reason why you shouldn't make a whole roomful of louvred doors in the space of a single weekend.

Louvres are an elegant feature in almost any room. They can be used in inside doors or cupboard doors, and are most attractive in shutters. The loudspeaker cabinets of stereo systems can also be faced with louvred panels, which let the sound through but hide the uninteresting cloth front that most cabinets have.

The only place where louvres are not suitable is outside doors (for obvious reasons), but even then you could draughtproof the door with a glass panel.

It is, of course, possible to buy ready-made louvred doors and shutters, but these are fairly expensive and come in a limited range of standard sizes. Making a louvred panel is not at all difficult, and although it can be a long job setting in each slat, this article will show you several short cuts that reduce construction time to a minimum.

Strictly speaking, a louvred door should be made by setting each slat individually into a pair of stopped housings cut at an angle into the inside edge of the door stiles (see Fig.1). You can imagine the time it would take to cut out each housing separately, and at the right angle. Furthermore, if you cut even one in the wrong place, you would have to throw away

the whole door stile, an expensive piece of heavy timber on which you would already have spent a lot of effort.

The way to avoid this laborious task is to make up a light rectangular frame separate from the door and set the louvres in that. Then the frame can be set in the door or shutter. Doors and shutters, incidentally, are made in exactly the same way and the only difference between them is one of size.

It is much easier to fix the slats in this kind of frame than in a door stile. They can just be pinned to it through the frame's outer edge. You can't do this with a door stile because it is 3in.-4in. (75-100mm) wide.

Shapes, sizes and spacings

The appearance of a louvred door can be altered quite a lot by changing the size and angle of the louvres and the way the louvred panel is set in the door frame. Before you start work, it is a good idea to make a scale drawing of the whole door, making it as realistic as possible, to ensure that you are satisfied with the proportions.

The possibilities are wide. For example, the front edge of each slat may be planed off parallel with the face of the door, which gives the louvred panel a smooth appearance (see Fig.2). Or it may be left at its original right angle to the face of the slat, which intensifies the contrast between light and shade in the panel and makes it look more serrated.

The louvred panel can be set in the door so that its surface is flush with the rest of the door, or it can be set in or made to project. Several possibilities are shown in Fig.3; the first one, where the slats are flush but their light frame is set back a short way, is probably the neatest as well as the easiest to build. It is proposed to set the slats in through housings to save trouble, so the louvre frame should not project beyond the front of the slats or the ugly ends of the housing slots will be visible. This could, however, be overcome by edging the frame with a piece of beading.

It is normal to set louvres with the lower edge of each slat towards you, which makes the panel opaque when seen from above (unless the slats are spaced wide apart). Shutters, however, should be the other way round if they are used to keep out direct sunlight or rain. In this way you will be able to look down through the slats into the garden or street, but people at the same level as you or above will not be able to look into the room. The spacing of the slats can be altered to make them more or less 'peep-proof' —see below for details.

The angle of the slats also makes a difference, both to their appearance and to how easy it is to see through them. The nearer they are to being horizontal the easier they will be to see through. An angle of 45° is a good choice, not just because it looks right but because it allows you to mark out the housings with an ordinary mitre try square. Angles nearer the vertical are often found in proprietary louvred doors, because

Opposite page. An unusual and very successful effect is created by mounting a pair of louvred shutters inside a window frame, where they can be seen when open.

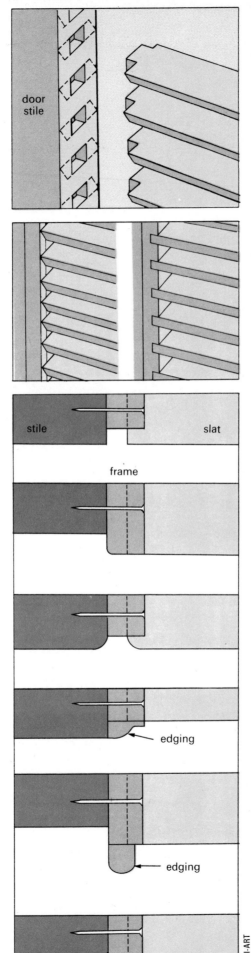

door stile

stile — slat

frame

edging

edging

TRI-ART

Fig.1 (left). Louvres should ideally be made by setting slats in stopped housings cut directly into the door stile. Of course, nobody bothers to do this today.
Fig.2. Two styles of louvre slats. The one on the left has its frame trimmed with an edging strip; the ends of the slats are planed flat to accommodate the strip.
Fig.3. Slats and their frames can be mounted flush or set forward or back.

they save wood. This is not really a problem for the amateur, however, since the saving is only a few pence per door.

If you want slats at an unusual angle for some reason, use an adjustable bevel gauge for the marking out, but otherwise proceed normally.

The size of timber required for the components varies with the use the door or shutter will be put to. A light wardrobe door could have a main door frame with the stiles and top rail made of timber as light as 2in. x 1in. (50 x 25mm) ; the bottom rail, which should always be deeper to give the door good proportions, should then be of 3½in. x 1in. (89 x 25mm) timber. The slats should be of timber ⅜in. (9.5mm) thick—this is a minimum thickness for any application—and 1½in.-2in. (38-50mm) wide, depending on the design.

Shutters should be a bit heavier than this. A hinged, useable shutter might have an outer frame of 4in. x 1in. (100 x 25mm), including the bottom rail, and ½in. (13mm) thick slats, which will be more resistant to warping and accidental damage. The slats should be 1½in.-2in. (38-50mm) wide, as before.

On the whole, the British use shutters very little—after all, there isn't much sun to keep out. If you live in Britain and want shutters for decoration only, there is no point in making them as strong as this, or in mounting them on real hinges. It is much simpler and cheaper to make them out of lighter materials, such as those for the wardrobe door, and screw them to the wall on either side of the window. Normally, open shutters would have the upper edge of each slat outermost, but a fake shutter set directly against the wall should be the other way round, both for appearance's sake and to stop it from channelling rain to the surface of the wall and making it damp.

Room doors should be heavier than shutters. 4in. x 1½in. (100 x 38mm) timber is about right for the outer frame, with a 6in. or 8in. (150-200mm) bottom rail. The slats should again be ½in. (13mm) thick, and as wide as is appropriate for the design.

In all these applications, the thickness of the timber making up the light inner frame that holds the slats should be the same : ½in. (13mm). It does not need to be strong, but it will have ¼in. deep housings cut out of it to take the slats, so this is a minimum thickness. The width of the inner frame will vary enormously with the style of louvred door you have chosen.

If you are replacing an existing panelled door with a louvred door, and the old door is in good condition, you might consider replacing the panels in it with louvred panels instead of replacing the whole door. This will give you a smart and unusual louvred door with four panels instead of one or two, and will allso save you the trouble and expense of building a whole new door from scratch. If you decide to do this, the best way to remove the old panels is to smash them up with a mallet and chisel and pull the pieces out of the grooves in which they are set. The smashing-up should be done as gently as possible so as not to damage the frame of the door. The grooves where the panels fitted will be covered by the light framing of the new louvred panels, so there is no need to fill them.

The outer frame

If you are making a complete new door from scratch, the first thing to make is the main outer frame. This is a solid but simple structure with fewer pieces than a conventional four-panelled door (see Fig.4). It has five pieces: left and right stiles and top, centre and bottom rails. The bottom rail should be 1½-2 times as wide as the other pieces, as already mentioned.

The four joints at the corner of the frame are haunched mortise and tenon joints. This joint is shown on page 34 in the DATA SHEET on joints. The procedure described there, however, is for the slightly angled joint needed for a step-ladder frame. Here, a plain right-angled joint is wanted, so no complex marking-out procedure is needed and you can do everything with a normal right-angled try square.

The two joints where the centre rail joins the stiles are ordinary through mortise-and-tenon joints, which are described fully in CHAPTER 25. They should be absolutely plain sailing if you follow the instructions there.

When making the door frame, pay particular attention to the squareness and exact size of the two rectangular spaces in the middle of it. You can always plane bits off the *outside* of the door if it doesn't fit its site. But if the louvre frame has to be made deliberately out-of-true to fit into a crooked rectangular space, you will have a lot of trouble.

The louvre frame

A typical louvre frame, consisting of a light

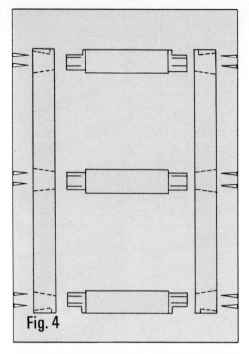

Fig. 4

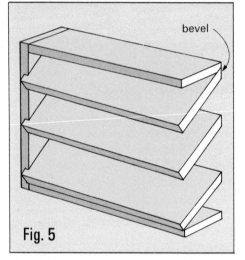

Fig. 5

½in. (13mm) thick framework and slats of the same thickness, is shown in Fig.5. The corners of the frame do not need to be strong, so they are just butt-jointed, glued and pinned. The only exception to this would be where a frame of this type has to stand on its own, as it might if it was used for a loudspeaker grille. Then, if you can be bothered to do them, tiny dovetails should be made to hold the frame together more positively (see the detailed instructions given in CHAPTER 11). The 'tails' of the asymmetrical joint should be on the top and bottom of the frame, so that assembling it locks the slats into their housings.

Do not make a frame of this type with mitred corners. They are just not strong enough.

The first stage in making a louvre frame is to make a really detailed scale drawing, showing all the measurements. This will both tell you how much wood to buy and save you from tiresome and expensive mistakes later.

There is a special technique for marking out louvres to fit into a space of a certain size. It is only suitable for calculation in *decimals,* however, not ordinary fractions. This is because if you start doing the calculations using six-teenths and thirty-seconds of an inch, you will need the mathematical ability of an Einstein to get through them without at least one mistake—and even one will spoil the whole procedure. Furthermore, even if you do avoid making a mistake, the result may well be in sixths or ninths of an inch, which are not marked on an ordinary ruler.

This doesn't mean that you have to work in millimetres if you are unused to them. Use tenths of an inch. Ordinary carpenters' rules don't have tenths of an inch marked on them, but school rulers do. They are very cheap and obtainable anywhere.

Before outlining the marking-out procedure, three points should be noted. First, the top rail of the louvre frame should be bevelled at its rear edge (see Fig.5) so that the top slat can overlap it by at least 2/10in. or 1/5in.) (5mm). Then, if

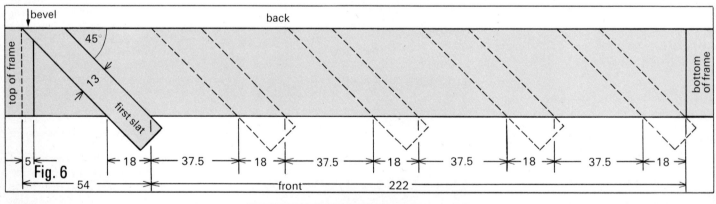

Fig. 6

either piece shrinks or warps, no ugly gap will be visible. If the front of the slats are flush with their frame, there should be a bevel at the bottom, too. All measurements should be made from the far side of the bevel, not from the flat inner face of the frame.

Second, a louvre frame, unlike any other frame with bars, has the same number of spaces as slats. A glance at Fig.5 will show you why.

Third, the number of slats needed to fill the frame (this number is given at step 3 of the

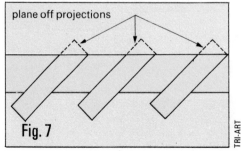

Fig. 7

Fig.4 (top of page). *The simplified door frame in which the louvred panels are set. It has haunched mortise-and-tenon joints at each corner and normal mortise-and-tenon joints at the ends of the middle rail.*
Fig.5. *A typical louvre frame. Note the bevel at the top, which prevents a gap from forming.*
Fig.6. *A marking-out diagram; its use is described on page 83 (opposite).*
Fig.7. *The rear edge of each slat should be planed flat after the frame is assembled.*

procedure below) is the minimum number that will make the louvred panel opaque when viewed from straight in front. If you want to make it more peep-proof, add at least one slat to every six that the calculations tell you you will need, and carry on with the subsequent steps using the increased number.

Marking-out formula

1. Make a scale drawing of the frame from the side, using Fig.6 as an example but altering it to your own measurements. Draw in the first slat, set at 45° or whatever angle you have chosen. Measure its total width along the frame—this is 54mm in the example, *including* the 5mm overlap where the frame top is bevelled, but *excluding* the part of each slat that projects out of the frame at the front.

2. Measure the remaining space from the bottom of the first slat to the other end of the frame (in this case, 222mm).

3. Divide the remaining space by the width of the first slat (222÷54=4.11). The result, taken to the nearest whole number, gives you the *minimum* number of slats you will need in addition to the first one (eg. 4).

4. Measure the diagonal thickness of a slat by holding your ruler parallel to the frame edge (a slat of 13mm timber will measure 18mm in this direction if set at 45°).

5. Multiply this measurement by the number of slats still to be drawn in (18 x 4=72).

6. Subtract the result from the remaining space (222—72=150).

7. Divide this figure by the number of slats still to go in to give the width of the spaces between them (150÷4=37.5).

8. Now you know the width of each slat measured along the frame (18mm) and of each

space between two slats (37.5mm). Mark these two measurements alternately right down your drawing to see if the slats fit exactly. If they don't, you have made a mistake. Transfer all these markings to the real frame sides, marking the two sides together to keep the slats absolutely level.

Assembly of the louvres

Now that you know how to set out louvres, everything else is easy. Cut the housings as marked, using a tenon saw and a chisel of the same width as the thickness of the slats. Don't make each housing separately. First make *all* the tenon saw cuts to a depth of $\frac{1}{4}$in. (6mm). Then chisel the wood out of all the housings. This 'production-line' technique saves a lot of time.

Fit the frame together 'dry' to make sure that it is (a) square, (b) the same width at top and bottom, (c) the right size to fit in the door or shutter. Measure the internal width between the pairs of housings to find the right length for the slats.

Now make up a rough jig to enable you to cut all the slats the same length. A typical jig would be a box like a mitre box, whose bottom is made of the same timber as a slat, so that it is the right width internally. It has a stop at one end and a slot to guide the saw at the other. Cut all the slats to length in this box. Do not plane

Below. How to add interest to a hallway: fit louvred doors and panels all round it. The mirror on the right gives the impression that there are even more louvres.

Above. This door is given a touch of distinction by its polished wood louvre panels, which stand out from the contrasting white-painted frame.

Below. The gentle, diffused light from a set of unpainted pine shutters softens the angular lines of the stark modern furniture in this living room.

BILL MACLAUGHLIN

MICHAEL BOYS

1

2

4

5

7

8

their edges at an angle, even if they are going to be angled later.

Glue and pin all the slats into their housings on one side of the frame. If the rear of the panel is to be planed flat, the slats should still project slightly beyond the rear of the frame so that none of the housing is visible (see Fig.7). Then fasten on the other side of the frame in the same way. One pin per slat is enough.

Slide the top and bottom of the frame into place between the sides. Glue them to the sides and the top and bottom slats, and pin them through the sides to hold them while the glue dries. Waterproof glue should be used for work that is to go outside.

Test each completed panel for square and leave it to dry. Then do any necessary planing on the slats and drop the panel into position in

1. Marking out the housings for the slats with a mitre try square and dividers.
2. Marking the depth of the housings with an ordinary marking gauge.
3. Sawing the sides of the housings. Do the whole lot in one go for accuracy.
4. Chiselling out the housings with a chisel held horizontally, bevel side up.
5. The box-shaped jig used to ensure that all the slats are cut to the same length.
6. Pinning the slats to one side of the frame; one or two pins per slat are enough.
7. Planing the back of the slats off flush with the frame. You can plane the front too.
8. A few pins are enough to hold the louvre panel in its door; don't glue it in place.
9. The completed door fitted to a cupboard unit, which will be built in later.

the rectangular hole in the main frame of the door or shutter. The outside of the frame might need a bit of planing before it will go in, in which case you will have to punch all the nail heads below the surface to avoid ruining the plane iron.

When the panel fits, glue it in and secure it with a *few* pins—you might have to take it out later for repairs.

Finally, clean everything up with fine glass-paper, then prime, undercoat and paint it, or give it three coats of polyurethane varnish. Shutters have a great deal of wind and rain to contend with, and the more paint you put on the longer they will last.

You may find the instructions on hanging doors, listed in full in CHAPTER 16, useful for installing your new louvred door or shutter.

All timber floors (except parquet, wood block, ply or chipboard floors—see below) are made out of *floorboards* laid in parallel rows. These are supported from below by *joists*, which are heavier timbers running across the line of the boards at intervals. The ends of the joists are in turn supported by even thicker members called *wall plates,* which run just inside the outside walls of the house, and *sleeper plates*, which provide intermediate support (see Fig.1).

The components of the floor must all be reasonably strong to take the weight of people and furniture. The minimum thickness of each part, and the maximum distance between joists or plates that is compatible with safety, are laid down in the building regulations of each country or locality. Unfortunately, these minimum requirements vary widely from place to place, and in a general survey it is only possible to give average sizes and spacings, or the range within which these sizes and spacings fall.

Floorboards and joists

Floorboards are flat boards $\frac{3}{4}$in.-1$\frac{1}{4}$in. (19-32mm) thick and 3in.-8in. (75-200mm) wide. They may be made out of softwood or hardwood, though nearly all modern houses have softwood floors because they are cheaper. The boards are held down on the joists with nails 2in.-3in. (50-75mm) long, or sometimes with wire staples; screws are not normally used except for removable boards above electrical or plumbing installations. Old floors are generally nailed with special *floor brads* (see DATA SHEET on page 48), but nowadays oval wire nails are used.

In modern houses the floorboards themselves may also be joined to each other by tongue-and-groove joints in their adjacent edges, which brace and strengthen the whole surface. Older floors in British houses, however, tend to have plain-edged boards. In high-quality modern work, the boards are often 'secret-nailed' to the joists by passing the nails through the tongues at an angle.

Sometimes chipboard or thick ply sheet is used instead of floorboards. This type of construction is found only in modern houses, unless the floor of an older house has had its boards replaced by chipboard.

Joists are heavier than floorboards and are set on edge, which makes them less liable to bend under weight. They are normally 2in.-3in. (50-75mm) thick (though in old houses thicker joists may be found) and anything between 6in. and 11in. (150-280mm) deep, depending on their *span*, that is, the gap they have to bridge without any support. In Britain, where timber is very expensive by world standards, the tendency is to use small spans and light joists.

Where joists do not completely extend from wall to wall (for example, where a staircase goes through the floor), special joists running at right angles to the main joists, and supporting their ends, are used (see Fig.2). These are called *trimming joists,* and are thicker than the ordinary joists (called *bridging joists*). In good quality work, these are solidly fastened in place by *tusk tenon joints* where the tenon on the trimming joist passes right through the bridging joist and is secured by a large peg driven through its projecting end. In lower-quality work, this

ALAN DUNS

Timber floors and footings

In a British house with a suspended ground floor, the masonry foundations are topped with strong timber supports for the floor. In many parts of the world, there are houses where the foundations, too, are made of timber.

There are many types of timber ground floor found in various parts of the world, and they differ widely in the way they are supported. But all types have certain similarities, mostly in the construction of the floor surface and the parts immediately below it.

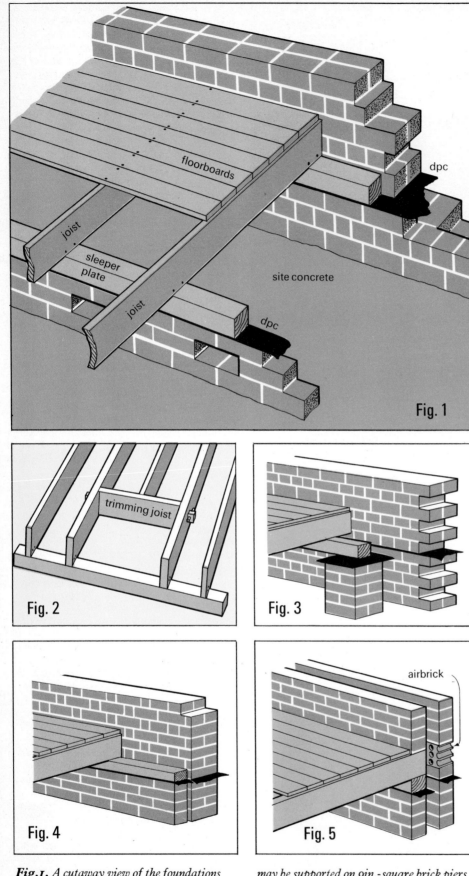

floorboards

dpc

joist

sleeper plate

site concrete

joist

dpc

Fig. 1

trimming joist

Fig. 2

Fig. 3

Fig. 4

airbrick

Fig. 5

TRI-ART

Fig.1. *A cutaway view of the foundations of a masonry house, showing how the timber parts fit on to the brick parts.*
Fig.2. *The ends of joists that do not reach all the way to the wall plate are supported by an extra-thick trimming joist.*
Fig.3. *The wall plate of a masonry house*

may be supported on 9in.-square brick piers close to, but not touching the wall.
Fig.4. *Sometimes the wall plate is set on a sleeper wall just inside the main wall.*
Fig.5. *In low-quality work, the joists and wall plate are set in the wall itself. They are kept from wet rot by airbricks.*

complex joint is replaced by a sheet-metal bracket called a *joist hanger,* which is also used for supporting upper floor joists.

Joists are spaced between 10in. and 18in. (250-450mm) apart. The stronger the floorboards, the wider the space between the joists.

Sometimes, joists have to cross a considerable distance, though they may be supported at several points along their length by *sleepers* (intermediate supports—see below). In this situation it may well be impractical to use very long joists, because of the extra cost. Joists can be joined above a solid support by the simple method of doubling them up, side by side. Where it is necessary for some reason to continue a joist along exactly the same line for its full length, without the slight offset caused by an overlap, the joists are butt jointed over the sleeper and reinforced with a *flitch,* or short length of joist nailed to the side of the joint. To give the joists proper support, at least 2in. (50mm) of each must rest on the sleeper on either side of the joint. Sleepers are generally 4in. (100mm) wide, so provided that the joint is above its centre there is no problem.

Joists are supported on heavy beams at each end called *wall plates.* These have a minimum size of 4in. x 2in. (100 x 50mm), but are much larger in old houses. Wall plates generally lie on their wider side in order to provide a better bearing surface for the ends of the joists. They do not have to be particularly rigid if they are supported along their entire length by the wall they lie against, as would normally be the case in masonry houses. The way a wall plate is attached to the wall varies widely (see below).

In masonry houses, wall plates generally run along only those walls where they are needed to support the ends of the joists—that is, along a pair of opposite walls in most cases. In timber houses, the wall plate (which is not the same as the bottom horizontal member of the wall) generally runs along one pair of walls; the other pair is supported by double joists (see Figs.8 and 9).

Wall plates on masonry foundation walls can be joined at corners, or anywhere along their length, with ordinary halving joints. This does not affect their strength, since they are continuously supported underneath and their real function is to provide something to nail the joists to. In older houses, the top surface of the wall plate is often notched or housed to hold the joists extra firmly. Sometimes, a special toothed joint called a *cog joint* is used. The joists are skew-nailed to the wall plate whether it is notched or not.

In a few masonry houses, metal wall plates are found instead of timber ones. They are flat metal strips 2in. to 4in. (50mm-100mm) wide and $\frac{1}{8}$in. to $\frac{3}{8}$in. (3mm-10mm) thick. In this type of construction, the ends of the joists are recessed into the brickwork of the wall to hold them steady, since they cannot be nailed to the metal plate. The plate itself is also set inside the wall between two courses of bricks.

Sleeper plates, the intermediate supports for long joists, are generally made of 4in. x 3in. (100 x 75mm) timber, the same size as wall plates. They run parallel to the wall plates, and the joists are nailed on in the same way. If a sleeper is supported along its whole length by a *sleeper wall* (see below), it can be jointed anywhere along its length like a wall plate. In most timber houses, however, the sleepers are only supported at intervals and in this case they must be either continuous or heavily reinforced at the joints.

Sleepers are generally placed under floors at about 7ft (2.1m) intervals. In theory, joists could span over twice this width in perfect safety, but using close-spaced sleepers allows thinner joists to be used, which saves wood (and money).

Parquet floors

Parquet and wood block floors are completely unlike conventional boarded floors. They are not a structural part of the house, but a surfacing material like carpet or linoleum, and may be laid on any type of floor. In fact, wood blocks are a popular way of disguising a concrete ground floor.

Parquet is a special type of floor made of oak blocks $\frac{1}{4}$in. (6mm) thick. Other types of floor may have blocks of other woods between $\frac{5}{8}$in. and 2in. (16-50mm) thick. They are never nailed down, but are glued down with mastic or asphalt. Sometimes they are raised a short way above the floor on small cork discs, which makes the surface more springy.

There is also a modern type of imitation block floor. This consists of small rectangles of veneer glued to a larger piece of chipboard. The chipboard pieces are laid like tiles, and (in theory, anyway) the joins between them are no more obvious than the joins between the pieces of veneer, so the effect of a parquet floor is created. This type of floor is not as hard-wearing as a real parquet one, but it is a lot cheaper.

Farther down

Although the floorboards, joists, wall plates and sleepers are much the same in all types of house, the way they are held up varies widely. There are major differences not just between masonry and timber houses, but also between different types of masonry and timber constructions. The only way to describe them is to go through them separately, one by one.

Masonry houses

There are several different constructions of the brick lower parts of a masonry house. The way the lower timber parts are arranged is, of course, heavily dependent on the conformation of the brickwork.

The most variable feature of a suspended timber floor in a masonry house is the way the wall plate is attached (or not attached) to the wall.

One method is to rest it on 9in. (230mm) square brick piers resting on the concrete surface layer under the floor (see Fig.3). These piers are generally set a few inches away from the wall. They are topped with bituminized felt or other damp course, and the wall plate is simply laid on top of the dpc. It is not fastened down; the joists hold it steady. Since the wall plate is only supported at intervals, it needs to be a bit thicker than normal. 4in. x 4in. (100 x 100mm) is usual.

Another method—and the standard one in modern British practice—is to rest the wall plate

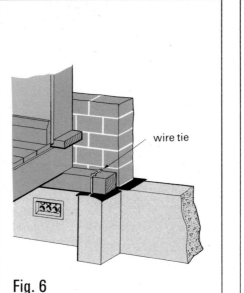

wire tie

Fig. 6

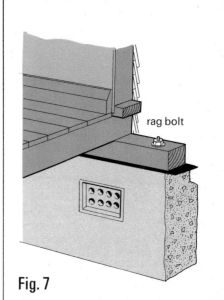

rag bolt

Fig. 7

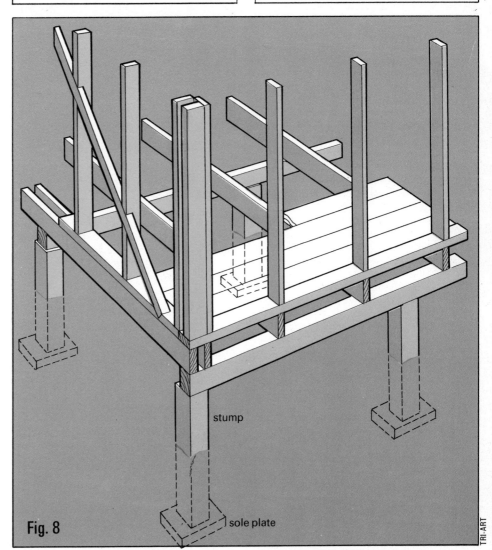

stump

sole plate

Fig. 8

TRI-ART

Fig.6. A common arrangement in Australian and New Zealand 'brick-veneer' houses: piers extending inwards from brick or concrete foundations support the wall plate, which is fastened on with wire set in the masonry.
Fig.7. In an all-timber house with concrete foundations, the wall plate supports the whole wall as well as the floor. It is attached to the concrete with rag bolts.
Fig.8. An older timber house may be supported on wooden 'stumps' buried in the ground and resting on sole plates to stop them sinking further. Note the typical double joist supporting the left-hand wall.

on a sleeper wall just inside the main house wall (see Fig.4). This wall is 4½in. (115mm—one brick width) thick, and does not quite touch the house wall. Again, it must have a dpc. Most often it is topped with bituminized felt and the wall plate is not fixed to it. A normal 4in. x 3in. (100 x 75mm) wall plate is used.

Sometimes, instead of building a separate sleeper wall, builders used to increase the width of the wall below the wall plate to provide a ledge on which it rests. This method is no longer used in Britain, although it and variations of it (e.g. piers attached to the inside skin of brickwork) are still widely used abroad.

In all these installations, the ends of the joists do not quite touch the house wall. This allows a free circulation of air around the ends and so protects them from rot.

Many houses can be found in which the ends of the joists and the whole wall plate have been recessed into the wall (see Fig.5). In a cavity wall as shown here, there is still a certain amount of air space at the end of the joists, and air bricks are generally built in to improve the flow. But this system is more prone to rot than others, and is now almost never used.

In an installation of this kind, a metal wall plate is sometimes found. Occasionally (and in very low-quality work as a rule) the wall plate is omitted altogether. It is, of course, not strictly necessary to hold the joists up, but it does keep them all at the same level. Ordinary brickwork is slightly uneven, and this irregularity is transferred to the joists and so to the floor itself, if there is no wall plate. Sometimes small bits of slate or tile have been used to pack joists up to the right height. They generally crack or fall out after a few years, causing the floor to subside unevenly.

Joist hangers are sometimes bolted to the wall, or inserted into mortar joints, to hold up the end of each joist separately. This construction is, however, more usual for upper floors than for ground floors.

The sleepers that hold up the middle of the joists are supported on 4½in. (115mm) thick walls. These sleeper walls do not have to be very strong, because they are only holding up one floor and not the whole house. So they are laid directly on the site concrete, without proper foundations. Large gaps in the brickwork improve the ventilation of the space under the floor. These gaps often form a regular 'honeycomb' pattern.

Timber houses

Modern timber-framed houses often have brick or concrete foundations similar to those of masonry houses. This is always the case with brick-veneer houses, since solid concrete is absolutely necessary to hold up the outer skin of bricks. Some of the newest houses of this type have solid concrete ground floors as well, so that there is no timber below floor level at all.

A more usual arrangement is shown in Fig.6. Here, a 4½in. (115mm) thick concrete foundation wall runs all round the outside of the building to support the brick outer layer. Concrete piers, generally measuring 8in. x 4½in. (200 x 115mm), extend inwards from this wall at maximum intervals of 6ft (1.9m). These serve two purposes: to brace the wall and to provide a

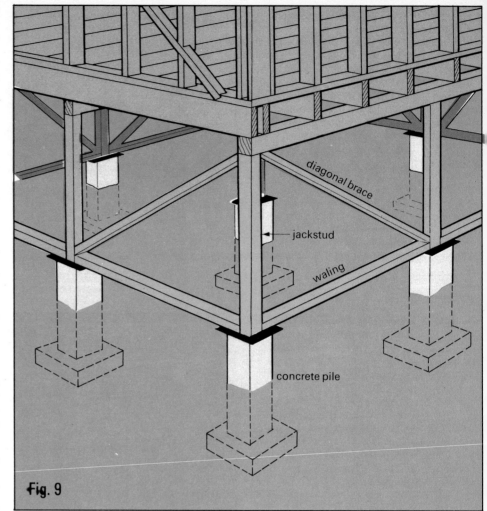

Fig. 9

Fig.9. *A more modern version of stump construction. Concrete piles support vertical jackstuds, which are braced upright with walings and diagonal struts. The jackstuds are nailed to the piles with ordinary nails.*

support for the wall plate. The plate is generally made of 4in. x 3in. (100 x 75mm) timber set on edge. It is fastened solidly to each pier by heavy No. 8 gauge wire bedded in the concrete and stapled around the top of the wall plate.

A house made entirely of timber, without any bricks at all, may still have continuous masonry foundations. These are generally made of concrete, though bricks are also found. The usual arrangement is shown in Fig.7. It consists of a single concrete wall 5in.-6in. (130mm) thick, topped with a bituminized felt damp course and with a 4in. x 3in. (100 x 75mm) wall plate bolted to it.

The classic foundation for a timber house, however, is made of piles set in holes in the ground. Modern houses have concrete piles; older ones were supported on timber 'stumps' 4in. or 5in. (100-130mm) thick, which may have a square or round cross-section depending on local practice.

A typical stump foundation is shown in Fig.8. The stumps are let into the ground to a depth of 15-24in. (380-610mm) and rest on wide *sole plates* to keep them from subsiding. They may extend between 6in. and 4ft 6in. (150mm-1.4m) above ground level to keep the

floor level above uneven ground. Note the typical double joist used instead of a normal wall plate on one pair of opposite walls.

Very tall stumps are sometimes fitted with diagonal braces running from stump to stump to keep them from sagging sideways.

The modern counterpart of this stump construction uses concrete piles (see Fig.9). These are generally 8in. (200mm) square for single-storey houses and 10in. (250mm) square for two-storey houses. They are set into the ground in the same way as stumps, and normally have a wider part at the bottom to act as a sole plate.

The wall plate may rest directly on top of the piles, in which case it is wired on with heavy wire set in the concrete. Where the floor is a long way above the ground, however, it is usual to top the piles with a timber framework—something like a masonry sleeper wall—made of timber the same thickness as the wall plate. The frame is firmly attached to the concrete with rag bolts or ordinary 3in. (75mm) nails, and is further strengthened by diagonal braces and *walings* (horizontal struts). The wall plates rest on top of the *jackstuds* (vertical members) as they would on wooden stumps.

Sleeper walls of the type found in Britain are most uncommon in timber-frame houses, even those with continuous masonry foundations. Sleepers are generally supported on stumps, brick piers or concrete piles set 4ft 6in. (1.4m) apart, and are attached to them in exactly the same way as wall plates.

Modern lines of a boxed in bath

The days are gone when baths were tall cast-iron structures with ornate exposed legs. The simple lines of a modern bathroom require the sides of a bath to be boxed in.

Boxing-in a bath is a comparatively simple job and can be done with a wide range of surfaces—ceramic tiles, plastic laminate, tongued-and-grooved timber boarding, or even gloss-painted plywood. None of these presents any serious

The bathroom before the bath was boxed in. The old box frame shown here was warped, and had to be discarded.

technical problems.

All these surfacing materials can be mounted on a simple but robust wooden frame fastened to the floor around the edge of the bath. The installation, however, has to meet various requirements.

First, the frame must be strong enough not to warp—this is a serious problem in the steamy atmosphere of bathrooms. The tendency of wood to warp in damp air can be reduced by painting all the parts with waterproof paint or varnish on all sides, so that the humidity of the wood remains constant.

Second, it must be properly fastened to the surfaces it touches, so that it will resist kicking, blows from mops when cleaning the floor, and so on. The frame can be nailed to a wooden floor or it can be fastened to a concrete floor with wall plugs and screws, or with masonry pins. Nearly all baths have at least one side or end against a wall, and the ends of the frame can be plugged and screwed to this too.

Third, the outer surface has to be reasonably watertight, so that water does not seep down behind it and under the bath where it cannot be mopped up. This is simply solved by setting the panel about $\frac{1}{8}$in. (3mm) back from the outer lip of the bath, so that any drips from it run down the front of the panel instead of seeping through its back and rotting the frame. At the same time, the join between the bath and the wall should be sealed, either with a 'bath trim kit' consisting of narrow tiles with an L-shaped cross-section or (more simply and cheaply) with the white, plasticine-like sealing strip obtainable from any hardware shop.

Fourth, the pipework under the bath must be accessible for maintenance. This includes not just the taps but also the trap in the waste pipe, which has to be cleaned out occasionally. The best solution here is to screw on the panels with 'mirror' screws, which have decorative covers on the heads so that you don't have to disguise them. Don't use too many screws; six or eight is ample for each panel if it has to be removed from time to time. (It is a good idea to inspect the floorboards under a bath for wet rot every few months.)

Materials

The framing should be made of 2in. x 1in. (50mm x 25mm) or 1½in. x ¾in. (38mm x 19mm) softwood throughout. The amount you will need of this, and all the other materials, depends on your particular bath and bathroom, so you should make a scale drawing of everything you are going to make before you buy anything.

The panelling material depends on what you are going to surface it with. An ideal material for tiling, painting or laminating is 13mm (½in.) WBP (water- and boil-proof) birch plywood, which will last for many years. Chipboard and hardboard are cheaper but less durable. If you do use them, choose exterior grade chipboard or tempered hardboard, both of which are more waterproof than the ordinary kind.

Other materials you can use are a good-quality ready-laminated chipboard (the edges should be given several coats of polyurethane varnish to make them waterproof) or any kind of tongued-and-grooved boarding (this should be thoroughly varnished on both sides—do the

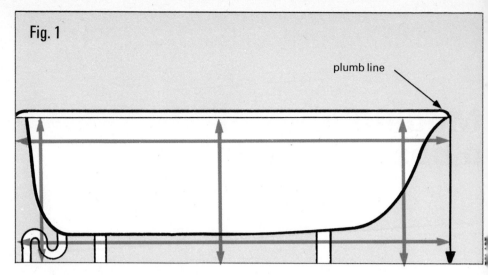

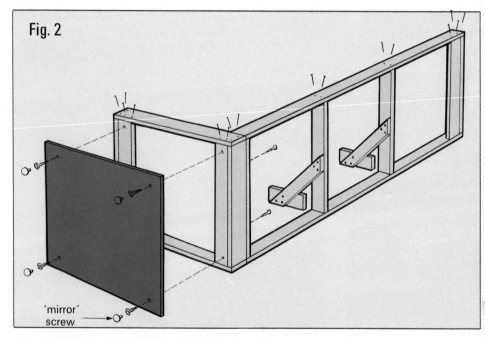

Fig.1 (above). The vertical distance from the bath rim to the floor, and the horizontal distance along the bath, should be measured in several places (marked with red arrows) to ensure complete accuracy.

Fig.2 (below). The basic frame for the bath. All types of panelling fit this frame. It can, of course, be built with as many side and end panels as you need to suit the layout of your own particular bathroom.

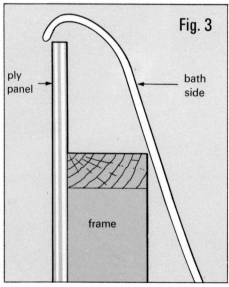

Fig.3 (left). A bath with sloping sides and a narrow rim may need a shallower frame than normal to fit into the limited space.

Opposite page: Fig.4 (top). The frame should be braced upright with a diagonal strut fastened to a block nailed to the floor. The nails can be driven in diagonally as shown; neatness is not important.
Fig.5 (second from top). Tongued-and-grooved boarding should be made up into a single panel by nailing it to battens. This panel can then be removed in one piece when you want to inspect the pipework of the bath.
Fig.6 (bottom). Ceramic tiles are heavy, and a tiled panel running along the whole of one side of the bath would be very difficult to remove and replace. The solution is to make a smaller, removeable inspection panel, and attach the rest to the panel permanently to the box framework.

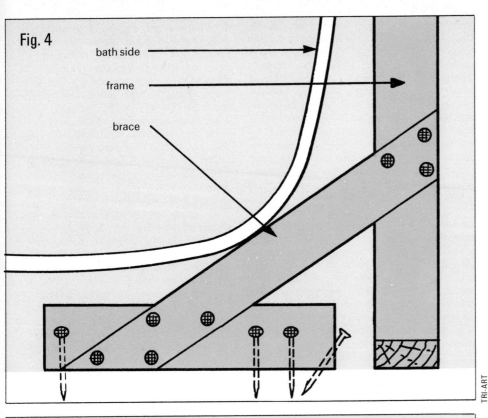

Fig. 4

bath side

frame

brace

TRI-ART

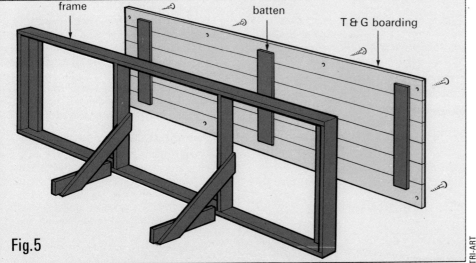

frame

batten

T & G boarding

Fig.5

TRI-ART

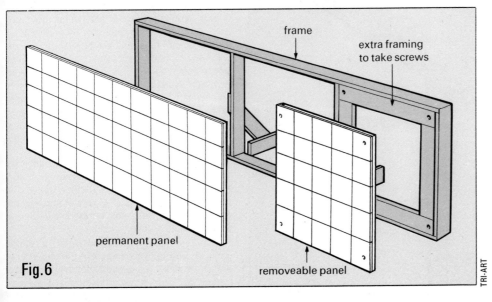

frame

extra framing
to take screws

permanent panel

removeable panel

Fig. 6

TRI-ART

back and ends before you put it on).

You will also need some chromed or stainless angle strip to neaten and protect the corners of the box, unless it is tiled or the bath has a wall at each end. Other necessities are surfacing material for the panels, if they are to be surfaced, and plenty of 2in. (50mm) oval wire nails, 2in. No. 10 screws, and 1½in. (38mm) 'mirror' screws—the kind with chrome-plated domed covers that screw into a hole in the flat head of the screw.

Measuring

The first thing to do—before you buy anything —is to measure the bath carefully. The space into which each frame must fit should be measured at several points, to allow for the floor not being quite even and the walls being slightly out of true (as they almost certainly will be, even in a well-built house).

Measure the height of the underside of the rim of the bath above the floor in at least three places (see Fig.1). Then measure the length of the outer edge of the rim of the bath. If the bath is set between two walls, measure this distance from wall to wall; if there is a wall at one end only, measure from that wall to a plumbline (or a small weight on a string) hung over the outside corner. If there is no wall at either end, use two plumblines. Any length beginning or ending at a wall should be measured both at floor level and at bath rim level to see if the wall slopes.

A typical frame for a box around a bath is shown in Fig.2. To find the length that each side of the frame should have, take the *shortest* measurement of the length of the bath, i.e., the horizontal distance measured at the height where the wall bulges out most. Subtract from this ⅛in. (3mm) or the thickness of the rim of the bath, whichever is greater; the thickness of the plywood (or T & G boarding) that you are going to cover the frame with; the thickness of the tiles or laminate (if any); and the width of the frame members (at each outside corner of the frame not touching a wall).

This last measurement should be subtracted on *one* side of each corner only, since it allows for the overlap of the frames where they meet at each corner. Note that the frame members are nailed together on edge and not flat (for extra rigidity) so that a frame of 2in. x 1in. timber is 2in. wide, seen from the end.

To find the height of the frame, take the shortest measurement from the floor to the lower edge of the bath rim and subtract ⅜in. (10mm)— this will make the frame easier to insert. The panel over it must, of course, be the full height and project above the frame a short way.

Measure also the horizontal distance from the inner edge of the bath rim to a point at the same level on the outer wall of the bath. This is to check that the frame will be narrow enough to fit into that space without the bath's outer wall pushing it beyond the outer rim of the bath. On most baths, there should be enough room. If there isn't, you can make the top of the frame lower (see Fig.3) so that it will fit—but don't make it more than 3in. (75mm) lower if you are panelling with 13mm (½in.) ply or chipboard, or about half that if you are using T & G boarding or hardboard. Otherwise, the panelling may curl at the top. If you cannot fit the frame in and still comply with these limits, you might cut away part of its rear edge to make it fit.

When you have sorted out the size of everything, make scale drawings and from them work out how much wood and other materials you will need. Allow a reasonable amount for waste, particularly with the tiles if you are buying any, because they often break when you are trying to cut them.

Order of work

The frames are so simple to make that no detailed instructions are required. There are no fancy joints, because they would be out of sight anyway, and because the frame is not required to be incredibly strong. A few points to watch: the pieces should be skew-nailed, i.e., the nails should be put in slightly crooked in opposed pairs. This makes them less likely to come apart. All the frame members are set on edge except for the inserts at each end, which should be set flat and flush with the front. The purpose of these inserts is to provide something to screw the panels to that is not dangerously near the end of the panels, and so likely to split them.

When the frames are made, mark the floor where they are to go by dropping a plumb line from the rim of the bath at various points. This will ensure that they are vertical—but remember that the frames are set back from the place where the plumb line hangs, so that there is room for the thickness of the panelling and the slight projection of the rim of the bath.

Fasten the frames to the floor in a suitable manner, and brace them upright with battens

running diagonally back from as high up the frame as possible to blocks fastened to the floor under the bath (see Fig.4). The blocks should be made of 2in. x 1in. or 1½in. x ¾in. (50mm x 25mm or 38mm x 19mm) timber, and fastened to the floor by very long screws sunk vertically through the top edge, nails driven diagonally through the sides, or small angle brackets or angle strips screwed to both block and floor.

You will probably find it easier to screw the corners of the frame together than to nail them, because it is difficult to hammer a nail sideways into a slightly flexible frame in close proximity to a bath. The ends of the frame must be screwed into plugs in the wall. If the wall is irregular, pack the gaps between it and the frame with scrap plywood.

When the frame is completely installed, cut each piece of 13mm (½in.) ply, if that is what you are using, to slightly more than the correct length and height. Then get a helper to hold it steady against the frame with its top edge 2in. (50mm) above the bottom of the rim of the bath —mark the back of the panel to help you to locate it correctly. Set a pair of compasses to 2in. (50mm) and use them to scribe the bottom of the panel to the floor, or use a 2in. (50mm) block and a pencil instead of the compasses. If you are in doubt about how to do this, see 'Marking for a true fit'

Fig.7 (below). An old-fashioned bath with round corners can be put into a square box by bridging the gap at the corners with a double-round-edged 'corner' tile.

Opposite page: Fig.8. Skew-nailing the frame together. Nails are quite strong enough for this type of construction; there is no point in wasting time on complex joints.
Fig.9. Nailing the diagonal struts to the frame. This frame has been set a short way above the floor to provide a toe recess underneath, which gives a little extra standing room to this very small bathroom.
Fig.10. Fitting the frames together at the corners of the bath. They can be nailed or screwed together, as you prefer.
Fig.11. Check that all the frame parts are straight and level before you go any further. The sloping panel mounted behind the taps drains splashes back into the bath.
Fig.12. The finished frame, a sturdy job that will stand up to years of hard use and constant dampness.
Fig.13. Fastening a laminated chipboard panel to the frame with 'mirror' screws.
Fig.14. The completed job. The bathroom has also been improved by building an airing cupboard round the hot-water cylinder, changing the wallpaper and laying a carpet.

If the wall is irregular, you will have to scribe the panel to that, too. This should be done after the panel is scribed to the floor, removing as little wood as possible. Trim the other end to length afterwards.

When the panels are the right shape, they can be painted or covered with plastic laminate, glued in place with a contact adhesive. Then they can be installed with four, six, or eight 'mirror' screws, depending on the length of the panel. Finish the corners with decorative angle strip and the job is complete. If, however, you are using T & G boards or tiles, read on.

Special panels

Tongued-and-grooved boards can be nailed direct to the frame if you like. Instructions on how to make them fit are given fully in CHAPTER 6. But if you have to remove them to inspect or repair something under the bath, it will be a great bore to prise them off one at a time.

A better idea is to nail them to vertical battens set a short way in from each end, and not quite reaching to the top and bottom of the 'panel' of boards. When the panel is laid against the frame, these battens will fit into the spaces between the frame members, and the boards themselves will lie flat against the frame (see Fig.5). The whole made-up panel can then be fastened on by mirror screws in the usual way. The outside corners can be finished with a metal angle strip or wood moulding to conceal the end grain of the boards, or bevelled at 45° to create a neat mitred corner (this is laborious, but probably worth it).

You can now apply tiles to the bath panelling. The tiles should be applied to a normal 13mm (½in.) ply panel. The only difficulty here is that the weight of the tiles makes removing the panels difficult, and you might break tiles in attempting it.

If you are content with only one removeable panel at the end of the bath, and the tiles are not too thick, then go ahead. Tile the end panel before you put it up, finishing the outside

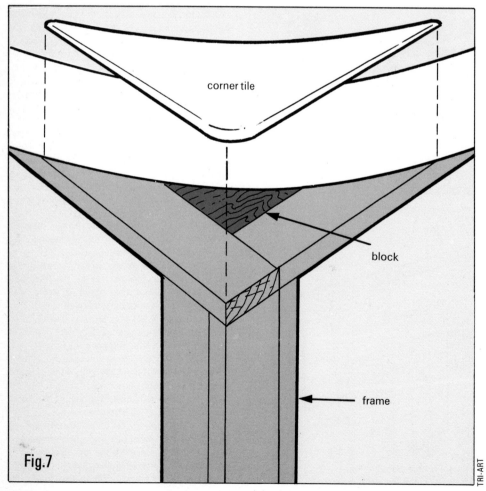

corner tile

block

frame

Fig.7

TRI-ART

8

9

10

11

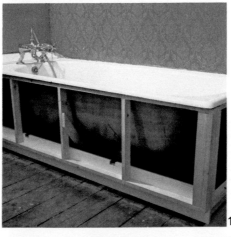

12

13

corner with round-edged tiles. Then drill holes (slightly oversize) for mirror screws, using a masonry drill, and put the panel up in the normal way.

If, however, the shape of the bathroom requires you to remove a long side panel to get at the pipes, it is a better idea to have only part of the side panel removeable, as shown in Fig.6. Fasten battens all round the inside edge of one bay of the frame, flush with the front, to provide something to fasten the removeable panel to. Install the larger, permanent part of the panel with ordinary countersunk screws, and tile and grout it in the usual way. Tile the removeable part of the panel before you put it up, making sure that the arrangement of the rows matches that of the permanent part. Then drill oversize holes in the corners and put the panel on with mirror screws. You can wipe grout into the join between the two panels if you like, but it will fall out the first time you remove the panel.

The only other problem you are likely to have is if you are boxing in a very old-fashioned bath with round corners. The best way to deal with this is to treat the bath as if it had square corners. Make the box the same length and width as the bath, so that it projects beyond the bath rim at the corners. Then insert a block behind the corners of the frame, flush with its top edge (see Fig.7) to bridge the triangular gap. Finish the projecting top corner of the box with a white 'corner' tile with two round edges, and its back cut to fit the curve (shown in Fig.7). These baths are nearly always white, so a white tile blends in and makes it look like a modern squared-off bath.

14

Versatile room dividers

Room dividers have many uses—when two children share the same room, for example, or when one room must serve two different purposes. And they can be both elegant and easy to make.

Very large rooms can often benefit from a partition. It may range from an elaborate wall structure to a simple screen, but the function of all partitions is essentially the same—to separate expansive areas into smaller, more contained ones.

Simple wall screens are especially useful for dividing a room into smaller areas that do not require absolute privacy. Frames may be constructed from timber battens and the screened panels filled with anything from cloth to decorative plastic panelling.

Estimating the size

The room partitions featured here are designed to fit floor-to-ceiling heights; this is both for strength and visual appearance. The frames were made from 2in. x 1in. (50mm x 25mm) finished softwood (also known as 'dressed' 'gauged' and 'planed-all-round') and separated into panels 2ft wide by 2ft high (610mm by 610mm). They were made to fit an area 6ft wide by 8ft high (1.8m x 2.4m). If your room is larger or smaller than this you will simply need to make additional panels—or fewer ones—according to the same directions. Widths have been calculated to fit even distances. If the height of your ceiling is uneven—ie, if it cannot be divided into 2ft areas—the frame should be constructed according to the alternative method suggested below.

In addition to the timber you will need a number of $1\frac{1}{2}$in. (38mm) and $\frac{3}{4}$in. (19mm) oval nails, $\frac{1}{2}$in. (13mm) scotia or quadrant moulding, 3in. (75mm) No. 8 screws and plugs, and a pva adhesive.

Building the frame

When working with finished timber, the dimensions of the wood are somewhat different from the sizes quoted. 2in. x 1in. will, in fact, be around $1\frac{7}{8}$in. x $\frac{7}{8}$in. or 48mm x 22mm. To allow the inner area of each square to be exactly 2ft sq—a size which cuts exactly out of most standard sheet materials—the actual dimensions for a '6ft x 8ft' frame will be about 6ft x $3\frac{1}{2}$in. x 8ft $4\frac{3}{8}$in. or around 1.9m x 2.5m.

It is probable that your ceiling will not be perfectly level so, when making your frame, you will find it easier to stop it about $\frac{1}{2}$in. (13mm) below the ceiling. The gap can then be filled with a packing strip of timber slightly narrower than the frame. From eye level, this gap will not normally be noticeable, especially if scotia or quadrant moulding (Fig.13) is used to hide it.

The timber frame

As can be seen in Fig.15, the frame consists of top and bottom *plates*, vertical members, called *studs*, which run between the two plates, and horizontal members, or *rails*, which run between the vertical members.

Begin constructing the frame by establishing the correct height for the vertical members. Square off the end of one of the vertical mem-

bers using a try square and marking knife, and cutting with a tenon saw or fine-toothed panel saw. Stand this piece in position next to the wall against which you are building the divider, keeping it as close to the skirting board as possible. Mark the upright so that it will fit ½in. below the ceiling. Cut the remaining vertical studs to the same height, making sure that the ends are all in square.

Hold the first upright against the skirting board and scribe off the necessary amount so that the upright will fit flush against the wall. Cut out the marked area with a coping saw.

If the skirting board is too thick you will not be able to scribe and cut the upright to fit over it. The way to get around this is to mark off the width of the upright on the skirting board, scoring the lines deeply with a marking knife. Then chisel out the board between the two marks so that when the partition is erected it will stand against the wall.

Next mark and cut the top and bottom plates to length (6ft 3½in. in this case). Join these four outer pieces of the frame together at the corners with *corner halving joints* (see Fig.10). The principles for making all the halving joints used to construct this frame are simple and are fully described in CHAPTER 5. Glue and nail these four joints firmly together using 1½in. (38mm) oval nails.

Once this has been completed and you have checked to see that the outer members are in square, you may fix the vertical studs in position. These should be 2ft (610mm) apart, measuring from the innermost edges (Fig.15). Fix these vertical pieces to the top and bottom plates using end halving joints as shown in Fig.11, 1½in. (38mm) ovals, and adhesive.

Now, cut the remaining horizontal members to the same size as the top and bottom plates. Mark out 2ft distances on these from the inner-most edges of each of the vertical members. Do this at the bottom of the vertical members, not midway. Measuring and cutting out the horizontal members in this way will help to straighten out any bows in the uprights. You will need to use a try square to see that all the angles formed between the cross members and the vertical ones are right angles.

Each cross rail should be fixed in position with halving joints (Fig.12). The outer joints will be end halving joints and the internal ones will be 'edge-on' halving joints. Check at all times that the angles are right angles by measuring the diagonals of each panel area. Glue and pin these cross rails into place, using 1½in. (38mm) oval nails for the outer joints and ¾in. (19mm) ovals for the inner joints. Allow a day for the adhesive to set.

Erecting the frame

Once the frame has been constructed it must be hoisted up into position; you will need at least two people to do this safely. First check the ceiling for the position of the joists. You can locate them by gently tapping a hammer along the ceiling. Areas along which joists run will emit a much less resonant sound than other areas. Make a final check with a bradawl. Remember that the joists may run either along the room or across it, and that they are usually at 16in. (407mm) centres. If the joists run in the same direction as the eventual position of the partition, you *must* fix the partition to one of them. So, unless you are certain where the joists are positioned you will have to be flexible within 16in. as regards the final installation. On the other hand, if the joists run at right angles to the partition, there will be no problem except, of course, in locating them and marking their position so that you will be able to place the fixings correctly.

Stand the frame upright in its correct position, so that the cut out portion of the first upright fits over the skirting board (or the upright fits into the rebated skirting board). Hold the frame in its exact position, against the wall, making sure that it is in square, and mark out four positions for drilling screw holes into the frame and the wall. These positions should be at the top and

Opposite page. Lightweight plastic panel-ling available in several colours and textures, is one attractive way of finishing your screen. **Centre** *and* **below.** *Fabric-covered soft-board is another—and offers enormous variety.*

bottom of the upright, near the outer plates, and at equidistant positions moving towards the centre. Someone must hold the frame for you while you drill. Use a power drill with a masonry bit set at slow speed and work carefully. Drill a hole about 2in. into the wall to accommodate a 3in. (75mm) No. 8 screw and wall plug. Continue doing the same for each position, inserting wood fibre, dowel or plastic wall plugs and countersinking the screws.

Now fit a packing strip of softwood, about ½in. thick between the top rail and the ceiling to make a snug even fit. Once this is done, check with a plumbob that your frame is upright, and adjust it at the base if it is 'out'. Then drill through the top rail and the ½in. packing strip into the ceiling at the points previously marked to indicate the position of the joist(s). Countersink the screws. The bottom plate can be screwed directly into the floorboards. Fix moulding around the top, if necessary (Fig.13), mitring it at the corners and then finish the frame with paint or varnish.

Alternative frame method

If your ceiling is unusually high—12ft-14ft— or is extremely uneven, or is an odd height, you may not wish to construct a frame to the full ceiling height. If this is the case, it would be possible to make the frame in the same manner as described, but you would have to allow for the outermost upright (the one farthest away from the wall) to extend to the full height of the ceiling and to be fixed to the ceiling joist by skew nailing (this is illustrated in CHAPTER 2). In this case, you will need an outer post of 2in. x 2in. (51mm x 51mm) for stability, and a matching inner one for appearance. The sides of the frame should be fixed to the wall with screws and wall plugs as described before.

Filling the panels

The choice of insert is mainly a matter of personal taste, but it should be something which is reasonably lightweight or the frame will not be able to support it. Another thing to consider is that the divider will be seen from both sides,

so the panel inserts will either need to be suitably finished on both front and back or some method of double covering will be necessary.

Cloth-covered panels

Any of the wide variety of fabrics that are suitable for use as wallcoverings can be used in the screen panel inserts but it is best to use a lightweight, fairly stiff, simply designed fabric. Dark fabrics or fairly heavy ones, such as felt or hessian, can be used to fill in some, but not all of the panel areas. If used exclusively, these fabrics can produce too dense an effect.

All fabric coverings will need to be tacked to a firm backing of some sort; ½in. (12.7mm) thick insulation board, obtainable at most builder's merchants, is quite suitable, since it is both firm and lightweight and is also available in a fire-resistant grade. (A similar material is called 'softboard').

The primary reason for using boarding is that both sides of the panel will display the fabric covering. To fill a panel, use a tenon saw to cut

Fig.1. *Using a mitre iron to cut scotia. For proper alignment on the iron, the length mark must be carried down the back of the wood.*

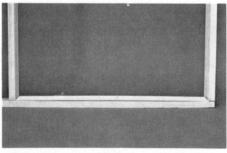

Fig.2. *Next, a tenon saw is used to trim the wood. Cut from the 'good' side towards the 'bad', so that any splintering is hidden.*

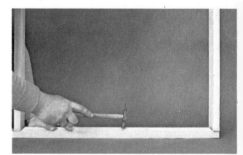

Fig.3. *With the offcut severed, you can check that the angle is correctly sawn—and not 'upside down' as for an external corner.*

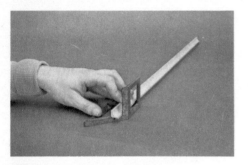

Fig.4. *A trial assembly of the first corner will show whether you are cutting correctly. Here, a sharper angle will be needed.*

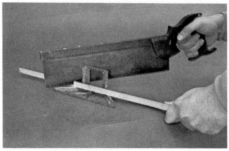

Fig.5. *For internal angles, as in this project, cut scotia a shade over-length and 'spring' it in to ensure a tight corner fit.*

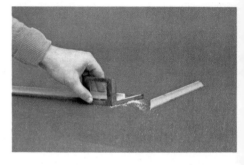

Fig.6. *Initially, tack the first length of scotia in the middle only. This allows for adjustment when fitting the other pieces.*

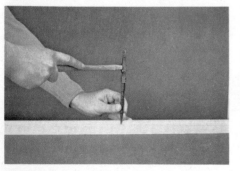

Fig.7. *All nails should be punched, and the holes filled with wood stopper (for varnish) or cellulose filler (for a painted finish).*

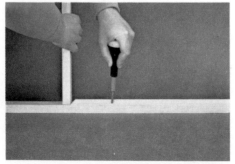

Fig.8. *A push-pin tool is handy for fixing mouldings. By pushing rather than driving the nail, it helps prevent the wood splitting.*

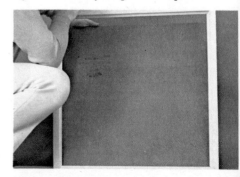

Fig.9. *When all the mouldings are fitted, test-fit the sections of panelling to make sure there will be clearance for the fabric.*

a piece of the board to fit *exactly* into the interior area of the panel (in this instance 2ft x 2ft), but first mark out the area on the board and check to see that it is in square by measuring the diagonals. Test the fit by inserting the board into the frame—it should fit snugly, but should not have to be forced into place. Trim off any uneven sections if necessary.

The material should now be cut to fit this board—two pieces for each panel—with ¾in. (19mm) extra left on all sides to overlap the edges. If the material is a bit too lax. starch it lightly to give it body. Make sure that the surface of the board is free from dirt and bumps, and then spread a piece of the material across, smoothing out any wrinkles with your hands. Keep the material centred across the board so that the overlap on each edge is equal and, using a staple gun, tack the material to one edge of the insulation board. Staple it securely across the edge about six to eight times, keeping the material taut; do not, however, stretch the cloth. Continue stapling the material around the

remaining edges, making certain that you do not distort the weave of the cloth. Now trim off the overhang on each edge. Edges do not have to be perfectly neat, since they will be covered by the moulding.

Do exactly the same with the second piece of cloth on the opposite side. Once you are certain that the material is securely fastened, you can position it in the panel.

Mitred moulding

In order to hold the panel material securely inside the frame—whether it be cloth, or special panelling pieces—moulding will need to be cut and mitred to fit the inner panel area. Each panel will need four pieces of moulding, one to run along each side. ½in. (13mm) thick scotia or quadrant moulding should be mitred to the correct size (follow the directions in Figs.1 to 9) and fixed to the edges of each panel with ¾in. (19mm) moulding pins. Cut each piece of moulding slightly oversize so that it can be sprung into position. The moulding should be finished to match the frame before it is installed.

First, fix the moulding to the outer edges of each panel area that you are covering, tapping the pins in just below the surface of the moulding. Insert the covered board *behind* the moulding and pin it lightly to the top and bottom of the moulding to hold it in place. Now fix the moulding around the edges of the panel area on the opposite side, so that the covered board is fixed squarely and securely *between* the lengths of moulding. The moulding will form a kind of rebate for the insert and will cover the edges of the covered board by ½in. (13mm) all round.

Alternative fillings

Cloth-covered panels are only one of the many materials that may be used to fill the panel areas. You can also use hardboard to fill the gaps. Locally-available ranges vary somewhat, but you may find both board with an attractive perforated pattern and another kind with a textured surface. This comes in 2ft (610mm) widths and needs only to be cut into squares to fit the panels. The squares should be fixed in place between the moulding as directed for the cloth-covered insulation board.

If desired, these hardboard panels may be used in long sections rather than in square sections. To do this, construct the frame with the outer members and inner vertical members only —no cross members are needed. It is helpful, however, if the inner area of the frame—from upper rail to bottom rail—is exactly 8ft (2.44m) or less in length, since the hardboard comes in a standard height of 8ft. Cut and mitre the moulding to fit the dimensions of 2ft x 8ft, remembering to cut each piece slightly oversize so that it can be sprung into place. Fix the moulding in place as described earlier, using ¾in. moulding pins, and position the panelling between the sections of moulding as described

Left (*from top*). *Details of the halving joint at the extreme corners of the frame; on an outside edge; and where two rails cross. The bottom illustration shows how packers are used to fix the screen to an uneven ceiling, and a moulding used to cover the gap.*

above. The hardboard can be painted or finished as desired.

Modern plastic materials are also available for use in room dividers (Celotex Venetian panels are one of the best known proprietary examples). This material is usually translucent and comes in a variety of colours, textures and designs. It can be cut with any type of small-toothed hand saw. Since it tends to expand slightly, it should be cut just slightly undersize.

These panels can be fixed in place using mouldings as for the other materials. If you wish to seal them into place to prevent rattling, use a mastic sealing strip or even self-adhesive foam strip around the edges. Usually such plastic-type panels do not come in sections larger than 2ft x 6ft. Besides being lighter than glass, they are much less liable to breakage.

Fibreglass and plastic acrylic, such as Perspex, are other possibilities, but rather costly ones. Alternatively, you may decorate plain cloth panels with variously designed appliqués, or decorate only some of the panel areas.

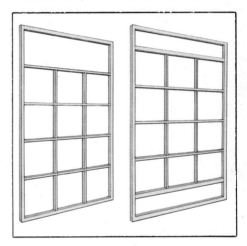

Fig.14 (*above*). *Two ways of setting out the frame for ceilings whose heights do not match the standard module of the panelling material.*
Fig.15 (*below*). *The horizontal and vertical members are all cut in continuous lengths, then half-lapped to fit over one another.*

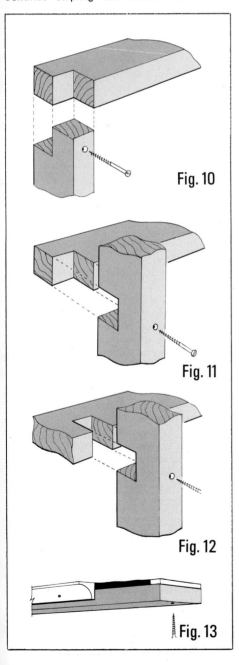

Fig. 10

Fig. 11

Fig. 12

Fig. 13

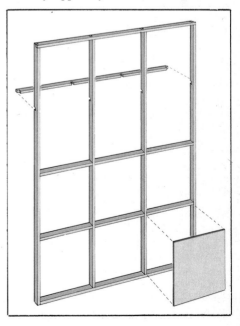

Building a flat roof

Roof construction seems one of the more difficult of do-it-yourself carpentry jobs—until you try it. In fact it is perfectly straightforward. For flat roofs and gabled roofs in particular, no elaborate angles or joints are needed; the finish must be neat, but not nearly as precise as in (say) furniture making; and what might look like a complex structure can turn out to be quite simple, once you understand what each component is there for.

Of all the common types of roof—flat, lean-to, gabled, hipped and mansard—the flat roof is the simplest. And, since the same lengths of timber serve as both rafters and ceiling joists, it is also the least expensive.

Pitching a flat roof

Flat roofs are never truly flat. If they were, rainwater would not drain off and, sooner or later, it would penetrate the roof covering. And there are few more dramatic—or disheartening—events in housebuilding than what happens when a large volume of water, filtering through a leaky roof into a 'pond' between the ceiling joists, suddenly bursts through the ceiling and floods the room below !

In Britain, the minimum *pitch,* or slope, permitted is 1in. in 5ft. But a steeper pitch, around 1in. in 3ft, is better anywhere, and essential in areas subject to heavy rain or to gale-force winds, which can blow water *up* a slight slope.

The lean-to roof

In Britain, the building regulations state that a roof can slope by as much as 10°—about 1in. in 5½in.—and still qualify as a 'flat' roof.

Above that pitch, it becomes a *lean-to* roof. On garages and workshops, where a steeply-sloping ceiling is acceptable, this is built in the same way as a flat roof. But on living accommodation, where a flat ceiling is desirable, both ceiling joists and rafters are needed. So the lean-to roof is then built by the same methods as those for a gabled roof (CHAPTER 39 describes this) except that an extra set of wall plates (see below) is necessary where the joists and rafters meet the wall of the existing house.

Parts of a flat roof

The main components of a flat roof are :
Wall plates. These two heavy pieces of timber are fixed to opposite walls of the structure to support the ends of the rafters, which are nailed to them. (In some countries, a wall plate bolted to the side of an existing wall is known as a *ledger.*)

Rafters/ceiling joists. These are also heavy pieces of timber, running from one wall plate to the other and forming the main support for the roof covering. The bigger the span—distance from one wall plate to the other—the bigger the rafters used. The higher end of a rafter is called the *head;* the lower end the *foot.*

Noggings. These are short lengths of timber nailed between the rafters to stiffen them and stop them twisting. Their depth matches the depth of the rafters.

Strutting. An alternative to nogging, this consists of lighter pieces of timber fixed between the rafters in a herringbone pattern; that is, each pair of struts forms an 'X' shape between two rafters.

Soffits. These are the coverings—of timber, plywood or asbestos-cement—fixed to the underside of the rafters where these protrude beyond the walls of the building. They neaten the exterior appearance, help form a watertight seal around the ends of the rafters and—not least important—stop birds from nesting under the eaves.

Fascias. These are wide boards fixed around the outside edge of the roof to neaten its appearance and to provide 'nailing' for the roof guttering.

Sarking. This name is sometimes used for the continuous boarding which covers the rafters, and to which the roof covering (roofing felt, lead, etc.) is fixed.

Planning your roof

Rafters in a flat roof usually cover the area below across its shorter dimension. On an extension measuring 12ft by 8ft (3·66m x 2·49m), for example, they normally run from one of the 12ft. walls to the other. This means that there are two quite different methods of constructing the roof.

When the rafters run in the same direction as the slope of the roof:

In this case, you must decide whether you want a dead-flat ceiling or one with a slight slope.

If you want a flat ceiling, the wall plates are fixed in place so that both are level, and the rafters are also installed flat. The slope on the roof is imparted by fixing *firring pieces* on top of the rafters (Fig.1).

If a sloping ceiling will do, on the other hand, one wall plate is fixed higher than the other so that the rafters slope automatically (Fig.2).

When the rafters run at right angles to the slope of the roof:

In this case, the roof slope is imparted by fixing the firring pieces, not on top of the rafters, but on top of the wall plates (Fig.3). This means

that each successive rafter is automatically a little higher than the one before it—and also, of course, that a flat ceiling is impossible.

So the first thing you must decide is which way you want the rafters to run. And if, for example, your 12ft x 8ft extension is joined to the house across its 8ft wall, and you want a flat ceiling, you will find you have no option but to run the rafters across the 12ft span. This will mean larger, and somewhat more expensive, rafters.

Finishes for flat roofs

At the planning stage, you must also decide what type of finish your roof will have, since the kind of fascia/soffit combination you use will affect the placing of the outside rafters. The most common types of finish are :
The flush finish

For this finish (Fig.4), the outside pair of rafters are kept flush with the side walls, and the ends of the rafters are also trimmed off flush. The fascia boards are fixed direct to the sides and ends of the rafters, and must be deep enough to cover both the rafters and the top ½in. or so of the brickwork or wall cladding.

For this finish, it is usual to 'sink' the wall plates in the top course of brickwork, as shown in the diagram; otherwise, the fascia would have to be very deep indeed and it would look rather ugly.

The boxed-in finish

For this finish (Fig.5), the outside pair of rafters are laid just *inside* the inner walls. Then short pieces of rafter, called *stub noggings*, are cut, laid across the walls at right angles to the rafters, butted against the rafters and skew-nailed in position. The stub noggings provide support for the soffits and the fascia, while the outside pair of rafters—being just inside the walls—are handily placed to receive the ceiling lining.

Rafter sizes

Local authorities in different countries differ as to the safe dimensions for a rafter spanning a given length. But the British sizes given below are close enough for you to use on your preliminary drawings—and if a larger size is wanted the building inspector will soon tell you !

Sizes of rafters for a flat roof, if the rafters are spaced at 16in. centres :
Up to 7ft 9in. span, use 4in. x 2in.
Up to 9ft 8in. span, use 5in. x 2in.
Up to 11ft 4in. span, use 6in. x 2in.
Up to 13ft 4in. span, use 7in. x 2in.
Up to 15ft 3in. span, use 8in. x 2in.
Up to 17ft 1in. span, use 9in. x 2in.

These sizes are for roofs to which only limited access—for maintenance and repair—is required. If you want to use your roof as, say, a sun-deck, you will generally need rafters 'one size larger' than those given.

Fixing the wall plates

Wall plates (except in timber-frame houses, where they form part of the wall) are usually of

An unusual but attractive finish for a flat roof. The rafter ends are left uncovered to reveal the neatly laid continuous boarding, or sarking, which covers the rafters and supplies a fixing to the roof covering.

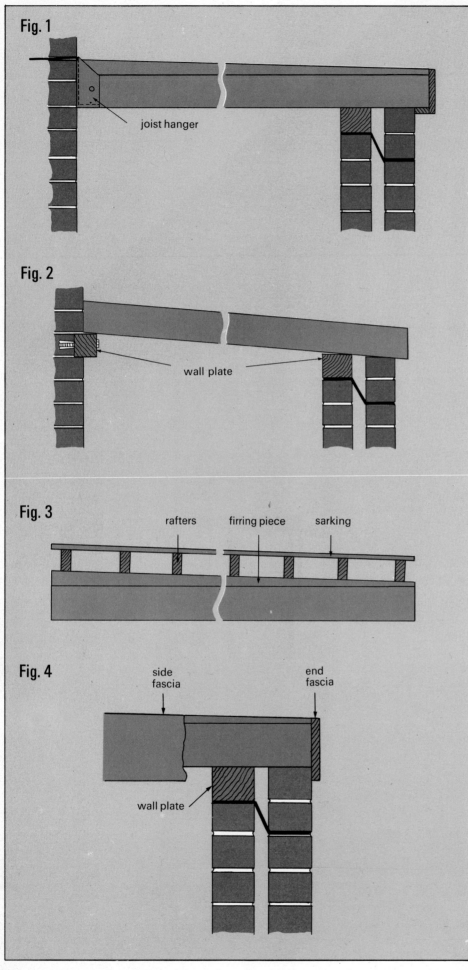

Fig. 1

joist hanger

Fig. 2

wall plate

Fig. 3

rafters   firring piece   sarking

Fig. 4

side fascia   end fascia

wall plate

4in. x 3in. (100mm x 75mm) timber, so that their cross-section matches one course of bricks. They are fixed in place by rag bolts mortared into the brickwork.

The first job is to fix in place the plate or plates which are set into the inside skin of the cavity wall. Begin by cutting the timber to length and then, unless you are using timber which has been 'Tanalised' or similarly treated, apply a lavish coating of woodworm and dry rot preventative. Put both plates side by side while you mark on them the positions that the rafters will occupy; this job is most easily done at ground level!

Stand the plate on edge beside the rag bolts and mark off on the plate the positions of the bolts. Drill holes at these points in the plate, ease the plate in position over the bolts, and tighten firmly.

If one of your plates has to be fixed to the side of an existing wall, its strength will be greatly increased if it is partly embedded in a brick course as well as being bolted in place. First, measure the height at which you want the plate, and mark the corresponding course of bricks with chalk. Using a bolster and club hammer, chip away no more than one-third of the thickness of the bricks—that is, about $1\frac{1}{2}$in. or 38mm from a standard brick.

Next, drill No.10 holes in the plate at 1ft (305mm) intervals along its length. Hold the plate in position (you will need a helper) while you check with a spirit level that the channel you have cut in the brickwork is level. If necessary, insert temporary packing pieces in the brickwork to level the plate. Then mark the positions on the wall where the screws will enter, drill for 4in. or 100mm No.10 screws, insert fibre or plastic wall plugs, and screw the plate home. Fill with mortar any gaps above and below the plate and, when the mortar has hardened, remove the packing pieces.

The firring pieces

If your firring pieces are to go on top of the plates, fix these next. Otherwise, fix your rafters first and then the firring pieces.

Since it is difficult to cut a firring piece to a sharp taper, make its thinner edge about $\frac{1}{2}$in. or 13mm thick and increase the other end correspondingly. For example, an 8ft (2.44m) long firring piece, cut $2\frac{1}{2}$in. (64mm) thick at one end and $\frac{1}{2}$in. (13mm) thick at the other, will give you a slope of 1in. (25mm) in 4ft (1.22m).

Cutting firring pieces by hand is a long,

Fig.1. Setting wall plates level and using firring pieces on all the rafters gives the necessary slope and a flat ceiling. An alternative to the wall plate at the house wall is joist hangers—square-sectioned metal supports which are bedded in a mortar course to form a box-like support for each rafter.
Fig.2. If you do not require a flat ceiling, the slope of the roof can be achieved by setting one wall plate higher than the other.
Fig.3. If the rafters are to run the same way as the slope of the roof, fix a firring piece on each wall plate.
Fig.4. The flush finish. Here the end rafters are flush with the side walls and the feet of the rafters are trimmed off flush.

TRI-ART

laborious job. If you cannot buy them pre-cut from a timber-yard—and British timber yards usually carry them in stock—you would be wise to hire a hand-held power-saw—which, incidentally, will also make short work of cutting all the other heavy timber in this job.

The firring pieces are fixed in place simply by nailing to the plates or rafter tops, as appropriate.

Cutting the rafters

The next step is to cut the rafters to size.

If you are going to use a *flush* finish, begin by squaring the end of one piece of timber, laying it in position, carefully marking the right length, marking a vertical line with a pencil and spirit level, and cutting it to size. Then cut all the remaining rafters from this first one. Do not measure the third rafter from the second, fourth from the third, and so on—you may make a progressive error and be well off line by the time you cut the last one. If you are going to use a *boxed* finish, square one end only of all the rafters, and leave the other end over-size. They will be cut to length later.

Mark on the rafters the positions that the nogging will occupy. Then place the rafters on the marks you have ready on the plates, and skew-nail them through both sides with two 3in. or 75mm nails.

Next, if your rafters are overhanging, run a builder's line (a length of nylon fishing line is fine for this) across each row of rafters, and mark where each has to be trimmed off. Use a builder's level, upright, to ensure that your trimming cuts will be vertical. Trim off all the unwanted ends. The reason for doing this, instead of pre-cutting the rafters to length, is that you will automatically correct any variation in the overhang caused by, for example, one of

Fig.5. *The boxed-in finish. The end rafters are laid inside the walls and stub noggings provide fixing for the fascias and soffits.*

your walls having a slight 'wander' in it.

Fixing the nogging

The nogging is cut from short lengths of timber the same depth as the rafters, and spaced at 2ft or 600mm centres.

To save time, cut out together, and to the same length, all the nogging except those pieces which will go between the last two rafters. In this case, since the rafters are at 16in. or 400mm centres, the nogging will be 14in. or 350mm long, or slightly longer if you are using planed or dressed timber.

Fix in place all these identically-sized pieces of nogging, skew-nailing them into the rafters through the *sides* of the nogging. Then measure the lengths for the pieces in the last row, cut them to size, and fix them individually.

Fixing the boarding

The main objective with the boarding on top of the rafters is to get as smooth a surface as possible, so that puddles of water cannot collect on your roof. Flat-sawn timber 1in. (25mm) thick will do, but tongued-and-grooved boards $\frac{3}{4}$in. (19mm) thick, or a $\frac{7}{8}$in. (22mm) thick high-quality impregnated chipboard, would be better.

Lengths of timber can be fixed at right angles to the rafters but, if you care to take the trouble, fixing them diagonally is better. This braces the roof by creating a series of triangles, and also means that, should the boards begin to 'cup' with time, the ridges thus created are running down, and not just across, the slope of the roof.

Fixing the fascia and soffit

Fascias can be made from random-length boards, but any joints should be over a rafter or stud-nogging end. Joints should be splay-cut—that is, cut at an angle so that one overlaps the other—so that any shrinkage in the boards will

not create an ugly gap.

Paint all sides of the fascia boards with primer before you fix them on, using plenty of paint at joints and on end-grain. Fix with galvanized nails.

If you are using tongued-and-grooved boards for your soffits, fix these using the methods given in CHAPTER 6.

If you are using asbestos-cement sheets, cut them to size by scoring them deeply with an old file or chisel, and then snapping the sheet over the edge of a length of timber.

Different methods of fixing are used for asbestos-cement sheets in different countries, because the density of the sheets varies. In Britain for example, you must drill holes in the sheets with a masonry drill and fix them with screws; in Australia, on the other hand, the sheets are softer and can be nailed in place with galvanized flat-headed nails. If in any doubt, ask the merchant from whom you buy your sheets.

Finishing off

There are several types of roof covering suitable for a flat roof. Transparent plastic sheets, usually corrugated, and bituminous roofing felt are the most common. Whichever one you choose however, you must be careful that, where the roof abuts an existing wall, you provide adequate *flashing* between the old wall and the new roof.

This is a sheet of roofing felt or metal, let into a mortar course immediately above the roof where it joins the house wall, providing a run-off for rainwater.

Select a joint about 6in. or 150mm above the roof, and with a cold chisel and hammer rake out some mortar to a depth of 2in. or 50mm. Insert the flashing, wedging it with small pieces of brick if necessary, and run the flashing down so that it covers at least 6in. of roof. Fill the joint with a good bricklaying mortar and leave for two or three days to set.

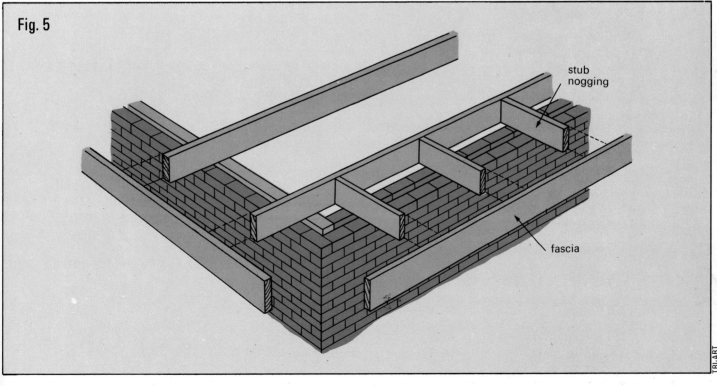

Fig. 5

stub nogging

fascia

TRI-ART

DATA SHEET

Screws and bolts

Screws and bolts provide enormous holding power, but are simple to fix. The types shown here are the ones you are likely to come across when fixing both wood and metal, together with the most commonly used accessories.

Screws—common types

1. Countersunk wood screw. For general use; head let in flush with wood surface.

2. Pozidriv head countersunk screw. Fixed with special non-slip screwdriver.

3. Raised head countersunk screw. For fixing door-handle plates, etc., to wood; decorative head designed to be seen.

4. Round head screw. For fixing hardware without countersunk holes to wood.

Screws—special

5. Coach screw. Extra-large wood screw with square head; tightened with spanner.

6. Self-tapping screw. For sheet metal; cuts its own thread as it is screwed in; has slot, Phillips (cross), or Pozidriv head.

7. Dowel screw. For invisible fixings; two pieces of wood twisted together to tighten.

8. Handrail screw. For 'pocket' screwing; head screwed on from side with screwdriver.

9. Cup hook and screw eye. Large number of shapes and sizes available.

Screws—accessories

10. Flat washer. For round head screws; spreads load to give a strong grip.

11. Screw cup—raised type. For countersunk or raised head countersunk screws; spreads load, improves appearance.

12. Screw cup—socket type. For countersunk screws; hammered into pre-drilled hole for a completely flush fixing.

Bolts

13. Machine screw. Not a screw, but a bolt. Small sizes only; available with (1 to r) round, pan, cheese or countersunk heads.

14. Machine bolt. Large sizes only; available with hexagonal or square heads.

15. Coach bolt. Large bolt with a square collar under the head that stops it from turning when the nut is done up.

16. Rag bolt. For bolting wood or metal to concrete; jagged head is set in wet concrete and holds bolt firmly when concrete dries.

Nuts

17. Hexagonal nut. Commonest type, available in a wide range of sizes.

18. Square nut. This type available in large sizes only, e.g. for coach bolts.

19. Flat square nut. Small sizes only; thinner than 18 in proportion to width.

20. Handrail nut. Used on handrail screw (8) and in other places where nuts have to be tightened from the side in a small space.

21. Wing nut. Tightened by hand; for uses where nuts must be undone quickly.

22. Domed nut. Decorative nut, generally chromium-plated.

23. Locking nut. For places where vibration might make nuts undo; has fibre ring inside to make it hard to turn.

Bolts—accessories

24. Flat washer. Same as 10; used in same way; also makes nuts easier to turn.

25. Single coil washer. For metal fastening only; spring shape prevents bolts from undoing.

26. Internal and external tooth washers. Gripping teeth keep bolts from undoing.

27. Timber connector. Used between pieces of wood bolted together; teeth prevent slippage.

Screws—accessories

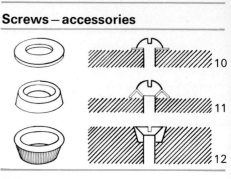

Bolts

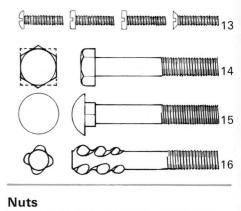

Nuts

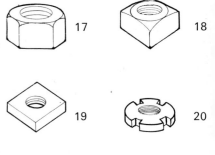

Bolts—accessories

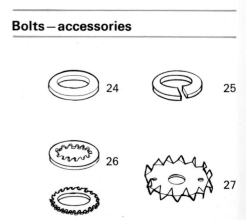

Screws—common types

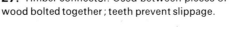

Screws—special

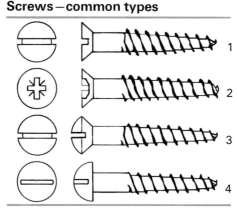
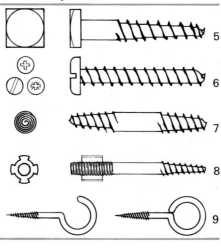

Door and window frames: how to repair them

Door and window frames are very alike in their construction. Both are tough, and will last for years if properly painted. But when they do go—for example if they are forced by a burglar—here is how to mend them.

Door frames are fairly simple pieces of woodwork in most buildings, and are not hard to repair. Even if an entire frame has to be replaced from scratch, the job is well within the range of a competent amateur—though in a masonry house it can be a fairly messy one.

An important reassurance: no part of the door frame assembly ever holds up the wall above it in any normal building. The job of supporting the wall is done by a separate lintel above the frame. The lintel may be made of wood, as in timber-framed houses and older British masonry houses. Or it may be a flat or segmental (shallow-curved) brick arch, or (in modern masonry houses) a reinforced concrete beam. In any case, it is entirely separate from the door frame.

Types of door frame

The main part of a door frame, and the part which carries the weight of the door, is the *casing*. This may be of three types, but the simplest is the *plain casing* (see Fig.1), which is found in nearly all modern houses, masonry or timber.

103

A plain casing is made out of fairly solid timber, seldom smaller than 4in. x 3in. (100 x 75mm), and it may be much wider than this, particularly around front doors, or in old houses with thick walls. It may be rectangular in cross-section, but often has a rebate in one edge into which the door fits when closed. Wide plain casings—they can be over 10in. wide in houses with thick masonry walls—often have a rebate on both edges, simply to improve their appearance.

Plain casings without rebates are most commonly found in newer houses. These have a separate *stop* consisting of a lighter strip of timber nailed around the inside of the casing to provide something for the door to close against.

The top horizontal part of the casing (known as the *soffit casing*) normally extends the full width of the door aperture, and in masonry houses, often a few inches into the brickwork on either side—but not so far as to undermine the lintel. The two side pieces (or *jamb casings*) extend up the sides of the door aperture and, if they are rebated, are attached to the underside of the soffit casing by a rebated joint (see Fig.2). This joint serves the dual purpose of holding the side pieces in place to counteract the weight of the door, and of allowing the rebate (if any) on the edge of the casing to continue around the corner without interruption. A mitred corner would perform this second function just as well, but would loosen if the wood shrank, allowing the door to sag.

This construction is not invariable. The rebated joint may be omitted, or the jamb casings may run to the top of the doorway and hold the soffit casing between them. But the method described is the commonest for a rebated casing. Casings without rebates may have mortise-and-tenon joints, or several other kinds of joints.

In masonry houses, plain casings are generally attached to the doorway by being screwed to small pieces of hardwood set between the bricks. These may be *pallets*—flat boards the thickness of a mortar joint, put in when the doorway is built. Or they may be *plugs*—smaller wedges driven into holes cut into the mortar with a special plugging chisel. The first method is typically found in better-quality work. Sometimes pallets are made of lead sheet instead of wood, so that they are rotproof. In low-quality work, softwood plugs made of old floorboards may be found.

In timber houses, the casings are nailed to the studs on either side of the door opening. *Packers*—odd bits of wood cut to the right thickness—are fitted between frame and studs so that the frame is not forced out of plumb as the nails are driven (see Fig.5).

These are not the only methods of fastening casings to the doorway. There are two other types of casing, which are normally held on in a different way. They are *skeleton* and *framed* casings (see Fig.3).

Both these types of casing are commonly found in older masonry houses, where even the partition walls are 9in. (230mm) thick or more. They are not, however, used on front doors as a rule, however thick the wall is, because a front door needs the extra solidity of a plain casing.

A skeleton casing consists of a ladder-like frame the same width as the thickness of the wall. The two sides, or *stiles*, of the frame are bridged by frequent horizontal *rails* mortised into them. The frame is covered by a flat panel whose edges are set back from the edge of the frame to form a rebate into which the door fits. A door would be mounted at one side of this type of casing, so that the strain could be taken by one of the stiles.

A framed casing is a higher-quality piece of equipment, typically found in well-built old houses. It, too, has a frame and panels, but the frame is heavier and generally rebated instead of having a nailed-on stop. The panel fits into grooves on the inner edge of the frame. The joint between panel and frame is often decorated with a moulding.

Skeleton and framed casings are not normally attached to pallets or plugs. Instead, they are fastened to *rough grounds* and *backings* (see Fig.4). Rough grounds (rough because they are not seen, and do not have to be highly finished) are mounted flat against the wall on both sides of the doorway, so that they sandwich the wall between them. They are held there by the backings, timber strips running across the inner edge of the doorway between the grounds and joined to them with a strong single dovetail joint. These pieces provide a firm base to which the casing can be nailed or screwed.

Rough grounds are the same thickness as the plaster on the walls. They provide a convenient limit for the plasterer to work up to. Their outer edge normally has an undercut bevel to hold the edge of the plaster to the wall.

In all the forms of construction mentioned so far, there is an untidy area at the edge of the door frame where the plaster on the wall ends and the woodwork begins. This join is masked by an *architrave*, a moulding lying flat against the wall and running all round the top three edges of the door frame. The architrave is attached to the rough ground if there is one, or to the pallets or plugs set in the brickwork. Its corners are mitred for neatness and because it is a purely decorative feature carrying no load.

Front doors in masonry houses do not generally have an architrave on the outside, though one on the inside is usual. The normal installation has a heavy plain casing narrower than the thickness of the wall. The inner edge of the casing is normal; the outer edge does not reach the level of the outside face of the wall. In this way, the minimum amount of wooden frame is exposed to the weather.

In timber-clad houses, however, both the inside and outside of the front door frame have an architrave. The outside one is made weathertight by a *cap* over the door and strips of *scribing* down each side (Fig.5).

Builders often set the front door casing in place when the walls of a new masonry house are only three or four courses high. They then brick up around the frame. This makes the initial building easy, but if you want to replace the frame later you will find it jammed in place by the tight-fitting brickwork and by little projecting bits of mortar around the edge.

Removing an old frame installed in this way will involve a lot of chipping at the mortar and may spoil the look of the brickwork.

Window frames

Many windows, particularly casement (hinged) windows, are set into masonry walls by the same method as front doors, that is, a plain casing set back from the wall surface on the outside, and with an architrave on the inside. A glance at your windows will tell you if they are made in this way. If they are, then their frames can be repaired using the same method as for door frames. Much more detailed instructions on how to repair window frames are, however, given in CHAPTER 24. This deals with sash windows, too, where the frame is significantly different.

Architrave repairs

Architraves, in spite of their imposing name, are purely decorative (see Fig.6) and, usually, fixed in place with nails. They tend to wear out faster than the rest of the door frame because they are on the edge of the wall and are frequently hit by trays, suitcases, boots and children. Fortunately, they are simple to take off and replace.

Modern houses tend to have narrow, plain architraves—3in. x $\frac{3}{4}$in. (75 x 22mm) is a typical size. When one of these is damaged, it should be replaced rather than repaired. Cut along the join between architrave and casing with a sharp knife to break the paint seal. Then insert an old wide chisel under the architrave and tap the handle with a mallet to loosen the joint. When you can get the chisel quite far into the gap all along the architrave, prise the timber off by *twisting* the chisel, not by levering upwards. This will reduce damage to the casing, and is also less likely to snap the chisel blade.

Replace the architrave with a new one exactly the same width, or you will have to alter the skirting boards to fit. It is risky to cut the angled corners of the architrave in a mitre box without first trying them in position, because if one of the sides is slightly curved, or if the doorway is slightly out of square, the corner will 'gap' in an ugly way. So begin by cutting the side pieces slightly over-length, and 'tacking' them in place a bit out from the wall. Slide in behind them the length of material from which the top piece will be cut. Mark the points at which the outside

Fig.1. A plain casing with a single rebate, cut away at the top to show its cross-section. It is nailed to pallets or plugs set in the mortar joints of the brickwork.

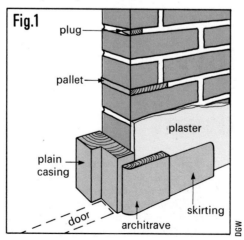

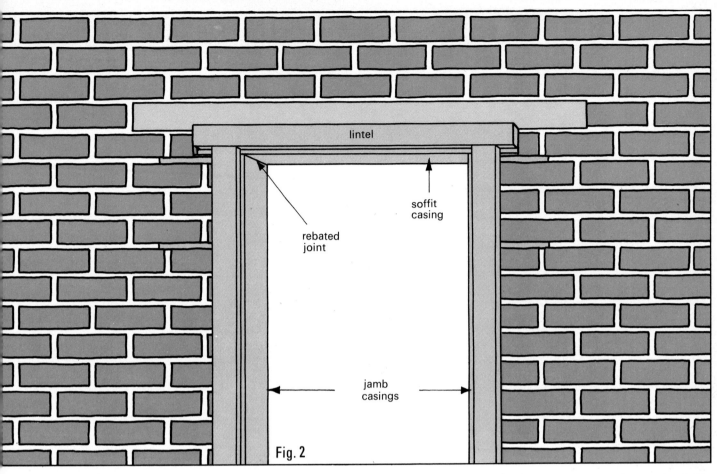

Fig. 2

Fig.2 (above). The soffit casing is mounted below the lintel, but does not carry any weight.

The jamb casings are rebated into it.
Fig.3 (below). Two types of casing often

found in old houses: the skeleton casing (left) and the more complex framed casing (right).

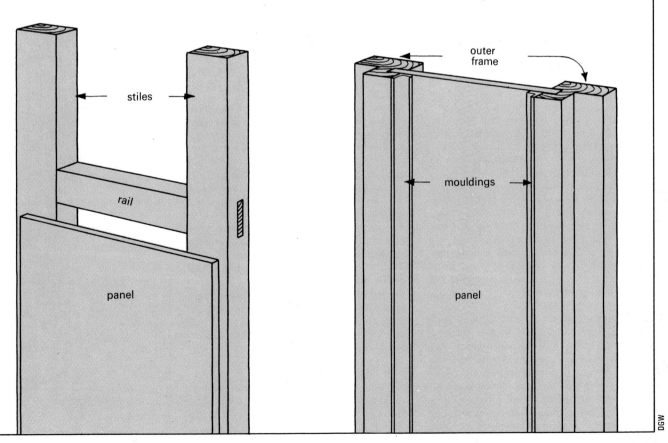

Fig. 3

DGW

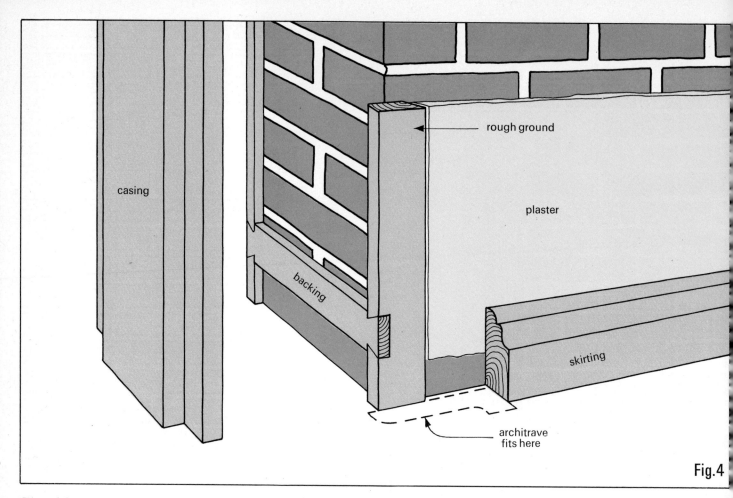

casing

rough ground

plaster

backing

skirting

architrave
fits here

Fig.4

Fig.4 *(above). Wide casings are generally mounted on rough grounds and backings, which provide firmer support than plugs or pallets.*

Fig.5 *(right). Timber-framed houses have a cap and two pieces of scribing to stop water from seeping around the front door frame.*

edges of the side pieces meet the top edge of the top piece. Then take all three pieces down, put each in turn in a mitre box, and cut to 45°.

When you come to erect the architraves, nail one side; then the top; then the other side. If, as occasionally happens, the architrave boards are much wider than the door frame, hold each corner joint together with one nail, driven through from the top piece into the side. Punch all nail heads below the surface, and fill the holes before painting.

Architraves in large older houses tend to be decorative mouldings 6in. (150mm) wide or more. Often, these mouldings are obsolete and it is impossible to duplicate them. The alternatives are then :

1. Replace the old moulding with plain timber or another moulding the same width.

2. 'Steal' an architrave from a little-used room, replacing it with a plain one.

3. Replace only the damaged portion of the architrave with a hand-made section cut to the right profile.

This last method is quite difficult because it must be done accurately. A non-matching section, however small the discrepancy, will show up clearly. You will need a combination plane with a good assortment of blades.

Make a template out of stiff card to record the exact profile of the moulding—or you can use one of the 'instant shape tracers' made out of sliding metal rods set in a clamp; a good one is

called a 'Mimic'. Then use the shaped blades of your combination plane to reproduce this profile exactly on a strip of plain timber of the correct width. It is best to make a far longer piece than you need, so that you can choose the best section for your repair, or keep the rest for future repairs.

Cut out the damaged portion of the architrave and cut a new piece to fit exactly into the gap. The join will be less obvious if the ends are cut at a slant. The best way to make the new piece fit is to tack it in position over the old architrave and cut through both new and old wood simultaneously with a fine, sharp tenon saw. Don't make two cuts at different slants with the new piece pinned on in the same place, or it will be the wrong length. Measure the length of the cut-out section and the new piece carefully before making the second cut.

The idea is to make the joint as accurate, and therefore invisible, as possible.

Some very wide architraves are built up from several mouldings. It may be possible to reproduce them exactly from standard mouldings glued and pinned together. This will save you a lot of trouble.

Stop repairs

In modern door frames with separate, nailed-on stops on the inside of the casing, a damaged stop is best replaced rather than repaired. It can be prised off in the same way as an architrave.

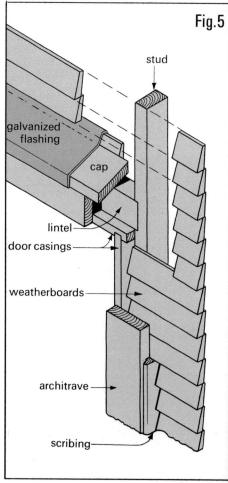

Fig.5

stud

galvanized flashing

cap

lintel

door casings

weatherboards

architrave

scribing

Take particular care not to damage the casing.

Marks on the casing near the stop can be covered by replacing the original stop with a wider one. Note that it can only be wider on the side *away* from the door, or the door will not shut.

In door frames where the door fits into a rebate in the casing, and so the stop is integral with the door frame, damage is best repaired by inserting a new piece, as described in the next section.

Casing repairs

The casing of a doorway is normally fairly robust and unlikely to suffer more than superficial damage. It can nearly always be repaired by patching, rather than replacement.

If you do have to replace a casing entirely, for example because it is rotten, the first step is to remove all the paint from those places where the mounting screws are likely to be. The architraves and other fittings should be removed as well, to save them from damage.

When all the screw heads are exposed, remove the screws (they may have to be chopped out) and work the casing loose. You may have to use a crowbar, but try to avoid damaging the wall covering. A soffit casing with its ends set in a brick wall may be very hard to remove. A good plan would be to saw it into

Fig.6 (below). An architrave projects well beyond the edge of the casing. It is nailed on around its inner edge only; a diagonal nail often holds the outer corners together.

three, remove the middle part first and then tackle the ends separately.

Copy the old casing with new wood. This is very simple with a plain casing, and possible with a skeleton casing. Copying a framed casing, however, is a long and tiresome job nearly as intricate as making a panelled door. Wherever possible, patch a framed casing without removing it.

When you are installing the new casing, you will probably have to slice bits off it here and there to get it to fit. The original builders probably did the same when putting in the first casing, so don't let it worry you. Finish the job by screwing the new casing on (not through the old screwholes), refitting the architraves and painting everything.

Patching a casing is easier. The damaged section should be cut out with the saw blade slanted inwards at 15° so that the new piece is held in as if by a dovetail joint (see Fig.7). This will enormously increase the durability of the repair. The slant should be kept constant on old and new pieces by the careful use of a bevel and a marking knife. Accuracy is very important.

To insert a new section in any part of a plain casing, first mark out the area to be removed. Try to remove as little wood as you can—certainly not more than half the thickness of the casing. The slant of the ends must be arranged so that the new piece can be slid in sideways. Cut down the slanted ends (just inside the marked lines) with a sharp tenon saw. Make several rough saw cuts almost as deep between the first pair, and then chisel out the wood to be

removed, bit by bit, leaving the cutout with a neat flat bottom.

Mark out the new piece to fit exactly, and cut it out very slightly oversize to allow for adjustments. Then pare it down with a very sharp chisel until it can just be knocked into the space, but is still slightly too thick so that the outer surface still stands slightly proud. Remove the new piece and apply glue liberally to the inside of the cutout and sparingly to the new piece. Then knock it in. When it is finally in place, a good deal of glue will squirt out of the joint. Wipe it off the surrounding woodwork before it dries.

Finish the job by planing the new piece down level. If you are patching a moulded area, you will need a combination plane to match the shape of the mouldings. It is easiest to shape the piece when it is firmly glued in place.

If the panel on the front of a skeleton casing is damaged, you can remove and replace it without removing the frame. This cannot be done with a framed casing, however.

If the frame of a framed casing is damaged, it can be patched in the same way as a solid casing. A damaged panel cannot be taken out, or a new one inserted, without dismantling the frame. But you can patch a panel by sticking a piece of plastic laminate over it. Provided the piece reaches the edge of the frame on all sides, it will be invisible when it is painted.

Fig.7 (below). When a casing or architrave is patched, the new piece that is inserted should have its ends cut at a two-way slant to hold it firmly in place.

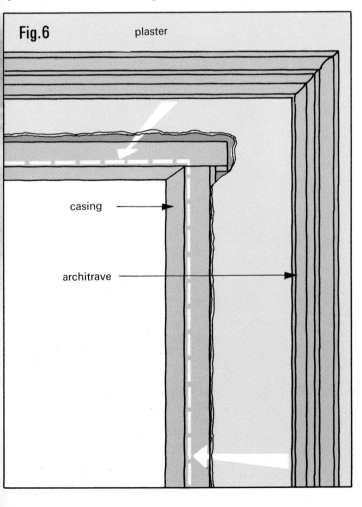

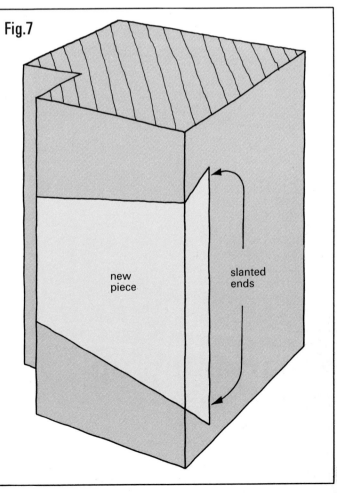

Smartening up old floors

Floors in old houses tend to be covered with stains, dents, cracks and layers of old paint. Yet underneath all these surface defects, the planks are generally sound, and the floor can be made to look as good as new.

The best way to restore a floor like this is to sand the surface flat. The majority of the defects are removed, the sound wood underneath is revealed, and at the same time it is smoothed so that it can be polished.

Floor sanders shaped like vacuum cleaners, and which can be operated from a standing position, can be hired from tool hire shops or flooring firms. The daily rate is not expensive, and sanding sheets and other necessities can be bought at the same time. Many firms will, upon request, deliver and remove the machine.

It is essential to wear very old clothes when using a large sander, since it throws up a good deal of dust and dirt. It is also a good idea to wear a face mask, to avoid inhaling dust.

Before you arrange to hire the machine, check

that your floor is not suffering from dry rot or any other condition that will involve you in replacing all or some of the boards. Check also that the boards are still thick enough to sand—they may be worn very thin around doors or in other heavily-used areas.

The minimum acceptable thickness depends on the type of boards and how far apart the joists are. Square-edged boards must be thicker than tongued-and-grooved ones, which interlock and to a certain extent hold each other up. The closer together the joists are, the thinner the boards can be. For example, square-edged boards on joists at 16in. (400mm) centres must not be thinner than $\frac{3}{4}$in. (19mm). Tongued-and-grooved boards on joists at 11in. (280mm) centres can be as thin as $\frac{1}{2}$in. (13mm)—though you will have to be careful not to over-sand them if they *are* this thin.

If any of the boards are too thin, they will have to be replaced. Try not to replace them with new boards; even after old and new have been sanded together, there will still be a marked difference in colour between them. You will almost certainly be able to get matching old boards from a demolition contractor. If this fails, you could take boards from a carpeted room in your house and fill the gaps there with new boards.

Preparation

Floorboards in old houses are often so badly shrunken that there are large gaps between them. If there are gaps all over the floor, running the full length of each board, probably the only thing to do is to take up the boards one by one and move them sideways. This will create a large gap at one side of the room which can be filled with an extra board or boards. Floorboards, whether square-edged or tongued-and-grooved, should be pressed hard against their neighbours and held there while being nailed down. This can be done most easily with flooring cramps, hired from tool hire firms. An alternative method is to protect the edge of the board with a strip of wood the same thickness as the board (and grooved if it is a tongued board), and then to lever the board into place with a stout chisel work into the joist (see the illustration in CHAPTER 6).

Smaller gaps can be filled by making appropriately sized hardwood fillets with a wedge-shaped cross-section, and forcing them into the cracks with a mallet.

Some boards may be split. If the split is really bad, the board may need replacing. Moderately bad splits can be repaired by taking up the board (you may have to break off the tongue), cutting out the split area and inserting a new piece cut to shape. This piece will, of course, have to stretch between at least two joists to have proper support. A simple, clean split can be quickly mended by breaking off the split part, cleaning the broken surfaces, and glueing the piece back in place with pva adhesive. If you nail it, make sure that no nails project above the top surface of the plank.

If some of the floorboards have been frequently taken up and put back (to reach pipes or wiring, for example), they may be full of messy-looking jagged or split nail holes. These can be repaired with a proprietary wood-filler.

Another method for very large holes is to drill them out and insert a piece of dowel.

On heavily-worn floorboards the knots, which are harder than the surrounding wood, may be sticking out. You can cut them down level with a plane, 'Surform' or similar tool.

It is essential before any sanding is done to punch *all* the nails in the floor below the surface. This is a boring task, but not particularly strenuous. If lino or a carpet has ever been tacked to the floor, there will probably be a lot of tacks left in it. They can easily be removed with an old chisel and mallet or a pair of pincers. After you think you have removed or punched down everything, double-check the whole floor area. One projecting nail will rip up a sanding sheet, or may even ruin a very expensive hired sander.

If the floor is painted, the sander will remove paint perfectly well, even if it is thick. Unfortunately, the machine cannot sand right to the edge of the floor (see below). If there is only one coat of paint on the floor, you do not have to bother about those edges the machine cannot reach. If there are several coats (which is much more likely), you will have to use paint stripper or a blow torch to get the paint off. When the stripper or torch has softened the paint, scrape it off with a shavehook or some similar scraper.

Parquet floors

Parquet floors have their own preparation problems. Damaged blocks may have to be replaced (matching blocks can generally be obtained from a demolition contractor) and loose but sound ones stuck back. Parquet blocks are hardly ever nailed down. They are stuck down with mastic, or sometimes asphalt, either direct to the floor or to little cork, plastic or wooden discs pinned to the floor. In any case, the blocks should be stuck back with what was used to fix them originally.

If the parquet was not laid when the house was originally built, the chances are that it has been laid with a cork strip between it and the skirting to allow it to expand with changes in humidity. This strip may need replacing. Where original parquet extends under the skirting, no strip is needed.

There is a modern type of parquet floor which comes in large pieces, each appearing to consist of many individual blocks. In point of fact, the blocks are not blocks at all, but pieces of veneer stuck to a chipboard backing with tongued-and-grooved edges. This type of floor can be sanded, but it must be done gently. Serious damage can be repaired only by replacing an entire chipboard 'tile', though you can patch the veneer if the damage is only on the surface.

The only thing remaining to do before you can start sanding is to find a large hardboard or metal sheet to protect the skirting from damage by the heavy sanding machine.

Types of sander

The floor sanding machines you can hire will sand up to within a few inches of the skirting, but no nearer. You will have to sand the edges and any awkward corners in some other way. You could do it by hand in a small room, but it would be exhausting. A disc sander of the type that fits on to a power drill will do it quickly and

thoroughly, but may leave circular 'swirl marks', which you may consider unsightly. Special flexibly-mounted discs are made that reduce swirl marks, but probably the best solution is to use a domestic orbital sander, which can be hired from the same firm that supplies the floor sander.

The floor sander you hire should be the smallest size available—unless you live in a mansion. The hire firm will normally supply you with plenty of coarse, medium and fine sanding sheets to fit the machine; you pay only for the ones you use. They will also give you advice on how to use the machine, but basically it is no harder to operate than an upright vacuum cleaner. Like a cleaner, it has a dust bag that collects most of the wood it removes from the floor. The only point to watch when using it is that the flex should be kept well away from the machine or you might sand through it. It is a good idea to hang the flex over your shoulder while working.

Getting down to it

Start sanding with coarse abrasive sheets, working along the length of the boards, and not across them. The sheets must be fastened securely to the revolving drum on the machine or they will come to pieces. Continue with coarse sheets until the worst of the dirt and old paint has come off the floor, then switch to medium to smooth it off. Do not over-sand the floor, or the boards will become dangerously thin.

Once the floor is in a reasonably clean condition, go over the edges with the smaller sander until they match the middle. Then, if you want a polished floor, put a fine sheet on the big sander and go over the floor repeatedly with it. If you persist, it will become smooth and shiny. Finishing the edges to the same standard should not be too hard with an orbital sander fitted with a fine sheet. Sweep the floor carefully afterwards to remove all dust.

To protect the floor, it should be given two or three coats of polyurethane sealer, which must be allowed to dry thoroughly between coats. Dilute the first coat with 20 per cent turpentine substitute. This seals the timber and gives a smoother surface. Sand with fine paper after this first coat. Then use either a proprietary wood filler or putty to fill the nail holes. If you use putty, tint it with paint tinters to a colour a little *darker* than the floor timber—darker filler shows up less than one which is too light.

Remember to start painting on the side away from the door and work towards it—this may sound like an unnecessary piece of advice, but it is surprising how many people forget and have to climb out of the window. When the last coat of sealer is dry, a good application of wax polish completes the job.

Warning

One final point: the wood dust from the dust bag can be put on the garden only if the timber has not been treated with a preservative. And **NEVER PUT IT ON THE FIRE** or even let it get near one. Fine wood dust is a dangerous and powerful explosive. It should be thoroughly wetted before disposal, and put where there is no possibility of it catching fire.

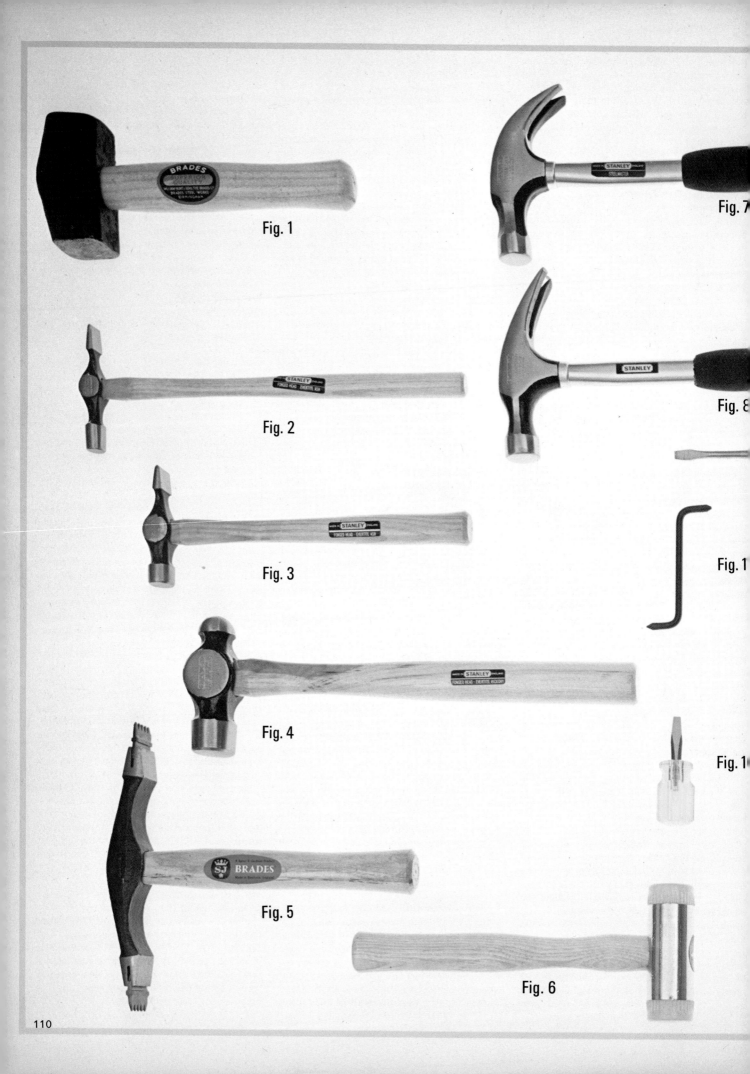

Fig. 1

Fig. 2

Fig. 3

Fig. 4

Fig. 5

Fig. 6

Fig. 7

Fig. 8

Fig. 1

Fig. 1

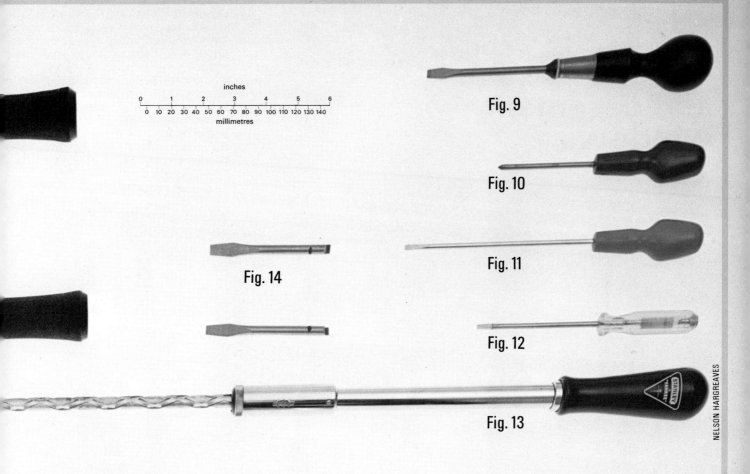

inches
0 1 2 3 4 5 6

0 10 20 30 40 50 60 70 80 90 100 110 120 130 140
millimetres

Fig. 9

Fig. 10

Fig. 11

Fig. 14

Fig. 12

Fig. 13

NELSON HARGREAVES

DATA SHEET

Hammers and Screwdrivers

The right tool for the job makes all the difference—saving time, tempers and often money as well. The range of choice for even simple tools such as hammers and screwdrivers is extremely wide, and each one is designed with a particular task in mind. This DATA SHEET will help you match tool to task.

Hammers range in function from those used for heavy demolition work to those appropriate to fine nailing. In addition, each type of hammer comes in various weights.

Fig.1. Club hammer. 2½-4lb (1130-1800g). Used for general heavy hammering, particularly in building and demolition work. In conjunction with a bolster chisel it is used for cutting bricks, shaping paving stones, knocking through brickwork and so on. The *sledge hammer* (not shown) has a straight sided head, a 3ft handle, weighs between 4 and 14lb (1.8-6.4Kg) and is used for driving metal stakes, demolition work and so on.

Fig.2. Pin or telephone hammer. 3½-4oz (100-110g). Used for tacks, panel pins, fine nailing and bradding. The wedge shaped end is used for starting small nails while holding them between your fingers.

Fig.3. Warrington or cross pein hammer. 6-16oz (170-450g). Used for general nailing, joinery, and planishing or metal beating.

Fig.4. Ball pein or engineer's hammer. 4oz-31lb (110-1360g). Used for metal working. The round end is used for starting rivets, for example. This is the hammer to use for *masonry nails* as its hardened steel face will not chip.

Fig.5. Scutch or comb hammer. Used for trimming and shaping common or hard bricks which would damage a brick trowel. The combs can be replaced after wear.

Fig.6. Soft-headed hammer. Used in metal beating and in general work where it is important not to damage a surface. The soft head also avoids the possibility of a spark setting off an explosion. Replaceable heads may be made of plastic, lead, copper or leather.

Fig.7. Claw hammer. 16-24oz (450-570g). Used for general purpose carpentry, particularly for driving and removing nails. When taking out nails, make sure the nail head is well into the claw and lever evenly.

Fig.8. Ripping claw hammer. Used similarly to the claw hammer in work where speed rather than care is essential.

Screwdrivers, too, have a range of functions and sizes. Match the screwdriver tip as closely as possible to the screw slot to prevent damage to either.

Fig.9. Standard slotted screwdriver. Used for general screwdriving of single slotted screws.

Fig.10. Crosshead screwdriver (Pozidriv or Philips). Used with cross slotted screws to provide greater purchase and positive location.

Fig.11. Parallel tip screwdriver. Used in engineering, and otherwise, when the screw sits inside a recess of the same width.

Fig.12. Electrical screwdriver. The insulated handle contains a neon indicator which lights when the blade is touched against a live source. You must ensure that the insulation is safe for the voltages you intend to check.

Fig.13. Archimedean (or Yankee) spiral ratchet screwdriver. Used for general purpose screwdriving. Pushing the handle home automatically drives or removes screws. When locked, at length or closed, the ratchet allows screws to be driven or removed without taking the blade from the slot. **Fig.14.** The chuck can take blades of different widths, and even drill bits.

Fig.15. Double-ended cranked screwdriver. Used for driving awkwardly-placed screws.

Fig.16. Stub screwdriver. Used in confined spaces. You can grip the square shank with a spanner to give greater purchase.

Repairs to sash and casement windows

Windows are among the most troublesome of problems in home maintenance. They can be difficult to open or close; glass may become loose and need replacing or refixing. A badly fitting window can be a source of draughts and discomfort, as well as making the home less secure. Timely maintenance can prevent these problems from getting out of hand. This article shows how to set about repairs on the two most common types—sash and casement.

Lack of maintenance is the usual cause of deterioration in softwood timber windows, causing them to jam and refuse to open and close properly. If paint is not renewed, it ceases, sooner or later, to fulfill its essential protective function and will flake and deteriorate, allowing the timber to become saturated and swell in wet or damp weather. Tenons may rot and break, and glue joints come apart. In severe cases of deterioration, the only solution is to discard the window sash and fit a new one, since wet rot may have irreparably harmed the timber fibres.

Ideally, repairs should be tackled during dry weather. In damp conditions, apart from your discomfort in working and letting cold into the house, timber will remain swollen and the trouble difficult to rectify.

Where a number of windows require attention, remove one window at a time and carry out inspection, repair and replacement. A piece of 500-gauge polythene can be tacked in place across the window gap as a temporary protection. Wrap the polythene round thin battens, or hardboard, to prevent it from pulling away from the nails.

With care, it may be possible to remove upstairs windows from inside, and also fix polythene, without using a ladder.

Where a ladder is needed, check that it is sound. Stand it at an angle of about 30° and on a firm base. Ensure that all rungs are firm. Steady the ladder firmly by sash lines fixed to it, and secured to a No. 14 screw eye driven into a convenient point on a soffit board, or tied round a window mullion (Fig. 1).

Lightweight scaffold towers are a useful aid for this type of job. These can be hired and can be quickly assembled by slotting the frames together. They can be moved around on wheels to the desired position, where the wheels can be locked.

Types of window

The two basic types of window are the *casement* window and the double-hung *sash* window—although the latter term is misleading, since the movable part of any window is called the 'sash'. Deterioration in a casement window is apparent because it will not close fully. Sash windows will stick and not slide properly and inspection will normally show distortion, sometimes causing windows to crack or break; this is often accompanied by deterioration of the sash cords, which have to be replaced.

The main operations are removing the windows; removing the glass; dismantling the frames; cleaning up the joints; glueing and repegging the joints; checking for squareness and general alignment; removing old paint from the frames; repriming and repainting; reglazing; and, finally, rehanging. If necessary, broken or rotted tenons may have to be remade.

Removing casement windows

If you are removing an upstairs window single handed, support the window by a sash cord or a strong clothesline before you loosen the hinges. The cord may be tied to a fanlight, handy drainpipe, or a sound gutter support. This will help to prevent hazards such as windows falling out and becoming wrecked—or even hitting someone below.

Remove the screws fixing the window to the frame. Those fixing the hinge to the window are more easily removed once the window is taken out.

Before attempting to remove the screws holding the hinges, remove all paint from the grooves in the ends of the screws. This ensures that the screwdriver can get a good grip in the screw, avoiding slipping and damage to the screw head, which may then jam and have to be drilled and filed out. Clearing the screw head is best done with a spiked tool, such as a sharpened 4in. nail.

If the hinge screws prove difficult to remove, try tightening them first before undoing them. If this fails, a few sharp taps with a mallet on the end of the screwdriver might do the trick, or a nailpunch may be driven at an angle against the outer end of the screw groove to free it. Penetrating oil left to soak in will help to ease rusted screws.

Once you have removed the screws, place a pad on the ground below the window and lower the window on to this. The best pad is a sack filled with straw, rags or similar. Remember, a window sash may be heavier than you think, so have some help handy 'just in case.'

Removing sash windows

Sash windows, correctly known as *double-hung sashes* or *box windows,* operate with cords, pulleys and weights, which counterbalance both inner and outer sash while they slide up and down. One end of the cord is nailed to a groove in the side of the sash, and the other is attached to a weight hidden in the frame.

The pulley wheels are attached to the *pulley stiles*—the upright sides of the frame which hide the weights. Part of each pulley stile consists of a removable piece of wood known as a 'pocket', which fits flush with the stiles and serves as an access hatch to the weights. These pockets may be screwed in.

Carefully remove the fixing bead round the inside edge of the window frame. Start in the middle of a long bead by gently prising it away from the main frame by about an inch (25mm). You can use an old chisel for this. Next, tap the bead smartly back into position; the pins holding it should pop up through the surface of the wood, to be removed with pincers. (A piece of thin ply between the pincers and the timber surface will prevent damage to the timber). If this does not work, drive a wedge in the middle and use the chisel to lever progressively towards the ends of the bead.

Next, remove the parting bead between the sashes by using an old chisel to ease it out of its groove.

Now you can take out the lower sash and rest it on the window sill. Before going any further, mark the front of the sash with a pencil to show where the ends of the sash cords come. Make a corresponding mark on the frame.

Next, remove with a pair of pincers the nails holding the sash cords—but keep hold of the cords so that the weights at the other end do not crash down behind the stile boards. The inner sash can now be removed and stood aside. Repeat the marking procedure for the outer sash.

Finally, unscrew the pocket covers in the frame (or lever them out if they are not screwed,

but wedged in place); remove the covers; and take out the weights by pulling them through the pocket openings. The window detail is shown in Fig. 2.

Removing the old glass

The most useful tool here is a glazier's hacking knife for removing the old putty. This has a flat back for tapping in the glazing sprigs—the tiny, diamond-shaped pieces of metal which hold the glass in position. Alternatively, use an old screwdriver or chisel to clean out the putty, and drive the sprigs below the surface of the wood with a small hammer.

First, chip out the old putty from in front of the glass, then remove (or drive home) the glazing sprigs. Lift out the glass (you will need old gloves to handle it). Then clear out the $\frac{1}{8}$in. or so of putty around and behind the glass, so that you are down to bare wood.

Old glass which is brittle and needs replacing can be broken out into a large bag or a paper sack. Use pliers to remove jagged pieces from around the edges.

Dismantling and repairing windows

First remove all window furniture—catches and so on—following the procedure above for removing tough screws if necessary.

For tenon joints, remove the wedges in the joints by drilling a bore hole down the middle of the wedge and then using a slim chisel to prise out the bits (Fig. 3 shows details of this type of joint).

For dowelled tenon joints, remove the dowels by drilling them out, using a drill of the same size as the dowels.

Next, mark the timber on each side of each joint with a letter or number. This will make it easy to identify the correct section when reassembling the sections.

Tap the joints apart by holding a block of wood against the frame and tapping them with a mallet. This must be done carefully in order to avoid damage.

Remove all the old glue from the joints by using an old chisel or scraper or by brushing the joint with boiling water to soften the glue. Clean the joint with fine wire wool.

Repairing tenons

Broken or damaged tenons should be cut off and replaced by a new tongue. This is done by replacing the tenon with a hardwood fillet, half of which becomes the new tenon, and the other half of which is inset into the rail (horizontal member of the window sash).

First, measure the length, depth and thickness of the old tongue. Next, mark out a piece of hardwood whose depth and thickness is the same as the old tenon's, but whose length is twice that of the old tenon plus $\frac{1}{4}$in. (6mm). For example, if the old tenon is 2in. (51mm) long, the fillet should be $4\frac{1}{4}$in. (108mm) long. The extra $\frac{1}{4}$in. waste is allowed so that, when you reassemble the sash, it projects right through the mortise hole and is sawn and planed off to make a flush, flat surface.

Next, set a mortise gauge to the width of the tenon and mark it back along the rail. Cut off the old tenon. Continue the tenon lines across the end grain. Measure out where the

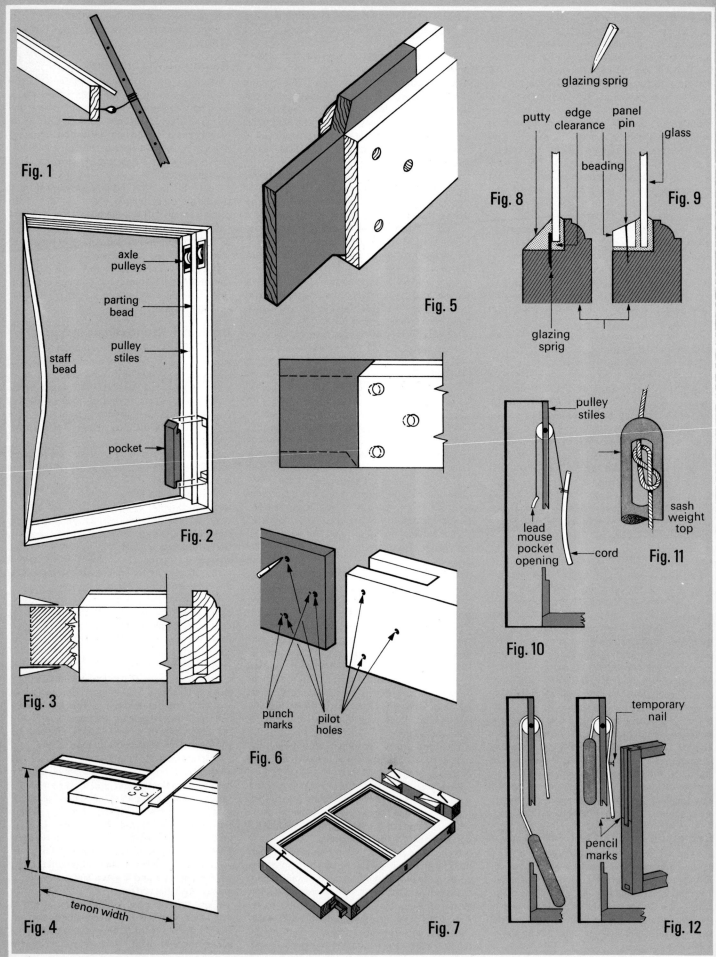

Fig. 1

Fig. 2
- axle pulleys
- parting bead
- pulley stiles
- staff bead
- pocket

Fig. 3

Fig. 4
- tenon width

Fig. 5

Fig. 6
- punch marks
- pilot holes

Fig. 7

glazing sprig

Fig. 8
- putty
- edge clearance
- glazing sprig

Fig. 9
- panel pin
- beading
- glass

Fig. 10
- pulley stiles
- lead mouse pocket opening
- cord

Fig. 11
- sash weight top

Fig. 12
- temporary nail
- pencil marks

114

fillet will be fitted into the rail, as in Fig. 4, using a rule. Place the rail in a vice and, using the techniques described in CHAPTER 5 for making the halving joint, cut out the unwanted section. Remember to saw on the waste side of the line. Now remove the waste timber in the middle with a coping or bow saw and finish off with a firmer chisel of the appropriate width.

The new tongue is fixed into the rail by three $\frac{3}{8}$in. (10mm) dowels (Fig. 5). First, drill three pilot holes through the rail so that these just mark the hardwood tongue. Then remove the fillet from its position and, using a nail punch, mark new points about $\frac{1}{32}$in. (1mm) on the outside of the three marks (Fig. 6). (Drilling the holes off-line in this way will help tighten the joints.) Now enlarge to $\frac{3}{8}$in. the holes in the rail, taking them right through to the other side, and drill matching $\frac{3}{8}$in. holes through the fillet. Slightly point three oversize lengths of dowel. Coat the end of the tongue, and the dowels, with an exterior grade of glue, tap the tongue into place and firmly hammer in the dowels. After the glue has set, cut off the excess dowel and plane smooth with the surrounding surface. The new tenon may now be haunched (cut back) as necessary to fit the mortise (Figs. 3 and 5).

Reassembling the sashes

The sashes can now be reassembled. Coat the tenons with adhesive and slide them into position in the mortises. Great care is necessary to see that the sashes are square. You can check the corners with a try-square, but a more accurate method is to measure from corner to corner across the diagonals; if the sash is square, the diagonals should measure exactly the same.

Once all four sides of the sash have been assembled, cut new hardwood wedges the same thickness as the tenon, glue them, and drive them in from the outside, above and below each tenon (Fig 3). To hold the work steady, and square, while you do this use sash cramps if you have them. If not, you can improvise cramps by nailing blocks of wood to a floor, as in Fig. 7, and using wedges to tighten the joints. Where large frames are being cramped, use wedges at both ends. Blocks and wedges should be clear of joints to allow for movement.

Or you can make a 'tourniquet' of rope, tied right round the sash and twisted tight with a piece of wood. Before you leave the adhesive to dry check again that the sash is square, and remove excess glue.

Sometimes excessive paint causes sashes to stick, and this is a good opportunity to remove and renew it. Strip the old paint, reprime and undercoat, and apply two top coats of paint.

Replacing the glass

Avoid using old or weathered glass for replacement glazing, as this is very difficult to cut—it usually gives a ragged cut edge. Glass becomes brittle as it ages and tends to discolour.

You may wish to cut your own glass, but usually a glass supplier or handyman's shop can cut it for you. Most windows need 3mm sheet glass (24oz). For larger windows, 4mm (32oz) glass may be needed.

Measure carefully for the new glass, using a steel tape. The measurement is made from the inside edge of each rebate to the inside edge of the opposite one; then you subtract $\frac{3}{16}$in. (3mm) all round to give an adequate clearance. Too tight a fit may make the glass crack.

A steel glass wheel is satisfactory for most glass cutting and works out cheaper than the traditional glass cutter's diamond. You need a large, flat surface to cut glass on. A felt-tipped pen can be used to mark guide lines on the glass, and a long straight edge or 'yardstick', or a home-made T-square, is needed to guide the cutter accurately.

First clean the glass. Then lubricate the line of the cut with either water or turpentine. To cut, use a firm stroke, holding the cutter vertically. Never back-track, since the glass is then unlikely to break along the cut line. After the surface has been scratched, put a strip of wood, or the yardstick, beneath the glass under the score line.

Place your fingertips as close as possible to the line and press down slowly and firmly on both sides. This should give you a clean break. If you have to trim any surplus from the glass, scratch a further line and gently break off the waste in small bites with a pair of pliers, with emery cloth in the jaws.

It is best to hold the cut sheet in a fold of newspaper or rag. Never stand it on or against a rough surface such as concrete, without protecting the edges from becoming chipped.

Before glazing, apply pink or white lead primer to all timber rebates to protect the wood and prevent oil in the putty from being sucked out.

As a rough guide, allow about 4oz-5oz (113-142 grammes) of putty for each foot of frame, but always have an extra 1lb handy for contingencies. In some putties, there is a tendency towards excess oiliness and over-softness of the material, particularly if it is bought in a polythene or plastic wrapper. To remove the excess, the putty should be wrapped in newspaper which will absorb the oil.

The putty should be rolled in the hand until malleable. Use linseed oil to soften it if necessary. Next, line the rebate of the frame with bedding putty to a depth of about $\frac{1}{4}$in. (6mm) by 'rolling' it from a ball of putty in the hand.

Place the pane gently into the frame, bottom end first, and holding it by the edges. Press it in at the edges; *never* from the centre. This pressure will squeeze out surplus putty, leaving a bed to a depth of $\frac{1}{16}$in. or $\frac{1}{8}$in. (2mm-3mm). With heavier panes, you may need to put a couple of pieces of matchstick at the bottom to keep the pane from sliding down and displacing the putty.

Secure the pane by tapping the sprigs into the side of the sash, hard against the glass, at about 12 in. intervals. Keep the hammer sliding down the glass as you use it, so that you do not knock the glass and break it.

Now that the glass is in place, with putty behind and all around it, you need a strip of weathering putty around the outside. Feed it from a ball of putty in your left hand while you use your right hand to spread it, at an angle of about 45°. Fig. 8 shows the finished sections.

If the putty shows signs of sticking to the putty knife, keep the knife moist with water.

Fixing glazing beads

If you are using glazing beads instead of exterior putty, use rather less putty to line the rebates. Prime the inside surface of the glazing beads and let them dry. Use only $\frac{1}{16}$in. or so of putty between the beads and the glass, and pin the beading to the sash with panel pins. Then trim the putty at a slight angle to allow water to run off (Fig. 9).

Finishing off

On the inside of the pane, trim off surplus putty by cutting at a slight angle. This helps to stop condensation from collecting.

Both inside and outside, finish off by brushing over the putty with a soft paint brush. Clean any smears from the glass or surrounding woodwork with methylated spirits.

Putty should not be painted for about four weeks after it has been applied. When painting the frame, carry the paint line just beyond the putty and on to the glass to seal the joint and prevent water from getting between the putty and the glass.

Replacing sash cords

If the sash cords need replacing, buy pre-stretched waxed cords; otherwise you will have to allow about an inch (25mm) for stretching in use.

Begin with the outer (upper) sash. As well as the cord, you need a length of string and a flat piece of lead made into a 'mouse'. Roll the lead right round the end of a 5ft (1.52m) or 6ft (1.83m) length of string at about the thickness of a cigarette but half as long. Bend the lead 'mouse' slightly in the middle and feed it over the groove of the outer pulley wheel until the mouse falls down behind the stile. Tie the new sash cord to the other end of the string. The cord can now be pulled over the wheel and out through the pocket opening, and the mouse removed (Fig. 10).

Tie the sash cords to the top of the weights. Either use a flat-finish knot, or bind the loose end of cord, so there is no 'lump' to interfere with the window-opening action (Fig. 11).

Pull the weights up about 2in. (50mm) from the bottom, and half drive a nail through each cord into the pulley stile to hold the weights temporarily in position. Cut each cord level with the pencil marks on the stile (Fig. 12).

Now position the outer sash so that you can fit one of the cords into its groove. Align the end of the cord with the pencil mark on the sash edge, and fix it with four or five clout nails, starting at this point (Fig. 12).

Once both cords are fastened, take the temporary nails out of the cords and stiles, and lift the sash into position. Give a trial run by sliding the sash vertically.

The two weights for the inner (lower) sash are corded in the same manner, except that the weights are pulled up almost to the pulleys.

The pockets can then be replaced, the parting head sprung back, and the inner sash lifted back. So that the sash slides smoothly, run candle wax in the two channels and on the edges of the staff and parting beads.

Left. A Dutch door from the kitchen to the garden prevents children tramping in and out on a wet day and yet provides extra ventilation

a middle horizontal rail, can be copied as a Dutch door.

Standard British doors are 6ft 6in. x 2ft 6in. (1.98m x 0.76m), but there are many variations. The size of the door you build will obviously depend on the size of the door you intend to replace. The construction involves quite advanced jointing techniques and very accurate rebating.

Construction

A Dutch door consists of a frame composed of four horizontal members, or rails, and two vertical pieces, or stiles, which run the whole length of the outsides of the door. The top rail of each part of the door is made from timber of the same size. For standard doors and all but very large doors pieces of 4in. x 1½in. (102mm x 38.1mm) timber are ideal. The bottom rail of the top part of the door is slightly wider than the rail it meets to allow for a ½in. (12.7mm) matching rebate to be cut. 4½in. x 1½in. is ideal for this rail. The bottom rail of the finished doors should equal the finished width of the two middle rails—8in. x 1½in. (203mm x 38.1mm) being about the right size. The bottom rail is double haunched mortised and tenoned into the stiles, and the other three rails are single haunched mortised and tenoned (Figs.3 to 4).

The space between the rails and the stiles is filled with tongued and grooved boards, or 'matching'. These are pinned to rebates cut into the inside edges of the stiles and rails. Dutch doors are usually made with braces—diagonal pieces of timber the same width as the stiles, placed on each half of the door along the matching. The braces run parallel to each other, are fixed to what will be the back of the door, and their top faces, when fixed, are flush with the top faces of the stiles and rails. Braces are not essential but they do give extra strength—provided they run *upwards* from the hinge side.

A matching rebate is cut into the two middle rails, and across the stiles that meet them, to provide a weather-tight joint where the two halves of the door meet.

Setting out

If the two halves of a Dutch door were made separately, they would almost certainly not be parallel when they were hung. So you make the whole door in one piece, using stiles which are over-length, and cut it in two when construction is nearly complete. This means that you must set out the height of each half by measuring over the *rails,* not by measuring down the stiles. Remember to allow an extra ½in. for the overlap in the middle; your doors will 'shrink' by this amount when you rebate them together.

The stiles should be cut about 2in. (50.8mm) too long. This will allow for ½in. (12.7mm) waste at each end and 1in. (25mm) in the middle. The inch in the middle allows adequate room for waste. The gap in the middle of the door will resemble a narrow 'letter box' when the door is assembled. The rails must also be cut slightly over-size; the waste is removed after the mortise and tenon joints are completed.

Dutch doors for a farmhouse look

Dutch doors, traditionally seen in farmhouses and rustic country cottages, can be both an attractive and functional addition to various rooms in the more conventional home.

Dutch doors are doors that are separated into two pieces across their width. This enables one half to be opened independently of the other. Traditionally Dutch doors were ledged and braced but any design, providing it incorporates

At this stage the areas of the joints in the stiles and rails can be marked. Lay the two stiles together with their long edges butting. Measure and mark a point in the middle of the stiles' length. On each side of this point measure and mark $\frac{1}{2}$in. (12.7mm) towards the ends of the stiles. Square lines through these points.

All measurements for the areas of the joints must be made from these squared lines. For the area of the joints in the upper part of the door mark from the top squared line. To mark the area of the joints in the lower part of the door measure from the other squared line.

From the respective squared lines measure and mark half the length of the finished door towards the end of the stiles. From this point marked in the top part of the door measure and mark 4in.—the width of the top rail—back towards the centre of the stiles. From the points marked near the ends in the bottom part of the door measure and mark 8in. (203mm) back towards the centre of the stiles. This indicates the width of the bottom rail. Returning to the central squared lines, mark off towards the ends of the stiles the width of the two middle rails— $4\frac{1}{2}$in. (114mm) for the rail in the top part of the door and 4in. (102mm) for the rail in the lower part of the door.

Working from the middle, mark out each rail using the same method as for the stiles. The first pair of squared lines should mark the length of each rail between the stiles; what is left over (4in. and a bit) is for the tenons, which run right through the stiles and protrude slightly on the other side.

Now lay the rails and the stiles together in the positions they will occupy in the finished door. Mark the top surfaces and the edges that are to be rebated. This will avoid the danger of cutting joints or rebates the wrong way round.

Cutting the mortises

The next step is to cut the mortises in the stiles. Fig.4 shows the shape of the haunched mortise and tenon which will later be cut on the ends of every rail (except the bottom rail) in the finished door. The mortises should be cut to accommodate this shape. The tenon is one third the thickness of the rail—in this case $\frac{1}{2}$in. (12.7mm). The tenon also has a stepped shoulder which is equal to the depth of the rebate which will later be cut on the inside edge of the stiles and rails. The depth of the rebate, given the measurements stated earlier, is $\frac{1}{2}$in. (12.7mm). The haunch in the tenon is about one third the length of the tenon—which equals the width of the stile. So the mortise has three depths, the main part of the tenon going right through the stile, the stepped shoulder entering to a depth of $\frac{1}{2}$in. (12.7mm), and the haunch entering to a depth of about $1\frac{1}{3}$in.

Carefully mark out the mortises on the ends of each stile, referring to the data in Figs.3 and 4. In the case of this complicated joint, do not cut the whole mortise yet. Cut the part that accommodates the main piece of the tenon but simply mark out the area of the haunch and the stepped shoulder. These can be cut to depth after the full shape of the tenon has been cut.

The single haunched tenons can now be cut. The shape and dimensions of these are shown in Fig.4. Then finish cutting the mortises, trying

the tenon in the joint from time to time until the stepped shoulder and haunch are cut to the right depth.

The next step is to cut the mortise and tenon joints in the bottom rail and bottom of the stiles. Fig.3 shows the shape and dimensions of these double haunched mortise joints. The tenon has two tongues, a stepped shoulder and a haunch.

First mark out the position of the mortises. Cut only that part of the mortise that will receive the two tongues of the tenon that go right through the stile.

Then cut the tenon. Score a line with a handyman's knife and straight edge along the squared lines you have previously marked on the ends of the bottom rails to indicate the width of the stiles. Set a marking gauge to one third the thickness of the rail. On the narrow edge of the rail score a line from the squared line to the edge of the rail, with the marking gauge. Continue this line on to the end grain and along the bottom edge to the squared line. Repeat this process with the block of the gauge flat against the opposite face of the rail.

The tenon can now be cut to the shape and size shown in Fig.4. On the side that is not to have the rebate, saw down the scored line

Above. *For a children's room Dutch doors give necessary contact with the rest of the house at night but also prevents children wandering.*

MICHAEL BOYS

through the end grain. Stop the cut when you reach the squared line. Then saw down the squared line through the face of the rail until you reach the original cut at right angles. Remove the waste. On the opposite face—the one at right angles to the edge to be rebated— mark inwards a distance that equals the depth of the rebate. This will indicate the size of the stepped shoulder. Square a line through this point and on the two edges. Saw away the waste as before.

Next mark out the positions of the two tongues on the existing single tenon. From the top of the tenon mark it into quarters along the end grain. Square lines through these points onto the face of the tenon. Mark the distance of the haunch, which is one third the length of the tenon, from the original squared line towards

the end of the tenon. Cut out the waste down to this line to the shape shown in Fig.4.

Now complete the mortise that will receive the double haunched tenon.

Cutting the rebates

The inside edges of the rails and stiles are rebated to receive the tongued and grooved matching. The rebates are cut to a depth that equals one third the thickness of the timber— $\frac{1}{2}$in. (12.7mm) if $1\frac{1}{2}$in. (38.1mm) timber is used. Their width along the wide surface of the pieces should be about $\frac{1}{2}$in.—giving you plenty of room to pin the matching in place.

The rebates can be cut the whole length of the inside edges of the rails with an ordinary rebate or plough plane. But along the edges of the stiles the rebates run to $\frac{1}{2}$in. inside the squared lines that were marked to show the area of the joints. This will form a corner between the rebated stiles and rails. On the ends of the stiles mark a distance of $\frac{1}{2}$in. from the original squared lines towards the ends. From the squared lines that denote the position of the middle rails mark inwards $\frac{1}{2}$in. towards the central waste area. Square lines through these points part of the way across the top surface and on the edge to be rebated.

The rebates can now be cut in the stiles between these points. Stopped rebates are difficult to make with either an ordinary rebate plane or a plough plane. This is because the body of the plane projects about 3in. or 75mm in front of the blade and about 5in. or 130mm behind it. This means that you cannot stop the rebate accurately at the point required. A special type of rebate plane, called a bullnose rebate plane, is specially made for stopped rebates. Or you can do most of the job with an ordinary rebate plane, and finish off with a chisel.

Assembling the door

The skeleton framework of the door can now be fitted together. Assemble the door on a perfectly flat surface, and check that the two parts of the door are the correct size. (Remember the $\frac{1}{2}$in. rebate still to come in the middle!) When satisfied glue the parts together with a waterproof glue such as Cascamite. Do not use pva adhesive as this is soluble in water and is, therefore, not weatherproof. Check that the door is square with either a large square or by measuring the diagonals. These will be exactly equal if the door is square.

The next step is to drive thin wedges from the outsides of the stiles into the mortise and tenon joints with a mallet. Do this before the adhesive dries. The wedges will make a tight fit between the mortise and the tenon. If the door is not square the fault can be rectified by driving the wedges home with extra force at suitable corners.

Cramp the assembly using sash cramps with waste wood blocks between the shoes of the cramp and the edges of the stiles. Wipe excess glue from the surfaces of the doors.

Cutting the braces

The length of the braces will depend on the size of the door. Their width should equal that of the stiles, and their thickness should fill the space between the matching and the back of the

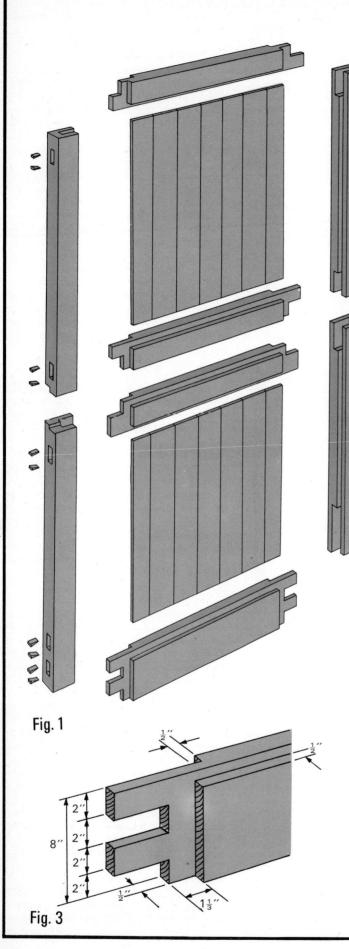

Fig. 1

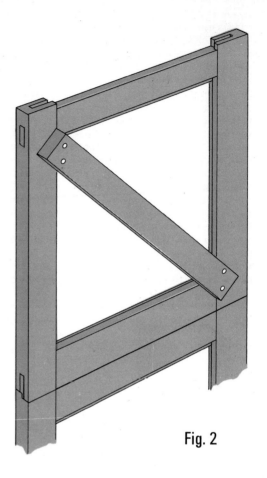

Fig. 2

Fig.1. *An exploded view of one style of Dutch door. The construction, particularly the shape of the joints, is the same in most cases. Braces, if they are to be used, are fixed along the back of the infill matching.*

Fig.2. *To mark the shape of the braces, nail them to the opposite face of the door to the one to which they are finally fixed. Turn the door over and mark the shape of the braces.*

Fig.3. *The double haunched tenon that is cut on the bottom rail. The dimensions given are for a standard sized door.*

Fig.4. *The single haunched tenon that is cut on all the other rails. Again the dimensions are for a standard sized door.*

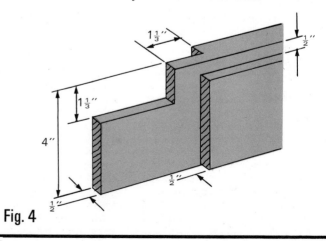

Fig. 3

Fig. 4

frame, so that stiles, rails and braces are all flush. Cut the braces several inches over-size. Lay the braces across the rails so that they 'cover the corners', and lightly nail them in position. Turn the door over, and direct-mark the braces by running a marking knife around the corner. With a saw and smoothing plane cut down to these lines. Fig.2 shows the braces nailed across the rails. Now remove the braces until matching has been fixed.

Now sand the back surfaces of the matching with either an orbital (not rotary) sanding device fitted to an electric drill or glasspaper wrapped around a wood block.

Fitting the matching

The tongued and grooved matching can now be fitted.

Cut the T & G matching to the required length. Prime the ends of the matching (which fit into the rebates) and the tongues and grooves with a waterproof sealant. Remove the groove edge from the first piece of matching and place this piece into the rebate, butting the inside of the stile, with the tongue side outwards. Pin through the surface of the matching into the stiles and rails with galvanized nails, cramping the boards as shown in CHAPTER 6.

Now fix the braces. They can be glued into place first. Then nail them to the matching, nailing through its surface. Pin the braces to the stiles and rails by angling the nails.

Separating the two parts

The assembly can now be cut in two. Separate the two components of the door by sawing through the stiles into the middle waste area. Saw away any waste that protrudes from the ends of the stiles and remove any parts of the wedges and tenons that stick out at the joints.

The rebates in the meeting rails

Cutting the rebates in the meeting rails is the final step in the construction of a Dutch door. Set the rebate plane to half the thickness of the meeting rails. Take the top half of the door. Cramp a waste block to the end to which you will be planing. This will avoid damaging the end grain of the stile. Lay the body of the plane along the face of the middle rail that will be the back of the door. Cut a rebate along the rail and two stiles to a depth of $\frac{1}{2}$in.

Then cut the rebate in the lower part of the door. The process is the same, but the body of the plane must lie on the surface of the rail that will be in the front of the finished door. Cut this rebate to a depth of $\frac{1}{2}$in. (12.7mm) also.

Finishing the door

Sand the stiles, rails and braces perfectly smooth. The two parts of the door can either be painted or varnished. If they are to be painted, apply a coat of knotter before applying the undercoat. The finish must be waterproof.

Hanging the door

Each half of the door is hung with two 3in. (50mm) butt hinges. Cut the positions of the hinges with care, first on the door, then on the frame. Fix the bottom door first. The top door can then be hung, but take care to ensure an accurate fit. Fit each part of the door with bolts.

Above. *This Dutch door's finish attractively contrasts with that of the table to add an extra touch of old fashioned charm to this room.*

Below. *Here the Dutch doors, together with the table, chairs and tiled floor, give this otherwise modern kitchen a farmhouse look.*

Make a military chest

If you need more drawer space and are contemplating building a chest of drawers, then you should seriously consider making a miltary chest. It takes a little longer to construct, but a military chest is more versatile, attractive, and just that bit different.

The military chest was really years ahead of its time—and is still an up-to-the-minute piece of furniture. It is probably the earliest example of unit furniture, because in fact it is two units that can stand together, or apart, either as a four-tier chest of drawers or as a pair of chests that might double as seating space. Not only that, in the past it also doubled as luggage! This versatility means a military chest could be an attractive addition to a modern home.

Origins of the military chest

Military chests first became popular as a convenient method of storage for soldiers and gentlemen making a sea voyage, from Britain to India for example, for long terms of office. It is designed in two sections, which makes it simpler to handle when moving. (This is still an advantage today if you are contemplating a do-it-yourself home removal.) The top section rests on the lower section when the chest is in use. The chests were enclosed in a heavy canvas bag while on voyage to protect the surface from scratches. On arrival they would be promptly installed as units of furniture.

The handles are always made of brass, with brass corner brackets, and all the attachments are inset for protection in transit. There is provision underneath for detachable feet.

Often the top unit was a military *desk*, or contained a dressing table. You will find some examples in books about antiques and you may see specimens in antique shops. These will give you some alternative design ideas.

The originals were invariably made from teak, mahogany, or similar exotic timber; but the one shown here used more readily available—and more economical—pine.

Construction

This chest is 36in. in length, 18in. deep and 16in. high (914mm x 457mm x 406mm), but the dimensions can easily be adjusted to suit your particular requirements. You can make two at once to provide the two sections of a four-drawer chest.

The woodworking joints on an original chest

(Left). This impressive military chest is an example of all that is best in traditional design, and will be the envy of your friends.

would almost certainly be dovetailed, but in this project the construction has been simplified and the joints are rebated, glued and screwed. For appearance the screw heads are sunk and the recesses covered with plugs of dowelling or plugs of matching wood extracted with a power drill attachment such as a Stanley Screw-Mate. The plugs are planed down and sanded smooth.

The rebated joints are cut with a router attachment such as a Stanley Bridges 1045 on a hand power drill as shown in Fig.4, but the same result can be achieved using either a bench saw or portable electric circular saw.

The chest is 18in. deep. It is difficult, to say the least, to buy wood of this width, so for the top, bottom and side panels two planks, each 9in. wide, are butted and glued along their long sides and cramped tightly together while the glue sets.

To do this, lay a pair of planks on a flat surface with their long edges touching. Arrange this so that the faces with the most attractive grain are on the same side—this will be the outside of the chest—then check that the butting edges fit together with no unsightly gaps. If there are any high spots that prevent the edges butting evenly, plane or sand them down.

The edges must now be glued with a woodworking adhesive such as pva. For this you will need at least two sash cramps, preferably three. If you have no sash cramps you can improvise by using strings and wedges.

Set out two sash cramps and lay two planks over them as shown in Fig.3. Apply adhesive along both long edges, place waste blocks or strips of wood between the outer edges of the planks and the jaws of the cramps to prevent the jaws marking the cramps, then tighten the cramps steadily. If you have a third cramp, place it in between the other two, but running *over* the planks. This will prevent the planks raising or 'jack-knifing' when the lower cramps are tightened.

The planks must fit together perfectly with their surfaces completely level. If there is some uneven alignment, loosen the cramps a little, place a waste piece of wood on the raised plank and tap it lightly with a hammer. Then re-tighten the cramps.

Wipe any excess adhesive from the join, using a soft damp cloth. Otherwise any glue left on the surface of the wood will show as a white patch through the polyurethane finish that is applied later. Leave for the adhesive to set.

Making the carcase

First cut and fit the carcase (the top, bottom and ends) lengths. As you can see in Fig.5, the ends fit in between the top and bottom panels.

Although no joints have been cut yet, briefly dry-assemble the carcase to check that the frame is square.

Next cut the rebate recesses in the top and bottom panels to take the end panels. These are cut to the same depth as the thickness of the butting end panel, leaving a ¼in. or 6mm lip. This is shown quite clearly in Fig.14. In this case the rebates were cut with a router, which in fact cuts a groove. To make a rebate, a groove of the required depth is cut along the end of an edge as shown in Fig.4, then another groove is cut out at right angles to the first, creating the 'L' shaped rebate recess for the end panel to fit into.

Briefly dry assemble the carcase and with a pencil lightly mark the four edges that will be at the back of the chest. Dismantle the carcase and cut a ¼in. or 6mm deep rebate, ¾in. or 19mm wide round the inside edges of the rear. This creates a recess into which the plywood back fits, as shown in Fig.13A.

Spread adhesive in the rebate recesses of the ends of the top and bottom panels, fit the end panels in place and stand the frame on one end, with the opposite end cramped as shown in Fig.6. With the cramps in position, drill the countersunk screw holes at approximate 3½in. or 89mm intervals, then drive the screws firmly in position and fill the screw recess with wood plugs as shown in Fig.6. Repeat with the opposite end, square the carcase and leave for the glue to set.

The runners and cross member

The cross member—the centre front in the cutting list—must be housed into each of the end panels at the front. This in effect makes the carcase stronger and keeps the drawers apart. It is located exactly half way up each end panel.

Place the carcase on its back on a flat surface and, using the cross member for direct marking, measure half way up each end panel. The cross-member must house down into the depth of the panel so that it is seating flush with the front, and the ends must house into the thickness of the panels leaving ¼in. or 6mm on the outside, the same as with the rebate recesses.

When you have marked the joints, cut them out with a sharp wood chisel. Then glue the ends into the recesses, securing the member with a countersunk screw into each end through the panel. There is no need to plug this screw recess because the head will be covered by an angle bracket.

Next fit the middle drawer runners. These are fixed level with the cross member, and the front of each runner is cut away so that it is housed *round* the cross member as shown in Fig.13. The cut away part is marked by direct marking—butt it against the cross-member—and two cuts made down its length with a tenon saw, then chiselled out.

Line the runners up with the aid of a square and screw in position as shown in Fig.7.

Now fit the bottom drawer runners in position. These are only glued and pinned in position in the bottom corners. Fig.7 shows one being pinned.

The drawers

These are made in exactly the same way as the carcase except that the front panel, which is

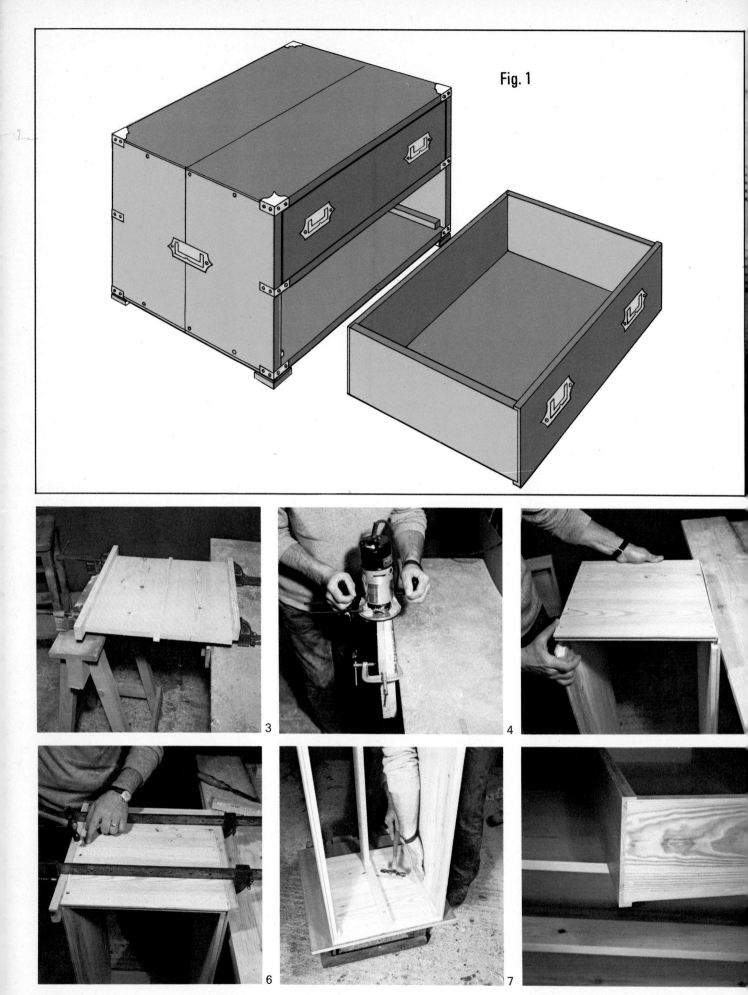

Fig. 1

3

4

6

7

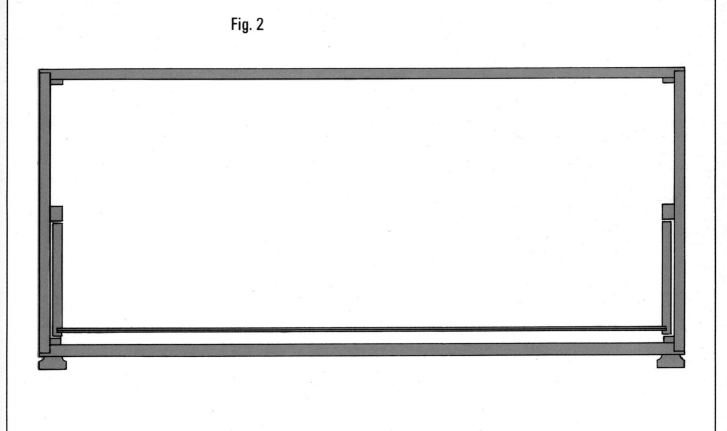

Fig. 2

Fig.1. *The complete unit. All brass fittings, including handles, are recessed flush with the surface.*

Fig.2. *Front view of the chest carcase with runners and legs. The sides and base of the lower drawer are also shown.*

Fig.3. *To join two planks of timber, spread adhesive along butting edges and hold together with sash cramps until the glue sets.*

Fig.4. *One way of cutting a rebate is to cut a groove with a router, then cut another groove at right angles.*

Fig.5. *This shows how the top and bottom panels are rebated to take the side panels, which just butt into place.*

Fig.6. *Three aspects of construction. Sash cramps are in place; screws driven in; and wood plugs have been fitted.*

Fig.7. *The drawer runners and centre front member in position. One end of the middle runners is cut away as shown in Fig.13-A.*

Fig.8. *Side front of one of the drawers. Note how the side panel is recessed into the front panel, which is cut away to provide a rebate which is stopped at each end.*

Fig.9. *Locate the drawers so that they are flush at the front, then nail battening round the inside back to provide stops.*

Fig.10. *Use each corner bracket as a template to mark its own outline, then chisel out to the depth of the brass.*

Fig.11. *There is no need to use corner brackets at the bottom corners. Angle brackets are easier and cheaper to fit.*

Fig.12. *Placing the back in position. This is simply glued and pinned.*

9

10

11

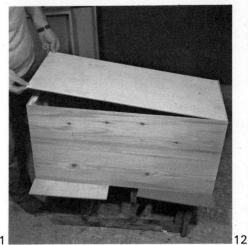
12

123

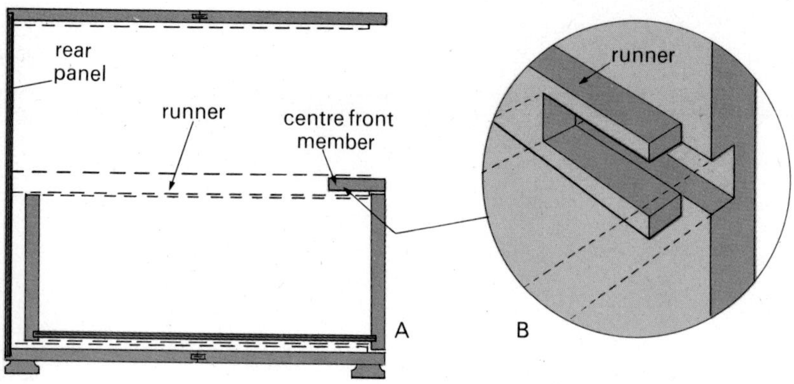

Fig. 13

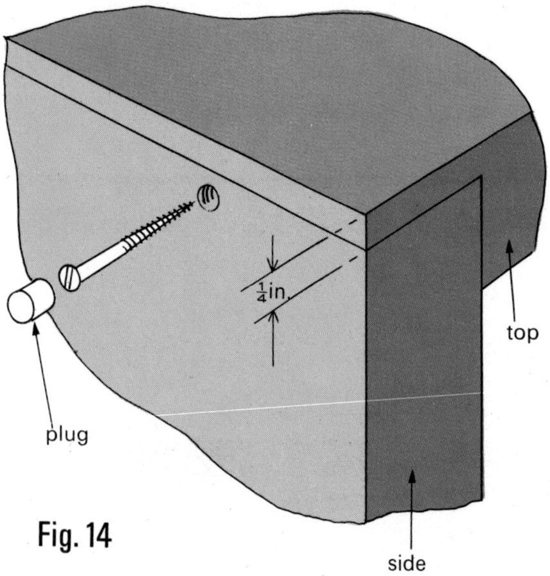

Fig. 14

Fig.13(A). Side view of the chest. The rear panel has been glued and pinned in place and the centre front member and runners fixed in position. (B), shows how the front end of each middle runner is cut away to allow the centre front member to house through.
Fig.14. Front corner section of the carcase, showing the joint used.

larger than the sides and back, has a rebate on each side which is stopped at each end. Fig.8 shows this quite clearly. To do this, lay one of the side panels against the end grain of a front panel so that it lays centrally, that is with the same amount of end grain showing at each end, and $\frac{1}{4}$in. or 6mm from the front of the panel, and mark round the side panel on to the end grain of the front. With the router, cut two right angled grooves, stopping just short of each end, then chisel the rest out.

Mark and cut the rebates to take the side panels on the rear panel, then dry assemble the drawer to check for squareness. This is easier if you lay the front panel on its face, stand each side panel into the stopped rebates, then place the rear panel on top.

If everything fits, mark a line round the inside of the drawer, $\frac{3}{8}$in. or 10mm inwards from the bottom. Dismantle the frame and with the router cut a $\frac{1}{4}$in. or 6mm wide groove, about $\frac{1}{4}$in. deep, round the marked line. This will house the edges of the drawer bottom panel.

Now check that the drawer fits properly before you fix the joints. Place the front panel in position in the front of the chest and, from the back, insert the two side panels in the stopped rebates, slide the bottom panel through the housing slot, then place the back panel in place. If there are any badly fitting parts, these can be planed or sanded down.

Dismantle again, place the front panel face down on a flat surface, spread glue over the joints, assemble the frame, drill screw holes and drive the screws home as shown in Fig.8. The bottom panel just slides in place and is not glued or pinned. This avoids any stress problems caused by expansion and contraction. Repeat for the other drawer.

When the adhesive in both drawers has set, slide the drawers into the chest so that the front panels are flush with the front of the chest.

Finally, glue and pin some 'drawer stops' in place at the back of the chest as shown in Fig.9, to ensure that the front stops flush. Then glue and pin the rear plywood panel in place, driving a pin in every 2in. or 51mm.

Handles and brackets

These are all inset, and to ensure a perfect fit each one is direct marked and cut individually.

Lay a corner or angle bracket in position and mark the outline on the chest lightly with a pencil. The area inside the mark is then cut away with a chisel to a depth equal to the thickness of the brass. Figs.10 and 11 show this being done.

Traditional military chests had a corner bracket at each corner, top and bottom. However, as modern chests rarely have to suffer the buffeting of an India passage, corner brackets are normally fixed only round the top, where they can be seen, and angle brackets are fixed round the bottom. It's really a matter of personal choice—but the latter method is cheaper and entails less work.

The handles are marked and cut in exactly the same way.

The position of the handles is also a matter of personal preference. Some people like them placed more towards the outer edges of the drawers, and some slightly towards the middle.

Finishing

Coat the chest with a 50/50 solution of clear polyurethane and turpentine. When dry, rub down with the finest steel wool, wiping afterwards with a soft cloth damped with turpentine to remove steel wool dust. Repeat, and when dry finish with a coat of neat polyurethane varnish.

You are now the proud owner of a modern military chest that will be the envy of your neighbours. Of course you must now make a second one—unless you only need two drawers. In any case, before you make another one study alternative designs used in antique varieties.

Your next effort might incorporate some of these ideas in modern form. The occasional writing desk would certainly be a good idea for many small homes. Or how about a small cocktail cabinet for the 'top deck'?

Cutting list

Pine:	inches:	millimetres:
4 top and bottom	36 x 9 x 1	914 x 229 x 25
4 ends	$15\frac{1}{2}$ x 9 x 1	424 x 9 x 1
1 centre front	35 x 4 x 1	889 x 102 x 25
4 drawer sides	$15\frac{3}{4}$ x $6\frac{1}{8}$ x 1	400 x 156 x 25
2 drawer backs	$34\frac{3}{8}$ x $6\frac{1}{8}$ x 1	883 x 156 x 25
2 drawer fronts	$34\frac{3}{8}$ x $6\frac{5}{8}$ x 1	883 x 168 x 25
Hardwood:		
4 top and bottom drawer runners	16 x 1 x $\frac{1}{2}$	406 x 25 x 13
2 centre drawer runners	16 x 1 x $1\frac{1}{4}$	406 x 25 x 32
4 feet	3 x 3 x 1	76 x 76 x 25
2 drawer bottoms	$33\frac{3}{4}$ x $15\frac{3}{4}$ x $\frac{1}{4}$	857 x 400 x 19
2 drawer reinforcing bottoms	$14\frac{3}{4}$ x 3 x $\frac{1}{4}$	375 x 76 x 19
Plywood:		
1 back	$35\frac{1}{2}$ x $15\frac{1}{2}$ x $\frac{1}{4}$	857 x 400 x 19

These sizes are for finished dimensions and do not include any allowance for waste. All pinewood should be ordered 'dressed'.

Also required for each chest: 4 inset drawer handles, 2 inset side handles (same, only larger), 8 corner brackets and 2 angle brackets —all in brass.

This free standing bar and the wall of sliding cupboards faced with mirrors have been designed to give a modern look to this recreation area. The layout of the back of the bar can be seen in one of the mirrors.

Easy to build cocktail bar

If you do a lot of entertaining at home, you may find yourself coping with makeshift catering arrangements—tables that aren't large enough, nowhere to keep the glasses, and so on. Build your own bar, however, and you can keep all your drinks and glasses together and pour a drink without having to move from one spot. The days of making-do will be over.

You can design your bar to suit your requirements exactly, so that it can take mainly bottles of wine and spirits or crates of beer. And you can make it just the right size, too, so that it fits your living room and stores away unobtrusively after use.

Bars tend to be very personal things, and a design may well please one person but not another. So a simple and readily-adaptable design for the basic carcase of a freestanding

bar is described here; it is shown in Fig.2. There are also a number of ideas for features that will give your bar a character of its own, and these are illustrated in Fig.1.

Design

The carcase, or basic structure, of this bar is rectangular and made from sheets of manufactured board, so that it is surprisingly easy to construct and can be made in any size to fit your particular room. It can be freestanding in the middle of the room, joined to the wall at one end or, if you fit it with castors, can be pushed out for use and stored unobtrusively.

The unit is given a more open and less box-like appearance by cutting away the bottom of the front panel to leave a recess. This gives plenty of foot room if you want to stand up against the bar—or for an authentic touch, a tubular foot rest can be fitted as shown in Fig.2.

The actual size of the bar you build will depend on the size of your room, the number of

Fig. 1

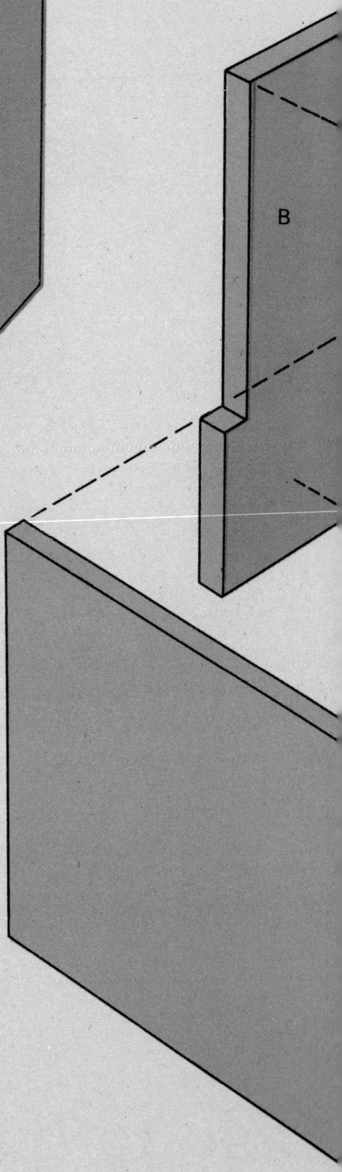

bottles and glasses you want to store and whether you want it to be a feature of your room or to be as inconspicuous as possible. The basic structure can be made to any reasonable size you want. But if it is to be exceptionally large, it should be braced by inserting a number of intermediate formers parallel with the sides and dividing the inside into separate areas, or you should construct two shorter units and stand them side by side. Although the dimensions are infinitely variable, the following measurements are intended as a guide:—

The height of the bar top depends on a number of factors. If you want to sit behind it, the bar top can be lower than if you want to be able to stand up at it. Or you may want it to match the height of the existing furniture and so continue the visual line around the room. In most cases, you will probably find that somewhere between 3ft and 3ft 6in. (0.91m—1.06m) is a convenient level.

The depth of the bar, that is, the distance from back to front, can vary too, but it must be deep enough for the unit to be stable and yet shallow enough so that when serving behind it you can easily reach to the front edge. In practice, something around 2ft (0.6m) will probably suit you.

The height of the recess at the bottom of the panel is entirely at your discretion, but note that in this design the bottom shelf (marked C in Fig.2) also forms the top of the recess. You may want the shelf to be a specific height so that, for example, a crate of beer can be stored underneath, and in this case the recess will be the same height as the top of the crate. You will need at least 1ft (0.30m) clearance to fit a foot rest, and 18in. (0.46m) should give sufficient space to store crates of beer under the shelf.

Carcase—general construction

The carcase is made from six pieces of board arranged as shown in Fig.2. Blockboard or chipboard ¾in. (19mm) thick or ½in. (13mm)

ply can be used, but remember that if you choose chipboard you must plug the screw holes with fibre plugs or dowel, as described in CHAPTER 40.

To join these pieces of board, glue strips of 1in. (25mm) square softwood along the internal angles between the boards and screw through these into both pieces from the inside. (See 'Assembly', below, for details). Panel pins driven in from the outside will provide additional strength, without marking the surface noticeably, but you are unlikely to need these except in a very large structure.

The front piece (A) provides much of the rigidity of the carcase, as it overlaps the edges of the sides, top and bottom shelf (pieces B, D and C). The front piece is therefore the full length of the bar and its width is the full height of the bar less the height of the recess at the bottom.

The side pieces (B) are as wide as the depth of the bar from front to back, less the thickness of the front, and as long as the height of the bar, less the thickness of the top, which overlaps them. A long strip is cut out from the top front corner of each side as wide as the thickness of the front panel and reaching down to the top of the recess.

The shelf (C) runs between the side pieces and from the back edge of the bar to where it meets the front piece. It is as long as the bar, less twice the thickness of the board used for the sides, and is usually as wide as the depth of the bar, less the thickness of the front piece—but you can make it narrower and stop it short of the back edge so that you don't knock your shins on it when serving from behind the bar.

Fig.1. This easy-to-build bar has been fitted out with a refrigerator, space for beer crates and shelves for a variety of glasses. The horizontal racks are ideal for bottles of wine and the holes in the bar top for bottles of spirits. These features could be altered to suit your needs: a waste bin may be more useful than the refrigerator and the wine rack could be extended downwards as in Fig.3.

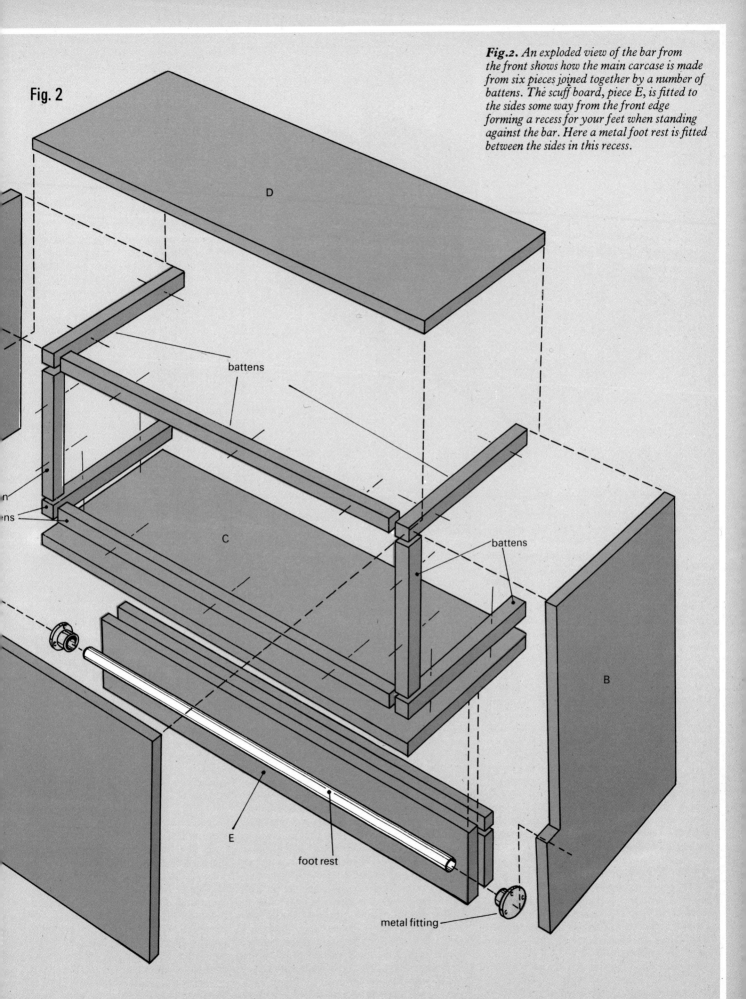

Fig. 2

Fig.2. *An exploded view of the bar from the front shows how the main carcase is made from six pieces joined together by a number of battens. The scuff board, piece E, is fitted to the sides some way from the front edge forming a recess for your feet when standing against the bar. Here a metal foot rest is fitted between the sides in this recess.*

D

battens

C

battens

B

E

foot rest

metal fitting

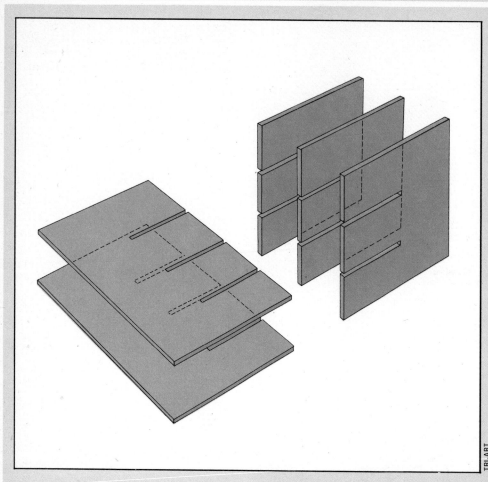

each piece. Now, before the glue dries, stand the unit on its feet and check that everything is square—if necessary, use sash cramps to hold it in position. Then drive in the rest of the screws from the inside through the battens.

When the adhesive is dry, remove any cramps and smooth the joins with sandpaper. The basic carcase is now nearly ready for finishing and covering—but first add any extra shelves or other features that you need (see below).

Additional features

You can make this bar hold most of the things you need without resorting to fixtures on the wall behind. The space below the bottom shelf can accommodate a crate or two of beer if you have made it high enough. In addition you need room to store glasses, to hold wine and spirits, a waste bin, a space for the ice bucket, and perhaps for a washing-up bowl full of hot water. If the bar is really elaborate and permanently installed in a suitable place, a fully-plumbed sink set into a hole in a shelf below the top is extremely useful, but for most people this will be too ambitious.

A handsome foot rest can be made from proprietary metal tube towel rail mounted between standard end fittings, and hung from the bottom shelf in the middle with another standard fitting as shown in Fig.2.

A vertical divider of the type shown in Fig.1, parallel with the end pieces and stretching from the bottom shelf to the bar top adds greater strength to the unit and can support the ends of half-width shelves. It can be set between battens as in Fig.1, or, if you don't want the battens to show from the back, screw down through the bar top and up through the bottom shelf into this divider.

If one side of the divider is fitted out with shelves for glasses, as shown, the space on the other side can be fitted with a waste bin, wine bottle rack, or anything else you need.

There are two ways of adapting a space to take wine or spirit bottles. Wine bottles are best stored horizontally so that the cork remains moist. This allows you to store the bottles on a shelf, or a number of shelves set close together, supported just below the bar top on battens, as shown in Fig.1. Vertical dividers made of thin plywood stop the bottles from rolling about. If you want to store a lot of bottles, you can make a set of interlocking plywood shelves as shown. Remember that bottles vary in length and diameter, so check the size of the bottles you are most likely to store. Stick a batten at the back of the shelf at a suitable distance from the edge —this stops the bottle going back too far so you can't reach it.

Spirit bottles are best stored upright, because the spirit tends to rot the corks. One way, as shown, is to cut circular holes in the top of the bar so that the bottles of spirits can be placed in them and supported by the shelf beneath. Position the top shelf so that sufficient of the bottle extends above the top of the bar to allow you to get hold of it easily (and also to see which bottle it is). If you cut these holes near the front edge of the bar it prevents people from leaning on the bar along its whole length, and leaves the back free for serving.

The top piece (D) is the full length of the unit and as wide as the depth of the bar, less the thickness of the front piece, and the *scuff board* (E) is as long as the shelf and as wide as the height of the recess.

Plan the pieces for your bar against the sizes of boards obtainable in your area. If you plan the bar carefully you may be able to make it largely from standard-sized pieces of board and save yourself cutting a lot of straight lines. If you do have to cut out many pieces, use a power bench saw if possible, for the greatest accuracy.

At the same time, remember that it may be cheaper to cut all the pieces out of a large board. When calculating the amount of board you need, include enough to make any of the extra shelves described below under 'Additional fittings'. Also buy sufficient battening to brace all the joints.

The edges of the pieces in this design are clearly visible so you should cover the whole bar when it is finished with veneer of a covering such as plastic laminate or one of the quilted self-adhesive plastics available (CHAPTER 42 gives full details of veneering and instructions on how to apply it).

Carcase assembly

Mark and cut out the pieces shown in Fig.2 to the dimensions you have chosen, as well as the pieces for any additional shelving. Check that the corners are all square and that the two side pieces (B) are identical—otherwise the whole bar will be out of line.

Check by direct measurement that the front panel fits into the rebates in the side pieces and projects beyond their tops by the thickness of

Fig.3. Exploded view of a wine rack to be fitted between shelves. Parallel slots are cut and chiselled half way across the boards as shown and the boards slotted together.

the top piece. The bottom shelf and the scuff board must both be the same length and shorter than the length of the top piece by the thickness of the two side pieces.

Measure and mark the positions of the battens on the pieces as shown in Fig.2—the battens are placed on the inside faces of the pieces and nearly all of them level with the edge except where shown. Cut the battens to length and drill holes for the screws both ways through the battens alternately at roughly 3in. (75mm) intervals. Hold the batten against the board where it is to fit and mark through the screw holes on to the board. Drill small pilot holes at this point with a small drill or bradawl—or in the case of chipboard, drill holes for, and insert, the fibre plugs to take the screws. Apply pva adhesive to one side of each batten and stick it to the board. Then screw through the pre-drilled holes and allow the adhesive to set.

Now assemble the pieces in the following order. Place the front panel downwards on the floor with one short end against the wall, then place a side panel on it leaning against the wall and glue and screw it in place with two or three screws only. Next, glue and screw the bottom shelf in place—this fits against the front and side panels, so that from this stage the carcase can support itself. Then fix on the second side, the top piece and the scuff board, again with only a few screws.

So far you have used only a few screws to

Installing a bow window

A bow window does a lot for your home: the smaller panes give a house character in this age of functional picture windows, and it makes the room behind it brighter and gives it an illusion of spaciousness. It is surprisingly easy to replace an existing window with a new bow window—or, for that matter, to enlarge the existing window space and put in a bigger bow window, or even to knock through a blank wall and add a bow window from scratch.

There are two kinds of window that project outwards from a wall; these are generally distinguished by being called a bow window and a bay window. With a bow window, which is a section of a circle in shape, only the frame itself usually projects out from the surrounding wall, and the wall itself is perfectly flat, as shown below. With a bay window, in which straight sections form the bay, the curve of the window frame is continued down the wall, and this projecting wall has its own masonry foundations. Both types of window give more light and space, but fitting a bow window is much easier, because it does not involve any disturbance of, or addition to, the foundations of the house.

Fitting a bow window involves little more work than replacing an existing window with one of a similar type. The opening is enlarged to take the new frame and a new, longer lintel is fitted across the opening to support the wall above. The frame is then set in place and the wall rebuilt around it. Finally, the space at the top and bottom of the window frame is boarded over. If you follow the instructions given here, you will be surprised at how simple the job really is.

Planning

When you fit a bow window to your house you are altering its external appearance, and in Britain and most other countries this means that you should apply to your local authority before you start work. In Britain you have to do this twice: once for planning permission and once for building permission. The initial stage involves submitting a dimensioned drawing of the alteration to your planning authority.

You will probably be fitting a ready-made bow window, rather than making the frame yourself. Bow window frames can be bought ready-assembled and primed from most builders' merchants. They come in a limited number of sizes, so check which sizes are obtainable locally before your plans get too advanced.

Correct siting of the window is also important. Be careful that you do not place it so near another wall or door that there isn't sufficient wall between them. Leave at least 18in. (450mm) of wall between the extreme edge of the assembly (normally the end of the lintel) and any existing feature. Also try and position the window so both it and the lintel fit neatly above and below a horizontal row of bricks.

Lintels

If you are enlarging a window opening or making a new opening in the wall, you must insert a strong lintel into the brickwork at the top of the opening to take the weight of the wall above.

It is important to check, and indicate on your plan for the authorities, whether the wall in which the window is being fitted is load-bearing. This is normally determined by the way the joists of the floor above run in relation to the wall; whether their ends rest on the wall you are knocking through (in which case it is loadbearing) or whether they run parallel with the wall (in which case the wall is not loadbearing, unless the joists of the floor above rest on it). When you knock through a wall, especially a loadbearing one, it can collapse unless it is shored up effectively. You can do this with special adjustable steel props or with timber. The load carried by the wall must be evenly transferred to the floor.

The size of the lintel you use is very important, and the Building Inspector will insist on checking that it is strong enough for the load on that part of the wall from above. If the bow window is to lie below an upper floor or floors, you will need a stronger lintel than if you were fitting one to a bungalow. The strength of the lintel also depends upon whether it is concrete or steel, and upon its width and depth.

Only a professional engineer could work out all the factors involved accurately. Fortunately, however, there is a rule-of-thumb method for calculating the size, and in any case the inspector will tell you if you have worked it out wrong. The rule states that the lintel should be as wide as the wall into which it is set, should be 1in. (25mm) high for each 12in. (300mm) span and, if it is concrete, should be reinforced with

Left. This bow window was installed as shown on the following pages, and completely transforms a small terraced house.

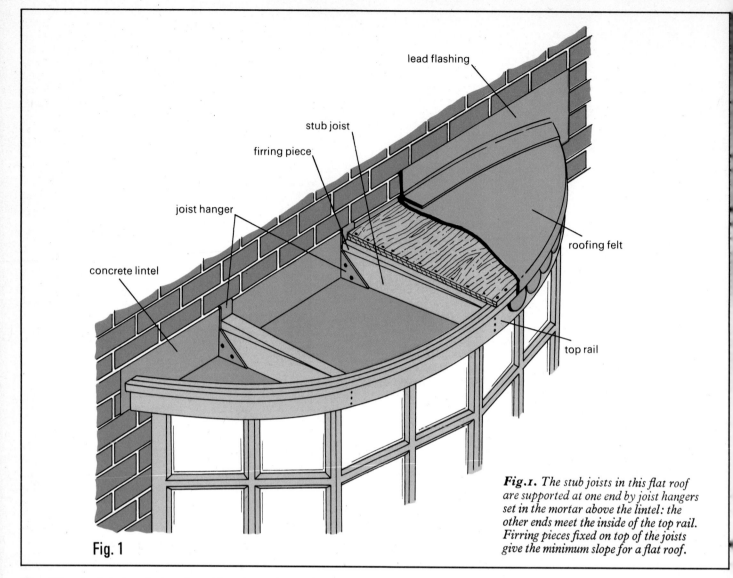

lead flashing

stub joist

firring piece

joist hanger

roofing felt

concrete lintel

top rail

Fig.1. The stub joists in this flat roof are supported at one end by joist hangers set in the mortar above the lintel: the other ends meet the inside of the top rail. Firring pieces fixed on top of the joists give the minimum slope for a flat roof.

Fig. 1

$\frac{5}{8}$in. (16mm) diameter steel rod positioned near the bottom. All lintels must be long enough to project into the brickwork on either side of the gap by $1\frac{1}{2}$ times their own width from front to back.

In a cavity wall, a lintel must be inserted in both inner and outer walls, or a wide lintel set across both walls, bridging the cavity. If the second course is chosen, a dpc must be inserted above the lintel and slanting down from the inner wall to the outer one to give maximum protection against damp.

Filling in

There is always a gap between the inner top and bottom edges of a bow window frame and the outer edge of the wall into which it is being fitted (see Fig.3). The actual size of this gap depends on the width of the window being fitted, and this may affect the method you choose for filling in the space. Some are shown in Figs.2 and 3, and described below.

A flat roof can look very attractive above a bow window; part of its charm lies in its visual simplicity, because it doesn't detract from the pleasing basic shape of the window. It is extremely easy to build, since it consists only of a framework covered with boarding. The only point to remember is that it must (by law as well

as in practice) slope from back to front by at least 1 in 40 to keep rainwater from collecting on the top.

The construction is shown in Fig.4. A 4in. x 3in. or 100mm x 75mm wall plate is fixed to the outer wall of the building at such a height that the stub joists attached to it will run down at a 1 in 40 slope and rest their other ends on the top rail of the window frame. This normally results in it being placed against the bottom of the lintel, which makes it rather hard to fix in place; there is no convenient attachment point for it.

The way you support this wall plate depends on what the lintel is made of. If it is a steel lintel, you can drill it and attach angle brackets at, say 1ft (300mm) intervals, to which the plate can be screwed (see Fig.2). A reinforced concrete lintel should not be drilled if you can avoid it. It is not illegal, but is hard to do properly and might weaken the lintel if done messily. The solution with this type of lintel is to forget about the wall plate, and hang the joists on steel joist hangers hooked over the top of the lintel and set in the mortar joint (see Fig.1). These hangers are available in a large range of sizes, so you should be able to find one with the right 'drop'.

All steel that comes into contact with con-

crete must be either galvanized or thoroughly coated with red-lead paint. If this is not done, a chemical reaction will be set up that will completely destroy the steel in a few months.

If you prefer, the 1 in 40 slope can be given to the joists by nailing firring pieces to their tops, instead of sloping the joists themselves. The gaps at the ends of the joists must be covered with a flush-fitting fascia board of the same depth as the joists themselves, plus the thickness of the boarding covering them.

The boarding fitted over this framework may be of plywood (exterior grade), asbestos sheeting or tongued-and-grooved boards. The underside of the roof is lined with plasterboard nailed direct to the framework. The gap between the inner and outer boards can be filled with an insulating material such as glass fibre wool; this is particularly recommended if you are double-glazing the window.

The same system can be used to fill the gap found at the bottom of the window frame. The wall plate can, however, be screwed to plugs set directly in the brickwork, which will save you trouble. The top piece of boarding should be a solid piece of timber to form an internal sill; exterior-grade plywood will make a sound weatherproof underside. Insulation can be inserted or not, as you prefer.

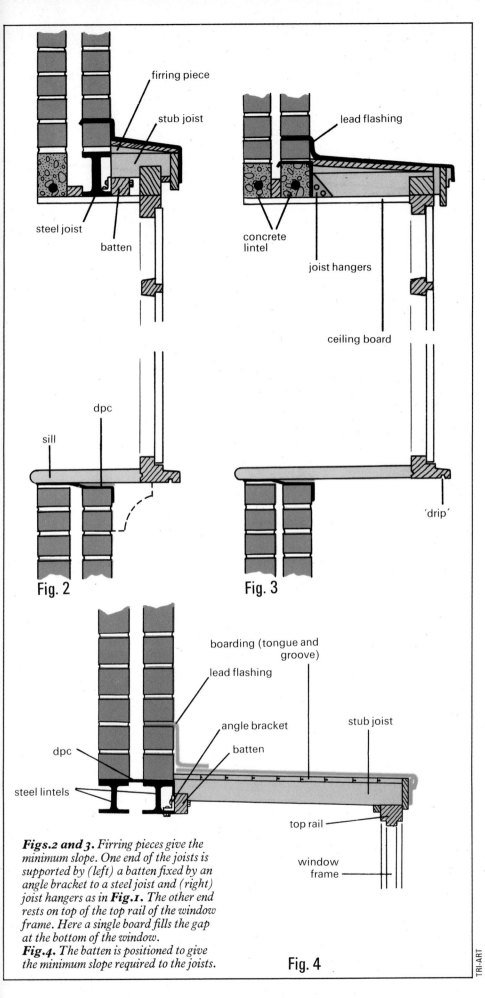

firring piece

stub joist

steel joist

batten

Fig. 2

dpc

sill

lead flashing

concrete lintel

joist hangers

ceiling board

'drip'

Fig. 3

dpc

steel lintels

boarding (tongue and groove)

lead flashing

angle bracket

batten

stub joist

top rail

window frame

Fig. 4

Figs.2 and 3. Firring pieces give the minimum slope. One end of the joists is supported by (left) a batten fixed by an angle bracket to a steel joist and (right) joist hangers as in Fig.1. The other end rests on top of the top rail of the window frame. Here a single board fills the gap at the bottom of the window.

Fig.4. The batten is positioned to give the minimum slope required to the joists.

TRI-ART

A sloping roof can be constructed in a similar way from a framework of battens and covered with boarding as described above. The top ends of the joists will be well above the level of the lintel, so they can simply be skew nailed to an ordinary wall plate plugged and screwed to the brickwork.

Both of these types of roof must be covered with either felt or lead to make them weatherproof. The top edge of the lead or, if felt is used, a separate lead flashing overlapping the top end of the felt, must be let into the wall in a line of mortar between the rows of bricks immediately above the lintel. British legal requirements for roofing felt are described in CHAPTER 21.

Tools and preparation

You will need a club hammer and bolster for knocking out bricks to enlarge the window space; and if the wall is loadbearing, you will need lengths of timber and folding wedges, used at the base of the timber struts, to shore up the wall. Other requirements, apart from the usual carpenter's tools, are a spirit level, a plumb line, and some pieces of old roofing slate to wedge in around the window frames.

The window frame will come without any glazing, so don't forget to order some glass of the correct size, and to buy putty and other necessaries for the glazing. Your glass merchant may be prepared to cut the glass to size—if not use a glasscutter and straight-edge.

Once you start, there will be a great deal of plaster and brick dust flying around and making a mess. So clear everything out of the room, or cover it with polythene sheeting and roll back the carpet for at least 10ft (3m); or screen off the rest of the room with polythene stretched over a timber frame.

Mark out on the outside wall the area the window will occupy, trying to align it with as many mortar joints as possible to save you the work of cutting bricks. Also try to line up the head of the new window with the head of the adjoining doorway or window, which will neaten the appearance of the outside of the house. Fig.10 shows the lintel lined up with the top of the soldier arch over the doorway.

Do all this the day before you begin knocking through, and also check that you have enough materials and tools for the job before you begin. In this way, you should be able to get the bow window in position and largely finished in one day, or perhaps two, and you will reduce the time your house is left with a large hole in the wall.

Knocking through

Before you start knocking through a wall or extending an existing window aperture sideways, make sure you have adequately supported the wall above with steel props or 4in. timber supports. But if you are using an existing opening and not replacing the lintel, or extending an existing opening downwards, there is no need to fit any supports in place.

You can now start the job of knocking through and inserting the lintel, taking care, again, to support the wall above. If you are using joist hangers hooked over the top of the lintel, remember to insert these into the mortar joint above the lintel before the mortar dries.

5

6

8

9

Fig.5. A simple sash window to be replaced by a primed, factory made bow window.
Fig.6. The outline of the new window is drawn on the wall, the sash window removed and the brickwork knocked away.
Fig.7. A concrete lintel is carefully lifted into position.
Fig.8. A framework of battens and joists is constructed above the window and boarded over to give a sloping roof.
Fig.9. The underside of the roof covered with plasterboard and the gaps around the window bricked up ready for plastering.
Fig.10. The final stage before the last coat of paint.

Fitting the window frame

Once the lintel is firmly fixed in place, lift the window frame into position and insert wooden wedges underneath it until it is in exactly the correct position in the hole cut in the wall.

If there is a large gap between the bottom of the frame and the row of bricks directly beneath, fill it with bricks cut lengthways to fit into the space, remembering to leave a gap for the mortar joints.

Mark the position of the mortar joints in the brickwork at either side of the frame on to the frame itself. You can then later drive nails halfway into the outside of the frame at these points to make a firm bond between the window frame and the brickwork.

Take the frame out of the hole in the wall. If necessary, because of a large space below the frame, brick up the space under the window frame to the level of the top of the wooden

wedges. (If you are in a hurry, you can leave out a couple of bricks and use the wooden wedges to support the window frame while you mortar it into place and wait till the mortar is dry). Fasten the lower and upper (if any) wall plate to the wall.

Drive some 4in. or 100mm nails halfway into the outer edge of the frame at the lines drawn to show the position of the mortar joints. Paint the outer edges of the frame with as many coats of undercoat as you can stand putting on (it should already be primed). These edges can never be repainted, so the more paint there is on them, the better.

Put the frame back in the wall and check with a spirit level and plumb-line that it is set absolutely straight, then wedge it firmly with pieces of slate.

Bricking up

Replace all missing bricks all the way round the frame; the edges of the masonry should ideally finish about $\frac{1}{8}$in.-$\frac{3}{16}$in. (3mm-5mm) from the frame all round. You should then fill this gap with mastic, which is sold in inexpensive disposable 'guns'. Alternatively, you can fill the gap with mortar, but it is difficult to obtain a lasting watertight seal by this method.

Finishing off

Cut the stub joists to length by direct measurement and skew nail them in place between the top of the window frame and the wall plate or joist hangers. Nail a fascia board on to the ends of the joists and cover their tops with boarding. Cover the whole roof with two

layers of roofing felt and a lead flashing, as shown in Fig.1, or alternatively with lead alone. The flashing must run up to the row of bricks just above the highest point on the roof; there, it should be let into a horizontal mortar joint along its entire length. Rake out the mortar, bend the lead into the groove and make good with more mortar. Further details of this type of roof construction are given in CHAPTER 21.

Nail any insulating materials, such as glass fibre blanket, to the underside of the roof, and then nail the plasterboard in place.

Fill in underneath the window in a similar manner, but here there is no need for roofing felt or lead flashing. The bottom of the assembly can be boarded with exterior grade ply and the joint between this and the wall sealed with more mastic. The ply should be thoroughly primed, undercoated and painted to finish the job, but before you do this, make sure that there is a 'drip' under the edge of the window frame to stop rainwater from trickling horizontally along the underside of the bow window sill and soaking the wall behind it. This drip can be either a groove or a ridge. If there is none, you should nail on a strip of narrow beading all the way round the lower edge of the frame just in from the front.

Finally, glaze and paint the window and make good the plaster inside the room. The inner edge of the window opening can be simply and neatly finished by nailing an architrave all round the inside of the frame. The shelf below the window on the inside will make a most attractive window seat for use in summer if it is upholstered.

All about panelled doors

A well-proportioned panelled door has an appeal which centuries of change in building fashions have left undented. Unfortunately, buying new panelled doors is expensive. But you can restore an old one to its former beauty—or, failing that, make your own 'panelled' doors from cheap flush ones.

Repairs and alterations to panelled doors do not require any advanced carpentry techniques, but any changes made demand careful planning. Panelled doors, like most articles of furniture, have a proportional unity.

Alterations to panelled doors

Before making any alterations, consider carefully how the door is constructed, particularly the types of joint used in the top and bottom rails. In older doors, single mortise-and-tenon joints were usually used in the top rail, and double mortise-and-tenon joints in the bottom rail. The tenons in these doors passed right through the stile. In newer, mass produced panelled doors, the same joints are generally used, but they are *stub* mortise-and-tenon joints, that is, the tenons pass only part of the way through the stiles. Some modern doors have dowelled joints.

Shortening doors

However the rails and stiles are joined together, a panelled door can easily be shortened if the amount of wood to be removed from the top and bottom of the door is no more than $\frac{1}{4}$in. (6mm). Remove the wood simply by planing the ends of the door, working 'outsides to middle' so you do not tear off the edges. Do not remove more than $\frac{1}{4}$in. or you may cut into the joints.

NIGEL MESSETT

Shortening a door by a greater amount involves a lot more work. You will have to partially dismantle the door. The method of doing this differs depending on whether the door joints are mortise-and-tenon or dowelled.

To shorten a panelled door without spoiling the proportions, move the top and bottom rails in equal distances down the stiles towards the middle rail.

For a door with dowelled joints, cut down the back shoulder of the joint and into the dowels with a fine-toothed tenon saw. Carefully break the remainder of the glued joint. If the door has a central vertical member, or *muntin*, you will have to cut through the muntin where it is joined to the rails. To do this, you will have to remove the panels. Since you will have to cut new panels to match the new size of the door the old panels, which are usually set into a groove in the inside edges of the door members, can be broken with a few bangs of a hammer and the pieces pulled out. This process, and the fitting of new panels, is described below.

You will have to cut the muntin to size before you fit the rails in their new position. Muntins are normally stub-tenoned into the rails, even on dowelled doors. You can cut a new tenon on the end of the muntin and dig out the wood in the old mortise in the rail. Alternatively, you can make the joint into a dowelled joint. The method of making such a joint is described below.

The next step is to move the rail down the stiles towards the middle of the door by the required distance. If the rail is too tight a fit in its new position, the door will not be square. In this case, shave the ends of the rail with a chisel. This process is known as *easing*.

The next step is to cramp the rails and stiles in their new position and drill holes for new dowels. Drill from the outside edge of the stiles into the end of the rails. If you are going to varnish the door, cut the new dowels about ½in. (13mm) shorter than the depth of the holes. Uncramp the door and insert new panels the same thickness as the old ones and cut to the right size.

When making dowelled joints you must slightly flatten one side of the dowel along its whole length. If you do not do this, the air in the drilled hole will not allow the dowel to be pushed home. Round one end of the dowel, apply glue to it and push the rounded end into the hole.

Fill the remainder of the hole with a tapered wooden plug, glued in place. When the adhesive has dried on all the plugs, plane off their protruding ends.

Doors can be planed easily if they are laid on edge and wedged in an upright position, using pairs of folding wedges.

Making doors narrower

To reduce the width of a panelled door with dowelled joints, you will have to remove an equal amount of wood from both ends of each rail. If the door has glazing bars, however, they are usually stub-tenoned into the stiles even though the rails are dowelled. In this case the stub tenon will have to be recut. HOME DECORATOR 11 describes the method of cutting mortise and tenon joints.

If the door is to be shortened in both width

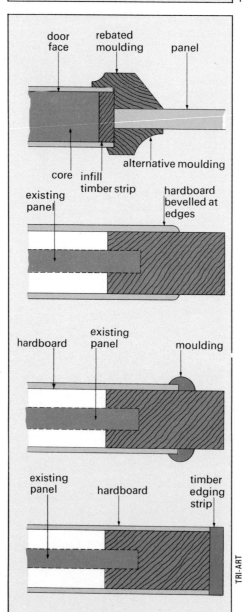

Fig.1 (*left*). *Before and after: a door with a damaged panel held in a groove cut in the door frame members, and with a new panel inserted. After breaking out the old panel and filling the groove with stopping, you hold the new panel in place with wood moulding.*

Fig.2 (*below left*). *Four ways of converting an old panelled door into a 'new' door. The top illustration shows how hardboard panels can be let into holes cut in the door, and their edges neatened with cover moulding. The other illustrations show three ways of making flush doors from panelled ones, using hardboard and wood edgings or mouldings.*

and height, saw through all the joints. Remove the required amount from each rail to make the door narrower and mark out on the stiles the new positions of the rails. Cut new stub tenons if and where necessary.

In reducing a door in width and height you may have to fill in any unwanted mortises. Do this with a wooden block, cut with a slight taper and just longer than the depth of the unwanted mortise. Apply adhesive to the block and knock it into the mortise with a mallet. When the adhesive has dried, plane off any part of the tapered wooden block that protrudes.

Doors with mortise-and-tenon joints

To shorten doors where the tenons run right through the stiles, you will have to dismantle the door almost completely. You will have to remove both stiles to enable you to get the tenons on the rails into their newly-cut mortises.

First chisel or drill out the wedges from the mortises in both stiles. Then break the glued joints. Older glues, and many newer glues such as pva, are water soluble and the joint can easily be broken after applying hot water. Knock the stile from the door using a mallet and a waste block to protect its surface. This will probably damage the panels beyond repair, so new ones will have to be cut to the correct size (see below).

The next step is to fill the old mortises with tapered wood blocks as described above. Mark out the areas for the new mortises and cut them. Fit the rails into the new mortises in the stiles and check that the door is square. Remove the rails, apply adhesive to the joints and assemble the door with all panels in place. Knock wedges into the mortises. Cramp the assembly together with sash cramps. If the door is now a little out of square, as it may be, this can be corrected by applying extra cramping pressure at one end of the door (if this doesn't work you can always plane it afterwards). Allow the glue to dry, then cut away the projecting ends of the stiles and any pieces of the wedges that protrude.

If the door is to be made narrower, the process is the same except that new tenons and not mortises have to be cut.

If the door has already been hung before alteration, you will have to plane down any cut-outs made for hinges, or, if the door is not being reduced in width, fill them with flat wood blocks. The mortise cut to house a mortise lock can be filled with a rectangular sectioned tapered wooden block glued in

In the figures: door frame / wood filler / moulding / panel housed in groove / replacement panel / damaged panel / moulding / door frame — 1

door face / rebated moulding / panel / core / infill timber strip / alternative moulding / existing panel / hardboard bevelled at edges / hardboard / existing panel / moulding / existing panel / hardboard / timber edging strip — TRI-ART — 2

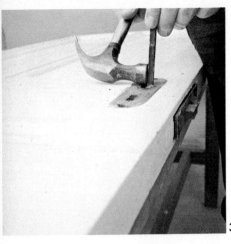

6

3

4

6

7

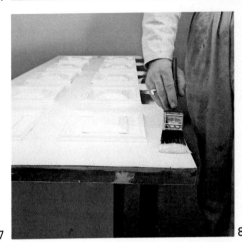

8

place. A cylinder lock hole, made to accommodate a Yale-type lock, can be filled with two wide, tapered dowels knocked in from both sides of the door.

Lengthening and widening doors

The only way panelled doors can be lengthened or widened is to attach pieces of wood to the tops or sides of the door. The door can only be enlarged a little in this way. The joins will be visible, but if you work carefully they will not be too conspicuous.

To lengthen a panelled door, apply a strip of timber to the bottom edge of the bottom rail of the door. The join can be disguised by fixing a metal or plastic kick plate to the bottom rail.

To widen a door, fix strips of wood half the thickness of the required increase in the width to each stile. To do this plane the outside edges of the stiles to remove any dents or rounding at the corners. With a chisel, cut back the ends of the tenons so that they are about ⅛in. (3mm) below the surface of the stiles. This is done so that any movement in the stiles does not affect the strips. The edge of each strip that is to butt against the stile should be perfectly square. The strips should be cut a little too wide and too thick. Glue them in place and cramp them to the door. When the adhesive has dried, plane the strips flush to the door and to the required width.

Flushing panelled doors

It used to be popular to flush old panelled doors to give cleaner lines and a 'lighter' look.

Imitation panelled doors can be built up from old doors, hardboard, mouldings—and patience.

Fig.3. If the old lock is stubborn, its own centre shaft is a useful lever for removing it.
Fig.4. Carefully measure the depth of the panels to accept softwood packing strips, which help stop the hardboard buckling.
Fig.5. Next, sand smooth both the packing strips and the rest of the door frame.
Fig.6. Using hardboard pins. These have shaped heads which bury themselves in the board, avoiding the need for laborious hole-stopping.
Fig.7. Carefully align your pre-made panels, and fix them on with adhesive and panel pins.
Fig.8. Undercoating the door before stopping any fine cracks gives a long-lasting finish.

It is not done so often now from a purely fashionable point of view, but it is a good way of disguising extensive damage to panels.

The process involves simply glueing and pinning a hardboard panel to both sides of the door. The edge of hardboard is rather unsightly, however. It can be finished in three ways which are shown in Fig.2.

The first is to bevel the edges of the hardboard and fix it in place on the door so that the sides of the panel are 1in. to 2in. (25mm to 51mm) from the edges of the door. The second method involves positioning the panel in a similar place and pinning a rebated wood moulding of a type called *cover bead*, around the edges of the panel. Various kinds of moulding are shown in CHAPTER 37. The third method is

more time consuming. Plane about ¼in. (6mm) from each edge of the door. Glue and pin the panel in place with its edges flush with the planed edges of the door. Then glue strips of timber onto the planed edges of the door. They should be just thicker than the amount of wood removed from the door and as wide as the new thickness of the door. Plane the strips down to size and pin them in place to strengthen the joint. Punch the heads of the panel pins just below the surface of the hardboard and wood strips and fill the holes with wood filler.

Repairing panelled doors

The most common damage to panelled doors are splits and breaks in the panels, and dents or similar damage to rails and stiles.

Broken or badly split panels should be removed and replaced. Panels are generally held in place by rebates, or grooves, cut into the edges of the members that enclose the panel. They may be finished with strips of moulding around the points where the panels meet the rails, stiles and the centre vertical dividing pieces known as *muntins*.

To remove a damaged panel, first remove the moulding around the panel, if there is any. You can do this by sliding a chisel between the moulding and the door frame and prising the moulding off. The damaged panel can be cut away, but since it is damaged there is no need to treat it gently. Break it in several pieces with a hammer; the pieces can then be pulled away. Any remains still stuck in their grooves can be cut away with a saw.

You will not be able to put the replacement

piece into the groove, so fill this with wood filler. Smooth the filler flush with the inside edges of the door members. Cut the replacement panel. This panel is held in place by new pieces of moulding which should be the same as that bordering other (undamaged) panels (if this is unobtainable, remove the original pieces carefully so that you can replace them). Cut new pieces of moulding oversize and mitre their ends so that they are the right length. Glue and pin four pieces of moulding in place on one side of the filled-in-groove. Glue the panel in place and then fix the remaining four pieces of moulding in the same way (see Fig.1).

If the damaged panel was simply housed in the groove and not bordered by moulding in the original door you can replace it in the manner described above, introducing strips of moulding to hold the replacement panel in position. You will, however, have to apply strips of moulding around the other panels or the door will look odd.

Damage to the outer edges of stiles or rails, such as dents or splintering, can be repaired by cutting away the damaged area and replacing it with a dovetail-shaped piece of wood. This is known as *patching* and is basically the same process as described fully in CHAPTER 22 for repairing damage to the edges of architraves.

Splits in rails or stiles can be repaired by running adhesive into the fault, wrapping the damaged area with newspaper and cramping up tightly with a G cramp and waste blocks.

Fig.9 (below). *The success of imitation panelled doors depends on their proportions. For exterior doors 6ft 6in. x 2ft 9in., you might like to try: A, 5in.; B, 5in.; C, 8in. For interior doors 6ft 6in. x 2ft 6in. A, 4in.; B, 5in.; C, 8in. will 'balance' well.*
Fig.10 (below right). *Panels are made up from hardboard, shaped offcuts and picture mouldings.*

Fashion considerations, or the fact that you have altered the dimensions of the door, may require a change in the furniture of the door, that is, handles, knockers and so on. In this case, the holes cut for them may have to be filled. This can be done by simply glueing tapered wood plugs in the holes and planing them flat.

The inner edge of the stiles, rails or muntins may become damaged where the panels are held in a groove and not bordered by moulding. This damage can be disguised easily by applying strips of rebated moulding around the edges of the panels to cover the damaged corners.

Imitating panelled doors

Flush doors can be made to resemble panelled doors, and panelled doors made to look more elaborate, by glueing and pinning strips of moulding or small panels with a design built on to them onto the door. Making a raised panelled door, where the panels project beyond the frame, or one where the panels are flush with it, is straightforward. Converting a flush door into a sunken panelled door—the usual type, where the surface of the panels is below the surface of the stiles and rails—is considerably more complicated.

The simplest way of making a flush door resemble a panelled door is to pin and glue pieces of moulding to the surface. A more elaborate method is to make a number of panels of various types of moulding pinned to hardboard. These can be glued in suitable positions on the door.

When imitating a panelled door with mouldings alone, the first step is to mark out roughly the areas where the frame and panels would fall on a real panelled door. Average sizes of these features are: Top rail 100mm (4in.) bottom and middle rail 200mm (8in.), muntins 75mm (3in.).

Using these measurements mark out the 'panelled' areas of the door with a soft pencil or masking tape. Masking tape will give you a better idea of what the finished door will look like. Use a large try square to ensure that all the angles you mark are right angles. Mark out and cut three of the pieces of moulding that will enclose a square or rectangular area. Pin the three pieces lightly in place and then cut and apply the last piece. Do this with the other panels. If the door looks right, remove one·

strip of moulding at a time, apply glue and pin it firmly to the door. Punch home the pin heads, fill the holes and rub down the moulding with glasspaper when the filler and glue have dried.

A dramatic effect can be achieved by applying fabric to the 'panels' enclosed by the moulding. HOME DECORATOR 26 tells you how to do this.

A method of giving a more elaborate look to a door is to build up, on squares or rectangles of hardboard or plywood, frames of moulding to resemble ornate panels. The various types of moulding available are illustrated in HOME CARPENTER 38. The design of these panels is a matter of taste. An attractive design is to place moulding around the edges of the hardboard or plywood panels with a thin rectangle of wood with bevelled edges placed centrally on the panel. The panels are glued and pinned to the door.

Converting a flush door into a sunken panelled door is a more complicated process. You will have to cut out square or rectangular sections of the door with a coping saw. To do this, mark out the areas of the door that are to be cut away. You must be careful, however, not to interfere with the stiles and rails, which are there but cannot be seen. Tapping the door with your knuckles will give some indication of the whereabouts of these pieces. Mark out the door well within the estimated area of these pieces. Drill small holes at all four corners of each marked out area. Cut out the areas with a coping saw, which should be stuck right through the door so that it removes the core as well as the plywood surface of the door. A variety of materials are used for the core of flush doors—paper or cardboard arranged in a 'honeycomb' pattern, straw and in some newer doors, polystyrene foam. With a chisel, cut back the filling inside the cut-out areas to a depth of about $\frac{1}{2}$in. (13mm) from the edge of the ply. This will enable you to position strips of $\frac{1}{2}$in. timber between the two outer surfaces of the door, flush with the sides of the cut out area. Then put plywood panels in the cut-out areas and fix them with strips of moulding as described above. The edges of the cut-out areas will probably be a bit messy, so arrange your mouldings to hide them (see Fig.2). This is the most elaborate way of imitating a panelled door, but the only one that gives an entirely 'real' effect.

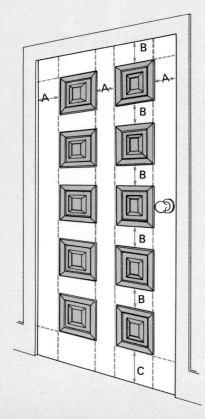

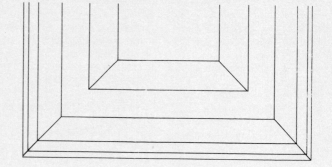

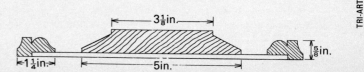

3⅛in.

1¼in.　5in.　⅝in.

TRI-ART

Tailor made
kitchen units : 1

Fitted kitchen units are one of the most popular DIY projects. For simplicity of construction, most commercial units are made up from prefabricated parts, but if you do the job yourself you will not only be able to introduce a distinctive design of your own, you will also be able to incorporate better materials and still save about one third of the price.

Manufactured units, however well made, can be produced only in a limited number of sizes. Making your own units means that you can 'tailor' the units to fit exactly into the space available in your kitchen.

General construction details

Most home-built fitted units consist of a framework of timber over which cladding of some sort is fixed. Although this is a satisfactory method of construction, the measuring, cutting and fitting of the frame does require a degree of technical competence.

This method uses, where possible, man-made boards such as chipboard or blockboard. The thickness and rigidity of these materials eliminates the necessity for framing many pieces of timber, and reduces the cutting to the squaring up of several boards.

The boards are available in a wide range of sizes, and if the unit is designed around the board sizes that are available in your area, you can eliminate a lot of sawing. These boards are usually veneered in different woods, or are surfaced with a plastic laminate. The latter is

particularly suitable for the tops of units because the laminate will withstand hard wear much better than wood veneer. Initially, the laminated boards will cost slightly more than the type with a wood veneer, but when the veneer has been treated with at least three coats of poly-urethane varnish—essential for kitchen furniture—then the difference in price almost vanishes.

Chipboard with a wood veneer is easy to cut with a fine-toothed panel saw. The edge that is exposed by sawing is covered over with an iron-on veneer strip specially made for this purpose and sold in rolls of the correct width.

Plastic-laminated chipboard is more difficult to cut, and although this can be done with a fine-toothed panel saw, a bench power saw makes a better job of it. Fit the saw with a hollow-ground cabinet saw blade with very fine teeth—22 or 24 to the inch. Any chipboard that is exposed by sawing can be covered with wood veneer strip if the edge is out of sight, for example at the back of the unit, or it can be covered with a strip of matching laminate that will have to be cut to size with a handyman's knife. If your retailer has the facilities, ask him to do this for you, because small strips of laminate chip easily.

The basic construction is a box, as shown in Fig.1, with butted joints that are either pinned and glued, or joined with screws and angle brackets. There are several proprietary fitments for making square joints, but you will have to decide whether these fittings are suitable, because they could in certain circumstances interfere with the fitting of drawers.

There is a wide variety of hinges available for fitting the doors, and of course this would be dictated to a certain extent by the doors you fit, which could be inset, flush, or sliding. A good hinge to fit is plastic or brass piano hinge. This hinge runs along the whole length of the door, distributing the weight and stresses evenly. It is sold in long strips and is easily cut to length—and you do not have to make housing joints to fit it.

Although any sort of handle can be fitted to the doors, this unit has inset handles made from 'L' or 'J' section aluminium strip as shown in Fig.7. This is cut with a hacksaw, and can be drilled quite easily with a hand-drill. If possible, use aluminium screws, so that the screw heads will match the strip.

Although screws are used for certain joints, care must be taken not to screw down too hard in chipboard, which has limited holding strength. The best method of screwing into chipboard is by drilling holes large enough to take fibre plugs such as Rawlplugs. The plugs are then glued into the holes with a woodworking adhesive, and provide a holding area almost as strong as solid wood.

Whenever nails or pins are used in chipboard, they should be dovetailed for maximum holding power.

Fig.1. Although these three units are different in appearance, they are all constructed the same way. The shell in each case is identical, but the interiors and external fittings vary slightly.

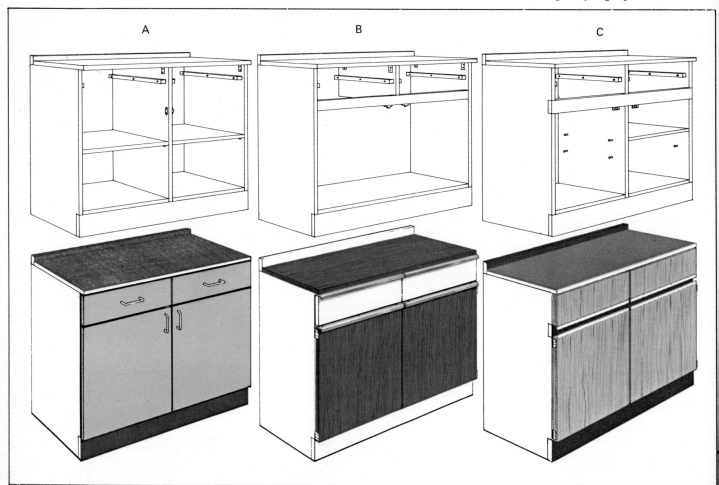

Planning and design

When you build your own units, you have the opportunity of making furniture to your own design and achieving something that is a little different and unobtainable in any shop. So give the design some careful consideration. Obtain brochures of the types of board available in your area so that you can select the veneer or laminate—or a combination of both—to suit your kitchen. The brochures will also list the dimensions of available board, so that you can plan the sizes of your units.

First list your requirements in terms of measurements. Decide on an approximate height for the working surfaces of the units, and the horizontal length into which they must be fitted, along with the necessary depth. You can then study the brochures and plan the unit.

Fig.2. *Prefabricated drawer kits only require glueing and fitting together.*
Fig.3. *When tapping joints together, a block of wood placed across the working surface will prevent unsightly hammer marks.*
Fig.4. *The drawers are faced with a panel of chipboard glued and screwed to the front.*
Fig.5. *One of the side panels. The battens for the plinth, bottom shelf and drawers have been screwed in place, and the recesses cut for the plinth and both cross members.*
Fig.6. *The unit top is held in place with angle brackets or similar fittings after the cross members and plinth have been fitted.*
Fig.7. *Fitting the drawers. Aluminium angle strip can be used in place of handles.*

If you want to incorporate drawers in the unit(s), then this might alter the design aspect. This unit uses one of the many prefabricated drawer kits on the market, which saves a lot of time and is only fractionally more expensive than making your own. Using this method, you will have to obtain the drawer sizes first so that the unit is built with sufficient clearance for the drawers to be fitted. But if you are making the drawers yourself this point is unimportant as they can, if necessary, be fitted after the rest of the unit has been made.

Cost will obviously be a consideration. As mentioned, wood veneered chipboard costs almost as much as plastic laminated chipboard if you varnish the wood properly, so this is really only a question of which type of surface you prefer. However, if you want to paint the finished units, blockboard would be a much cheaper alternative to chipboard. The disadvantage of blockboard is that it is not sold in as wide a variety of panel sizes as chipboard, and so it must be accurately cut down to size. This is not much bother if you are used to cutting squared angles accurately, but otherwise you will have to ask your DIY shop or timber merchant to do the cutting for you. In most cases they will charge you for this, which increases the cost of the unit; and they will rarely cut the panels as precisely as you require.

If you are clever with your calculations, you will be able to design a unit that requires very little cutting. Where it is necessary to cut a board, try to ensure that the cut edge is hidden from sight. For instance, in this unit a recess is

cut out of the bottom front edges of the side panels, but the exposed chipboard is covered by the 'kick panel' or plinth which fits into it at each end, and the side edges of most panels are not cut at all.

Making the drawers

The use of prefabricated drawer kits, while simpler from the aspect of construction, has one disadvantage in that you are limited to the sizes in the available kits. However this is not quite as serious as it appears. As shown in Fig.4, the actual drawer is faced with a much larger chipboard panel. This means that you can get away with a drawer that is slightly smaller than the drawer opening by increasing the horizontal thickness of the batten used as a drawer runner on either side.

The alternative is to go all the way and build the drawers yourself. The method of doing this is described in CHAPTER 14.

Marking and fitting the shell

The shell is the unit minus doors, drawers and shelves.

The only involved piece of cutting in it—and even this is relatively easy—is in the sections marked A in Figs.8-9.

Mark, and cut if necessary, the three A sections. Ideally these should be constructed from standard chipboard panels, veneered on all surfaces and edges. But in your area chipboard might be sold in a variety of widths and only one length (usually about 8ft or 2.5m), in which case you will have to do some cutting. Make

2

3

4

5

6

7

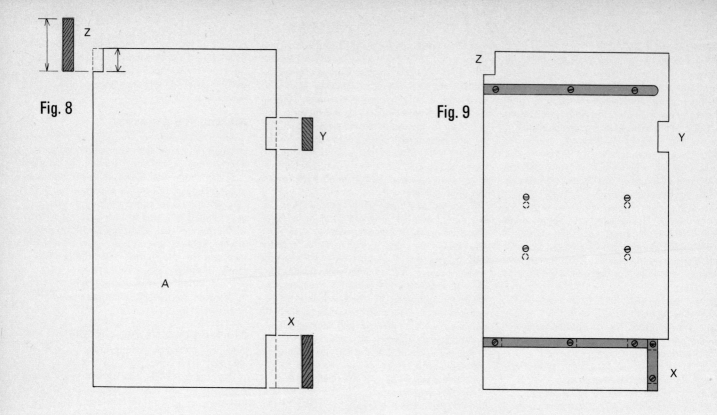

Fig. 8

Z

Y

A

X

Fig. 9

Z

Y

X

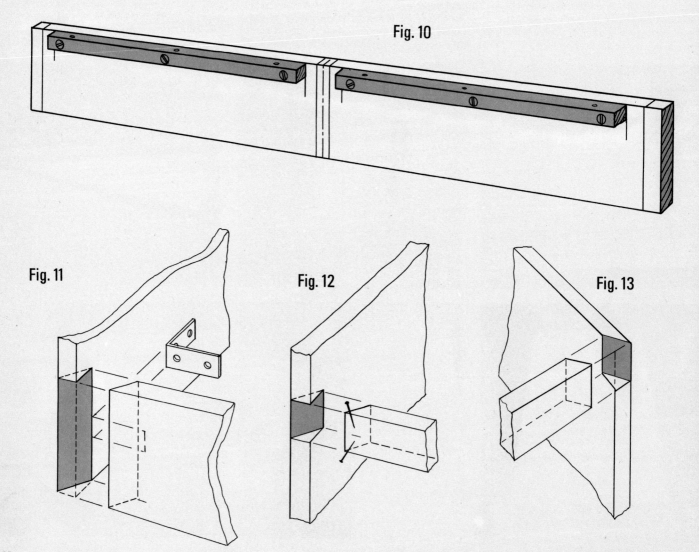

Fig. 10

Fig. 11

Fig. 12

Fig. 13

sure that each section or panel has absolutely square edges by using a try square at the corners and measuring the diagonals. This applies throughout the construction of the unit.

There are three recesses to cut in each A section, to house joints X, Y and Z. These are marked and cut, as shown in Fig.8, to the thickness and depth of each piece that is to be inserted. The height of the top edge of joint Y is dictated by the depth of the drawers you are fitting. The height of the bottom edge of joint Z depends on the amount you want the splashback to project.

When the cutting has been done, trial-assemble the unit by inserting sections C, D and B (Fig.14) into their recesses, to enable you to check that the unit is square.

With a try square and straight edge or rule, mark the positions of all shelf and drawer supports, remembering to mark both sides of the centre A partition.

Drill holes for the shelf support fittings.

Fig.8. The side panels—these are identical to the centre panel if one is fitted—must be recessed to take joints Z, Y and X.

Fig.9. Hardwood battens are screwed to panel A to provide support for the plinth and bottom shelf, and runners for the drawers.

Fig.10. The rear of the plinth or kickboard has hardwood battening screwed on to provide a fixing surface for the bottom shelf.

Figs.11-13. Cross-members need not be housed straight through; they can be mitred and fitted as shown if you do not want to cut away any of the surface veneer or laminate.

Fig.14. Front view of the complete unit. This version has a centre partition, but as you can see in Fig.1, this is not essential.

Fig.15. Three different types of drawer runner. The top version requires grooved drawer sides, but the other two do not.

Cut the drawer runners to length, and drill and countersink them to take No. 10 screws. Smear glue on the backs of the runners, and secure with screws of a length ½in. or 12.5mm longer than the thickness of the runners, set properly in glued-in wall plugs to take the weight of the drawer.

Weight of the drawer

The bottom shelf supports are attached next. These can be of 1in. x 1in. or 25mm x 25mm ramin, as shown in Fig.10, or you can fit metal angle brackets of the type used to fix the top panel F in place. In any case, screw on short vertical 1in. x 1in. or 25mm x 25mm battens flush with the front surface of the recess for joint X to take the kick panel, as shown in Figs.5 and 9.

Trial-assemble the unit again, and check that panel F fits properly. Lay the angle brackets that will hold the underside of F to the sides of the A sections temporarily in place, and with a bradawl mark out the positions of the screws.

The inside face of each end A panel, and both sides of the internal A panel, should now appear as shown in Fig.5.

Assembling the shell

Although you can do this by yourself, it is much easier if you have some assistance.

Lay section B down on a flat surface and glue and screw the A partitions to it as shown in Fig.1.

Gently stand the unit upright and glue and pin sections C and D in position. Use 2½in. or 65mm pins for this and pre-drill the pin holes in C and D with a 3/64in. or 1.20mm drill bit. Check the unit for squareness and leave it while the adhesive sets.

Fit the base shelves E in position, holding them in position by screwing into the underside through the ramin battening. Or, if you have fitted angle brackets, screw these to the shelves.

The unit top F, is now placed in position and screwed in place through its angle brackets.

The back of the unit is covered with a sheet of exterior grade hardboard, glued and pinned at 2in. or 50mm intervals. The proper fixing of this section is very important because it not only covers the back but also acts as a bracing for the whole unit.

Fix the shelf supports in position.

Doors and drawers

All that is left is to fit the fascia panels to the fronts of the drawers, hinge the doors, and fit handles and door catches.

The drawer fascias are fitted quite easily if you spread some impact adhesive over the front of each drawer panel and the back of each fascia. Fit the drawers in position, pushing them back as far as they will go. Place one fascia accurately over a drawer space, hold the fascia in position with one hand and, with the other hand, reach underneath the drawer immediately behind and slide it forwards until it touches the fascia. The impact adhesive will hold the fascia in position until you can screw it in place from the inside.

The doors are made from standard width boards, but you may have to cut the boards to length if you have not been able to design the unit to fit the appropriate sizes. If you have to cut the boards at all, cover the cut edges with wood veneer strip and place these edges so that they are at the door bottoms.

The placing of the door hinges is particularly important. Whenever door hinges have to be screwed into chipboard, it is essential to drill the screw holes and glue fibre plugs in position as described above, to hold the screws.

Finish off by cutting the aluminium angle strip for the handles, drilling and countersinking holes in it, and fastening it to the fibre plugs set in the edge of the door panels and drawer fascias.

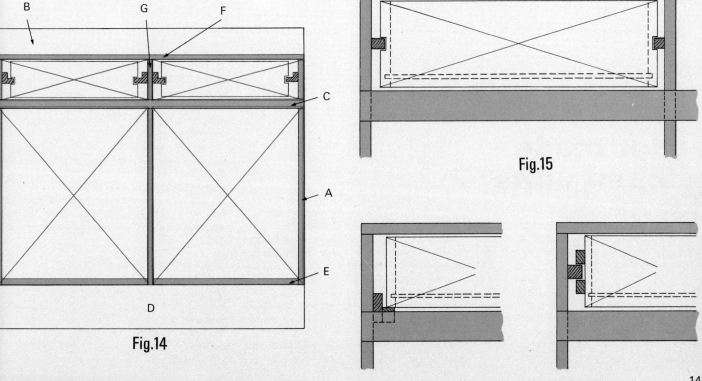

Fig.14

Fig.15

DON KIDMAN

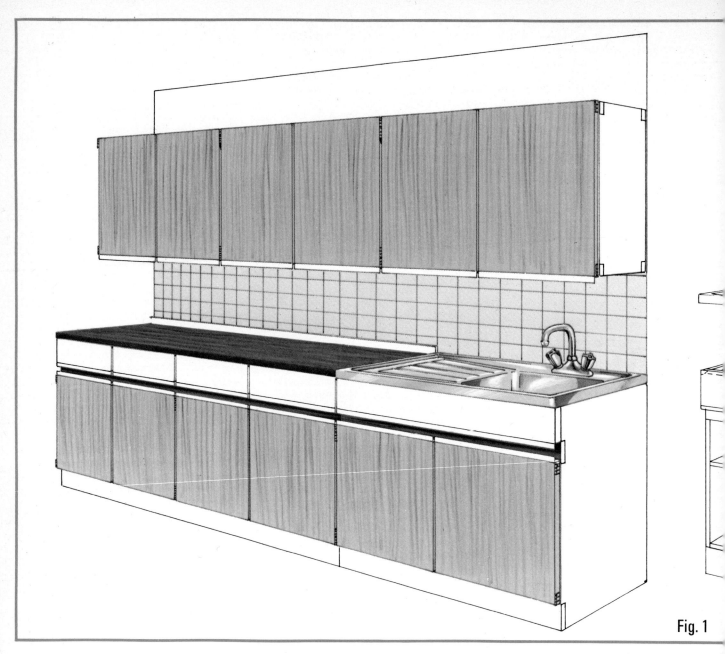

Fig. 1

Tailor made kitchen units : 2

When you have built the kitchen unit, the same techniques can be applied to make hanging wall units to match and a base to house the kitchen sink.

Building and fitting the sink unit will of course involve some basic plumbing, but this is not at all complicated—even if you want to change the location of your present taps. If not, the work only involves removing and replacing a few nuts and washers.

General construction details

The woodworking techniques involved here are virtually the same as those used in the first stages of this project, but some parts of the units have to be strengthened because of the different stresses involved.

For instance, the hanging wall cupboards are fixed to the wall by two cross-members at the back of the unit, and the weight of the unit and its contents creates severe strain on the side panels where the cross-members join

them. So these joints have to be stronger than in an ordinary freestanding unit. And the freestanding sink unit should always have a vertical partition wall for maximum strength, as shown in Fig.1, because even the smallest sink will hold the considerable weight of several gallons of water.

The sink itself can be fitted as a complete top, as shown in Fig.1, or inset as in Fig.2. With the second type, you do not have a draining board, although a portable one could be devised. In some cases, for example in a very small kitchen, this disadvantage could be more than offset by the increased working area.

The hanging wall unit

Resist the temptation to make these units too deep. As already mentioned, there is considerable strain on the points where the unit is fixed to the wall, and it is surprising how heavy it can become when filled with crockery and the like.

If you plan to tile the wall underneath the

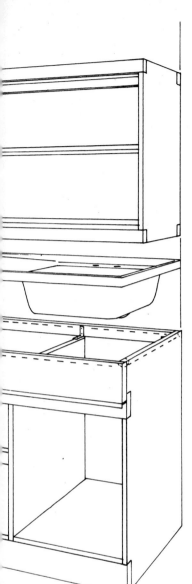

Fig. 2

DON KIDMAN

Fig.1. This shows a run of kitchen units, one of them fitted with a sink bowl and draining board; and hanging wall cupboards above. A construction outline is on the right. It is important that the sink unit has a central partition to add strength to the frame when the sink is holding the considerable weight of several gallons of water.

Fig.2. The sink bowl can be fitted flush with the work surface to save space.

hanging units, then try to arrange the distance between the top and bottom units to equal the number of whole tiles that come nearest to 20in. (505mm) as shown in Fig.1. This will save you the bother of having to cut tiles to fit.

It is not necessary to use expensive panelling for the top of the unit. Hardboard or thin plywood is sufficient. But the top must be screwed—not nailed—in position to add strength to the carcase. This applies throughout; all joints should be glued and screwed, using the fibre plug method described in the first part of this article.

Apart from the middle shelf, which is optional, and the doors, the hanging unit consists of 12 pieces: two sides and a base of laminated or veneered chipboard or blockboard; four lengths of 2in. x 1in. or 50 x 25mm hardwood for the cross-members; three lengths of 1in. x 1in. or 25 x 25mm hardwood for the supports underneath the base panel; and two hardboard sheets to cover the top and back.

To construct the unit, first cut out the recesses for the ends of the cross-members. As shown in Fig.4, these are all 2in. or 50mm high and 1in. or 25mm wide and located at each corner of each panel. Cut the recesses fractionally undersize and pare them down with a handyman's knife, using the end of a cross-member for direct fitting.

Cut the cross members to length, then glue and screw the 1in. x 1in. battening supports for the bottom shelf along the inside base of the side panels and along the inside edge of the front bottom cross-member. This side battening is fixed in position so that the top

edge is level with a line drawn between the tops of the recesses shown in Fig.4.

Trial assemble the unit, check for squareness, then cut the base panel or shelf to length and glue and screw it to the battens.

Drill screw holes through the ends of the cross-members, and also into the edge of the side panel to take the fibre wall plugs, and glue these in position. Note that the screw holes for the rear members must be dovetailed for extra strength, as shown in Fig.5.

When all the fibre plugs are set in position, assemble the sides, base and cross members. Check for squareness and leave for the adhesive to set.

Screw the hardboard rear covering in place. Don't be tempted to leave this part out, because it braces the whole carcase. If you don't want to see a hardboard panel when you open the doors, paint the hardboard or use plywood instead.

The hardboard top can be fitted at this stage but this will make it more difficult to screw the rear cross-members to the wall. If you

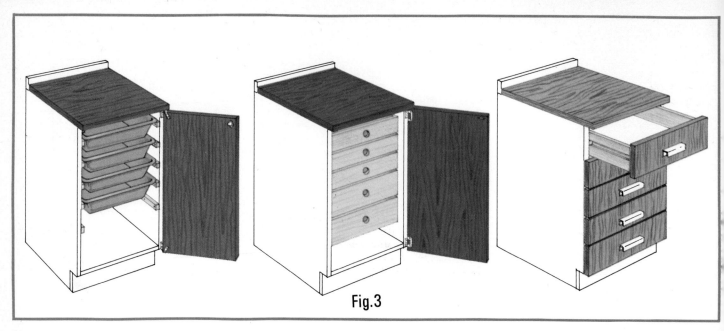

Fig.3

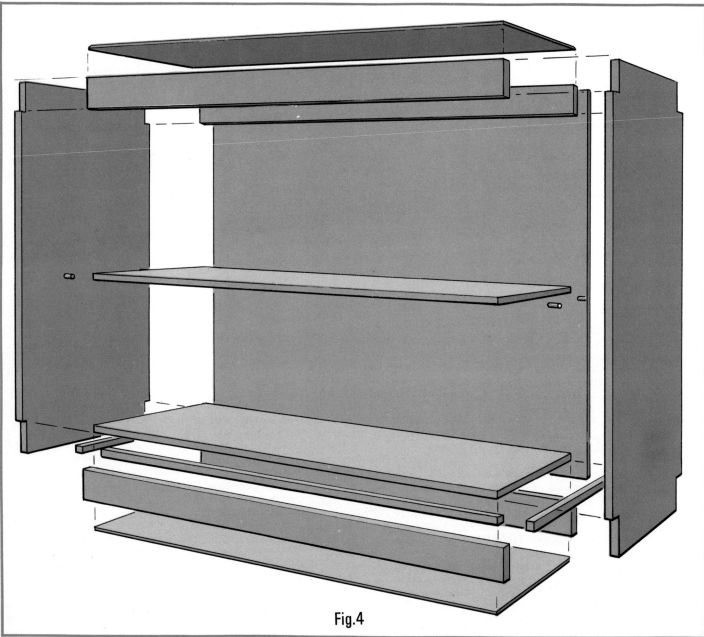

Fig.4

handle the unit gently, it is generally more convenient to drill holes for the top panel, then leave the fitting until the unit has been fixed to the wall.

The inside joints at each end of the top rear member must now be reinforced with two angle brackets, as shown in Fig.5.

Cut and fit the doors. The method for this has been described, but note that for these units the aluminium angle strip that forms the handle is placed underneath the bottom edge of the doors, in the same way as the handle fittings for the drawer fronts.

The unit is secured to the wall by 3in. or 75mm No.10 screws passed through the rear cross-members at 6in. or 150mm intervals. If you use good-quality masonry plugs or other wall fittings (your do-it-yourself store will advise), this size and spacing of screws will be quite adequate.

The sink top

Broadly, there are two types of sink; the

Fig.3. There are many variations you can make to the basic unit. Some of these are shown in the preceeding chapter. Here, the storage receptacles are simple slide-in trays or drawers. The handles shown are made from short lengths of aluminium angle strip.
Fig.4. Exploded view of the hanging wall cupboard. Because of the considerable weight the unit will hold when laden, all joints and the top, bottom and rear panels, must be securely screwed in place using fibre plugs.
Fig.5. The two rear cross members will take the most strain, so the securing screws must be dovetailed and the joints reinforced with brass or steel angle brackets.
Figs.6 and 7. Edge detail of two sink units.

integral bowl and draining board, shown in Fig.1, and the bowl that has to be inset into the surface, as in Fig.2.

When you are purchasing your sink top, bear in mind the possibilities of fitting a waste disposer which will be a great asset in the kitchen. A sink bowl to take a waste unit has a much larger drain hole than the usual kind, so it might be as well to purchase a bowl made to take a disposal unit in case you want to fit one in the future.

If you want to fit a sink that has an integral draining board, you must make sure that the external dimensions will fit the top of the unit. The unit shown in Fig.1, for instance, is 21in. or 533mm deep from front to back—the same as the width of the chipboard panels used for the construction of the unit base.

Some sink tops rest flush on the top of the unit, and are sometimes secured with screws or bolts passed through holes in a turned-in lip on the underside. But the usual kind has a rim that fits over the top outside edge of the unit. Both types are shown in Figs.6 and 7.

An inset bowl can be fitted in either of two ways. In one, the bowl is purchased already set in a sink top, with a watertight seal. The bowl fits flush with the work top and there are no raised edges whatever. This type, of course, has to be ordered to the dimensions you require. The other kind is simply a bowl with a flat flange round the rim. A hole of the same diameter as the inner rim of the bowl is cut out of a solid sink top, a sealing compound is smeared over the underside of the flange, and the bowl is dropped into position. This type needs a separate draining board higher than its rim.

To make a laminated board with a suitable hole to take a bowl, buy the laminate and

chipboard separately. Cut to identical sizes, then cut the hole in the laminate with a sharp knife. Glue the laminate to the chipboard, then cut out the chipboard hole with a fine toothed general purpose saw.

The area of wall behind the sink will have to be covered with a splash-proof surface of some kind. This usually takes the form of ceramic tiles as shown in Fig.1, though you could use a washable vinyl wallcovering.

The sink base

This is constructed in the same way as the unit described in the first part of this project, except that this unit has no drawers, and the top front part of the unit, where the drawer fascias would be, has a 6in. or 150mm wide length of chipboard running across it instead, as shown in Fig.1. It is essential to fit a central partition to support the sink, as already described. The more internal bracing there is, the better.

Plumbing

Unless you wish to change the location of your taps, this will only entail turning off the hot and cold water supplies at the mains. The next step is the disconnecting of the tap and drainage pipe fittings, replacing or re-fitting the sink, then re-fitting the taps and sink trap.

If the taps are to be relocated, then you will have to extend or shorten the existing pipework. This involves cutting and fitting pipes—the manufacturers of drainage pipes will supply information on these jobs.

If you do change the location of the taps, it might be necessary to knock through an outside wall to fit a new drainage pipe, and of course, make arrangements for the construction of a new drainage channel or soakaway to carry away waste water.

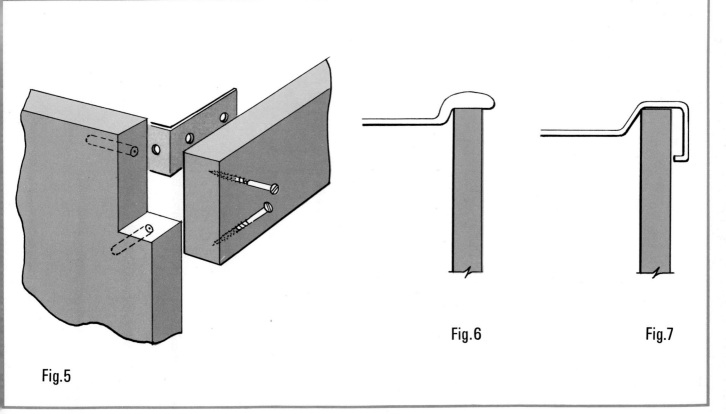

Fig.5

Fig.6

Fig.7

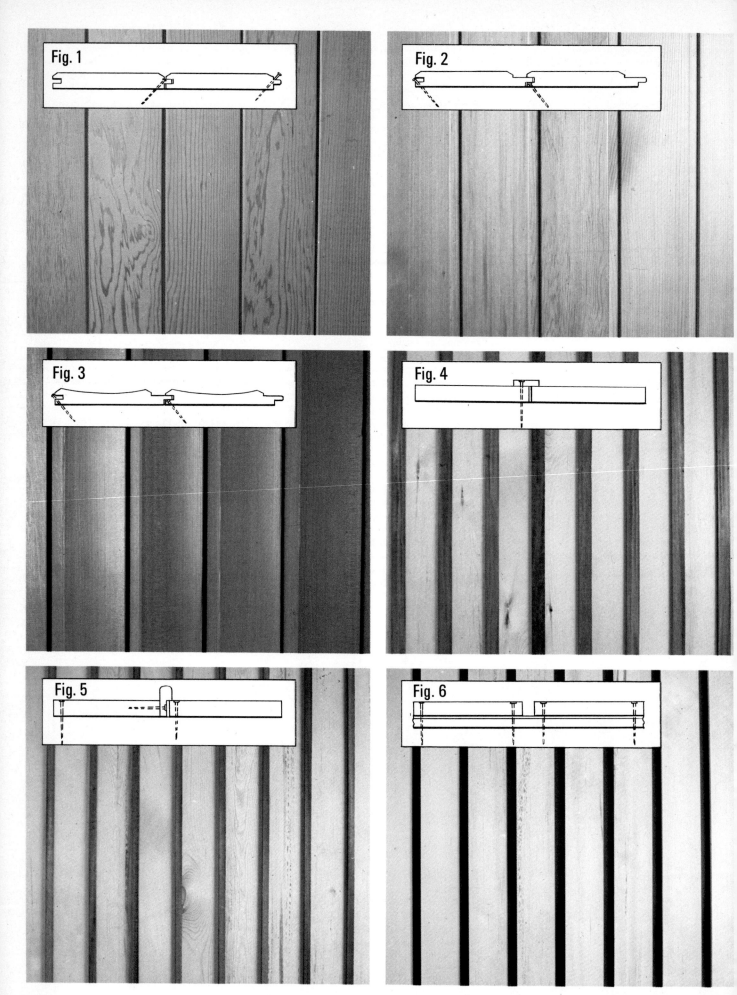

Fig. 1

Fig. 2

Fig. 3

Fig. 4

Fig. 5

Fig. 6

Timber panelling with a difference

The rich appearance of timber lining can be spoiled by careless application. Always check as you go along to see that boards are straight and joints are even.

Horizontal positioning

Horizontal T and G boards are fixed in the same general manner as vertical ones. It is best to position the first board an inch or two (25mm to 50mm) above floor level, with the tongue upwards. This board should be skew-pinned into the underlying battens through the surface of the timber about $\frac{1}{2}$in. (12.7mm) up from the bottom edge. It should then be skew-pinned through the battens along the edge of the tongue so that the groove of the next board will cover the pins. Use a spirit level over this first board to see that it is level.

Continue fixing the boards up to ceiling level, cramping each board and checking your boards every once in a while to see that they are level. If they are slightly out of line, you can make adjustments by cramping very closely where necessary. Just below the ceiling, leave a $\frac{1}{4}$in. (6.35mm) gap for air to circulate.

If you cannot buy boards which will fit the entire breadth of your wall, you will have to join two or more lengths. Use a *splay joint* (Fig.7), so that no gap shows at the joint. Stagger the joints so that they fall randomly across the wall.

Diagonal positioning

An unusual and often effective means of fixing boarding is diagonally. Visually, the best angle to fix diagonal boarding is at 45°.

Instead of beginning with short lengths of board in a corner, begin at a position along a wall where your first board will be a full length one, as in Fig.8 (you can save short offcuts to fill in the corners later).

To establish the length of the full-length boards required, cut 45° angles in two boards with a mitre block (Fig. 9). Be sure to cut these angles in the direction in which you want the

Opposite page. Internal timber lining comes in a variety of styles, using either T & G boards or cheaper square-edged planks. **Fig.1.** *Conventional, v-jointed T & G.* **Fig.2.** *Flat surfaced, extended tongue T & G.* **Fig.3.** *Concave surfaced, extended tongue T & G.* **Fig.4.** *'Board-and-batten'— hardwood batten over square-edged planks.* **Fig.5.** *Square-edged planks with moulding fixed to one board at joints.* **Fig.6.** *Square-edged planks fixed over hardboard which has been pre-painted in a contrasting colour.*

boards to slope. Position these boards one beside the other and hold them against the wall, adjusting them until they are straight and you get the correct length. Fix them together by nailing two short battens across them (Fig.10). These boards will give you a gauge from which you can measure the first full-length board. The others can be marked from this—but check as you go that the lengths do not need to vary slightly because the floor and ceiling are 'out'. If your walls are very high, it is not advisable to attempt to cover them in diagonal boarding, since you may not be able to buy long enough timber to avoid a jumble of joints.

For boards which are to slope from left to right, work from left to right across a wall, with the tongue on each board facing towards the right. Hold your first board in place with nails partly driven through the surface of the timber on the right-hand side only. This first board (A in Fig. 8) is fixed loosely so that later boards can be 'sprung' into position, as previously explained. 'Secret fix' the remaining full-length boards into position by skew-nailing them through the tongues and punching the nail heads below the surface of the timber. Cramp each board as you go along and check, occasionally, to see that all the boards are at the correct angle of 45°.

To fill the top left-hand corner (above board A in Fig.8) start by temporarily stacking a row of offcuts against the wall along the left-hand edge (you will need to hammer in a few nails to keep these boards up) until you can accurately judge the size of the board that will fit into the extreme corner (C in Fig.8). Cut this board, which will be a right triangle, about $\frac{1}{4}$in. (6.35mm) oversize along the two sides forming the right angle, and fix it in position. (Cutting the board oversize will ensure a tight fit later).

Once you have fixed board C into the corner, you can remove the offcuts from the wall and with boards which have been cut to the correct size, work progressively back towards board A, cramping each board along the tongue-side as you go. However, the last three or four boards should not be nailed into place at first, but 'sprung' into position. If the last board does not quite fit, the tongue-edge may be smoothed with a plane slightly so that it can be eased in. After these boards are in place, nail them through the surface and punch in the nailheads. Fill the holes with a wood filler.

To fill the bottom right-hand corner, follow roughly the same process. When you have six or seven boards to go, stack offcuts as you did before until you can ascertain the size of the corner piece (see Fig.8). However, do not fix

the corner piece first. Rather, work from left to right, springing the last three or four boards into place and surface nailing them.

Doors and windows

When fixing timber boarding around doors or windows, one of the most important considerations is to see that the unsightly rough edges of the planks do not protrude beyond architraves or flush edges. Usually, the thickness of the battens plus the thickness of the planks will be greater than the thickness of your architraves. If you have doors or windows which are set into walls without any architraves, you will encounter the same problem. And anyway, most elaborate moulded architraves will look awkward set against this sort of boarding.

Such problems can be solved by first removing all existing architraves. Try to pry them off from their external edges so as not to damage adjoining woodwork. Windows may present many more problems than doors, since you will have to remove not only the architraves but also the window sills (or trim them flush with the wall surface).

On *masonry* walls, replace the old moulding (or, in the case of doors and windows without any architraves, make a new moulding) with square-section timber (1in. x 1in. or 25mm x 25mm or whatever size necessary) which will be slightly thicker than the *combined* thickness of your battens and your planks (see Fig.11). The same procedure will work on *timber* walls, but only if 'nailing' is available around the door or window—either to existing studs or to battens which you provide.

When putting up vertical planks around a door, work progressively across one side of the wall from a corner to the door, then across the wall space above the architrave, and then across the wall on the opposite side of the door to the end of the wall. If you are planking around a window, follow the same plan—side, top, side—and then fill in the area across the bottom of the window. To fit boards around the corners of architraves, scribe and cut boards as in Fig.12.

When putting up horizontal boarding around doors, begin on one side of the door and work up the wall to the top of the architrave, butting the boards against the architrave as you go.

Then, work up the wall on the other side of the door in the same way. Finally, fix boards across the wall area above the architrave, staggering any splay joints which you may need to make. For boarding around windows, follow essentially the same procedure, beginning with full-length boards at the bottom of the wall and working up and around the walls on either side of the window and then across the top of the window. It is important that you stagger any splay joints across the wall so that they do not make an unsightly line.

Fixing the boards diagonally around doors and windows often is not visually pleasing, and problems can arise in matching the slope of the boards and the angles. Consider carefully before you attempt to fix diagonal boarding on a wall area broken by doors and windows.

If you do fix diagonal boarding, be absolutely sure that you measure and cut your boards so that they can be butted smoothly against any architraves and are all positioned at a 45° angle.

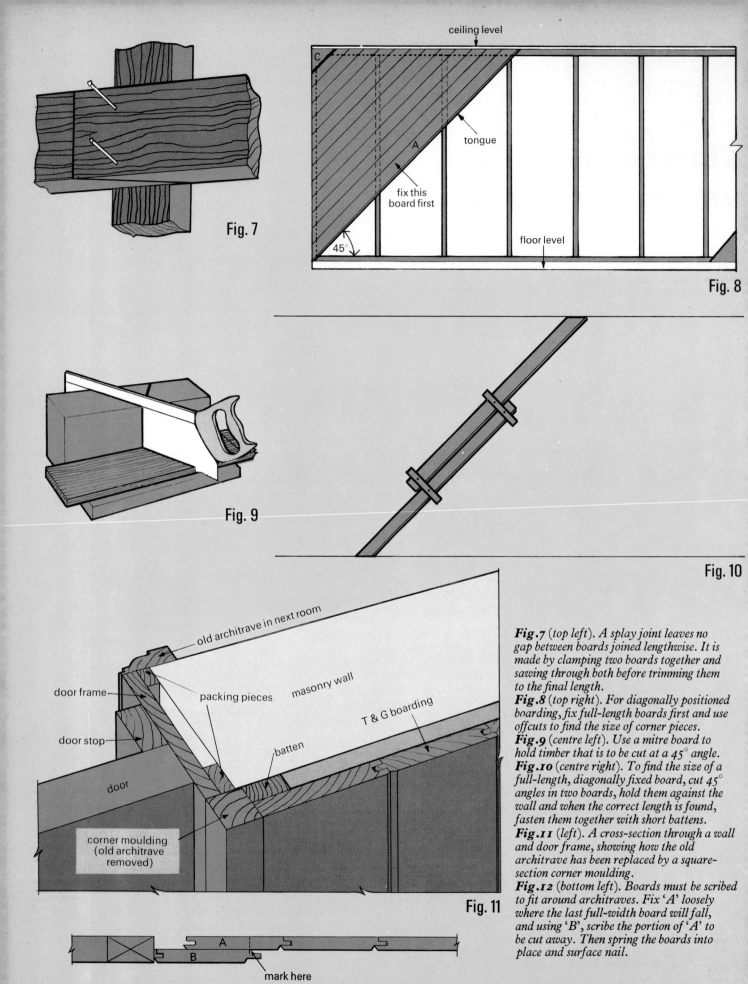

Fig. 7

Fig. 8

ceiling level

C

tongue

A

fix this
board first

45°

floor level

Fig. 9

Fig. 10

old architrave in next room

door frame

packing pieces

masonry wall

door stop

T & G boarding

batten

door

corner moulding
(old architrave
removed)

Fig. 11

A

B

mark here

A

B

Fig. 12

Fig.7 (top left). A splay joint leaves no
gap between boards joined lengthwise. It is
made by clamping two boards together and
sawing through both before trimming them
to the final length.
Fig.8 (top right). For diagonally positioned
boarding, fix full-length boards first and use
offcuts to find the size of corner pieces.
Fig.9 (centre left). Use a mitre board to
hold timber that is to be cut at a 45° angle.
Fig.10 (centre right). To find the size of a
full-length, diagonally fixed board, cut 45°
angles in two boards, hold them against the
wall and when the correct length is found,
fasten them together with short battens.
Fig.11 (left). A cross-section through a wall
and door frame, showing how the old
architrave has been replaced by a square-
section corner moulding.
Fig.12 (bottom left). Boards must be scribed
to fit around architraves. Fix 'A' loosely
where the last full-width board will fall,
and using 'B', scribe the portion of 'A' to
be cut away. Then spring the boards into
place and surface nail.

Good looking bed platforms

Bed platforms can be an attractive addition to any room. A platform covered in carpet can integrate easily into an old fashioned setting while a naturally finished timber platform com- plements the clean lines of a modern home setting. Whatever shape or finish you choose for your platform, the construction techniques are not beyond the least experienced woodworker.

HEIDEDE CARSTENSEN/STUDIO HUELSTA

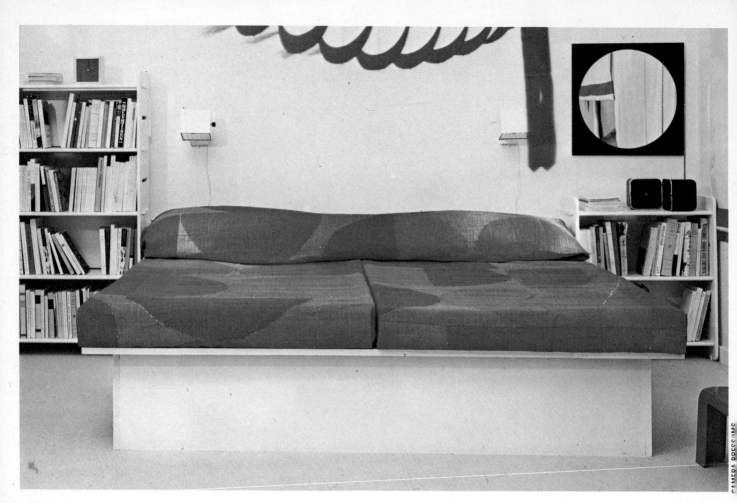

The basic construction of all bed platforms consists of the sides, the top and internal support struts. These are essential to prevent the top sagging. The method of strutting is the same whatever type of platform is built—the struts are evenly spaced, run the length and width of the box construction, and meet the box sides and each other at right angles. They are as wide as the distance between the floor and the underside of the top of the platform.

Design considerations

Before constructing a platform think hard about the shape of the room and the position the platform will occupy. Remember that the platform will be an almost permanent feature —even if it is not fixed to the wall and is free standing it will be too heavy to move with any ease.

It is a good idea to make a scale drawing of the room and position the platform on it. This will avoid mistakes in positioning the platform— the worst being not allowing sufficient space for the room door to open fully when the platform is in place.

The nature of the room in which it is to be used will influence the shape of the platform you choose. A rectangular bed platform will fit into any setting if it is finished suitably. A triangular platform would look odd in an old fashioned room and in a small room take up a great deal of space that could be better utilized. The height of the finished platform is a matter of taste but again the nature of the room should influence your decision. A very low platform will look out of place in a room with a

high ceiling whereas a high platform will tend to 'overpower' a low room.

Bed platforms can either be free standing or can be fixed to the wall. The advantage of free standing platforms is that they can be moved more easily than fixed platforms. Free standing platforms do, of course, involve using more materials than fixed platforms.

If possible construct the platform in the room in which it is to be used. It will be fairly heavy and will be awkward to move from place to place.

Materials

A variety of materials and combinations of materials can be used to build a bed platform.

—Timber is easy to work with, but it may prove expensive to make the whole platform with this.

—Timber and blockboard is again expensive, but the pieces can be easily fixed together and will be very strong.

—Timber and chipboard is cheaper and will make a platform of adequate strength.

—Chipboard only is not really practical. It is cheap and light, but fixing the parts together strongly enough will prove difficult.

—Timber with a $\frac{1}{2}$in. (13mm) hardboard top is workable, but the top may need extra support to prevent it sagging.

Finishing the platform

The way in which you intend to finish the platform will effect the type of wood material you use and how you fix the pieces together.

The finished platform can be carpeted over

with either the same type of carpet used on the floor or a contrasting one. This method of finishing thoroughly integrates the bed platform with the rest of the room. If this finish is used, the sides of the cabinet do not have to be particularly well finished—they could, for example, be made of chipboard with the constituent parts screwed in place through the outer face.

The sides can be covered in plastic laminate. Again fixing can be done through the outer surface of the sides before the laminate is applied. Fix the plastic laminate in the usual way, using a contact adhesive.

A natural solid timber finish will make a feature of your bed platform. The constituent parts should be screwed together into the inside face of the sides or fixed through the sides with brass screws. The sides can be sanded smooth and treated with several coats of clear polyurethan varnish.

Shape of the platform

A rectangular platform is the easiest to construct and its shape is conventional enough to fit all types of rooms. It can be made slightly wider than the bed mattress to allow space at each side for various bedside items such as a clock and bedside light.

Platforms that are constructed exactly to the mattress width can have a rim or lip incorporated in them. Here the top of the platform is recessed below the level of the top of the sides. The disadvantage of this design is that if the rim is more than a few inches deep, making the bed will prove difficult. It may be necessary to use a duvet or continental quilt as bedding

Above left. In this bed platform, the top extends beyond the sides. It has an attractive clean finish, though the butt joints at the corners are rather unsightly.
Above right. Bed platforms add an extra touch of distinction to the modern bedroom. The colours of the mattress cover and bolster are attractively mirrored in the blinds.

in this case. Triangular and tee-shaped platforms can also be constructed by adapting the basic construction techniques described in this article.

Free standing bed platforms

With rectangular bed platforms the sides are constructed and fixed together in a box shape first. If you use timber and the bed platform is to be over 12in. (305mm) high you may have trouble getting planks of this size. You can overcome this by planing the long edges of two planks square, applying glue and butting them together to give a plank of the required height. If chipboard is used there will be no problem getting boards high enough for the job.

If you intend to cover the sides of the platform they can be cut square and the ends simply fitted at right angles to each other. These joints will, however, look unsightly if a natural timber finish is intended.

One good way of making neat corner joints is to mitre the end edges of the sides. Cut the side pieces to the exact size required. Set a bevel gauge to 45 degrees and, with a pencil, mark inwards from the outside edge of the ends of all side pieces. It is a good idea to stand the

pieces together in a rough box shape—this will ensure that the mitres are marked in the correct way. Clamp a piece of waste wood to the end to which you will be planing to avoid knocking the corners off the ends, and plane down to the lines, holding the boards upright in a vice. Check that the mitres are flat by drawing a straight edge along their surfaces.

Other neat corner finishes can be achieved with exposed dovetail joints (described in full in CHAPTER 11) or rebated and butted joints (refer to CHAPTER 9). This last-named is probably the easiest to make.

If the sides are to be covered in plastic laminate then the shape of the corner joints will not matter. The platform may, however, have a rim with the top panel inset to take the mattress. From above, a joint made by butting the end edge of one piece to the end of the wide surface of another piece will look unsightly. In this case a hardwood edging strip, mitred at the ends, can be glued to the tops of the side pieces after they have been screwed together in a box shape.

If you are using a natural timber finish on the top of your platform, two of the sides will have to be rebated to accept the ends of the top planking. This is to avoid having a lot of end grain showing. The depth of the rebates should match the thickness of the planking. And you will have to cut the internal struts that much shorter.

Assembling the carcase

The method of fixing the sides together, and the internal struts to the sides and each other,

is to use wood blocks on the insides of the corners. Blocks of 1½in. x 1½in. (38mm x 38mm) hardwood are glued and screwed to the two pieces which meet at right angles. If it does not matter whether screw heads appear on the outer surface of the sides, the pieces are fixed through the sides, screwing into the wood blocks. If it does matter, you screw through the blocks and into the inner surface of the sides.

Start by fixing together the four sides to form an open box. As well as four wood blocks cut to size, you will need eight pieces of 2in. x 1in. (51mm x 25mm) timber the same length as the wood blocks, and four G cramps. With a coarse toothed saw, cut a groove lengthwise down each of these pieces of 2in. x 1in. Stand the sides of the box together, apply pva adhesive to two surfaces of each of the glue blocks, and put the blocks into place. Now use a pair of the 2in. x 1in. pieces on each corner as packing for the G cramps—the notches will stop them sliding off the corners (Fig.4). Make sure the box is in square, then leave the glue to dry.

Now fix the blocks more securely. Depending on the considerations given above, screw the blocks to the sides through either the blocks or the sides.

Fixing the struts

The next step in making the bed platform is to construct and fix the internal support struts. The space between the struts will depend on the type of material to be used for the top—a chipboard or ½in. (13mm) hardboard top will require more support than solid timber planks.

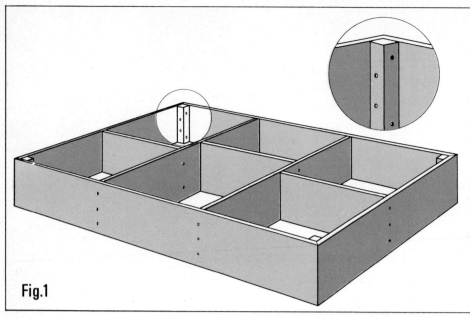

Fig.1

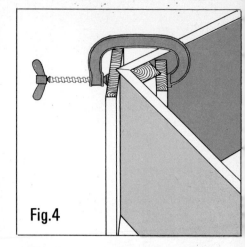

Fig.4

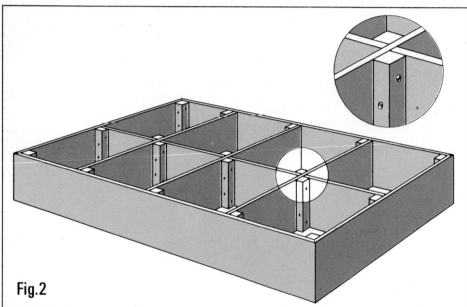

Fig.2

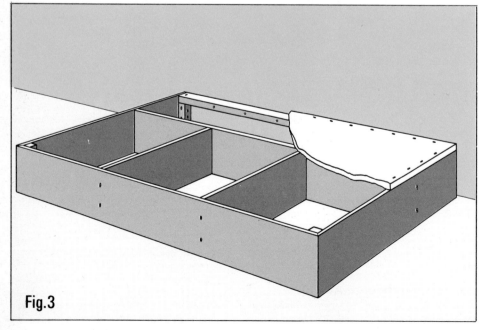

Fig.3

Fig.1. *The timber struts in this platform are staggered so that they can be screwed directly to the other struts. The struts are fixed to the sides from the outside of the box.*
Fig.2. *If chipboard struts are used it will be difficult to screw them to each other, so glue blocks are used at all the corners.*
Fig.3. *In a fixed platform, pieces of timber are fixed to the wall to support part of the top. The long strut, which in a free standing platform would be centrally placed, is offset so that the short struts can be fixed to it and not to the wall.*
Fig.4. *This method of glueing and cramping wood blocks at the corners ensures that they do not move out of place while the glue dries.*

If solid timber is used the struts can be placed about 2ft (610mm) apart, but space them about 18in. (458mm) or less apart for chipboard or hardboard.

For a simple rectangular platform the struts should be as deep as the sides of the box. For all platforms the struts should meet at right angles. Fig.1 shows an ideal method of placing struts within a solid timber box where screwing from the outer face of the sides is suitable. The struts that run parallel to the long sides are staggered to allow them to be screwed to the struts that run parallel to the short sides.

Fig.2 shows how the struts are placed in a chipboard box. Wood blocks are used at every internal corner as well as at the corners of the four sides.

The top board or boards can now be glued and screwed into place with countersunk screws. If one single sheet of chipboard or hardboard is used, cut it slightly oversize. Plane two of the sides that meet at right angles exactly square. Measure and mark, on the top of this board, the positions of the internal struts —this will tell you where to drive screws later. Spread pva adhesive on the top edges of the platform sides. Lay the top panel in place, marked side upwards, with the squared edges flush with two edges of the box. Screw the board to the sides and to the internal struts, the positions of which you have marked. Remove any waste from the top panel with a smoothing plane so that its edges are flush with the sides of the box.

If the top is to be formed of solid timber planks then they are fixed so that their long edges butt together. Cut each plank slightly

HEIDEDE CARSTENSEN/STUDIO UMSTAETTER

oversize. Square a line on the wide surface of each plank, close to one end. Saw and plane to these lines taking care not to damage the corners of the boards when planing.

The planks can either run the long way or the short way across the box. Running them the long way will involve less sawing and planing. Lay the first plank with its long edge and squared end flush with the sides of the platform and screw it into place with counter-sunk screws. Drive the screws into the edges of the side panels and into the supporting struts that run at right angles to the first plank of the top. Lay and fix each subsequent plank in the same way as the first. When all the planks are fixed remove any waste wood from the unsquared ends with a plane.

For a recessed mattress

A variation on the simple rectangular design is to construct the platform with a lip or rim. The mattress fits snugly between the sides and on the recessed top. In this case the internal supporting struts are not as deep as the box sides—they are of a depth sufficient to give you the depth of recess you require. Fix the sides together in a box shape in the manner described above and fix the internal struts in place at the bottom. Now place struts on the

inside surface of the platform sides so that their tops are level with those of the other struts.

The top panel or planks for this type of platform will have to be cut exactly to size before being screwed into place. When this is done fix the top in the manner described above.

Fixed platforms

If your bed platform is to stand against a wall you may decide to fix it permanently in place. To do this the top board or planks will have to be screwed to a support strut fixed to the wall and the side pieces fixed to the floor.

First, fix however many sides there are together, using wood corner blocks. Then mark the position the bed platform will finally occupy on the wall. Make the marks where the insides of the side pieces meet the wall at right angles. Draw lines through these marks at right angles to the floor. Along these lines measure and mark a distance that equals the depth of the side pieces of the platform, measuring from the floor. Draw a line through these marks parallel with the floor. Screw a length of $1\frac{1}{2}$in. x $1\frac{1}{2}$in. (38mm x 38mm) wood to the wall so that its top edge is exactly on these lines. Fix a block of wood to the end of each bottom edge of this piece, at right angles to it and running to the floor. Now fix the ends

Above. This brightly finished platform can be moved about on small castors.

of the sides that run to the open end of the platform to these wood blocks.

The next step is to position the strutting. The struts that run to the wall from the side of the platform parallel to it can be fixed to wood blocks screwed to the wall. Or, if you prefer, one of the internal struts that runs parallel to the open wall side can be moved further towards the wall than would be the case in a four sided platform. This will reduce the strength of the platform a little but the primary purpose of struts is to support the top. This arrangement of struts will do this as adequately as any other (see Fig.3).

The platform can now be fixed to the floor. Again the method of doing this is to use wood blocks—this time screwed to the floor and to the bottom of the inside of the sides of the platform. The number of blocks required will depend on the size of the platform. If, for example, the platform measures 6ft 8in. x 5ft (2033mm x 1525mm) six blocks $1\frac{1}{2}$in. x $1\frac{1}{2}$in. x 6in. (38mm x 38mm x 152mm) will be sufficient. Place two on each long side, each about 18in. (458mm) from the ends, and one on each short side, positioned near the centre.

153

Bargeboards, fascias and soffits

Fascias, soffits and bargeboards sound like exotic pieces of equipment. Perhaps you think you haven't got any. But the chances are that if you live in a detached house or a semi, you have them on your roof—and they probably need looking at.

Fascias, soffits and bargeboards are the facings of the eaves and gables of a house. They cover up the ends of the rafters and the gap between the top of the walls and the edge of the roof.

The positions of the different boards are shown in Fig.1. A *fascia* is set on edge under the lower edge of the roof covering, and is nailed to the ends of the rafters. Buildings with hip roofs have fascias all round; those with gable roofs have fascias along the horizontal sides only.

A *soffit* is a horizontal piece reaching from the lower edge of a fascia to the wall behind it. Some old houses with narrow eaves have no soffits; instead, the fascia is mounted directly against the wall.

A *bargeboard* is like a fascia, but runs up the slope of a gable instead of horizontally. For this reason, bargeboards are generally found in pairs. They frequently have soffits underneath them where the sloping roof edge projects beyond the flat gable front.

None of these pieces plays any part in supporting the roof. They are for weather protection and to neaten the appearance of the outside of the house. When they rot or break, they can easily be removed or replaced—and should be before the damage goes too far. A leaky fascia can admit rainwater to a house. Gutters are generally mounted on fascias, too. If the wood becomes rotten, heavy cast-iron fittings may fall off—a remote possibility, but a dangerous one.

Ladders and towers

One of the main difficulties in repairing the upper works of a house is reaching up there in safety. An ordinary ladder is sufficient for inspecting them, but not for repairs. This is because the pieces of wood you will be working with are large and heavy. You will almost certainly need a helper to hold them up while you fasten them in place—and two people on one ladder won't go.

The simplest, but not the most satisfactory solution, is to use two ladders, one for each person. They should be securely fastened in

Opposite page. The old houses in this village have a rich variety of bargeboards, fascias and soffits decorated with fretwork.

place at the top and bottom—otherwise you could have a serious accident.

The trouble with this method is that you will have to keep moving the ladders along the house, which will involve a lot of climbing up and down, tying and untying of ropes and a lot of other boring work. What you really need is a platform at roof level, so that two people can move about with reasonable freedom.

The cheapest way to achieve this is to go to a tool hire firm and hire two ladders considerably longer than the distance from ground to roof, some planks for a platform and a pair of special *ladder brackets.* These are large metal brackets that hook over the rungs of a ladder set at 60° to the ground and support a narrow platform two planks wide. The platform can be moved up and down the ladder by dismantling it and hooking the brackets on to different rungs.

A ladder scaffold offers a useful increase in mobility. But it has serious drawbacks. It is rather hard to climb on to, unless you have a third ladder to rest against the platform. Otherwise you have to climb round the edge of the ladder, which is awkward if you are carrying a plank. Also the entire structure has to be dismantled to move it to a new part of the roof.

A better idea, though slightly more expensive, is to hire a *platform tower.* This is a tower made of prefabricated scaffolding-like sections that slot together to reach to any height within reason. At the top, there is a generous-sized plank platform. The whole structure is mounted on wheels, so that it is easy to move around on a flat surface. The wheels lock with screws to hold the tower still. It can also be set up on uneven ground by means of adjustable *jacking bases,* which fit on in place of the wheels. The top platform is reached with an ordinary ladder.

Fascia repairs

Fascias can be of various types, and before starting work you should find out what kind you have.

They may be fastened direct to the ends of the rafters, without a soffit—this type of fascia is generally found in houses over 60 years old. The fascia may not quite touch the underside of the roof covering (Fig.2), in which case all you need to do is prise it off. Or it may hold up the bottom row of tiles or slates (Fig.3). In this case, removing the fascia will cause the tiles that are resting on it to sag. But they are (or should be) quite adequately fastened in place at the top, and will not fall off. Check that this is so by lifting up one tile and pulling at it to see if it is firmly fixed. If it comes away, you will have to remove the bottom row of tiles before you lever

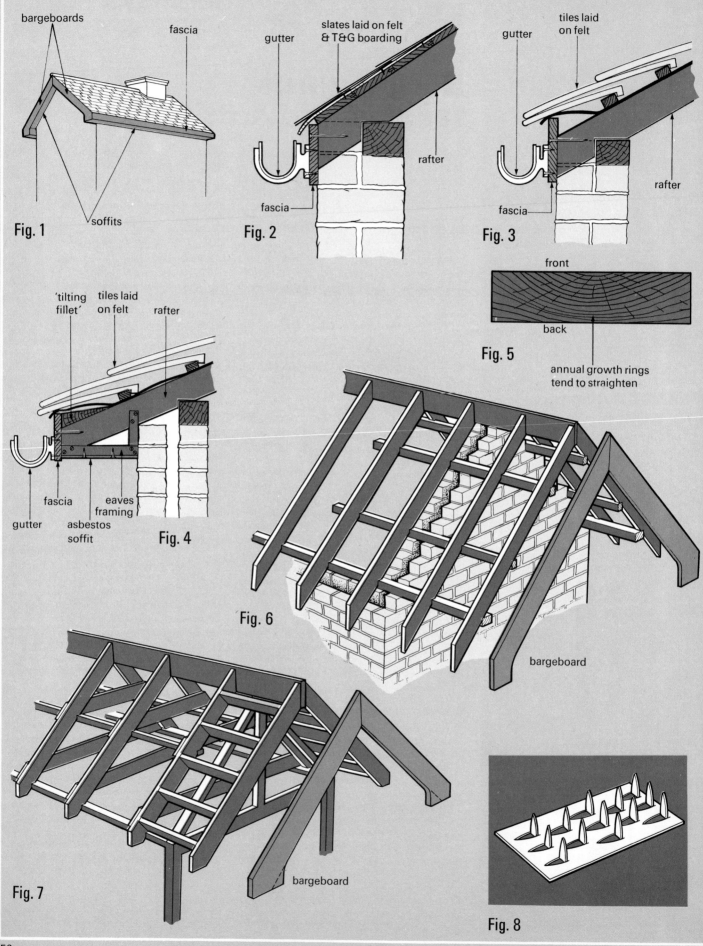

bargeboards

fascia

soffits

Fig. 1

gutter

slates laid on felt & T&G boarding

fascia

rafter

Fig. 2

gutter

tiles laid on felt

fascia

rafter

Fig. 3

front

back

Fig. 5

annual growth rings tend to straighten

'tilting fillet'

tiles laid on felt

rafter

fascia

gutter

asbestos soffit

eaves framing

Fig. 4

Fig. 6

bargeboard

Fig. 7

bargeboard

Fig. 8

he fascia off, and replace it afterwards.

Fascias with soffits behind them rest against (but are generally not nailed to) the light wooden frames that support the soffits (see Fig.4). Soffits in modern houses are generally made out of asbestos sheeting, which is fragile. In any case, the wooden frame that supports them should not be treated too roughly when you are prising the fascia off. If you are unlucky enough to have a fascia with tiles on top and asbestos below, you will just have to work extra slowly and carefully.

Fascias nearly always have gutters attached to them, and the brackets which hold them should be carefully unscrewed from the fascia and fastened to the new fascias after these are installed.

The order of work for replacing a decayed fascia is as follows. First, inspect the fascia and determine whether it needs replacing or just repainting.

Then, if it needs replacing, hire and erect a suitable scaffold. Unscrew the gutter brackets and carefully take down the gutter—you will probably need a friend to help you. While the gutter is down, you might as well mend and paint it.

Carefully prise off the old fascia, trying not to break it. There are several ways of doing this. You can use a hammer and nailpunch to drive all the nails right through, or drive wooden wedges up behind the fascia. Or use an old chisel to cut away enough wood around the nails to reach their heads with a crowbar or a claw hammer. Carry the fascia down, measure it, and order a suitable length of new timber in the same size, or in a size that can be cut to fit. Most fascias are 4in. or 5in. x 1in. (100mm or 125mm x 25mm).

Rake out all the old birds' nests and dirt between the rafters and inspect the bituminous felt (if any) under the tiles for holes. Patch it if necessary. Paint the exposed ends of the rafters with primer to protect them from rot.

Examine the new fascia. The annual growth rings of the tree it was cut from will show at the ends. The fascia should be installed so that the concave side of the rings is at the front (see Fig.5). When it warps (as it inevitably will), if it is this way round, the curvature it takes on will tend to straighten the rings and so press the top and bottom of the board against the wall, providing an efficient seal against moisture. Cut a small notch out of the back to mark it, then prime and paint the fascia on both sides, and,

Fig.1 (*opposite*). *A guide to where the various eaves facings of a roof are fitted.*
Fig.2. A fascia may be completely separate from the rest of the roof covering.
Fig.3. Or it may support a row of tiles.
Fig.4. A modern roof with wide eaves, an asbestos sheet soffit and a 'tilting fillet'.
Fig.5. Mount the new fascia this way round.
Fig.6. The roof structure of a typical British house, showing the bargeboard mounting and how the end rafter is supported.
Fig.7. The roof of one Australian type of timber house. The end rafter, on which the bargeboard is mounted, is supported by a ladder-like row of 'lookout rafters'.
Fig.8. A gang nail or ply plate.

most important, both ends, since the end grain of the timber is the most vulnerable to rot.

When the paint is dry, carry the fascia up. Hold it in position (pushing the tiles up to their original height if necessary) and nail it on with *one* large nail into each rafter, hammered through about 1in. (25mm) from the top edge. This will allow it to expand and contract with changes in humidity. Use galvanized nails for this, and all other outside jobs.

If the roof covering is unsafe or fragile, use screws in pre-drilled holes instead of nails to avoid breaking tiles or dislodging them by hammering.

Finally, screw the gutter back on, using a spirit level to ensure that it slopes down at least 1in. in every 10ft (25mm in 3m).

Soffit repairs

Soffits may be made out of asbestos sheet or timber boarding. The tendency in modern houses is to use asbestos, as a fire precaution and because it is cheaper. The soffits are mounted on an eaves framing nailed or screwed to the rafters (see Fig.4). This is generally made of 3in. x 1½in. (75mm x 38mm) timber in modern British houses. The asbestos sheet is normally ⅛in. (3mm) thick.

Asbestos is rotproof but fragile, and needs replacement only if it is broken. It is tricky stuff to work with, because if you press it too hard it cracks. The best saw to cut it with is a sheet saw, which has a replaceable hacksaw blade mounted on a thin sheet-metal backing so that there is no frame to get in the way when cutting along wide sheets.

An alternative method of cutting asbestos is to treat it like glass. Scribe a deep scratch along a straight-edge where you want to cut it; the tang of a file cuts as good a scratch as anything; or you can use an old, discarded chisel. Then lay the sheet down on the straight-edge so that the scratched line is immediately over it, and snap it along the line by pressing down hard on both sides of the straight-edge.

Holes can be drilled with an ordinary twist bit. With the British variety of sheeting, you have to drill holes for nails as well as for screws, because hammering a nail through the asbestos may well split it. With the softer variety used in, for example, Australia, you can nail straight through. But it is wise to drill holes at corners; otherwise they might crack off if you nail too near them.

To replace an asbestos soffit, first try to unscrew the old one, or pull out the nails if it is nailed on. Use the old soffit as a template to mark out the new one. If it is too badly broken to do this, measure the space where it fitted.

Cut the new soffit to shape and drill and countersink screw holes in it. If you are replacing several pieces, they should be butt-jointed, not overlapped, and both adjoining pieces screwed to the frame they meet under. It is essential to give asbestos adequate support, or it will just break again.

Install the new soffit, being careful not to over-tighten the screws or you may split the sheet. Use black japanned screws to prevent rust marks. Leave the new sheet to weather for six months, to get rid of the chemicals from the manufacturing process, before painting it.

Wooden soffits are easier to work with. Often, however, tongued-and-grooved boards are used. If you are replacing only one of these boards, you will have to cut off the tongue on both sides of the old board to get it out. This is best done by drilling a large hole in the old board and inserting a pad saw. Replace the board with a plain-edged one, pre-painted on both sides.

Sometimes, particularly in old houses, plain-edged boards are found. These are very simple to replace.

The eaves framing is sheltered from the weather, and is unlikely to rot until the rest of the roof does. If it is rotten or broken, simply replace the bad parts with new ones of the same size screwed in place.

Bargeboard repairs

Bargeboards are very similar to fascias except that they are sloping. They are fastened in various ways, and may be flush with, or projecting beyond, the gable end.

In houses with brick gables (this includes most British houses) a bargeboard is generally nailed to the end rafter of the roof, which is supported on timber strips running between the end rafter and the stepped top of the brickwork (see Fig.6). In the equivalent fixing for a timber gable, the overhanging roof is supported on small 'look-out rafters' parallel to the purlin (refer to main diagram in CHAPTER 39) and holding up the main end rafter. The bargeboard is nailed to the main end rafter (see Fig.7). Sometimes, in the case of a rigid roof such as a corrugated-iron one, the bargeboard replaces the main end rafter. In this case the last row of sheet roofing will have to be removed to gain access to the 'look-outs'—if the bargeboard has rotted, some of these will almost certainly need replacing too.

Whichever way the bargeboards are fixed, they are only nailed on and can easily be prised off. The angled joint at the top is often braced at the back with a *ply plate* or *gang nail* (see Fig.8), and cannot be dismantled until you have taken both boards down together. This is a two-man job, and best done by loosening the ends first and working towards the middle.

Some old houses have decorative barge-boards cut into intricate shapes. These can be copied with a power jigsaw by tracing the shape direct from the old board to the new one. Or you can put up a plain replacement. To get the correct angles at the top and bottom, the most accurate (if time-consuming) way is to nail one bargeboard temporarily in place, and use a spirit level held upright to mark both the apex and the cut-off at the bottom. Then you make the second board a 'mirror-image' of the first.

Even the plainest bargeboard generally has a wider part at the bottom end to hide the soffit. The best way to make this is to glue a piece on with urea formaldehyde glue and cut it to shape when the glue is dry, using a coping saw or power jigsaw if it is curved.

New bargeboards are installed in exactly the same way as fascias. It is best to prime the end-grain, then gang-nail both boards of each gable together at the correct angle and put them up in one piece. This gives extra strength, even if it does make them rather hard to lift.

Wet rot, dry rot and woodworm

Wet rot, dry rot and woodworm can seriously affect the structural stability and the value of your home. Once the first signs of attack are noticed you should take action to rectify the damage and remove its cause.

Timber is one of the most important materials in house building. Many houses, including a large number of older British houses, are timber framed, and in the great majority of homes the roof framing, the floors, doors, window frames and skirting boards are all made of timber.

Attacks on timber by wet rot, dry rot and woodworm are, therefore, extremely serious and unless they are checked quickly they will severely weaken the structural stability of the building. In order to know what to do about these timber attacks, it is necessary to understand their nature.

Woodworm

Woodworm is the collective name given to a variety of wood-boring insects whose larvae (grubs) feed on timber. In Britain, there are three main types of wood-boring beetle—the common furniture beetle (*Anobium punctatum*), the house longhorn (*Hylotrupes bajulus* among others), and the death watch beetle (*Xestobium rufovillosum*). Of these the first is by far the most prevalent. This is because the death watch beetle attacks nothing but old hardwood and the house longhorn only the end grain of softwood, but the furniture beetle attacks any timber. Not only does it do the most damage, therefore, but there is no limit to the area it will attack. Most houses have it in some degree.

In New Zealand, where it is known as 'borer', and in Australia anobium is just as common as in Britain. There are local varieties of woodworm, too—some of them highly destructive— but the techniques for dealing with them are the same as for anobium.

The difficulty with woodworm is that its presence is not noticed until some damage has been done. The furniture beetle lays its eggs in cracks in unpolished wood and when the larvae emerge from the eggs they tunnel into the wood. This process lasts about three years, at the end of which the adult beetle emerges from the wood. The exit holes made by the beetle are the first sign of the presence of woodworm.

Dry rot

This is a very serious form of timber attack. It is caused by a fungus (*Merulius lacrymans*) which spreads through porous materials and lives on the moisture within the holes, or hollow parts, of the grain of timber.

Below. *Part of a wall plate that has been subjected to a long attack of woodworm. Structural timbers seriously weakened in this way are dangerous and must be replaced.*
Inset, left. *A skirting attacked by dry rot. Dry rot will spread to sound timbers so you must remove the infected wood from the house.*
Inset, right. *Sheets of dry rot fungus.*

RENTOKIL

The fungus develops only in ideal conditions —in damp, badly-ventilated areas such as hollow floors, cellars and gaps behind skirtings. Timber attacked by the fungus becomes dry and crumbly—hence the name 'dry rot', which is something of a misnomer.

Wet rot

Wet rot is also a fungus growth and develops where timber is in contact with wet or damp surroundings. Wet rot is by no means as difficult to deal with as dry rot, and if it is treated in time, the damage can be kept to a minimum.

General treatment

Since the correct treatment for wet rot is considerably different from that for dry rot, it is essential to be able to differentiate between the two. Remember the type of conditions in which the two develop—wet rot where timber has been in contact with moisture caused by leaking pipes and water tanks or inadequate damp proofing, and dry rot in damp, still, un-ventilated areas. In general, dry rot is not often seen in houses built after 1945—this is because of improvements in construction techniques and, in Britain, the requirement under the Building Regulations that all new buildings should have a damp-proof course.

Both dry rot and wet rot are fungus attacks but dry rot is caused by one, and only one, particular type of fungus. The growths produced by this fungus appear as sheets of silver-grey or mouse-grey colour with patches of lilac and bright yellow.

In the case of dry rot, it is essential that all the affected timber and any timber within a radius of about 5ft of the damaged area be removed. The damaged timber should be burnt immediately— it is infectious to sound wood.

Any plaster surrounding the damaged area should be hacked away to a distance of 3ft or 1 metre with a bolster and club hammer. Use a wire brush to clean all surfaces thoroughly, including brickwork, surface cement, adjoining timbers and pipes. Collect the dust with a vacuum cleaner and remove it from the house.

Apply two coats of a proprietary liquid fungicide to all the surfaces you have brushed clean. Use dry, well-seasoned timber to replace the removed timber. Coat the new timber with fungicide, standing its ends in a bucket of fungicide for a few minutes so that the fluid can soak into the end grain. Methods of fixing re-placement timbers are described below.

You should also remedy the situation that allowed the dry rot to develop in the first place. Air bricks can be inserted in the walls to increase ventilation. The damp-proof course, if there is one, may be defective. You can install a new physical dpc but this a long job and a chemical dpc may be your best bet.

The treatment of wet rot is much simpler than that of dry rot. Once the initial cause of the dampness has been remedied and the timbers dried out you may not even have to cut away the damaged area. This type of rot is not infectious, and spreads only in wet conditions.

If the timber has been seriously weakened, however, you will have to remove the damaged area and replace it. You can test the extent of the damage by pushing a strong, pointed tool into the damaged timber—a bradawl is ideal for this. If the bradawl can be pushed right into the timber the rot has severely weakened the sub-structure of the timber and the rotted part will have to be cut away and replaced. Treat the replacement timbers with fungicidal fluid as described above.

If the damage is not severe, the existing timber can be left in place and strengthened in the manner described below.

The problem with woodworm, as stated earlier, is that the attack becomes apparent only after the adult beetle leaves the timber. Once exit holes appear you know that at least one generation of woodworm has attacked the timber.

A mild attack of woodworm can be dealt with by painting the damaged area with proprietary woodworm fluid, as described below. If the damage is severe, or if you can see the pencil-sized holes made by the larger varieties—which means that the inside of the wood will have been seriously weakened—the timber will have to be removed.

Furniture

This is not attacked by wet or dry rot, but is susceptible to woodworm. Furniture can be treated by brushing woodworm fluid on all the unpainted surfaces and injecting the fluid into the exit holes so that it penetrates deep into the wood. Pay particular attention to the bottoms of table and chair legs, which are usually left roughly cut and to the bases of wardrobes and cupboards which are often made from rather cheap material. Woodworm fluids will not penetrate paint but, if you intend repainting, you can mix an insecticide powder into the undercoat.

Ensure that you use the correct type of wood-worm fluid—some materials will damage pol-ished surfaces, others will not.

To treat pieces of furniture, first remove all dust and dirt from the article. Remove any drawers and shelves from the article, turn it up-side down and brush on the woodworm fluid, working it well into any cracks. Follow the manufacturer's instructions when applying the fluid. Treat any drawers and shelves.

The fluid, after this surface treatment, pene-trates to a depth of about $\frac{1}{8}$in. (3mm). To kill larvae deep in the wood this treatment should be followed by an injection treatment. Here the woodworm fluid is forced deep into the wood.

There are several types of proprietary injector available. A useful one consists of a soft plastic bottle with a nozzle fitted with a plastic washer near its end. The nozzle is inserted into the larger exit holes up to the washer, which forms a tight seal. The bottle is then squeezed, so that the fluid is pumped into the wood. If the job is done properly the fluid will be forced along all the galleries formed by the larvae.

Leave the article for a few days, then wipe off any unabsorbed insecticide from the surface with a dry cloth. Fill the exit holes with wood filler; if any new attack of woodworm occurs the new exit holes will then be noticeable.

Mouldings

If skirtings, architraves and picture rails are attacked by woodworm they can be removed, treated and replaced. (Details of how to do this are given in CHAPTER 37). If dry rot is present, they must be removed and burned.

You may wish to minimize the extent of dis-ruption caused by this process. Remove the damaged article from its fixing and coat the back, unpainted side with woodworm fluid. Brush the fluid onto the end grain and on to any fixing plugs and groundings. If you use this treatment you will not have to repaint the moulding after you nail it back in place.

If you intend to redecorate anyway, remove the damaged moulding. Strip the paint from its surfaces with a proprietary paint stripper or blowlamp. Brush woodworm fluid on to all the surfaces and inject it into the exit holes at 3-4in. (76-102mm) intervals. If the exit holes are not so conveniently placed, make new holes with a bradawl.

Leave the timber for a few days, then wipe unabsorbed fluid from the surfaces, refix the mouldings and paint them.

Doors and window sills

These timbers are particularly susceptible to wet rot, as they are constantly exposed to the weather. They may also be attacked by wood-worm.

Door sills are the bottom part of the frame of the door. They are sometimes called thresholds. They help provide a weatherproof seal between the bottom of the door and the ground surface just outside the door. Wet rot in door sills can usually be prevented provided the sill is regu-larly painted. If it is neglected, however, and rot sets in, it will have to be replaced.

This is not an easy process as the frame of a door is made in one piece, with the components firmly fixed together. To remove the sill, you will probably have to hack out some of the brick-work around the bottom of the door opening.

In older constructions, the sill is mortised and tenoned to the door jambs, the vertical pieces which frame the opening. The sill in these door frames extends beyond the outer edge of the jambs into the brickwork. These protrusions are called horns or joggles. In newer door frames, the jambs and sill are jointed together with a box joint as shown in Fig.3. These give a greater glueing area than mortise and tenon joints.

Modern sills do not have horns, however, and so are easier to remove than older sills. In the case of older sills, you will have to chip the horns from the brickwork. You may also, for either type of sill, have to remove and replace timbers in contact with the sill, such as archi-traves. Methods of removing and replacing these are given in CHAPTER 22.

The jambs are also likely to be damaged, so you may have to remove some of the lower part of each jamb. The first step is to saw through the jambs just above the damage. Cut away as much as you can of the damaged sill and chip out the horns, if any, with an old chisel and mallet. You can make a new sill if you like, but it is easier to buy one ready-made. Cut lengths of timber to replace the cut-away parts of the jamb.

Cut a tenon on the end of each new jamb piece and mortises in the new sill. Then make a joint between the undamaged part of the jambs and the new pieces. A scarf joint (i.e. a straight,

159

Fig.1. *Though no longer permitted in Britain at ground floor level, you may find that the wall plate and joist ends are bedded in a brick course in an older house. If a joist has been badly damaged by rot or woodworm, cut it away from the wall plate and replace it with a new timber supported by joist hangers.*

Fig.2. *A top and side view of the Common Furniture beetle and (below) a top view of the House Longhorn beetle. In Britain the Furniture beetle is by far the most prevalent wood boring insect. Cases of severe attack should be treated by the removal of the damaged timbers. Timbers less badly affected can be coated with woodworm fluid which is*

also injected into the timber through the beetles' exit holes. The House Longhorn is particularly prevalent in certain warm areas of Britain. This beetles' exit holes can be $\frac{1}{4}$in. in size.

Fig.3. *A box joint joining a door jamb to the sill. If the sill is rotten you will have to cut through the jambs to remove the sill.*

Fig.4. *In areas of Australia, New Zealand and America the most damaging wood destroying pest is the termite. In areas liable to termite attack no timber should be left in contact with the ground. Treated timber house supports should be topped with metal caps, fixed by one of the methods illustrated, to prevent termites reaching the floor timbers.*

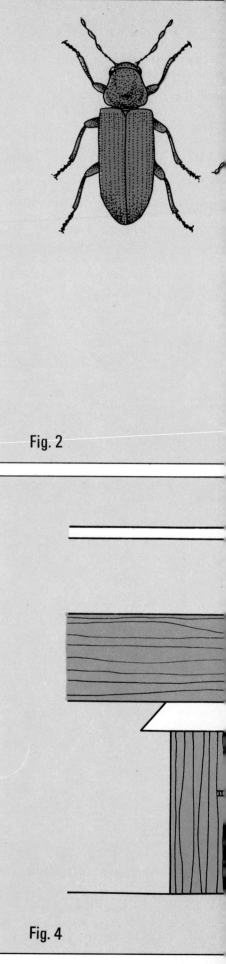

Fig. 2

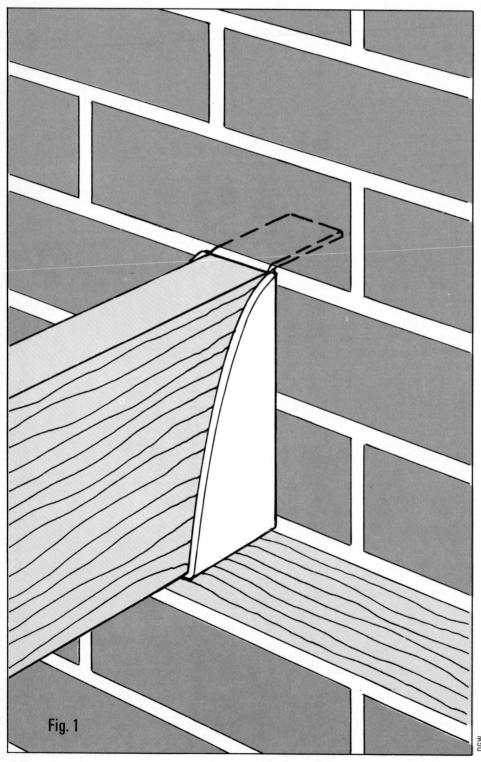

Fig. 1

DGW

Fig. 4

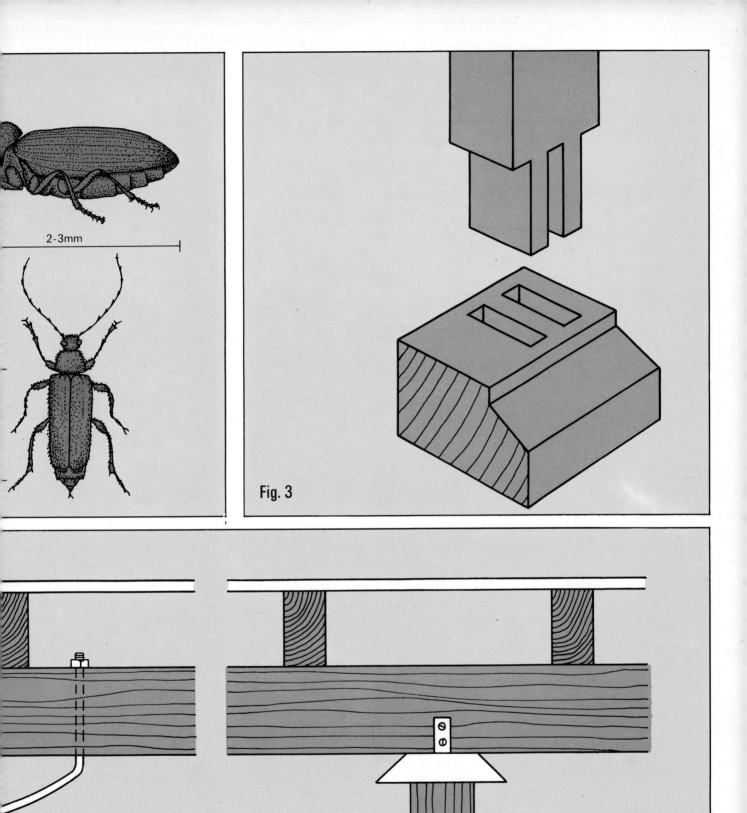

2-3mm

Fig. 3

but angled cut) is the easiest to make, though a halving joint is stronger. These joints should later be strengthened by screws.

Fit the new jamb pieces and the sill together, dry and check that the assembly fits into the space left by the removal of the old sill. If it does fit, take it out and glue the jamb pieces into the sill. Use a waterproof adhesive such as Cascamite, not a pva glue.

When the glue has dried, treat the assembly with fungicide or woodworm fluid, depending on the cause of the original damage. Knock wedges into the mortise-and-tenon joints. Slide the assembly into place. Put wedges under the sill to lift it up until the joint between the old and new jambs comes together. Screw this joint. Pack a fairly dry cement under the sill and into the gaps between the sill ends or jambs and the masonry.

If the door jambs are undamaged, you will still have to cut through them. Make the cuts where the top of the sill meets the jambs. This will have cut off the tenons or the tongues of the box joints. The new sill can be jointed to the jambs by means of false tenons, which are described in CHAPTER 5.

There are many variations in the design of window frames. Window sills can, in the main, be repaired in the same way as door sills, though some types of construction present particular difficulty. The box frame sill, for example, has jambs made up of a box-like section, each part of which is independently jointed to the sill. The only way to repair the sill successfully is to remove the window frame, study its construction and copy it.

Structural timbers

Damage to structural timbers is often revealed only when a house is sold and the new owner has it surveyed. Whether structural timbers are attacked by wet rot, dry rot or woodworm the remedy is often drastic, requiring the cutting away and replacement of the damaged pieces. Even to find the extent of the damage will involve considerable disruption. It may well be worth while to call in a firm specializing in insect and rot control to assess and rectify the damage—though this is expensive.

Wet rot is probably the least dangerous type of attack. If the wood is seriously weakened, it will have to be replaced. The method of assessing the extent of the damage was described earlier. If the timber is not badly damaged, it can be strengthened. This is done by glueing and nailing fresh timber to both sides of the damaged area after you have allowed the original timber to dry out. In the case of a joist, for example, nail pieces of 4in. x 1½in. (100mm x 38mm) timber to either side of the joist. The new timbers should extend a few inches either side of the damaged area.

The structural timbers most usually attacked by woodworm and wet and dry rot are ground floor timbers—joists, floorboards and wall plates. Roof timbers are not often attacked by dry rot as roofs are too airy and cold.

Woodworm in floor joists, wall plates and floor boards can be treated in situ but not if a large number of exit holes show that the attack has taken place over a long period. In this case, the timber will be seriously weakened and

dangerous, and should be removed and replaced. Timber damaged by dry rot should always be treated in this way because of the danger of infection.

Gaining access

To inspect joists and wall plates for damage you will have to remove some or all of the floorboards. If the floorboards are square-sectioned, remove them at intervals—about every fifth board—across the room. This will allow you to judge the extent of the damage with the minimum of disruption. If the floorboards are tongued and grooved you will have to remove them all, working from one side of the room. Lift the floorboards by forcing bolsters under their edges and levering upwards against the joist underneath.

Damaged joists

CHAPTER 19 gives full details of how joists are fixed to wall plates and the various positionings of wall plates relative to the house wall. The greatest problem, when removing and replacing joists, is presented when the wall plate and the ends of the joists are bedded into the brickwork (shown in Fig.5 of CHAPTER 18). In Britain, this type of construction is no longer permitted at ground floor level though it is still likely to be encountered in older houses.

To remove a damaged joist fixed in this way, first saw through the joist as close as possible to the wall. Remove the part of the joist bedded in the wall with a hammer and a bolster. Brush any dust and debris from the holes into a container and remove it from the house. In the case of dry rot, follow the process outlined above. Fill the holes with cement mortar and a half brick.

The new joist can be hung on joist hangers, which give greater protection from rot. These are sheet metal brackets with a box-like cross-section which holds, and is nailed to, the joist ends. At the top, the hanger has a metal prong which is bedded into a mortar course (see Fig.1). Fix the joist hangers in place.

The new joist should be treated with the necessary preservative—woodworm fluid or fungicide. The method of doing this is described above. Put the new joist on the hangers and nail through the hangers into the joist.

While you have the floorboards up it is a good idea to treat the other joists, even if they are undamaged. As an absolute minimum, treat the joists adjacent to the damaged joist and the area of the wall plate that was in contact with it.

If a proprietary insecticide is too expensive for you to use lavishly, Dieseline is a cheaper alternative. It penetrates deeply, smothering the larvae, but its protection is not so long-lasting.

If the damaged joist was attacked by dry rot, check the underfloor ventilation and install new air bricks if necessary. If wet rot was present, find the source of the dampness. If the dpc is faulty, replace it with either a physical or chemical dpc.

Damaged wall plate

If the wall plate has been attacked, the replacement is considerably more involved. There is no need, however, to replace the wall

plate in one piece and this simplifies the job. The replacement of a wall plate depends on how it is fixed to the wall. Whichever way it is fixed you will have to devise a means of supporting the joist ends while you remove and replace the wall plate. A few bricks, or car jacks set on blocks, will suffice.

Prop up several joists at a time and remove the part of the wall plate that supports them. If the wall plate is set on a sleeper wall, this will present no problem, but if it is bedded into the wall you will have to chip it out with a bolster and hammer. If the wall plate is supported on brick piers the lengths of timber that make up the wall plate should be jointed over the piers.

When one length of wall plate has been removed, brush away any debris. In the case of dry rot treat the brick surfaces near the old timber with fungicide. Check that the dpc has not been damaged by the removal of the wall plate. If it has been, replace it with a felt or lead dpc. Treat new timbers with woodworm fluid or fungicide.

Work progressively across the room, propping up several joists at a time. Lay the new lengths of wall plate on mortar. Remember to include a strip of damp-proof course between the mortar and the timber.

Damaged floorboards

Remove these in the manner described above and replace them with treated timbers. Fix the new boards with wire nails through the surface into the joists. Treat adjacent boards with the appropriate preservative, even if they appear sound.

Termites

The most dangerous wood boring insect in some parts of Australia and New Zealand is the termite, sometimes wrongly called the 'white ant'.

In areas likely to be infested with termites no timber should be left in contact with the ground around a house. This is because termites will make galleries through the wood and eventually reach the house timbers. Termites do not work in the light or in the open and if they have to cross open ground they make tunnels from earth and saliva. These can be seen and destroyed, whereas you cannot detect the fact that termites are eating through wood towards the house timbers.

If you are having a house built treat the soil in the area of the planned building with a proprietary insecticide. This poisons the soil and makes it impossible for termites to establish a colony. The foundations of the house should be brick or concrete—do not use timber within 18in. (457mm) of the ground.

Most houses in Australia and New Zealand are built on brick or concrete piers though some of the older houses in Australia are supported by timber piers. Whichever type of support is used the top of the piers should be covered with metal caps (see Fig.4) which will prevent the termites reaching the floor timbers. The tops of concrete or brick foundations of houses should also be capped with metal.

If you live in an area of termite infestation be constantly on guard for tunnels made across open ground by termites.

Garden fences

Aside from providing an attractive addition to your home, garden fencing can lend an air of privacy to your property. In some cases it may even offer some protection from the elements.

This fence is of a traditional design that not only looks handsome but also is quick and easy to build. It is faced with overlapping 'feather edge' boards nailed to horizontal *arris rails,* which in turn are set into 3in. x 3in. or 75mm x 75mm posts by means of mortise-and-tenon joints. Feather edge boards and arris rails are specially made for this type of fence from low grade timber, so the materials are cheaper than they might otherwise be.

The fence can be made of hardwood or softwood—with this grade of timber there is not much difference in price between the two. It can be painted or treated with a clear wood preservative, but an attractive effect can also be created by using old-fashioned creosote as a rot-proofer. This soaks into the rough, unplaned surface of the wood to give a slightly mottled medium brown colour with the grain showing through clearly.

The only disadvantage of creosote is its strong smell, which, though not unpleasant, hangs about for weeks.

HEDRICH-BLESSING

JOHN HOVELL

Above. *A fence with a difference. Paling stakes, drilled and 'threaded' to the main posts with dowelling.* **Below.** *Double-sided ranch style fencing, with the boards stepped alternately, forming a patio corner.*

Above. *Rustic fencing simply trellised to form an attractive boundary. The hedge forms an integral part and acts as both screen and background.* **Below.** *Plain ranch fencing painted in four harmonizing colours.*

HARRY SMITH

JOHN HOVELL

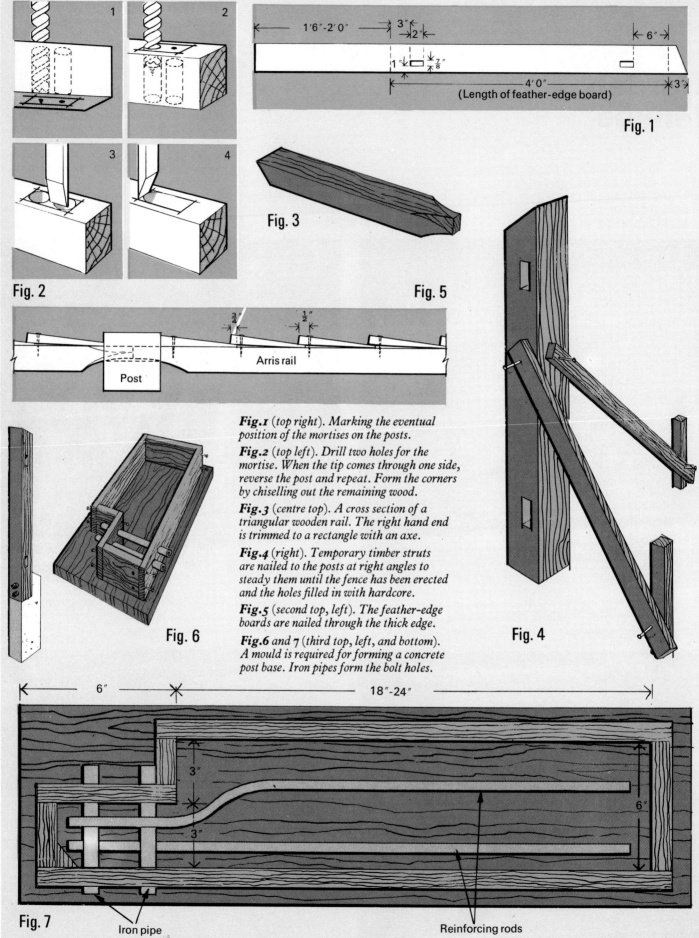

Fig.1 (top right). Marking the eventual position of the mortises on the posts.

Fig.2 (top left). Drill two holes for the mortise. When the tip comes through one side, reverse the post and repeat. Form the corners by chiselling out the remaining wood.

Fig.3 (centre top). A cross section of a triangular wooden rail. The right hand end is trimmed to a rectangle with an axe.

Fig.4 (right). Temporary timber struts are nailed to the posts at right angles to steady them until the fence has been erected and the holes filled in with hardcore.

Fig.5 (second top, left). The feather-edge boards are nailed through the thick edge.

Fig.6 and **7** (third top, left, and bottom). A mould is required for forming a concrete post base. Iron pipes form the bolt holes.

Fig. 1

Fig. 2

Fig. 3

Fig. 4

Fig. 5

Fig. 6

Fig. 7

Arris rail

Post

Iron pipe

Reinforcing rods

1'6"-2'0"

3"
2"

1"

7/8"

6"

4' 0"
(Length of feather-edge board)

3"

3/4"

1/2"

6"

18"-24"

3"

3"

6"

The normal height for this type of fence is 4ft 6in. (1.4m). A fence this high should have posts 8ft (2.5m) apart. Assuming you are sticking to these standard dimensions, you will need the following materials for each 8ft panel. Remember to buy one fence post more than the total number of panels.

Materials needed

. . . for each 8ft panel :—
Unplaned timber for the upright post :
1 length of 6ft 6in.-7ft x 3in. x 3in., or 2m-2.2m x 75mm x 75mm.
Standard arris rails with a triangular cross-section :
2 lengths of 8ft or 2.5m.
Unplaned timber for the 'gravel board' running along the bottom of the fence :
1 length of 8ft x 6in. x 1in., or 2.5m x 150m x 25m.
Unplaned timber for mounting the gravel board :
1 length of 1ft x 2in. x 1in., or 300mm x 50mm x 25mm.
Feather-edge boards :
27 lengths of 4ft x 4in., or 1.2m x 100mm.
These boards are generally sold in 8ft or 2.5m lengths, so you can simply cut them in half.
One pound or half a kilo of 2in. (50mm) galvanized nails. Ordinary nails rust and mark the wood.
Creosote, wood preservative or paint.
Special tools required :—
Small, sharp axe.
Ground auger (called a post-hole borer in some countries), which may be hired.

Planning the fence

Before buying any wood, it is essential to determine exactly how long the fence will be, and whether there will be any special problems in constructing it. It is a sensible precaution to draw a scale plan of the site and mark the position of the posts on it. This will not only tell you how many posts you need, but also ensure that none of the posts is to be placed in an impossible position. If you discover that one of the post sites is in solid rock, you can insert a shorter section in the fence so that the posts miss the obstacle. There will in any case be a short section at one end of the fence, unless you care to space *all* the posts less than 8ft apart to even up the spacing.

If the ground under the fence is uneven, ensure that there are no sudden changes in height in the middle of a section. The sections can be at any angle to the horizontal—or, better still, stepped to follow the contours of the ground—but obviously they cannot be bent in the middle.

The posts are going to be sunk 18in.-2ft (450mm-600mm) into the ground, so check that there is enough soil or loose rock to allow this all along the site.

Preparing the timber

First mark out and cut the posts. For a 4ft 6in. fence they can either be 6ft 6in. or 7ft long, depending on whether you mean to sink them 18in. or 2ft into the ground. The longer posts are recommended where the fence is to be set in soft soil.

To increase weather resistance the tops of the

The feather-edge boards are fixed after the gravel boards are fixed to the mounting blocks. The gravel boards are easily removed if they rot.

165

posts should be cut at an angle. This will prevent water from collecting on the top. Mark the holes for the mortises in the positions shown in Fig.1. The size of the mortises depends on the size of your arris rails, but standard-sized rails will probably allow you a maximum size of 2in. x $\frac{7}{8}$in. (51mm x 22mm). The closer to this size that you can make the mortises, the stronger the joints will be.

If there are any sharp drops in the ground under the fence, it may be necessary to cut the mortises lower on one side of a post than on the other to create a step in the fence. Slight irregularities can be taken care of by simply angling the arris rails, however. There is no need to angle the mortises—it is easier to cut the tenons at an angle.

The mortises should be cut by drilling two holes with a bit the same width as the mortise (see Fig.2). The wood between the holes and in the corners can then be taken out with a chisel. The holes should go right through each post unless, of course, the mortises on each side are at different heights.

The tenons can be made more quickly. First cut the arris rails to length and set aside a short offcut to practise on.

Shape the wood with a small one-handed axe, holding the wood in the hand and cutting as if sharpening a pencil. A more accurate way of making a tenon would be to use a draw knife. But it is a much slower method and accuracy is not really the most important thing here. Even if it does not quite fit, the shape of the tenon will act as a wedge to hold the arris rail steady. Leave one pair of rails with one unshaped end, so that you can adjust the length later.

Cut the feather edge boards to length. Also cut the 1ft length of 2in. x 1in. timber in half at an angle so that it forms two 6in. pieces with slanted tops. This will enable them to resist the weather, and also to fit snugly under the arris rail when they are nailed to the posts as gravel board mountings. Leave the gravel boards over-length for the time being.

Give all the wooden parts a generous coat of creosote or other preservative. The bottoms of the posts, which will be most exposed to damp, should be stood in a bucket of the liquid for a few hours, to make sure that it soaks into the wood.

Work on site

While the preservative is drying you can begin preparing the site. Hammer in stakes at both ends of the proposed length of the fence or, if the fence does not run in a straight line, at the beginning and end of each straight section. Tie some string firmly to the tops of the stakes. To prevent the string from getting entangled later with the uprights, the stakes should be about 2ft or 600mm higher than the eventual height of the uprights. This will be your guide for keeping the fence straight.

Dig the first hole at one end of the site. A ground auger, which is a kind of giant gimlet, will make the job much easier, but a perfectly good hole can be dug with a narrow spade. Make each hole slightly deeper than required and pack clean hardcore into the bottom to prevent the post from sinking.

The simplest way to space the second and subsequent post-holes is to lay arris rails end to end along the fence site and dig at the joins. If the preservative is still wet, however, you can just as easily measure the distance with a tape.

Erecting the fence

Fit the first post into its hole and put a little hardcore around its base to stop it slipping sideways. Then lock the post upright by nailing a pair of timber struts between the post and pegs set into the ground. The struts should be set at right angles to each other (see Fig.4).

Position the second post loosely in its hole. Then take a pair of arris rails and knock them into the mortises in the first post with a mallet. The flat side of the rails should normally face outwards from your property. Push the tenons at the other end into the mortises in the second post and drive them home by hitting the post. Check that the second post is upright (use a spirit level), ram in a little hardcore and prop the post upright with one temporary wooden strut at right angles to the line of the arris rails.

Carry on in this way until you have put up all the fence posts and arris rails. The last pair of rails should be trimmed to length on the spot. Apply preservative to the cut ends before inserting them in the mortises—there is no need to wait for it to dry.

Nail the gravel board mounting blocks to the fence in a vertical position one inch (25mm) from the flat side of the fence with their slanted tops resting against the arris rail. This will provide a valuable guide to whether all the posts have been sunk the same distance into the ground. A gravel board is to be nailed between each pair of blocks, so the ground must be level between the posts or there will be a gap under the fence.

Check all the posts for straightness using a spirit level, and for alignment by looking at the fence from one end. When you are satisfied, fill the holes to within two inches of the top with hardcore rammed well down. An alternative method which prolongs the life of the posts is to fill the holes with a rather dry concrete mix. Slope the top of the concrete so that water will run away from the post. Do not remove the bracing struts till the concrete has set hard.

Cut each gravel board to the exact length of the space between the pairs of posts and treat the cut ends with preservative. Then nail the boards in place so that their lower edges rest on the

AUSTRALIAN HOME BEAUTIFUL

AUSTRALIAN HOME BEAUTIFUL

AUSTRALIAN WOMEN'S WEEKLY

Top left. *An unusual fence of branches. These are nailed to top and bottom rails which are supported by preservative-treated poles.*
Top right. *Closely spaced ranch fencing.*
Bottom. *White-painted pallisade fencing looks simple and, at the same time, elegant.*

ground. These boards provide an easily replaceable base for the fence, and also prevent the feather edge boards from wet rot.

Finally, nail the feather edge boards to the arris rails. Each board should be secured by only two nails, one each into the top and bottom rails. This allows the boards to expand and contract with changes in humidity—an important consideration in outdoor carpentry. The spacing of the boards and the position of the nails is shown in Fig.5. The nails must go through the thick side of each board about $\frac{3}{4}$in. or 20mm from the edge. The boards should overlap by about $\frac{1}{2}$in. or 13mm.

The best way to space the boards equally is to cut a small wood block $\frac{1}{2}$in. or 13mm narrower than the width of the boards (this will be 3$\frac{1}{2}$in. or 90mm if you are using standard-width boards). Use this block and a pencil to step out the distance along the arris rails, but remember that *all* the width of the last board will show.

Extra-strong posts

The fence posts already described are quite strong and should last for years if properly treated with preservative. But in areas where the soil is unusually damp, or attack by pests is a problem, you may prefer to make concrete bases for the posts and bolt the wooden part to them above ground level.

The formwork (mould) for the posts is shown in Fig.7. It should be a wooden box lightly nailed together so that it can be taken apart to release the post. A couple of iron pipes can be passed through holes in the side of the mould to form bolt holes for the attachment of the post. Two short reinforcing rods should also be inserted. The whole inside of the mould, particularly the

Fig.8 and 9 (top left and right). *Mortises are not necessary for ranch-style fencing. The boards are simply screwed to the posts.*
Fig.10 (bottom). *Feather-edge boards can be mounted horizontally by fixing them to battens on the sides of the posts.*

pipes, should be heavily greased to stop the concrete from sticking to it. Old sump oil from a car is good enough for the job.

The mouldings should not be removed for three days, and should be treated with care for a further four days. Obviously, you will need several sets of formwork if post bases are to be produced at a reasonable rate.

An even stronger fence can be made with solid concrete posts. In this case the formwork should be in the shape of one complete post, with reinforcing rods the whole way up. Remember to insert a couple of 2in. x $\frac{7}{8}$in. (50mm x 22mm) wood blocks to mould the mortises.

Other types of fence

The feather-edge board fence described here is sturdy and long-lasting, but not particularly smart. However, the same building technique can be used to make a more attractive fence for the front of a house.

Ranch-style fencing is made by nailing or screwing 6in. x 1in. or 150mm x 25mm boards to the sides of the fence posts. No mortises are needed. The boards can be fastened either on alternate sides or all on the same side with alternate boards stepped up on small wood blocks to give a varied effect. One panel of each type is shown in Figs.8 and 9, but in a real fence the joints in the horizontal boards would be

staggered to make the fence stronger.

The horizontal boards can be fastened edge-to-edge as shown to make a solid fence, or spaced apart to make it possible to see through. Screws used in its construction should be the galvanized or black japanned type; plain steel screws rust and mark the wood, and brass ones are too expensive. Needless to say, this type of construction is unsuitable for concrete posts.

This type of fencing looks best painted. But this means that you will not be able to creosote the timber, as creosote stains paint. So you will have to buy timber pressure-treated with preservative to resist wet conditions. To make the job weatherproof, the knots in the wood should be sealed with 'knotting' and an undercoat applied to the separate pieces *before* erecting the posts or putting the fence together.

A fence can also be made with horizontal feather-edge boarding nailed to 2in. x 1in. or 50mm x 25mm battens running down the sides of the posts (the same way as the gravel boards were mounted on the original fence). The horizontal boards will need to be nailed to vertical stiffeners between the posts (see Fig.10) to make the structure more rigid. These stiffeners are not posts and should not touch the ground.

This type of construction looks best with 'waney edge' boarding, which has the bark left on one edge to give a rustic effect.

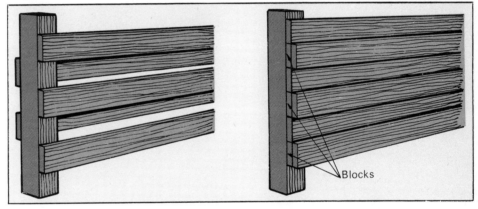

Blocks

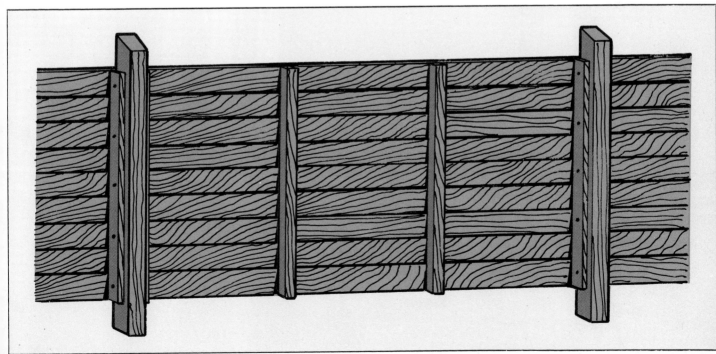

Repairs to skirtings and cornices

Damage to skirtings, architraves, picture rails and cornices can be among the most unsightly in the home. Dents and cracks, particularly to architraves and skirtings, are very common, especially in a home where children are allowed a free rein with their toys. More serious damage, such as woodworm, can occur to all these features; in this case the damaged area should be removed as soon as possible to prevent the trouble from spreading.

In older houses, these features were made from wood moulding with a decorative front. In modern houses, architraves and skirtings are generally made of square-section timber, though skirtings are sometimes bevelled on their top edge. In all homes the timber used is softwood—only public buildings have hardwood mouldings. Plastic skirtings, and fibrous plaster, polystyrene and heavy paper cornices, are also used. Architraves and picture rails are always made of timber, however.

Victorian houses tend to have elaborately shaped mouldings, unlike modern houses, where simple uncluttered lines are usual. The main photograph shows a cross-section of a traditional and a more modern skirting.

The size of materials used for mouldings varies. Older skirtings and architraves tend to be considerably heavier than their counterparts in modern houses. In all houses, the size of each moulding is scaled in proportion to that of the others. So if you replace any piece of moulding, the new timber should be the same dimension as the old. If they are not, you will upset the proportions of the room.

The main techniques to master when replacing or repairing these features are accurate mitring and scribing. At some corners mitring should be avoided, because ugly gaps will be left as the skirtings shrink. The cross section of one piece should be scribed on to the other. The outline made is cut out and the boards are fitted so that the shaped end of one board fits over the square-cut end of the other.

Skirting

Skirting has two functions. Visually, it provides a decorative finish to the corner of the wall and floor, thus making the angle less harsh. Functionally, it protects the surface of the wall where it is most vulnerable to scuff marks and knocks.

Wooden skirting in brick houses is nailed in place through its surface, either to small wooden blocks known as *groundings* or to pieces of batten that run the whole length of the wall. Where the wall is made of concrete, groundings are used, but here fixing presents a problem as the groundings have to be set into the wall. Modern pneumatic hammers are used by some builders to fire hardened pins into the concrete to fix the groundings to the wall. This is a complicated procedure, however, and most houses with concrete walls have plastic skirting fixed in place with a strong impact adhesive.

The groundings or battens used for wooden skirting are as thick as the plaster or plasterboard wall surfacing. The wall surfacing ends just below the top edge of the skirting. If groundings are used, they fit snugly between the bottom edge of the wall surfacing and the floor and are fixed with masonry pins.

In timber-framed houses, skirtings are laid over the top of the lining material and are nailed into the studs.

Plastic skirting, as found in houses with concrete walls, is also used extensively in modern housing developments on walls surfaced with plasterboard.

Damage to skirting boards may be localized—a dent, break, or crack in one part of their length—in which case the damaged area can be removed and replaced. Damage may also be general, as in the case of woodworm, and here the entire length of skirting may have to be removed. Even if woodworm is localized it is advisable to remove considerably more of the skirting than the damaged area. This is because the surface holes show only where the woodworm beetle has emerged ready to lay more eggs; the damage done during the grub stage extends over a far greater area.

Removing damaged skirting

Where damage is general the method of removing a length of skirting is to prise it away from the wall and the timber groundings or batten with an old chisel. Push the chisel into the small gap between the top back edge of the skirting and the wall. Tap the handle of the chisel with a mallet or the *side* of a hammer until the blade enters to a considerable depth. Then place a thin wooden wedge behind the chisel so that its edge is close to the edge of the skirting. Twist the chisel. Do not lever it forward, or the blade may break. Repeat this process at various points along the length of the skirting until it comes away from the wall.

In certain cases, you will have to remove more than one length of skirting, even if only one is damaged. This is because the ends of the pieces are not generally mitred together at the corners, but scribed and shaped to fit as mentioned above. Consequently one board can be held in place at its ends by the shaped ends of the two other boards. You may have to remove three boards just to remove and replace one length of skirting, even if the other two are sound. To fit a new section of moulding by this method, consult the Data Sheet on page 18, which gives two methods.

If your floor is uneven it may also be necessary to scribe and shape the bottom edge of the replacement skirting. If this has to be done you will have to buy a board deeper than the other skirtings in the room. This is because you will be making the new board shallower by shaping its bottom edge. The procedure for scribing the skirting to the floor is also described on page 18. Cut the new piece slightly over-length and fit it in slightly diagonally as near as the wall as possible to scribe it.

Fixing new pieces of skirting around fireplaces and in bay windows presents no problem providing you remember a few basic points. Whether the new skirting is square or moulded, it will have to be mitred at all outside corners. If, for example, one angle in a bay window is 135°, the two pieces of skirting that meet must have a mitre of half this angle—67½°—in their ends. Mitre boxes do not cater for this type of angle, so

mark the angle with an adjustable bevel gauge and cut it carefully to shape with a saw. If you cannot do this because the skirting has a rounded top, mark the angle on a flat topped piece of timber, clamp it to the skirting length with G-cramps and saw through both pieces of wood together. Inside corners, whatever the angle or shape of the moulding, should be overlapped, scribed if necessary, and butt-jointed. Square-section skirtings need not be scribed.

Gaps between floor and skirting

In new houses, as they dry out, the skirting boards often shrink to leave gaps between the floor and the skirting. These are both unsightly and draughty. To remedy this, nail strips of fairly lightweight moulding to the floor so that one of the square faces butts the skirting board. Fixing the moulding to the floor, and not to the skirting, allows for further movement of the skirting. When fixing this moulding, mitre or scribe the pieces at corners, according to the considerations given above.

Alternatively, you can make an even neater finish—at the cost of considerable effort—by filling the crack with a cellulose filler such as Polyfilla. British Polyfilla is produced with pva already added; if the brand you buy does not, use pva adhesive and water mixed 'half and half' to mix the filler with.

Where damage to skirtings is localized, removing the damaged pieces is rather more involved. It involves cutting away the damaged section while the main part of the length of skirting is still in place. To do this, first prise the part of the board near the damaged area away from the wall, using an old chisel in the manner described above. Then wedge a piece of wood, 1in. (25mm) thick if possible, otherwise thinner, between the skirting and the wall, on the left hand side of the damage. Place a mitre block, preferably not a double-sided mitre box, against the skirting. If necessary, place pieces of packing underneath the mitre block so that its top edge is flush with the top edge of the skirting.

Now make a mitred cut, sloping so that the handle of the saw is offset to the left. Use a tenon saw set in the mitre block. You will have very little room for the saw blade, so work carefully. When the cut is about 1in. deep, remove the mitre block. Continue the saw cut to the floor.

Now jam the wedge between the board and the wall on the other side of the damage. Make another cut, repeating the process described above, but with the tilt of the blade the other way round, so that the new piece will hold the ends of the old skirting down. Remove the damaged piece of skirting. There may not be any groundings behind the damaged piece of skirting, in which case you will have to cut two to size from a piece of softwood. The thickness of the new groundings should be that of the overhanging wall surfacing and the height should be that of the brickwork exposed by the removal of the damaged skirting.

When you have cut two groundings, knock each one into the gap between the mitred ends of the skirting still attached to the wall, and the wall. Position them so that half their width is exposed. Using masonry nails, fix the new groundings to the wall.

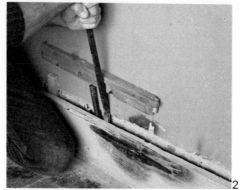

The next step is to cut a board to replace the damaged skirting. First cut a piece of board a little over length. Hold it against the skirting so that it bridges the gap between the mitred ends of the existing skirting. Carefully mark on the replacement piece the point where the mitred ends of the skirting run to the replacement piece. From this point make a rough pencil mark on the replacement piece to indicate the direction of the mitre. This mark is not used as a guide when cutting—it simply ensures that you do not cut the mitre the wrong way by accident.

Using a mitre box, cut the mitres on the ends of the replacement piece, being careful to get it the right length. Put the new piece in place against the wall. Apply firm downward pressure to its top edge—you can do this by resting one end of a plank on the top edge with the other end on the floor and kneeling on the plank. Nail both the replacement piece and the existing skirting to the groundings. Punch the nail heads just below the surface of the skirting. Fill the holes with wood filler and paint the replacement piece to match the surrounding skirting.

Architraves

Architraves are decorative surrounds to any opening. They provide a finish to the sides of the opening, covering up the wall surfacing and the frame within the opening. They are most commonly seen around doors and sash windows.

Architraves are generally of timber and are very commonly mouldings with a shaped cross-section. In older houses, the architraves are often made from fairly elaborate moulding, but the architraves in modern houses tend to be fairly lightweight square-section timber. At corners, architraves are mitred—this is acceptable as they are not load-bearing pieces. Architraves are nailed to rough grounds—pieces of timber that cover the end of the wall where it runs to the opening—and to the casing, the timber that frames the opening at right angles to the rough grounds.

Architraves are more susceptible to damage than other timber components around an opening. They are on a corner and thus more vulnerable to bumps and kick marks. Replacing and patching architraves, both frequently-under-

Fig.1. To patch a damaged skirting, first remove the plaster just above the damaged area.
Fig.2. Carefully prise the damaged area from the wall with a crowbar or an old chisel.
Fig.3. Knock wood blocks behind the skirting to hold it away from the wall.
Fig.4. With a flooring saw and mitre block begin to cut through the skirting. When the cut is about 1in. deep remove the block and continue sawing right down the skirting.
Fig.5. Mark the mitres on the replacement piece with a bevel gauge.
Fig.6. Mitre the ends of the new piece with a bench saw set at an angle or . . . .
Fig.7. . . . with a handsaw and mitre block.
Fig.8. Fix new groundings to the wall, if necessary, with masonry nails.
Fig.9. Apply firm downward pressure to the new piece and nail it in place.
Fig.10. The new piece nailed in place and all gaps and holes filled with wood filler.

taken jobs, are described in full detail in **CHAPTER 22.** This chapter also describes how to copy unobtainable mouldings with an 'instant shape tracer' and combination plane. The problem of duplicating the obsolete mouldings in old houses is often encountered in the repair of architraves, and also with skirtings and other fittings. The task of duplicating mouldings is time consuming but not difficult.

Picture rails

These are rarely used in modern houses but are commonly seen in houses built before 1939. They are not, of course, susceptible to dents but, like all household timbers, can be attacked by woodworm. Picture rails should be scribed or mitred at corners, as with skirtings.

The rails are generally fixed direct to the plaster of old houses with cut nails—nails with a square section and rectangular-shaped heads. Usually the nails were 1½in. (38mm) long and the fibrous material that was mixed with the plaster provided a secure fixing for them. Hardwood picture rails are found in the opulent timber-panelled rooms of large Victorian houses; these are built into the panelling. Unless your home is really 'stately', you are unlikely to have a room like this.

Use an old chisel to remove a picture rail that is cut-nailed to the plaster. Since the picture rail is not nailed to timber grounds or battens you cannot avoid damaging the plaster behind it. To avoid damaging the plaster above or below the picture rail, use a thin waste piece of wood against the wall at the points where you will be prising the rail away with the chisel.

If possible, avoid jointing picture rail moulding along its length. The joints, unless they are very neatly cut, will be conspicuous. Use a mitre box to cut slanted ends on the new pieces. If necessary, rub down the ends with glasspaper and, having cut-nailed the new rail in place, fill any gaps with filler.

You may, of course, wish to remove the picture rail and not replace it. If you do this you will have to fill the holes left by the nails with cellulose filler. You should be careful here, however. The decorative mouldings give a certain proportional unity to a room and picture rails also tend to lower a room. If your room is very small, removing the picture rail will make the ceiling appear too high.

Cornices

Cornices are curved pieces of material that form a neat finish and disguise the harshness of the wall and ceiling angle. Various types of materials are used for cornices—plaster, wood, polystyrene foam and heavy paper. The most common type in new British homes is plaster coving; where timber is inexpensive, you are more likely to find a wooden *scotia* moulding.

Damage is unusual to these materials as they are well out of reach of the normal traffic in the home. But wood is susceptible to woodworm, and the softer materials such as polystyrene can become dented or broken during redecorating or cleaning.

Fibrous plaster, polystyrene and heavy paper cornices are stuck on with proprietary adhesives. Wooden scotias are nailed in place, and can be removed in the same way as picture rails.

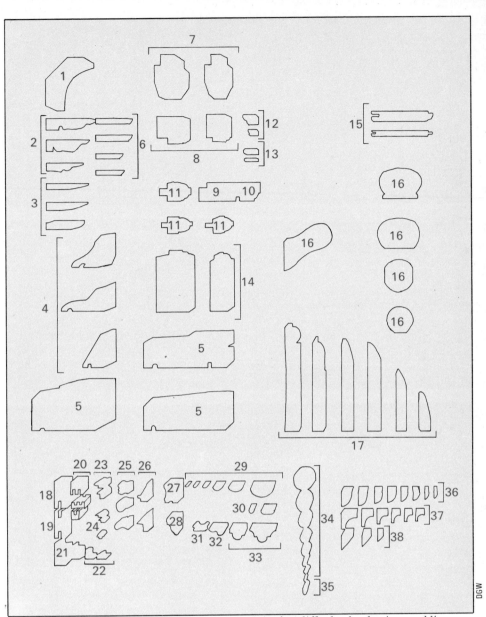

Cornices made from other materials can be pulled away by hand.

At right angled corners these materials should be scribed and cut to shape so that one end of one piece fits neatly over another. Polystyrene should be cut with a handyman's knife and the other materials with a coping saw.

When joining these materials along their length or at outside corners, mitre their ends. In doing this, you must be careful to hold the cornice in the mitre box in the same position that it will occupy on the wall. First offer the length of cornice to the ceiling. Mark a point on the end section through which an imaginary angle of 45° from the point where the wall and ceiling meet will run. Try to be as accurate as possible in estimating this.

Then place the cornice in the mitre box. Line up the mark on the end section with the exact corner of the base and the side of the mitre box. If the mitre box is too wide, pack it with waste wood so that the cornice stays in position during mitring. Then cut the mitre.

It is not worthwhile mitring polystyrene cornices to join them along their length. The material is fairly thin and can be neatly butt-jointed.

It is often difficult when buying moulding to find out the correct term for the particular type of material you require.

The photograph at the start of this chapter shows many of the mouldings available. The diagram above is a key to the photograph. The types of moulding shown are :

1 Ceiling cove (expanded polystyrene) 2 Ogee architrave 3 Architrave C.A. 4 Door and window weather mouldings 5 Sills 6 Ovolo door stop 7 Greenhouse bar 8 Stile 9 Top sash meeting rail 10 Bottom sash meeting rail 11 Glazing bar 12 Stop bead 13 Parting bead 14 Bottom rail 15 Tongued, grooved and veed matching 16 Hand and banister rails 17 Skirtings 18 Single end groove moulding 19 Double end grooved moulding 20 Top and bottom grooved moulding 21 Rebate moulding 22 Flat corner moulding 23 Round bead P.F. and hockey stick 24 Rebate half round moulding 25 Cupboard and tray handle 26 Picture mouldings 27 Weather moulding under sills 28 Base moulding 29 Half round beading 30 D moulds 31 Cable cover 32 Ogee panel moulding 33 Double Astragal 34 Dowel moulding 35 Perdu 36 Quadrant 37 Scotia 38 Triangle moulding

Power tools : 1

One of the dullest and slowest jobs in carpentry is making a large number of identical pieces — sawing the same shape over and over again, hand-drilling row after row of holes, sanding everything to shape, and so on. If you have to do this, you may easily lose interest. So why not speed up the routine work with a power tool ?

Power tools greatly speed up some of the most time-consuming work in carpentry, such as drilling, sawing and sanding. Anyone who intends to do a lot of carpentry would be well advised to invest in some kind of power tool, which would soon pay for itself in time saved.

Many types of specialized power tools are made, such as power saws, orbital sanders, lathes and so on. But the average woodworker can save some of the money required to buy this costly equipment by buying a power drill and a range of attachments to fit it.

Power drills

Handy power drills do a lot more than just drill. A huge number of fittings can be attached to the basic drill unit, enabling it to do almost anything that can be done by a specialized power tool—perhaps not quite so fast or accurately, but certainly well enough for general use.

Basically, a power drill is a compact electric motor fitted with a projecting shaft at one end on which is mounted a *chuck*—a revolving clamp that grips and drives drill bits or other attachments. The motor unit is held in the hand by a pistol grip, and the motor is started by pressing a 'trigger' at the top of the grip. For safety reasons, the motor stops if pressure is released on the trigger, but most drills have a locking pin that can be engaged to hold the trigger in the 'on' position.

Electric power is supplied to the drill by a cable that enters the machine through the bottom of the handle. On all modern drills, a complex system of insulation is built in to keep the user from getting an electric shock.

The motor is cooled by a built-in fan that draws air through slots in the side of the drill. These slots must be kept uncovered and free of sawdust, or the motor may overheat and burn out.

Many drills can be adjusted to run at different speeds. The normal type is a two-speed drill geared to run at up to 1,000 rpm and 2,500-3,000 rpm. These two speeds are suitable for most household jobs, and a two-speed machine is probably the best type for the householder to buy.

Variable-speed drills, where the speed can be infinitely varied by an electrical device, are also made, but these are specialist tools. It is false economy to buy a single-speed drill and a separate electrical speed reducer, because although single-speed machines are cheaper, the cost of the two units together will be higher than that of a good two-speed drill.

The most suitable speeds for various woodworking and other operations are shown in Fig.12.

Drills come in various sizes, which are graded by the capacity of their chuck—i.e. the largest drill bit that can be fitted into it. Common sizes are $\frac{1}{4}$in. (6mm), $\frac{3}{16}$in. (8mm), $\frac{3}{8}$in. (10mm) and $\frac{1}{2}$in. (13mm). The larger machines have more powerful motors. A medium-sized machine—say, $\frac{3}{8}$in.—should be adequate for all ordinary jobs, though the smallest may be too light for some.

An indispensable accessory that every drill user will need is an extension cable. This enables him to use the tool in places remote from a power outlet. Cables are available in standard lengths from 25ft (8m) to 300ft (100m), or you can make up your own. The longer the cable, the thicker it needs to be to prevent power loss. Heavier machines also need thicker cables. Recommended cable sizes are shown in Fig.13. In some countries, though not in Britain, you must also have an isolating transformer if using a power tool out of doors; the shop that supplies the drill can advise you.

Drill bits and fittings

Many types of drill are sold for cutting different sizes and shapes of hole in different materials (see Fig.14). The 'everyday' sort are *twist bits,* used for drilling all sizes of hole in metal, and holes in wood up to $\frac{1}{4}$in. (6mm) in diameter. The smallest common size of twist bit is $\frac{1}{16}$in., and sizes increase in steps of $\frac{1}{64}$in. up from this.

Larger holes in wood are drilled with *Jennings bits,* which have a wide spiral to remove the surplus wood, and a centre spur or spike to keep the cut accurate when it is being started. *Forstner* bits must be used in a drill press. They cut neat, flat-bottomed holes, but they have to be cleaned out more often than auger bits. *Dowel bits* are like twist bits with a wood-drill-shaped point for extra accuracy.

Very large holes are drilled with *flat bits* [up to $1\frac{1}{4}$in. (32mm)] or *hole saws* [up to 3in. (76mm)]. The flat bit has a flat, spade-shaped cutter with a central spur to hold it in place. The hole saw has a revolving toothed ring attached to a central twist bit—the ring removes wood like a revolving pastry-cutter. Different sizes of ring are available.

Very long holes, such as those up the shaft of standard lamps, are drilled with *shell* or *parrot-nosed augers.* They are generally used on a lathe, and not in a hand-held drill.

Other types of bit include *countersink bits,* for countersinking screw holes, and *drill-countersinkers* or *'screw sinks',* which are specially shaped to drill and countersink (or counterbore) a hole for a particular size of screw.

A *plug cutter* is often used in conjunction with a 'screw sink' to conceal screw heads in wood. The 'screw sink' is used to counterbore a screw

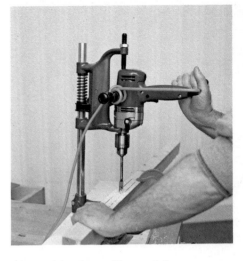

Fig.1. *A bench stand is one of the most useful accessories for your drill. It allows you to make perfectly accurate vertical holes in wood, metal or plastic.*

Fig.2. *A jigsaw attachment. Here, a cut is being started in the middle of this wooden door by tipping the saw on its nose and gradually lowering the blade into the wood.*

Fig.3. *A more powerful integral jigsaw. Here, the saw is being slid along a wooden straight edge to make a straight cut in a sheet of plastic laminate.*

Fig.4. *When sanding a flat surface, you should hold the rubber disc at an angle to the wood to minimise swirl marks.*

Fig.5. *The same disc can also be used, with practice, to sand rounded objects. Note how the cable is being held away from the disc.*

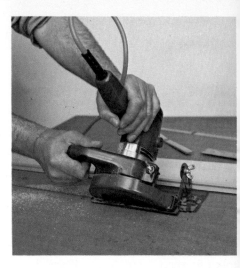

Fig.6. *A drill-powered circular saw being used to cut a bevel, or mitre, along the edge of a piece of timber.*

Fig.8. *An easy way of sharpening chisels without a grinder. First mark and cut slots in a fine-grade sanding disc . . .*

Fig.9. *. . . then apply special disc cement to the revolving sanding plate and press the sanding disc on to its tacky surface.*

Fig.10. *Start the motor and hold the chisel tip to the underside of the disc. It will not catch in the slots.*

hole—ie, to recess the screw head some way into the wood—and then a plug like a short length of dowel is cut from a matching piece of timber, glued into the recess over the screw head, and planed flat to give an almost invisible result.

For drilling hard masonry, a *hammer attachment* to a drill is useful. This makes the bit vibrate up and down as it revolves. A *percussion bit* should be used with the attachment. For drilling without hammering, special *masonry bits* are made—they look like twist bits but have cutting tips made of a special hard alloy.

Glass and tiles are drilled with a *spear point drill,* which also has a hardened tip.

Special *right-angle* and *flexible drive shafts* are made to allow drilling in awkward corners that could not normally be reached.

Drilling techniques

Whatever you are drilling, the position of the hole should be clearly marked before you start, and a small indentation made in the work-piece with a centre punch (or, at a pinch, nail-punch or big nail), to stop the drill from wandering in the first few seconds of work. Clamp the workpiece down securely, or it may start to revolve.

It is essential that the drill should be at right angles to the surface to be drilled. You can line it up with a try square before you start—though of course the drill always tilts a bit once you start drilling.

Simple drill guides are made (the Wolf 'Drillrite' is an example) that hold the drill at right angles to any flat surface. Or you can buy a drill stand, which holds the drill vertical on a frame. The drill can be moved up and down by a lever. The workpiece is placed underneath on the base of the stand (see Fig.1).

Drill bits should be prevented from over-heating through friction. If they become too hot, the metal loses it 'temper' and becomes soft. This is a particular problem with ordinary carbon steel twist bits. Special 'high-speed' steel bits, made for drilling hard metals, are more resistant—but also more expensive. Masonry bits are very prone to overheating.

When drilling wood with a twist bit, remove it occasionally to check that the spirals are not clogged with wood dust, which can lead to overheating. When drilling any metal other than brass or cast iron, lubricate the drill bit frequently to cool it. Use oil for steel, turpentine or paraffin (kerosene) for aluminium, turpentine for glass and water for mirrors. When drilling glass, make a small pool of lubricant around the hole in a plasticine ring.

Thin metal should be clamped to a wood backing when being drilled to reduce dis-tortion and keep the drill from jamming as it breaks through to the other side. A piece of thin sheet metal revolving with a drill is extremely dangerous.

Circular saw attachments

These fittings for power drills are very popular, because sawing by hand is a time-consuming business.

Two types are made: *hand-held* ones consist of a 5in. (130mm) or 6in. (150mm) blade, a frame to hold drill and blade steady and allow

Fig.7. *A hole saw cutting large circles out of an aluminium sheet, which is firmly clamped to a wooden backing.*

Fig.11. *The rapidly passing slots allow you to see, through the disc, whether you are holding the blade at the right angle.*

Fig.12   Speeds for two-speed drills

High speed: 2500-3000 rpm	Low speed: up to 1000 rpm
Drilling: *wood up to $\frac{3}{8}$" diameter* *steel up to $\frac{1}{4}$" diameter* Circular saw Jigsaw Sanding Grinding Hedge trimming	Drilling: *wood over $\frac{3}{8}$" diameter* *steel over $\frac{1}{4}$" diameter* *Masonry* Screwdriving Polishing Paint mixing

Fig.13   Cable sizes for extension cords

For 200-250V drills

Length of extension cable (ft & m)	Current consumption of drill (amps)						
	0-1	5-9	10-14	15-19	20-24	25-30	
25ft (7.5m)	A	B	B	C	D	E	
50ft (15m)	A	B	B	C	D	E	
100ft (30m)	A	B	C	D	D	E	size of cable required
150ft (45m)	B	C	D	E	E	—	
200ft (60m)	C	D	E	E	—	—	
300ft (90m)	C	E	—	—	—	—	

For 110-160V drills

Length of extension cable (ft & m)	Current consumption of drill (amps)						
	0-4	5-9	10-14	15-19	20-24	25-30	
25ft (7.5m)	A	B	B	C	D	E	
50ft (15m)	A	B	C	D	D	E	
100ft (30m)	B	D	D	E	—	—	size of cable required
150ft (45m)	C	D	E	—	—	—	
200ft (60m)	D	E	—	—	—	—	
300ft (90m)	D	—	—	—	—	—	

Cable sizes

Letter	Amperage	cross-sectional size (sq mm)	British size
A	6	0.75	24/.20
B	15	1.5	30/.25
C	20	2.5	50/.25
D	25	4	56/.30
E	42	6	84/.30

it to be slid across the wood to be cut, and a fixed top and retractable bottom blade guard. There is also a *saw table,* or bench-mounted circular saw, where the blade projects upwards through a flat table top.

Unfortunately, neither machine is satisfactory for all types of job. Partly, this is because a circular saw requires a great deal of power to drive it—in fact, rather more power than can be provided by even the largest drill motor. There is a serious danger of overloading the motor to such an extent that it burns out. A drill-driven saw should, therefore, only be used for light work such as battens, mouldings and plywood, and not kept too constantly in use.

Another reason is that, on many jobs—for example, repair work, or where you are fitting architraves or other mouldings—it is necessary to keep removing the drill bit and swapping it for a saw-blade. Often this slows you down to the point where a hand-saw would be quicker.

So that if you intend to do carpentry on a serious scale, a better alternative is to buy a proper *bench saw* with an adequate motor,

which will do everything that a drill-driven saw table can do—and more—faster and more safely. The use of this tool is fully described in CHAPTER 48. It is used in exactly the same way as the smaller, less powerful saw table, so only the use of the hand-held type of saw is described here.

Using a hand-held circular saw

Saw attachments should only be used on medium- or large-sized drills, and then only for work that is unlikely to overstrain the motor. The 5-inch blade gives a depth of cut of 1½in. (38mm), and the 6-inch blade one of 1⅞in. (48mm) when set up normally on the machine, and this is about the maximum depth of cut the motor will stand. If the motor shows signs of slowing down or jamming, stop work immediately or you may burn it out on the spot. It is essential that the motor should be kept running at a high speed all the time to keep it from being damaged. Do not press the saw forward too hard, and always start the motor before the blade touches the wood, so that the speed of the

motor stays up. You need a straight edge, and some practice, to bring in the blade at exactly the point where you want to cut; sighting straight down the blade will make it easier.

Saw cuts can be kept straight by nailing a batten to the wood you are cutting, and running the saw along it; or by using the adjustable *rip fence* on the saw, which guides it parallel to the edge of the wood.

Four types of blade are available: the *rip blade,* with coarse teeth, for cutting along the grain; the fine-toothed *cross-cut;* the *planer blade,* which gives an extra-neat result, and the most useful type, the *combination blade,* which cuts at any angle to the grain. Sharpening and maintaining the blades is fully described in CHAPTER 48.

These blades will not cut metal, so when using the saw on old wood it is essential to remove all nails and screws. To prevent the blade catching on anything underneath the wood, and to reduce the strain on the motor, set the depth gauge of the blade to only slightly more than the thickness of the wood you are

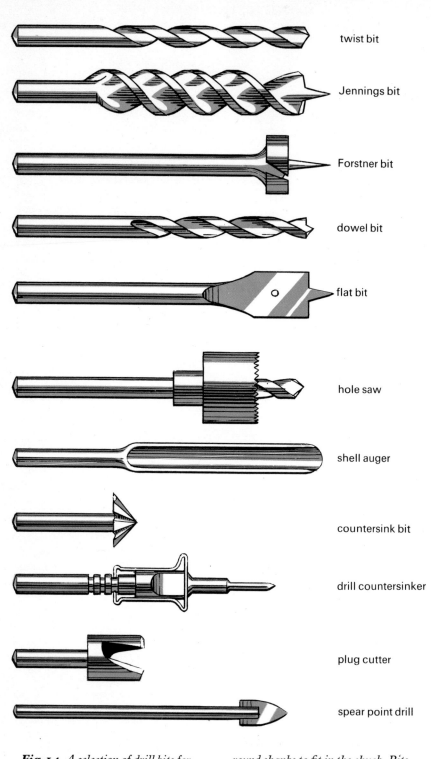

twist bit

Jennings bit

Forstner bit

dowel bit

flat bit

hole saw

shell auger

countersink bit

drill countersinker

plug cutter

spear point drill

Fig.14. *A selection of drill bits for use with power drills. They all have round shanks to fit in the chuck. Bits for handbraces have square shanks.*

thick.

Jigsaws should not be pressed forward too hard, or the highly tempered blade may snap. But they should be held firmly down on to the material they are cutting to resist the down-stroke of the blade.

The blade is narrow enough to cut $\frac{1}{2}$in. (13mm) radius curves, but will not turn a right-angled corner. It can, however, be started in the middle of a piece of wood by tilting the machine forward on its nose and gradually lowering the blade into the wood until it is upright (see Fig.2).

Jig saws are available both as power tool attachments and as integral tools, hand-held or bench-mounted with the blade pointing upwards.

Sanders

Several types of sander can be fitted to a power drill. The most commonly used is the *disc sander.* A flexible rubber disc is mounted in the chuck of the machine and an abrasive paper disc is fastened to it with a recessed central screw.

The sander is used at an angle, so that only one side of the disc touches the surface being sanded (see Fig.4). If the disc is laid flat against the surface it produces circular marks called *swirl marks,* which may be deep and difficult to remove. Even with the disc used at the correct angle, slight swirl marks are unavoidable.

A special type of disc called the 'Swirlaway' reduces these marks to a minimum. The disc is made of metal, and is flat and completely rigid. To give it flexibility in use, the shaft on which it is mounted can be bent at a slight angle while it is turning.

The *drum sander* consists of a wide revolving drum made of stiff foam rubber, with an abrasive belt fastened around its edge. It makes no swirl marks, but can only be used for sanding small objects or narrow strips of wood. On large, flat surfaces it tends to give an uneven result.

The *orbital sander,* on the other hand, can be used to give a perfect finish to any surface. It has a large, flat sanding pad covered by an abrasive sheet. This moves to and fro in a small circle without revolving, so it leaves no swirl marks at all. Orbital sanders are available both as attachments and as integral tools.

The abrasive discs, belts, and sheets for all these tools are available in coarse, medium and fine grades as well as special types such as 'wet-and-dry' and 'preparation' for rubbing down paintwork.

Other attachments

Many highly specialized attachments are available for power drills. These include *rotary files* for finishing the edges of metal sheet, *polishing pads,* made of lambswool, that fit over the rubber sanding disc, *wire brushes* for removing rust from metal, *screwdriver attachments,* useful when a large number of screws have to be driven, and even *paint stirrers* and *hedge trimmers.* Among the most useful are *grinding wheels,* which can save a lot of time in sharpening knives, chisels and plane blades. Special extra-tough wheels are made for sharpening masonry drills.

cutting. A circular saw blade cuts on the up-stroke, so setting the blade as shallow as possible gives a neater result by flattening the angle at which it cuts.

If the blade of the saw wanders off the cutting line, do not twist the saw to straighten the line. This may jam the blade in the cut, with disastrous results. Take the saw out of the cut, go back a few inches and cut along that section again.

Jigsaws

A power-driven jigsaw is used in the same way as a hand-held coping saw—that is, for cutting curves and complex shapes. Its blade is small and pointed and moves rapidly up and down with a stabbing motion. Various types of blade are available for cutting wood, plastic and sheet metal, but it will not cut very thick boards or sheets. It can manage a 2in. (50mm) thick softwood board, or hardwood half as

Building a gable roof

Apart from flat roofs, gable roofs are the simplest type of roof to construct. With the correct techniques and approach even the least experienced carpenter can handle the job.

A gable roof is a pitched roof with vertical ends, as opposed to a hipped roof, which has sloping ends.

The angle of slope, or *pitch,* of the gable roof, can be between 20° and 60°. The steeper slopes are more efficient in dispersing rainwater, but are generally used for purely decorative effect.

Some angles of pitch will spoil the look of the roof. An angle of 45° somehow looks odd, whereas any angle between 50° and 60° seems normal.

The design of the roof will depend on a variety of factors, the most important being the building regulations that apply in your case. In Britain, for example, the Building Regulations lay down standards for all types of construction and these must be adhered to exactly. Local authorities may also insist on new erections conforming to certain other requirements—your gable roof may have to conform with the design of others in your street, for example. In historic towns the local regulations are likely to be particularly restrictive.

Components of a gable roof

The wooden framework of a complete gable roof for a brick house is shown on the following pages. Its equivalent for a timber frame house is shown in CHAPTER 41. Some of the terms you will encounter when planning your roof are:
Wall plate: in a brick house, a piece of timber, usually 4in. x 3in. or 100mm x 75mm, built into the top of the brickwork along the long walls. It is bedded in cement mortar and supplies a fixing point for the foot of the rafter on either side of the roof. In a timber house it is the top component of the timber frame, usually 4in. x 2in.
Common rafter: one of the main support timbers of the roof, which run in pairs between the wall plates and the ridge board and at right angles to

This open gable roof is not supported by collar ties or joists. The supports that are there—purlins, rafters, and struts running to the chimney breast are, therefore, of heavier timber than would otherwise be needed.

them. The size depends on the spacing between rafters, and the span and loading of the roof.

Ceiling joists: timbers that run parallel to the short walls of the house, horizontally from wall plate to wall plate. The feet of the rafters are fixed to the ends of the joists as well as to the wall plates. Their size depends on their spacing and span, and the load they carry.

Ridge board: the highest point of the roof, this is a piece of sawn timber which runs the full length of the roof. It is usually 1¼in. (31mm) thick and its depth is sufficient to accommodate the angled ends of the rafters plus a bit standing proud above the rafter tops. The rafters are nailed to the ridge board.

Purlin: an intermediate support timber that is as long as the wall plates and runs parallel to them. Purlins are nailed to the inside edge of the rafters, usually about half way up their height.

Collar ties: pieces of timber that run horizontally between pairs of rafters parallel to the short walls. They are nailed to about every fourth rafter.

Struts: supports that run diagonally from the purlins to a suitable surface, such as an internal dividing wall, to provide extra support. On this surface, the struts are nailed to pieces of timber called *sole plates.*

Fascia: a length of prepared timber approximately 6in. x 1in. (150mm x 25mm); the size depends on the size of the rafters. It is fixed to the foot of the rafters to provide a finish here. The rainwater gutter is fixed to the fascia.

Soffit: a timber, plywood or asbestos cement covering which is fixed to the underside of the rafters where these protrude beyond the walls of the building. It provides a watertight seal and a neat finish.

Bargeboards: a pair of boards like fascias except that they are sloping and are fixed to the last rafters at the gable end of the roof.

Eaves: this describes the whole area of the ends of the rafters.

Tilting fillet: a piece of timber with a wedge-like cross-section fixed near the foot of the rafters. Its top edge is flush with the top of the fascia board. It lifts the ends of the roofing tiles slightly to provide a good fitting and firm ends.

Battens: 2in. x 1in. or 50mm x 25mm sawn timbers which are nailed to the top edge of the rafters parallel to the ridge. The roofing tiles or slates are fixed to the battens. Their spacing depends on the size of the tiles or slates.

'Look-out' rafters: timber supports for the end rafters of a roof that oversails (projects beyond) the gable walls. They are fixed at right angles to the common rafters. They do not run the whole length of the roof but are nailed to the side or underside of the first rafters inside the gable walls.

Hanging beams or runners: used to brace ceiling joists, especially over long spans. They bind the joists together and prevent them from twisting. Hanging beams run parallel to the long sides of the roof, and are fixed to the joists by small vertical *hangers* which are placed on alternate sides of the hanging beam. Hangers are often 2in. x 1in. or 50mm x 25mm.

Sarking felt: bituminous coated felt nailed to the rafters under the battens. It adds waterproofing to the roof and aids heat insulation.

Roofing tiles: the traditional finish for gable roofs used to be slates, but these have generally been superseded by concrete tiles with a coloured finish. The tiles are fixed to the battens by hook-like lugs called *nibs,* and sometimes by nails passed through moulded holes in the tile. Each tile overlaps the one below it by half its length, so that the roof is two tiles thick.

Eaves tile: a shorter tile to start off the roof covering. Its size is that of the other roofing tiles minus the overlap. The area of each ordinary roofing tile visible when the roof is complete is known as the *margin.*

Ridge tile: a special tile shaped to cover the apex of the roof over the ridge board, and seal the gap between the topmost tiles on either side of it.

Approaching the job

Building a gable roof is relatively straightforward if approached in the correct manner. It is however, a long and heavy job which is hard to do single handed. A great deal depends on correct positioning of the timber and it is particularly important that the ridge board is in square. You should have at least one helper.

You will be working at a considerable height from the ground in most cases. Building a gable

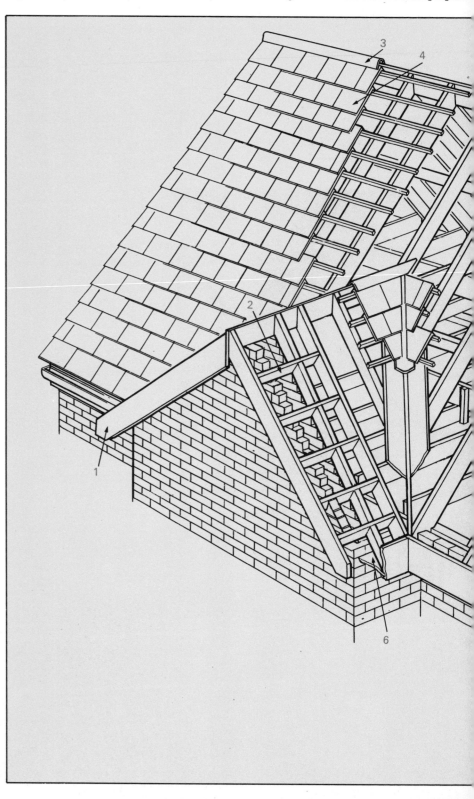

roof on to a garage, however, will not present too many difficulties in this respect and a work platform constructed of two stepladders and a sturdy plank may be sufficient if it is properly braced. The garage, however, may be too high to allow you to use this makeshift support, and if you are building the roof on a two-storey house you will need a higher and more efficient work platform.

A platform tower, which can be hired from tool hire firms, will enable you to reach the job. This is a tower made of prefabricated scaffolding-like sections that slot together to reach any reason-able height. At the top there is a good size plat-form made up of planks. The whole structure is mounted on wheels so that it moves around easily. The wheels can be locked to hold the tower still. The tower's work platform is reached by an ordinary ladder.

Setting out the wall plates

Once planning and building permission have been obtained, and the walls of the building (but not the gable ends) are complete to the top, mark out the positions of the joists on the wall plates. By the time you come to start the roof you will know the size and the spacing of the joists. Mark their positions on the wall plates by laying the two wall plates together on the ground with their long edges butting. Draw lines to indicate where one edge of the joists will meet the wall plate. On one side of these lines make a pencil cross. This will ensure that you do not nail some of the joists on the wrong side of the pencil lines.

The wall plates can now be fixed in place on the brickwork. Be careful to position them correctly—if the roof is to oversail the gable walls all the parts of the wall plates that protrude must

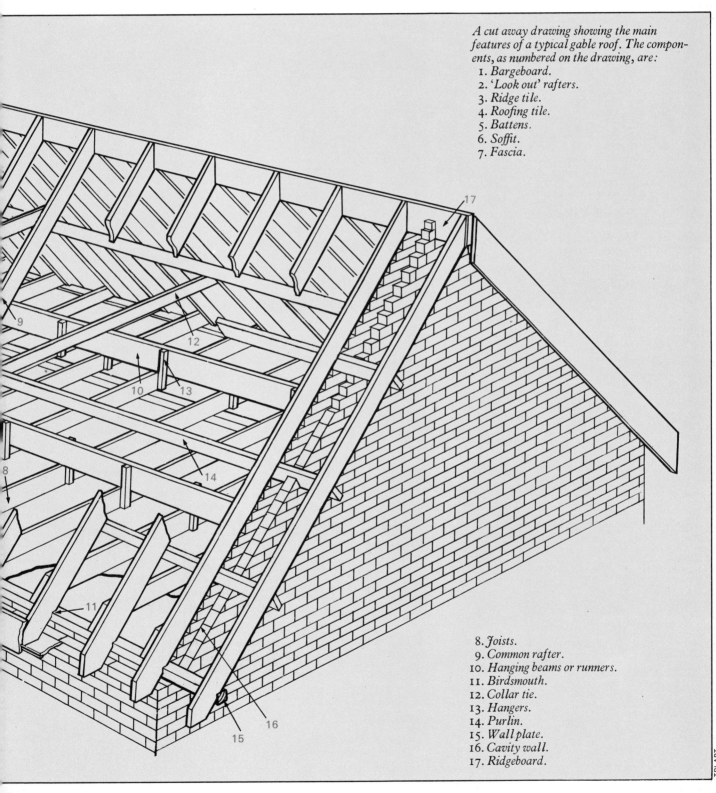

A cut away drawing showing the main features of a typical gable roof. The components, as numbered on the drawing, are:
1. *Bargeboard.*
2. *'Look out' rafters.*
3. *Ridge tile.*
4. *Roofing tile.*
5. *Battens.*
6. *Soffit.*
7. *Fascia.*

8. *Joists.*
9. *Common rafter.*
10. *Hanging beams or runners.*
11. *Birdsmouth.*
12. *Collar tie.*
13. *Hangers.*
14. *Purlin.*
15. *Wall plate.*
16. *Cavity wall.*
17. *Ridgeboard.*

TRI-ART

179

be of equal length. The wall plates are fixed to the long walls of the building because the joists, which meet the plates at right angles, usually run the shortest distance across a roof. In a brick cavity wall, the wall plate is bedded in cement mortar on top of the inside course. Figs.1 and 2 shows a cross section of the eaves of a gable roof and the position of the wall plate. If there is an internal dividing wall running parallel to the ridge of the roof, top it with a sole plate the same size, and fixed in the same way as, the wall plate. This will provide a midway support for the ceiling joists and reduce their span and—hence, the size of timber needed.

The joists

In Britain the sizes of ceiling joists are listed in the Building Regulations. Four standard spacings are listed, but the most useful and most commonly used is 16in. (407mm). The chart given below lists sizes of joists spaced at 16in. centres. It will enable you to make a reasonably accurate dimensional drawing to take to your

Fig.1. A cross-section of the eaves of a gable roof. Here the rafters oversail the wall. An angled cut made at the bottom of the foot of the rafter provides a fixing for the soffit board.
Fig.2. An alternative finish at the eaves. The rafters end flush with the outer skin of the wall. A soffit is not needed as the fascia seals the rafter ends against the weather.

local authority. It is only a rough guide, but close enough that you will not have to completely re-design.

For dead loads of between 5 and 20lbs per sq ft (the normal range in ordinary timber and tile roofs):

Size of joist (in.)	Maximum span between the wall plates
3 x 2	6ft 2in.
4 x 2	8ft 3in.
5 x 2	10ft 4in.
6 x 2	12ft 2in.
7 x 2	14ft 3in.
8 x 2	16ft 3in.
9 x 2	18ft 4in.

The length of the joists should be sufficient to allow a small overhang at the two long walls to enable the rafters to be nailed to them at a later stage. Cut all the joists to the required size —any slight variation in their length when fixed will not be noticeable when the roof is finished. Skew-nail the joists in place at the positions marked on top of the wall plates. (In a timber house, for reasons given below, the rafters *must* be immediately over the studs, so the joists must be just beside these).

Setting out the roof

The most difficult part in building a gable roof is to set out the various components correctly. The task requires precise measurement and marking—a trial and error approach to this sort

of job will be costly and frustrating.

When you have designed your roof make a scale drawing of it. Use a scale of 12:1—1in. on the scale drawing will thus equal 1ft in the roof. This will enable you to calculate the span and the height of the roof accurately, which you will need to do to execute the most difficult job— setting out the rafters. If you are using metric measurements, the scale should be 10:1.

Size of rafters

In Britain, the size of timbers used for roof rafters is governed by the Building Regulations. These list sizes of rafters for roofs with a pitch of between 35° and 40° and for roofs with a pitch of 40° or over. The chart below gives rafter sizes and lengths for roofs pitched at 40° or over, for a 16in. (407mm) spacing of rafter. For roofs pitched at between 35° and 40° the permitted span is 2 to 3in. shorter. Use the chart as a guide to draw up your dimensional plan to present to the building inspector.

For dead loads of between 5 and 20lbs per sq ft:

Rafter size (in.)	Maximum span across the building
1½ x 3	7ft 3in.
1½ x 4	9ft 9in.
1½ x 5	12ft 2in.
2 x 3	7ft 11in.
2 x 4	10ft 7in.
2 x 5	13ft 2in.

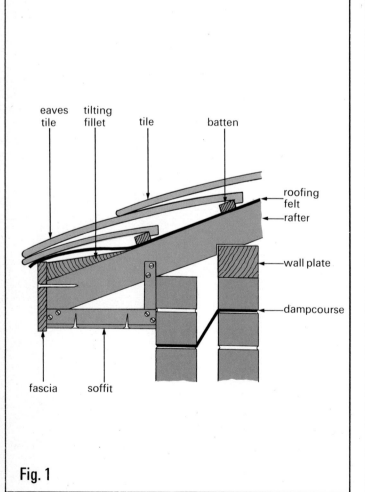

Fig. 1

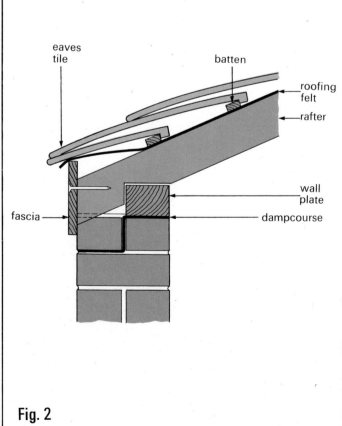

Fig. 2

It is essential, when building a gable roof, to set out the components accurately. This is particularly so in the case of the rafters, where a trial-and-error approach will be both costly and frustrating.

Setting out the rafters

The method of setting out a rafter is shown in Fig.3. The method is the same whether you want the roof to oversail the long walls or whether you want it to end flush with these walls. The only difference is the shape of the foot of the rafters (see Figs.1 and 2). [In the case of the former, the foot will have to be cut so that it has one vertical surface to take the fascia and one horizontal surface for the soffit or its supporting frame. In the case of the latter, the foot of the rafter has a single angled cut made so that the fascia can be fastened on vertically. More details on fascias and soffits and their fixing are given in CHAPTER 34.

To set out the rafters, lay a long piece of timber (marked 'A' in Fig. 3) on a level piece of ground and position wooden pegs along its edges so that it stays in position. Near one end of this piece make a pencil mark. From this mark, using your scale drawing to obtain the correct dimensions, measure and mark a distance equal to half the span of the roof. The span of the roof is the distance between the outside edges of the two wall plates. Next take a second piece of timber, 'B', a few feet longer than the height of the roof, and peg it to the ground at right angles to 'A'. Position it so that its end butts the second marked line on timber 'A'. One edge of 'B' should be inside the second line by a distance which equals half the thickness of the ridge board.

The next step is to measure and mark, on these pieces of timber, the position and shape of the wall plate and ridge board. Then take a piece of the timber you intend to use for the rafters. Cut it to a length a couple of feet longer than that needed—remembering any overhang that you may require at the eaves. You can judge the length by reference to your scale drawing or by measuring the distance between the marked positions of the ridge board and wall plate on the two pieces of timber that are pegged to the ground.

The rafters of a gabled roof fit over the wall plate by means of a *birdsmouth,* a triangular-shaped cut, made near the foot of the rafter. This ensures that the weight of the rafter presses

directly downwards on the top surface of the wall plate and not on its outside corner. The birdsmouth should never be cut deeper than one-third the width of the rafter.

Now take the over-length rafter and lay it diagonally across the two pieces of timber pegged to the ground. One end of this rafter should run to and just pass over the marked position of the ridge board. If you are using normal ridge tiles on your roof, there will be a U-shaped gap under their centres to allow the ridge board to project 1-2in. (25-50mm) above the tops of the rafters without lifting the ridge tile off them. Allow for this projection when fitting the rafters to the ridge board; the deeper you can make this board the better, because it will add to the strength of the roof.

Near its other end, the rafter should pass over the marked position of the wall plate. The part of the marked position of the wall plate that is covered should not be more than one-third the width of the rafter, because of the limitation on the depth of the birdsmouth. When you have correctly positioned the over-length rafter, lightly nail it to the two pieces of timber.

Then mark out where the birdsmouth will be and the angle at which the rafter meets the ridge board. Use a straight edge to do this, sighting what can be seen of the previously marked areas as a guide. If your roof is to oversail the walls at the eaves, you will also have to mark the bottom corner at the foot of the rafter so that a surface can be cut that will be parallel to the joists in the finished roof. If these eaves are to be flush with the long walls there is no need to cut the foot of the rafter to shape. Ensure that the bottom end of the rafter is cut slightly over-length—the excess wood can be trimmed off when all the rafters have been fixed in place. The method of doing this is described in CHAPTER 21.

The next step is to remove the rafter from the pieces pegged to the ground and cut out the birdsmouth and the angle at the top of the rafter and, if necessary, the surface at the foot of the rafter to which the soffits will later be fixed.

Now make another rafter, marking it by laying the first rafter on the top of it. Keep the *top* edges of the two boards flush so that, even if there is a variation in the depth of the boards, the distance above the birdsmouth will be equal. Mark the second rafter using the first as a guide and then cut it to shape.

Now try these two rafters on the walls of the building. Place a piece of scrap wood the same thickness as the ridge board between the tops of the rafters. With lengths of battens, temporarily prop the rafters in place in the same manner as is used later for fixing the first set of rafters. This is described below and shown in Fig.7. Check that the rafters slope at about the pitch you require—it is unlikely that the angle will be perfectly accurate. If the angle is badly out, the two rafters have been cut to the wrong length and you will have to do the setting out process again.

If the angle is right, take the two rafters down. Mark the first one 'Pattern' and use this to mark out all the other rafters. These can now be cut to shape and placed in convenient positions on the ground around the building. Remember

when using the pattern to have its top edge flush with the top edge of the rafter being marked out. Then, even if the width of the rafters differs, the height above the birdsmouth will be the same.

Setting out the ridge board

The length of the ridge board depends on whether you want the roof to oversail the end walls or not. If you do, it should oversail the walls by the same amount as the wall plates. The depth of the ridge board must be at least the depth of the angled cut made on the top ends of the rafters, and preferably more, so that the top of the ridge board stands proud of the tops of the rafters.

It will involve less work if the ridge board is one single length of timber. If you cannot get a timber long enough, the pieces that make the ridge board should be scarf jointed together before you set it out (see Fig.5 for how to make this joint).

Setting out the ridge board involves marking on it the positions the tops of the rafters will occupy in the finished roof. You must work accurately but, since the rafters are in opposite pairs, you only have to mark one side of the board.

First mark out the positions of the rafters on the wall plate. The placing of the joists will determine the rafter positions. One face of each rafter, when fixed, touches one side of each joist and is nailed to it. To be equally spaced, the rafters must later on be nailed to one side (the same side) of each joist. Mark a line on the wall plate away from the side of the joist to a distance equalling the thickness of the rafter. Do this on the same side of each joist. Make a cross between the marked lines and the side of each joist as shown in Fig.4.

Now mark out the position where the rafters will meet the ridge board in the finished roof. To do this, lay the ridge board at right angles across the joists just over the wall plates. Position the ridge board accurately and lightly nail it to the joists. Place a straight edge across the ridge board lining up with the side of each

joist from which the position where the rafters meet the wall plate was marked. Draw pencil lines to indicate the sides of the joists on the ridge board. On the side of the pencil line *away* from the joist, make a cross (see Fig.4). When the ridge board is erected the top ends of the rafters will cover these crosses and one edge of each rafter will run along the pencil lines.

Erecting the roof

The most difficult part of this operation is to fix two pairs of rafters and position the ridge board correctly at the same time. The two pairs of rafters should be those at the ends of the roof, but *inside* the house walls. (If the roof is to oversail the end walls, do not fix the rafters on the tips of the wall plates first. These are nailed in place later.)

To fix two pairs of rafters and the ridge board in place, first lay one pair of rafters on the ground in roughly the position they will occupy in the finished roof, leaving a gap wide enough for the ridge board between their top ends. Nail a piece of batten across each rafter near the top so that the rafter tops and length of batten form a triangle. The batten should be placed far enough from the apex of the triangle so that the ridge board, when slotted into the gap, will occupy its desired position when resting on the batten. Use one nail only to nail the batten to each of the rafters. This will allow some play in the assembly during the positioning. Repeat this process with the other pair of rafters.

Lay one pair of rafters on the joists at one end of the roof so that the apex of the triangle they form points towards the opposite end wall. At the other end of the roof, position the rafters on the wall plates on the marked positions and nail them lightly in place. You

Fig.3. To set out the first rafter, peg two lengths of timber to a level piece of ground. Mark on them the shape and planned position of the wall plate and ridge board. Lay a piece of the timber you intend to use for the rafters across these two points. Mark the position of the wall plate and the ridge on the rafter.
Fig.4. Mark the points at which the rafters will meet the ridge board before you fix the ridge in place. Do this by laying the ridge on the joists just over the wall plate. Mark a pencil line at a point that indicates one side (the same side) of each rafter.
Fig.5. The ridge board can be jointed along its length with a scarf joint and gang nails.
Fig.6. The method of fixing one pair of rafters to the ridge board. The first rafter is nailed in place from the opposite face of the ridge. The second rafter is skew-nailed in place.

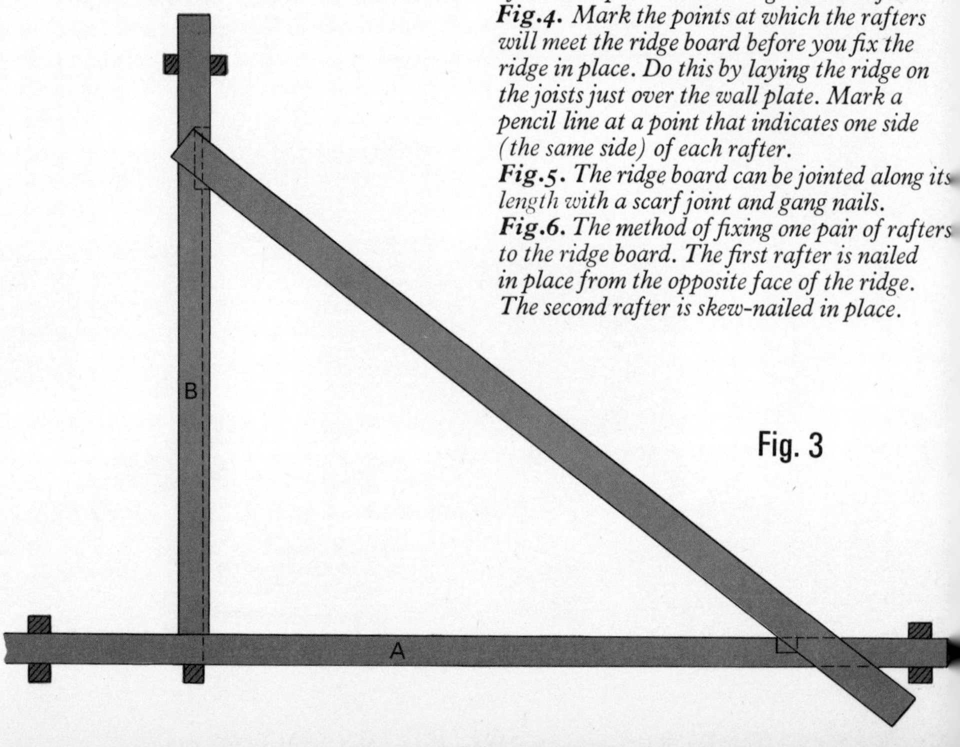

Fig. 3

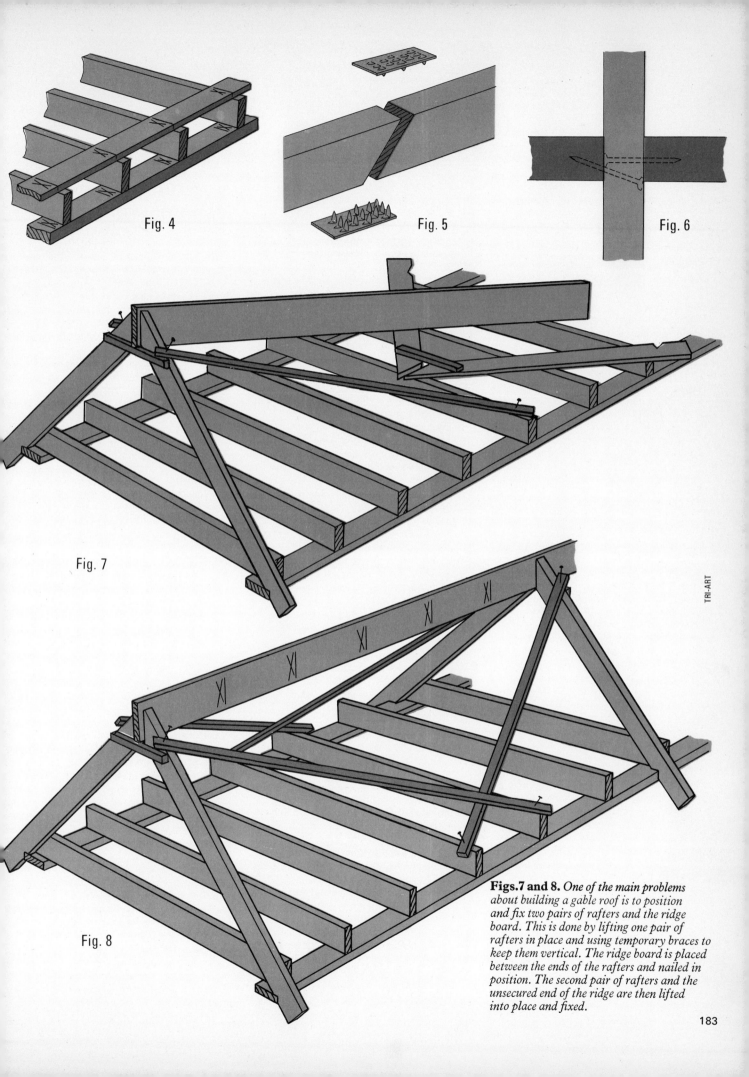

Fig. 4

Fig. 5

Fig. 6

Fig. 7

Fig. 8

TRI-ART

Figs.7 and 8. *One of the main problems about building a gable roof is to position and fix two pairs of rafters and the ridge board. This is done by lifting one pair of rafters in place and using temporary braces to keep them vertical. The ridge board is placed between the ends of the rafters and nailed in position. The second pair of rafters and the unsecured end of the ridge are then lifted into place and fixed.*

will need some assistance to do this. Next, nail a long temporary support brace to each rafter near their tops and to each end of one of the joists some distance away (see Fig.7). The birdsmouth cut in the rafters should fit over the wall plates.

Lift the ridgeboard into place so that one end is between the top ends of the rafters that have been temporarily fixed in place. The other end should rest on the joists at the other end of the roof.

Now lift the second assembly of rafters up and secure it in position with support braces. Slide the ridge board along the channel formed by the ends of the rafters and the battens until it occupies the correct position. Once the ridge board is in place, skew nail the feet of the four rafters firmly to the wall plates and to the adjoining joists. Then nail the tops of the rafters to the ridge board. Now remove the battens and the support braces and check that everything is straight.

Once two sets of rafters and the ridge board have been fixed in place, the fixing of the other rafters is simple. Lift each one to the job and nail it in place on the position marked on the wall plate and ridge board. One rafter of each pair can be nailed to the ridge board from its opposite face. The second rafter of the pair is skew nailed to the ridge board (see Fig.6).

The next step, if the roof is to oversail the end walls, is to provide some additional support for the rafters which are positioned outside the end walls. In a brick house, this is done by nailing lengths of timber to the sides of the first two rafters inside the end walls, and passing out through notches in the top of the brick gable—which must, of course, be built up to its full height at this stage.

To build a brick gable end, the outline of the brickwork must first be determined. To do this, tie a length of string to the end of the ridge board and take it to one edge of the wall that runs parallel to the ridge. Tie the other end of the string to a masonry pin and knock it into a convenient mortar course. Do the same at the other side of the roof. The lengths of string now show the required outline of the brickwork at the gable ends.

When the lines are in place you can start to build up the brickwork in the usual way. The end bricks of each course have to be cut so that they follow the slope of the lines. You can cut bricks with a bolster and club hammer. If the gable ends are to be finished with a tile verge the bricks should be cut carefully to ensure as neat a finish as possible. If you intend finishing the gable with a bargeboard, though, you do not have to be so careful—any small irregularities in the outer profile of the bricks can be filled with mortar to the string line.

In a timber house the gable ends are filled in by 3in. x 2in. framing, the top members of which carry the short lookout rafters.

Use timber the same size as the rafters for these pieces, space them at the same intervals as the rafters, and nail them to the rafters inside the end wall. Place them so that each is supported by one of the brick steps in the end wall.

In all roofs, the tops of the end brick walls have to be covered so at least one rafter has to

be outside the end walls. If the roof is not to oversail these walls the inside face of this rafter is butted against the outer surface of the end wall.

Other supports

The next step is to provide greater internal bracing for the roof structure. This is done by means of purlins, collar ties and struts. The size of purlins is governed in Britain by the Building Regulations but if you plan your roof for 9in. x 2in. purlins you will not be far wrong. Purlins run the whole length of the roof and are nailed to the under side of the rafters. Usually one purlin is used for each side of the roof and they are positioned about centrally along the length of the rafters. At their ends, purlins are built into the inside leaf of the cavity wall of the brick gable, so they give extra support to the end rafters. Where they run into the brickwork they must be wrapped in building felt as a precaution against rot.

Next, install the collar ties and diagonal struts. Collar ties can be the same size as the rafters and nailed horizontally between pairs of rafters. The maximum spacing is between every fourth pair of rafters, but you may prefer to put in more than that for extra strength.

If the house has a central internal dividing wall running parallel to the ridge board, struts should be fixed to the collar-tied rafters running from the intersection of collar-tie, purlin and rafter to a 4in. x 3in. or 100 x 75mm sole plate bedded in mortar along the top of the wall exactly like a wall plate. The struts should be firmly skew-nailed to the sole plate.

If no partition wall is available to take the ends of the struts, these are nailed to hanging beams or runners, fixed to tops of the joists and running at right angles to them. They should be bigger than the joists—exact sizes involve a lot of engineering calculation, but design for 9in. x 2in. and you will have a starting point—and set on edge. Most roofs that require these supports have two, one in each half of the roof. Fasten them to the joists with hangers, usually 2in. x 1in. pieces of timber, which are nailed at the corners of the hanging beams and the joists on alternate sides of the hanging beams.

The fascias and soffits

The methods of fixing and the materials used for these components of a roof are described in full in CHAPTER 21. But note that, in a timber house, the soffit support boards are nailed to the ends of the rafters and to the studs—this is why the former must be above the latter.

At the verge of a gable roof two types of finish can be used. The first, mentioned briefly above is to cut the end bricks of each gable course carefully and smooth them over with mortar prior to tiling. An alternative which is more common in older British houses, is to fit a bargeboard. These are lengths of timber like fascias, except that they run up the slope of a gable rather than being fixed horizontally. The bargeboards are not part of the roof support—they simply give a weatherproof finish at this point of the roof. Bargeboards and their fixings are dealt with in CHAPTER 34.

The tilting fillets should also be installed at this stage. These run the whole length of the roof

and are fitted in the V-shaped intersection between the top of the fascia board and the feet of the rafters. Not all roofs require a tilting fillet, but their purpose in those that do is to lift the eaves tiles or slates slightly and to provide a firmer support for these tiles.

Once the basic components of the roof are in place, it is advisable to treat all the timbers with a preservative to prevent attacks of dry rot and woodworm. Some local authorities insist that roof timbers be treated in this way.

The roof covering

The gable roof must, of course, be covered with some type of waterproof material. Slates were once in widespread use but they are less common nowadays and tend to be expensive. Tiles made from cement and coloured a dull green or red or dark brown are more usual. To supplement the waterproofing qualities of both tiles and slates a bituminous roofing felt is nailed to the rafters before the tiles or slates are applied.

Nail the strips of roofing felt across the tops of the rafters, working from the eaves towards the ridge board so that the overlaps point 'downhill'. Lay the first strip so that it overhangs the long wall a little way and overlap the joints between the strips of felt on all the successive strips. To apply the felt you will need to build a cat ladder.

A cat ladder allows you to clamber up and down the slope of a roof in reasonable safety. It is simply a ladder made of square timber with rungs about 15in. (380mm) apart. It has a block of wood, 4in. x 2in. (100mm x 50mm), nailed to it at the top so that it can be hooked over the ridge. The cat ladder is secured by tying it to the main ladder—the one you used for access to the roof—or, if possible, by lashing it to a convenient chimney. It is a useful piece of equipment for all roofing jobs.

When the felt has been applied, fix battens to the rafters, parallel to the long wall. Both slates and tiles are fixed to these battens which are 2in. x 1in. pieces of timber. They can be jointed along their length if necessary, providing you do this over a rafter. The spacing of the battens depends on the size of tile or slate used; both materials are fitted so that they overlap. The space between the lowest batten and the fascia board is narrower than the space between one batten and another. This is because the eaves tile is narrower than the other tiles.

Slates are fixed to the battens with zinc nails—two to each slate is usual. Tiles hang on the battens by means of nibs, small protruding pieces on the underside of the top of the tile. Nail holes are provided in each tile. Apart from the eaves, end, and ridge tiles, though, it is not usual to nail every tile in place. Except in exposed conditions only every fourth tile is nailed, usually with copper nails. When covering a roof with tiles or slates work upwards from the foot of the rafters, fixing the eaves course first. This will ensure that the overlap points 'downhill'. The waterproofing qualities of the tiles are enhanced if the joins between them that are at right angles to the wall plates are staggered from course to course. At the ends of the roof (nearest the gable walls) a tile 1½ times the length of the ordinary tiles is used.

Shelves and how to fit them

If you are pressed for storage space in your home, extra shelves should prove a godsend. They take up far less floor space than cupboards, and can hold almost as much.

Shelving is the most versatile of all storage methods. Shelves can be built with any degree of strength to support the heaviest objects. Adjustable shelves can be moved up and down in a few minutes to take objects of any height. At the same time, things stored on shelves are always visible and accessible, and do not have to be hunted for as they would if stored in drawers or cupboards.

Shelving can be an important decorative feature, too. Room-dividers in modern houses are often made entirely out of shelves, on which ornaments, books, or hi-fi equipment can be arranged. Glass shelves fastened to walls make an ideal setting for the display of prized possessions, particularly since the glass allows the objects to be viewed from below.

Many kinds of shelving unit are available ready-made, in a wide range of sizes and strengths. They take only a few minutes, and absolutely no skill, to set up and are instantly adjustable. In most systems, the brackets that support the shelves slide up and down metal tracks that are fixed to the wall, or occasionally free-standing.

Ready-made shelving systems, however, do have serious drawbacks. For one thing, nearly all of them are quite expensive. For another, in most of the systems the shelf brackets and frames are large, noticeable and ugly. Furthermore, most ready-made shelving will carry only light or medium loads, and the stronger it is, the uglier.

It might be well at this stage to define what is meant by light, medium and heavy loads. A light load on a shelf is 10lb per foot length (15kg

Below. A simple white-painted shelving unit can set off your crockery or ornaments to their best advantage.

PHOTO AND TEXT

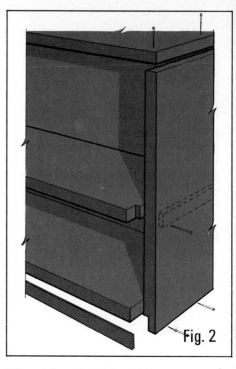

Fig. 2

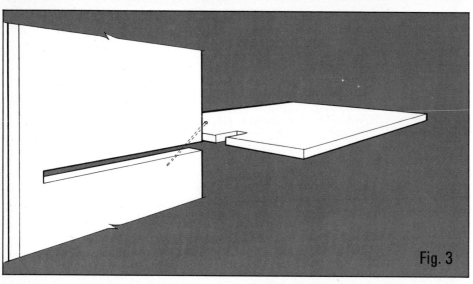

Fig. 3

Fig.1 *(above, left). Boxed-in shelves.*
Fig.2 *(above). Housing joints are often used to make this kind of shelving.*

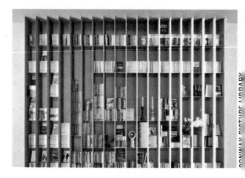

Fig.3 *(above, left). Cheap, light 'egg-box' shelving made of plywood can give a dramatic effect, as in* **Fig.4** *(above).*

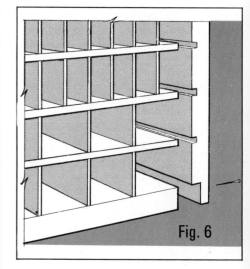

Fig. 6

Fig.5 *(above, left). Vertical spacers strengthen shelving and give it variety.*
Fig.6 *(above). The shelves are supported by housing joints, the spacers pinned.*

Fig.7 *(below, left.) Proprietary shelving brackets support specially-made timber shelves.*
Fig.8 *(below). Details of the support.*

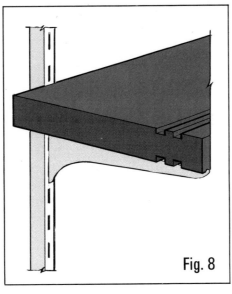

Fig. 8

Fig.9 *(below, left). Glass shelves are ideal for ornaments.* **Fig.10** *(below). They can be invisibly fixed on clear plastic 'buttons'.*

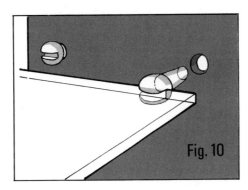

Fig. 10

Fig.11 *(below, left). Hanging shelves supported by roof beams are strong enough to take heavy loads—and there are no awkward brackets.* **Fig.12** *(below). How it works.*

Fig. 12

per metre) or less. An example would be light ornaments or a shallow stack of magazines stored horizontally. A medium load, such as that created by paperback books or large glass storage jars, is up to 20lb per foot (30kg per metre). A heavy load may be as great as 40lb per foot (60kg per metre), and might be made up of large hardback books or records stored on edge. These are much heavier than you might think.

Unless you intend your shelving for a particular use that never changes, it is probably not a good idea to buy or make light-duty shelving. It is all too easy to set up a lot of flimsy shelves with the intention of storing a few magazines on them, and gradually build up the height of the stacks until the shelves collapse. On the other hand, the sturdy metal framing of a heavy-duty ready-made system looks out of place in most living rooms.

The way out of this quandary is to build your own shelving. It can be as strong as you like, and in many cases the brackets or fasteners holding up the shelves can be made completely invisible. Where this is not possible, careful design of the brackets can at least give a 'clean' appearance.

Home-made shelving is normally not adjustable. This, however, is less of a drawback than it would be for a bought system, for you can design it for your particular needs and then it will not need to be adjusted. In practice, most people who buy adjustable shelving never alter the settings anyway.

Invisible fixings

There are two types of 'invisible' fixing for shelves: those that are unseen from above, used for shelves below eye level, and those which are genuinely invisible from any angle. The first kind is easier to build.

Shelves that run the full length of a wall or alcove, and which can be supported at each end by other walls, are much easier to fix unobtrusively than free-standing shelves with open ends. Small glass shelves in alcoves can be held up by virtually invisible clear Perspex supports that plug into holes in the wood or plaster at each end (see Fig.10).

A wooden shelf mounted below eye level can rest on horizontal wood strips plugged and screwed to the wall (see Fig.18). Provided these strips do not come right to the front of the shelf, and their ends are trimmed at an angle, they will not be noticeable. A long shelf can also be given extra support by running a strip along the back. If it is more than 6ft or 2m long and carries heavy loads, one or more brackets may be needed in the middle of the shelf to stop it from twisting and sagging. These brackets can also be hidden—see below.

A shelf running between solid walls and mounted above eye level can be fixed in such a way that nothing shows at all. The supporting strips at each end of the shelf are made either of very narrow wood strips (narrower than the thickness of the shelf) or of aluminium angle strips. Instead of resting on the strips, the shelf is grooved at the ends and slides on to the strips, effectively concealing them (see Fig.19). If the grooves are 'stopped' (do not reach all the way to the front) nothing will be visible.

Grooves in the ends of shelves should be cut with a plough plane, if you have one. The end of a piece of blockboard is hard to plough neatly because the joints between the blocks impede the plane blade. The best way to do it is to make deep cuts with a marking knife to mark the edges of the groove, then to set the plane blade very fine and alter its setting very slowly.

If you don't have a plough plane, the grooves can be made just as well with a narrow mortise chisel the same width as the groove.

This method is very suitable for blockboard shelves, because they are quite thick and will conceal a wide, strong supporting strip. It is important that blockboard shelves are made with their internal blocks running *along* the shelf, or they will have little strength. These shelves are normally edged to hide the blocks and make the front look neater. In this case, the groove can be cut right across the shelf and its front masked with edging strip.

All these techniques can also be applied to

Fig.13 (left). A highly original shelving idea: three wooden shelves drilled at the corners and hung from thick, knotted ropes. But you need plenty of confidence to put a tall, fragile oil lamp on them.

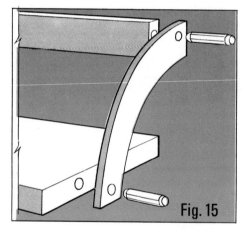

Fig.14 (left). If you can't hide brackets, why not make a feature of them? Fig.15 (above). The curved plywood brackets are held to the shelves by dowels.

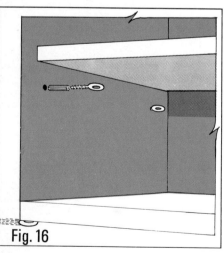

Fig.16 (above). Shelves look good in alcoves, and are easy to install there.

Fig.17 (above). One of the simplest alcove mountings: screw-eyes and wall plugs.

shelves mounted around inside and outside corners (see Fig.20). The shelf on one side of the corner acts as a brace for the shelf on the other side. However, both ends must be firmly attached to their mounting and not just resting on it, for the force exerted by pressing down on one end of a corner shelf may lift the other end. A shelf resting on wood strips can simply be screwed to them. One slotted into invisible mountings is harder to fix, unless the mounting strips are very wide and can have a screw passed through them from above. It may be easier to plug and screw the shelf to the wall instead. A small 'pocket' cut out of the less visible side of the shelf, with a screw passing through it into the wall at an angle is one solution (see Fig.21).

Free-standing shelves

Shelves which do not have their ends supported by a wall are harder to fix unobtrusively. Most people putting up this kind of shelf settle for small, neat brackets, but if you feel you must have invisible fixings, there are solutions to the problem.

The simplest method is suitable only for timber-framed stud walls—common in the United States, Australia and New Zealand. Few houses in Britain have this type of wall, except in the 'box room' over the stairs, but a few recently-built houses have stud partition walls. Large coach screws—at least 9in. (230mm) long and $\frac{3}{8}$in. (9mm) thick—are screwed into the studs, which are generally 16in. (400mm) apart. Once they are firmly screwed in, their heads are sawn off. Holes the diameter of the screws are then drilled into the shelf from the back edge and the shelf is then slid on to the screws (see Fig.23). This fixing method is very strong, provided the timber for the shelves is twice as thick as the screws, and provided the screws project about two-thirds of the width of the boards.

Another similar method for brick or breeze-block walls uses steel angle brackets—the flat solid steel kind, not the U-section type made of sheet metal. The horizontal parts of the brackets are slotted into the shelf as the coach screws were. The only difference is that the slots in the shelf are rectangular, rather than round. These slots are made by drilling several holes and cutting out the wood between them with a long, narrow chisel. It is easier to make the slots too wide and insert narrow pieces of wood as a wedge to hold the shelf firm to the brackets.

The other half of the bracket is harder to hide. One solution is to plug and screw it to the wall and hide it with a backboard. If there are three or more rows of shelves and the backboard runs behind them all, it can be quite a decorative feature.

A more satisfactory way of hiding the brackets is to recess them into the wall $\frac{1}{4}$in.-$\frac{1}{2}$in. (6-13mm) and cover up the recess with cellulose filler. A neat, shallow channel can be cut in a plaster wall with an ordinary carpenter's chisel, though you will have to sharpen it afterwards. The blade should be held at an angle so that its cutting edge always points towards the centre of the channel. Then, if the blade slips, it will damage the plaster *inside* the channel instead of making a long gash in the wall. Once the channel is cut, use proprietary plugs and screws to fix the bracket to the wall.

As brick is much harder to cut than plaster, the above method is probably not worthwhile for a brick wall.

Brackets should not be placed too near the ends of shelves or they will make it liable to sag in the middle. A proper position for a pair of brackets under a free-standing shelf is roughly one-quarter and three-quarters of the way along it. With this arrangement, neither the middle nor the ends is very far from a solid support. A shelf should always be fixed rigidly to its brackets to stop it from tipping up if the end is pressed down.

Featured fixings

If you cannot hide the fixings of your shelves, the best thing to do is to bring them out into the open and make a feature of them. One way of doing this is to buy a ready-made shelving system, which has the great merit of being adjustable. If this doesn't appeal to you, there are many good-looking fixings you can make yourself.

If you have period furnishings, plain timber brackets are probably the most suitable. A typical design, intended to be made out of $\frac{5}{8}$in. (15mm) thick hardwood, is shown in Fig.22. The shape can, of course, be varied to taste, provided that the vertical depth of the bracket is at least half the width of the shelf. The bracket is best fastened to the back plate with a mortise-and-tenon joint as shown, but can be screwed on from the rear if you prefer.

One of the simplest ways of holding up shelves, and one that looks particularly good with modern furniture, is to run vertical boards up the ends of the shelves to turn them into a wall-mounted box (see Fig.1). All the shelves except the top one should be attached to the vertical boards by stopped housing joints, and the top shelf rebated at each end. (CHAPTER 3 describes how to cut both these joints.) This construction, which makes the shelves look like a bookcase, is very strong. (In good carpentry, shelves are never supported by just the strength of nails driven into the ends.) A backboard, even of hardboard, fitted behind the unit makes it even more stable, by acting as a brace. In a long unit, short vertical 'spacer' boards can be put between the shelves to hold them apart. An attractive random effect can be created by placing these boards at irregular intervals.

There are many other methods of giving your shelving an interesting appearance. For example, the method illustrated in Fig.13 uses heavy rope to hang the shelves from rings at the top of the wall. The rope is knotted under each shelf; the height of the shelves can be adjusted by reknotting the rope. This method is too flexible for fragile ornaments to be put on the shelves, but it is ideal for books or magazines.

One of the most convenient types of shelving consists of large open-sided boxes than can be stacked on each other. As long as the boxes are not stacked too high, they provide a strong, stable storage space that can be rearranged to any shape. If all the boxes are made the same height, but some are twice or three times as wide as the others, an enormous variety of arrangements can be made to suit any use.

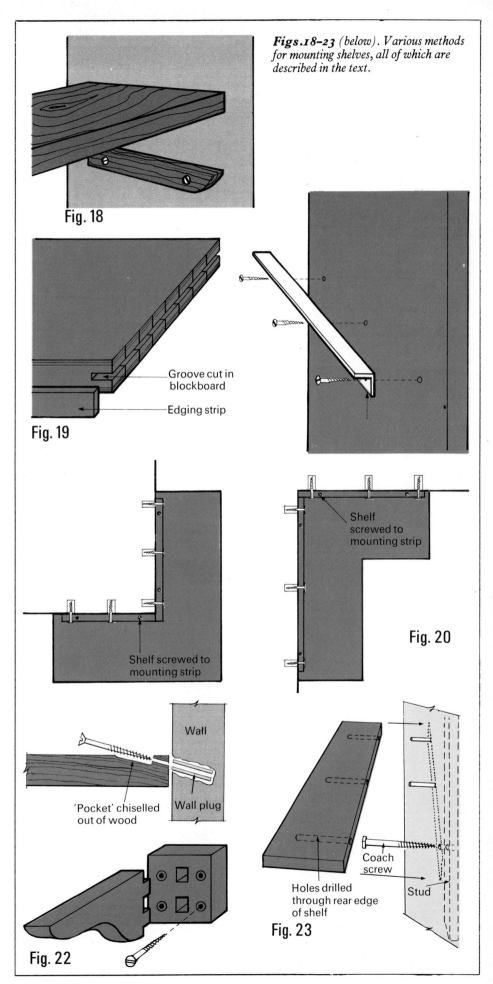

Figs.18-23 (below). *Various methods for mounting shelves, all of which are described in the text.*

Fig. 18

Fig. 19

Groove cut in blockboard

Edging strip

Fig. 20

Shelf screwed to mounting strip

Shelf screwed to mounting strip

Wall

'Pocket' chiselled out of wood

Wall plug

Coach screw

Holes drilled through rear edge of shelf

Stud

Fig. 23

Fig. 22

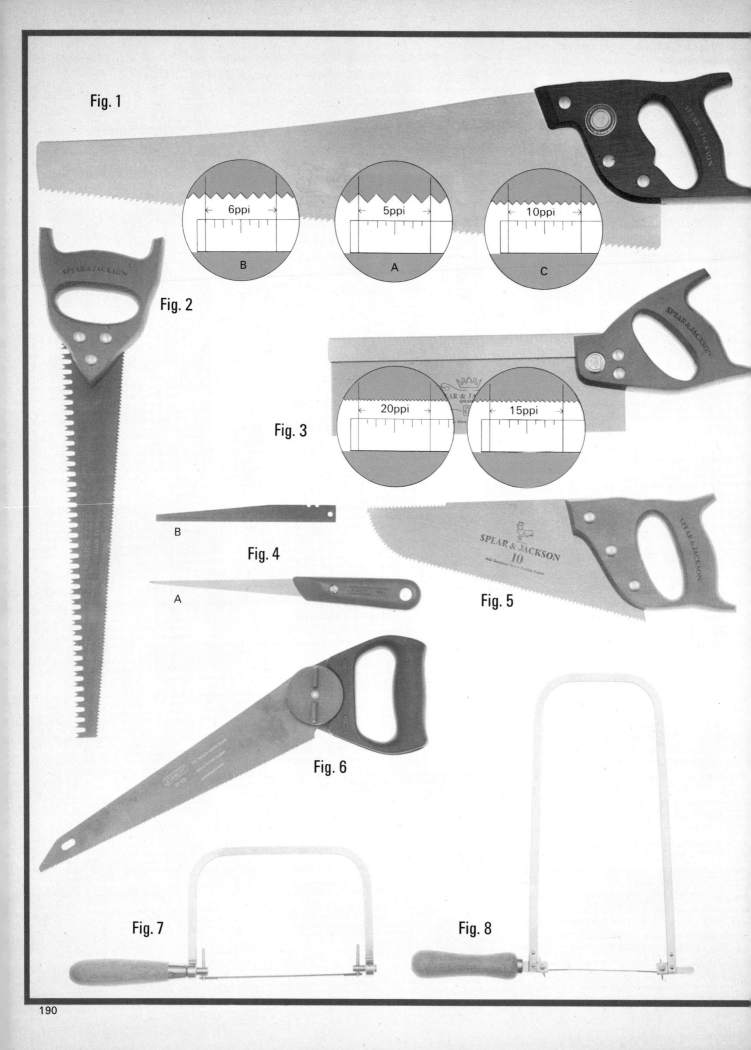

Fig. 1

Fig. 2

6ppi
B

5ppi
A

10ppi
C

Fig. 3

20ppi

15ppi

B

Fig. 4

A

Fig. 5

SPEAR & JACKSON
10

Fig. 6

Fig. 7

Fig. 8

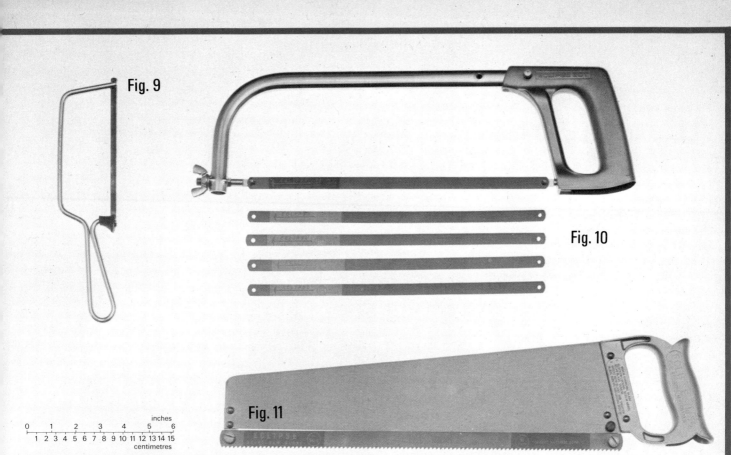

Fig. 9

Fig. 10

Fig. 11

inches
0   1   2   3   4   5   6
1 2 3 4 5 6 7 8 9 10 11 12 13 14 15
centimetres

NELSON HARGREAVES

DATA SHEET

Saws

Efficient and easy cutting is a prime requirement of all do-it-yourself jobs. There are a wide range of saws available to enable you to do just this—and this DATA SHEET tells you all about them.

The type of saw you use for a job depends on the material you are using, how accurate the cutting needs to be and where the job is located. Knowing which saw to use will simplify all do-it-yourself jobs.

Knowledge of a few technical terms will help explain the DATA SHEET:

Points per inch (ppi) refers to the number of saw teeth to the inch along the saw blade. Woodworking saws with a small number of ppi are suitable for cutting softwoods and those with a larger number should be used for sawing hardwoods.

The *kerf* is the name given to the width of the saw cut.

The *gullet* is the distance between one saw tooth and the next. The gullet carries sawdust out of the kerf to make the task of sawing easier. Saws suitable for cutting softwoods have larger gullets than those suitable for hardwoods—this is because softwoods tend to produce more waste material than hardwoods.

Fig.1. Hand saw. There are 3 types of hand saw: **A.** Rip saw. 26in. (661mm) long with 5 ppi. It is used for cutting softwoods working *with* the grain. The teeth are chisel edged to shave off the fibres of the grain. The large gullet carries the sawdust out of the kerf. **B.** Cross cut saw. 24in. to 26in. long (610mm to 661mm) with 6, 7 or 8 ppi. The saw is used to cut across the grain on hardwoods and softwoods and for working with the grain on very hardwoods. The knife point shaped teeth gives the sharper cut needed when working across the grain. **C.** Panel saw. 20in. to 22in. long (508mm to 558mm) with 10 ppi. The panel saw is used for fine cross cut and jointing work and for cutting plywood, blockboard and hardboard. The teeth are a similar shape to those of a cross cut saw.

Fig.2. Double sided saw for cutting greenwood. One side is fine toothed for cutting slender plants and the other has large open gullets to carry away sawdust when cutting larger timber. It is usually Teflon coated to stop it sticking in sappy greenwood.

Fig.3. Tenon or back saw. 8in. to 14in. long with 13, 14, 15, 16 or 20 ppi. It is used for jointing and for cutting across the grain on small pieces. The back may be brass or steel. The saw with 20 ppi is for cutting dovetails. Its blade is

thin to give greater accuracy. All cuts made with a dovetail saw should be along the grain as it performs a ripping action.

Fig.4. A. Saw knife or pad saw with a keyhole blade. **B.** Metal keyhole saw blade. Both are used for cutting small irregular shapes in the middle of a board.

Fig.5. Flooring saw. 6 to 10 ppi. The rounded nose allows you to cut into floorboards without damaging adjacent boards.

Fig.6. General purpose saw. The teeth are hardened and tempered. It is used for cutting wood laminates, plastic, mild steel, rubber, asbestos etc. It is a handy odd job tool but is not recommended for first class, accurate work. The handle is adjustable to enable work in awkward places and positions.

Fig.7. Coping saw. It has very fine teeth and is used for cutting tight curves. Tension is applied to the replaceable blade by tightening the handle.

Fig.8. Fret or piercing saw. It is similar to coping saw but is deeper to allow work with larger boards. There are many types of blade available, the choice depending on what material you wish to cut.

Fig.9 Junior hack saw. General purpose saw for light metal work.

Fig.10. Adjustable frame hack saw. It can take 10in. to 12in. (254mm to 305mm) blades. Blades are available in range of ppi from 14 to 32.

Fig.11. Sheet saw. This is available with 12in. (305mm) blade with 14 to 32 ppi for cutting metal or 16in. (407mm) blade with 6, 10 or 14 ppi for cutting thicker building material such as asbestos cement, insulation slabs and metal covered plywood. It is more accurate for cutting straight lines than general purpose saw.

Anatomy of a timber frame house

The timber-framed house is a traditional method of building in several parts of the world—Canada, the United States, Scandinavia and Australasia, to name some. It uses a timber framework clad in timber or asbestos cement outside, and timber panelling or plasterboard inside.

Another variation uses a timber frame plus an outside skin of brickwork to form a cavity wall. It is called *brick veneer*.

One disadvantage of the all-timber house is that, although no more a fire risk internally than a masonry one, it could transmit fire more easily from one house to the next. So countries which use it insist that space is left between houses or, where houses or flats are built in terraced rows, that continuous masonry walls be built between each dwelling.

Another disadvantage is that when the exterior needs redecorating, the whole surface has to be painted or varnished.

Advantages are that the comparatively light-weight construction makes alterations or additions easy, and that whole houses can be moved if needed. In New Zealand, for example, a common activity is to double the area of a bungalow by lifting it bodily by 8ft or 9ft and adding basement rooms underneath. And California has 'used house lots' where houses, due for demolition for road development, can be bought for removal to the owner's own plot.

1. Foundations. Most commonly of poured reinforced concrete, although brick piers on concrete bases also used.

2. Blocks or **stumps,** concrete, 14in. (355mm) x 8in. (203mm) x 6in. (152mm). Used at intermediate points between perimeter foundation walls. Concrete piles, or brick piers on concrete bases, also used.

3. Damp-proof course of bitumenized felt.

4. Jack studs, 4in. x 3in. (102mm x 76mm), skew-nailed into tops of blocks. Spaced at 6ft centres along line of sleeper plates.

5. Wall plates or **bearers,** 4in. x 3in. (102mm x 76mm), bolted to foundations.

6. Sleeper plates or **bearers,** 4in. x 3in. (102mm x 76mm), in rows 4ft 6in. (1.37m) apart.

7. Floor joists, 6in. x 2in. (152mm x 51mm), at 16in. (407mm) centres. Note the double joists to carry an exterior wall frame.

8. Plates, 4in. x 2in. (102mm x 51mm). Horizontal top and bottom members of the frame. Half-housed at corners to help tie frame together.

9. Studs, 4in. x 2in. (102mm x 51mm). Main vertical load-bearing members. Usually butt-jointed by nailing through top and bottom plates.

10. Nogging or **dwangs.** Rows of short timbers nailed horizontally between studs to straighten and stiffen them, and to provide nailing for wall linings. Two or three rows are usual in housing work. Usually same thickness as studs.

11. Braces. Inserted to turn the frame into a series of triangles—a shape which cannot easily be distorted—to prevent frame from *racking* sideways out of shape. Usually cut from timber of same dimensions as rest of frame, and butt-jointed in place, but lighter, cut-in braces are sometimes housed into sides of studs instead.

12. Sill trimmer, 4in. x 2in. (102mm x 51mm).

13. Lintels. Used to carry the weight of the roof, or upstairs floor, where the row of studs must be broken—e.g., for a window opening. Width of timber usually matches the thickness of the studs; height depends on the span. Always housed into studs on either side so that the weight is firmly supported.

14. Jack studs. Support top plate above lintel.

15. Weatherboarding, usually cut from 8in. x 1in. (203mm x 25mm) or 6in. x 1in. (152mm x 25mm) timber, although many other horizontal and vertical varieties also used.

16. Soakers, metal, to help waterproof vulnerable end-grain at mitred joints.

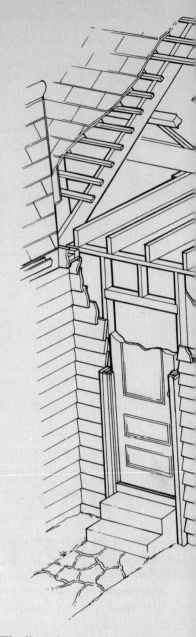

Note: The dimensions given are average only, but further details are given in later chapters on specific projects.

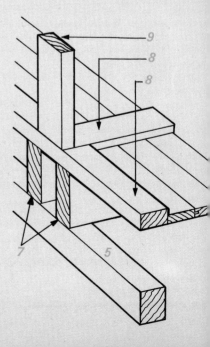

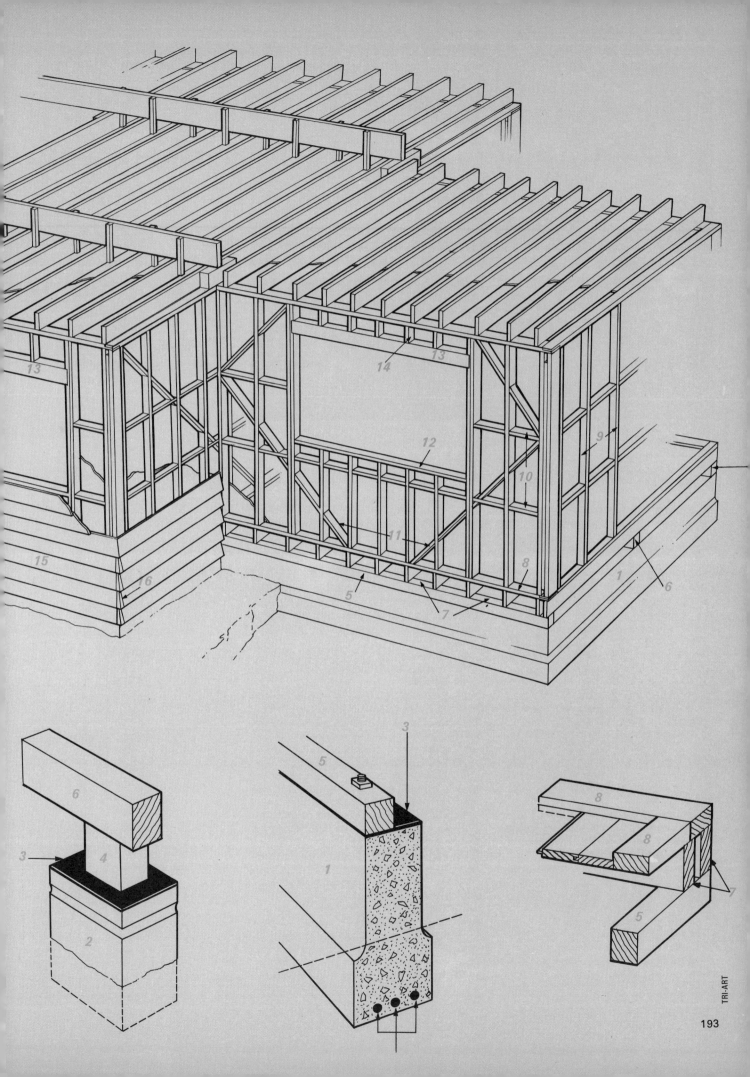

The **gable roof** comes in two main varieties —the *overhanging* gable (on left of illustration) and the *flush* gable (on right of illustration), although compound roofs using both styles are not uncommon.

A gable roof has exactly the same surface area as a hip roof covering a building of the same size, providing the pitch, or slope, is the same. But the total cost of materials is somewhat higher, because the gable end itself must be bricked up or panelled.

However, a gable roof wastes less roofing materials than a hip roof, because it avoids the need to cut ends at an angle. And it is somewhat easier for an amateur to build.

The structural layout is basically the same, wherever a gable roof is built. Sizes of components do vary, but those below are typical.

1. Top plate or **wall plate**. In a timber-framed wall, the top member; in masonry construction, fixed to top course of brickwork. Commonly 4in. x 2in. (102mm x 51mm).

2. Ceiling joists. Usually fixed with intervals of 16in. (406mm) or 18in. (458mm) from the centre of one to the centre of the next. Depths vary according to the distance being spanned, and the density of locally-available timber. Usually nailed to . . .

3. Common rafters. Full rafters, running from ridge board to wall plate, over which they are fitted by a *birdsmouth* cut. Usually 4in. x 2in. or 6in. x 2in. (152mm x 51mm).

4. Hanging beams or **runners.** Used to strengthen ceiling joists, especially over long spans, by binding them together to spread the load; also to prevent joists twisting.

5. Hangers. Used to fix joists to hanging beam, to which they are placed on alternate sides. Often 2in. x 1in. (51mm x 25mm).

6. Purlins or (where over-rafter purlins also used) **under-purlins.** Nailed to underside of rafters to support and stiffen them. Usually 4in. x 3in. (102mm x 76mm) in new work.

7. Struts. Fixed to hanging beams, if any, or direct to top of partition wall, to support purlins.

8. Collar ties. Link pairs of rafters to help prevent roof splaying. Often fixed to every second pair of rafters.

9. Ridge board. Usually 1½in. (38mm) thick. Depth made to accommodate ends of common rafters, plus a small upstand at the top projecting into ridge tiles.

10. Tiling battens. Size and spacing depends on kind of tile used; 2in. x 1in. (51mm x 25mm) common. Where sheet roofing is used instead of tiles, battens are replaced by sarking (continuous boarding) or purlins (3in. x 2in. cross-members at about 2ft intervals).

11. Tiles.

12. Soffit or **soffit rafter.**

13. Battens.

14. Fascia board. Used to neaten the ends of rafters, and to support guttering.

15. Soffit lining. In this case, of asbestos cement, housed in rebate in fascia board; but tongued-and-grooved boards often used.

16. Valley rafter.

17. Jack rafters. Short rafters, in this case running from hip rafter to valley rafter, but also used between hip rafter and top plate.

18. Valley boards. Wide boards—9in. x 1in. (229mm x 25mm) to 12in. x 1in. (305mm x 25mm)—carrying valley gutter.

19. Valley gutter. Often galvanized sheet iron.

20. Creepers. Short lengths of rafter supporting overhanging gable.

21. Cladding. In timber-framed construction, this is most often of timber, asbestos cement panelling or aluminium sheeting. In masonry construction, of course, brickwork runs up to cover the gable end.

22. Barge boards. Fulfil same purpose—giving a neater finish—as fascias. Only difference is that these are fixed 'slantwise.'

23. Guttering.

Fig.3 (below). *Details of a chimney breast in a timber-framed house. All the timber must be kept clear of the brickwork by an inch or so.*

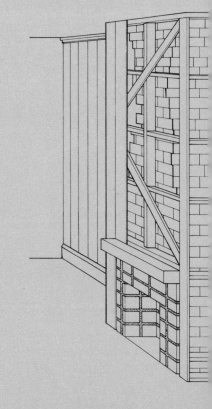

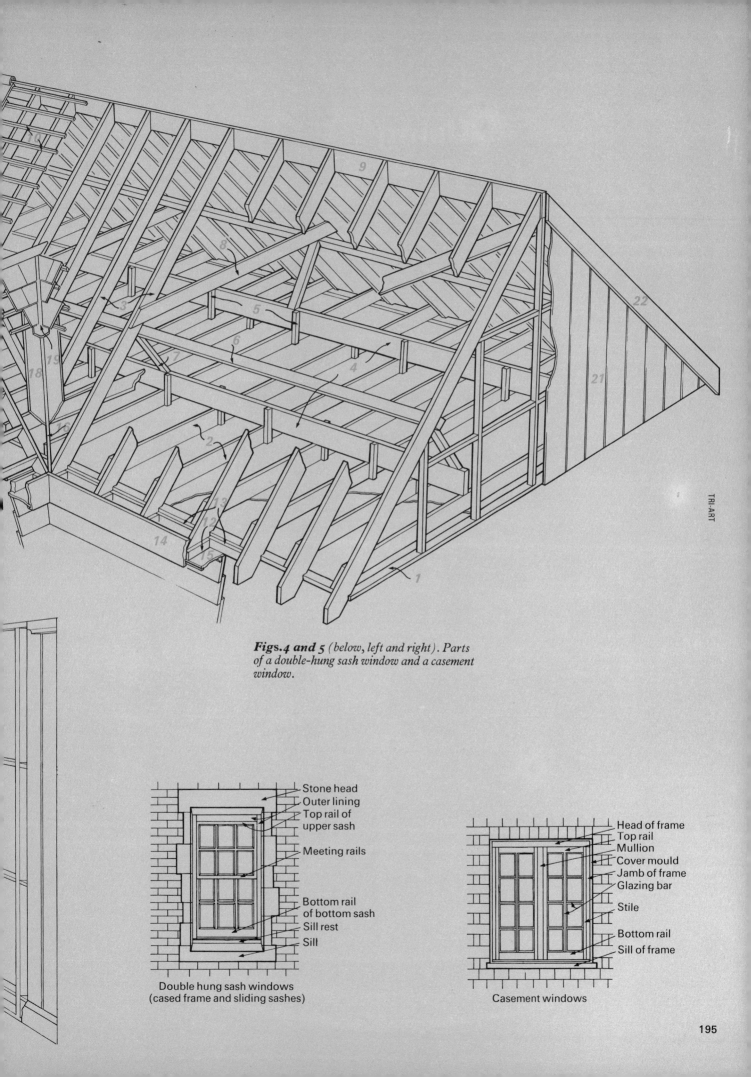

Figs. 4 and 5 *(below, left and right). Parts of a double-hung sash window and a casement window.*

Double hung sash windows (cased frame and sliding sashes)

- Stone head
- Outer lining
- Top rail of upper sash
- Meeting rails
- Bottom rail of bottom sash
- Sill rest
- Sill

Casement windows

- Head of frame
- Top rail
- Mullion
- Cover mould
- Jamb of frame
- Glazing bar
- Stile
- Bottom rail
- Sill of frame

Using veneers

The price of wood gets higher every year, particularly of expensive and decorative hardwoods. As a result, more and more articles that would once have been made of solid mahogany or teak are now built from cheap softwood and covered with a decorative hardwood veneer, giving much the same effect as solid wood if it is properly done. Some decorative woods are too fragile or unstable to use solid, and these have to be applied in veneer form. Sooner or later, you will probably want to apply some veneer yourself. Here is how to do it.

You can apply veneer successfully by hand without much specialised equipment, even though special heated presses are used by many professionals. But try to avoid veneering anything except flat surfaces to begin with; special formers are usually necessary with curves such as those found on a number of old cabinets. If curves must be veneered, you can achieve reasonable—but not first-class—results by sticking the veneer on with contact adhesive.

Buying and handling veneer

Veneer is quite hard to find in shops, and you may have to spend quite a while looking for it. The ideal place is, of course, a specialist veneer dealer, but there are very few of these even in large cities. If you can't find one, the next choice is a large timber yard that sells hardwood as well as ordinary softwood. Many of these also handle veneer, though not exotic types. Antique dealers who restore their own furniture always have a few sheets of veneer around, and may agree to sell you some. And failing all these, larger art and handicraft shops sell small pieces of veneer for marquetry.

A number of veneer-like products are sold in Britain. Some have a backing that gives greater stability to the extremely thin veneer and others a coat of glue on one side. Always follow the manufacturers' instructions carefully when using these proprietary products to ensure the best possible results.

Specialist veneer shops generally insist on selling you a large amount of veneer at a time; the standard size of sheet is 6ft (1.85m) long and 10in.–15in. (250mm–380mm) wide. Veneer is very fragile and particularly easy to split, so you may have some difficulty taking a piece this size home on a train or bus. It should be carefully rolled into a loose cylinder; this is only possible with standard 1/40in. (0.7mm) thick veneer, however. Antique furniture has much thicker veneer, and if you are matching this you will be in trouble. It is completely unrollable—though slightly less likely to split.

Methods of veneering

Veneer can be stuck down with scotch glue; pva adhesive or contact adhesive. Scotch glue is a solid substance when cold, and only becomes liquid and adhesive when heated. As it cools, it soon becomes too thick to flow around easily, so it has to be kept hot during

use. In contrast, pva adhesive is a water-based glue which flows easily at all times and in normal conditions takes many hours to set. Contact adhesive makes both surfaces stick fast on contact; but does not hold as strongly as the other two types. Because of the differences between these adhesives, the method of applying the veneer differs in each case.

The principle of the *traditional scotch glue method,* correctly called *hammer veneering,* is to spread hot, liquid scotch glue on both surfaces, lay the veneer in place, and work excess glue out from underneath it by scraping the surface with a special *veneer hammer,* as in Fig.7. This produces a smooth, flat finish. The use of the veneer hammer is very important, because otherwise the glue remains where it is laid and gives a rippled surface. If the glue dries before you have finished smoothing the veneer, it can be reheated by ironing the surface of the veneer with a heavy iron. The glue holds the veneer firmly in place from the moment it is applied, but takes about two weeks to finish setting and gain its full strength.

This method is the only practical one for covering large areas—say two square feet and above. Always use scotch glue when re-veneering part of an article already veneered with scotch glue—if pva adhesive and scotch glue are used side by side the pva will not stick.

The *pva and G cramp method* is best for small areas no more than 2ft (0.6m) wide, and for curly, wavy or burr veneers, which are hard to lay flat. The base wood and the veneer are both coated with pva adhesive. The veneer is put in position and a thick, flat board cramped in place on top of the veneer. Since this type of glue flows easily, the excess will be forced out by the pressure of the cramps, and as long as the cramped-down board is really flat, the veneer will have a perfectly smooth surface. The cramps are essential to prevent the veneer lifting during the fifteen or so hours pva adhesive takes to dry; they must be arranged so as to exert an equal pressure all over the board. But as an even pressure can be exerted for only a distance of about 1ft (0.3m) from a big cramp with a block under it, the greatest width that can be adequately veneered by this method is about 2ft (0.6m). You can veneer long strips of this width by using several cramps.

In the *pva and steam iron method,* the veneer is stuck to the wood base with pva adhesive as before, but no cramps are used to hold the veneer in place. Instead, the veneer is ironed in place with an electric steam iron for a few minutes. This both forces out any excess adhesive and speeds up the drying time, so that the veneer stays in place and the whole job is dry in a couple of hours. But it is very easy, by careless ironing, to leave a lump of glue under the surface of the veneer. This lump cannot be ironed out later, as with the scotch glue method, for heat causes pva adhesive to harden. Furthermore, this method requires a lot of ironing, so that in practice only small areas are ever veneered in this way.

Contact adhesive is too thick for normal use, and not very strong. Lumps cannot be ironed out, and often cause the surface of the veneer

to be rippled. But if a curve has to be covered some success can be had with this method—though the finish may be far from perfect.

Therefore, use the scotch glue method when covering large areas or when repairing articles previously veneered with scotch glue. For small areas, use the pva and G cramp method on surfaces where it is possible to apply G cramps. If this is not possible, use the pva and steam iron method. Try not to use contact adhesive at all, except as a last resort.

Removing old veneer

If you are re-veneering an old piece of furniture, remove the old veneer before re-covering it. First take any remaining polish off the surface by roughening it with coarse sandpaper or wire wool, or scratching it with a chisel. Lay hot wet rags all over the surface and apply a very hot iron to boil the water. Continue until the veneer begins to peel, adding water as necessary. When it does, take an old carving knife or chisel and work it under the edges. The veneer will be easy to lever off. Finish the preparation by scraping the softened glue from the base wood. Wash it with methylated spirits.

Scotch glue method

You will need to work as quickly as possible when veneering by this method, so have the following tools and materials ready and within reach.

1. Sufficient scotch glue. The glue may be in the form of a solid sheet or small balls known as *pearls,* or in a semi-liquid state.

2. A glue pot. You can use two different-sized tins; one should fit inside the other with at least 1in. (25mm) space all round it. Fill the larger pot with a few inches of water and drop a few bolts or stones of equal size into the bottom. Better, make a wire support for the smaller tin. Put the scotch glue in the smaller tin and place it in the larger tin on top of the bolts. This allows the glue to be heated without any risk of burning.

3. A source of heat. Any type of stove, but preferably not electric, will do; the double boiler described above prevents overheating.

4. A veneer plane (illustrated in Fig.1) or coarse sandpaper wrapped round a flat block.

5. A veneer hammer (illustrated in Fig.1).

6. A sharp knife, a chisel, and a metal rule.

7. A clean rag and hot water.

8. Various grades of sandpaper down to flour grade.

When you have assembled all these things, clean the surface to be veneered. Then, if veneering a piece for the first time, roughen it with a veneer plane or coarse sandpaper, both used at an angle of 45° to the grain, to give a good key for the glue. If the surface is particularly absorbent, for example in the case of very coarse-grained wood, size it with watered-down scotch glue—this will prevent so much glue being absorbed that the veneer does not stick properly.

Now match the pieces of veneer to give the most attractive grain pattern. Use the knife and metal rule to cut them so that they are about 1in. (25mm) oversize around the edge of the surface to be covered. If two or more pieces are being laid next to each other, lay them in place with

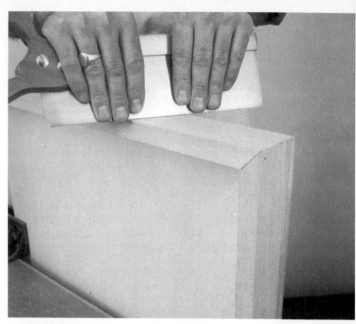

1

3

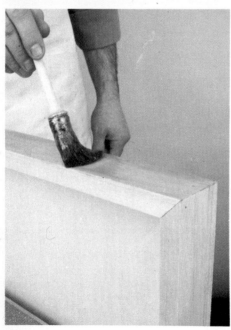

5

the edges overlapping by an inch. Then cut through the centre of the line of the overlap along a steel rule, cutting through both pieces at once. Be sure to hold the knife vertical. Discard the offcuts and stick the pieces edge-to-edge with ordinary brown paper tape (Fig.4).

Heat the scotch glue till it melts, and add a little water to keep it thin. Damp the veneer on both sides. Spread the glue evenly but as thinly as possible over the adjoining surfaces of both the wood case and the veneer. Work quickly as the glue soon thickens. Lay the first sheet in place. Take the veneering hammer and draw it over the veneer parallel with the grain but with the blade slanted at approximately 45 degrees to it. Ways of using the hammer are shown in Fig.11. Always use a scraping movement with the veneer hammer and never a tapping movement, as this would mark the surface. Try to keep an even pressure on the hammer at all times. Then clean off any lumps of excess glue around the edges with a hot wet cloth.

The scotch glue may set before the veneer

Fig.1. A veneer plane (bottom) has a finely toothed blade for slightly roughening the surface to be veneered. Alternatively you can use medium sandpaper. The veneer hammer (top) used to smooth the veneer in place has a brass smoothing edge. Some hammers have a hardwood edge, but the edge must be smooth.

Fig.2. A tenon saw can be used instead of a veneer plane to roughen the surface.

Fig.3. Two sheets of veneer are matched with the grain running in the same direction. The edges are overlapped by approximately 1in. (25mm) and a sharp knife and metal rule used to cut through both pieces down the centre of the overlap to give a neat join.

Fig.4. Sheets of veneer can be bought cut from the same section of tree and then matched together (or quartered) to produce a very attractive pattern. Here the edges have been taped before cutting to prevent these delicate veneers from splitting.

Fig.5. Hot, molten Scotch glue is applied with a brush to the edge of the piece—work as quickly as possible before the glue dries.

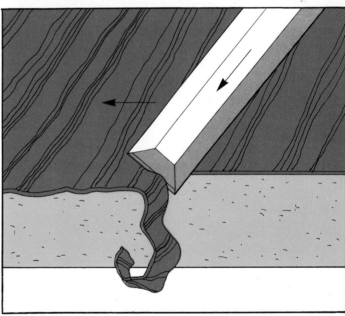

Fig.6. *Here pva adhesive is brushed as evenly as possible onto the face of the wood.*
Fig.7. *Here an edge is veneered by the Scotch glue method. The veneer is smoothed in place by even strokes with the veneer hammer: an even pressure must be applied at all times. Any excess glue will be forced out at the sides. If the glue sets before the veneer is smoothed it can be remelted by ironing with a steam iron—but keep the surface moist.*
Fig.8. *Veneer stuck with pva adhesive is ironed in place with a steam iron. The pressure of the iron smooths the veneer and the heat hastens the setting process of the adhesive-but unlike Scotch glue, pva adhesive once set, can not be loosened by reheating.*
Fig.9. *The overlapping edges of the veneer are trimmed with a chisel: note the combined downwards and sideways movement.*
Fig.10. *Battens provide a more robust edge than a strip of veneer and can make a nice contrast with the veneered top. Here the battens are stuck and pinned in position and then trimmed with a plane before veneering the top.*

has been scraped completely smooth, but you can soften the glue so that it can be worked again by ironing it with a warm iron. Always keep the surface slightly damp to allow the veneer hammer to slip easily over it and to prevent the veneer from being scorched by the iron. But try not to reheat the glue more than necessary, as you may dry out the veneer and cause contraction cracks.

When you have smoothed over the whole piece, check the surface for bubbles or ripples. Go over the whole area carefully tapping it with your finger nails. If it sounds hollow anywhere, there is an air bubble underneath. If the surface is uneven, but does not sound hollow, there is a lump of glue under it. To remove these faults, iron that area and slit the surface in the direction of the grain with a razor blade or modelling knife. Work over the area with the veneer hammer to squeeze out any air or excess glue. Then stick a piece of brown paper over the cut. This prevents it from opening up and air being drawn back beneath the veneer. For the same reason stick brown paper round all the edges of the

sheet of veneer, using a little scotch glue.

Leave the veneer to dry for two weeks. Then trim the edges, being careful not to damage the surface. If the veneer overlaps a corner, use a chisel to trim it to size as shown in Fig.9. Dampen and remove any brown paper stuck to the surface. Sand the whole surface lightly with the grain with fine sandpaper, followed by flour grade. Spread colour-matched filler, such as Brummer stopping mixed with methylated spirit, over the whole surface to seal the grain and hide the joins, and rub down again. If you are re-veneering part of an old article, stain the new veneer to match the old. French polish the surface to finish the job.

The pva and G cramp method

Have the following ready: pva adhesive, a mixing pot, a sharp handyman's knife, a chisel, sandpaper in various grades, a large sheet of brown paper, a flat, thick, smooth board large enough to cover the veneer, and sufficient G cramps.

Remove the existing veneer (if any) and clean the surface with sandpaper, but do not roughen it as described above. Match the veneers and cut them out oversize, but do not wet them. If you are laying two pieces side by side, do not overlap them. Cut the adjacent edges along a steel rule so that they can be butted accurately against each other.

Water down the pva glue—one part water to 5 parts pva. Spread it evenly over the top surfaces to be joined—keep it off the top—and place the veneer in position. The adhesive is very fluid so that the cramps will press any excess adhesive out at the sides of the sheets. A veneering hammer is not therefore used.

Lay the sheet of brown paper over the veneer and put the flat board on top of it. Cramp the board in place with at least one cramp every 2ft (0.6m). The brown paper prevents the veneer from sticking to the board. Tighten the central cramps first, then the outer ones, so as not to create a bubble. Leave to dry for approximately 24 hours, then remove the cramps and board. Trim the veneer, sand and finish as before.

The pva and steam iron method

Have ready pva adhesive, a mixing pot, handyman's knife, chisel, sandpaper, clean rag, water and an electric iron, preferably a steam iron, set to 120°F (50°C).

Prepare the surface, cut the veneer and glue it on as in the previous method. Then iron the veneer in place, starting from the centre of each piece of veneer and working to the edges. Never stop moving the iron and try to apply even pressure all over so that you finish with a smooth finish to the veneer—indentations caused by the iron will be plainly visible. Keep the surface moist, so that the veneer is not scorched. A steam iron will do this for you. The adhesive will dry in a few minutes—you should be able to feel when this happens. Once it has dried, nothing can be done to iron out bubbles or lumps—the adhesive cannot be softened as with scotch glue.

Other methods

In Britain and some other countries, a special plastic 'glue film' is sold in sheets. This is laid under the veneer, which should be moistened on the outside only, and the film melted through the veneer with a cool electric iron. A veneer hammer is used on the softened film exactly as with scotch glue, though in practice less smoothing will be necessary.

This method is simple and effective, and reasonably economical. It should not, however, be used for veneering surfaces that are going to be subjected to heat, such as radiator shelves.

Veneer can also be stuck on with contact adhesive, but only as a last resort when all other methods are impossible. Simply spread both surfaces as thinly and evenly as possible with adhesive, leave it for the time recommended by the manufacturer to become tacky (normally 10 minutes) and press it into place. A veneer hammer is useful for pressing it down, but you can't use it for removing lumps of glue under the veneer. If there are any lumps, they will have to stay. Air bubbles can be removed by the method described above.

Modern thixotropic contact adhesive gives you a few seconds' grace to slide the veneer into the right position before you press it permanently into place. If you have to use this method at all, buy this kind of adhesive.

Fig.11. *The veneering hammer in the Scotch glue method is run over the surface in the general direction of the grain but at 45 degrees away from it. When quartering, work from the centre towards the edges.*

Edge and back treatment

When two surfaces at right angles to each other—such as the edge and face of a table top—are being veneered, one piece of veneer must overlap the other. This join will later be filled and sanded smooth, so it will not be very obvious. But you should make the surface that is seen most overlap the surface that is seen least—for example, the veneer on the top of a table should overlap that on the edges. In this case veneer the edges first, allowing the veneer to overlap both sides of the edges.

Leave the job to dry for two days and then trim the pieces to size (see Fig.9) so that the top of the table is smooth all over. Then veneer the top of the table and leave it for two weeks to dry thoroughly.

An attractive method of finishing the edges of a table is to fix strips of solid wood matching the veneer to the edges with glue and the very thin panel pins which are called *veneer pins*. This method gives a more robust result, since the edges of a veneered table are most easily damaged. But the top veneer must not overlap the edging strip, or the different rate of expansion of table and edging will split it.

If veneer is applied to one side only of a board, the veneer will create considerable stresses on that side, causing the wood to *bow* or *warp*. To prevent the board from doing this, cover the other side with a veneer of equal thickness. To keep the cost low, a cheaper veneer can be used for the backing.

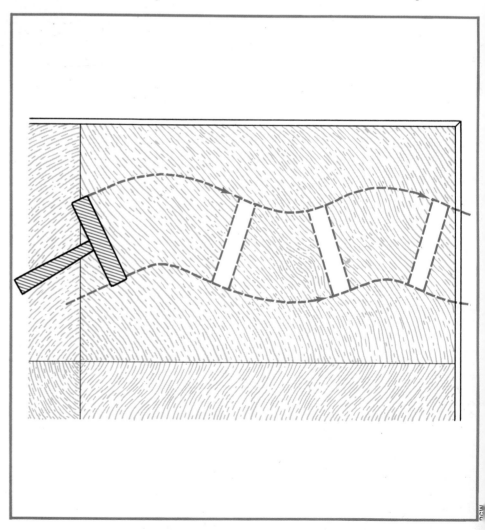

Versatile
gate legged table

A gate-legged table is an especially useful item of furniture in modern homes where rooms may have several uses, or where the dining area is on the small side. When the end leaves are folded down, the table takes up a minimum of space and can be stored against a wall. But with one or both leaves opened up there is ample space for as many as eight people to sit at it.

The gate-legged table shown here is easy to build and has been designed to meet as many different seating requirements as possible. Since the top can be altered to three different sizes, any number of people from two to eight can find it exactly the right size for them. The centre section is wider than on many gate-legged tables; this allows the legs on either side of the table to be spaced far enough apart for you to sit with your feet between them. An extra bonus is

that the single cross strut between the legs in the centre of the table (part H in Fig.1) is designed not to get in the way of your feet.

Design and materials

The design of this table is most attractive, but at the same time thoroughly unusual; it is intended to be made out of plywood throughout, including the frame. This apparently strange choice of material turns out to be very practical for two reasons. One is that plywood is far less likely to warp than solid timber and so, because there is no need for rigid framing under the leaves, the construction is much simplified. The other is that the whole of the table is designed so that it can be cut from one standard-size sheet of ply. There is no attempt to hide the striped edges of the ply in this design: instead, a feature has

Below. This versatile gate legged table makes a useful sized breakfast table when one leaf is extended. Made from birch ply, it has been covered with a polyurethene varnish tinted with red dye to give a bright finish.

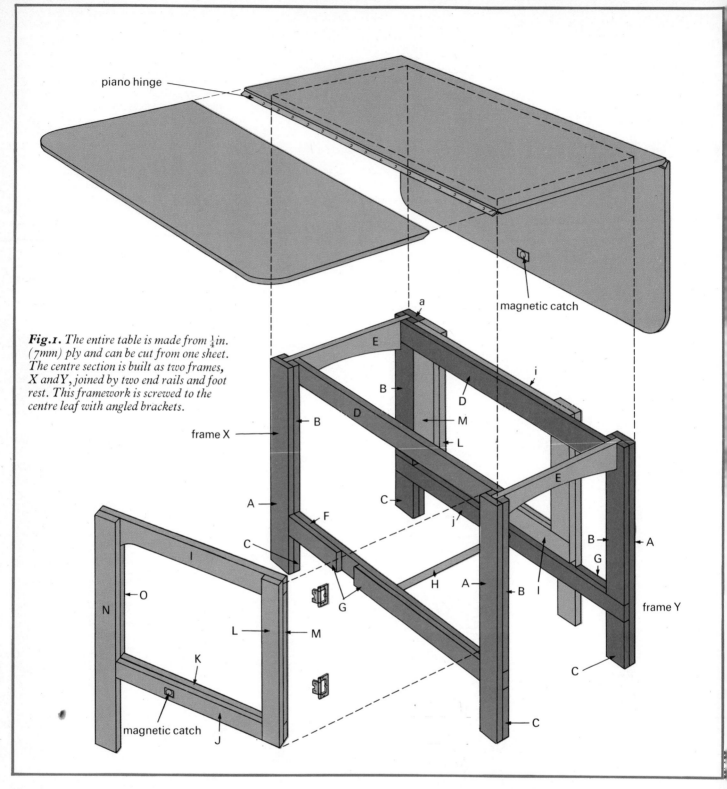

piano hinge

magnetic catch

Fig.1. *The entire table is made from $\frac{1}{4}$in. (7mm) ply and can be cut from one sheet. The centre section is built as two frames, X and Y, joined by two end rails and foot rest. This framework is screwed to the centre leaf with angled brackets.*

a

E

B

D

M

L

frame X

B

D

A

F

C

C

i

E

j

B — A

G

I

H

A

B

I

N

O

frame Y

L

M

K

C

magnetic catch

J

C

been made out of these edges, so that they contrast with the plainness of the flat surfaces.

If you have no power bench saw, however, and want to avoid sawing all the frame pieces to their finished width by hand, you can make the legs and framework from solid planed timber. This alternative will also save you trouble if you are going to paint the table or apply laminate or veneer sheets with edging strips, so that the striped effect is lost.

In the table shown here, the foot rest is made out of round dowel to suit the contours of the feet. If you prefer, however, you can make this

piece, too, out of two thicknesses of ply cut 1½in. (38mm) wide. There will be enough ply to spare in the large sheet for the two extra parts.

The join between the end leaves and the centre piece always presents a problem in gate-legged tables. Sometimes the edges that meet are left square, but this results in an unsightly right-angled groove between them when the leaves are down. In this design, the hinged edges are cut at an angle of 45° (see Fig.1) and screwed together with lengths of piano hinge. This produces neat external corners when the leaves are down, and there is no groove visible.

When the flap leaves are extended, there is a groove on the underside between the centre piece and the two leaves, but as this is below eye level it is hardly noticeable.

The leaves and centre section are fixed to the piano hinges so that the folding edge of the hinges is about level with the upper side of the table top. As a result, when the leaves are dropped, they will be supported by their outer edges, and so will hang slightly out of the vertical. Again, this is hardly noticeable, but you could correct the slight error by fitting magnetic catches to the inside edges of the leaves and the cross struts of the gate legs (see Fig.1). Small circular magnetic catches can be obtained that can be dropped directly into drilled holes, and hardly show at all.

The end leaves in this design have been left square, with only the corners rounded off. But with skill and patience it would be possible to mark and cut them to an oval shape—make sure, however, that this oval is at no point smaller than the arc through which the leg pivots when it is opened.

Details of construction

The top of the table consists simply of two leaves hung from the centre piece. The framework beneath consists of four legs, two hinged gates and a number of cross pieces, all of which are joined with halving joints, most of them just glued together, though a few need screws as well. The framework is assembled as one piece and then screwed to the top with metal angle brackets.

All the legs and cross struts are made out of two thicknesses of $\frac{3}{4}$in. or 19mm ply stuck together. (A useful hint: knock a few headless panel pins almost the whole way into one of the surfaces to be glued together so that their tops bite into the other piece and prevent the two pieces from slipping around when they are cramped together.)

All the pieces of ply could be glued together before the halving joints are marked out, and the joints then marked and cut in the conventional way. The method described here, however, is simpler, since almost no joints have to be chiselled out. The lengths of ply are cut out as in Fig.3 and glued together as in Fig.2 below, so that the correct shapes for the halving joints are preformed and no cutting has to be done. The only exception to this is with the cross strut on the main frame, which is made out of pieces F and G. Here, it is advisable to cut out the two pieces G in one length and glue them to piece F. Then, when the whole frame has been put together, the joint to take the gate leg can be cut by direct measurement to ensure accuracy.

Choice of timber

All the parts for this table can be cut from one standard-sized 8ft. x 4ft. or 2.4m x 1.2m sheet of $\frac{3}{4}$in. or 19mm ply by arranging them as shown in Fig.3. You will find that buying this one large sheet is cheaper than buying a number of smaller, different pieces. If you can't obtain this size from a DIY shop, try your nearest timber yard.

Ply can be bought in various woods and grades: the grade denotes the number of knots in the sheets. Birch ply is a good choice; it has a plain, light-coloured surface that will take a good polish. But there is no reason why you should not use a more exotic type. The British grades for birch ply are as follows.

Grade BB is the best grade of ply and has no knots in either side. It is more expensive than the other grades, but if you are going to varnish the table, and want a perfect finish all over, this is the grade to use.

Grade BB/CP is of average quality and should have one perfect side free of knots. There will have been some knots in the other side, but these should have been removed and filled before you buy it. Sheets of this grade are less expensive than BB and perfectly suitable for this job, since you can arrange for the perfect side to be on top of the table.

Grade BB/C is cheaper still ,and was used in the table shown here. The knot holes are neatly filled, so that when the table is sanded and varnished, a reasonable standard of finish is obtained.

Lower grades: sheets of ply of any lower grade than BB/C will have a number of unfilled knots (there may even be holes where the knots have fallen out) and are completely unsuitable even if you are going to face the table with veneer.

Plywood should be stored flat and not on edge; otherwise it will twist and the edge may be damaged. Check that the sheet you buy is flat, that the edges (or at least two adjacent ones) are sound, that the veneers of ply that make up the sheet are firmly stuck together and that no knots have fallen out.

Materials and tools

The equipment needed to make this table can be very simple. The minimum requirements are pva adhesive, a number of G cramps, some panel pins, various grades of sandpaper, some wooden wedges as described below, a tenon saw and a rip saw. It will simplify the assembly if you also have three sash cramps which will open to the width of the frame (that is across the narrow side) plus about 6in. (150mm)—this adds up to about 22in. (560mm). But you can do without them at a pinch by holding the frame together with tightly wound string and wedges as described in CHAPTER 44.

A power bench saw for cutting the leaves to shape and bevelling their edges at 45° will save you a great deal of time and effort, and it is strongly recommended that you use one.

Lengths of piano hinge should be used for joining the end leaves to the centre piece, since they support the leaves along the whole of their length and don't have to be recessed into the wood. The hinge for this table should be 1in-1½in. (25mm-38mm) wide when opened out flat.

Each gate leg should be hung from two flush hinges (see Fig.2); these, too, can be screwed in place without cutting them in. If you plan to have a circular-section foot rest between the legs, you will need a length of 1½in. (38mm) hard-wood dowel.

Marking and cutting

Choose the best side of the sheet of plywood for the top surface of the table. Find the best two adjacent edges, ensure that they are at right angles, and measure from these to mark out the first piece, as shown in Fig.3. Alternatively, use a large set square to mark out two straight lines at right angles to each other, and measure and mark from these. Then cut along the marked lines by one of the following methods.

A *power bench saw* is the simplest means of cutting the 3ft. (1m) sides on the leaves of the table. It should be fitted with a fine-toothed 'planer' blade, which gives an accurate straight

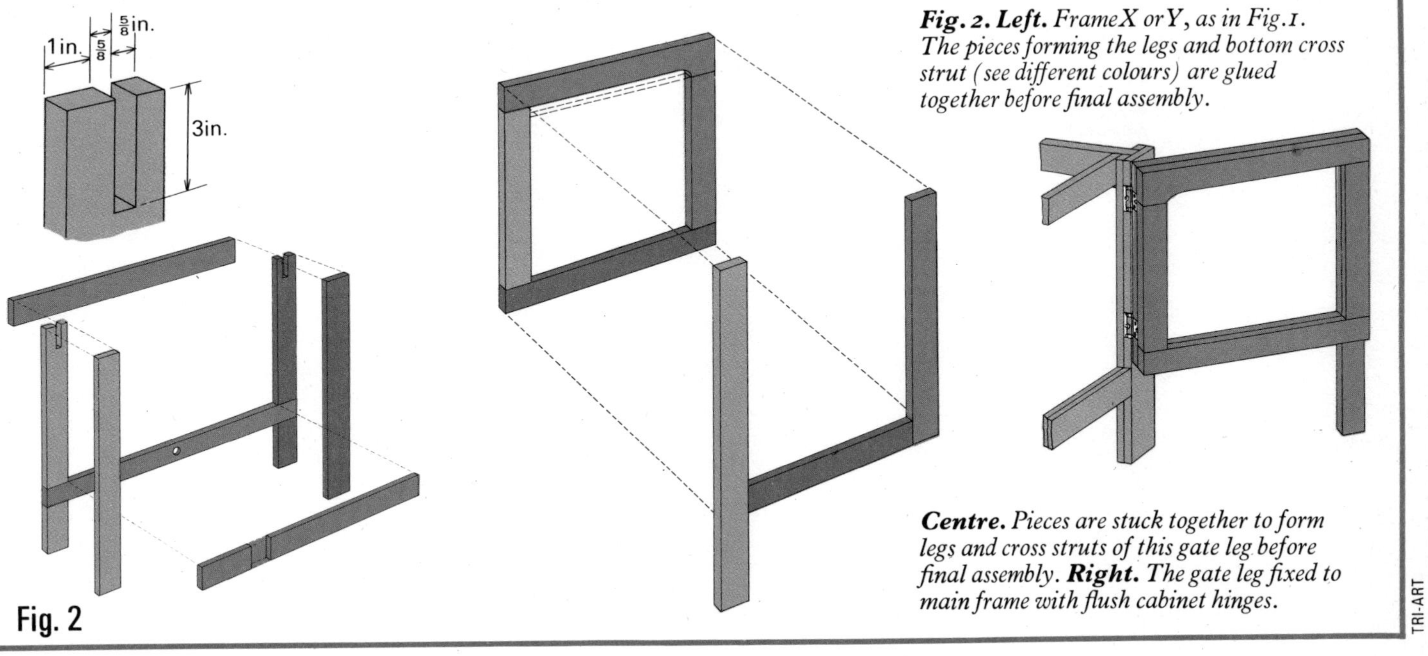

Fig. 2

Fig. 2. Left. Frame X or Y, as in Fig.1. The pieces forming the legs and bottom cross strut (see different colours) are glued together before final assembly.

Centre. Pieces are stuck together to form legs and cross struts of this gate leg before final assembly. Right. The gate leg fixed to main frame with flush cabinet hinges.

TRI-ART

edge that can easily be finished with sandpaper. The 45° edge needed where the leaves meet can also be cut accurately in this way.

Using a *hand saw* takes more time and a lot of patience, but in the absence of a power bench saw it is the only alternative. When you have marked out the first piece, rest the sheet on edge on the floor in front of your work-bench and grip it in the vice with the cutting line vertical. Carefully cut down the waste side of the line, constantly checking that you are keeping to the line on both sides of the wood. The curved edge of pieces E and I can be cut with a keyhole or pad saw, or you can modify the design and cut a straight line instead.

To obtain the 45° bevelled edges for the leaves, first cut them square and then plane them to size using a triangular former with an angle of 45° on top as a guide.

The three main pieces of the table top should all be arranged so that the grain on their surface runs the same way. But only mark out one piece at a time, using a pencil, and then saw along the waste side of the pencil line. If you achieve a perfectly straight edge, you can use that as the edge of the next leaf; otherwise you should plane it straight first. If you marked all the pieces out at once, the thickness of the saw cuts would reduce the size of each piece when cut out. Cut out all the pieces in this way, then finally saw and chisel out the housing groove in the top of the four corner legs as shown in Fig.2.

The foot rest stretches between the two horizontal struts that lie across the width of the table and braces each pair of legs. Each of these struts is made from the thicknesses of ply, and the foot rest should be set into a mortise cut in the inner thickness only. Whether this mortise takes the form of a 1½in. (—38mm) square or a

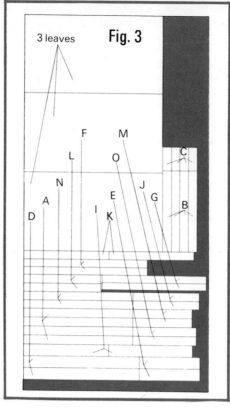

Fig.3. The pieces for the table (see cutting list alongside) can be cut from one sheet of ply size 8ft. x 4ft.

1½in. diameter circle depends on whether you are using a square or circular-section foot rest. Anyway, cut the mortise at this stage, using a chisel or hole saw as appropriate.

CUTTING LIST

All pieces are made of ¾in. or 19mm ply, except where stated.

Main frame	inches	millimetres
legs :		
4 pieces (A)	28¼ x 2¼	717 x 57
4 pieces (B)	20¼ x 2¼	514 x 57
4 pieces (C)	6 x 2¼	152 x 57
top struts :		
2 pieces (D)	29½ x 3	749 x 76
2 pieces (E)	16½ x 3	419 x 76
bottom struts :		
2 pieces (F)	32 x 2	813 x 51
2 pieces (G)	27½ x 2	699 x 51
Gate legs		
top struts :		
2 pieces (I)	22 x 3	559 x 76
bottom struts :		
2 pieces (J)	17½ x 2	445 x 51
2 pieces (K)	22 x 2	559 x 51
inner legs :		
2 pieces (L)	20¼ x 2¼	514 x 57
2 pieces (M)	15¼ x 2¼	388 x 57
outer legs :		
2 pieces (N)	28¼ x 2¼	717 x 57
2 pieces (O)	16¼ x 2¼	413 x 57
Top		
3 pieces	20 x 36	508 x 914

Foot rest (H)

1 piece of 1½in. (38mm) dowel, 16⅜in. (416mm) long.

'Doubling up'

There are only six pieces in the finished framework which are made of a single thickness of ply: the top cross strut in each of the gates and the four pieces at the top of the frame which are screwed to the table top (parts I, D and E in Fig.1). Take these six pieces and keep them completely separate from the rest.

The remaining pieces of ply have to be 'doubled up' by glueing two thicknesses together to give them extra strength. To do this, first match the two halves of a piece together, then take one of the halves and hammer three or four small panel pins halfway into the inner face. Cut their heads off fairly close to the wood with a pair of pincers. Provide yourself with a clean, wet rag, then spread pva adhesive over the inside face of both halves. Press the pieces together. (If necessary, place a piece of wood on top of them and hammer it to make the headless panel pins sink into the other piece. They will hold the pieces firmly in place while the cramps are set.)

Wipe off any surplus adhesive immediately with the rag. Any adhesive left on the surface would only become noticeable when you varnish the surface, but by then it will be too late to do anything about it. Sandwich the pieces between a couple of bits of scrap wood and hold them together with G cramps; wipe them again with the cloth and leave them for 2-4 hours to dry. Repeat this with the other

Left. When both leaves of the gate legged table are extended it becomes a good sized dining table—and there is plenty of space to sit with your feet between the centre legs.

204

pieces; the more G cramps you have, the more you can do at once.

When the adhesive has set, clean up all the edges. If you have cut the pieces accurately in the first place, you can probably smooth them down with sandpaper wrapped around a wood block. But if they are far out, you will need to plane them. Try to remove as little wood as possible—plywood is such unpleasant stuff to plane that you will need no encouragement to do this.

Assembling the framework

The rectangular framework under the centre of the table consists of two flat frames (marked X and Y in Fig.1) joined by the foot rest and the two top cross struts.

The two frames X and Y consist of two legs and a bottom cross strut (each made from two thicknesses of ply) and a top cross strut (one of the single pieces of ply previously set aside).

Trial assemble the four pieces in each frame flat on the floor with the joints in the legs facing upwards, and check that the top strut does not cover the housing in the top of the leg. This top cross strut should be screwed to the two legs, to hold the pieces firmly in position and drill screw holes through the strut and part of the way into the leg.

Now apply adhesive to all the joints, assemble the frame and cramp it up until the adhesive is dry. Remember to wipe off any excess adhesive at once and check that everything is square. Repeat this with the other frame.

Once both the frames are assembled and dry, take them, the two top cross struts and the foot rest (parts X, Y, E and H in Fig.1) and make a trial assembly with the frame upside down, so that the four top struts are resting on a flat surface to hold them steady.

Dismantle the pieces, apply adhesive to all the joints (six joints and twelve surfaces) and reassemble them cramping the joints with sash cramps, or alternatively use some suitable improvised cramps. Check that the whole frame is square, using a piece of string to check that the two diagonals in every rectangle in the frame are equal in length.

The gate legs

Take the four parts which make up each gate leg: that is, the two legs and the top and bottom cross struts. Glue the joints and assemble the frame in the way previously described for frames X and Y. The legs of each frame should be laid on a flat surface with the cutouts for the halving joints uppermost.

When the adhesive has set, screw the gate legs to the main frame as shown in Fig.2. Make sure that the top and bottom of each gate is level with the top and bottom of the frame. Don't try to line up the horizontal cross struts so that they meet—they have been designed to be a short way apart to prevent them from sticking. Just screw the hinges directly in place: there is no need to cut them into the wood.

Now mark the position where the longer upright leg of the gate crosses the bottom cross strut of the main frame on each side, and cut half way through the strut with a tenon saw to form the sides of a recess for it. It should then be fairly easy to form the recess by separating the

two thicknesses of ply with a chisel inserted between them. Use the chisel, held bevel side up, to clean out any debris in the recess.

Final assembly

Place the centre piece of the table top and the two end leaves side by side on a flat surface with the angled edges towards each other. Half open the piano hinges and lay them in the two V-shaped grooves. The hinges should go as far into the V groove as possible while the edges of the leaves continue to meet. Mark the position of the screw holes in the hinges on to the edges of the leaves. Start the holes with a bradawl, then screw the hinges in place. The screws must not be too long, and must be inserted at the correct 45° angle, or they may break through the table top.

Take the main frame and place it upside down on the centre piece. Measure carefully around it to make sure it is set straight and exactly the same distance from the sides and ends. Then fix it in place with screws and angle brackets, again

being careful that the screws don't break through the surface of the table top.

Round off the bottom edges of the legs slightly with sandpaper or a file to avoid any danger of them splitting when the table is dragged along the floor. Screw a small block of wood to the underside of each leaf in the right position to act as a stop to prevent the gate leg from opening too far. Hold the end leaves and carefully turn the table on to its feet, but be careful not to strain the piano hinges in the process.

Finish the table with varnish or a covering of veneer or plastic laminate. The edges of plywood are notoriously hard to finish neatly so if you are varnishing or painting the surface, be particularly careful to sand the edges of the ply very smooth. The flat surfaces should also be sanded with flour grade paper to give a silken-smooth finish.

Below. *With both gate legs closed and the leaves down this gate legged table becomes an extremely stable and useful sized occasional table.*

Elegant
tea trolley

This richly elegant tea trolley in oiled teak will be an attractive addition to your dining room. With its trays covered in hard-wearing plastic laminate it is also extremely functional. The real beauty of the trolley, though, is that it is very easy to make with its few basic joints.

A tea trolley is easy to build and all the jointing involved is straightforward. The trolley in the photograph is made from teak, but you may wish to use a different hardwood to match the rest of the furniture in your kitchen or dining room. Afrormosia looks much the same as teak and is cheaper, though it is not quite so easy to work with.

The trays of the trolley are made of chipboard and covered in plastic laminate. The colour of the laminate used is a matter of taste, but the very dark slate green on the trolley in the photograph blends attractively with the colour of the teak. The trays are edged with teak.

Preparing the trays

The first step is to cut the chipboard for the trays. These are 31in. x 18in. x ¾in. (787mm x 457mm x 19mm). Cut the trays slightly oversize. Clamp the two trays together in a vice and plane the sides and ends exactly square and to size. Check that the trays are square by measuring the diagonals.

The teak side members of the trays are jointed to the long sides of the chipboard sheets by means of a ½in. x ¼in. (13mm x 6mm) plywood fillet. This is glued into grooves cut in the edges of the chipboard and the inside face of the side members.

Cut the grooves in the long sides of the chipboard with a combination plane. The groove runs along the centre of the long edges and is ¼in. (6mm) wide and ¼in. deep.

Applying the laminate

The trays of the trolley are covered in plastic laminate. The underside of the trays is also covered, since if you covered the top only the trays would be likely to warp and twist. The pieces of laminate on the bottoms of the trays are called 'balancers' in the cutting list. A good quality laminate should be used for the top, 'working' surface of the trays; a cheaper quality can be used for the balancers.

Cut the four pieces of laminate to size. The balancers only are glued in place at this stage. Spread contact adhesive over the surfaces to be glued and let it go tacky. Then put the pieces together and clamp them.

When the adhesive has dried, carefully plane the edges of the balancers flush with the edges of the chipboard. Do this with the two trays held together in a vice. Try to avoid removing any chipboard from the edges. If you do accidentally remove any, make sure that you have not put the edges out of square, and run the combination plane along the groove to make sure that it is still ¼in. (6mm) deep.

Buying the hardwood

You should buy the timber for the trolley from a timber merchant who specializes in hardwoods. Ask for timber that is machined and planed to exact widths; it is called 'PAR' in Britain and 'dressed' or 'gauged' elsewhere. The lengths, however, are only approximate, so when you order the timber, give an exact width but add 1in. or 25mm to the lengths given in the

Left. Good looking and efficient, this tea trolley will add interest to your dining room and simplify the job of serving meals.

cutting list, just to be certain. Before you order the timber, ask your dealer whether he will exchange any pieces with unsightly blemishes. Most reputable merchants will do this.

The side members

The strips of timber that run along the long side of the trays have a finished size of 32in. x 1½in. x ¾in. (823mm x 38mm x 19mm). They are 1in. (25mm) longer than the chipboard panels to allow for strips of edging ½in. thick to be inserted between their ends to cover the short edges of the tray.

The side pieces have a groove cut in their inside face. This holds part of the plywood fillet that is used to joint the chipboard trays to the side members. The ¼in. x ¼in. (6mm x 6mm) groove begins ⅜in. (10mm) up from the bottom edges of the side pieces. Cut it with a combination plane, its fence set to ⅜in.

The next step is to glue edging strip to the short sides of the trays. Use pieces of 1in. x ½in. (25mm x 13mm) timber for this—they can be cleaned off flush with the shelf top and with the bottoms of the side pieces later. The ends of the edging strip should be cut slightly over length to protrude ⅛in. (3mm) beyond the chipboard at each end. Glue the strips in place, cramp them and allow the glue to dry.

You can now apply the top sheet of laminate. Glue it in place over both the chipboard and the teak end pieces, and trim its edges off flush with the sides and ends of the tray. Then apply a thin coat of wax polish to the laminate. This prevents excess glue from sticking to the surface of the trays later on.

Now cut the overlap off the edging strip so that its ends are flush with the grooved sides of the tray. Then continue the groove cut in chipboard through the ends of the edging strip. Do this carefully with a saw and a chisel, not with a plane, which might rip off the edging strip.

Jointing the sides to the trays

A ½in. x ¼in. (13mm x 6mm) plywood fillet is used to join the side pieces and trays together. The fillet is glued into the groove cut in the chipboard tray, glue is applied to the groove in the side piece and the components are pressed together.

Before you do this, clean up the inside edges of the side pieces, sand them smooth and polish them. These surfaces will not be so accessible when the side pieces are fixed.

Cut the plywood fillet 1½in. (38mm) shorter than the length of the trays. Spread adhesive on the fillet and in the grooves. Push the fillet into place so that its ends are ¾in. (19mm) from each end of the tray. Then push the side pieces and the tray together. Cramp the assembly and place it on a level surface while the adhesive dries.

The next step is to cut 1in. x ½in. x ¾in. (25mm x 13mm x 19mm) plugs of teak, or whatever hardwood you are using. These fill the small gap left at the ends of the side pieces by the groove, and also add strength to the edging. Taper the ends of the plugs slightly and chamfer one corner a little, as you would do for a dowel. Then spread adhesive on the plugs and tap them into the small gaps with a mallet. When

the glue has dried, carefully saw off and plane down any parts of the plugs that protrude, and clean up all the timber pieces.

The trolley legs

The finished dimensions of the trolley legs are given in the cutting list. The sides of the trays and the legs are jointed together by means of halving joints. The position of these joints is shown in Fig.11. The legs at the back of the trolley are jointed to a handle that runs above the surface of the top tray, so they protrude above the top tray. The front pair of legs end flush with the top of the tray sides. A cross rail is jointed to the bottoms of each pair of legs.

Cut-outs for the halving joints must be made in the sides of the trays and the legs. The ones in the sides are 3/16in. (5mm) deep and 1½in. (38mm) wide, and start 3½in. (89mm) from the ends of the side pieces. Those cut in the legs are ¼in. (6mm) deep and 1½in. (38mm) high. Mark out the cut-outs in the two shelves while they are held together in a vice. They should be 'marked tight', to allow for any reduction in the width of the legs caused by cleaning them up. Mark and cut according to the techniques described in **CHAPTER 5**.

To avoid wobbles when the trolley is finally assembled, process all four legs together through as many stages as possible. Start by cutting them just over length. Lay them together in a vice. Square a line near one end. From this line measure and mark on the legs their finished length—28in. (711mm) for the back legs and 24½in. (623mm) for the front legs. Square lines through these points. All measurements for the positions of the joints must be made from the lines squared near the ends of the legs. Fig.11 shows the positions of the joints on the back and front legs. Make the cut-outs with a tenon saw and chisel.

The handle

The legs at the back of the trolley protrude above the top shelf, and are jointed at their tops to the handle. This runs between the two legs above the surface of the top tray. The joint used is a *comb* or *box* joint (a near relative of the dovetail, but easier to make) which provides a greater glueing area than most other joints and adds an attractive touch to the finished trolley.

The box joint is shown in Fig.7. The handle end of the joint consists of two tongues; these fit into two slots cut in the top of the leg so as to leave three tongues of wood protruding. Thus, the whole joint consists of five tongues; these should be of about equal width for the sake of appearance. In this case, the tongues on the handle are 5/16in. (8mm) wide and ¾in. deep. The tongues on the legs are slightly thinner—9/32in. (7mm) approximately—and the same depth.

Cut the handle just over length. Square lines near the ends of the timber to indicate the finished length. From these squared lines, measure back towards the centre of the rail a distance of ¾in. (19mm). Square lines through these points.

Use a marking gauge to mark out the box joint, as in Fig.8, working from these squared lines towards the ends of the timber. Carefully saw down the lines made with the marking gauge, using a tenon saw. Then make diagonal cuts

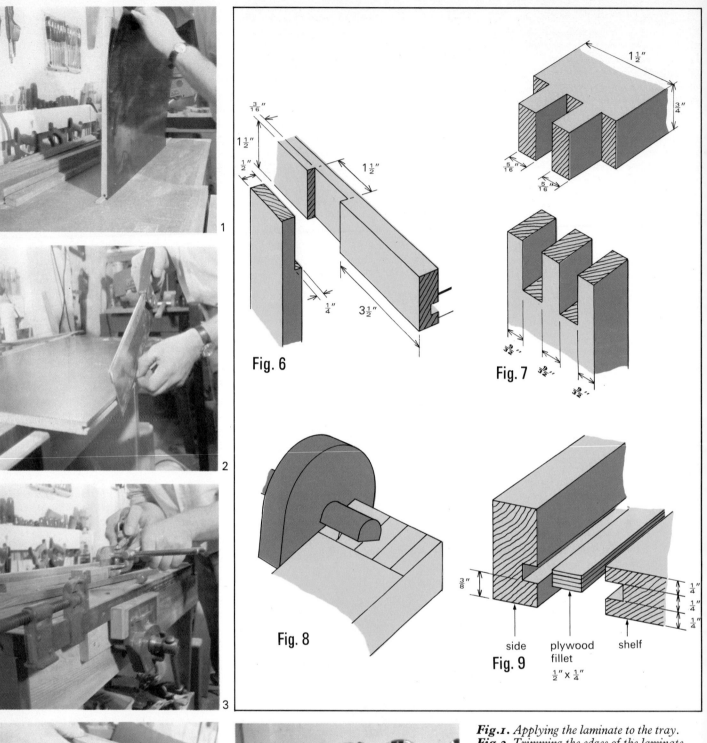

Fig. 6

Fig. 7

Fig. 8

Fig. 9

side   plywood fillet $\frac{1}{2}$" x $\frac{1}{4}$"   shelf

Fig.1. Applying the laminate to the tray.
Fig.2. Trimming the edges of the laminate.
Fig.3. Cutting the groove in the tray side.
Fig.4. Fitting the side piece to the tray with a plywood fillet which is glued in place.
Fig.5. Fitting one of the back legs into the halving joint cut in the side piece.
Fig.6. The dimensions of the halving joint that is used to join the side pieces of the trays to the front legs.
Fig.7. The box or combed joint between the trolley handle and the back legs.
Fig.8. The box joint is marked out with a marking gauge. The timber is divided into five more or less equal widths.
Fig.9. The dimensions of the groove cut in the trays and sides, and of the plywood fillet.
Fig.10. An exploded view of the tea trolley.

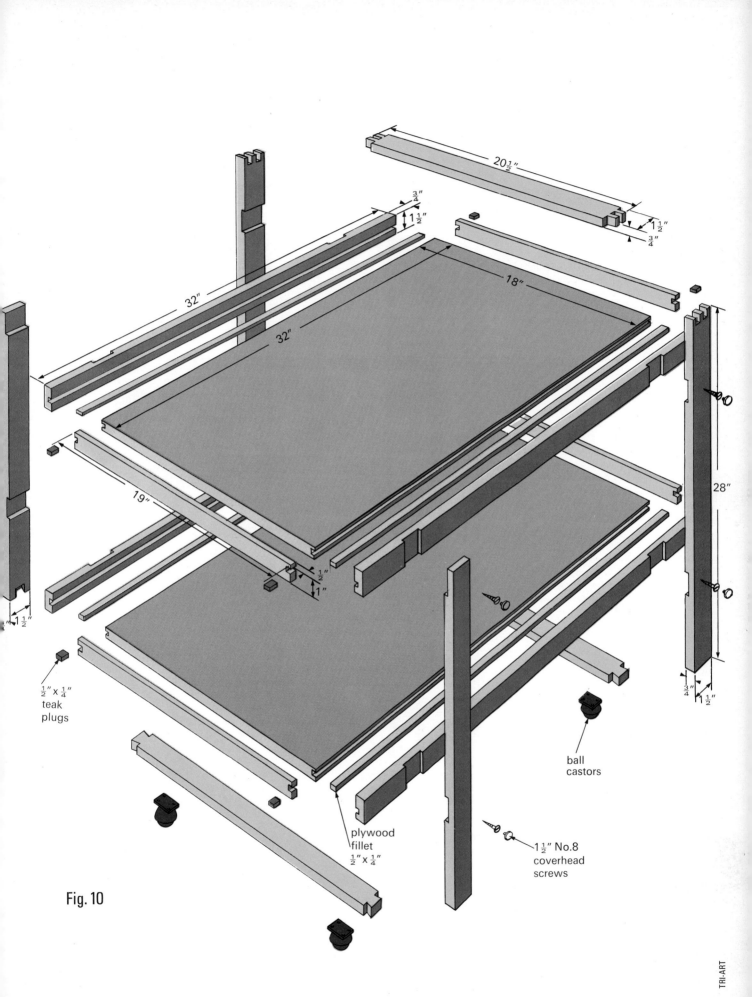

$20\frac{1}{2}''$

$\frac{3}{4}''$

$1\frac{1}{2}''$

$1\frac{1}{2}''$

$\frac{3}{4}''$

32"

32"

18"

19"

28"

$\frac{1}{2}''$

1"

$\frac{1}{2}''$

$\frac{3}{4}''$

$1\frac{1}{2}''$

$\frac{1}{2}'' \times \frac{1}{4}''$
teak
plugs

ball
castors

plywood
fillet
$\frac{1}{2}'' \times \frac{1}{4}''$

$1\frac{1}{2}''$ No.8
coverhead
screws

Fig. 10

between the first saw lines. This will leave you with a small triangle of waste wood which can be removed with a chisel. Instead of measuring twice, use the sides of the joint on the handle to direct-measure where the legs are to be cut. This is more accurate.

The cross rails

Both pairs of legs have cross rails connecting their bottom ends. The cutting list gives the dimensions of these rails. The legs and the cross rail are jointed with a single dovetail joint, as shown in Fig.12.

First cut the rails exactly to size. Square a line around the rail $\frac{9}{16}$in. (14mm) from each end. From each side of the rail measure inwards along this squared line a distance of $\frac{3}{8}$in. (10mm). Mark these points. Set a bevel gauge (this tool is similar to a try square, but has one adjustable arm) to 10° and from the marked points draw two lines running outwards to the corners of the wood. Cut this joint to shape with a tenon saw.

Now saw through the legs along the squared lines that indicate their finished length. Use the part of the joint cut on the cross rail as a template to mark out the leg. Cut this part of the joint with a sharp chisel.

Assembling the trolley

Assemble the trolley only after you have cleaned up and polished all the inside edges of the trolley members. This should be done now because the pieces will not be so accessible when the trolley is assembled.

Apply adhesive to the halving joint cut-outs on the insides of the legs. Push the legs and trays together. Cramp this assembly; this is best done with sash cramps, but if you do not have any, bind the assembly with loops of strong twine. Force wooden wedges under the twine where it runs over the joints.

Apply glue to the joints on the handle, cross rails and legs and push the pieces together. Check that the whole assembly is square by measuring all the diagonals; opposite diagonals should always be equal, or your assembly is out of square. If it is, cramp the entire assembly with sash cramps—you will need at least six—or with the string and wedge method.

Finishing the trolley

Clean up where necessary the outer surfaces of the trolley members with a smoothing plane. Remove those parts of the box joint that protrude. Sand the trolley smooth with glasspaper.

Now, at the points where the legs are jointed to the tray sides, drill holes for 1½in. (38mm) No. 8 steel 'mirror' screws with decorative heads. Countersink the hole and fix the screws. Fig.10 shows this screwed joint.

Clean off the wax polish on the laminate surfaces of the trays with turpentine substitute.

Apply one coat of cellulose 'sanding sealer' to the trolley members. Then apply teak oil, following the manufacturers' instructions, or an alternative finish.

Fit castors to the legs, following the fitting instructions for the type you have. Ball castors are the most efficient and elegant, but you can use the cheaper wheel castors if you prefer.

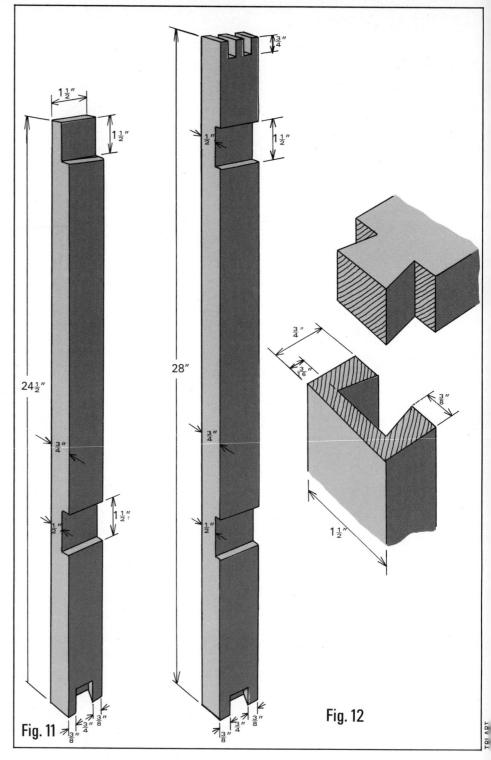

Fig. 11. *The front and back legs of the trolley showing the overall dimensions and the size and positions of the joints.*

Fig. 12. *The bottom cross rails are jointed to the front and back legs of the trolley with a single dovetail joint.*

Cutting list

Hardwood (finished sizes)	inches	millimetres
4 side pieces	32 x 1½ x ¾	823 x 38 x 19
2 legs	28 x 1½ x ¾	711 x 38 x 19
2 legs	24 x 1½ x ¾	623 x 38 x 19
3 crossrails and handle	20½ x 1½ x ¾	521 x 38 x 19
4 edging strips	18 x 1 x ½	457 x 25 x 13
8 plugs	1 x ½ x ¼	25 x 13 x 6
Chipboard		
2 trays	31 x 18 x ¾	787 x 457 x 19
Plywood		
4 fillets	32 x ½ x ¼	823 x 13 x 6
Plastic laminate (sizes allow for trimming)		
Tray tops	32½ x 18½	835 x 470
Balancers	31½ x 18½	810 x 470

Also needed
8 mirror screws 1½in. x No. 8, 4 castors, ½ pint contact adhesive.

Mansard roof

A roof that is the right size and shape does more than keep the water out; it gives proportion to the house and makes it look right. Too many roofs are so shallow that the box-like shape of the house becomes too noticeable. So give your house a roof with a difference, a mansard roof.

A mansard roof provides everything at once. Because of its height, for example, it makes the house look better. But the real trick is that it is higher even than it looks. The amount of space beneath a mansard roof is really surprising. You will be able to fit virtually another floor of spacious rooms within the roof structure.

Each side of a mansard roof has two slopes (see Fig.2); first a steep slope up from the eaves, and then a more gradual slope to the top or ridge of the roof. The lower, steeper slope provides a large amount of space within the roof—sufficient for as many rooms as on the floor beneath, although they would be a little smaller.

Many large older buildings have this type of roof—because it gives an extra storey without affecting the skyline too much—but it is equally suitable for the smaller and more modern home.

Below. *This mansard roof adds character to the house, and there is almost as much floor space as in a house with the same number of floors and a conventional roof.*

Sometimes a mansard roof is built on top of a single floor, creating the appearance of a bungalow but giving the space usually associated with a house. A variation of this roof is also used in some chalet bungalows.

A mansard roof creates severe stresses on the joists across the base of its upper section (see Fig.1), so it is best not to use this roof for a span, from back to front, of more than 30ft. (10m). It is, however, suitable for most medium-sized houses.

The mansard roof really consists of an upper and lower section. The lower section is a box-like structure stretching upwards from the wall plates and ceiling joists of the house itself to the upper joists (see Fig.1). The upper section is like a gabled roof with its own joists, ridge board and so on set on top of the lower section. Read CHAPTER 39 carefully—this gives instructions on how to build a gabled roof. The same components and methods used for constructing a gabled roof are used, or adapted, in erecting a mansard roof.

A mansard roof is generally designed so that the five 'points' of the eaves, the ridge and the joins between the slopes fit on a semi-circle (see Fig.2). François Mansart, who developed this style of roof, thought this gave the best proportions.

If a mansard roof is drawn to fit into a semi-circle, a roof with a 20ft (7m) span will give headroom of approximately 5ft 9in. (1.8m)—but this depends on the size of the timber used. As a rough guide, the headroom is usually approximately two-sevenths of the span.

Note, however, that in the Building Regulations in Britain, 'wall' means any part of a roof which slopes at less than 20 degrees to the vertical. Under these rules, a wall has to be constructed of different materials from those of a roof. Therefore plan your mansard roof so that the lower slope has a pitch of not more than 70 degrees from the horizontal. In other countries, check the regulations that cover roof building before designing the roof.

You will probably want to make maximum use of the room under the roof instead of treating it just as a larger-than-usual storage space. This means building in some windows. When designing your windows, ensure that they conform to any building regulations. In Britain, the building regulations specify that each room must have a window space equal in area to at least one tenth of the floor area. Regulations in other countries may differ, so again check before you start. Then draw the position and structure of the window on the plans and work out how to keep it in style with the rest of the house. A typical dormer window suitable for setting into a mansard roof is shown in Fig.4 and 5.

Draw a plan and elevation of the roof you intend to build, and then submit it for the approval of your local authority or building inspector (CHAPTER 39). If you are planning a conventional mansard, with the five points or 'corners' planned to lie on the circumference of a semi-circle, the two lower rafters between the eaves and the joins between the slopes must be the same length as each other, as must be the upper two in the gable section.

Fig.2 shows how to set about designing a roof of this type. First draw a semi-circle with a compass so that the diameter represents the roof span—set the two arms to a distance representing half the roof span using a scale of 1in. to 1ft, or if using metric measurements a scale of 10:1. Divide the semi-circle into ten equal parts—use a protractor and measure steps of 18 degrees from one side to the other. The ridge is at the centre; the joins between upper and lower sections can be placed three steps round the semi-circle from here.

This straightforward way of drawing a cross section of the roof ensures that the roof will look right. But if greater headroom is required, the lower slopes can be extended, or if greater width is needed they can be reduced in length. But do not move the lower slopes so much that they slope at more than 70° to the horizontal, otherwise the 'roof' will become a wall!

Components of a mansard roof

The components of a typical mansard roof with vertical ends are shown in Fig.1, and the function and sizes of most of them are described in CHAPTER 39. These are: wall plates, ceiling joists, rafters (but only those of the upper slope), purlins, ridge board, collar ties, struts, fascias, and soffits. A mansard roof can have the slope continued round the end, as with a hipped roof, but this is not usual. Components of the mansard roof that have not been described previously include:

Pole plate: a piece of timber (there are four in Fig.1) running the length of the house on top of the outside long walls, and along the join between slopes. The lower pole plate rests on the lower joists and holds the bottom end of the lower rafters. The upper pole plate rests on top of the studs and holds the bottom end of the upper rafters.

They are usually the same size as the wall plates described in CHAPTER 39, that is 4in. x 3in. or 100mm x 75mm.

Stud: this piece of timber supports the lower and upper rafters where they meet, and completes a triangle between each lower rafter and ceiling joist. They are usually the same size as the pole plates, and form the framework for the internal walls.

Upper joists: these timbers run in the same direction as the lower joists in the original ceiling, see Fig.1, from front to back of the house. Their size depends on their spacing, span and the load they carry, as with a conventional gabled roof. Guidelines for the sizes are found in CHAPTER 39.

Lower rafters: these are the same size as the upper rafters and run from the bottoms of the upper rafters to the lower pole plates.

Scaffolding

Always have adequate scaffolding (see page 155). Remember that a mansard roof is taller than a comparable gable roof and the scaffolding needs to be that much higher. Be especially careful when working on the upper section of the roof—there are many timbers beneath that could injure you if you fell. If a mansard roof is added to the top of an existing terraced house, you may need to seek specialist advice for adequate scaffolding.

Construction

The roof shown in Fig.1 and described below is built from individual lengths cut and individually fitted in place. The upper and lower rafters form a continuous line seen from the front of the house; the tops of the lower rafters butt against the bottoms of the upper rafters. But they could be staggered slightly. Alternatively, the upper section could be made from prefabricated gable trusses fitted in position.

Lower section

The sizes of the wall plates and lower joists and how to fit them are covered in CHAPTER 39. But remember to mark the position of the joists on the wall plates before fixing the wall plates in position. With a cavity wall, the wall plates can be placed on top of the inner or outer skin as long as they are of brick or similar construction. But do not place them on the inner skin if it is built of breeze blocks, as this is not a strong enough support.

The method of erecting the lower section is a further application of the method of erecting a gable roof described in detail in CHAPTER 39. The triangles formed by the studs and the lower rafters are erected on the lower pole plates along both the long walls and propped in place while the upper pole plates are fitted on top.

First, cut the timber for the lower pole plate to length. Do not mark the positions of the lower rafters on the pole plates as you can line them up later with the lower joists (the rafters lie directly over the joists and the studs to one side of the joists). Fit the pole plate in position on top of the rafters and skew-nail it in place.

To position the studs, measure from the plan the distance of the edge of a stud from the pole plate, and mark this distance from the pole plates along one lower joist at each end of the roof. Then use a straight length of timber to draw a line between these two points, cut the runner to size and nail it along this line. Again from the

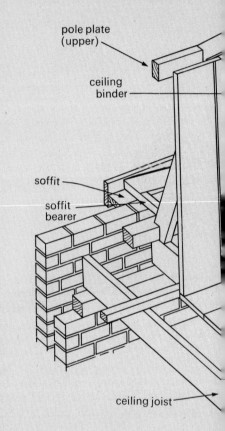

Fig.1. *The framework for a mansard roof is shown here set on a cavity wall. The inner wall is brick and takes the weight of the ceiling joists. The roof is continued beyond the edge of the outer wall by nailing the soffit bearers and sprockets to one side of the lower rafter as shown, and gives a pleasing shallower slope to the end of the roof*

Labels in Fig.1: pole plate (upper), ceiling binder, soffit, soffit bearer, ceiling joist

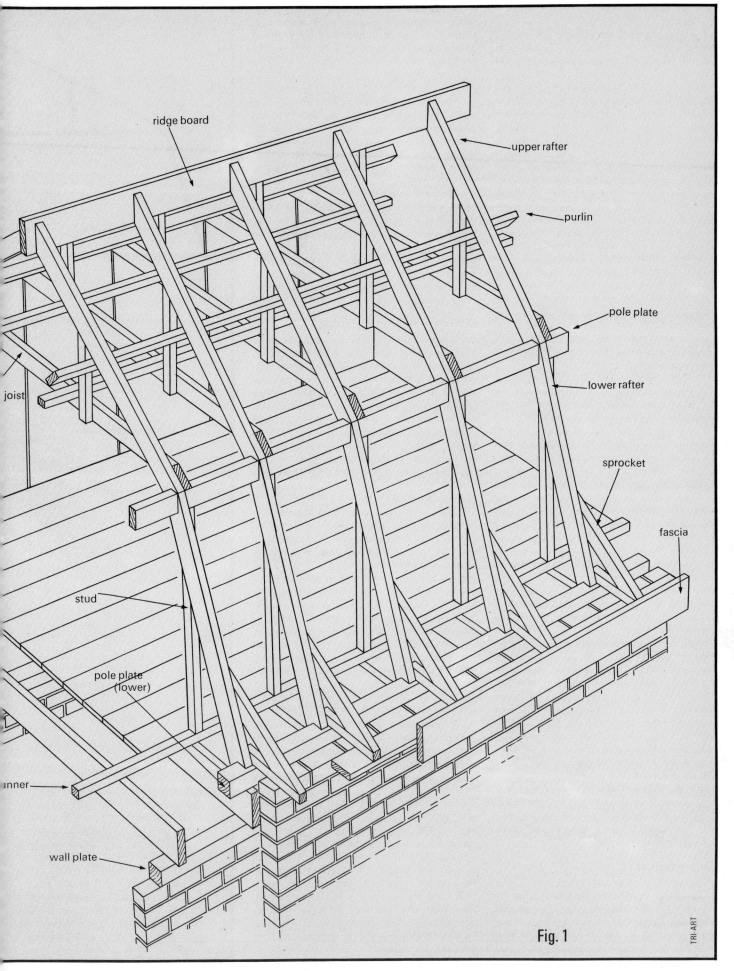

ridge board

upper rafter

purlin

pole plate

lower rafter

joist

sprocket

fascia

stud

pole plate
(lower)

runner

wall plate

Fig. 1

TRI-ART

plan, measure the height of the studs and cut them to size.

The length of the lower rafters is measured in the same way as for the gabled roof (see CHAPTER 39). Fix a length of wood to the ground and from one end measure the distance of a stud from the wall plate. Butt a stud at right angles against the wood at this point and fix it to the ground. Place a short length of the timber used for the pole plates on top of the stud to allow for its thickness. Then take a piece of timber for the lower rafters somewhat longer than the rafter is to be—you can measure its length roughly from the plan—and place it to form the third side of the triangle. Mark and cut the rafter to shape, birdsmouthing (CHAPTER 39) both ends to fit over the pole plates. The rafter should be long enough to overlap the stud. Nail a short length of timber across the stud and rafter to make a triangle that will hold the frame in shape.

Take this frame onto the roof and check to see if it fits. Place the lower end of the rafter over the pole plate and the stud over the runner. The rafter will lie directly above the ceiling joist. Check that the stud is vertical and that the slope of the rafter is as designed. Alter your triangle if necessary. Then copy it to make the remaining triangles.

To erect these frames and the upper pole plate, simply use the same method as with the rafters on a gabled roof in CHAPTER 39. Put one frame in position at one end of the roof with the stud next to a joist, and the rafter on the pole plate and directly above the joist. Check that the frame is still upright and support it temporarily with a batten by nailing one end of the batten to the top of the stud, and the other end to a nearby joist. Rest another frame flat on the joists at the other end of the roof with its 'feet' towards the end of the roof. Place the upper pole plate in position in the birdsmouth on the frame that is held upright by the battens. Then lift the other end of the pole plate, raise the second frame into position and place the pole plate in the birdsmouth on top of that frame. Check for squareness and nail both frames permanently to the joists. Then fill in with the intermediate frames.

The upper joists lie above the upper pole plate. They are generally laid on top of the pole plates and nailed in place alongside the rafter, as in Fig.1. In an alternative arrangement, they can be butted against the lower end of the upper rafter as in Fig.3 and held in place with a sheet of ply—approximately 12in. to 18in. (300 to 450mm) long, 4in. (90mm) wide and $\frac{1}{2}$in. (13mm) thick—glued and nailed to either side. This arrangement is found in many pre-fabricated trusses.

Nail one joist in position between the upper pole plates at front and back of the house. Check again that the entire framework is square, and then fill in the intermediate joists. Then build up any end walls to this level.

Upper section

The upper section of rafters, purlins and trusses is then cut and erected (see CHAPTER 39 for details). When this framework is completed, brick the ends up right to the ridge. Usually the roof extends over the top of the wall but, especially in a terraced property, the walls may

be built to project above the roof line to prevent rainwater from draining on to a neighbour's property. In this case the top of the wall will require a coping to prevent water entering the brickwork. (See Conversion, below.)

Tiling

Cover the roof with roofing felt, nail battens in place on the rafters and tile the roof (as described briefly in CHAPTER 39). Start from the eaves and work towards the ridge. On the lower, steeper slope you should nail every tile or slate in place, and not every third tile as you can do on the upper slope.

After the last row of tiles is laid on the lower slope, a piece of lead or zinc should be nailed in place as a soaker or apron (see Fig.3). This is to provide a watertight joint between the two different slopes of tiles. Nail it to the battens and rafters with galvanized nails at the top edge and mould the lower part round the lower row of tiles. Then nail the first row of tiles on the upper slope in place.

Fitting a dormer window

A dormer window is the most convenient way of providing the lighting necessary to turn the roof space into a room. The dormer window, as shown in Fig.5, lies between the top and lower pole plates. Leave out sufficient of the lower rafters to leave space for the window. Check that the studs forming the inner and outer face of the window are vertical and that the 'flat' roof shown here has a slope away from the main roof of at least one in 40 so that rainwater runs off into the gutter. The horizontal battening between the inner and outer studs should be halved or notched into them.

The flat roof and sides of the window should be boarded and covered with a minimum of two layers of roofing felt (see CHAPTER 39 for a brief description). Lay strips of lead or zinc in the corners where the dormer window and the roof join so that the water flows down into the gutter. The sides and top of the window can be tiled if you prefer; every tile hung on the sides of the dormer window must be nailed in place. In this case, the top of the window should continue the slope of the upper part of the roof instead of being flat; the junction of top and sides should be fitted with a soaker as described above.

Conversion on a terraced house

If it is possible to obtain planning permission —and the co-operation of your neighbours—a mansard roof is an ideal way of adding an extra floor to the top of a flat-roofed or shallow-roofed terraced property. If there is a large chimney stack with a dividing wall reaching high above the flat roof, it is possible to let the pole plates and ridge board into it without disturbing the neighbouring property. However, it is normally necessary to build up the dividing wall to a sufficient height, and this will invariably mean disturbing the edge of the neighbouring roof. Flashing will have to be built into the neighbour's side of the party wall to provide a watertight joint with the roof. Because of these potential difficulties check carefully that your local authority will grant you permission before you plan too far ahead.

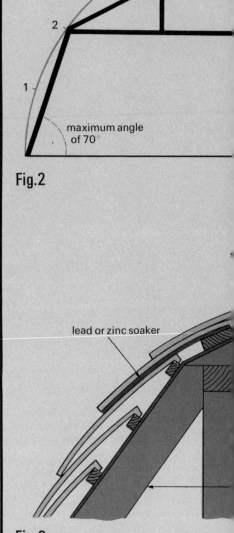

Fig.2

lead or zinc soaker

Fig.3

Fig.2. A mansard roof is traditionally designed to fit into a semi-circle which is divided into ten equal sections.

Fig.3. A lead or zinc soaker fitted between a couple of tiles makes a watertight join where the lower and upper rafters meet. Here the upper joist is fitted by the alternative method: it does not extend over the upper pole plate as in Fig.1., but is cut at an angle so that it meets flush with the bottom end of the upper rafter. A sheet of $\frac{1}{2}$in. (13mm) ply is nailed over both sides of the join as found in many factory made trusses.

Fig.4. Side view of a typical dormer window. The flat roof must slope at least 1 in 40.

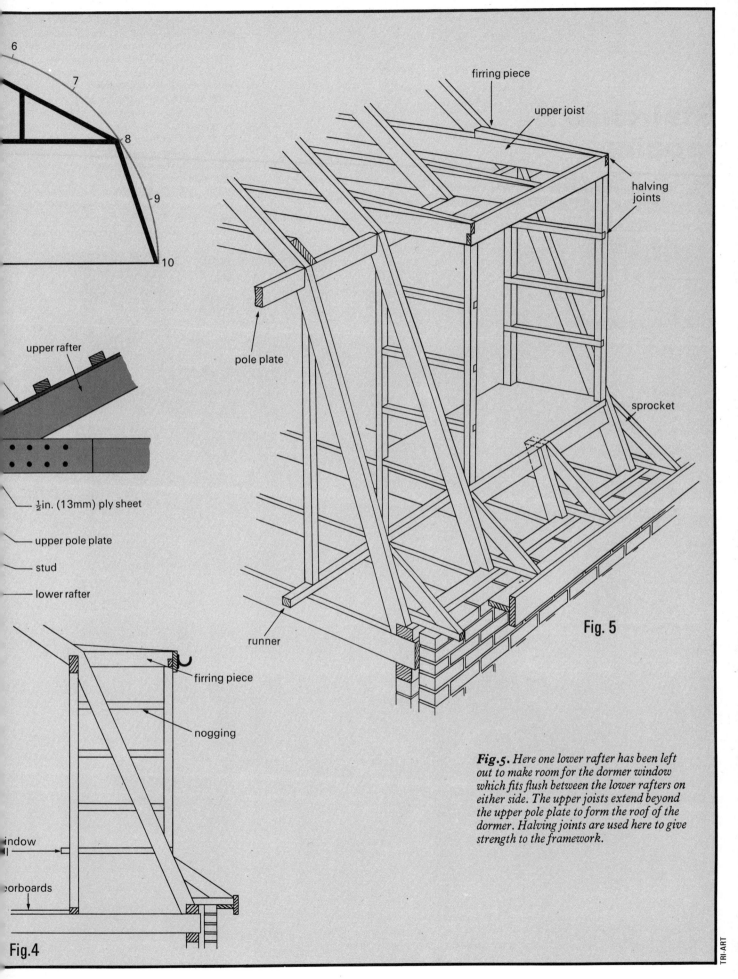

6
7
8
9
10

upper rafter

½in. (13mm) ply sheet

upper pole plate

stud

lower rafter

firring piece

nogging

...indow

...orboards

Fig.4

firring piece

upper joist

halving joints

pole plate

sprocket

runner

Fig. 5

Fig.5. *Here one lower rafter has been left out to make room for the dormer window which fits flush between the lower rafters on either side. The upper joists extend beyond the upper pole plate to form the roof of the dormer. Halving joints are used here to give strength to the framework.*

TRI-ART

Staircase repairs

Staircases are strong things. They are almost impossible to break in normal use, they do not generally suffer from rot, and as a rule the worst that can happen to them is that the handrail comes loose or some of the steps start to creak. Here is how to deal with both these faults, and some others.

Staircases are not difficult to repair. But it is essential first to know how they are constructed, because nearly every part of a staircase supports, and is supported by, some other part. And if you remove the wrong part you may easily bring the whole structure crashing down.

All wooden staircases are fairly alike in construction, but there are three main types. The *closed-string staircase* (Fig.1) is the cheapest type, easier to make and repair and generally found in newer houses. The *cut-string staircase* (Fig.2) is better-looking but more complicated and expensive to build. It would typically be found in a house built before the first world war. The *open-riser* staircase is built like a stepladder, with treads but no risers. It is most commonly found in open-plan architecture.

The closed-string staircase

The main load-bearing components of a closed-string staircase are the *strings* or *stringers,* a pair of straight-sided pieces of wood running up each side of the staircase. The *treads* and *risers* (horizontal and vertical parts of the steps) are fastened into the strings by housing joints.

Most staircases run along a wall, and have one *wall string,* which is solidly fastened to the wall and is about 1⅛in. (29mm) thick, and one *outer string,* which has to be stronger and so is about 1⅜in. (35mm) thick. The outer string is held in place by being inserted into the vertical *newel posts,* one at each end of each string, by a set of large angled mortise-and-tenon joints. The newel posts are bolted strongly to the floor joists.

Some staircases are completely free-standing and have 'outer' strings on both sides. Others have a wall on both sides and two wall strings. But in both cases, the rest of the construction is completely normal.

The two main methods of treads and riser construction are shown in Fig.4. They can be tongued and grooved together, in which case it is impossible to remove one tread without dismantling the entire staircase. Or they can be screwed together, in which case it might just be possible to remove and replace one tread from below—though it would involve chiselling out the rear of the housing and a lot of other arduous work. The screwed construction is not as strong as the tongued-and-grooved method.

The joint between each tread and the riser below it is reinforced by a triangular glue block with 3in. (76mm) long screws passed through it. These blocks are, of course, used only in the inside angles on the *underside* of the step. If they were used on the top they would get in the way of your feet.

The method by which the treads and risers are held firmly to the strings is found only in stair construction. They are jammed into their housings by narrow wedges driven *along* the groove of each housing, so that they are held firmly against the upper side of the housing (see Fig.1). The lower side of the housing, against which the wedge rests, is cut at a slant to accommodate it. The purpose of this wedging is to jam each tread and riser so firmly in place that it cannot rock or creak. If a stair creaks, it is generally a sign that the wedges have come loose under it.

The bottom step of a flight of stairs generally projects beyond the newel post. It is normally a completely separate unit from the rest of the stairs, and can be levered off without much difficulty if, for example, you want to repair the floorboards near it.

Vertical *balusters* are set in mortises in the top of the outer string to support the *handrail.* The tops of the balusters are sometimes inserted in mortises under the handrail, sometimes nailed or fastened by brackets into a groove cut all along the underside of the rail. The ends of the handrail are strongly fastened to the newel posts, generally by a mortise-and-tenon joint unless the handrail is a curved, decorative one of the type found in many old houses.

If there is a handrail on the wall side of the stairs, it is generally just fastened to the wall on

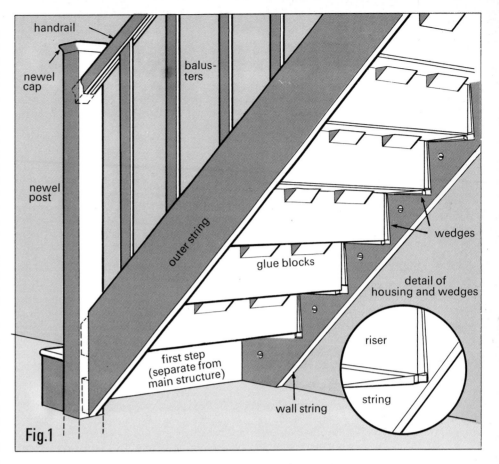

Fig.1 (above). A closed-string staircase, seen from below to expose the structure.

Fig.2 (below). A cut-string staircase, exploded to show its intricate joints.

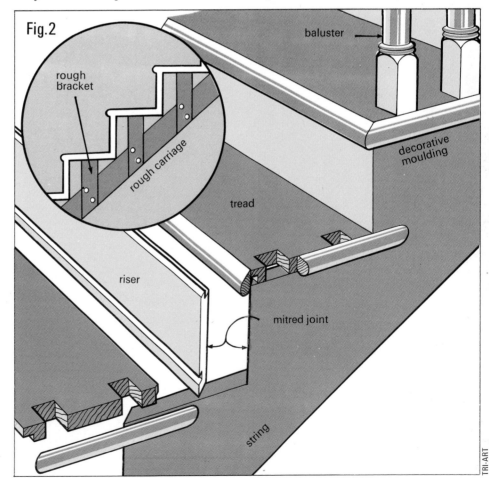

217

brackets, and plays no part in the construction of the stairs. Sometimes there is a newel post fastened to the wall at the bottom to match the one on the outer string. It is just decorative, however, and can be removed if necessary. Removing the real, outer newel post would deprive the outer string of its support and might easily cause the whole flight to collapse.

The cut-string staircase

In a cut-string staircase, the wall string is the same as that of a closed-string staircase. The outer string, on the other hand, is completely different. It is cut away to the profile of the treads and risers (see Fig.2). The treads rest on it, instead of being housed into it. They are finished with decorative end mouldings that project a short way beyond the string, which gives the outer side of the staircase a very elegant appearance. The risers are mitred into the strings so that no end grain shows.

The balusters are not mortised into the strings, because the tops of the strings are not exposed. Instead, they are inserted in cutouts in the outside ends of the treads, so that their outer sides are flush with the ends of the treads. The outside of the assembly is covered by the decorative end moulding of the tread, giving the cutout the effect of a mortise.

Since the outer string is largely cut away, it is not nearly as strong as a closed outer string. For this reason, there is a strong additional support called a *rough carriage* running down the centre

Fig.3. (*above*). *An old cut-string staircase painted in contrasting colours to make the ornamentation stand out.* *Fig.4* (*below*). *Details of tread and riser construction.*

of the flight. It consists of a heavy piece of timber, probably 4in. x 2in. (100mm x 50mm), just touching the bottom corner of each step where tread and riser are joined. As an extra support for the treads, timber blocks called *rough brackets* are screwed to the rough carriage, and reach up from it to the underside of each tread. The word 'rough' is used because the assembly is not seen, and does not need to be finished to the same standard as the rest of the staircase.

Obviously, this type of staircase is much more complicated than a closed-string one. The cutting to shape of the outer string, the mitred joints of string and riser, the decorative mouldings on the treads and the rough carriage all take extra work. This explains why a cut-string staircase is seldom found in a modern house.

Repairs

As you may already have gathered, major structural repairs or alterations to a staircase are out of the province of the amateur handyman, and should only be done by a professional. Furthermore, in most countries (including Britain) planning permission is required for all work on the loadbearing parts of a staircase, other than extremely minor renovations.

This does not mean that you cannot substantially improve the appearance of a tatty old staircase. But it does outlaw some projects— for example removing the risers to create a modern-looking 'open tread' staircase. People quite often attempt to do this, but since the risers contribute to the strength of the stairs, removing them is a recipe for disaster.

Squeaky or loose treads

Treads often squeak when they are stepped on, and it is not a sign that they are about to collapse. But when the problem gets worse, and they can actually be felt to move under your feet, it is time to do something about it.

The cause of the problem is nearly always loose wedges. The glue blocks may be loose as well. Both have to be reached from underneath, however, and this may cause difficulties.

Where stairs run above a cellar or a hall cupboard, the underside is exposed and easy to reach. But where the lower side of the stairs can be seen from one of the inhabited parts of the house, it is generally covered with lath and plaster. This must be removed to repair the stairs—a really messy job that covers everyone and everything with plaster dust and the filth of ages from inside the staircase.

One consolation for having to perform this unpleasant task is that you can replace the plaster with plasterboard, painted chipboard or

tongued-and-grooved boarding. Next time the stairs need attention, it will be quite simple to remove this covering.

Cover everything with dust sheets and rip out the old plaster with a club hammer and bolster. It is a good idea to wear a motor-cyclist's crash helmet and goggles, and a handkerchief tied round your nose and mouth.

When the dust has settled, look over the underneath and find all the loose wedges. Remove them one at a time and glue them back. If they are shrunken, warped or broken, cut new ones, taking care to copy the slope of the original wedge exactly. Reglue any loose glue blocks and tighten their screws. Make sure that all surfaces you glue together are clean and dry. If you find a cracked tread, strengthen it with a metal angle bracket screwed to the tread and nearest riser.

Newel posts are very firmly fixed and seldom need attention. If they do come loose, take up the floorboards and inspect the way the posts are fastened to the joists. It should be possible to reinforce the joints with wood blocks or steel angle brackets screwed into the corners.

Sometimes the mortise-and-tenon joint between the outer string and the newel post becomes loose, loosening all the treads and risers with it. You can't take it apart, so the only thing to do is to brace it with $1\frac{1}{4}$in. (32mm) square wood blocks glued and screwed into the inside corners. Knocking shallow wedges into the gap might work, but it might also split the newel post if it is not strong.

Replacing the handrail

The only structurally important parts of the handrail and baluster assembly are the newel posts. These should never be removed or weakened, but the rest of the structure is easy to repair or alter.

A few years ago people used to dislike the ornamental balusters of old houses, and board them up with hardboard or plywood to create the effect of a solid wall. This type of balustrade may or may not be to your taste, but it does have the disadvantage of making the stairs dark, and thus dangerous, unless they are well lit from above.

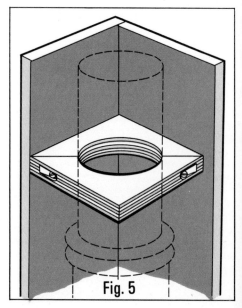

Fig. 5

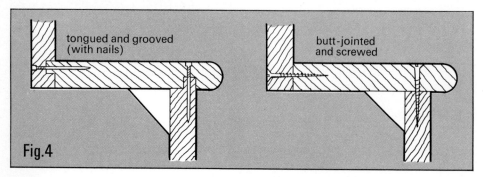

tongued and grooved (with nails)

butt-jointed and screwed

Fig.4

Today, most people appreciate old balustrades with turned balusters, but if they are in very bad condition, there is no alternative but to take them out and replace them. You might be able to get some more of the same type from a demolition contractor. Otherwise, there is a type of replacement that you can easily make yourself (see Fig.7). It looks like a 'ranch-style' fence and goes well with most modern furniture, but is not suitable for curved stairs.

The construction differs slightly for closed-string stairs (where you will probably want a single rail with the outer string finished to match) and cut-string stairs (where two rails will look better).

The first step is to remove the old handrail and balusters, and, in the case of a cut-string staircase, to fill the holes where the balusters fitted. This will present a problem only if the treads are finished in polished wood, which you might have some trouble matching. Glue in small square blocks and plane them flat.

Next, box in the newel posts to give them a square section (unless they are square already). Use solid timber, or you will have trouble hiding the edge. Most newel posts have a square base, to which the timber can simply be screwed, but at the top you may have to make a 'yoke' out of thick plywood (see Fig.5) to provide something to screw the timber to.

If the newel post is too tall, saw the top off. Otherwise, put a square block in the top of the 'box' and pin it in place from the sides. You can screw a polished hardwood cap to the top of the posts if you like.

To box in the outer string of a closed-string staircase, first remove all projections such as electric cables. Then cover the outside of the string with the thinnest timber you can find in the necessary width—or you could use veneered plywood. Cover the inside with a strip of the same material scribed to the shape of the steps. This is a boring job but not difficult. The strips need only be pinned in place, since they are not carrying a load. Finally, cover the top of the string with a strip to hide the mortises. This strip must be solid wood, because the edges will show. If you have used veneered ply for the sides, the top should be in the same material as

Fig.5 (left). *A round newel post can be boxed in by means of a thick plywood 'yoke'.*
Fig.6 (below). *How to mend a worn nosing with a glued-on hardwood strip.*

the veneer; the idea is to create the appearance of a solid string matching the rails.

Finish the new balustrade with a rail or rails made of solid 6in. x 1in. (150mm x 25mm) boards screwed to the inside (wall side) of the newel posts. Allow plenty of extra length when buying them, because the ends will be cut at a slant.

Of course, there are many other designs for replacement handrails. One that is *not* recommended is replacing it with a rope. If you stumble and fall against it, it gives outwards and downwards and you tend to go over it head first.

Worn nosings

A *nosing* is the rounded front part of a tread. On uncarpeted stairs, the nosing wears away, particularly in the middle. Replacing the tread entirely is very difficult and not worth the trouble. A better idea is to cut away the nosing and patch the tread with new wood (see Fig.6). Do not cut the wood right back to the riser, or you will weaken the joint there, particularly if it is a tongued-and-grooved joint.

The best tool to use for cutting away the old nosing is a spokeshave. Cut a flat surface, glue a wood strip to it (hardwood is best) and cut the strip to shape with the same tool when the glue is dry.

A worn bottom step can be replaced entirely if it is the separate, non-structural kind. But be careful to make the new step exactly the height

and width of the old one. If it is different, it will alter the *going* (slope) of the stairs at the bottom, which might make people trip up at the unexpected change.

Finishes

If your stairs are structurally sound but covered in tired old paint, you can transform them simply by stripping off the paint. Scrape off a paint sample and see what kind of wood there is underneath. If it is hardwood, as old stairs often are, you are in luck. Unless it has been stained, which you can discover only by scraping a piece clean, it will look magnificent if it is wax-polished. Even an ordinary softwood staircase will look very good if carefully cleaned and given three coats of polyurethane varnish.

The intricate mouldings of an old staircase are best cleaned with chemical paint stripper (open all windows first!) and a combination shave-hook. The treads, risers and strings can be finished with an orbital sander (or less well with a disc sander) when you have removed most of the paint. The rails and balusters must be hand-sanded.

If you have a really ornate staircase, and you aren't frightened of over-decoration, you might even bring out the relief on the mouldings with contrasting paint on the highlights (see Fig. 3).

Fig.7 (below). *Details of the 'ranch fence' conversion for handrails and balusters.*

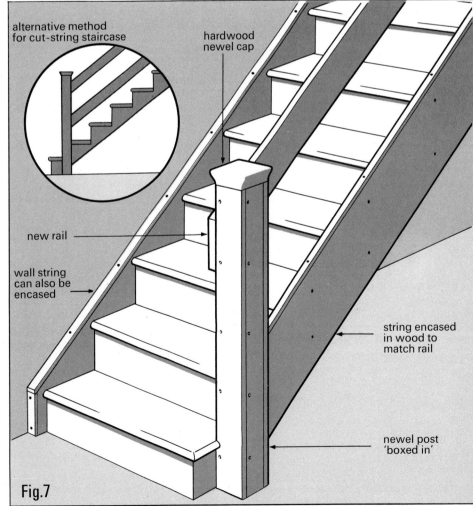

alternative method for cut-string staircase

hardwood newel cap

new rail

wall string can also be encased

string encased in wood to match rail

newel post 'boxed in'

Fig.7

TRI-ART

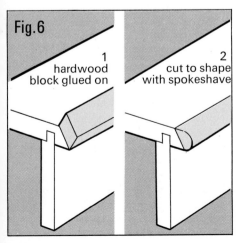

Fig.6

1 hardwood block glued on

2 cut to shape with spokeshave

Easy to build ledged and braced doors

Ledged and braced doors are usually seen outside the home where their strength provides necessary security on garages, sheds and other outhouses. If constructed carefully and well designed, though, a ledged and braced door can add an interesting and attractive touch inside the home.

The basic construction of ledged and braced doors is simple. The face of the door consists of vertical lengths of timber, called battens, which are butted together along their long edges. They are held together by ledges, horizontal pieces which are as long as the door is wide. Most of these doors also have braces, pieces of timber that run diagonally between two ledges. These always run *upward* from the hinged side; they give added strength to the door.

There are many designs for ledged and braced doors, some of which are shown in Figs.2-6. If the door does not have to be particularly strong—for a cupboard, say—you can do away with the braces. You can use only two ledges, one near the top and one near the bottom of the door.

Another variation is a framed, ledged and braced door. This has stiles and rails jointed together, with the battens glued and pinned into a rebate cut on the inside edges of the stiles and rails. The construction of this type of door is basically the same as that described in CHAPTER 25 for making Dutch doors though, of course, the door is not cut in two.

Most British doors are $1\frac{1}{4}$in. (31mm) thick, and if your door frame will only take this size you can build the door to this thickness. Doors on outhouses, however, need to be fairly solid for security, and for one of these you may wish to increase the thickness to $1\frac{1}{2}$in. (38mm); you can then use $\frac{3}{4}$in. (19mm) timber for all the pieces, which will be more convenient and less wasteful than using two different thicknesses of wood. The width of the timber depends largely on the design you choose but 4in. (100mm) is a common size for ledged and braced doors. Doors made from wider boards tend to look heavy and unattractive.

Tongued-and-grooved boards are often used for battens. These help to provide a weathertight seal. Square-edged boards can be used but these are not as weatherproof, especially when they shrink and gaps appear between them.

Basic construction

The first step in the construction of most designs of ledged and braced door is to butt the edges of the battens together. You will first have to decide how many battens you need to make up the door. You may have to cut some of the battens narrower than the rest. In doing this you must ensure that the arrangement of the battens is symmetrical. For example, if the door width is 2ft 6in. (762mm) and you intend to use 4in. (100mm) battens, this width will be approximately bridged by seven 4in. and one $2\frac{1}{2}$in. (63mm) battens. The door would look odd if you simply put the $2\frac{1}{2}$in. batten at one edge of the door. In this case you should use eight 4in. battens, cut two of them down to just over 3in. (75mm) and put one at each side of the door.

Cut the boards a little too long and the outside boards just over width. If you are using T & G boards, paint the tongues and grooves before you begin the assembly of the door. (But see 'Designs with a difference' below.) Paint the edges of square-sectioned timber also. This makes the door more weatherproof.

The battens should be fitted together tightly and the ledges nailed to them. To do this, you will have to cramp the boards together. Two or three sash cramps would do the job, but you may not have any. An alternative is to nail a long, reasonably straight piece of timber to the floor parallel to the skirting. Do not drive the nails right home. The distance of this piece from the skirting should be the planned width of the door plus, say, 2in. (50mm).

Cut four wedges, each of which should be a little narrower than 2in. (or whatever distance you have chosen). Lay the battens on the floor between the nailed-down strip of timber and the skirting, then force them together with the wedges, used as 'folding wedges' in two pairs (see Fig.7).

Fixing the ledges

Now mark out on the battens the finished length of the door and the position of the ledges. To do this, mark a line across the battens in the middle of their length. Take all measurements from this line. On each side of the line, measure half the planned height of the door. Square lines through these points across the battens.

Now mark the lines that will indicate the position of the ledges. If you intend to use three ledges the middle one should run across the centre of the door. On each side of the central squared line mark a distance equal to half the width of the middle ledge. Square lines through these points. The top and bottom ledges can

Right. An attractive, naturally finished ledged and braced door. An interesting design variation is the use of narrower timber for the braces than is used for the ledges.

be between 1in. and 3in. (25mm-75mm) away from the top and bottom of the finished door. They should not be farther away, or the ends of the battens may become damaged when the door is in use. Mark out the positions of the top and bottom ledges from the central squared lines.

Before assembling the door further you will have to decide how the braces, if they are to be used, will be jointed to the ledges. If you intend to use simple butt joints you can go ahead and fix the ledges, as described below. If you want to notch the braces into the ledges, as shown in Fig.3, you will have to cut the ledges to shape before you fix them. The distance of the point where the braces meet the ledges from the ends of the ledges is a matter of design. Fig.3 shows one design and indicates the positioning and size of the notches.

Once the ledges have been cut to shape, you can fix them to the cramped-up battens. *Lightly* pin the ledges to the battens in the marked positions. Use oval nails to do this, nailing through the edges of the ledges into the battens. Release the cramps, or knock out the wedges if you are using them, and turn the assembly over. Place rough pieces of wood underneath the ledges to hold them away from the ground.

Now nail through the battens into the ledges. Use nails about $\frac{1}{4}$in. (6mm) longer than the combined thickness of the ledges and battens. Nail through the door into the rough pieces with oval nails. Then turn the door over, knock off the rough pieces and *clench*, or bend over, the nail points with a nail punch. This pulls the ledges and the battens together tightly. Remove the oval nails that were used to fix the ledges temporarily to the battens.

Ledged and braced doors sometimes sag a little when hung. You can reduce this distortion by screwing the central and the two outside battens to the ledges as well as nailing them.

The door can now be cut to size. Saw along the marked lines that indicate the top and bottom of the door. Plane off the excess wood on the long sides of the outside battens.

Fitting the braces

If you have designed your door with braces, these can now be cut to size and shape and nailed in place. Remember that braces add to the strength of a door only if they run *upwards* from the hinged side.

If the braces are to butt against the ledges, mark on them the points where the brace ends meet the ledges. Cut the braces slightly over length and nail them temporarily *over* the ledges, so that they cover and protrude beyond the points marked on the ledges. Near the end of the brace lay a straight edge and line it up with the edge of the ledge—the edge to which the brace will run. Draw a line along the straight edge. Repeat the process at the other end of the brace. Remove the brace from the assembly. With a tenon saw, cut down the lines marked at the brace ends.

Once you have cut the brace to shape and tried it for fit, cut the other brace to length in the same manner. Lightly pin the braces to the battens and follow the procedure outlined above to enable you to nail through the battens into the ledges. These nails should be clenched too.

Insert braces

If the ledges have a V-shaped notch cut into them, cutting the braces to shape will be a little more difficult. It involves reproducing the V shape on to the end of the braces, but at a different angle (see Fig.8). To do this, mark a line along each ledge to indicate the maximum depth of the V, and across each ledge through the point of the V. Nail the braces lightly in place over the ledges and draw a line to indicate the edge of the ledge. Now mark on the brace the maximum depth of the V and the position of its point. The place where these two lines cross will be above the point of the V. Draw two lines from this point to the line indicating the edge of the ledge. Repeat this at the other end of the brace. Remove the brace and cut it to shape.

If you have cut the V shape in the ledges accurately, you can use the first brace to mark out the second. If in doubt, though, repeat the process outlined above. Nail the braces in place.

Designs with a difference

There is a wide variety of designs for ledged and braced doors. Many of the variations are small, but the less conventional designs can be attractive as well as functional.

A simple variation is to use two different widths of batten for the door face, placed alternately across the door. The assembly is exactly the same as for a conventional door. Make sure that the arrangement of the battens does not spoil the symmetry of the door.

Fig.1 shows a door with a diamond-shaped window in the centre of the top half. The hole for the window is cut after the ledges are fixed, but before the braces. The braces must be positioned so that they do not obscure the window.

To make this type of door lay the battens together in the manner described above and cramp them together. Mark out the position of the ledges. Then mark out the diamond shape. Its size is largely a matter of taste, but it should not be too large or the door will lose some of its rigidity. An attractive size for a door 2ft 6in. (762mm) wide is 12in. (305mm) along the vertical and 8in. (203mm) along the horizontal.

Assemble the door in the manner described above. Mark out the diamond with a pencil. At the four corners, drill a $\frac{1}{4}$in. (6mm) hole. The diamond shape can then be cut out with a power jig saw or, if you do not have one, a pad saw.

An alternative is to cramp the battens and mark out the position of the ledges. Do not fix them yet. Mark out the diamond shape and number each of the battens. Release the cramps. The battens in the centre of the door will have part of the diamond marked on them. Cut along the lines with a tenon saw. Reassemble the battens in their correct position, lining up the pencil marks that indicate the position of the ledges. Re-cramp the battens and assemble the door in the usual way.

If you intend to cut the diamond by this second method, and you are using T & G boards, you should not paint the tongues and grooves before the initial assembly. If you do, it will be difficult to get them apart again. They can be painted when you reassemble them after the diamond has been cut.

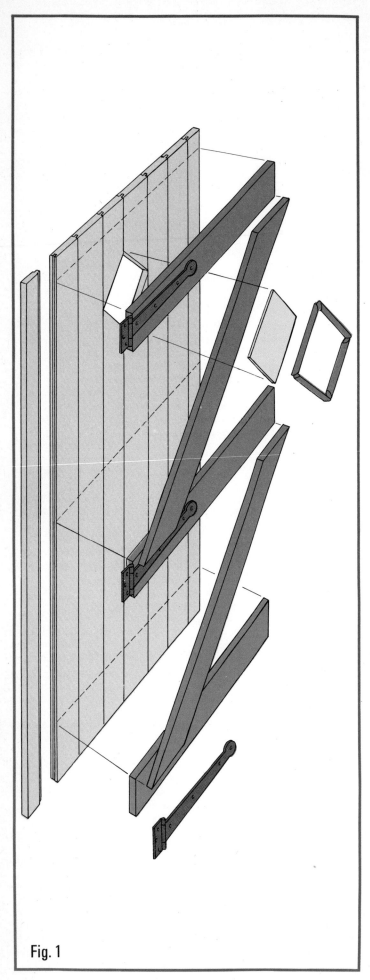

Fig. 1

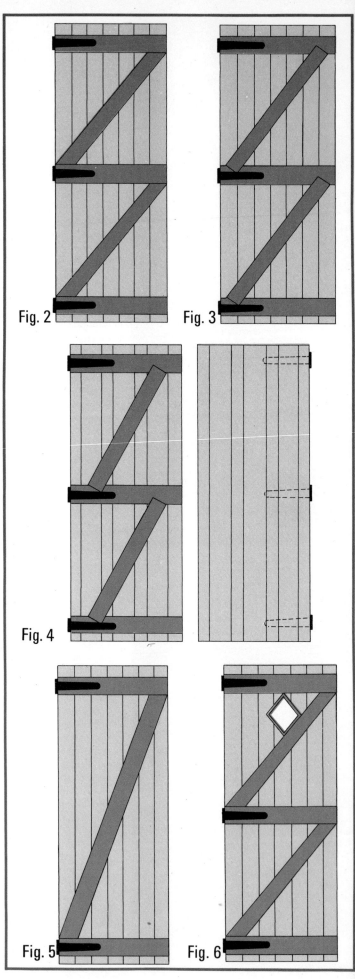

Fig. 2

Fig. 3

Fig. 4

Fig. 5

Fig. 6

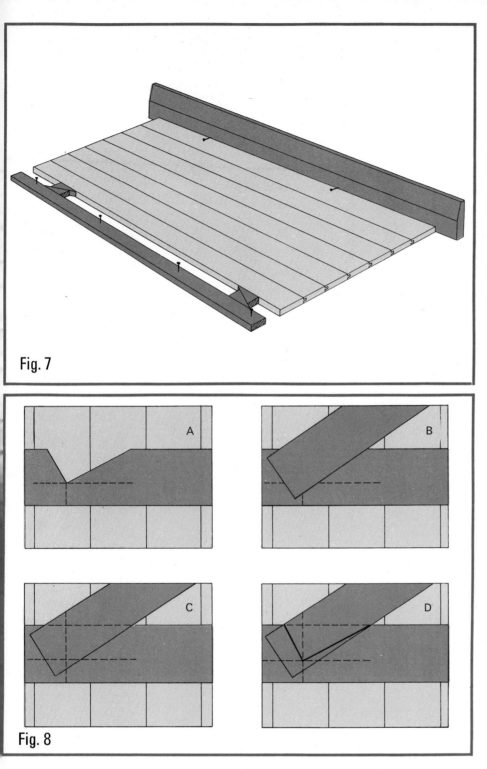

Fig. 7

Fig. 8

Fig. 9

TRI-ART

Fig.1. An exploded drawing of one design for a ledged and braced door. The diamond-shaped window is held in place with putty and strips of moulding. The braces can be positioned so that they do not obscure the window.
Fig.2 to 6. Five designs for ledged and braced doors. The basic construction requirements—the braces must run upwards from the hinged side and the door must be symmetrical—allow plenty of scope for designs with a difference.
Fig.7. One method of cramping the door battens while you fix the ledges. A piece of timber is nailed to the floor. Pairs of wedges are knocked in place between the timber piece and the door edge. This pushes the door firmly against the skirting board.
Fig.8. If the braces are to be inset in the ledges, cut the ledge to shape and fix it to the door. Mark it as shown in A. Lay the brace over the ledge (B). Sighting the marks on the ledge, draw intersecting lines on the brace (C). Draw lines joining up this intersection with the points where the brace meets the edge of the ledge (D). Then remove the brace and cut along these lines.
Fig.9. Where security is not really important a thumb latch will hold the door closed.

Once you have cut out the diamond, you can reassemble the rest of the door, including any braces. These do not have to run right to the ends of a pair of ledges, so you can avoid obscuring the cutout for the window. When the door is assembled and cut to size, fit a glass pane into the window.

You can cut the glass for the door yourself using a glasscutter and a straight-edge but your glass merchant may be prepared to do the job for you. Fit strips of wood moulding around the sides of the diamond cut out from one side of the door to give a firm fixing for the window. Then fix the glass in place with putty. If the sides of the diamond-shaped cut out have been irregularly cut then rebated moulding will

disguise this. The moulding is pinned in place —the method of fixing the moulding is basically the same as that described in CHAPTER 29 for fitting new panels into panelled doors.

Hanging the door

Ledged and braced doors are hung with tee hinges. These are shown, fixed in place on the door, in Fig.1. The long part of the hinge is screwed to the ledges. If the door is fairly heavy and has been built from thicker timber than that suggested above a heavier type of hinge, known as a Scotch tee hinge, may be necessary. The method of hanging doors is fully described in CHAPTER 16.

You will also need to fit some kind of lock,

bolt or latch to the door so that it closes securely. A barrel bolt is the most commonly used on ledged and braced doors. These are made from iron, brass or bronze, but for purely functional purposes an iron bolt is sufficient. The length of barrel bolts varies between 75mm and 380mm (3in.-14in.) but a 150mm (6in.) bolt is sufficient for most types of ledged and braced door. The plate of the bolt is screwed to the door and the metal socket or staple is fixed to the door frame. The bolt is pushed into this socket to secure the door. If the door frame is thick, the bolt can slide directly into a hole drilled in the frame.

A thumb latch will hold the door closed, but does not lock it. The components of a thumb latch are shown in Fig.9. A rim lock is the most secure way of locking the door. These are easy to install, the main part of the lock being screwed to the door and the keep, or smaller part, to the door frame.

Power tools : 2

Anyone who has used both a hand tool and its drill-powered equivalent will appreciate the fantastic saving of time and effort that a power drill brings. Sooner or later, however, he will become dissatisfied with the performance of some of the accessories of his power drill, and graduate to integral tools, as used by professionals.

Integral tools are designed in one piece for one purpose, instead of being a makeshift adaptation. Many have more powerful motors than those of drills, and as a result work faster and more efficiently than their equivalent drill attachments.

In many cases, an ordinary power drill with an attachment is quite good enough for amateur use. For example, the amateur carpenter would not dream of buying a full-size integral drill press instead of his power drill. But with other tools, bolt-on attachments to power drills are inadequate. This is particularly true with circular saws. A drill-driven saw will simply not cope with the strain of cutting large pieces of hardwood. So the first integral tool that many amateurs buy is a proper bench saw.

The bench saw

Circular saws of this type have powerful motors—at least $\frac{1}{2}$hp—and large blades ranging from 6in. (150mm) to 12in. (300mm) in diameter. The blade turns much faster than the one on a drill attachment, which not only speeds up the saw's cutting rate, but also gives a cleaner result.

However, both integral bench saw and drill-driven saw table are used in exactly the same way, and if you have a drill-powered saw, you can use these operating instructions provided that you do not overtax the tool's limited power.

*Opposite. Some of the many ways of using a bench saw. **Fig.1** (above, left). A push stick is used to protect fingers from the revolving blade. The saw is a lightweight drill attachment. **Fig.2** (above, right). Cutting a mitre on a more powerful integral bench saw, using its built-in protractor. **Fig.3** (below, left). Cutting a bevel. A straight-edge is laid along the rip fence to make the cut more accurate. **Fig.4** (below, right). Using the same saw to make the second cut of a large rebate.*

A bench saw consists of a flat table top through which the saw blade projects. Wood is slid over the table towards the blade, which is adjustable for depth and angle of cut and protected by a slide-away guard that reduces the risk of you cutting your fingers off—though this is still a tool that must be used with great care.

Wood is fed into the saw at the correct angle by using one of two *guide fences*. One of these, the *rip fence*, is parallel to the saw blade, but can be set any distance away from it by sliding it sideways in a groove up the edge of the table. Wood is slid along it into the blade for straight cutting parallel to the edge, generally along the grain. The other fence, the *crosscut guide*, is for cutting across the width (and grain) of wood at any angle. It does not lock in position, but moves from the front to the back of the table by sliding in a slot parallel to the blade. On the front of the guide there is a protractor. This is set to the desired angle, and the wood is rested against it. Then wood and guide are pushed together towards the blade, which cuts the wood at the angle the protractor is set to.

Both guide fences can be removed entirely if necessary, so that large sheets of hardboard or plywood can be cut without anything getting in the way. It is as well to check the angle of the rip fence from time to time. If it is not exactly parallel to the blade, it may cause the blade to jam when making a cut in a long piece of wood. Some, but not all, bench saws have slip clutches that disengage the motor when this happens, to stop it from burning out.

Of course, the saw is not restricted to making cuts straight along or across wood. It is an extremely versatile tool.

Sawing techniques
Small pieces of wood

It is dangerous to feed small pieces of wood into the blade with your hands, because your fingers get uncomfortably close to the blade and the slightest slip may cause a serious accident. Wood is very likely to slip on a bench saw, because the tremendous torque of the blade tends to wrench it aside if you are not holding it firmly. This is a particular problem when using the crosscut guide at an angle.

Small pieces should be pushed towards the blade with a *push stick*—a short lath with a V shape cut out of the end so that it can hold the piece of wood firmly (see Fig.1). It doesn't matter if the push stick gets cut, because you can make another in seconds. Fingers are not so easily replaced.

Mitring and firring

Mitring, or cutting wood at a 45° angle to make a mitred joint, as described in CHAPTER 38,

can be done quickly and accurately. To cut a mitre across the face of a piece of wood—as if making a picture frame—set the protractor on the crosscut guide accurately to 45°. Then lay the wood against the guide and slide the guide and wood together down the table into the saw blade (see Fig.2.)

As a general rule when crosscutting, wood should be held with both hands on one side of the blade, and the offcut allowed to fall away freely. If you push from both sides, the pressure tends to close up the cut around the blade, causing it to jam and 'buck' dangerously. If you must hold both sides, curve the wood slightly with your hands to hold the cut open.

To cut a bevel, or mitre along the edge of a piece of wood—as if making a box with mitred corners—set the blade at a 45° angle. Many saws have built-in protractors here, too, to ensure accuracy. On some bench saws, the table tilts

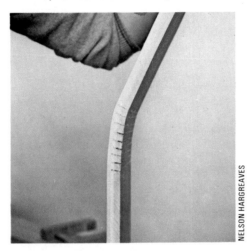

NELSON HARGREAVES

Fig.5. A bench saw is particularly useful for kerfing—bending a piece of wood into a curve by making rows of deep cuts in it.

instead of the blade. Slide the wood and crosscut guide towards the blade in the normal way, but grip the wood extra firmly (see Fig.3).

Firring is cutting a very shallow taper on a long length of wood so that it is a few inches narrower at one end than the other. It is used, for example, in cutting rafters for flat roofs to create a slight slope for drainage.

Firring is best done by making an adjustable jig out of two moderately long battens. Set them face to face and fasten them together by a hinge at one end and a slotted metal strip fastened with wingnuts at the other. By moving the free ends a distance apart and locking them at this distance with the strip and wingnuts, the jig can be set at any shallow angle (see Fig.10).

In use, the jig is slid along the fence together with the wood to be cut. This method is particularly convenient when a large number of identical pieces have to be cut.

Housing joints

Housings and other grooves can be cut very simply (but also very accurately) by setting the saw blade to the required depth of cut and cutting the sides of the groove first, using the fence to keep them straight. Then slide the fence away and remove the wood between the cuts by repeatedly passing the wood over the saw blade. Mark the extent of the groove on

top of the wood, or you may cut past the edges. Except with very wide grooves or housings, this method is faster than chiselling by hand, although for a stopped housing you will have to cut the last inch or two by hand, since the curved saw blade cannot reach the inside corner of the housing. It is also more accurate, because the depth of cut is constant all over the groove.

When cutting tenons, wood can be removed in the same way.

Rebates

There are two ways of cutting rebates on a bench saw. One way is to cut along one side of the rebate, using the fence to ensure accuracy, and then turn the wood through 90° and cut the other side (see Fig.4).

This involves two operations for each rebate. A faster way is to mount the blade on 'wobble washers'—a pair of angled washers that make the blade wobble from side to side as it revolves. As a result, the blade cuts a wide groove instead of a neat line. The width of the groove is restricted by the size of the slot in the saw table, because if the blade 'wobbled' too far it would cut the table. But you can always make several passes to cut a wide rebate.

When you have set the blade on its washers, fasten a piece of old battening to the fence to protect it and move it until the blade just brushes the battening at the apex of its wobble. Now any piece of wood that is slid along the battening will have a rebate cut out of it the same width as the wobble of the blade—or narrower if you adjust the blade to cut farther into the temporary battening fence. The depth of cut can still be adjusted in the normal way.

Great care should be taken when using wobble washers, because the oscillation of the blade makes it even more dangerous than an ordinary circular saw blade. At all costs, keep your fingers well away from it and use a push stick to move the wood you are cutting.

Kerfing

Kerfing is a special technique that enables a piece of solid wood to be bent in a curve. Rows of parallel cuts are made across the wood on the inside of the curve through half to three-quarters of the wood's thickness, and all the way along the part that is to be curved. The wood can be bent (see Fig.5)—though it helps the process if you wet it or steam it as well. Use a crosscut or planer blade to make the cuts; a combination blade is too coarse and will give a messy result.

Kerfing reduces the strength of wood sharply, and should not be used for load-bearing frames. It is also only suitable for outside curves—that is, with the saw cuts on the narrower radius; the wood *could* be bent the other way but the surface would probably wrinkle unattractively. But when used correctly, kerfing produces a neat curve that is impossible to make by any other method.

Maintenance of blades

Blades should be kept clean and as sharp as possible. After using a blade, rub a little oil or vaseline over it to stop it from going rusty. If any rust does form, take it off with wire wool. The smoother the surface of the blade is kept, the faster it will cut because there will be less friction between blade and wood.

Circular saw blades are very easy to sharpen

yourself. You *can* have them sharpened professionally, and some shops run an exchange service, sharp blades for blunt, but you only need a big flat file and a quarter of an hour to do just as good a job as they can.

Rip, crosscut and combination blades have teeth with squared-off outer ends filed at an angle. Alternate teeth have opposite angles. It is these angles that wear down, and all you need to do is file them back to their original shape. Do not file any of the other surfaces of the teeth or bend them.

Planer blades have straight-cut, pointed teeth which should all be filed straight across, filing the rear edge of each tooth. Otherwise, they should be treated in the same way.

Power saws are sometimes fitted with abrasive cutting wheels for sawing asbestos sheet and other materials. When these become blunt, they cannot be sharpened, but must be replaced.

The bench grinder

One of the most useful tools in any workshop is the bench grinder. It enables all edge tools to be resharpened in an instant—and sharp tools make for easy work. If you have a grinder attachment for a power drill, you will have to set it up every time you want to sharpen something —which is often. In practice, this means that you will not sharpen things often enough. So a bench grinder, which is not particularly expensive, is a good investment.

Another advantage of an integral bench grinder is that it has two revolving shafts—one on each end of the motor. Chisel and plane blades are sharpened in two operations; grinding, to get the blade the right shape, and honing, to put an edge on it. Different grinding wheels are needed for each operation, so having both of them on the same machine speeds up work considerably.

Sharpening is done against the front curved edge of the grinding wheel, and not against the flat circular face. The wheel revolves so that the front edge moves downwards. This keeps sparks and fragments of metal or abrasive from being thrown upwards into the eyes (but it is still a wise precaution to wear goggles). Adjustable tool rests are provided in front of each wheel to hold blades steady while they are sharpened.

Cutting wheels come in various grades. For most jobs, a medium wheel for grinding and a very fine one for honing should be all you need. Special extra-tough wheels are made for honing the hardened tips of masonry drills.

Fig.6 *(top left). Sharpening a chisel on a bench grinder. The blade is held steady against the tool rest and moved from side to side to keep the edge straight and even.*
Fig. 7 and 8 (second and third from top). The hand movement for sharpening a twist drill has to be learned. The drill is laid against the wheel with the front of its cutting edge touching (first picture) then turned clockwise and slid forward and up the curve of the wheel (second picture).
Fig.9 (bottom). Shaping a curved end on a piece of wood with a bench sander—this one is a power drill attachment.

NELSON HARGREAVES

The wheels are fastened to their shafts by nuts screwing down on to the threaded ends of the shafts. The wheel on the left has a left-hand thread to stop it from coming undone in use. The wheel on the right has a normal right-hand thread.

Sharpening chisel and plane blades

Chisel and plane blades, though completely different in shape and use, are sharpened in exactly the same way. In both types of blade, the preliminary grinding to shape of the edge of the blade should give the ground surface an angle of 25° to the flat face of the blade. Then it should be honed at the slightly greater angle of 30°. The 5° difference saves you from having to hone the whole ground surface. Only the tip is honed (see Fig.11).

To sharpen a blade, first lay it on the tool rest of the grinder with the point touching the stationary wheel, and measure the angle where the point touches. Move the blade until the angle is 25°, and memorize the position of the blade. Now take the blade away, start the wheels and lay the blade lightly against the coarse wheel. High speed and light pressure are the secret of good grinding. Move a wide blade from side to side across the wheel, so that its whole edge is ground evenly.

Grind on one side only until the blade is properly shaped, when the length of the ground surface should be 2½ times the thickness of the blade. Every few seconds of grinding, remove the blade from the wheel and dip it in cold water to stop it from overheating. An overheated blade 'loses its temper' and turns blue. If this happens, grind off the blue part.

The freshly ground surface will be slightly hollow in shape because of the curve of the wheel, but that doesn't matter. The next stage is to hone it.

Find the correct angle of the blade against the stationary wheel as you did before, except that it should be 30° and not 25°. Then start the grinder and lay the sloping side of the blade against the fine wheel—but only for a few seconds. The wheel will turn the edge of the blade over, producing a fine 'burr' on the other side. Cool the blade and lay the flat side *flat* on the wheel (i.e. not at 30°) for a few seconds to turn the burr the other way. Then turn the chisel round again and give the other side a few seconds at 30°. This will turn the burr again.

Continue doing each side alternately, using very light pressure and reducing the honing period each time. Eventually, the burr will break off, leaving a razor edge.

Blades can be honed several times before they lose their shape and have to be reground.

Sharpening twist drills

Twist drills and high speed drills can also be sharpened on a fine grinding wheel. The angles have to be watched carefully, but otherwise the job is not difficult. Do not cool twist drills in water, because the extra-hard steel might crack. Just try not to overheat them.

There are three important angles that must be maintained on a twist drill. They are marked A, B & C in Fig.12. Angle A, the angle of the cutting edge to the shaft, should always be 30°. Angle B, the angle of the sloping shoulder of the cutting edge to the horizontal, varies with the size of the drill. For small drills (from $\frac{3}{32}$in.

Fig.10 (*top right*). *An adjustable jig for firring. It can be set to a slope of (for example) 1 in 10 by measuring a 1in. gap 10in. along from the hinge. The hinge must be inset so that there is no gap when it is shut.*
Fig.11 (*below left*). *Sharpening angles for all types of chisel and plane blade.*
Fig.12 (*below right*). *Sharpening angles for twist drills—see the text.*

to $\frac{3}{16}$in. or 2.4mm to 4.8mm) it should be between 20° and 26°. For medium drills (up to $\frac{3}{8}$in. or 9.5mm) it should be between 10° and 15°. For large drills (up to $\frac{5}{8}$in. or 15.8mm) it should be between 9° and 13°. As a check on these two angles, if you have got them right, angle C, the angle of the front of the cutting edge to the chisel point of the drill, will always be 130°.

The correct way to sharpen a twist drill is to hold it near the point between the thumb and forefinger of the left hand, gripping it flexibly so that it can be moved about. Rest the left hand comfortably on the tool rest, as shown in Fig.7, and use the right hand to poke it through the improvised pivot you have made with your left hand until the cutting edge touches the wheel.

The front of the cutting edge should touch the wheel first, at such an angle that its whole length is in contact with the wheel. As soon as it touches, push the shank of the drill down with your right hand so that the cutting edge rises, simultaneously twisting the bit a quarter of a turn clockwise (see Fig.8). This movement is necessary to achieve the correct curve and angle on each cutting edge. You can practise on an old twist bit until you get it right. Once learned, it is never forgotten.

Sharpen both cutting edges of the drill equally so that the point is in the middle. When it is, check angle C, which should be 130°. If not, keep on until it is.

Special wood bits should not be sharpened on a grinding wheel, but with a small flat needle file with medium fine teeth. Aim only to preserve the original angle of the cutting edges; these bits are so large that sharpening them is a simple job.

Other integral tools

Most other integral tools are out of the amateur's domain. They are generally larger and more expensive than is suitable for amateur use, and many of them, such as the drill press or orbital sander, can be duplicated satisfactorily by drill-powered accessories.

One that you might come across is a *bench sander*—though even this can be duplicated fairly well with a power drill and a horizontal sanding stand (Fig.9). It consists of a vertical wheel faced with abrasive paper, and in front of it, a horizontal table equipped with guide fences like those of a bench saw.

The purpose of the tool is to sand the ends of pieces of wood at an exact angle—like a shooting board, only more accurate and faster. Only one side of the wheel is used, the side which is moving downwards as the wheel revolves. This holds the wood down flat on the table for maximum accuracy. The wood is fed past the guide fence, which can be set at 90° or 45° (for really accurate mitres) or any angle between.

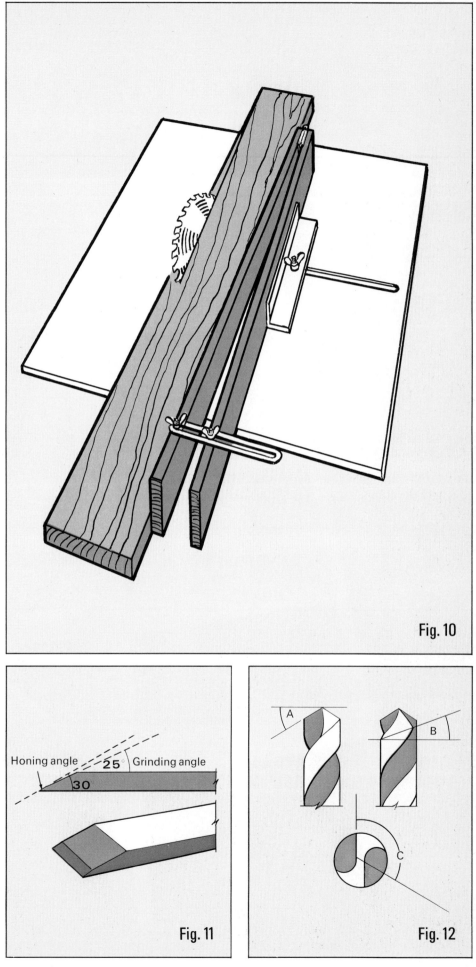

Fig. 10

Honing angle — 25 — Grinding angle
30

Fig. 11

A   B

C

Fig. 12

Sturdy stepladder to build

A stepladder is one of the most useful pieces of equipment in any household. It can be used for painting ceilings, reaching high cupboards, cleaning windows and supporting planks. The ladder described here is simple to build, but as sturdy as any bought stepladder—and of course much cheaper.

The design given here is for a stepladder about 3ft (0.9m) tall, a convenient height for general household use. If you want a taller ladder, all you have to do is extend the legs of the design downwards (so as to make the ladder wider as well as higher) and put in more steps. If the ladder is longer than about 4ft 6in. (1.4m) you should use heavier timber for the sides and rear frame, and put a diagonal brace in the rear frame for extra stability. Heavier hinges may also be needed.

This project introduces two variations of ordinary carpentry joints: the *angled housing joint* and the *haunched mortise-and-tenon joint*. It also has an unusual feature: because of the characteristic tapered shape of a stepladder, there are no right-angles and no verticals anywhere in the frame. Seen from the front, the sides slope in at 5° to the vertical; seen from the side, they slope at 20°. Achieving these slopes while keeping the frame symmetrical is not nearly as hard as it sounds.

Materials needed

The ladder is made throughout from ¾in. (19mm) thick timber, which is quite strong enough to support a heavy man if the ladder is kept to the height given here. All the pieces will eventually have their ends cut at an angle, so you will need to cut them out with a more generous allowance for waste than usual. The vertical members of the rear frame, for example, should be cut at least 1in. (25mm) over length. A point to watch is that the front vertical members, although 36in. (914mm) long, will use about 39in. (990mm) of timber because of their sloping ends—though you can reduce this by cutting them end-to-end out of the same piece of wood.

The timber required is as follows:
6ft 6in. (1.98mm) of 4in. x ¾in. (102 x 19mm),
4ft 3in. (1.30m) of 4½in. x ¾in. (114 x 19mm),
13in. (330mm) of 5⅜in. x ¾in. (137 x 19mm),
12½in. (318mm) of 3in. x ¾in. (76 x 19mm),
11⅜in. (289mm) of 2½in. x ¾in. (63 x 19mm),
6ft 10½in. (2.10m) of 1⅞in. x ¾in. (48 x 19mm)
. . . and a little scrap wood for making wedges for the mortise-and-tenon joints.

These dimensions include the large waste allowances needed for cutting angles, but not the normal waste allowance for the thickness of saw cuts, etc.

You will also need two 1½in. (38mm) 'back-flap' hinges, the screws for mounting them (normally ¾in. (19mm) No. 8s,) and a few feet of ordinary sash cord. The screws used in construction are 1¾in. (44mm) No. 8s; you will

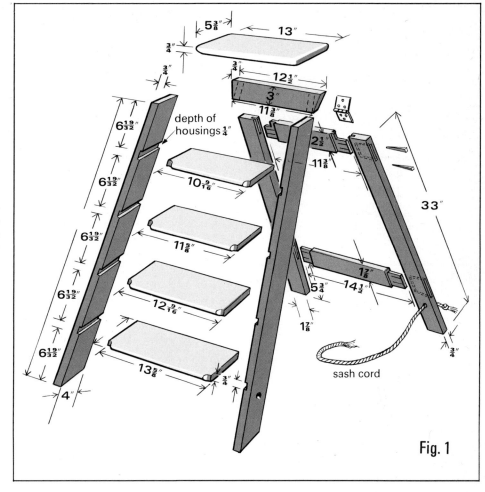

Fig. 1

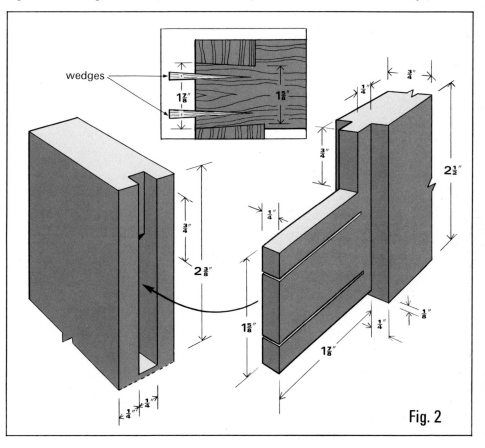

Fig. 2

Fig. 1 (above). An exploded view of the stepladder, showing all measurements.

Fig. 2 (below). The shape and dimensions of the haunched mortise-and-tenon joints.

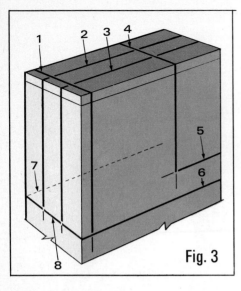

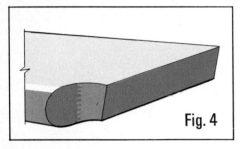

Fig.3. *When cutting the tenons, make the saw cuts in this order for greatest accuracy.*

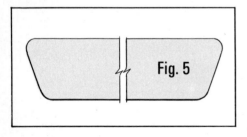

Fig.4. *A close-up of the end of a tread, showing the shape it should be cut to.*

Fig.5. *The top platform should be planed to this section to make it easier to lift.*

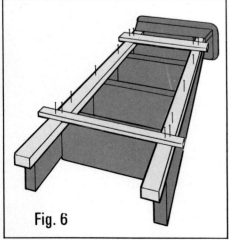

Fig.6. *The rear frame pieces are pinned to the front frame and marked directly from it.*

need two dozen. Use urea formaldehyde glue, which is waterproof—stepladders often get wet.

The front frame

The front frame, on which the steps are mounted, should be made first. Begin by marking out the vertical side pieces, which are called *stringers.*

The top and bottom of these pieces, and their four housings that carry the *treads* or steps, are slanted at an angle of 70° to the sides. This is done quite simply with a bevel gauge set accurately to 70° with a protractor. Use it like a try square, taking care to keep it the right way round. Mark the lines on the edges of the pieces with an ordinary right-angled try square, and use a marking gauge to mark the ends of the housings ¼in. (6mm) deep.

Cut the stringers to their exact length immediately, since other pieces will be measured against them later on. Saw down the sides of the housings, making them a tight fit, and clean them out with a ¾in. (19mm) chisel, or a router if you have one.

Now cut out the treads—but cut only the top and bottom ones to the length given ; leave the middle two ¼in.-½in. (6-13mm) over length for the time being. Put the top and bottom treads 'dry' into their housings. (If you have made the housings tight enough, they will probably need to be knocked in.) Cramp up the frame with sash cramps, or failing those, string twisted tight with pegs. Check the diagonals (NB: the corners are not at right angles, but the diagonals should still match). Now you can scribe the correct length of the middle two treads by laying them against the stringers.

The treads are ½in. (13mm) wider, from front to back, than the stringers. Their rear edges are planed off parallel with the rear edge of the stringers, which reduces the extra width slightly. The front corners should be chiselled off at an angle to fair them neatly into the front edges of the stringers, as shown in Fig.4. This planing and chiselling is best done before the frame is finally assembled, but keep fitting the tread into its housing while you are shaping it, or you might take off too much wood. The front edge of each tread should be planed to a semicircular profile at the same time.

When all the treads are shaped, glue the frame together and brace it with screws passed through the stringers into the ends of the treads —two to each end. Screws do not hold very well in end grain, but glue, screws and housings together should give ample strength.

Check the diagonals of the frame and leave it to dry. Meanwhile, cut out the top platform and the top rear piece with its angled ends (the exact angle is not important; it is just for decoration). Plane all the edges of the top platform off at a slight angle, so that the lower side is about ½in. (13mm) shorter and narrower each way than the top side (see Fig.5). Round off the edges and corners. Plane the ends of the top rear piece smooth, but do not round them off.

Glue and screw the top rear piece to the rear edge of the stringers, wide side up, and allow it to project about ⅜in. (10mm) above the top of each stringer. Then plane its top edge down at an angle to make it level and parallel with the

top of the stringers. Glue and screw the top tread in position, placing the rear two screws so that they pass through the top rear piece—this will give them extra grip. Set the completed front frame aside to dry.

The rear frame

The side-members of the rear frame are about 33in. (838mm) long, but cut them out 34in. (864mm) long to allow for later adjustments. The bottom cross-member is the same depth as the side-members, but the top one is 2½in. (63mm) deep.

Lay the front frame down on its face and place the two rear frame side-members on it in the position they will occupy, with their outer edges level with the outer edges of the front stringers.

The top ends of the rear side-members will not fit exactly against the lower edge of the top rear piece of the front frame, because they meet it at a slight angle. Plane the top ends so that they do fit, then lightly fasten each rear side-member to the front frame with three or four panel pins. Leave the head of each pin sticking out of the wood, so that they can be removed easily.

Lay the top cross-member down on the side-members with its top edge directly above the lower edge of the top rear piece (see Fig.6). Fasten it in place with two panel pins to each side. Do not drive them right in. Lay the bottom cross-member down in the same way, with its top edge level with the top edge of the bottom step, and pin it in place with two panel pins a side. Then draw pencil lines across each side-member along both sides of the two cross-members where they cross it. This will give you the angle and position of the mortises.

Remove the single pins holding the rear frame to the front frame, but leave the pairs of pins holding the rear frame together. Lift up the rear frame carefully, so as not to disturb it, and mark the cross-members where the side-members cross them. This marks the position of the tenons.

Dismantle the frame and square all the marks across the edges of the pieces. Then link the edge marks across the other side of the wood, but do not use a try square for this because the lines are not at right angles.

The haunched mortise and tenon

This type of joint is adapted for the top of a frame, where an ordinary mortise-and-tenon joint (see page 33) would not provide the necessary strength. The top of the tenon is cut away so that the mortise can begin below the top of the frame—if it reached to the top it would, of course, weaken the joint seriously.

Full details of the joint are given in Figs.2 and 3. The upper part of the tenon is not removed completely, but is cut back to leave ¼in. (6mm) to make a sort of tongue-and-groove joint. The tongue of the tenon and the slot of the mortise are ¼in. (6mm) thick, following the invariable rule that they should be one-third the thickness of the wood.

Mark out both tenons carefully and saw them to shape, making the saw cuts strictly in the order given in Fig.3 to ensure accuracy. Make two extra saw cuts in the ends of the tenons,

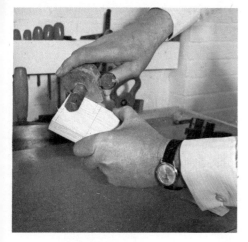

To make a haunched mortise-and-tenon joint, first mark out the tenon accurately, marking all the lines before you start cutting.

Next, saw down all the marked lines, tilting the saw blade alternately backwards and forwards to keep the cut straight.

Don't forget to cut a narrow strip off the lower edge of the tenon; this makes the joint more resistant to distortion.

The mortises are normal in shape except for the narrow groove running up from the top edge to the upper end of the wood.

A well-made joint should be such a tight fit that the pieces have to be knocked together to assemble it.

To complete the joint, hammer small hardwood wedges into the pre-cut slots in the tenons, then plane their projecting ends off level.

reaching almost their full depth. The wedges that hold the joint closed will be inserted into these cuts for maximum strength.

You will have noticed that the lower side of the tenon is cut away too—about $\frac{1}{8}$in. (3mm) is sawn off it. The normal tenons on the lower cross-member are treated in the same way on both sides. The purpose of this is to create a small ledge at the top and bottom of each tenon that will help it to resist being pulled out of shape by sideways strain on the ladder.

The tenons on the lower cross-members are conventional except for the $\frac{1}{8}$in. cutback at top and bottom. The shape and dimensions of these tenons are given in Figs.1 and 2. You can either make saw cuts in them for the wedges or insert the wedges at the top and bottom in the usual way, but the first method is probably a little stronger.

The mortises are not at right angles to the edge of the wood, but their angle is shown by the pencil lines you have already made. The pencil lines are, however, $1\frac{7}{8}$in. (48mm) apart, and the mortises only $1\frac{5}{8}$in. (41mm) wide. Place the drill $\frac{1}{8}$in. in from the pencil lines, then drill through the wood in the usual way. Clean out the mortises with a $\frac{1}{4}$in. (6mm) bevel-edged chisel, and use the same tool to cut the $\frac{3}{4}$in.

(19mm) long, $\frac{1}{4}$in. (6mm) wide and deep groove from the top mortise up to the top of the side-members.

When all the mortises and tenons have been made to fit each other, apply a generous coating of glue to the surfaces to be joined and assemble the frame. Knock wedges into the saw cuts, check the diagonals to ensure that the frame is straight and leave it to dry.

Final assembly

When the glue has set on the rear frame, plane off the projecting ends of the wedges and tenons and lay it on the front frame. Join the two frames together with the back-flap hinges, which should be placed so that the lower half of each hinge lies over the joint between the cross- and side-members of the rear frame—this will help to hold the joint together.

Now turn the stepladder over on its back, and with a pencil mark the length of the front legs on the projecting ends of the rear legs. Open out the frame and lay a long ruler across both legs at once on the pencil marks. Draw a line across both legs, and then, with a bevel gauge set at 70°, slant the line downwards across the edges of the legs—it should, of course, slant the opposite way from the front legs. Link the lines

across the back face of the wood with a ruler laid across both legs at once, as you did before. Then saw off the ends of the legs at this compound slant, which should ensure that they rest flat on the ground when the ladder is open.

Drill a hole in each leg a few inches from the bottom for the sash cord to go through—it doesn't matter exactly where, provided it is the same on both sides. Then set the ladder upright and get a friend to open the legs out until you can see that their slanted bottoms are resting flat on the floor. This should happen when the angle between the front and rear frames is 40°.

Knot the end of a piece of sash cord, pass the other end through the hole in the front frame, then through the hole in the rear frame, and pull it tight without disturbing the setting of the frames. Mark the cord where it emerges from the rear frame, close the ladder up and knot the cord slightly inside the mark, because the knot will be pushed along the cord as the ladder's weight tightens it. Repeat this procedure with the other cord, aiming to get it exactly the same length.

The ladder is now complete. Give it a quick once-over with glasspaper, but it is not worth varnishing it. Ladders always get filthy and covered with grease and paint, and besides, they are for using and not for looking at.

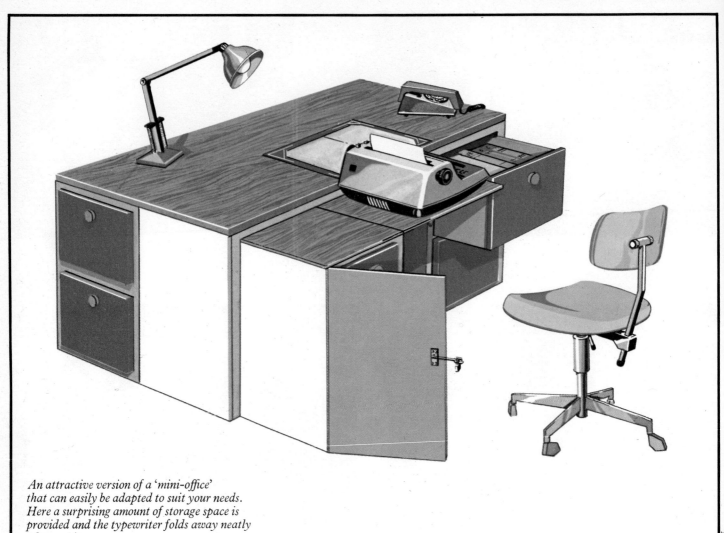

*An attractive version of a 'mini-office'
that can easily be adapted to suit your needs.
Here a surprising amount of storage space is
provided and the typewriter folds away neatly
when not in use.*

Mini-office
for the home

If you do work that involves writing or typing at home—whether running a small business, keeping your job records up to date or just coping with household bills—you probably find that your desk, and even the floor around, becomes a welter of loose papers and pencils. What you need is a properly arranged working area — makeshift arrangements never function well. The ideal solution is to build this 'mini-office'—a combination of a desk and a huge storage space, which folds up into a compact box when it is not in use.

The 'mini-office' described here is extremely easy to build, and the dimensions given can be altered if its size does not suit you. It has four enormous drawers and a pull-out cabinet with shelves for storing papers that you need to consult quickly. In addition, there is a hinged flap on which a small portable typewriter can be mounted permanently, so that it can be swung up ready for use in a moment. Any or all of these features can, however, be modified to suit your individual requirements.

Design

The 'mini-office' illustrated in Fig.1 is designed to fit into the right-hand corner of your room; the right side and back are therefore completely flat and free of drawers, shelves and cupboards. To fit it into a left-hand corner, simply build a mirror image of the design shown.

As the unit is shown, there is a set of drawers on the right-hand side of the front and a hinged cupboard on the left. When this cupboard is in the closed position, it is the same width as the drawers; this leaves a gap in the centre into which a chair can be pushed (a width of approximately 20in. (500mm) is adequate for most office-type chairs). If you want to make the whole unit lockable, enlarge the hinged cupboard so that when it is in the closed position, its door can be opened to stretch across the knee-hole of the desk and fasten on to it with a padlock, as shown in Fig.3. The drawers can be given separate locks of a conventional type. But don't make the cupboard over-large or it will place too great a strain on its hinges.

The cupboard swings open into the working position to give you an additional working surface on your left hand side. The special feature of this cupboard is the hinged flap fitted to its rear side. This can be lifted and bolted into the main frame, as shown in Fig.2. It will then be rigid enough to provide a typing surface for a lightweight typewriter. If you bolt the typewriter to the flap, you can leave it in place when you let the flap down and close the cupboard. This arrangement is particularly useful because you can arrange your typing surface to the level that best suits you: although this obviously varies between people and on the

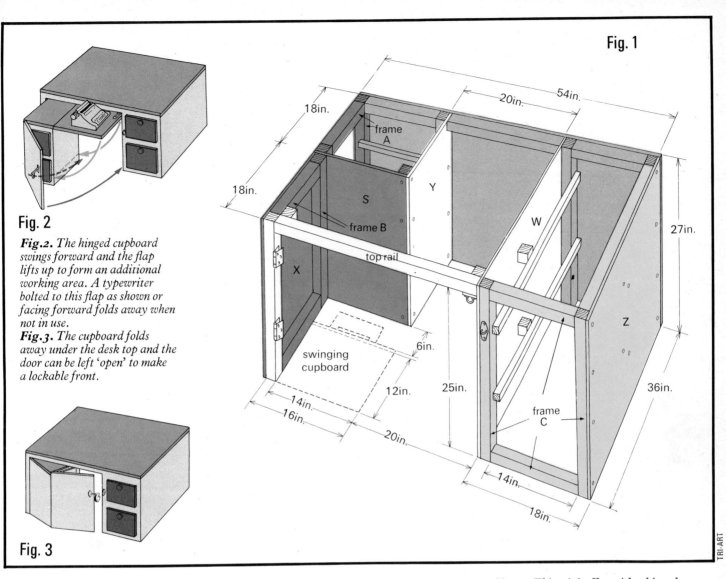

Fig. 2. The hinged cupboard swings forward and the flap lifts up to form an additional working area. A typewriter bolted to this flap as shown or facing forward folds away when not in use.

Fig. 3. The cupboard folds away under the desk top and the door can be left 'open' to make a lockable front.

Fig. 2

Fig. 3

Fig. 1

height of chair you use, 25in. or 25½in. (620mm or 633mm) is the usual recommended height, 2in. (51mm) less than the usual height of a desk top.

The back half of the left hand side is designed to be fitted with two more drawers or shelves, depending on your own requirements.

The dimensions shown in Fig.1 will give you a desk 54in. (1.35m) long and 36in. (0.91m) deep; and since this is a little deeper than many desk tops, a row of bookshelves made to fit along the back edge of the unit would still leave an adequate working area on the top.

Note that the whole depth of the right-hand side of the unit is available for drawers. You may not need drawers 36in. deep (which is very deep indeed for a drawer). In this case, you can make the drawers shallower from front to back and use the space that this releases for some other kind of storage space reached through the desk top, for example a locker for stationery or an inset waste-paper basket that can be lifted out to empty it.

If you have full-depth drawers, you should fit them with stops to prevent them from being pulled out the whole way, which would place a great strain on the runners. The best way of doing this is to nail a wood block to the inside of the top (for the top drawer) and to a batten fastened across the inside of the unit (for the

lower drawer) *after* the drawers have been inserted, so that the blocks catch on the drawer backs when they have been pulled out a certain distance.

Basic construction

A simple but effective construction system is used for this unit. The top and side panels are made from single sheets of manufactured board, which are joined by simply nailing them into lengths of 2in. x 2in. or 50mm x 50mm timber which run the length of the joins. The construction is further braced by three rectangular frames of the same timber, all of which are of identical size if you keep to the measurements given here.

The *top* gives essential rigidity to the unit and should be cut from a single sheet of 1in. or 25mm thick blockboard, which is fairly resistant to warping. Don't try to make do with thinner board or a weaker material such as chipboard, and don't use two pieces joined together; you won't get the same strength as from a single piece.

The *sides* should be cut from ¼in. or 6mm ply. Other materials are unsuitable. Don't use veneered ply or a board with a plastic-laminated surface, since you will spoil the surface by nailing through it.

All *the struts and frames* should be made from

Above. This mini-office with a hinged cupboard and a lockable front is built using an easily constructed carcase.

2in. x 2in. or 50mm x 50mm timber, as this will give plenty of room to nail into from two sides. The frames are assembled simply with butt joints and 4in. or 100mm nails driven in on the skew. The frames do not have to be very rigid, as they are either covered in boarding or braced by adjoining pieces.

All the vertical struts are the same height as the vertical frame members, which will speed up the cutting-out process.

Order of construction

Mark and cut all the *vertical struts* needed both for the frames and for the joins between the sides and make sure that they are all exactly the same length. Then construct the *frames*. Mark and cut the horizontal frame struts to size (with the measurements given here, they are all the same length) and skew nail through the uprights into the cross pieces to form the frames, which are marked A, B, and C in Fig.1. Check that the frames are square and push them into shape if they aren't. Don't cut any other horizontal struts yet.

Mark and cut the *blockboard top* and the *ply side panels* to size. Cut three end pieces the size

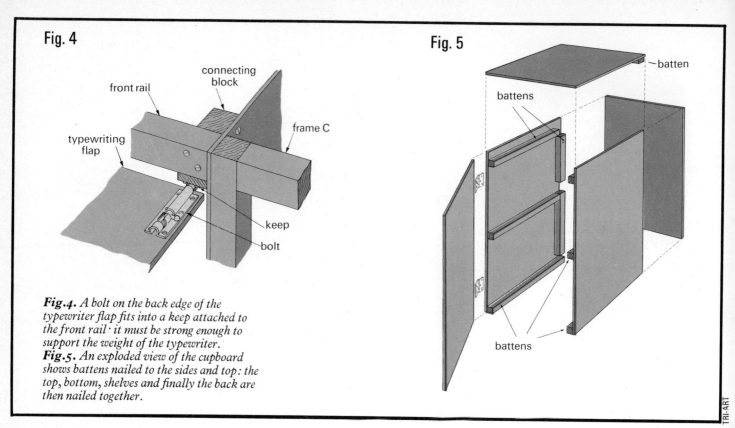

Fig. 4

typewriting flap

front rail

connecting block

frame C

keep

bolt

Fig. 5

batten

battens

battens

Fig.4. A bolt on the back edge of the typewriter flap fits into a keep attached to the front rail : it must be strong enough to support the weight of the typewriter.
Fig.5. An exploded view of the cupboard shows battens nailed to the sides and top : the top, bottom, shelves and finally the back are then nailed together.

of piece W, checking that the corners are square. Then cut one of the pieces exactly in half to form pieces Y and X. (This can only be done if frames A and B are the same size.) The remaining full-sized pieces are parts W and Z. Mark and cut the back piece to size.

Now partially assemble the parts as follows to give three sections capable of standing upright by themselves. For the *first section*, cover the face of frame B with plywood piece X, and fasten it on with 2in. or 50mm nails, which should be used for all ply-to-batten joints. Nail the plywood piece S to the side of frame B, then nail frames A and B together to form one end of the unit. Nail a vertical batten to the side of piece S that will be joined to piece Y.

For the *second section*, nail the piece of ply W to the frame C.

For the *third section*, take the piece of ply that forms the back and nail through the ply into the centre vertical struts (first mark the position of the struts on both sides of the ply, then place the struts on the floor and nail through the ply into them). Then nail the piece of ply Y to the left-hand centre strut (as seen from the front, but it will be on your right as you nail).

Now that the three sections will stand upright by themselves, the final assembly work can be done. First nail through the back into the two end sections with a few 2in. or 50mm nails : you will need a helper to hold the ends in place while you nail into them. Then nail the middle cross piece W in place.

Cut the front rail, a length of 2in. x 2in. 50mm x 50mm timber, to fit exactly between the inside edge of frame B and the side of piece W that faces towards it.

From the same timber, cut a couple of 2in. or 50mm long blocks to join the front rail to frame B and piece W. They will have to be put on with screws to achieve the necessary rigidity ;

two screws should pass into each side of each block and these should not be in line with each other or the wood may split. Use 3½in. or 90mm No.10 screws to fasten the front rail and frame B to the blocks, but 2in. or 50mm No.10 screws to fasten piece W to the right-hand block. Pre-drill the screw holes carefully, preferably using a 3/32in. or 2.40mm bit for the blocks and a 13/64in. or 5.15mm bit for the pieces that are to be screwed to them. Screw on the blocks, then screw the front rail to them.

Check the unit for squareness, nail through piece Y into the batten fixed to piece S, and add additional nails to all the joins between the pieces. Then cut and fit pieces of 2in. x 2in. (50mm x 50mm) around the top edges of the unit so that the top can later be screwed down firmly into them.

Shelves and drawers

Fit the drawer slides or shelf supports now, before you fit the top in place and while the inside of the unit is still accessible. For methods of making and fitting drawers refer to CHAPTER 14 and for details of how to fix shelves see CHAPTER 40. It will probably be easiest to fit the drawers on slides of 1in. x 1in. or 25mm x 25mm timber as shown in Fig.1, and hang the drawers by the 'three cleat' method ; they will then be slightly under width for the space but you can make them false fronts of ¼in. or 6mm ply to fit between the frame members. If the drawers are very deep, brace the centre of the slides with blocks as shown in Fig.1.

Fitting the top

The top should be cut to size and nailed—or better screwed—firmly in place at 4in. (100mm) intervals all round to keep the unit from twisting. If you cut the top larger than the walls of the unit to give an overhanging edge, make sure

that you leave the same amount overhanging all round, unless the unit is to fit flush against a flat wall without a skirting board.

Hinged cupboard

The hinged cupboard is also made from ¼in. or 6mm ply and 2in. x 2in. or 50mm x 50mm battens. Two solid ply sides are joined firmly by the battens to the shelves, top and bottom. The cupboard is held square by a ply back, which should be fastened to battens set all round the inside back edge of the cupboard.

Cut the two sides to size : the height is the same unless the typewriter flap is to be more than 2 in. lower than the desk top, in which case the side that is at the front of the cupboard when it is shut should be higher to bridge the gap between the cupboard and the top rail.

Nail battens to the sides as shown in Fig.5 ; then nail the top, the shelves and finally the back to these battens. Then cut and fit the cupboard door, fit a magnetic door catch and hang the cupboard on large, solid hinges, because it will have to take a certain amount of pressure.

Mount the typewriter flap at the same height as the cupboard top on a metal (not plastic) piano hinge and fit a large door bolt to support it as shown in Fig.4 ; the *keep* of the bolt (the socket side) may have to be mounted on a block to bring it down to the right level.

Finish

This useful unit can be finished with a variety of surfaces. If you are going to paint it, punch the nail heads below the surface and fill the nail and screw holes with stopping ; sand this down well before painting. For a stronger finish you can cover either the top or the entire unit with a plastic laminate, applied with one of the brands of contact adhesive that are available.

Repairing veneers

Veneered furniture is frail and easily damaged. Common causes include cigarette burns, knocks from children playing, and loose pieces of veneer catching on clothing and tearing away from the surface. All these produce minor local damage, which is best repaired by patching.

Making a new patch match the old veneer around it is quite difficult, but it is easier than the alternative, which is to re-veneer the whole article. And there are various tricks that will help you disguise the join between old and new.

Buying veneer

DIY and veneer shops sell veneer in a good range of woods, so that you should have no difficulty in getting a piece of veneer in the wood you want, or one very like it. The trouble is that they will almost certainly insist on selling you a whole sheet of veneer at once. This measures 3ft x 1ft 6in. (914 x 457mm) as a rule, which is almost certainly far more than you need for a patch. A sheet this size is quite expensive, particularly in a rare wood.

Before you commit yourself to paying for a whole sheet, try all the antique shops in your locality. Many of them repair their own furniture, and some *may* have an offcut of the veneer you want. It is worth trying, anyway.

Nearly all veneer is the same thickness: about $\frac{1}{16}$ in. (1.6mm). An exception to this is the veneer border around the leather tops of some desks and tables. Here, the veneer has to be the same thickness as the leather. In high-quality furniture, this may be as much as $\frac{1}{8}$ in. (3.2mm). Veneer in this thickness has to be specially ordered.

You will probably not be able to get veneer exactly the same colour as the veneer you are patching, so buy a lighter piece. You can always darken it, as described below, and applying polish will darken the wood anyway.

Always handle veneer carefully, particularly in large sheets. It splits very easily.

Cutting the patch

Most damage to veneered furniture is along the edge of a surface. This part is the most vulnerable to knocks and cigarette burns. It is also, fortunately, the easiest part to repair invisibly.

Wherever possible, repair damage to an edge by removing and replacing a straight strip running along the whole edge of the piece, with the grain of the veneer. In this way, the old and new pieces will be joined along the line of their grain, which conceals the join; and the join will be a straight line, which makes it very easy to fit. You can leave the outer edges projecting $\frac{1}{8}$in. (3.2mm) or so over the edge of the furniture and trim them later, after the glue is dry.

This method is only suitable for veneer with a fairly straight grain. Knotty veneer and veneer damaged at the end of the line of the grain, or in the middle of a surface, are better repaired by the following method.

This involves replacing the damaged area with a 'boat-shaped' patch, ie. an oval one with pointed ends, with the long diameter of the oval pointing along the general direction of the grain. This is the shape that will be least obvious when glued down. The more a join runs across the grain, the more it will show, so keep the ends of the oval as pointed as possible.

Find out the best shape and size for the patch by putting a piece of tracing paper over the damaged area and drawing 'boat' shapes on it until you find one that seems right. Draw a few lines along this shape to give the direction of the grain.

Use a piece of carbon paper to transfer the shape from the tracing paper to the new veneer, pressing very lightly and getting the grain running the right way by means of the lines on the tracing. Then cut the shape out, using a handyman's knife with a brand-new blade. Slope the knife sideways as you cut, so that the cut edge slants; the handle of the blade should point outwards at 45°. It is a good idea to cut the shape out slightly too large, as this will give you a chance to move it around over the damage to match the grain more exactly.

When cutting a straight strip of veneer, there is no need to slope the knife. Cut along a steel ruler or straight-edge to keep the line straight.

Take your oval strip of veneer and lay it down over the damaged area. Move it around until the grain matches best, then hold it in place with your left hand and draw round it lightly with a sharp pencil.

Now remove the patch and cut around the mark, just inside the pencil line and holding the knife at the same 45° angle as you used for cutting out the patch. Be sure not to cut out too much of the old veneer; if the patch proves too big you can cut it down, but if it is too small you will have to make a new patch. The slanting join will hide any small discrepancies, however.

Remove the damaged veneer inside the cut line with a *very sharp* narrow chisel, held bevel (slanted) side down. You should just chisel out the old veneer and the glue under it, without hurting the wood that the veneer is glued to. This is not as hard as it sounds. If your chisel is blunt, sharpen it. Large areas of old glue can be removed with hot water.

Try the patch in the hole and trim it to size if necessary. It is now ready for glueing in.

Glueing in the patch

Patches in veneer need to be glued in very strongly, and held in place while the glue dries. The right kind of glue is a white pva wood glue, but use scotch glue for large, difficult patches. The first kind can be attached without clamps if necessary (see below) but it is always best to clamp the patch down if possible.

The patch must be held down firmly. You could use a carpenter's G-cramp with a wood block under it. The block should cover the whole patch, or the edges will curl. A good improvised clamp for a horizontal surface would be a sheet of glass with three or four bricks carefully laid on top of it.

Apply glue thinly but evenly to the two surfaces to be glued, and press the patch in place. It doesn't matter if a bit of glue oozes out; wipe it off with a damp cloth. Put a sheet of brown paper over the patch to absorb the surplus, then apply the clamp and leave to dry for as long as it needs. The longer you can leave any type of glue, the better.

A patch glued with pva adhesive may be ironed in place with an ordinary electric iron set to 'warm'. When the adhesive is tacky, cover the patch with brown paper and run the iron back and forth until the glue is dry—this will probably take twenty minutes or half an hour.

If you don't have an iron or any clamps, you *can* stick the patch on with an impact adhesive (preferably the thixotropic kind, which allows you to slide the patch about). But the repair will not last for so long.

Finishing the patch

When the glue is thoroughly dry, pull off as much of the brown paper as will come off—damping the paper carefully helps. Then wrap some very fine glasspaper around a flat-surfaced cork or wood block and sand off all traces of paper and glue, carrying on until the surface of the patch is level with the veneer around it. Obviously, this will remove some of the polish from the surrounding veneer, but that doesn't matter. Always sand along the grain if possible. Finish the sanding with 'flour grade' paper (the finest of all), so that the surface is beautifully smooth.

If the surface you are repairing is very light-coloured, or the veneer has a coarse, open grain (examples of this type of wood include oak, ash, rosewood and sapele), you should seal it with a proprietary grain filler in the appropriate colour. Otherwise enormous amounts of polish will sink into the wood, discolouring it and making it very hard to achieve a good sheen. Rub the filler into the veneer and sand it smooth with 'flour grade' paper.

Before applying any french polish to the patch, make sure it will turn the right colour when it is polished. Ordinary 'white' (ie, uncoloured) french polish darkens wood slightly, but not much. As a rough guide, examine the area around the patch where the old polish has been sanded off. If it is not exactly the same colour as the patch itself, you will almost certainly need to stain the patch to match.

You can discover the difference that applying french polish makes to the colour of the patch by applying 10 or more coats (no fewer) to

an offcut of the veneer. For details of how to apply the polish, see below. There is no need to rub down between coats, however.

If you need to stain the patch, buy a good brand of ready-mixed spirit-based wood dye. The *depth* of its colour does not matter, because you can dilute it with methylated spirit, but the *tone* (ie, whether it is reddish or yellowish) does. Experiment to find the right dilution on offcuts of veneer, then paint the diluted mix on to the patch with a brush, being careful not to paint beyond the edge. Water-based wood dye is not suitable because it spreads out.

It is now time to polish the patch and the sanded area around it. French polish should be applied undiluted with a 'rubber' made of a small piece of cotton wool wrapped in a lint-free cotton cloth which has been slightly moistened with linseed oil. The purpose of the oil is to stop the cloth from sticking to the sticky polish. If it shows signs of doing this, put a little more oil on the cloth.

Rub the polish on, not too generously, with small circular motions. Let it dry for 20 minutes, then rub it down very lightly with 'flour grade' paper wrapped round a block. Apply the next coat, and go on doing this until the sheen matches the surrounding polish. This will take at least 10 coats, and more probably 20 or even 30.

Do not rub down the last coat of polish. Let it dry really thoroughly for two or three days, then complete the job with a good wax polish.

Some modern veneered furniture has a satin finish. This can be duplicated with a mixture of polyurethane varnish and turpentine substitute, as described at the end of CHAPTER 5.

Opposite page. The veneer on this antique desk lid was badly damaged along one edge, and a strip needed replacing completely.
1. The first step: removing the polish round the damaged area with a cabinet scraper.
2. Matching a piece of new veneer to the old wood. It should match the area from which the polish has been scraped off.
3. A good quick way of seeing whether the new piece will match when it is polished is to wet it—on both sides to prevent warping.
4. Removing the damaged strip of old veneer. The chisel is held bevel side up at the edge . . .
5. . . . and bevel side down farther in.
6. Delicate veneers should be dampened on both sides before cutting and held under a heavy straight edge to avoid splitting them.
7. The new strip will take hard knocks, so it is stuck on with scotch glue for extra strength.
8. Each piece of veneer is cut to length on the spot for maximum accuracy.
9. When all the pieces are in place, air bubbles are forced out by rubbing the veneer lightly with a Warrington or veneer hammer. It is then cramped in place for a while.
10. If you use pva glue, you can iron a patch on. The heavier the iron, the better.
11. A short straight-grained patch in an edge, as shown here, should be cut over-length in a wedge shape and gently knocked in sideways to hold it firmly. Trim the ends to length with a very sharp chisel or handyman's knife.
12. Burred (that is, knotty) veneer should be joined along the wavy line of its grain.

1

2

3

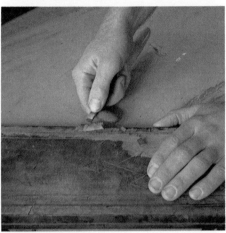

4

5

6

7

8

9

10

11

12

NELSON HARGREAVES

237

All about
man-made boards

One of the most noticeable features of modern furniture is its large, plain, flat surfaces, unlike those of older furniture, which is made of many small panels joined together.

This is because modern furniture is almost invariably made of man-made boards. These materials include plywood and blockboard (called coreboard in some countries) made from fairly large pieces of wood, and hardboard and chipboard, manufactured from compressed

wood chips. The second type is sometimes called particle board.

One important advantage of man-made boards is that they can be supplied in almost any size, whereas the maximum size of a plank of solid timber is limited by the width of the tree it is cut from. Another advantage of man-made boards is that they are free of the common defects of solid timber, such as shakes (splits), knots, warps and so on. Furthermore, they expand and contract far less with changes in humidity than solid timber does. The expansion

PAUL REDMAN

Above. Good-quality chipboard is strong enough for making shelves, and has an attractive appearance when varnished.
Left. Pegboard can be very useful in working areas, since almost anything can be hung on it. Wire brackets, as used in shop window displays, support shelves. All brackets and hooks can be moved anywhere on the board in an instant.
Below. This screen and saloon-type door are made of perforated hardboard, which can be bought in a variety of patterns.

FIDOR

of solid timber is the reason why traditional furniture has to be made out of many small panels—larger pieces, even if available, would be hard to fasten together in a way that allowed enough movement.

The final advantage is price. Nearly all man-made boards (except for some specialized types) are cheaper than an equivalent amount of solid timber of one of the 'dressier' sorts.

Plywood

Plywood is a flat board made of *veneers*, or very thin sheets of wood, glued together with a powerful adhesive. Each layer has its grain running at right angles to that of the layers on either side of it. The number of veneers depends on the thickness of the ply, but it is always an odd number because ply with an even number of veneers would warp. The thinnest ply, 0.8mm ($\frac{1}{32}$in.) in thickness, and the next few sizes have three veneers, and the thickest commonly found, 25mm (1in.) thick, has eleven.

Plywood comes in a vast range of types and finishes. It can be made of various woods, both hardwoods and softwoods. Common woods include birch and beech, which are both very strong, and West African and Gaboon mahogany, which are weaker but available with special water-resistant glue for outdoor use. The most weatherproof grade of all is called WBP, which signifies that it is 'water- and boil-proof'. This means that it will actually withstand boiling for some time without the veneers coming apart. Ordinary ply deteriorates quite fast in damp conditions.

Special types of plywood include resin-impregnated WBP, which is used for concrete shuttering; ply with decorative hardwood veneer on one face, used for furniture; and plastic-laminated ply, which is suitable for building kitchen units. There is also an unusual type made of three veneers with all their grain running in the same direction. This is used for making drawer sides. Ordinary ply has a little end grain showing whichever way it is cut; if this touched a drawer runner that fitted into a groove in the ply, it might make the drawer stick.

Cutting and finishing plywood

The thinnest grades of ply—up to 2mm thick—can be cut with an ordinary handyman's knife. Otherwise, ply should be cut with a tenon saw, although a panel saw can be used for very thick grades to save time.

The glue content of plywood causes tools that are used on it to become blunt much faster than if they were used to cut solid wood. There is nothing you can do about it except sharpen your tools more often.

The edge of ply is difficult to finish smoothly because of the end grain. An exposed edge should be protected from chipping and splitting with a solid wood edging strip whenever possible.

Plywood can be joined edge-to-edge very strongly in a way that would not be possible with solid wood. Thin plywood can be joined with a *scarf joint.* Clamp both pieces to a piece of scrap wood, with the edges that are going to be joined arranged in line side by side. The edges should be nearly, but not quite, projecting over

the scrap wood (see Fig.1). One piece of plywood should be one way up, and the other piece the other way up. Now plane down the edge at a very shallow angle.

Take the pieces out of the cramps and turn the upside-down one right side up. Finally, glue the slanted edges together and hold them with cramps till the glue sets. Pad the jaws of the cramps with scrapwood blocks, and put a layer of newspaper between the blocks and the ply to ensure that the blocks stick to it.

Thicker plywood can be joined edge-to-edge by ploughing a groove out of the adjacent edges and inserting a loose tongue to link them. The grain should run *across* the tongue. If ply of any thickness is to be bent, bend it to its final shape before joining any pieces.

In common with other man-made boards, plywood must always be painted on *both* sides, or it will twist and warp unless it is very solidly fastened down. If you stick plastic laminate to it, you should glue a 'balancer' layer to the back, for the same reason. Special cheap laminate is sold for this purpose.

Hardboard

Hardboard is made by pulping softwood and turning it back into a solid board by subjecting it to heat and great pressure. With nearly all types, no adhesive is added to the pulp, as the natural resins of softwood are sticky enough to hold the hardboard together.

Ordinary hardboard has one smooth, shiny surface and one embossed with a mesh pattern. Double-faced hardboard is also available for applications where both sides will be seen. Other types of hardboard include tempered hardboard, which is treated to make it weather-resistant, and enamelled hardboard, which is suitable for panelling kitchens and bathrooms. Plastic-faced hardboard is used in the same way, but is tougher and longer-lasting. Pegboard is punched with rows of small holes; special wire hooks fit into these and the board can be used for hanging up tools or kitchen utensils.

Medium hardboard is thicker than ordinary hardboard but less dense, and can be used, among other things, for notice boards and partition walls. Ordinary hardboard ranges in thickness from 3mm ($\frac{1}{8}$in.) to 6mm ($\frac{1}{4}$in.). Medium hardboard starts at 6mm and goes up to 13mm ($\frac{1}{2}$in.).

Cutting and finishing hardboard

All types of hardboard should be cut with a tenon saw, working from the face side. If you apply too much pressure to the saw, the board might chip or tear. The edges can be finished with an ordinary plane and sandpaper. Do not sand the surface—once the smooth top layer is broken it can never be replaced. However, the face should be slightly roughened if anything is to be glued to it. The textured back will take glue well without preparation.

Hardboard should be nailed down with special hardboard pins, whose heads are shaped to countersink themselves neatly into the surface, leaving a small dent that can easily be filled in. Never nail (or screw) *into* hardboard; nail *through* it into something else.

Hardboard should be primed before it is

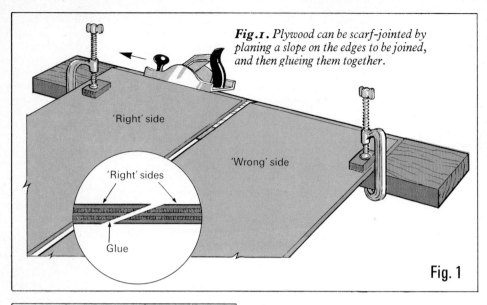

Fig.1. *Plywood can be scarf-jointed by planing a slope on the edges to be joined, and then glueing them together.*

'Right' side

'Wrong' side

'Right' sides

Glue

Fig. 1

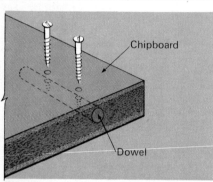

Chipboard

Dowel

Fig. 2

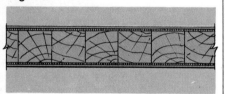

Fig. 3

'Lost head' nails

Fig. 4

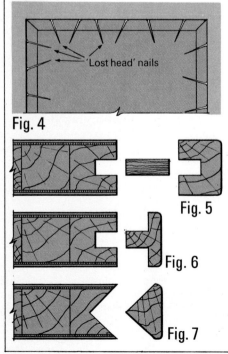

Fig. 5

Fig. 6

Fig. 7

Fig.2 *(left). A method of making strong fixings in chipboard.* **Fig.3.** *A cross-section of blockboard, showing how alternate blocks are reversed.* **Fig.4.** *Skew-nailing an edging to blockboard.* **Figs.5, 6, 7. Three other methods of edging blockboard.*

painted. Pink wood primer should not be used; special hardboard primer is available, but a cheaper method that is just as good is to paint it with emulsion paint thinned down with 20% water. This method is suitable for both gloss and emulsion paints, but gloss paint is not entirely suitable for hardboard since the face has a slightly lumpy texture.

Chipboard

Chipboard is made of wood chips, but unlike hardboard, it is mixed with adhesive, so that it can be made in much lower densities. It comes in a huge range of weights, thicknesses and finishes, and is probably the most adaptable of all man-made boards.

Standard density chipboard is quite cheap, because it is made out of odd scraps of wood from sawmills. It is not very strong and the surface is too rough to take paint well. It is generally used in places where it does not show, like the backs of cabinets or as a base for tiles. It can also be covered in plastic laminate.

'Painting grade' chipboard is basically the same material, but the surface is pressed flat to make it suitable for matt-finish paint. It is good for partitions or other uses where the surface will be seen.

'Exterior grade' chipboard is treated to make it water-resistant. It might not stand up to the weather if completely unprotected, but is ideal for roofing if covered with bituminized felt.

The strongest type of chipboard is 'flooring grade', which is nearly as strong as solid wood. Most local authorities will approve the use of 19mm ($\frac{3}{4}$in.) thick flooring grade chipboard for floors if it is supported at 400mm (16in.) centres, the usual joist spacing in modern houses.

Veneered chipboard is available with a good variety of decorative hardwood surfaces. It is extremely suitable for furniture-building, since it is both attractive and cheap. Plastic-laminated types are also available for working surfaces in

Top. *This suite of steam-bent furniture shows the sheer versatility of plywood.*

PAF INTERNATIONAL

HEIDEDE CARSTENSEN/STUDIO DIE WOHNFORM

Above. *Very thick plywood is used in the strong sides of these chairs and tables.*

kitchens. Both come with rolls of self-adhesive edging strip that matches the surface.

Cutting and finishing chipboard

Chipboard is quite easy to work but has one serious disadvantage : its high adhesive content makes it abrasive, so that it quickly dulls the edges of tools that are being used to cut it. But provided you sharpen your chisels and planes often, chipboard can be cut and worked much like solid wood. The lighter grades have a tendency to crumble if too much pressure is applied when sawing them.

It is impossible to adequately finish the edge of a piece of low-density chipboard neatly so that it can be primed and painted. The result looks like the end grain of cheap softwood, only worse. Even the densest grades have slightly messy-looking edges.

The solution is to cover the edge of the board either with one of the proprietary edging strips used for edging veneered chipboard, or a strip of solid timber. The second way is better, because the edge of chipboard is weak and likely to break off if struck, and a strip of real wood protects it.

Nails do not hold very well in the edge of chipboard. Fortunately, chipboard takes adhesive extremely well, and a plain glued butt joint is quite strong enough for all but the most severe applications.

If anything is to be fastened strongly to chipboard, it is not enough just to put screws in it, as they may tear out of the soft board. One method is to put a piece of solid wood behind the chipboard and screw right through into that. Where this is not possible, a neater method is to drill a hole into the board from one edge towards the place where the screw is to go in, and glue a dowel of the correct size into the hole. The screw can then be screwed through the face of the board into the side of the dowel (see Fig.2).

Chipboard, like any other man-made board, must be painted or covered with plastic laminate on *both* sides to prevent warping.

Blockboard and laminboard

Blockboard is a thick, strong board made of wood strips 19mm-25mm ($\frac{3}{4}$in.-1in.) thick, glued together between thick veneers of solid wood that give the board a smooth surface. Some types have one veneer on each side, with the grain running across the grain of the blocks. Double-veneered blockboard has two veneers on each side with their grain running at right angles to each other, so that it combines features of blockboard and plywood. It has a smoother surface than the single-veneered type, which may show traces of the rows of blocks through the surface veneer if it is polished or gloss-painted.

Blockboard is much stronger than chipboard and is ideal for uses such as heavy-duty shelving, where long, narrow strips of board have to bear great loads. When the board is used in this way, the grain of the blocks must run *along* the shelf, as in solid timber.

The grain of alternate blocks in blockboard is reversed to even out the pull of their expansion and contraction (see Fig.3). As a result, the board is exceptionally stable and unlikely to warp—unlike thick plywood, which warps almost as much as solid timber.

The edge of blockboard is very unsightly and must be covered with an edging strip, even if it is to be painted. Not only do the edges or ends of the internal blocks show, but there are occasional gaps between the end of one strip and the beginning of the next.

These gaps in blockboard cause another problem. When a decorative veneer is being applied to blockboard commercially, or when you are having veneer applied by a professional, as many amateur carpenters do, it is generally pressed on to the surface with a bag or vacuum press. In this process, the veneer is glued to the board, then pressed on by putting the board in a large bag and pumping air out of the bag, so that the pressure of the outside air presses the veneer hard on to the board. If there is a gap in the board, even under two layers of veneer, the all-over pressure will cause a hollow depression to form in the surface over the gap, spoiling the look of the job.

This problem is solved by using laminboard, the strongest and most expensive of all the man-made boards. It is like blockboard, but the strips in its inner core are only $\frac{1}{4}$in.(6mm) or even $\frac{1}{8}$in. (3mm) wide, and there are no gaps or other internal flaws in it. You would be unlikely to use laminboard except for very high-quality cabinet-making.

Cutting and finishing blockboard

Blockboard is more like solid timber than any other man-made board, even to the extent that it has a grain. It can be sawn, planed and drilled as if it were solid, except that sometimes you need to take extra care with the fine end grain.

The edging can be applied in various ways. The simplest method is to glue and nail it on, skew-nailing in alternate directions to make it hold more solidly (see Fig.4).

A neater method is to plough a groove in the edge of the board and in the back of the edging, and insert a loose tongue to link them (see Fig.5). This method requires an edging at least $\frac{1}{2}$in. (13mm) wide, because of the depth of the groove in it.

The width of the edging is normally no disadvantage, except in one case. If you are applying veneer to blockboard, and want the edging to be concealed under the veneer, you will run into problems with wide edging. This is because the edging strip expands and contracts with changes in humidity at a different rate from the blockboard. Since the join between edging and blockboard is under the veneer, the slight shifting of the edging strip during expansion will eventually crease or even split the veneer.

The solution is to use a much narrower edging strip, with wide rebates cut on each side of the back, to form a central tongue that fits into the grooved edge of the blockboard (see Fig.6). If you have a circular saw with a tilting blade or arbor, you can cut a V-shaped groove out of the edge of the blockboard and make or buy a triangular-section edging strip to fit into it (see Fig.7). If properly done, this method places the join between board and edging exactly along the corners of the board, and is the neatest method of all.

All these edging methods apply equally well to laminboard.

Above. A traditional, well proportioned, double ended hipped roof gives a very pleasing finish to this detached house.

Hipped roof : 1

A hipped roof provides an attractive symmetrical finish to a house. And though a hipped roof may appear a little more complex than a gabled roof to begin with, it is far easier to maintain than a comparable gable roof for there aren't any bargeboards or fascias to paint above the level of the eaves. Even building a hipped roof on a garage—or a house itself—is not that much more difficult than a gable roof. The instructions below show that its construction involves merely a few further techniques to those required for constructing a gabled roof.

The four sides of a hipped roof (three sides on a semi-detached house) all slope upwards and inwards towards the apex of the roof in contrast to a gabled roof where the two sides rise vertically and only the front and back slope. However, the slopes at either end of the roof do not normally meet but lie at either end of the ridge board as in Fig.1. Here the slope from the eaves on the long sides up to the ridge board are exactly the same as for a gabled roof, and the method of construction is identical. The only difference is that the slope on the long side is continued round the ends of the roof.

The pitch of the roof is usually the same on all sides but the slope on the sides may be different to the slope on the ends. There is no ruling as to what the slope of the roof should be —it can vary for aesthetic reasons, climatic conditions or with the materials used. As stated in CHAPTER 39 an angle between 50 and 60 degrees is usually acceptable.

Main components

The main parts of the hipped roof as shown in Fig.1 are the same as for the gabled roof as described fully in CHAPTER 39. With the hipped roof the ridge board extends beyond the common rafters by about 6 inches or so. The new components are as follows :

The hip rafters slope upwards from the corners of the roof to the ends of the ridge board and they are birdsmouthed at the top to fit beneath the ridge board ; the method of fitting the bottom end is described below. Hip rafters must be one continuous length of timber. As with common rafters, they should never be made from two pieces joined along their length. The size of timber varies as with common rafters, but if you mark timbers of 6 or

7in. x 1½in. (150 or 175mm x 38mm) on your plan the building inspector will correct you if you have overdesigned.

Jack rafters slope downwards from the hip rafters to meet the eaves, or wall plates, at right angles. These jack rafters are spaced so that they meet the hip rafter from either side at the same point. They should be the same cross section as the common rafters for which sizes are listed in CHAPTER 39.

To calculate the quantities of timber needed count each jack rafter along the long sides of the house as another common rafter and discount the jack rafters on the ends. This rough guide works because the shortest jack rafter plus the longest on each hip rafter equal the length of one common rafter, as do the next shortest and next longest and so on. It applies, however, only when the jack rafters are spaced at equal distances from each other and the roof has the same pitch on all sides.

Centre section

Cut, mark and fit the wall plates, joists, purlins, collar ties and struts as described for a gabled roof in CHAPTER 39. There are three main differences between a gable roof and a hipped roof, as described below.

Above. Hipped roofs are especially suitable for bungalows and are easy to maintain as there is no woodwork above the eaves. Here the garage is also covered with a matching hipped roof to make it 'belong' to the house.

The first compensates for the fact that the hip rafters exert considerable force upon the joint between the wall plates on adjacent walls of the house. Therefore one of the wall plates must be half lapped over the other as indicated in Fig.3 and both plates should be continued for 3in. (75mm) beyond the point where they overlap. This will prevent the wall plates being forced apart which could allow the hip rafter to slip.

The second is that the ridge board must overlap the last pair of common rafters at either end by a little more than the width of the hip rafters, that is about 6in. When the hip rafter is cut at an angle at the top, this angled end meets the side of the ridge board that extends beyond the last pair of common rafters.

The third difference is that you should cut the purlins longer than you have drawn them on your plan and fit these overlength purlins in position. Then when you fit the purlins at either end you can cut all the purlins to the correct length and angle at the same time.

End sections

When your centre section is completed this far check that it is square and rigid. Then fit the following pieces to turn the angle of the roof round the corner.

Hip rafters

The hip rafters set the angle of slope for the ends of the roof and support the jack rafters, so it is essential that you fit them properly. The instructions below give the right way to do it.

Take a length of timber for each hip rafter and cut the bottom end at an angle so that when in place the lower end of the timber will meet flush with the top horizontal surface of the wall plates (note that this is not the final cut). Then cut it slightly longer than the distance from the top of the wall plate at the corner of the house to the point where the ridge board and the end common rafter meet. Then hold the timber in place over and parallel with the position it eventually has to take, with the lower end resting on the wall plate in order to mark out the joints at either end.

There are three cuts to make to fit the hip rafter to the ridge board and end common rafter (see Fig.2) : a short horizontal cut to make a rebate under the ridge board, a vertical angled cut to fit the hip rafter to the ridge board, and another vertical angled cut to fit the hip rafter to the end common rafter. (On some roofs, where the hip rafter does not meet the common rafter, this third cut is unnecessary).

With a pencil, mark on the underneath and side of the hip rafter the horizontal plane of the bottom ridge board. Then, from the marked horizontal line, draw vertical lines parallel with the side of the ridge board on the side of the hip rafter. These lines should be an inch or so from the point where the marked horizontal line meets the inside edge of the hip rafter to provide a rebate when the joint is cut. Also mark lines on the sides, top and bottom of the hip rafter that are parallel with the side of the common rafter which it meets. Then cut out the slightly rebated joint shown in Fig.2. Check that the top end of the rafter fits and then mark and cut the lower end.

The foot of the hip rafter exerts considerable pressure upon the wall plate at the corner of the house, so use the method shown in Fig.3 to spread the weight as much as possible over the two adjacent walls. Here a length of wood, an *angle tie,* is notched and nailed into the two adjacent wall plates to form a right angled triangle. Another piece of wood, a *dragging beam,* stretches between the middle of the angle tie and the join between the wall plates. This beam supports the foot of the rafter and spreads the weight evenly onto both adjacent walls.

Cut the *angle tie* out of 7in. x 3in. (175 x 75mm) timber and make a hole in the middle to take the end of the dragging beam. Nail the angle tie in place. Then cut and nail a batten across the join between adjacent wall plates so that it is parallel with the angle tie.

The *dragging beam* is cut from the same size timber as the angle tie and rebated on either side at one end to pass through the hole already made in the angle tie. Then cut a groove in the underside at the other end of the dragging beam so that it fits over the strip of batten already nailed across the join between the wall plates. Make two saw cuts in the top of the dragging beam forming an oblique tenon as shown in Fig.4 to take the foot of the hip rafter. Then fit and nail the dragging beam in place between the angle tie and wall plates.

Place the hip rafter in position so that it fits tightly against the ridge board and end common rafter but with the foot against the side of the dragging beam; mark the outline of the oblique tenon cut in the dragging beam on the foot of the rafter and cut to shape. Now check to see whether this hip rafter fits the spaces for the other hip rafters: if so mark the other rafters from the first, but if not repeat the measurement by the direct method. Then nail the hip rafters firmly in position.

Fig.1. *The framework for the centre section of a hipped roof is the same as for a gabled roof. Here the hipped end of the roof slopes up from the wall plate (bottom left) to the ridge board (top right) in contrast to the vertical end of a gabled roof (for details of a gabled roof see* CHAPTER 39).
Fig.2. *The common rafters meet the ridge board at right angles, but the hip rafters are*

Jack rafters

Mark the positions of the jack rafters on the side wall plates so that they are spaced at equal distances from each other. This ensures that the two longest jack rafters on the end walls fall the same distance either side of the ridge board, but it is a point worth checking. Mark two lines on the wall plate for each rafter with a cross in between indicating clearly where the foot of the rafter is to be. Mark the top ends of the jack rafters on the hip rafters in the same way. Then rest a length of timber in place at a number of these points stretching from the wall plate to hip rafter and check that it lies at right angles to the wall plate.

Mark and cut the jack rafters to length individually. Lay a length of timber over the wall plate and hip rafter and mark it both for length and the angle of the birdsmouth. Then cut the first piece to length. Check to see whether the angles at the ends of the rafter fit all the way along the hip rafters; they should do. If so, cut one end of the next rafter from the first and then hold the timber in place while you mark it to length. Cut and nail all the jack rafters in position.

Purlins

You have already fitted the purlins on the longer sides of the roof in position so that they extend beyond the hip rafters. You must now cut the ends of these purlins to length at the correct angle and the purlins for the ends of the roof to size so that they meet in a mitre.

To cut the ends of the purlins already fixed in position, take a saw and lay it against the side of the hip rafter that faces the end of the roof. Then cut through the ends of the side purlins at the same angle as the side of the hip rafter.

To find the angle for the ends of the purlins take a piece of timber the size of the purlins and lay it on the outside of the end of the roof so that it overlaps the hip rafter at the level of the side purlin. Take a straight edge and continue the line of the side of the hip rafter (the side that you previously lay the saw against) around the side of the piece of timber. Cut to these lines to give you a template for marking the end purlin. Measure the length of the purlin either from your plan or from the roof itself, and cut the ends to the angle of the template. Then nail the purlins in place at either end of the house—nail at the ends first and then to all the jack rafters in between.

With the framework of your hipped roof completed you have met all the differences between the construction of a gabled and a hipped roof. There is a considerable amount of work still to be done such as covering the roof with felt, nailing the battens in place and laying the tiles in place but this is all described fully in CHAPTER 39.

birdsmouthed as shown to slip under and meet the ridge board at an angle.
Fig.3. *A plan (bottom) and side view (top) of the construction in* *Fig.4* *which shows how the force exerted by the foot of the hip rafter is spread over both wall plates. The dragging beam which supports the hip rafter stretches from the corner of the roof to the angle tie fixed to the wall plates.*

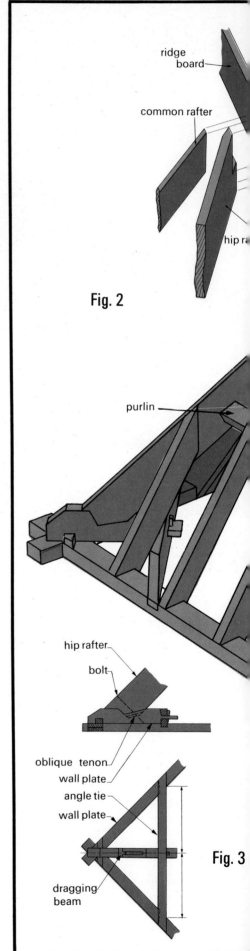

ridge board

common rafter

hip ra

Fig. 2

purlin

hip rafter

bolt

oblique tenon
wall plate
angle tie
wall plate

dragging beam

Fig. 3

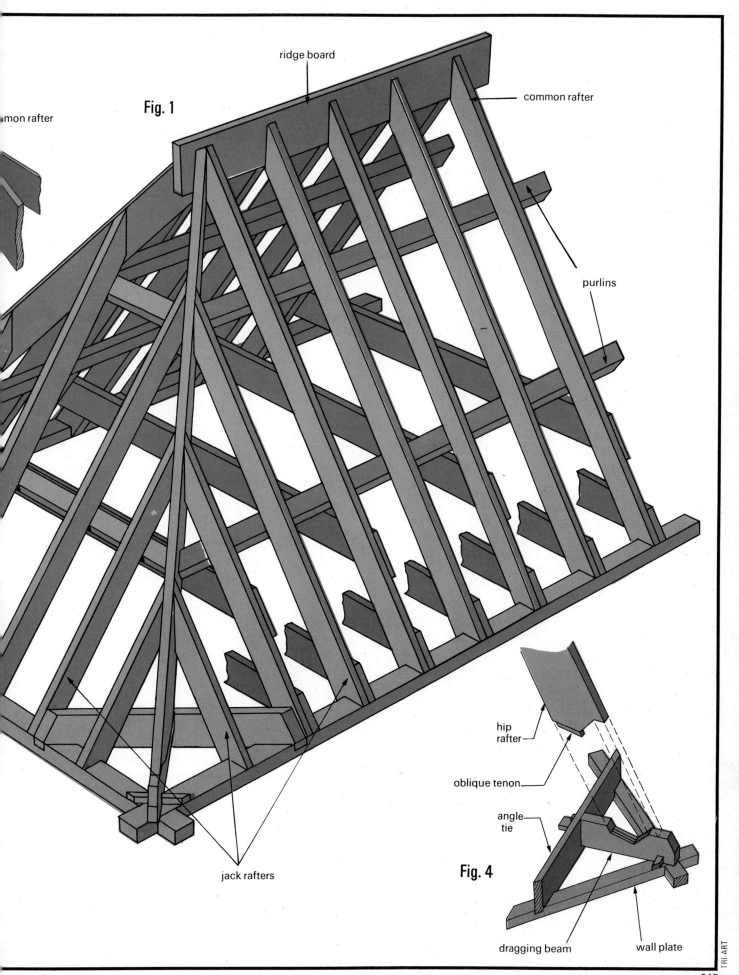

Fig. 1

ridge board

common rafter

mon rafter

purlins

jack rafters

hip rafter

oblique tenon

angle tie

Fig. 4

dragging beam

wall plate

TRI-ART

245

Hipped roof : 2

Many houses are constructed to plans that call for a roof that turns through a right angle. Few additional techniques are necessary when building or repairing such a roof beyond those required for a simple rectangular roof, and yet they give you far greater scope in the type of house you can cope with.

You can roof over an interesting L shaped house, for example, or erect a new extension at right angles to the main roof if the original line of the house cannot be extended. These techniques can be adapted to other situations such as building a sloping roof over a bay window—even if your house is in the middle of a terrace.

The extension that is built at right angles to the main part of the roof, can itself be hipped or gabled ended. But the join between the extension and the main part of the roof must necessarily follow the line of a hipped roof (see Fig.1). In order to build two parts of the roof at right angles to each other you must first familiarize yourself with the techniques described for building a gable roof (CHAPTER 39 tells you how to build a gable roof) and a hipped roof (see CHAPTER 53).

The few differences between a roof which turns through 90 degrees and a simple rectangular roof are the positioning of the valley rafter (which is essentially the same as the hip rafter reversed), the method of providing a watertight joint between the two slopes of the roof directly above the valley rafter, the method of joining the ridge boards and the order of construction. These are discussed in the same order below.

Hips and valleys

The two sections of the roof meet to form an internal corner between the outside of the walls of 90 degrees and an external corner of 270 degrees (see Fig.1).

The external corner where the two sections of the roof meet is the same as for the corner of a normal hipped roof and identical construction techniques are used.

At the internal corner the sides of the roof slope upwards and 'inwards' to the point where

Fig.1. Right. This L shaped roof structure combines a gable and a hipped roof: the major feature is in the join between the two sections at the hip and valley rafter.

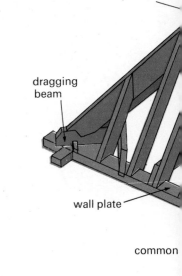

hip rafter

dragging beam

wall plate

common

Fig. 1

Left. Here the valley, that is the join between the two sections of the roof, has been made watertight with lead flashing before tiling the roof on either side.

the two ridge boards meet. The sides of the roof meet above the valley rafter which is in many ways similar to the hip rafter. This valley rafter slopes from the join between the wall plates in the internal corner up to the join between the boards—and if seen in a plan view continues the line of the hip rafter on the external corner.

The valley rafter differs from the hip rafter in two ways.

First, the foot of the valley rafter pushes both the wall plates and walls together and not apart as with a hip rafter on an external corner. Therefore, the valley rafter can be birdsmouthed directly over the join between the wall plates and does not have to be set in a dragging beam as with a hip rafter. The vertical face of the valley rafter at the birdsmouth does not have to be cut to fit around the right angle formed by the wall plates but can be a straight line cut which butts up against the corner formed by the wall plates.

Second, the jack rafters which run from the valley rafter up to the ridge board carry the weight of that section of the roof and transfer it to the valley rafter. The valley rafter should therefore be braced as much as possible at intermediate points along its length. Struts should

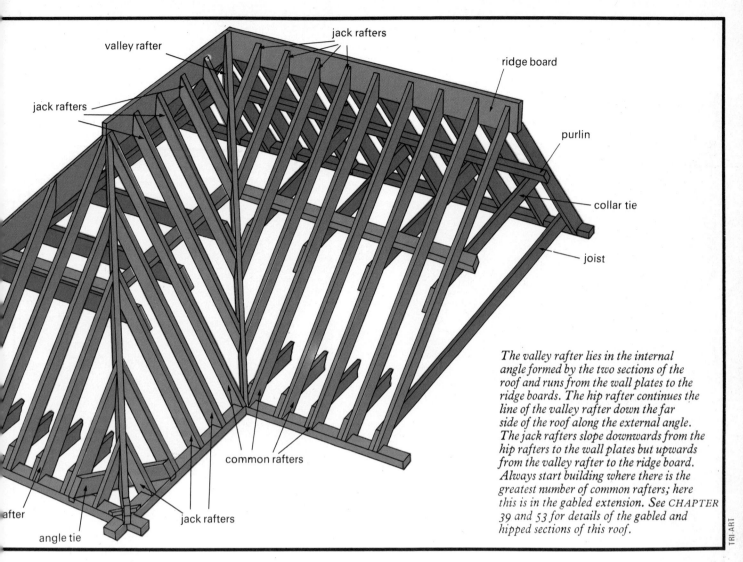

valley rafter

jack rafters

jack rafters

ridge board

purlin

collar tie

joist

common rafters

after

angle tie

jack rafters

The valley rafter lies in the internal angle formed by the two sections of the roof and runs from the wall plates to the ridge boards. The hip rafter continues the line of the valley rafter down the far side of the roof along the external angle. The jack rafters slope downwards from the hip rafters to the wall plates but upwards from the valley rafter to the ridge board. Always start building where there is the greatest number of common rafters; here this is in the gabled extension. See CHAPTER 39 and 53 for details of the gabled and hipped sections of this roof.

TRI-ART

run from the valley rafter down to the joists or ideally to runner joists so that the weight is distributed over a wider area (see Fig.1).

Valley gutters

The join between the two slopes of the roof in the valley can be made watertight in two ways.

The first method is to use special tiles which can be purchased for this join just as they can for the joins over the hip rafter. But since they are made in only a limited number of angles check that you can obtain some locally which are the same angle as the slope of your roof.

In the second method, lead flashing can be run down the join between the roofs along the line of the valley rafter producing a watertight gutter. In this method the roof tiles stop short of the join (see Fig.2).

In an open gutter the space left between the edges of the tiles on either slope is about 8in. (200mm). A valley board 1in. (25mm) thick and slightly narrower than the gap between the tile edges is nailed in place over the valley rafter and between the jack rafters so that it runs the length of the valley rafter and lies a couple of inches below the edges of tiles. Tilting fillets set either side of the valley board support the lower edge of the bottom row of tiles. The entire gutter, from just above the tilting fillet on either side of the valley board is covered with lead flashing from

the ridge board down to the wall plates. Any debris, leaves, moss and so on, that collects in an open gutter is relatively easy to clean out.

In a secret gutter there is only about a 1in. (25mm) gap between the edges of the tiles so that the gutter is barely noticeable, but the gutter itself is correspondingly smaller than the open gutter. There is no valley board providing a wide flat base to the gutter: instead the tilting fillets are nailed in place either side of the valley rafter leaving only a relatively narrow V shaped gutter between. This is then covered with lead flashing as previously described. If the roof is not boarded all over, but only battened ready for tiling, a board (called lier board) must be fitted either side of the join between the two slopes to provide a firm base for the lead flashing.

Join between the ridge boards

Various joints can be used at the ends of the ridge boards. A simple butt joint, however, is normally sufficient since the hip, valley and common rafters all meet at this point and make a strong joint.

Order of construction

Start by fixing the wall plates around the walls and setting the joists in place as described in CHAPTER 39. Remember, though, to half lap the wall plates in the corners as described in CHAPTER 53 to give extra strength in the corners.

The wall plates should also be overlapped in the internal corner where the valley rafter meets the wall plate.

Then mark on the joists the positions of the common rafters as described fully in CHAPTER 39. Mark also the line of the ridge boards and the points where they end. One end of each ridge board is above the wall plate with a gabled roof or at the intersection of the hipped rafters with a hipped roof. The other end of each ridge board is at the point where they meet—but remember that with a butt joint one ridge board ends where it meets the second but the second continues to the far side of the first.

The construction of a roof which turns through 90 degrees is really the construction of two roofs: first build the main framework of one of the roofs and then build the main framework for the other roof while using the framework of the first as partial support.

The best place to start building is that part of the roof where the greatest number of full length common rafters run from the wall plates up to a ridge board. This is not necessarily the main part of the roof; for instance if the main part of the roof is hipped at both ends while the extension is gabled the largest number of full length common rafters may fall in the extension.

Now build the framework for the first section of the roof. Follow the instructions given in CHAPTER 39 for a gabled roof or read CHAPTER 53

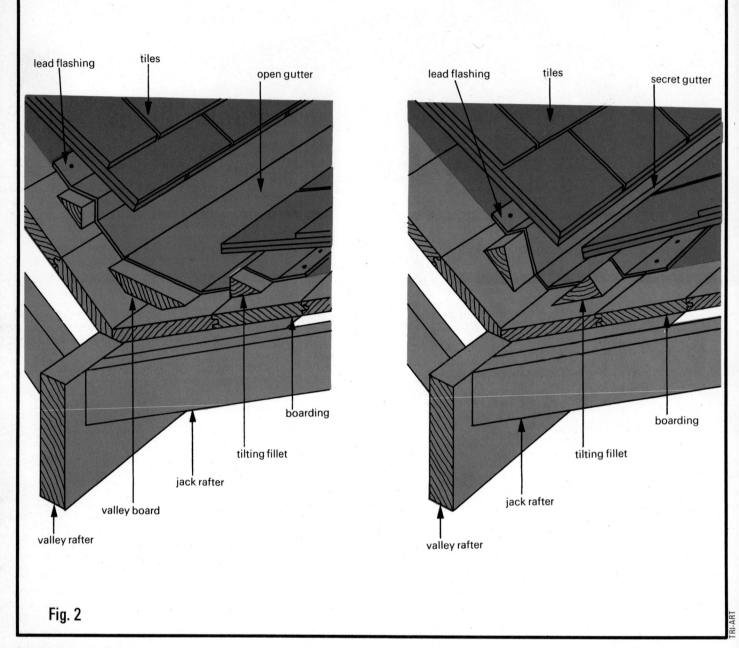

lead flashing · tiles · open gutter

boarding

tilting fillet

jack rafter

valley board

valley rafter

lead flashing · tiles · secret gutter

boarding

tilting fillet

jack rafter

valley rafter

Fig. 2

TRI-ART

for a hipped roof. Once the common rafters and ridge board are in position check that the framework is square and add collar ties and struts to make the framework rigid.

Then erect the framework for the second section of the roof so that the ends of the ridge boards for both sections meet. Place the pair of common rafters at the end of the second part of the roof in position and brace them with temporary supports. Place the end of the ridge board in the birdsmouth in the common rafters as described fully in CHAPTER 39. Position the pair of common rafters nearest the intersection of the two roof sections flat on the joists, place the other end of the ridge board in the birdsmouth and raise the rafter into position. Check that the ends of one of the ridge boards meets the side of the other, and then nail this butt joint firmly in position. Fix the other common rafters and hip rafters in position.

Hold the valley rafter above and parallel with

Fig.2. The construction of two types of gutter over the valley rafter. The bottom of the tiles are supported by a couple of tilting fillets. In an open gutter (left) there is about 8in. (200mm) between the tiles, so the tilting fillets are spaced some distance apart and a valley board fitted. In a secret gutter (right) there is only 1in. (25mm) gap between the edges of the tiles and the tilting fillets are set at either side of the valley rafter.

its eventual position and cut as for the hip rafter. Make sure you allow enough to cut a birdsmouth in the bottom end to fit over the wall plates. Nail the rafter in place and fit extra support struts in position underneath.

The jack rafters are then cut and fitted between the hip rafter and wall plates, and between the valley rafter and ridge board.

Once the framework is completed all that has to be done is to fit tiling battens and roofing felt

and tile the roof as previously described. If you are using lead flashing to make the join between the sides of the roof in the valley watertight, fit the valley boards, tilting fillets and flashing in position before you start tiling.

Valley over bays

In a number of older terraced houses a sloping gabled roof projects from the middle of the main roof out over a bay as in Fig.3. Very often the ridge board on this extension is considerably lower than the ridge board of the main roof. This type of sloping roof is largely decorative and not intended to house another room in the loft. Therefore its construction is fairly simple.

The main roof structure is built in the normal way with common rafters running from the wall plates to the ridge board where the extension is to be fitted. A couple of valley boards (in place of rafters) are then nailed to the common rafters so that they slope upwards from the wall plates to

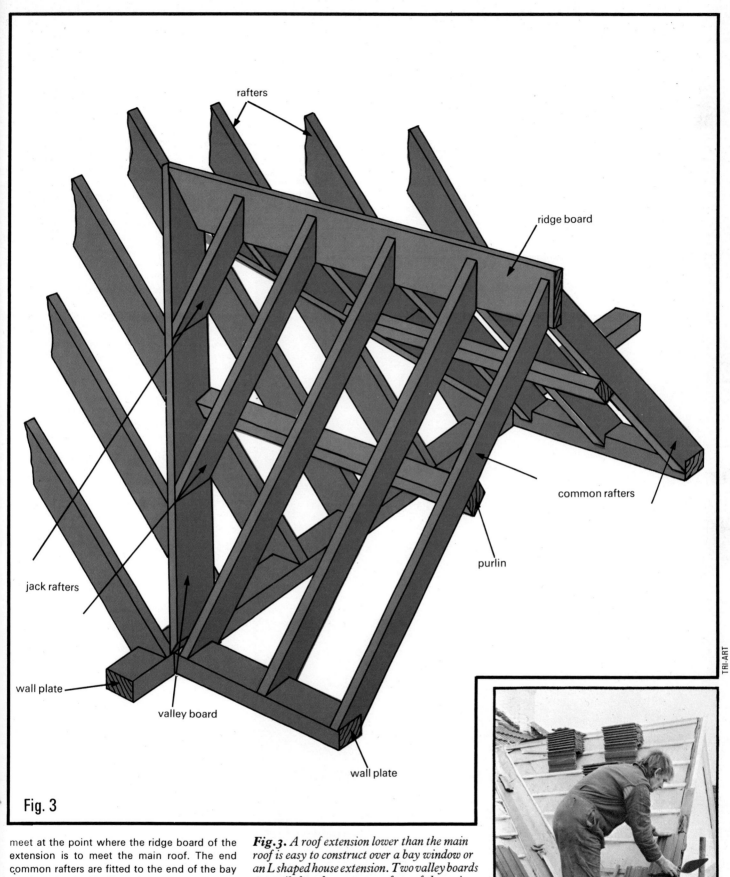

rafters

ridge board

common rafters

purlin

jack rafters

wall plate

valley board

wall plate

TRI-ART

Fig. 3

meet at the point where the ridge board of the extension is to meet the main roof. The end common rafters are fitted to the end of the bay window (as in Fig.3) and the ridge board is fitted and nailed to the valley boards where they meet. The jack rafters are then cut and fitted to run between the ridge board and valley board. When tiled, this type of sloping roof over a bay provides a pleasing break to an otherwise plain roof line.

*Fig.3. A roof extension lower than the main roof is easy to construct over a bay window or an L shaped house extension. Two valley boards are nailed to the common rafters of the main roof so that they run from the wall plates to the top of the roof extension. The method of construction is then the same as for a gabled roof. **Right.** An L shaped roof with a gabled end to the extension. The gutter is completed and the roof battened ready for tiling.*

Stylish
open riser staircase

Simple and stylish, an open riser staircase will add a note of distinction to your home. With the right techniques you can build yourself an attractive and streamlined staircase.

The building of an open-riser staircase is a major construction job which has to be carried out accurately to achieve a good result, as well as to conform to any building regulations that apply in your case. It is a long and heavy job,

and you may need assistance at certain stages.

There are two basic designs for open risers. The most common one is where the steps, or *treads,* are supported at their ends by *strings,* timber pieces that run the whole length of the staircase. Housings are cut into the strings to accommodate the treads. In the second design the treads are supported from underneath by means of long timber pieces called *spines.*

For either design a power saw is virtually a necessity and for the first design a power-driven router, to cut the housings in the strings that take the ends of the treads, is a great advantage. An alternative method of cutting the housings is, however, given below. An electric orbital sander will considerably simplify the job of finishing the staircase.

Hardwood is the ideal timber for the staircase, 10in. x 1½in. or 250mm x 40mm being a size that will give solid construction. Softwood can be used, but unless it is an unusually strong type such as parana pine or British Columbian pine, the size should be increased slightly. For example, if common redwood or whitewood is used, a size of 10in. x 2in. or 250mm x 50mm is more suitable. These sizes apply to strings or spines and treads alike, unless the treads are unusually wide.

Technical terms

You will need to understand a few technical terms when planning your staircase (see Fig.1).

Going is the horizontal distance between the front edge of one tread and the front edge of the next.

Rise is the vertical distance between the face on one tread and the face of the next.

The pitch line is an imaginary line drawn through the top facing edge of each tread. This indicates the angle at which the staircase slopes.

Construction requirements

In Britain, all new constructions must conform to the requirements laid down in the Building Regulations. In the case of open risers, the requirements are complicated but the basic ones are that:

each step must be level,
all steps must be of a similar rise,
the going of each step must be the same,
each step must overlap the next, on a plan view, by 16mm (⅝in.) as shown in Fig.1.

In addition to these basic items there are more complex requirements.

Sufficient headroom must be provided. Measured vertically from the pitch line, the clearance must be at least 2m (6ft 6in.) to the ceiling. Measured at right angles to the pitch line, the clearance must be at least 1.5m (5ft) to the ceiling (see Fig.4).

All staircases must be enclosed on both sides either by two walls and two balusters or by a wall on one side and a baluster on the other. In the case of a baluster or railing, this must be at at least 840mm (33in.) high, measured vertically from the pitch line. At landings the minimum height is 900mm (35in.).

RICHARD EINZIG

Left. An attractive and solid open riser, its timber used perfectly to match the rest of the room. Here the treads are fixed to the strings with metal angle brackets.

In Britain, the Building Regulations also dictate the sizes of the rise and the going. There are two sets of regulations applying to private open-riser staircases, i.e. those in domestic use and 'common' open risers—those used in public buildings. Be sure to consult the correct set. For private open riser the minimum going is 220mm and the maximum rise is also 220mm.

In addition, your staircase must conform to a certain formula. The sum of the going of a step plus twice its rise should not be less than 550mm (22in.) and not more than 700mm (27½in.).

The pitch of the staircase will also dictate the rise and going you use. Private open risers must not have a pitch of more than 42° to the horizontal. Therefore you cannot work to the maximum rise of 220mm and the minimum going of 220mm as this will give you too steep a pitch.

It is illegal in Britain to have an open-riser staircase leading to an attic unless there is some alternative means of leaving the attic, such as an external fire escape.

There is no simple formula for planning open-riser stairs. Take all the considerations given above into account when making your dimensional drawing for presentation to your local planning officer. He will tell you whether or not your planned staircase meets all the requirements.

Measuring the stairway

If your open riser is to replace an ordinary staircase you may be able to use the same dimensions for the new construction as were used for the old. For example, the rise of the old staircase may be suitable to allow you to position the new treads in the same place as the old. You cannot, of course, simply remove the riser from an ordinary staircase to give you an open riser staircase. This would make the whole structure come loose and fall apart.

If the dimensions do not conform, or the staircase is a new feature, then the first step is to measure the overall length of the stairway.

To do this, measure accurately the distance between the floors that the open riser is to connect. You must make sure that you allow for any slope on the floor (see Fig.3), or your height measurement will be out. Make a scaled and dimensioned drawing showing these two levels. Take the maximum permitted rise between one step and another and divide this into the overall rise—the distance between the two floor levels. This will give you the minimum number of treads you can use. From this, you can calculate the minimum overall going of the staircase—the horizontal distance between one end of the staircase and the other.

Once the overall rise and going have been calculated check that the headroom this construction will allow conforms to the regulations. To do this, first mark on the lower floor the position of the bottom of the planned staircase. From this point, to the edge of the upper floor level, stretch a length of string, fixed at the ends with nails. Measure the headroom from this string, both vertically from it and at right angles to it. Use a steel tape rule to do this.

If the headroom is too tight, reduce the overall going if you can. If there is plenty of headroom, you may wish to increase the size of the treads or decrease the rise between each of them to, ideally, about 7½in. This will make the staircase easier to ascend and descend.

Having made these calculations, check that they conform to the formula for private open risers given earlier. For example, if the overall rise is 2.20m the number of rises will be ten, with an individual rise of 220mm. If the overall going is 2.50m this will give you ten goings at 250mm individual going. Twice the individual rise is 440mm. This, plus one individual going adds up to 690mm. This figure is more than 550mm and less than 700mm, so this particular design conforms to the requirements.

The final step in ensuring that the staircase conforms to the British Building Regulations is to check the pitch of the staircase. It must not exceed 42°. You can do this simply by laying a chain-store protractor on your scale drawing.

Design considerations

There are two basic designs of open-riser staircases. In the first the ends of the treads are housed in channels cut in the strings, or long timber side supports. In the second the treads are supported from underneath by means of spines. Triangular blocks of wood are fixed to the top edge of the spines so that the treads are horizontal. The use of strings gives better fixing for the handrails and balusters—but this is not an insurmountable problem if you want spines.

If you design your staircase with spines, you must use more than one spine. If only one spine

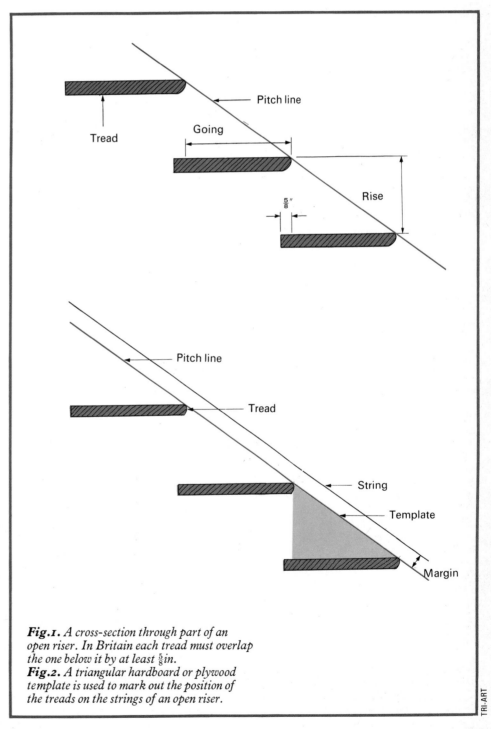

Fig.1. A cross-section through part of an open riser. In Britain each tread must overlap the one below it by at least ⅝in.

Fig.2. A triangular hardboard or plywood template is used to mark out the position of the treads on the strings of an open riser.

Pitch line

Tread

Going

Rise

⅝"

Pitch line

Tread

String

Template

Margin

TRI-ART

is used, the treads would create excessive leverage on the spine if you put your weight on one end of them.

Setting out the tread supports

In both types of staircase, the angles for making out the supports to show the positions of the treads have to be determined. This is done by using *similar triangles*. A similar triangle is one that has the same angles as another triangle but is larger or smaller than it.

In this case, the distance between the treads is estimated by drawing a similar triangle to that formed by the planned pitch of the staircase, the floor and a vertical line to the floor from the upper floor (the one to which the staircase will run). The two sides of the triangle that meet at right angles should be as long as the planned rise and going of the individual treads.

Make a template, sometimes known as a pitch board in this context, to match these sizes. This can be cut from hardboard or plywood.

If strings are used to support the treads the next step is to mark the distance you require between the top edge of the treads and the top of the strings. This distance is known as the *margin*. Mark it lightly with a marking gauge, or with a pencil and a strip of wood cut to the width of the margin. Along this line mark off distances that equal the longest side of the triangular template you have cut.

Then lay the template along the marked line between the stepped off points, with the longest side against the line. Draw a line on the string along the bottom edge of the template. This will indicate where the top edge of the tread will come (see Fig. 2).

Then mark on the strings the cross section of the treads. Use a piece of the material you intend to use for the treads as a template. Mark out this section tight—the timber will be cleaned up later and it is desirable that the treads should fit tightly into the strings.

If spines are to be used to support the treads, step off the length of the longest side of the triangular template on to the top edge of the spines. Do this with the planks laid together and their faces butting. Square lines through these marked points. This will indicate where the top edge of the triangular support blocks should meet the spines.

The triangular template can also be used to mark the angle at which the support pieces, either strings or spines, meet the floor. Lay the template on the pieces at the correct point with the longest side parallel to the top edge of the support piece. The side that indicates the going on the template gives the required angle for the line where the support piece meets the floor. The side that indicates the rise on the template gives the angle for a vertical end to the support pieces, for example for the mortise-and-tenon joint used where a string is inserted into a newel post.

Housing the treads in the strings

The next step, if the treads are to be supported by strings, is to cut the housing joints on the inside face of the strings. The housings should be a minimum of 13mm ($\frac{1}{2}$in.) deep. You can cut them with a power router and a jig, if you have one, and it will save you a lot of time.

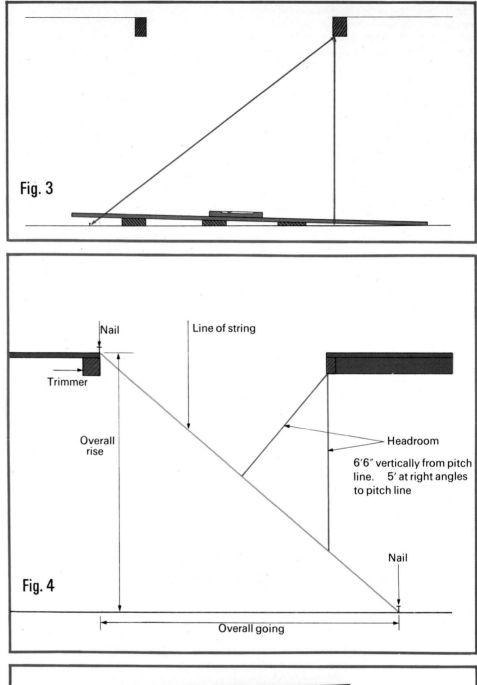

Fig. 3

Fig. 4

Nail

Line of string

Trimmer

Overall rise

Headroom

6'6" vertically from pitch line. 5' at right angles to pitch line

Nail

Overall going

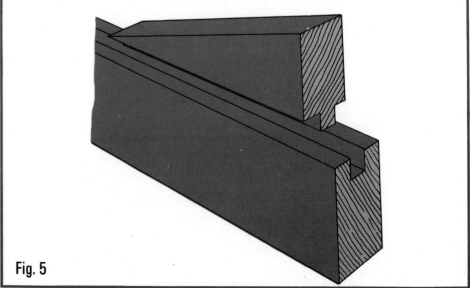

Fig. 5

TRI-ART

Figs.3 and 4. In Britain you must provide a minimum headroom above your open riser staircase. Measured vertically from the pitch line the clearance must be at least 2m (6ft 6in.). Measured at right angles from the pitch line the clearance must be 1.5m (5ft). But you must allow for any slope in the floor when taking these measurements. Lay a plank on the floor and pack it until it is level. Check this with a spirit level.
Fig.5. Where spines are used to support the treads, wooden blocks are glued and screwed into grooves cut in the spines.

If you do not have such a tool, you can cut the housings by drilling a series of holes within the areas marked out for the treads. These holes can be cut with an electric drill or a handbrace and bit. In either case it is advisable to use a depth stop to keep all the holes an even depth and avoid the necessity of having to even up the housings later.

A depth stop can be a piece of wood with a hole drilled in it that fits around the bit the required distance from the tip. Stop the wood from moving up the drill with a piece of adhesive tape. Alternatively, a proprietary type of stop that bolts onto the bit can be used.

Drill the holes so that their edges are almost touching. Remove the waste with a chisel and mallet. Carefully shape the front of the tread section to a rounded shape with the chisel; the fronts of the treads should be rounded off to save your shins.

The treads can now be cut to length. Each tread should be fitted individually to a particular housing. Number the ends of each tread and each housing so that there is no possibility of mixing up the pieces. The treads and housings can be marked as No.1 left, No.1 right, No.2 left, No.2 right and so on.

Assembly of the staircase

When you have cut the housings and numbered them the strings and treads can now be fitted together as a unit. You may need some assistance to do this, because of the weight of the strings. You will also need two low stools or saw horses and some sash cramps.

Lay one string on the stools or saw horses with the face with the housings uppermost. Position the treads in the housings as numbered. Lay the other string on top of the tread ends with the housings downwards. Align the treads with their housings, then apply glue to the upper ends of the treads. Knock the upper string onto the tread ends. Cramp the assembly. When the adhesive has dried, turn the assembly over and knock the other string off the treads. Apply adhesive to the ends and knock the string back down onto the treads. Then cramp the assembly up again.

The next step is to screw the treads to the strings. To achieve a good finish you can either use brass screws and cups or you can use ordinary steel screws counterbored below the surface of the strings. The cylindrical gap between the screw head and the surface of the string can be filled with plugs cut with a plug-cutter. These are glued and tapped into the countersunk holes and arranged so that the grain matches that on the string. Any part of

Figs.6 to 8. Three ways by which strings can be jointed to the newel post and the newel post fixed to the floor.
Fig.6. Here the newel post is let in below a timber floor and the strings are double mortise and tenoned to the newel post. Timber dowel pins strengthen the joint.
Fig.7. In a concrete floor the newel post is fixed with a galvanised mild steel dowel.
Fig.8. Here the string is let in below a timber floor and butts against blocking or a joist. The string and banister rail are housed into the newel post and dowel pinned.

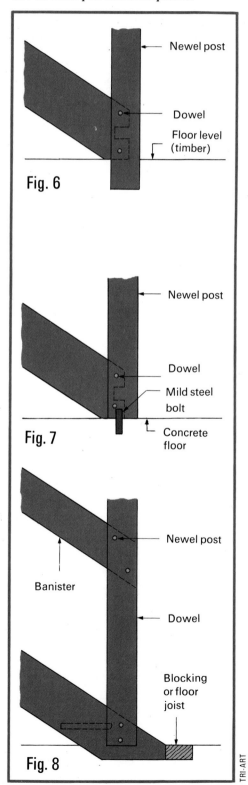

Fig. 6 — Newel post, Dowel, Floor level (timber)

Fig. 7 — Newel post, Dowel, Mild steel bolt, Concrete floor

Fig. 8 — Banister, Newel post, Dowel, Blocking or floor joist

TRI-ART

the plugs that protrudes can be cleaned off with a smoothing plane when the glue is dry.

Once the assembly is complete, the strings can be cut to the size required. At the top, the strings are fixed to a timber *trimmer*—a piece of wood slightly heavier than the floor joists, and which will normally be in place already on the upper floor. The angled end of the top of the strings butts against the side of the trimmer and is screwed in position. At their bottom end, the strings should be left a little overlength for the time being.

At the bottom, the strings are fixed to newel posts. There are several methods of fixing these to each other and of fixing the newel post to the floor. Figs. 6-8 illustrate these. In the first, the strings are double-mortised into the newel post and a timber dowel pushed through the tenon and the newel post. In the case of a timber floor the newel post can be set into the floorboards so that its bottom end rests on the concrete underlayer of the floor. There should be a damp course between post and concrete. The second method involves the same joint between the strings and the newel post, but the newel post is fixed to the floor by means of a mild steel dowel. This method is only suitable if the floor is concrete. In the third method, the strings and handrail are housed into the newel post. These are then screwed together. In this construction, the newel post ends at floor level but the strings are inset below the floorboards with their ends butting a floor joist, or a specially inserted timber block between the joists if these run the wrong way. Refer to CHAPTER 46 for further information about the usual methods of fixing newel posts to the strings, and the floor.

Supporting treads with spines

This construction method involves supporting the treads from underneath by means of spines. The setting out of the spines was described earlier.

The treads, in this type of design, are supported by triangular wooden blocks whose size depends on the going and rise of the treads. Their shape is similar to the triangular template cut earlier. The blocks are housed in a $\frac{1}{2}$in. x $\frac{1}{2}$in. (13mm x 13mm) groove cut along the centre of the top edge of the spines. Cut a tongue on the bottom side of each block (the wastage caused by this means that the blocks will have to be cut out slightly larger than your template). Glue the blocks into the groove so that their top edges are in line with the stepped-off pencil marks made earlier with the template. Screw the treads to the blocks with brass screws and cups, or fix them with timber dowels.

The fixing of this design of staircase to the floor and trimmer is the same as that for a staircase constructed with strings, except that the spines are not attached to a newel post. If a newel post is needed for the handrail, it should be separate.

Balusters and handrail

The method of fixing these is described fully in CHAPTER 46. Remember that in Britain the Building Regulations require the handrail to be a certain height. The requirements are described above under 'Construction requirements'.

Index

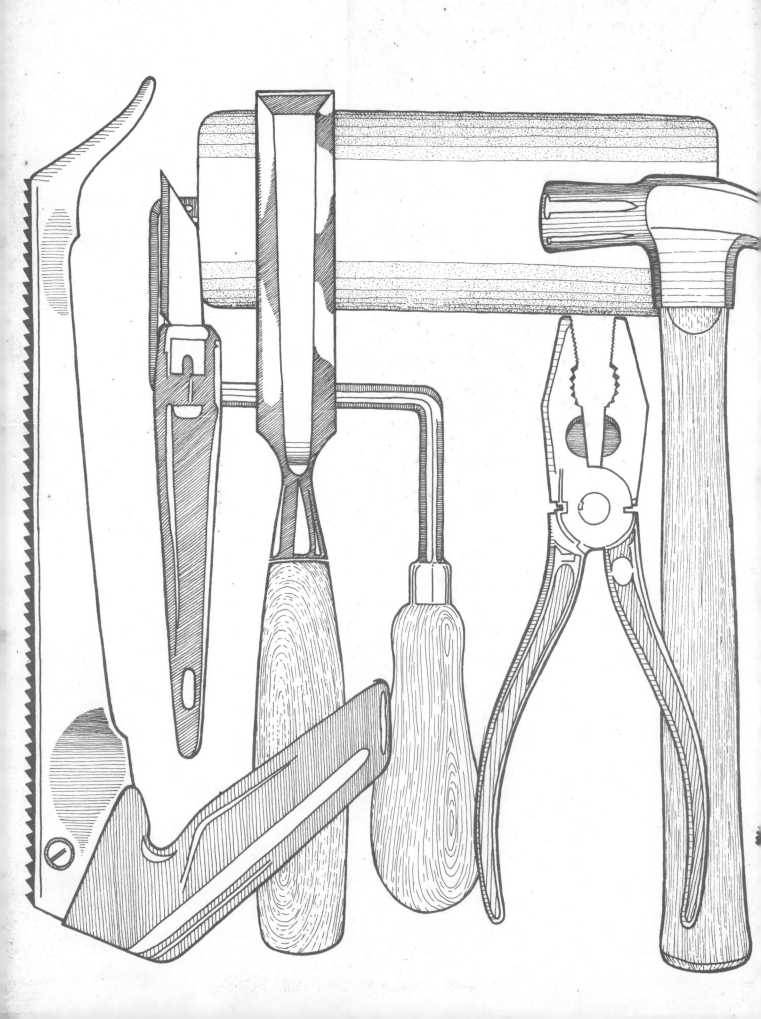